Contemporary Moral and Social Issues

BLACKWELL PHILOSOPHY ANTHOLOGIES

Each volume in this outstanding series provides an authoritative and comprehensive collection of the essential primary readings from philosophy's main fields of study. Designed to complement the *Blackwell Companions to Philosophy* series, each volume represents an unparalleled resource in its own right, and will provide the ideal platform for course use.

Contemporary Moral and Social Issues

An Introduction through Original Fiction, Discussion, and Readings

Thomas D. Davis

WILEY Blackwell

This edition first published 2014
© 2014 John Wiley & Sons, Inc

Registered Office
John Wiley & Sons, Ltd, The Atrium, Southern Gate, Chichester, West Sussex, PO19 8SQ, UK

Editorial Offices
350 Main Street, Malden, MA 02148–5020, USA
9600 Garsington Road, Oxford, OX4 2DQ, UK
The Atrium, Southern Gate, Chichester, West Sussex, PO19 8SQ, UK

For details of our global editorial offices, for customer services, and for information about how to apply for permission to reuse the copyright material in this book please see our website at www.wiley.com/wiley-blackwell.

The right of Thomas D. Davis to be identified as the author of the editorial material in this work has been asserted in accordance with the UK Copyright, Designs and Patents Act 1988.

Library of Congress Cataloging-in-Publication data is available for this book.

ISBN 9781118625217 (hardback); ISBN 9781118625408 (paperback)

A catalogue record for this book is available from the British Library.

Cover image: © AN Protasov / Shutterstock
Cover design by Nicki Averill Design and Illustration

Set in 10/12pt Bembo by SPi Publisher Services, Pondicherry, India
Printed in Malaysia by Ho Printing (M) Sdn Bhd

1   2014

To my wife, Diane,
with much love
and many thanks
and
in memory of Augie

Contents

Part VIII   Genetics   377

Preface

Contemporary Moral and Social Issues: An Introduction through Original Fiction, Discussion, and Readings (CMSI) begins with value theory, moral theory and contemporary political philosophy before moving on to five areas of "applied ethics": world poverty, abortion, the treatment of animals, the environment and genetic engineering. Each chapter contains a short story I wrote to introduce a particular moral or social issue, my discussion of that issue, and a selection of relevant readings from classical and contemporary sources.

Most instructors won't need to be convinced of the value of stories in getting students interested in ideas, especially ideas related to ethics. The question is likely to be: Why use this philosopher's stories? Part of the answer is that I'm pretty good at writing fiction: In addition to being a published novelist, I've been writing and publishing philosophical stories for a long time. My text, *Philosophy: An Introduction through Original Fiction, Discussion, and Readings*, was in print for 35 years. A number of stories from *Philosophy* have been anthologized in other texts.

The rest of the answer is that these stories are a solution to a problem that is likely to frustrate any instructor trying to use a piece of literature to introduce a philosophical topic. The literature may be exciting and relevant but it will almost certainly be philosophically unsophisticated. How then does one move from the literature to a philosophically sophisticated discussion without losing the initial student interest created by the literature? On the other hand, my stories hint at the issues philosophers will want to cover, issues that are then brought out in the discussion sections.

Here are some examples of the stories in CMSI: "The Trainers," where it turns out an alien race that saved the humans from extinction is now raising those humans for food, using the same justifications we use with animals; "People of the Underground" where the people holding out against the genetically engineered "Clenes" make the preservation of "true humanity" seem of dubious value; "The River" where a Westerner in an isolated outpost is faced with a steady stream of people who will die unless he makes Peter Singer-style sacrifices to save them; and the satiric "Divided States of America" in which the mid-twenty-first-century United States is dividing up into four separate countries based on caricature versions of liberalism, conservativism, libertarianism and socialism.

In the applied-ethics discussions I have done something I think too few texts do—give the students a basic grounding in the relevant factual issues. Personally I find classroom discussion of applied ethics hopeless unless students have a basic grasp of the related facts and the ongoing factual controversies (together with the evidence on each side). Otherwise student comments like, "I heard aid doesn't work," or "My minister says there are three hundred thousand partial-birth abortions every year," or "My friend's uncle raises pigs for Hormel, and he says the pigs get treated just fine" end up derailing the ethical discussion.

For instance, in the World Poverty chapter, the "Facts and Factual Issues" section covers:

- World poverty: basic facts
- Financial aid and economic growth
- Food aid and the "Green Revolution"

- Trying to find out what works
- What, if anything, can individuals do to help?

And in the Abortion chapter:

- Abortion: definition and statistics
- Abortion methods
- Development of the embryo/fetus
- Legal status of abortion
- Religious positions
- Public opinion

Within the limits of philosophical respectability, I have tried to make the discussions conversational, readable and personal. For example, at the end of the first chapter, following a discussion of biases in our reasoning and our tendency to talk issues only with people who agree with us, I write:

> It would be nice to think that you'll take advantage of this text to consider differing points of view; then, because you feel more comfortable with the issues, you'll be less inclined to avoid moral and political discussions with those who disagree with you.
>
> I can be as dogmatic and pig-headed as the next person. That's why I was surprised and pleased when I looked back and realized I'd changed my mind on a lot of issues in the course of researching and writing this text— sometimes making a slight shift of position, sometimes a major one. The changes came from both a more in-depth look at the ethical arguments and a more in-depth look at the factual disputes connected with those arguments.

One thing I urge you to do is to note, after reading this book, where you might have changed your mind, becoming certain where you were less certain before or becoming uncertain where you'd felt certain before.

If all your thinking remains exactly the same after you've read and discussed the issues in this text, we both will have failed.

The readability standard is applied to the selection and editing of the classical and contemporary sources. Often anthologies include whole chapters or articles when only parts of them are relevant: Where I could shorten the readings without distortion to emphasize the essential points I have done so. The standard sources are here, from Aristotle, Bentham and Kant to John Rawls, Robert Nozick and Peter Singer. However, a lot of non-philosophers are included to broaden the scope of the text, as for instance: *Time* magazine editor Claudia Wallis on the "new science of happiness"; psychologist Jonathan Haidt on biases in our reasoning as well as on virtue ethics in positive psychology; historian Patrick N. Allitt on conservativism and sociologist Paul Starr on liberalism; law professor Noah Feldman on the Free Exercise and Establishment clauses of the First Amendment; *New York Times* columnist Nicholas Kristof on world poverty; political speechwriter Matthew Scully on animal welfare (from his marvelous book, *Dominion*); and biophysicist Gregory Stock, political scientist Francis Fukuyama, and environmentalist Bill McKibben on the promises and dangers of genetic engineering.

Acknowledgments

Warm thanks to the following people at Wiley Blackwell: former Philosophy Editor Jeff Dean who liked my proposal and helped me through the review process; Jennifer Bray, who led me cheerfully and competently through the tortuous permissions process; Lindsay Bourgeois for help with publicity and Nicki Averill for her great work on the textbook cover; and Leah Morin and Graham Frankland for their expert editorial help.

I would like to thank the three reviewers for their support and helpful comments: Dean Kowalski, University of Wisconsin-Manitowoc; Mark D. White, College of Staten Island/CUNY; and Matt Lawrence, Long Beach City College.

I would like to thank the Teaching Company for permission to use excerpts from a few of their terrific courses. And special thanks to my PhD wife, Diane, for expert editing and many helpful conversations.

Source Acknowledgments

The author and publisher gratefully acknowledge the permission granted to reproduce the copyright material in this book:

From *Time* magazine, Jan. 9, 2005. Copyright TIME INC. Reprinted/translated by permission. TIME is a registered trademark of Time Inc. Inc. All rights reserved.

From *Anarchy, State, and Utopia*, by Robert Nozick. New York: Basic Books, 1974, pp. 42–5. Copyright © 1974 Robert Nozick. Reprinted by permission of Basic Books, a member of the Perseus Books Group.

From *Choosing Children: Genes, Disability and Design*, by Jonathan Glover. Oxford: Clarendon Press, 2006, pp. 87–93.

Reproduced with permission from *Questions of Value*, by Patrick Grim. Chantilly, VA: The Teaching Company, 2005, Transcript, part I, lecture 3. © 2005 The Teaching Company. Reproduced with permission of The Teaching Company, www.thegreatcourses.com.

Reproduced with permission from *Ethics: Discovering Right and Wrong*, 4th ed., by Louis P. Pojman. Belmont, CA: Wadsworth, 2002, pp. 6–9. © 2002 Wadsworth, a part of Cengage Learning, Inc. Reproduced by permission. www.cengage.com/permissions.

From *The Evolution of Morality*, by Richard Joyce. Cambridge, MA: MIT Press, 2006, pp. 70–2. © 2006 Massachusetts Institute of Technology, by permission of The MIT Press.

From *Sentimental Rules: On the Natural Foundations of Moral Judgment*, by Shaun Nichols. Oxford: Oxford University Press, 2004, pp. 4–7.

From *The Happiness Hypothesis: Finding Modern Truth in Ancient Wisdom*, by Jonathan Haidt. New York: Basic Books, 2006, pp. 59–71. Copyright © 2006 Jonathan Haidt. Reprinted by permission of Basic Books, a member of the Perseus Books Group.

From *An Introduction to the Principles of Morals and Legislation* (1789), by Jeremy Bentham, ch. 1.

From *Utilitarianism* (1861), by John Stuart Mill, ch. 2.

From *Practical Ethics*, by Peter Singer. Cambridge: Cambridge University Press, 1979 © 1980 Cambridge University Press, reproduced with permission.

From Kant, *Critique of Practical Reason* (originally published 1788), trans. Thomas Kingswill Abbott (1909).

Reprinted by permission of the publisher from *A Theory of Justice*, by John Rawls, pp. 11–15, 60–1, Cambridge, MA: The Belknap Press of Harvard University Press, Copyright © 1971 by the President and Fellows of Harvard College.

From *Anarchy, State and Utopia*, by Robert Nozick. New York: Basic Books, 1974, pp. ix, 6, 28–33, 150–63.

Reproduced with permission from "Rights" by Jeremy Waldron in *A Companion to Contemporary Political Philosophy*. Oxford: Blackwell Publishers, 1993, ch. 33.

From *The Nicomachean Ethics*, by Aristotle, trans. James E. C. Weldon (Macmillan, 1897), Books I and II.

From *The Happiness Hypothesis: Finding Modern Truth in Ancient Wisdom*, by Jonathan Haidt. New York: Basic Books, 2006, pp. 163–70.

Reproduced with permission from "The Idea of a Female Ethic." In *A Companion to Ethics*, ed. Peter Singer. Oxford: Blackwell, 1993, pp. 491–6.

From *Being Good: A Short Introduction to Ethics*, by Simon Blackburn. Oxford: Oxford University Press, 2001, pp. 37–43

Reproduced with permission from George Lakoff, *Moral Politics: What Conservatives Know that Liberals Don't*, University of Chicago Press, 1996, pp. 248, 260–1.

Reproduced with permission from "The Challenge of Cultural Relativism," in *The Elements of Moral Philosophy*, 5th ed., by James Rachels/Stuart Rachels. Boston, MA: McGraw-Hill, 1999, ch. 2.

Reproduced with permission from *The Animal Rights Debate*, by Carl Cohen and Tom Regan. Oxford: Rowman & Littlefield Publishers Inc, 2001, pp. 3–14, 61–3.

From *Dominion: The Power of Man, the Suffering of Animals, and the Call to Mercy*, by Matthew Scully. New York: St. Martin's Griffin, 2002, pp. x–xii, 15–17, 24, 28, 127–8. © 2002 by Matthew Scully. Reprinted by permission of St. Martin's Press. All righs reserved.

Reproduced from "Is Humanity Suicidal?" by Edward O. Wilson. © 1993 by *The New York Times*. Courtesy of E. O. Wilson.

Excerpts from *The Hot Topic* by Gabrielle Walker and Sir David King. Copyright © by Gabrielle Walker and Sir David King 2008. Reprinted by permission of Houghton Mifflin Harcourt. All rights reserved.

From *Cool It: The Skeptical Environmentalist's Guide to Global Warming*, by Bjorn Lomborg. New York: Alfred Knopf, 2007, pp. 4–9.

From *America and the New Global Economy*, by Timothy Taylor. Chantilly, VA: The Teaching Company, 2008, pp. 177–82. © 2008 The Teaching Company. Reproduced with permission of The Teaching Company, www. thegreatcourses.com.

Reproduced with permission from *People or Penguins: The Case for Optimal Pollution*, by William F. Baxter. New York: Columbia University Press, 1974. Columbia University Press

From "Is There a Need for a New, an Environmental Ethic?" by Richard Routley (later Richard Sylvan). This essay was originally published in *Proceedings of the XV World Congress of Philosophy*, Varna, Bulgaria, 1, 1973, pp. 205–10.

From *Respect for Nature: A Theory of Environmental Ethics*, by Paul Taylor. Princeton, NJ: Princeton University Press, 1986, pp. 44–6, 60–8. © 1986 Princeton University Press. Reprinted by permission of Princeton University Press.

From "The Search for an Environmental Ethic," by J. Baird Callicott. Reproduced with permission from *Matters of Life and Death: New Introductory Essays in Moral Philosophy*, 3rd edn., ed. Tom Regan. New York: McGraw-Hill, 1993, pp. 363–8, 372.

Reproduced with permission from *Deep Ecology, Living as if Nature Mattered*, by Bill Devall and George Sessions. Salt Lake City, UT: Peregrine, 1985, pp. 2–11.

Reproduced with permission from *Babies By Design: The Ethics of Genetic Choice*, by Ronald M. Green. New Haven, CT: Yale University Press, 2007, pp. 5–9.

Excerpts from *Redesigning Humans: Our Inevitable Genetic Future*, by Gregory Stock. New York: Houghton Mifflin Co., 2003, pp. 2–5 and 8–13. Copyright © 2002 by Gregory Stock. Reprinted by permission of Houghton Mifflin Harcourt Publishing Company. All rights reserved.

From *What Sort of People Should There Be?* by Jonathan Glover. Middlesex, UK: Penguin Books, 1984, pp. 45–56. Reproduced by permission of Penguin Books Ltd and courtesy of Pr J. Glover.

Excerpt from "Policies for the Future" from *Our Posthuman Future: Consequences of the Biotechnology Revolution*, by Frances Fukuyama. New York: Picador, 2002, pp. 206–18. Copyright © 2002 by Frances Fukuyama. Reprinted by permission of Farrar, Straus and Giroux, LLC.

Reproduced from *Enough: Staying Human in an Engineered Age*, by Bill McKibben. New York: Henry Holt and Company, 2003, pp. 181–91.

From *Beyond Therapy: Biotechnology and the Pursuit of Happiness*, by The President's Council on Bioethics, United States Government Printing Office, October 2003.

Every effort has been made to trace copyright holders and to obtain their permission for the use of copyright material. The publisher apologizes for any errors or omissions, and would be grateful to be notified of any corrections that should be incorporated in future reprints or editions of this book.

Part I

Introduction
Values

1

Values

Fiction

Too Much

Julia put her feet up on the coffee table, maneuvering a copy of *People* magazine across the glass surface with one foot until the magazine rested under her heels. On the end table was a mug of herb tea she'd put there a moment before. Wine would have tasted better, but with Julia being five months pregnant, she wouldn't be having alcohol for a while. She took a sip of tea, put the cup down, and leaned back against the sofa cushions.

The digital clock on the DVD player read 4:05. Still a little over an hour before Brian came home with Timmy. This was her private time between a day of teaching and an evening with her family, and it was time she valued to an absurd and slightly guilty degree. She never did anything special, but maybe that was the point. The TV was on low—to the news—the not-yet-opened mail was scattered around her, and a pad and pen lay at hand for notes and lists—whatever occurred to her that needed writing down. What made her feel guilty was knowing she could have picked up Timmy an hour earlier from Brian's parents' house and spent the extra time with him. Still, Grandma Elizabeth loved having Timmy, and Timmy had such fun with her; anyway, Julia would have the evening with her son. This hour of solitary quiet had come about early in the pregnancy when Julia had been feeling sick and overwhelmed; really it had been Brian and his mother who'd pushed it on

her. Now, even though she was feeling better, she was reluctant to give it up.

Julia took the rubber bands off the two thick bundles of mail on her lap and let the items spill over onto the sofa cushions. She saw a letter from her friend, Stephanie and opened it eagerly. Stephanie and Julia had been friends in college and had roomed together during a junior-year semester abroad in Florence. Italy had been such a magical place: The two of them had reveled in their time there, spinning out romantic fantasies about what they were going to do with their lives. Stephanie had come the closest to living out those fantasies. The letter told how she'd just come back from a business trip to Paris for her employer, a software company. There were descriptions of two quaint little restaurants and allusions to a stranger Stephanie had had dinner with.

Julia sighed. It was impossible to read a letter from Stephanie without fantasizing about *what if*. Julia had no real regrets. She loved her husband and her child and couldn't imagine giving them up. Though, in a way, she almost had. In one of those odd coincidences that seem to happen to friends, Julia and Stephanie had both gotten pregnant the last semester of senior year. Stephanie had been involved in a casual relationship and arranged to have what for Stephanie had been a second abortion. She assumed Julia would also have an abortion: After all, the two women had been making plans for a summer abroad together. Julia had

Contemporary Moral and Social Issues: An Introduction through Original Fiction, Discussion, and Readings, First Edition. Thomas D. Davis.
© 2014 John Wiley & Sons, Inc. Published 2014 by John Wiley & Sons, Inc.

almost let herself be carried along by Stephanie's assumptions. But Julia hadn't been in a casual relationship: She'd been dating Brian for two years and was in love with him; the two had been talking about marriage. In the end Julia hadn't gone through with the abortion. She wasn't proud of the way she'd handled the decision. She was glad she hadn't had the abortion—it was unthinkable now that Timmy was here—but she wished she'd had the courage to make the decision all on her own. Instead, she'd told Brian and let his reaction determine hers (he'd insisted on marriage). Looking back, she realized she'd been under Stephanie's spell and needed Brian as a counterweight. Stephanie had been angry and had become distant for a time, though later the friendship had resumed.

Though Julia had no real regrets, it was hard not to feel *something* like regret when reading Stephanie's letters. Actually, when Julia and Stephanie got together to talk, and it got late, and the wine had gotten to both of them, Stephanie would get down and let on about the lonely parts of her life. But nothing came across but the adventure in Stephanie's letters.

Anyway, Julia still had her own dream—put away—not for now, but much later, after the children were older—when she and Brian could go to Italy together for a couple of months. They'd visit lots of museums and churches and then she'd set up her easel and lose herself in painting Tuscan landscapes. The Italians had a lovely phrase for such a far-off dream—"sogno in cassetta"—a dream in a drawer. Meanwhile she'd just keep teaching her art classes at the local high school and painting local scenes when she could find the time.

Julia opened three bills, set the payment slips and return envelopes aside, and threw the waste paper into the open grocery bag she'd set on the floor next to the couch for that purpose. She'd pay the bills a little later when she got her checkbook out of her purse in the kitchen.

It was nice that opening bills was never traumatic. She and Brian made decent incomes but, more to the point, managed to live within them. Julia was middle-class in a way she knew her parents didn't quite approve of, yet just enough of their socialist ideas lingered in her superego to make her feel guilty at

the idea of luxury. Brian, who was in the business of making money for other people, was also conservative in his spending habits.

Not that they didn't *want* things. She and Brian could daydream over home listings, travel brochures, catalogs, and TV commercials like everyone else. But neither of them was obsessed with those things. It helped that their closest friends—all with small children—were also fairly modest in their spending habits. Of course, that might be one reason those people *were* their closest friends.

She and Brian did know people—some of whom they liked—who were very different when it came to money and possessions. It seemed those people were always obsessing over styles, how much things cost, who else had what, and what was "in." They were always talking about what they'd just bought and what they wanted to buy next—cars, furniture, entertainment systems, clothes, wines, whatever. Julia and Brian found such people uncomfortable to be around—partly because Julia and Brian couldn't really participate in their conversations, partly because such talk got boring after a while, and, partly, she was sure, out of envy.

Were those people happy? Julia laughed at herself: She knew that was the age-old question of those lower than others on the financial ladder. It was what sold *People* magazine: The fascination with wealth and fame plus the satisfaction of learning that people at the top had lots of painful problems.

What about the money-focused people Julia knew? Like a lot of obsessive people, they did seem frantic, but they never seemed bored. In addition to striving for money and "things," most of them were fixated on "self-improvement"—mostly physical—with the latest exercise classes, equipment, outfits. They weren't exactly materialists—they liked a New Age dimension in everything from workouts to management styles. One or two she knew were religious, but their religions seemed to focus on self-development—God as personal trainer. They didn't do much for other people, but then, Julia had to admit, neither did most people. Some didn't want children, but some did: No doubt those who did would be obsessed with having their children have, and be, the best.

Julia shook her head. She knew she was wildly overgeneralizing. It was so easy to caricature people in order to dismiss them. Anyway, how had she gotten on this subject? And why? Could her interest in those people show she was really more envious than she liked to admit? For that matter, how happy was *she* really?

At moments like this, Julia sometimes imagined a little beeper going off—a signal that she should write down what she was doing and how happy she was at that moment. The thought came from a psychological experiment her friend Reina had told her about, where people actually had to write down their moods when their individual beepers went off. Apparently the idea of the experiment had been to get a series of in-the-moment descriptions of people's moods, rather than to rely on their later memories of how they'd been feeling.

The idea of the beepers had a comic dimension—it gave new meaning to the phrase "coitus interruptus"—though, in spite of the interruptions, "having sex" turned out to be high on the happiness list. According to the experiment, though, people were happiest while eating. When Reina had told her that, Julia had laughed, switched hands with her sandwich, and given her friend a high five across the cafeteria table. The meaning of life solved, at last!

Julia wondered how her life would get summed up if she were part of that beeper experiment. She *thought* she was happy. At least, pretty happy.

Julia began looking through the rest of the mail. She noticed a newly arrived flyer from Catholic Charities, and she let out a groan, thinking about the coming weekend. It was going to be one of the rare get-togethers that involved both Brian's parents—Elizabeth and Charles Burke—and her own—Viktor and Anna Hasek. Together the Burkes and the Haseks were like oil and water—or, better, gasoline and matches. There'd been a big flare up during their second get-together, and things were still smoldering.

The Burkes were conservative Catholics. Charles, a successful stockbroker, seemed to take the Church's line on everything—except for its suspicion of laissez-faire capitalism. Charles dismissed that suspicion as the bias of the "dear, old men" who were better at theology than economics, who were too removed from the world to know how things really worked. Charles said that the Church talked about dividing

goods as if those goods fell like manna from heaven, rather than having to be created by a system that needed incentives to function and was bound to lead to inequalities.

Julia had held her breath during Charles' little speech that evening, watching her mother, Anna, take on that slight reddening in her cheeks Julia knew to be a warning sign. Julia had tried to catch her mother's eye, though she knew it was no use. Anna, who was an avowed socialist—not to mention a feminist and atheist—wasn't likely to take this nicely, and Anna wasn't one to be quieted for the sake of some ideal of family calm.

When Charles had paused for breath, Anna asked him how the "dear old men" who were too removed from the world to understand capitalism still managed to be such experts on women's reproductive rights. Charles had tried to laugh this off, soon saw it was no use, and started to argue in a reasonable tone that became less reasonable under Anna's barbed replies. Soon the two of them were off. Viktor and Elizabeth had at first tried to be peacemakers, but were soon pulled into the argument on the sides of their spouses.

Once the words "communistic" and "fascistic" had begun to appear, Julia and Brian knew they'd better get the argument stopped fast. They'd managed it somehow, but the four older adults had been more sullen than conciliatory during the rest of the mercifully short evening. A year had passed before Julia and Brian had dared get both sets of parents together again. The next two or three events had gone okay but they'd had to tiptoe around topics so carefully—even then there'd been little jabs here and there—that Julia had found the evenings very uncomfortable. As far as Julia was concerned, she'd be happy never to have her parents and her in-laws together again. Sometimes it was just impossible to avoid, though, especially when there was a grandson in the picture.

A tricky matter for this week was the menu. Elizabeth wanted to bring much of the dinner—a gesture that would normally have made Julia grateful. But Julia didn't want Elizabeth doing so much unless Julia's parents made a contribution. The problem was that for most of her adult life, Anna had refused to cook "on principle." Sometimes Julia thought she had the only Italian mother in existence who neither cooked nor believed in God. Julia wasn't sure how she herself felt about God, but she knew she loved to cook—at least when she had the energy—and she sure loved to eat. Fortunately, growing up, Julia had lived close to her maternal grandmother. Primetta had been a beautiful, caricature Italian grandmother, whose big bosom smelled of gardenias when the scent wasn't overwhelmed by garlic and rosemary, Primetta with her big hugs and glorious meals that Julia had reveled in. Julia loved and respected her mother—she realized she had some of her good traits—but her mother's unorthodoxy could be troublesome on occasions like this. Julia supposed she could do the usual and have her father buy the dessert and bread. Not the wine, though: Julia's parents (again, on some principle) went for inexpensive wines—"dago reds," her Italian mother liked to call them, in some kind of reverse snobbishness. Julia could just imagine the pained expressions such wines would bring to Charles' face; Julia didn't need that complication.

A flicker from the TV set caught her eye. The regular news was on now, with a report of rioting somewhere—the Middle East, it looked like. Julia kept telling herself she needed to be better about keeping up with the news. Brian was good about keeping up. Maybe it was a guy thing—no, that wasn't right. She knew plenty of guys who were just as vague about what was happening in the world as she was. Maybe a business thing—people afraid they would lose investments or miss out on opportunities if they didn't keep up with what was going on in the USA and abroad.

Now and then Julia would make a resolution to be better informed: She'd promise herself she'd look at the main section of the newspaper every day, or at least read a news magazine every week. But the resolve never lasted long. When she did sit down with the newspaper or a news magazine, she'd find herself diverted by cooking or travel or art or film reviews— the things that really interested her. And those were the sorts of things she and her girlfriends talked about—that and their children.

The regular news could be so *boring*. Julia laughed at herself, realizing she was sounding like some of her students. Julia always told her students that the way to make something not-boring was to learn about it— give yourself a chance to get interested. Julia knew her own boredom was partly lack of background. Unless

you kept up on the news, there were too many obscure references to people and places. It was always as if you were starting in the middle of a story and had no real idea why what was happening was happening, or who it was happening to.

She glanced at the DVD clock: Most of her hour was gone. She glanced over the rest of the mail and saw that it was more flyers from various "causes." No matter how often she and Brian asked their parents not to put them on mailing lists, and no matter how many times the parents agreed, it didn't seem to do any good. Or maybe it was just that these lists got passed between so many groups that there was no way to get the mailings stopped now.

Julia remembered years ago responding to an AIDS charity solicitation at the end of a very moving novel. It had produced a flood of follow-up solicitations from all sorts of organizations. Marrying Brian was a little like making that AIDS donation: It put the two of them on the mailing lists of all the organizations and charities favored by Brian's parents. Though it wasn't only the Burkes. There was an almost equal number of solicitations her parents were responsible for. Maybe they didn't want Julia led astray by the right-wing and religious causes of the Burkes.

Julia remembered the car one of the seniors had been driving to high school the previous year. On the right side of the trunk he'd pasted a bunch of right-wing stickers and on the other side, a bunch of left-wing stickers. In the center of the trunk, he'd pasted a familiar sticker that read, "Don't follow me, I'm lost." That car trunk had been a big conversation piece in the teachers' lounge, with the teachers volunteering other phrases that might have been used for the center sticker. The two suggestions Julia could remember were "Stuck in the Middle with You" and "I've Got My Own Problems."

That was how Julia always felt in the midst of these solicitations—vaguely lost, somewhere in the middle, and swamped by the complications of her own life. That, and sort of guilty.

She picked up a flyer from the Animal Welfare Institute and another from the Humane Farm Association. Strangely enough, the one responsible for the animal literature was Elizabeth, the conservative Catholic. Julia had always thought of animal issues as vaguely "leftist"— though she wasn't sure why, given that her two socialist parents had no interest in animals, personally or morally. Charles, like Julia's parents, was dismissive of the whole idea: Julia had thought this was one issue on which Anna and Charles might actually agree, but he'd made the mistake of dismissing it offhand as a "female thing," which, of course, had set Anna off.

Elizabeth wasn't against killing animals for food, but she was dead set against factory farming (which, judging from the photos in the Humane Farm Association booklet, did look pretty awful, Julia had to admit). Elizabeth bought only "free range" meat at the local whole foods market, and urged Julia to do the same. Julia did do that sometimes, when she was shopping in that part of town, though the free-range meat cost a lot more. She could tell herself that her family didn't eat *that* much meat—that they ate a lot of fish and simple pastas. Mostly she didn't like to think about the whole thing.

Julia and Brian had gotten on the mailing lists of competing organizations like NARAL Pro-Choice America and the National Right-to-Life Committee. Some of the anti-abortion literature reminded Julia of the anti-factory farming literature—really gross-out stuff. When Julia had mentioned this to the Burkes, Elizabeth had welcomed the comparison, saying they were both terrible crimes. But Charles had gotten angry, saying that the comparison was offensive. Killing innocent children who had souls and were made in God's image was *nothing* like raising dumb animals for food—animals God had given us dominion over for just that purpose. Julia had been glad to get off that subject.

Julia shook her head: Where did people get the energy for so much anger and so much arguing? Sometimes it seemed to Julia that she had just enough energy to make it through her normal day.

Still, she did wish she knew more, had more definite positions of her own. What positions she did hold seemed sort of in the middle, and she couldn't say that much about why she held them, other than that the other positions seemed too "extreme." She supposed she had a conciliatory personality, wanted people to get along with each other, whether in her home or in society as a whole. She hated the way so much of American society seemed made up of people screaming at each other.

On the other hand, sometimes she felt she was too passive. It could really be annoying getting preached at, whether about religion or politics or some social cause. Sometimes she wanted to object to something someone was saying or at least question it, but she knew if she did she'd quickly get buried under the other person's arguments and information. She really wished her beliefs were more definite, that she had clearer reasons for why she held them. She knew that would make her feel more mature, more substantial as a person. If only it didn't take so much time and effort to get to that point.

She was starting to gather up the mail when a brochure from Save the Children slipped out. The children's faces had always gotten to Julia—especially since she'd become a mother—and she really liked the idea that a contribution would go toward helping a particular child. A few years ago, Julia had signed up to contribute for one child for a year—it was only $24 a month—and told herself she would try to add another child at the end of that year. But like things you buy on the installment plan that sound so easy, the payment hadn't been easy, and it seemed as if she was always scrounging for that $24 at the end of the month, always wanting that money for something else. She hadn't renewed at the end of the year and had let it slide ever since. She definitely wanted to start contributing again.

Julia saw that it was five o'clock. She'd better get moving. She put Stephanie's letter aside to read again later, and picked up the rest of the mail in one armload to throw in the trash. She'd get something started for dinner—did she ever imagine, as a student in Europe with its late dining times—that one day she'd be eating dinner at 5:30? Then she'd play with Timmy, have Brian put him to bed, check e-mails and phone messages, call Elizabeth about this weekend, and her father about his dinner contribution, and decide what she herself would cook. Then there'd be the homework to grade. Sometimes there was just too much to do.

On the TV screen some politician was talking excitedly about…what?…stem cell research. Julia sighed: That was one more topic that Julia was vague on. There was just too much to think about, too much to understand.

Too much.

Questions

1. How would you describe Julia as a person? What is she doing with her life? What are her likes and dislikes, values, dreams and so on?

2. How would you characterize the differences between the lifestyles of Julia and her friend Stephanie? Does Julia envy her friend? Do you think Julia wishes she'd chosen Stephanie's lifestyle?

3. How would you characterize Julia's attitude toward money and toward the lives of the people she knows who have more money than she does?

4. What are some of the issues over which Julia's parents and her in-laws argue? What are Julia's attitudes toward those issues and the intensity with which the older adults approach those issues?

5. Do you have definite views on some of those issues over which Julia's parents and in-laws disagree (abortion, our treatment of animals, etc.)? Sketch your own views.

6. What are some of your major life goals? Your major values?

2

Values
Discussion

Too Much

Julia is a high school art teacher, a wife, and a mother. She's an artist: We don't know how serious she is about her own work or whether she has talent; we do know she likes to paint and dreams of going to Tuscany some day to do landscapes.

When Julia was in college, she spent a semester abroad with her friend, Stephanie, and was planning to go back to Europe with her after college. Both friends got pregnant in their senior year, Stephanie as a result of a casual relationship, Julia as a result of serious relationship with Brian. Stephanie got an abortion, remained single, and now travels abroad, living what seems to Julia rather an adventurous life. Julia decided against the abortion, married Brian, and settled down to teaching and family life. She doesn't regret the way her life has gone—she loves her husband and son—but sometimes she does envy Stephanie. Her friend's letters are full of exciting places and events, though Julia also knows from late night talks with Stephanie that there's a lonely side to Stephanie's life that doesn't come out in the letters. Perhaps Stephanie sometimes envies Julia, as Julia does her.

Julia loves to cook when she has the time, and she enjoys going through cooking magazines. She likes to read art and book and film reviews. She finds the news boring; she doesn't feel good about this, especially since she always tells her students that the way to find

something not-boring is to learn about it and give yourself a chance to get interested. Julia has made a few resolutions to keep up with the news, but hasn't really followed through.

Julia is facing the prospect of an evening with her parents and in-laws—not a nice prospect since the older adults don't get along and argue a lot about morality and politics. Brian's parents are conservative Catholics, who are against abortion and for a free market with minimum government interference. Julia's parents are socialists and firmly for women's rights. Brian's mother, Elizabeth, is for animal welfare, something her husband dismisses as sentimental and Julia's parents have no interest in.

Julia hates the fact that the older adults argue, as well as the fact that they all push their positions on Julia and Brian. There's a battle of the brochures going on, with Julia's mail full of solicitations for various causes, many with a far-right or far-left political slant.

Julia feels overwhelmed by the causes thrust at her, imagining how much thought and energy it would take to be so involved. She once committed to make a small monthly payment to Save the Children but found making the payment a struggle; she opted out when her year was up. She tells herself vaguely she should start again.

A lot of what concerns Julia in the story is values—her own values and those of others. Insofar as you can judge from the story, what are Julia's values?

Contemporary Moral and Social Issues: An Introduction through Original Fiction, Discussion, and Readings, First Edition. Thomas D. Davis.
© 2014 John Wiley & Sons, Inc. Published 2014 by John Wiley & Sons, Inc.

There are some things you might say here: She values her husband and son; she values painting. But asking about someone's values can be a bit confusing. Are we to say that Julia values cooking or simply that she likes to cook? Does she value painting in general or just for herself? And what about keeping informed about current events or donating to Save the Children? Does the fact that she doesn't keep up mean she doesn't really value those things? What about her feelings of obligation regarding both those activities? What kind of value conflict is the tug of war between her desires and her feelings of obligation?

We'd better lay some groundwork regarding values.

Values

When one talks about one's "values," one is likely to be talking about one's more important values—career goals, personal ideals, moral values. But in its broadest meaning—as when one talks of "facts versus values"—the word value covers not only moral values and personal ideals, but also likes and dislikes, preferences, and emotional reactions.

Whether peach ice cream is (tastes) better than chocolate ice cream is a "value judgment"; who got the biggest scoop is a "factual judgment." (We could resolve the factual matter by weighing the scoops.)

Whether the roller coaster is "scary-fun" or "terrifying" is a value judgment; how many minutes the ride takes and how many feet of track there are would be factual judgments.

Claiming abortion is wrong would be a value judgment; claiming that two million abortions are performed in the United States in a year would be a factual judgment—one we could decide by gathering statistics.

To call a judgment "factual" is not to say that it is true; actually, the claim that two million abortions are performed in the USA every year is false. The latest data from the US government for 2001 indicate the figure is well under a million. To call a judgment "factual" is only to say that it's the sort of judgment that might be resolved through empirical evidence. Predicting the abortion figure for 2025 would be a factual judgment; we'd have to wait for the figures, but eventually we should have them.

Often the fact/value distinction is put forward with the implication that all values are subjective and irrational, in contrast to the "hard facts." That is not the intention here. We're only saying that the fact/value distinction is a familiar one and that we want to look at the range of judgments that tend to be placed in the broad "value" category.

It's not as if all judgments are wholly evaluative or wholly factual. After all, the value judgments given above are about actual things—ice cream and roller coasters and abortion. Some words have both a factual and evaluative aspect. If you call someone "generous," I know you are praising her for giving time or money to others. If you call someone courageous, I know you are praising her for taking some risk, overcoming some fear. Once I learn how much she gave or what risks she took, I may disagree with your assessment, but at least I know the kind of thing you are taking about.

How should we define the word "value"? Here's what one philosopher has to say about that:

> …"What does the word 'value' mean in English?" There is no easy answer
>
> …Concepts of value are related to ways of life. That is, when we talk about a person's values, we make implicit reference to his hopes, aspirations, plans, and self-conception. All these latter things are complicated, and, of course, can vary from person to person….
>
> At the beginning we can think of values as those things worth having, worth doing, or worth being….

Since value judgments often refer to standards or norms, they are sometimes called "normative" judgments.

A distinction can be made between personal values and moral values. The distinction is rough and not always reliable, but it will do for a start. We'll talk about personal values first and moral values later.

Personal Values

Some distinctions

For the moment, let's think of personal values as those that come into play in contexts where our interests don't conflict with the interests of other people or with codes (like religious codes) that prohibit or require certain behaviors of us.

The category of "personal values" covers different types of values. Some examples:

1. Likes/dislikes; attitudes; emotional responses
This category would include your tastes in food, clothes, music—what you like and dislike. It would cover your attitudes toward the people you enjoy being with and those you'd just as soon avoid, the kinds of activities you enjoy and those you're not much interested in. It would include things you're excited by and things you're afraid of. Some of the many value terms we might use of items in this category are *likeable, lovable, awesome, boring, fun, exciting, scary, sexy, delicious*, and *satisfying* (as well as the obvious *good* and *bad*).

From the story, we know that Julia loves cooking (and eating), likes reading and talking about travel, art and films, and doesn't like reading or watching the news. Apparently she likes teaching well enough, though she'd rather paint if given the opportunity.

Julia loved her grandmother, loves her husband and son; she loves her parents, though they can be annoying. She likes her in-laws, but hates the tension when her parents and in-laws are together.

2. Life goals and ambitions
Our decisions often become more important and more difficult when we're dealing with what we want our futures to be. It doesn't seem to be in our natures to value future goods as strongly as present goods. Delayed gratification takes work.

We need to decide what kind of lives we want for ourselves in the near and farther future and then plan and live accordingly. If we want to be musicians or athletes or scholars or physicians or lawyers, we're going to have to plan and train, disciplining ourselves in ways we may not like for the sake of becoming what we want to be.

In formulating and implementing life plans, there are bound to be trade-offs. You want to be successful at something, but you also want time for close friendships, family relationships, and leisure activities. How do you fit this all into your life? Can you, in fact?

Regarding the story, if we put aside for now the moral question of abortion, we can imagine a decision between two lifestyles: Julia's more settled life with a husband and child and Stephanie's more adventurous life without ongoing close relationships. Whatever life one chose, there would certainly be moments of wondering what the other life would have been like.

Julia and Brian have chosen to live rather modestly and within their means. They feel good that they don't have any serious debt, but there are times when the more expensive lifestyles of some of their acquaintances look pretty attractive.

3. Ideals
There are ideals that are clearly in the domain of morality, such as being charitable or kind. But there are other ideals that don't *necessarily* have anything to do with morality—such as the ideals of knowledge or self-acceptance or great success. Ideals can be an aspect of one's ambitions—for instance, if one aspires to be a great athlete or a great scientist. Or ideals may be something we appreciate and encourage in others: Think, for instance, of the physical klutz who admires athletic process, the plain person who admires style and glamour, or the science buff who admires the great scientists.

Julia doesn't convey any obvious ideals in the story—though, one might assume she has a certain ideal of being a good wife and mother. She retains a dream of going to Tuscany to paint someday—perhaps there's an ideal lifestyle implied there.

Ideals can be things we want to live up to—adjusting eating habits and exercise to achieve a healthy or attractive weight, training/practicing to achieve a certain competence at basketball or golf or running. Ideals can also plague us for the ways in which we fall short—the way an ideal of physical attractiveness plagues a lot of people. The ideal of being informed about what's going on in the world certainly nags at Julia: It's one of those things she thinks she should be doing, but never does.

A friend might take a therapeutic approach with Julia and advise her to work on discarding the ideal of being informed; instead Julia should focus on what she enjoys doing. We all have to come to terms with what we are and aren't, especially if we're hounded by an overbearing superego and too much sense of failure. On the other hand, it could be argued that there are things we ought to keep striving for and that accommodating the more easy-going parts of our nature can be a failing. This could be especially true if there is a moral dimension to the ideal in question— if, say, staying reasonably informed were the responsibility of each citizen in a democracy.

What about Julia's on-and-off impulse to give money to Save the Children? Do we really want to tell people, "Well, giving to charity obviously doesn't come naturally to you, so just accept that and forget about giving"? Maybe that's being too accommodating.

What are the things you think are worth having or doing? If you were going to start making a list you might include such things as good health; a satisfying family life; healthy, well adjusted children; friends; a well paid, reasonably enjoyable job; a good education; fun activities; being part of a community; having a great entertainment system; and, so on.

Since at least the ancient Greeks, philosophers have made the distinction between something being good as an end (an "intrinsic good") and good as a means (an "instrumental good"). It's not a hard and fast distinction: Things can be good both as means and ends. Having some fun might be good in itself; it might also be good as a means, if you're taking care of someone and the quality of your care is slipping because you're getting tired and depressed and need a break. Knowledge is good as a means if it contributes to one's welfare and that of others; knowledge has also been thought to be good in itself by many people throughout history. Much the same could be said about belief in God.

We reason about both ends and means. We need to decide what kind of life we'd like, what our chances are of obtaining it, and what kind of preparation we need in order to have the best chance of attaining it.

Occasionally—maybe at two in the morning—you might find means-end talk taking a philosophical turn. You might ask yourself—or find someone else asking you—what you *really* want out of life, what is it you really want beyond all the specific goals you've set yourself. In such cases the tendency is to keep asking of any proposed answer, "But why do you want *that*?" or "What do you want *that* for?"

"Why do you want money?" "Well, for one thing, I could buy a sports car." "Why do you want a sports car?" "I don't know, I just do: It would make me feel good."

"Why do you want to get married?" "I think I need that kind of relationship to be happy."

Pressing such questions often ends up with such answers as "feeling good" and "happiness." After all, you'd think the other person was nuts if she asked you, seriously, "Why do you want to feel good?" and "Why do you want to be happy?" It's easy to conclude that when it comes to personal values, the one thing people really desire or value for its own sake is happiness, and that anything else they desire is as a means to that. However, this claim becomes less obvious when you examine it more closely—as we shall do now.

Happiness as the ultimate personal value

Below are three definitions of happiness. (*These are intended only as samples*, for purposes of contrast.)

D1.   Happiness = pleasant experiences (without unpleasant ones)
D2.   Happiness = many more pleasant than unpleasant experiences and an overall feeling of satisfaction
D3.   Happiness = what people desire

The statement, "The one thing people desire for its own sake is happiness," will mean something different depending on which meaning of happiness we substitute:

S1.   "What people desire for its own sake is having pleasant experiences (without unpleasant ones)"
S2.   "What people desire for its own sake is having many more pleasant than unpleasant experiences and an overall feeling of satisfaction"
S3.   "What people desire for its own sake is what they desire for its own sake"

S1 seems implausible: People would hardly struggle hard for goals or struggle to make relationships work if all they desired was pleasant experiences.

S2 looks better. People don't try to avoid all unpleasant situations, but it does seem they are looking for more pleasant than unpleasant experiences as well as an overall feeling of satisfaction.

S3 is a tautology—true, but totally unhelpful. Obviously people desire what they desire. We want to know what specific thing or things they desire.

Few people would get confused by statement *S3* as given. But frequently people will change their meaning of "happiness" in arguing that happiness is the only thing people want for its own sake. Suppose you start by defining happiness in terms of pleasant feelings; I then bring up a case in which a person put herself through great pain to help another person; you then say, "But that's happiness to her!" In the course of this brief exchange you have committed the logical fallacy of shifting meanings in the middle of your argument—from happiness-as-pleasant-feeling to the happiness-as-whatever-people want.

S2 looks like the most reasonable of the three statements. So we need to ask: "Are feelings of satisfaction or pleasure the only things people desire for their own sake?"

The following hypothetical situation will serve as a test: Imagine you've worked really hard for some dream career, forgoing lots of pleasures in pursuit of it. Now it looks as if your work and deprivations will pay off: You've been hired for that dream job, which will start in two months, offering you all the material rewards you have put off.

However, unknown to you, you have an inoperable brain aneurysm that will burst in the next two months, killing you quickly. Until the aneurysm bursts, there will be no symptoms. This terrible fact is known only by your physician and your parents.

Would you want to be told?

I can imagine a chorus of "No!"—given the way I've set up the situation and the degree of bitterness the hypothetical "you" would likely feel. But whatever your own response, some people, perhaps reluctantly, would say, "Yes." They would prefer knowing to being deceived. They might want to experience a few of the things they've missed, even though they'd be living in a state of anxiety. They might want to say their goodbyes to family and friends. (If you're tempted to say that being miserably aware would be *happiness to them*, remember that's the empty meaning of "happiness" above in *D3*.)

The relative value of pleasurable illusion versus not-so-pleasurable reality was the basis of a thought experiment proposed by philosopher Robert Nozick (see Readings) in 1972. Borrowing a concept from science fiction, Nozick asked his readers to imagine an "experience machine" that could program the brain to have a lifetime of vivid, pleasurable experiences with no pain.

> Superduper neurologists could stimulate your brain so that you would think and feel you were writing a great novel, or making a friend, or reading an interesting book. All the time you would be floating in a tank, with electrodes attached to your brain.

Let's hypothesize that the machine is reliable, that the technology is sound, and that the machine is being offered as a public service by people you trust. Would you want to be hooked up to such a machine for the rest of your life?

Nozick says people would reject such a machine and argues as follows:

> What does matter to us in addition to our experiences? First, we want to *do* certain things, and not just have the experience of doing them.... A second reason for not plugging in is that we want to *be* a certain way, to be a certain sort of person. Someone floating in a tank is an indeterminate blob....Thirdly, plugging into an experience machine limits us to a man-made reality, to a world no deeper or more important than that which people can construct. There is no *actual* contact with any deep reality, though the experience of it can be simulated. Many persons desire to leave themselves open to such contact and to a plumbing of deeper significance....

Philosophers who present Nozick's thought experiment usually agree with Nozick that obviously "we" would reject such a machine. But that conclusion may not be so obvious these days given the growing fascination with virtual reality (even cybersex).

Talk of the experience machine is going to remind most of us of the 1999 movie, *The Matrix*. Human beings lie in pods; their bodies are being used to extract energy to power a devastated world run by intelligent machines that turned against their human creators. The humans in the pods are programmed with a simulated fantasy world. It's not as happy as Nozick's world, but rather a construct of the world of 1999. Even at that, Cypher, one of those who have escaped the simulated world, would rather go back to the simulation than face the harsher reality.

Building on Nozick and *The Matrix*, let's imagine a series of hypothetical worlds as follows: In all cases, there's an experience machine that will program you with a very pleasant life. But imagine that outside the machine lies a continuum of realities that range from wonderful to horrible. The most interesting question is, Where, if anywhere, on the continuum would you opt for the machine? Where, if anywhere, on the continuum would you opt to have your newborn child plugged in?

I think it's likely that if reality were bad enough, a lot of people would choose the machine for themselves and their children.

However, the central conceptual point still holds: Even though good feelings may be all-important to some people and very important to all of us most of the time, they are not the only things we desire and value. At a minimum, having contact with reality, being free, and having real accomplishments and relationships also matter. Happiness is not our only intrinsic personal value.

For the rest of our discussions, we will use the word happiness to refer to "subjective well-being," or "SWB" as psychologists dub it. The phrase is still a bit vague, but the point is to have a phrase that indicates subjective happiness so we don't get confused by other possible meanings of the term.

In recent years, researchers have taken an increased interest in studying SWB. The research is relatively new and sometimes controversial. But it is interesting to see what it implies for our personal lives. Further, the research is starting to be used as the basis for social policy proposals.

Happiness research

British psychologist Richard Layard defines happiness (SWB) as follows:

> By happiness I mean feeling good—enjoying life and wanting the feeling to be maintained. By unhappiness I mean feeling bad and wishing things were different....
>
> When it comes to how we feel, most of us take a longish view. We accept the ups and downs and care mainly about our average happiness over a longish period of time. But that average is made up from a whole series of moments....

How is happiness measured? One method is to ask people how happy their lives are, but there's the danger their generalized assessment might not correctly reflect the sum of their moods. One corrective is to ask people to divide the previous day into episodes, write down what they were doing and with whom, and rate each period for happiness—thus trying to evoke more specific mood memories. Another technique is to give people beepers that will be set off at random times: When the beeper goes off, people must write down what they are doing and how much they are enjoying it. (This is the type of study that fascinates Julia.)

People's reports on happiness have been collected over a number of years. According to researchers, these reports correlate well with how family and friends rate them on happiness scales.

What has the research on happiness tended to show? Let's structure our summary according to a "happiness formula" proposed by psychologist Martin Seligman.

$$H = S + C + V$$

H stands for your level of happiness. *S* stands for your biological "set range"—the range of happiness levels within which you are likely to fall given your genetics and environmental background; *C* stands for the circumstances of your life that you can't control at a given time; and *V* stands for the factors you can voluntarily control.

Since the 1980s there has been a growing body of evidence (primarily from studies of identical twins raised in different environments) that there is a considerable genetic component to our capacity for happiness. The evidence indicates a "set range," a range of mood in which an individual is likely to fall. For example, suppose Maya tends to fluctuate between "sort of unhappy" and "sort of happy." Maya might get really happy if she fell in love or won a tennis match or get really unhappy if bad things happened. However, she would always tend to return to her set range.

C (the circumstances you can't control) would include gender, age, basic looks, IQ and some aspects of one's health. Contrary to what most of us would expect, studies indicate that none of these factors has that much effect on happiness. Men and women tend to be equally happy or unhappy; people's happiness levels tend to remain rather stable throughout their lives, even in spite of declining health; and there isn't much of a correlation between happiness and basic looks, IQ or health.

V (factors over which you have some voluntary control) would include career, marriage, friendships, recreation, hobbies, charitable activities, and church attendance. The word "voluntary" has to be taken a bit loosely: Some people are going to find it easier to get into a satisfying relationship, find good friends, and find a good job. In fact, these things come easier to happy people than unhappy people—accounting for part, but only part, of the correlations.

If you were to consult the research with an eye to deciding how to live the happiest possible life for you—that is, to live a life that would give you a level of happiness near the top of your own "set range"— the recommendations would go something like this:

1. Get married or at least establish an ongoing intimate relationship;
2. Involve yourself with friends and a community;
3. Cultivate whatever religious or spiritual impulses you have;
4. Find work you enjoy and activities you can get engrossed in;
5. Try to make a good salary, but don't obsess about money or possessions;
6. Carve out for yourself as much leisure time as is compatible with the above activities;
7. Try to avoid comparing yourself with others, especially those who have more; live and hang out in places where unfavorable comparisons aren't forced upon you.
8. Give to others, joining with like-minded people in some giving activity.

Certain things on the list—marriage, family and friends, interesting work, and engrossing activities— will tend to feel worthwhile in themselves, whatever else is going on. So will having our basic needs met with adequate food, shelter, clothing, and security. Money and material goods matter, but above a certain level they tend not to affect our feelings of happiness/unhappiness (or, at least, affect those feelings to a diminishingly small degree). Further, the happiness we get from money and

material possessions is at risk of getting undermined by certain familiar psychological processes.

One such process is *adaptation*. Getting a raise, a promotion, a nicer car, a bigger house, or the latest gadget will make us happier, but not indefinitely, and maybe not even for long. After a while we adapt to what we have and will need more or better to maintain whatever happiness we have derived from them. Some researchers refer to this as the "hedonic treadmill"— where we have to keep running to stay in place: We need more to maintain the same level of happiness.

Often we are unaware of how pervasive adaptation is: We tend to get lured on by the illusion that if we just had more of this or that, we'd be happy. Being too much taken with this illusion can lead to frustration and a sense of emptiness.

Not only are money and material goods subject to adaptation; they are also what economists call "positional goods." How much we value them will depend in part on how much we have in relation to other people. It might be better to talk about a positional *dimension* to goods since that need be only one aspect of their value. We do enjoy our incomes, our houses, and our cars, but how happy they make us depends in part on how they compare to what our relatives, neighbors or coworkers have. If your house were suddenly transported from a modest neighborhood to a richer one, you would feel less happy with it.

Let's now consider personal values other than happiness.

Other personal values

Imagine you are a space traveler and come across two separate planets with very different civilizations:

On the first planet, "Planet Primeval," people live at a very basic level of civilization, comparable, say, to the transition between the hunter-gatherer stage and early agriculture. Thanks to an abundance of vegetation on this planet, people have a fairly easy life, though there are enough diseases to keep the population relatively stable. They have no writing, their music is only basic chants (and perhaps simple notes on a lute), and insofar as their mythological conception of the world attempts to convey the nature of the physical universe (as opposed to the spiritual), you can see that their myths are almost completely false.

On the second planet, "Planet Progresso," people have complex literature, music, and religion; advanced science and technology; architecture that is both functionally and artistically sophisticated; a complex social structure; and, a general picture of the universe that is much closer to the one your even more advanced civilization has developed.

Let us suppose that the people on Planet Primeval and those on Planet Progresso live comparably happy lives. If that supposition seems at all problematic to you, we can add additional suppositions that help balance out the happiness: We might imagine that the people on Planet Primeval live peacefully with each other and harmoniously with the physical world. We might suppose that on Planet Progresso competition, stress, and maybe occasional threats of war offset the real benefits for human happiness of greater wealth and more advanced medicine.

By hypothesis, if happiness were our only value, we'd have to say that both worlds were equally good or worthwhile. But many of us would say that Planet Progresso was the better world in that it exemplifies a greater development of human capacities. To use a term that has become popular in philosophy and psychology in recent years, the people on Planet Progresso have reached a higher level of human "flourishing."

The flowery-sounding word "flourishing" (which does in fact come from the Latin word for flower) is one of several attempts to come up with a word that doesn't really exist in English—a word that covers the development of certain worthwhile human capacities such as intelligence, inquisitiveness, adventurousness, courage, sensitivity, freedom, love, and spirituality.

"Excellence" conveys part of the meaning, but not all: It would be a stretch to talk about a sensitivity to the natural world in terms of excellence. Also, we want a term that allows for the development of individual capacities that may not achieve "excellence" in any objective sense.

"Self-development" conveys part of what we're after, but the phrase is too subjective: People sometimes talk about "self-development" when they are involved in flaky fads that don't necessarily involve challenge or produce a more admirable person.

"Character development" is another term that comes close.

The point of the two-planets fantasy is to show that a case can be made for viewing human flourishing, as well as happiness, as being intrinsically good.

Philosopher Jonathan Glover (see Readings) talks about using "binocular vision" to evaluate one's life, by which he means evaluating it on two levels or from two perspectives. One is an interior perspective, where I might wonder how happy I am and what I might do to be happier. The other is from an exterior perspective, where I might wonder how I'm doing in terms of developing my capacities, what I'm making of my life and relationships.

We can use such bi-level vision in evaluating others as well—evaluating them empathetically as to how they feel about their lives and evaluating them externally as to how their lives are in terms in terms of self-development and success. You can imagine parents saying about a child, "Well, he hasn't done much with his life, but at least he seems happy." Or: "She has accomplished so much, but I wish she enjoyed her life a bit more."

A third perspective will be added when we get to morality—as we are about to do. Think back to our example of the planets: I suspect there were some of you who felt that Planet Primeval was the better planet because its inhabitants lived peacefully with each other and in harmony with the physical world. I didn't bring that up at the time because we were focusing on the non-moral; however, a full evaluation of the planets would necessarily touch on happiness, flourishing, and various moral qualities. In this we would be balancing all three dimensions—using "tri-level" vision.

Moral Values

Moral values/issues in the story

Let's talk about Julia's moral values and those alluded to in the story?

Julia obviously wants to be a good wife and mother and is trying to make the effort to get along with her parents and in-laws. No doubt she wants to be a decent person living a decent life.

However, in terms of the great moral and social contests of the day, Julia is pretty much on the sidelines: She's a bit embarrassed about being so uninvolved and uninformed, but basically she's not that interested. She's focused on her own life, which feels hectic enough to her. She's amazed at people—such as her parents and in-laws—who have the time, energy and interest to be knowledgeably involved in the moral and political issues of the day.

A number of those larger issues are alluded to in the story, mostly in connection with the views of the parents and the mailings the parents are responsible for.

Julia's father-in-law, Charles, is an enthusiast of a free market system with a minimal level of government interference—including minimal government efforts to redistribute money to the poor. Charles is a Roman Catholic: However, like a lot of conservative American Catholics, he rejects the Church's view of social justice, believing the Church is naive about how wealth is created. Julia's parents, Anna and Victor, are socialists, wanting a social system that favors much greater equality and substantial help for the poor. The issue of world poverty is alluded to in reference to Julia's sympathy for starving children, though she quit making contributions to Save the Children after a year.

Julia wrestled with the question of whether or not to have an abortion, though there's some indication that her internal debate had more to do with a decision on lifestyle (marriage and family versus the single life with Stephanie in Europe) than the moral question of abortion. Charles is definitely anti-abortion, his opinion being in accord with the official Roman Catholic view. Julia's parents support abortion rights.

Elizabeth is concerned with the ethical treatment of animals. She isn't against killing animals for food, but she objects to the way animals are currently raised for food in factory farms. None of the others—Charles, Anna, or Viktor—has much sympathy with this issue.

I think we would all recognize the above as moral issues. The question is, What makes them *moral* issues rather than a different kind of issue? What are moral values versus personal values? What is morality?

What are moral values?

We will be discussing moral theory in the next chapter. Here we're only after a preliminary characterization of morality.

We will be using the terms "moral" and "ethical" interchangeably, as synonyms. Perhaps these words have different associations for you: "Morality" might suggest sexual restrictions, while "ethics" might suggest the code of a professional society. However, the two terms are synonyms and we will treat them as such.

When we're trying to decide what's moral versus immoral, or ethical versus unethical, we're doing what's called "normative ethics"—reasoning about what's right and wrong, just and unjust. When we're trying to characterize the moral versus the *non-moral*, we're doing what's called "metaethics"—getting "above" (normative) ethics to see what it's all about, trying to determine the meanings of ethical terms, trying to determine the logic of moral/ethical discourse and how it differs from, say, the aesthetic, legal or scientific.

A proper definition of morality should be broad enough to cover different sorts of moral views; it should be neutral, not slanted toward one view or another. When it comes to favoring one moral view over another, we should rely on argument, not definition.

Defining "morality" is no easier than defining "values." However, if we stick to generalities, we should be able to come up with some uncontroversial characteristics.

Remember the earlier quote about values being things "worth doing or worth being." We can build on that quote for the first of our general statements about morality.

1. *Moral values are those values that concern what people in general ought to do or be.*

There are a couple of shifts here from the simpler definition of value. We're now talking about *people in general*—not just me or you. And we've added the word "ought," introducing the element of obligation.

The eighteenth-century philosopher Immanuel Kant (see Readings, Part II) distinguished between hypothetical imperatives and categorical imperatives. A hypothetical imperative has the form, "If you want A, you ought to do B." "If you want to impress Mia, you ought to dress a little better." "If you want Lars to do you that favor, you ought to offer him something in return." With the hypothetical imperatives if you don't want to impress Mia or have Lars do you a favor, then the "oughts" don't apply. Kant thought that moral judgments were *not* hypothetical imperatives, but rather categorical imperatives. It wasn't that you weren't supposed to kill if you wanted to be liked or to avoid jail: It was, Don't kill, period.

Kant also took the word "categorical" to mean that moral rules such as "Do not lie" allowed no exceptions. We won't follow him in that. Virtually no one believes it is always wrong to kill or lie; we believe it would be acceptable to kill in self-defense or lie to a killer to throw him off. But once we've added the appropriate exceptions to our moral principle, "It's wrong to lie except when...." we can treat the resulting statement as categorical, not hypothetical.

There are some moral acts we would consider "above and beyond the call of duty," acts to which philosophers have given the horrible technical name "supererogatory" (from a Latin term meaning, roughly, "pay extra"). Still, "above and beyond" assumes a basic level of duty or obligation.

You will sometimes come across the phrase "personal morality." However, strictly speaking, there is no such thing as personal morality—not in the sense of a morality that only applies to a particular person. Values and standards you apply only to yourself are personal, not moral, values. Moral values are standards you think people in general have an obligation to try to measure up to.

Here are some other things we can say about morality.

2. *Moral judgments are not simply judgments of self-interest; they must take account of interests other than those of the speaker.*

At least to some degree, morality constrains self-interest. How much we think morality constrains self-interest will depend on what we think is in our self-interest and what we think is morally prohibited. But there will be some constraint. No matter how minimal one's morality, almost everyone would agree it would be morally wrong for me to kill a person for her property just because it was in my interest to do so.

We'll see that some philosophers try to justify morality to the individual as being in her long-term self-interest. However, there's still a big difference between trying to justify the whole institution of morality in terms of self-interest and trying to justify individual moral decisions in terms of it. A recruiter might convince me that it's in my long-term self-interest to join the Army: That doesn't mean I won't have to take some unpleasant orders once I've enlisted.

3. *Morality involves rules, but differs from other systems of rules such as law and etiquette.*

We often justify calling a particular act wrong by appealing to general rules such as "Do not kill" or "Stealing is wrong." Analogous prohibitions are incorporated into laws against murder and theft. There are a number of similarities between law and morality: Both are authoritative and involve sanctions; both often use similar language—for instance, terms like "duties" and "rights."

However, there are differences as well. Law in our society involves detailed written rules and regulations which are backed by the power of the state and enforced through criminal and civil penalties. Morality, insofar as it isn't incorporated in law, has a more abstract sort of authority, is not written out in such detail (if it can be considered written at all), and tends to be enforced through blame or praise (or, in one's own case, through guilt or pride). Morality is one of the perspectives we take when we formulate or critique laws.

There are some moral wrongs we wouldn't expect or want to be prohibited by law. Most people consider malicious gossip to be wrong, but it would be too difficult, costly and intrusive to make a law against it. Sometimes what the law prescribes or prohibits has to do simply with custom and order rather than morality. It doesn't matter which side of the road people drive on, just as long as it's the same side.

Rules of etiquette resemble rules of morality in governing human interactions, and some violations of etiquette can result in shame, or at least embarrassment. Certainly there are people to whom etiquette and fashion seem all-consuming. No doubt there are many hosts who would rather have as a guest someone who was convicted of fraud than someone who slurps his soup. However, most of us would agree that our most important moral rules supersede our most important rules of etiquette and fashion.

Note that violations of etiquette could overlap with morality insofar as they involve intentionally hurting another's feelings.

4. *Moral judgments can be made of persons or institutions. When made of persons, they can be made in terms of acts, intentions or character.*

Laws or social institutions can be judged just or unjust. So with the acts of the individual.

Historically, different moralities have had different emphases on acts, intentions, and character. For some of the ancient Greek philosophers, including Aristotle, the central emphasis of morality was on developing character traits that in today's view would be both moral (like being a just person) and non-moral (being a contemplative person).

Many religious moralities have treated intentions and even thoughts as morally crucial. In Matthew 5:28, Jesus said, "whoever looketh upon a woman to lust after her hath committed adultery with her already in his heart." The fear of damnation through impurity of the heart is part of what caused Martin Luther such anguish and led him to seek salvation through faith, not works.

On the other hand, some moral systems—for instance, utilitarianism, which seeks to promote the greatest happiness of the greatest number—emphasize acts; intentions have a secondary role. It's *what* you do, not *why* you do it, that really matters.

The foregoing statements about morality should be uncontroversial because they are minimal and general: As stated earlier, we want a neutral definition of morality; it would violate the idea of definition to try to define "morality" in a way that favored a particular moral view.

There are some things a neutral definition of morality can give us. If a person is using moral language to do nothing more than justify what is in her self-interest, she really isn't engaged in moral reasoning. Also, as in any reasoning, a person's moral judgments can be discounted if they are inconsistent or don't accord with the facts. The consistency requirement may yield some weak version of the Golden Rule: Judge others as you would judge yourself.

However sometimes definitions of morality include controversial characteristics that don't belong in a definition. One such characteristic is *universality*—the idea that moral rules apply to all human beings.

Kant claimed that moral rules were necessarily universal and could be recognized by subjecting them to a test we can think of as the ultimate Categorical Imperative: *Act only according to that maxim by which you can at the same time will that it should become a universal law.* The idea of moral rules as universal can be found in many religions, in the ancient Greek Stoics, and in many modern thinkers before Kant.

However, social contract theorists and cultural relativists argue that moral rules apply only within a particular society or culture. Some animal advocates and environmentalists argue that morality applies *to all human beings and beyond*—to animals or insentient natural things. The point is not that you should agree with these claims, but that such issues need to be settled through argument, not definition.

Another troublesome idea is that moral rules must be *impartial*. This idea is uncontroversial if we're talking about the kind of formal impartiality that, say, traffic laws have. For the law to treat one driver differently than another driver, there must be general and relevant reasons for the differential treatment—that the one driver is driving under the influence or exceeding the posted speed limit. Moral rules would hardly be rules if they weren't impartial in this sense.

But what about my feeling that it is morally acceptable for me to be partial to the welfare of myself, my family, and my friends as against the welfare of strangers—whether people in my society or in other parts of the world? Some philosophers will argue that such partiality—at least to the extent most of us practice it—is morally wrong. We don't want to try to settle that issue through definition.

This question of impartiality relates to a larger question of moral theory, namely how demanding morality is or should be. Some moralists claim that morality demands almost everything of us—our total devotion to God or to the poor. Others argue that morality demands almost nothing of us—just that we follow some basic rules and otherwise leave each other alone. Still others argue that while morality allows us considerable freedom to live our lives our way, it still demands more than most of us seem willing to give.

There's a related issue here of obligation and motivation. If morality demands too much, too few people will follow it: Morality becomes like a general marching into battle with no force behind him, his troops all having deserted. On the other hand, if what passes as morality fights no battles and demands almost nothing, one has to wonder if it really *is* morality: Humans are far from perfect; isn't the point of morality to at least push us to be better?

We will pursue these issues throughout this text, starting with the next chapter on moral theory. There we will discuss three different types of ethical theory, which we will call perfectionist ethics, sympathy ethics, and reciprocity ethics. We will view those ethics from three different metaethical perspectives: the God perspective, the idealized human perspective, and the unidealized human perspective.

However, before we move on, let's discuss briefly what psychologists tell us about in-built biases each of us brings to our moral reasoning.

Biased moral reasoning

There's a lot psychological research that shows that our reasoning is soaked through with self-serving bias. As psychologist Daniel Gilbert says in his book, *Stumbling on Happiness*:

> ... if you're like most people, then like most people, you don't know you're like most people. Science has given us a lot of facts about the average person, and one of the most reliable of these facts is that the average person doesn't see herself as average. Most students see themselves as more intelligent than the average student... Ninety percent of motorists consider themselves to be safer-than-average drivers.... Ironically, the bias toward seeing ourselves as better than average causes us to see ourselves as less biased than average too. As one research team concluded, "Most of us appear to believe that we are more athletic, intelligent, organized, ethical, logical, interesting, fair-minded, and healthy—not to mention more attractive—than the average person."

To a certain degree, a biased view of ourselves seems healthy—a crucial component in self-esteem: One

study indicates that the most accurate self-assessments come from people who are chronically depressed.

On the other hand, self-serving bias can play hell with our ethical thinking. As psychologist Jonathan Haidt points out (see Readings), it makes us think we deserve more than we do—leading to disputes with others—and it keeps us from taking responsibility for our actions.

Further, self-serving bias distorts our view of the world and hence colors our ethical judgments about it. We tend to exaggerate how much of our good fortune is the result of our merit and the degree to which other people's misfortunes are their fault.

Another bias is shown in the way we protect our beliefs to an irrational degree, both consciously and unconsciously. We see what we want to see and miss what we don't want to see. We focus on evidence that supports our beliefs and quickly reject any counter-evidence. We prefer the web sites, television shows, radio shows and newspapers that support our beliefs. We are susceptible to political sloganeering that turns opponents into caricatures and makes some simplistic position seem the only reasonable one.

Evidence gathered by Diana Mutz in her book, *Hearing the Other Side*, indicates that, compared to the citizens of eleven other countries, Americans are above average in the frequency in which they talk politics, but least likely to discuss politics with those holding different views. Interestingly, and depressingly, the richer and more educated Americans are, the less likely they are to have political discussions with people who disagree with them. (Part of the reason for this is that wealthier/better educated Americans tend to have greater choice about where they live; as Bill Bishop points out in his book, *The Big Sort*, Americans tend to move to communities with people most like themselves.)

It would be nice to think that you'll take advantage of this text to consider differing points of view; then, because you feel more comfortable with the issues, you'll be less inclined to avoid moral and political discussions with those who disagree with you.

I can be as dogmatic and pig-headed as the next person. That's why I was surprised and pleased when I looked back and realized I'd changed my mind on a lot of issues in the course of researching and writing this text— sometimes making a slight shift of position, sometimes a major one. The changes came from both a more in-depth look at the ethical arguments and a more in-depth look at the factual disputes connected with those arguments.

One thing I urge you to do is to note, after reading this book, where you might have changed your mind, becoming certain where you were less certain before or becoming uncertain where you'd felt certain before.

If all your thinking remains exactly the same after you've read and discussed the issues in this text, we both will have failed.

Notes and selected sources

Values

NOTES:

"What does the word 'value' mean…" From C. Dyke. *Philosophy of Economics*. Englewood Cliffs, NJ: Prentice-Hall, 1981, pp. 15–16.

Happiness as the ultimate personal value

NOTES:

Robert Nozick's discussion of the experience machine in his *Anarchy, State and Utopia*. New York: Basic Books, 1974, pp. 42–3.

Happiness research

SOURCES:

Jonathan Haidt. *The Happiness Hypothesis: Finding Modern Truth in Ancient Wisdom*. New York: Basic Books, 2006.

Richard Layard. *Happiness: Lessons from a New Science*. New York: Penguin, 2005.

Martin Seligman. *Authentic Happiness: Using New Positive Psychology to Realize Your Potential for Lasting Fulfillment*. New York: The Free Press, 2002.

NOTES:

"By happiness I mean…." Layard, pp. 12–13.

Reports on happiness, Layard, pp. 17–20.

Genes and happiness, Layard, pp. 55–60; Haidt, pp. 31–4.

Set point, predicting happiness, "formula," Seligman, pp. 45–50.

Adaptation, Layard, pp. 48–9.

Positional goods, Haidt, pp. 98–101; Layard, pp. 43–8.

Other personal values

NOTES:

Binocular vision re values from Jonathan Glover: *Choosing Children: Genes, Disability and Design*. Oxford: Clarendon Press, 2006, p. 93.

What are moral values?

NOTES:

A brief version of Immanuel Kant's discussion of the categorical imperative can be found in his *Fundamental Principles of the Metaphysic of Morals*. Trans. T.K. Abbott. New York: Prometheus Books, 1988. First Section.

Biased moral reasoning

SOURCES:

Bill Bishop. *The Big Sort*. Boston, MA: Houghton Mifflin, 2008.

Cordelia Fine. *A Mind of Its Own: How Your Brain Distorts and Deceives*. New York: W.W. Norton & Co., 2006.

Daniel Gilbert. *Stumbling on Happiness*. New York: Alfred A. Knopf, 2006.

Jonathan Haidt. *The Happiness Hypothesis: Finding Modern Truth in Ancient Wisdom*. New York: Basic Books, 2006.

Diane Mutz. *Hearing the Other Side*, Cambridge: Cambridge University Press, 2006.

NOTES:

"…if you're like most people…." Gilbert, p. 229.

Self-serving bias, Haidt, pp. 69–71.

Depression and self-assessment, Fine, p. 23.

Definitions

(Terms are defined in the order in which they appeared in the text.)

1. *Values*: Those things worth having, worth doing, or worth being. "Value" covers moral values, personal ideals, likes/dislikes and preferences.

2. *Factual judgment*: The sort of judgment that might be resolved though empirical evidence; "factual" here does not mean "true." (Factual judgments are contrasted loosely, and somewhat controversially, with value judgments.)

3. *Intrinsic good*: Something being good as an end. Contrasted with,

4. *Instrumental good*: Something good as a means. (Something can be good both intrinsically and instrumentally.)

5. *Happiness*: Subjective well-being (SWB).

6. *Set range*: A range of mood in which an individual is likely to fall (according to some psychologists).

7. *Adaptation*: Getting less happiness from something we've gotten used to having.

8. *Hedonic treadmill*: The idea that we must keeping getting more to maintain the same happiness level.

9. *Positional goods*: Those goods whose value to us depends on what others have.

10. *Flourishing*: Developing certain worthwhile human capacities such as intelligence, inquisitiveness, adventurousness, courage, sensitivity, freedom, love, and spirituality.

11. *Ethical* (synonym *moral*): A complex and much debated term designating a certain class of values. (See text and readings for a loose set of definitional characteristics.)

12. *Normative ethics*: Relating to what's right and wrong, just and unjust.

13. *Metaethics*: Relating to the general characteristics of all normative ethical judgments (in contrast to legal judgments, aesthetic judgments and so forth.)

14. *Hypothetical imperatives*: They state what you ought to do *if* you want to achieve something else.

15. *Categorical imperatives*: They state what you ought to do, *period*.

16. *Supererogatory*: That which is "above and beyond the call of duty."

17. *Utilitarianism*: That ethical system which says that an act is right if it promotes the greatest happiness of the greatest number.

18. *Universality* (in ethical theory): The idea that moral rules apply to all human beings

19. *The Categorical Imperative*: Kant's idea that morality requires us to "Act only according to that maxim by which you can at the same time will that it should become a universal law."

Questions

(Please explain your answers, making specific reference to relevant passages in the discussion.)

1. Explain the fact/value distinction. Are all judgments either wholly evaluative or wholly factual? Explain.

2. Explain the difference between intrinsic and instrumental goods. List some instrumental goods you would like to have and explain in what way they are instrumental.

3. What is the problem with the claim that happiness is the only ultimate (intrinsic) personal value?

4. Explain Nozick's "experience machine." What is this bit of science fiction supposed to show?

5. According to the current psychological research, what sorts of things are likely to have a substantial effect on people's happiness? What sorts of things are not?

6. How are the fictional planets Primeval and Progresso characterized? What is this bit of science fiction supposed to show?

7. What is the idea of "flourishing"? What are some related ideas?

8. Glover talks about evaluating a life using "binocular vision." What does he mean by this?

9. Explain the following distinctions: moral vs. nonmoral; metaethics vs. normative ethics.

10. Explain Kant's distinction between hypothetical and categorical imperatives. How do moral judgments fit in this scheme?

11. According to the text, what are some general noncontroversial characteristics of moral judgments?

12. According to the text, which of the following supposed characteristics of morality are controversial? Explain.
    (a) Moral rules apply to all human beings
    (b) Moral rules indicate what people ought to do or be
    (c) Moral rules sometimes constrain self-interest
    (d) Moral rules require that we treat everyone alike

13. According to psychologists, our reasoning is full of self-serving bias. What are some of the advantages of this? What are some of the disadvantages?

3

Values
Readings

TIME

Claudia Wallis writes about the "new science of happiness"

Sugary white sand gleams under the bright yucatan sun, aquamarine water teems with tropical fish and lazy sea turtles, cold Mexican beer beckons beneath the shady thatch of palapas—it's hard to imagine a sweeter spot than Akumal, Mexico, to contemplate the joys of being alive. And that was precisely the agenda when three leading psychologists gathered in this Mexican paradise to plot a new direction for psychology.

For most of its history, psychology had concerned itself with all that ails the human mind: anxiety, depression, neurosis, obsessions, paranoia, delusions. The goal of practitioners was to bring patients from a negative, ailing state to a neutral normal, or, as University of Pennsylvania psychologist Martin Seligman puts it, "from a minus five to a zero." It was Seligman who had summoned the others to Akumal that New Year's Day in 1998—his first day as president of the American Psychological Association (APA)—to share a vision of a new goal for psychology. "I realized

that my profession was half-baked. It wasn't enough for us to nullify disabling conditions and get to zero. We needed to ask, What are the enabling conditions that make human beings flourish? How do we get from zero to plus five?"

Every incoming APA president is asked to choose a theme for his or her yearlong term in office. Seligman was thinking big. He wanted to persuade substantial numbers in the profession to explore the region north of zero, to look at what actively made people feel fulfilled, engaged and meaningfully happy. Mental health, he reasoned, should be more than the absence of mental illness. It should be something akin to a vibrant and muscular fitness of the human mind and spirit.

Over the decades, a few psychological researchers had ventured out of the dark realm of mental illness into the sunny land of the mentally hale and hearty. Some of Seligman's own research, for instance, had focused on optimism, a trait shown to be associated with good physical health, less depression and mental illness, longer life and, yes, greater happiness. Perhaps the most eager explorer of this terrain was University of Illinois psychologist Edward Diener, aka Dr Happiness. For more than two decades, basically ever since he got tenure and could risk entering an unfashionable field, Diener had been examining what does and does not make people feel satisfied with life. Seligman's goal was to shine a light on such work and encourage much, much more of it.

To help him realize his vision, Seligman invited Ray Fowler, then the long-reigning and influential CEO of the APA, to join him in Akumal. He also invited Hungarian-born psychologist Mihaly Csikszentmihalyi (pronounced cheeks sent me high), best known for exploring a happy state of mind called flow, the feeling of complete engagement in a creative or playful activity familiar to athletes, musicians, video-game enthusiasts—almost anyone who loses himself in a favorite pursuit. By the end of their week at the beach, the three had plans for the first-ever conference on positive psychology, to be held in Akumal a year later—it was to become an annual event—and a strategy for recruiting young talent to the nascent field. Within a few months, Seligman, who has a talent for popularizing and promoting his areas of interest, was approached by the Templeton Foundation in England, which proceeded to create lucrative awards for research in positive psych. The result: an explosion of research on happiness, optimism, positive emotions and healthy character traits. Seldom has an academic field been brought so quickly and deliberately to life.

What makes us happy

So, what has science learned about what makes the human heart sing? More than one might imagine—along with some surprising things about what doesn't ring our inner chimes. Take wealth, for instance, and all the delightful things that money can buy. Research by Diener, among others, has shown that once your basic needs are met, additional income does little to raise your sense of satisfaction with life. A good education? Sorry, Mom and Dad, neither education nor, for that matter, a high IQ paves the road to happiness. Youth? No, again. In fact, older people are more consistently satisfied with their lives than the young. And they're less prone to dark moods: a recent survey by the Centers for Disease Control and Prevention found that people ages 20 to 24 are sad for an average of 3.4 days a month, as opposed to just 2.3 days for people ages 65 to 74. Marriage? A complicated picture: married people are generally happier than singles, but that may be because they were happier to begin with. Sunny days? Nope, although a 1998 study showed that Midwesterners think folks living in balmy California are happier

and that Californians incorrectly believe this about themselves too.

On the positive side, religious faith seems to genuinely lift the spirit, though it's tough to tell whether it's the God part or the community aspect that does the heavy lifting. Friends? A giant yes. A 2002 study conducted at the University of Illinois by Diener and Seligman found that the most salient characteristics shared by the 10% of students with the highest levels of happiness and the fewest signs of depression were their strong ties to friends and family and commitment to spending time with them. "Word needs to be spread," concludes Diener. "It is important to work on social skills, close interpersonal ties and social support in order to be happy."

Measuring our moods

Of course, happiness is not a static state. Even the happiest of people—the cheeriest 10%—feel blue at times. And even the bluest have their moments of joy. That has presented a challenge to social scientists trying to measure happiness. That, along with the simple fact that happiness is inherently subjective. To get around those challenges, researchers have devised several methods of assessment. Diener has created one of the most basic and widely used tools, the Satisfaction with Life Scale. Though some scholars have questioned the validity of this simple, five-question survey, Diener has found that it squares well with other measures of happiness, such as impressions from friends and family, expression of positive emotion and low incidence of depression.

Researchers have devised other tools to look at more transient moods. Csikszentmihalyi pioneered a method of using beepers and, later, handheld computers to contact subjects at random intervals. A pop-up screen presents an array of questions: What are you doing? How much are you enjoying it? Are you alone or interacting with someone else? The method, called experience sampling, is costly, intrusive and time consuming, but it provides an excellent picture of satisfaction and engagement at a specific time during a specific activity.

Just last month, a team led by Nobel-prizewinning psychologist Daniel Kahneman of Princeton University unveiled a new tool for sizing up happiness: the day-reconstruction method. Participants fill out a long diary and questionnaire detailing everything they did on the previous day and whom they were with at the time and rating a range of feelings during each episode (happy, impatient, depressed, worried, tired, etc.) on a seven-point scale. The method was tested on a group of 900 women in Texas with some surprising results. It turned out that the five most positive activities for these women were (in descending order) sex, socializing, relaxing, praying or meditating, and eating. Exercising and watching TV were not far behind. But way down the list was "taking care of my children," which ranked below cooking and only slightly above housework.

That may seem surprising, given that people frequently cite their children as their biggest source of delight—which was a finding of a TIME poll on happiness conducted last month. When asked, "What one thing in life has brought you the greatest happiness?", 35% said it was their children or grandchildren or both. (Spouse was far behind at just 9%, and religion a runner-up at 17%.) The discrepancy with the study of Texas women points up one of the key debates in happiness research: Which kind of information is more meaningful—global reports of well-being ("My life is happy, and my children are my greatest joy") or more specific data on enjoyment of day-to-day experiences ("What a night! The kids were such a pain!")? The two are very different, and studies show they do not correlate well. Our overall happiness is not merely the sum of our happy moments minus the sum of our angry or sad ones.

This is true whether you are looking at how satisfied you are with your life in general or with something more specific, such as your kids, your car, your job or your vacation. Kahneman likes to distinguish between the experiencing self and the remembering self. His studies show that what you remember of an experience is particularly influenced by the emotional high and low points and by how it ends. So, if you were to randomly beep someone on vacation in Italy, you might catch that person waiting furiously for a slow-moving waiter to take an order or grousing about the high cost of the pottery. But if you ask when it's over, "How was the vacation in Italy?", the average person remembers the peak moments and how he or she felt at the end of the trip.

The power of endings has been demonstrated in some remarkable experiments by Kahneman. One such study involved people undergoing a colonoscopy, an uncomfortable procedure in which a flexible scope is moved through the colon. While a control group had the standard procedure, half the subjects endured an extra 60 seconds during which the scope was held stationary; movement of the scope is typically the source of the discomfort. It turned out that members of the group that had the somewhat longer procedure with a benign ending found it less unpleasant than the control group, and they were more willing to have a repeat colonoscopy.

Asking people how happy they are, Kahneman contends, "is very much like asking them about the colonoscopy after it's over. There's a lot that escapes them." Kahneman therefore believes that social scientists studying happiness should pay careful attention to people's actual experiences rather than just survey their reflections. That, he feels, is especially relevant if research is to inform quality-of-life policies like how much money our society should devote to parks and recreation or how much should be invested in improving workers' commutes. "You cannot ignore how people spend their time," he says, "when thinking about well-being."

Seligman, in contrast, puts the emphasis on the remembering self. "I think we are our memories more than we are the sum total of our experiences," he says. For him, studying moment-to-moment experiences puts too much emphasis on transient pleasures and displeasures. Happiness goes deeper than that, he argues in his 2002 book Authentic Happiness. As a result of his research, he finds three components of happiness: pleasure ("the smiley-face piece"), engagement (the depth of involvement with one's family, work, romance and hobbies) and meaning (using personal strengths to serve some larger end). Of those three roads to a happy, satisfied life, pleasure is the least consequential, he insists: "This is newsworthy because so many Americans build their lives around pursuing pleasure. It turns out that engagement and meaning are much more important."

Can we get happier?

One of the biggest issues in happiness research is the question of how much our happiness is under our control. In 1996 University of Minnesota researcher David Lykken published a paper looking at the role of genes in determining one's sense of satisfaction in life. Lykken, now 76, gathered information on 4,000 sets of twins born in Minnesota from 1936 through 1955. After comparing happiness data on identical vs. fraternal twins, he came to the conclusion that about 50% of one's satisfaction with life comes from genetic programming. (Genes influence such traits as having a sunny, easygoing personality; dealing well with stress; and feeling low levels of anxiety and depression.) Lykken found that circumstantial factors like income, marital status, religion and education contribute only about 8% to one's overall well-being. He attributes the remaining percentage to "life's slings and arrows."

Because of the large influence of our genes, Lykken proposed the idea that each of us has a happiness set point much like our set point for body weight. No matter what happens in our life—good, bad, spectacular, horrific—we tend to return in short order to our set range. Some post-tsunami images last week of smiling Asian children returning to school underscored this amazing capacity to right ourselves. And a substantial body of research documents our tendency to return to the norm. A study of lottery winners done in 1978 found, for instance, that they did not wind up significantly happier than a control group. Even people who lose the use of their limbs to a devastating accident tend to bounce back, though perhaps not all the way to their base line. One study found that a week after the accident, the injured were severely angry and anxious, but after eight weeks "happiness was their strongest emotion," says Diener. Psychologists call this adjustment to new circumstances adaptation. "Everyone is surprised by how happy paraplegics can be," says Kahneman. "The reason is that they are not paraplegic full time. They do other things. They enjoy their meals, their friends. They read the news. It has to do with the allocation of attention."

In his extensive work on adaptation, Edward Diener has found two life events that seem to knock people lastingly below their happiness set point: loss of a spouse and loss of a job. It takes five to eight years for a widow to regain her previous sense of well-being. Similarly, the effects of a job loss linger long after the individual has returned to the work force.

When he proposed his set-point theory eight years ago, Lykken came to a drastic conclusion. "It may be that trying to be happier is as futile as trying to be taller," he wrote. He has since come to regret that sentence. "I made a dumb statement in the original article," he tells TIME. "It's clear that we can change our happiness levels widely—up or down." Lykken's revisionist thinking coincides with the view of the positive-psychology movement, which has put a premium on research showing you can raise your level of happiness. For Seligman and like-minded researchers, that involves working on the three components of happiness—getting more pleasure out of life (which can be done by savoring sensory experiences, although, he warns, "you're never going to make a curmudgeon into a giggly person"), becoming more engaged in what you do and finding ways of making your life feel more meaningful.

There are numerous ways to do that, they argue. At the University of California at Riverside, psychologist Sonja Lyubomirsky is using grant money from the National Institutes of Health to study different kinds of happiness boosters. One is the gratitude journal—a diary in which subjects write down things for which they are thankful. She has found that taking the time to conscientiously count their blessings once a week significantly increased subjects' overall satisfaction with life over a period of six weeks, whereas a control group that did not keep journals had no such gain.

Gratitude exercises can do more than lift one's mood. At the University of California at Davis, psychologist Robert Emmons found they improve physical health, raise energy levels and, for patients with neuromuscular disease, relieve pain and fatigue. "The ones who benefited most tended to elaborate more and have a wider span of things they're grateful for," he notes.

Another happiness booster, say positive psychologists, is performing acts of altruism or kindness—visiting a nursing home, helping a friend's child with homework, mowing a neighbor's lawn, writing a letter to a grandparent. Doing five kind acts a week, especially all in a single day, gave a measurable boost to Lyubomirsky's subjects.

Seligman has tested similar interventions in controlled trials at Penn and in huge experiments conducted over the Internet. The single most effective way to turbocharge your joy, he says, is to make a "gratitude visit." That means writing a testimonial thanking a teacher, pastor or grandparent—anyone to whom you owe a debt of gratitude—and then visiting that person to read him or her the letter of appreciation. "The remarkable thing," says Seligman, "is that people who do this just once are measurably happier and less depressed a month later. But it's gone by three months." Less powerful but more lasting, he says, is an exercise he calls three blessings—taking time each day to write down a trio of things that went well and why. "People are less depressed and happier three months later and six months later."

Seligman's biggest recommendation for lasting happiness is to figure out (courtesy of his website, reflectivehappiness.com) your strengths and find new ways to deploy them. Increasingly, his work, done in collaboration with Christopher Peterson at the University of Michigan, has focused on defining such human strengths and virtues as generosity, humor, gratitude and zest and studying how they relate to happiness. "As a professor, I don't like this," Seligman says, "but the cerebral virtues—curiosity, love of learning—are less strongly tied to happiness than interpersonal virtues like kindness, gratitude and capacity for love."

Why do exercising gratitude, kindness and other virtues provide a lift? "Giving makes you feel good about yourself," says Peterson. "When you're volunteering, you're distracting yourself from your own existence, and that's beneficial. More fuzzily, giving puts meaning into your life. You have a sense of purpose because you matter to someone else." Virtually all the happiness exercises being tested by positive psychologists, he says, make people feel more connected to others.

That seems to be the most fundamental finding from the science of happiness. "Almost every person

feels happier when they're with other people," observes Mihaly Csikszentmihalyi. "It's paradoxical because many of us think we can hardly wait to get home and be alone with nothing to do, but that's a worst-case scenario. If you're alone with nothing to do, the quality of your experience really plummets."

But can a loner really become more gregarious through acts-of-kindness exercises? Can a dyed-in-the-wool pessimist learn to see the glass as half full? Can gratitude journals work their magic over the long haul? And how many of us could keep filling them with fresh thankful thoughts year after year? Sonja Lyubomirsky believes it's all possible: "I'll quote Oprah here, which I don't normally do. She was asked how she runs five miles a day, and she said, 'I recommit to it every day of my life.' I think happiness is like that. Every day you have to renew your commitment. Hopefully, some of the strategies will become habitual over time and not a huge effort."

But other psychologists are more skeptical. Some simply doubt that personality is that flexible or that individuals can or should change their habitual coping styles. "If you're a pessimist who really thinks through in detail what might go wrong, that's a strategy that's likely to work very well for you," says Julie Norem, a psychology professor at Wellesley College and the author of The Positive Power of Negative Thinking. "In fact, you may be messed up if you try to substitute a positive attitude." She is worried that the messages of positive psychology reinforce "a lot of American biases" about how individual initiative and a positive attitude can solve complex problems.

Who's right? This is an experiment we can all do for ourselves. There's little risk in trying some extra gratitude and kindness, and the results—should they materialize—are their own reward.

Questions

1. According to the various psychologists, what things do and don't contribute significantly to people's happiness?
2. What is Lykken's "set point" theory? What is his evidence for this theory?
3. According to the various psychologists, what are some proven "happiness boosters."

Robert Nozick discusses his case of the "experience machine"

[...] Suppose there were an experience machine that would give you any experience you desired. Superduper neuropsychologists could stimulate your brain so that you would think and feel you were writing a great novel, or making a friend, or reading an interesting book. All the time you would be floating in a tank, with electrodes attached to your brain. Should you plug into this machine for life, preprogramming your life's experiences? If you are worried about missing out on desirable experiences, we can suppose that business enterprises have researched thoroughly the lives of many others. You can pick and choose from their large library or smorgasbord of such experiences, selecting your life's experiences for, say, the next two years. After two years have passed, you will have ten minutes or ten hours out of the tank, to select the experiences of your *next* two years. Of course, while in the tank you won't know that you're there; you'll think it's all actually happening. Others can also plug in to have the experiences they want, so there's no need to stay unplugged to serve them. (Ignore problems such as who will service the machines if everyone plugs in.) Would you plug in? *What else can matter to us, other than how our lives feel from the inside?* Nor should you refrain because of the few moments of distress between the moment you've decided and the moment you're plugged. What's a few moments of distress compared to a lifetime of bliss (if that's what you choose), and why feel any distress at all if your decision *is* the best one?

What does matter to us in addition to our experiences? First, we want to *do* certain things, and not just have the experience of doing them. In the case of certain experiences, it is only because first we want to do the actions that we want the experiences of doing them or thinking we've done them. (But *why* do we want to do the activities rather than merely to experience them?) A second reason for not plugging in is that we want to *be* a

certain way, to be a certain sort of person. Someone floating in a tank is an indeterminate blob. There is no answer to the question of what a person is like who has long been in the tank. Is he courageous, kind, intelligent, witty, loving? It's not merely that it's difficult to tell; there's no way he is. Plugging into the machine is a kind of suicide. It will seem to some, trapped by a picture, that nothing about what we are like can matter except as it gets reflected in our experiences. But should it be surprising that what *we are* is important to us? Why should we be concerned only with how our time is filled, but not with what we are?

Thirdly, plugging into an experience machine limits us to a man-made reality, to a world no deeper or more important than that which people can construct.[1] There is no *actual* contact with any deeper reality, though the experience of it can be simulated. Many persons desire to leave themselves open to such contact and to a plumbing of deeper significance. This clarifies the intensity of the conflict over psychoactive drugs, which some view as mere local experience machines, and others view as avenues to a deeper reality; what some view as equivalent to surrender to the experience machine, others view as following one of the reasons *not* to surrender!

We learn that something matters to us in addition to experience by imagining an experience machine and then realizing that we would not use it. We can continue to imagine a sequence of machines each designed to fill lacks suggested for the earlier machines. For example, since the experience machine doesn't meet our desire to *be* a certain way, imagine a transformation machine which transforms us into whatever sort of person we'd like to be (compatible with our staying us). Surely one would not use the transformation machine to become as one would wish, and thereupon plug into the experience machine! So something matters in addition to one's experiences *and* what one is like. Nor is the reason merely that one's experiences are unconnected with what one is like. For the experience machine might be limited to provide only experiences possible to the sort of person plugged in. Is it that we want to make a difference in the world? Consider then the result machine, which produces in the world any result you would produce and injects your vector input into any joint activity. We shall not pursue here the fascinating details of these or other machines. What is most disturbing about them is their living of our lives for us. Is it misguided to search for *particular* additional functions beyond the competence of machines to do for us? Perhaps what we desire is to live (an active verb) ourselves, in contact with reality. (And this, machines cannot do *for* us.) [...]

Questions

1. What is Nozick's experience machine? What is Nozick's point in imagining such a machine?

2. Nozick discusses other hypothetical machines. What do these machines do? What is Nozick's point in discussing them?

Note

1. This point was suggested to me by Mr Thom Krystofiak.

Jonathan Glover discusses the dual values of happiness and flourishing

[...]

In the history of philosophy there have been repeated attempts to give a clear and convincing account of a good human life. Here I will draw on two dominant traditions. In one tradition the key concept is human flourishing. [...]. But the idea of human flourishing may not fully capture the good life. For the other tradition, the key concept is happiness. This has its limitations too. Both terms are used in different ways, sometimes contrasting with each other and sometimes overlapping. I will suggest that the best account of the good life comes somewhere in the overlap between some versions of human flourishing and some versions of happiness.

[...]

Is there anything general that can be said about what human flourishing is? The good life for human beings is unlikely to be the same as the good life for chickens or for crocodiles. Our nature is different from theirs. Which aspects of our nature are most important for what the good life is?

A minimal, Darwinian view of human flourishing might specify only the physical and psychological functions needed for survival and reproduction. But, obviously, having these functions is compatible with having an awful life.

An alternative is the 'normal-functioning' version of human flourishing. This explains flourishing in terms of having the physical and psychological functions possessed by a 'normal' member of the species. These functions may have evolved because of their contribution to gene survival, but they are now seen as needs for different reasons. For instance, Philippa Foot says that human beings need the mental capacity for language and that they need 'powers of imagination that allow them to understand stories, to join in songs and dances—and to laugh at jokes'.[1]

Although there are questions about the boundaries of normality, this account of flourishing is useful as a contrast with disability. But it is inadequate as an account of the good life. People with disabilities can have good lives and people without disabilities can have bad ones. And the account seems too conservative. It seems to place no value on enriching people's lives

From *Choosing Children: Genes, Disability and Design*, by Jonathan Glover. Oxford: Clarendon Press, 2006, pp. 87–93.

in ways that take them above normality. The list of human goods tends to be drawn up on the basis of human life as we know it. There may be capacities, activities, and experiences that, being as yet untried, have not made it onto the list. We might still value them if we encountered them.

One danger of an account of this sort is that it may leave out how life feels. A life rich in the normal human capacities may still not be a flourishing life if the person takes a jaundiced or depressed view of it. The cards you are dealt make a difference, but so does how you play them.

Both the Darwinian and the normal-functioning accounts of human flourishing are too narrow. This makes it attractive to move towards an account in terms of certain 'human goods', things that contribute to what we understand a good human life to be.

Martha Nussbaum gives one account of these human goods.[2] She includes health, nourishment, shelter, sex, and mobility, as well as being able to use the senses and to imagine, think, and reason. Her account includes family and other relationships, attachments and love. Also on the list is living a life one has thought about and chosen, in one's own surroundings and context. There is also laughter, play, and living in contact with the natural world. One strength of such a list is that it gives an account of what is recognizably a good life for us rather than for Martians.

Martha Nussbaum's approach is a liberal version of Aristotelianism. It is not confined by the idea of normality. Her version takes account of how life seems to the person who lives it. And she explicitly recognizes that any list of distinctively human characteristics must be open-ended, to allow for the possibility that 'some as yet unimagined transformation in our natural options will alter the constitutive features, subtracting some and adding others'.[3]

The main alternative to the 'human-flourishing' account of the good life is the utilitarian account in terms of happiness. This has the advantage of being based from the start on how people feel about their lives. But, notoriously, accounts of happiness given by utilitarians have sometimes been too narrow.

The simplest account of happiness is the 'experience' version. Jeremy Bentham gave this its classic expression: 'enjoyment of pleasures, security from pains'.[4] Obviously pleasure is an important part of the good life. And pain often makes life less good. But the experience version is far too narrow to capture the good life. Robert Nozick's classic 'experience-machine' thought experiment neatly makes the point. Imagine some future machine that can stimulate the brain to give any set of experiences. The machine's programming can be adapted to the tastes of the particular person. As a result, people can be offered a lifetime of experiences of intense pleasure and no pain. Would you be willing to be hooked up to such a machine for the rest of your life?

Most people asked this question say 'no'. Sometimes this is for reasons that are practically important but philosophically superficial. Can we really rely on the technology? How do we know the programmer is benevolent? Do we not need a bit of bad experience to heighten the pleasure by contrast? As this is a thought experiment, we can just postulate reliability, benevolence, and just the right small dose of bad experience needed to maximize the pleasure.

But people say 'no' also for deeper reasons, reflecting features of the good life that go beyond blissful experience. Nozick lists three of these. We want to do things, not just passively to receive experiences. We care about the kind of person we are. But someone floating in a tank has no characteristics: 'plugging into the machine is a kind of suicide'. And we also want to be in touch with a reality that is not artificially constructed by people.[5]

Over many years I have asked people their reactions to the experience machine, and have been struck by the way that even those who have not read Nozick's book often make his objections. This suggests that many people have ideas of the good life that make Bentham's experience version seem narrow.

The thought experiment is a powerful counter-example to the experience version of the good life. But it is no objection at all to a different utilitarian account. This sees happiness as the satisfaction of desires. The more people's desires are satisfied, the greater their happiness. (Though the satisfactions [sic] of stronger desires counts more.) If some of our strongest desires are to be active rather than passive, to be a certain sort of person and to be in touch with a reality that is not man-made, the experience machine will not give us happiness.

Compared to the experience account, the desire–satisfaction version allows for more aspects of the good life. But in turn it is too simple. The desires people have may be based on ignorance or on mistaken beliefs. So perhaps happiness should be seen as the satisfaction of informed desires: not the ones people actually have but those they would have if they only knew.

This still may be too narrow an account of happiness. Happiness can come from things that surprise us: things not thought of and so not desired. The account may also be too broad. The satisfaction of some informed desires may not be relevant to happiness. James Griffin gives the case of meeting someone on a train who tells me his ambitions. I form a strong, informed desire for his success, but never hear of him again. His later success satisfies my informed desire but leaves my life unchanged. On the other hand, my desires for the success of my children, are usually relevant. As Griffin says, we need to include only those informed desires that 'enter our lives' in the way this contrast brings out.[6]

There are also 'pathological' desires—for instance, those of misers or kleptomaniacs—which seem so distorted that losing them might be better for the person than satisfying them. Perhaps 'informed' desire could be stretched to exclude these cases. But the central issue seems to be the warping or distortion of the desires rather than any lack of information. [...]. John Elster's idea of adaptive preferences ('sour grapes') and Amartya Sen's thoughts about the scaled-down preferences of women in some developing countries are relevant here. To accommodate this, the desire version of happiness has to be liberalized to include some kind of evaluation of the desires themselves. And this requires some judgement about how rich different kinds of life are. Happiness is not just contentment or satisfaction, but also requires a certain richness of life.

Both the versions of the good life (as human flourishing and as happiness) start off too narrow. They become more plausible as they are liberalized. The liberalizing tends towards convergence. The Aristotelian version has to take account, not just of 'functioning' seen objectively from outside, but also of how a life seems to the person living it. It also has to become open-ended, allowing for changes possibly going beyond current views of human flourishing. The utilitarian version has to bring in some evaluation of experiences or desires. And this evaluation is likely to be linked to some idea of a rich human life.

Often it is not easy to assess how good a life someone is having. What the person says is obviously central, but may not give a complete picture. People claiming to be glad to be alive may not be telling us everything. They may be protecting their own self-respect, not wanting to be pitied. Even accurate and truthful reports need interpretation. There is the problem of how far the person's preferences and judgement have been shaped or distorted by the kind of life they have had. We need other sources of information too.

When we see the world in three dimensions, our visual system detects depth partly by combining information from both our eyes, and works out distances from the discrepancy between them. To see to the depths of a person, we need the equivalent of binocular vision: the person's own perspective and other perspectives for comparison.

The binocular vision we need corresponds to two strands of the good life. One strand is about the fit between what you want and value and what your life is like. Part of having a good life is being happy, in the (limited) sense of being reasonably content with how your life is going. The second strand is about how rich your life is in human goods: what relationships you have with other people, your state of health, how much you are in charge of your own life, how much scope for creativity you have, and so on.

Questions

1. According to Glover, an account of the good life must take account of what two dominant traditions?

2. "The good life is a life of happiness, defined as the satisfaction of desires." According to Glover, Nozick's experience machine argument doesn't count against the claim quoted above. Why not? According to Glover, what does count against this claim?

Notes

1. Philippa Foot, *Natural Goodness* (Oxford: Clarendon Press, 2001), 43.

2. Martha Nussbaum, 'Aristotelian Social Democracy', in Gillian Brock (ed.), *Necessary Goods: Our Responsibilities to Meet Others' Needs* (Lanham, MD: Rowman & Littlefield, 1998), 135–56.

3. Ibid. 146.

4. Jeremy Bentham, *The Principles of Morals and Legislation* (New York: Hafner, 1948), ch. 7.

5. Nozick, *Anarchy, State and Utopia*, 42–5.

6. James Griffin, *Well-Being: Its Meaning, Measurement and Importance* (Oxford: Clarendon Press, 1986), 16–26.

Patrick Grim asks what makes a life good, distinguishing between "lives to envy" and "lives to admire"

[…]

There are radically different ways in which a life can be thought of as good. What I want to do is to disentangle two of those ways; two major, but ultimately conflicting senses in which one can seek to make one's life a good life.

There are, first of all, lives that we envy. There are, in fact, many types of enviable life. One kind of life we might envy is a life of adventure; a life filled with the joys of exploration, perhaps, or the ecstasies of discovery. There are lives that glow with a sense of accomplishment, lived with boldness and gusto. Who wouldn't want such a life? Now there, we think, is a good life. That's the kind of life you'd want for yourself; that's the kind of life you'd wish for your children. We can all think of people who seem to have enviable lives. Bill Gates might be on that list, for some people at least, or Johnny Depp. More seriously, consider the remarkable life of Benjamin Franklin. We have a successful businessman and publisher; he's applauded worldwide for his inventions and for his fundamental discoveries regarding electricity. He's a towering statesman. He's a father. He's also one of the founding fathers of our nation. Now there was a life.

Reproduced with permission from *Questions of Value*, by Patrick Grim. Chantilly, VA: The Teaching Company, 2005, Transcript, part I, lecture 3. © 2005 The Teaching Company. Reproduced with permission of The Teaching Company, www.thegreatcourses.com.

Enviable lives that we can imagine feeling from the inside, as it were, and we envy that feeling. Wouldn't it have been great to be Teddy Roosevelt; to feel the bravado, the energy, the curiosity and the ambition of pursuing that life? That looks like a bully life. Abraham Lincoln's life doesn't look nearly so attractive from the inside. Despite his jokes, his is a life pervaded with a deep melancholy. Trapped in a bitter marriage, seeing a son die, rising to the presidency only to face the bloodiest war the country had ever seen. When you look at photographs of Lincoln in 1860 and when you look at photographs of him five years later, it could be a different man; he looks like he's aged 20 years in those five. And, of course, his life ends with an assassin's bullet. Who would wish that life on their children? Some lives are worthy of envy and some are not. Those are what I'm calling enviable lives.

But enviable lives are not the only kind of good life. There's another kind of good life—there are also *admirable* lives; lives the living of which we admire. It is on this list that Lincoln's life belongs, for example. Although it was far from enviable, far from a life we would want to live from the inside, Lincoln's life was surely a life that was well spent. Without Lincoln, without Lincoln's life, without that life, some basic moves toward the abolishment of slavery in our country, some basic moves toward justice, either wouldn't have been made, or wouldn't have been made so soon. It is on this radically different list of admirable lives that belong biographies of self-sacrifice and biographies of dedication to others. Maybe FDR's life belongs on that list, complete with its polio and its pain and with the horrors of the depression and of World War II. Maybe the lives of Ghandi [sic] or Martin Luther King belong on that list, the list of the admirable lives.

It is here that should be listed those lives dedicated to some greater cause; lives often full of suffering, incumbent on trying to further that greater cause. These are the lives we admire. We wish our lives could have the impact and the consequence of those. But we often know that those lives were far from pleasant. Much as we admire the accomplishments that come with those lives, the accomplishments that those lives represent, we don't envy the living of those lives.

There is a phrase in Aristotle's *Nicomachean Ethics* [...] "let us consider whether happiness is among the things that are praised or rather among the things that are prized." That's the distinction I am after, though I'm not talking about happiness, but about lives, or about lives as a whole. [...] Aristotle, in the passage just quoted, applies it to happiness. That sounds radically different; but in fact, in the end, it is not so very different.

The core term in Aristotle, the core term throughout the *Nicomachean Ethics*, is "eudaimonia." [...] Eudaimonia is what the *Nicomachean Ethics* is really all about; it's about what eudaimonia is, and how you go about getting it. The term is standardly translated as "happiness." If you translate eudaimonia as happiness, since the *Nicomachean Ethics* is all about eudaimonia, what that would tell you is that one of Aristotle's central concerns is what happiness is and how we are to obtain it. But, as many translators of Aristotle will tell you, happiness is an extremely poor translation for the original Greek term, eudaimonia. A much better translation is "well-being." So the *Nicomachean Ethics* isn't all about happiness; it's about well-being. Some people suggest the term "human flourishing." If you translate eudaimonia as human flourishing, then the central concern of Aristotle's *Nicomachean Ethics* is what human flourishing is and how you obtain it. So Aristotle is talking about whether eudaimonia, or human flourishing, in this passage we just quoted, he's talking about whether eudaimonia, human well-being or human flourishing, is something to be praised or something to be prized. That's not ultimately so distant from what I am asking, in asking whether it is an enviable life or an admirable life that makes something a good life.

[...]

Much of the ethical tradition in ancient Greek and Roman philosophy, which was carried over into medieval philosophy, is an attempt to paint a consistent picture of the good life that brings these two ideals— the enviable and the admirable—together in some kind of harmony. Throughout Greek and Roman, and later medieval, philosophy, you find the pursuit of the *summon bonum*—the highest good, or the good life— as something that's somehow going to combine these two aspects, the enviable and the admirable in a life. One attempt at reconciling those two things appears in Plato's dialogue the *Republic*. What I have called "the admirable life" is what Plato calls "the life of virtue." What I have called "the enviable life" is what Plato calls the life that is "good for its bearer." So, the "life of virtue," the life that's "good for its bearer"; the admirable life, the enviable life. In the *Republic*, Plato's attempt is to insist that these two kinds of lives are ultimately the same; that it is the admirable life that is really the enviable life; that it is the "life of virtue" that is ultimately the life that's "good for its bearer." Plato's attempt is to equate the two—the enviable and the admirable life, the "life of virtue" and the life that's "good for its bearer." I think there's something right in Plato's attempt, and something admirable in Plato's attempt to equate those. But I think there's also something that's definitely wrong.

What is right is that aspects of an admirable life contribute to a genuinely enviable life. In fact, aspects of an admirable life may even be necessary for a genuinely enviable life. Here's the argument: could one rationally, and on reflection, envy a life that was dedicated purely to the pursuit of the bearer's own pleasure, to the pursuit of pleasure of the person whose life it was? Could one rationally and on reflection envy a life that was self-centered in that sense? I don't think so. [...] What we've imagined there is the ultimate Playboy life; and would that be enough for a genuinely enviable life? Well, it certainly wouldn't qualify as enviable in comparison to a life which also contained elements of achievement and joys of genuine accomplishment, or moments of human sharing.

And the crucial truth about all those things—about achievement, genuine accomplishment, moments of human sharing—is that they all involve some aspect of self-sacrifice. [...] A fully enviable life, a life that's fully acceptable even from the inside, must have at least some of the marks of self-sacrifice in pursuit of something larger. That's what I think is right about Plato's effort at reconciling the admirable and the enviable [...].

What's wrong, I think, in Plato is the attempt to equate the two categories, the claim that they are simply one and the same. What's wrong is the insistence that it is the purely admirable life, and only the purely admirable life, that is truly enviable. In the *Republic*, Plato seems, to have wanted that to be true. It would have been so clean and neat for it to be true if these were to be equated, if they were one and the same. But in the end, I think, we have to admit that Plato's picture doesn't ring true of life as we know it. A simple observation shows that the two forms of good in a life, or the two forms of good life can't be strictly identified; they can't be strictly equated. The simple observation is this: that a truly admirable life can, nonetheless, be far from enviable. You can have a fully admirable life and not have an enviable life. A life can be deeply admirable, and yet constitute pure torment from the inside that could be a life filled with essentially nothing but the toll of self-sacrifice. That doesn't mean, of course, that that kind of life would be without value, or even that it was perceived as without value from the inside. In terms of one category of value, the category of the admirable, that would be the supremely good life. But it might still be a life devoid of value from the other category, from a different category. A life can be admirable in the highest degree, and enviable to almost no degree at all.

[...]

[...] What if we could teach ourselves to value only the admirable? What if we could teach ourselves to value only the virtues of self-sacrifice? Then maybe our lives could be stable in value. That sounds like the path of sainthood, perhaps; of complete virtuous self-denial, the path of asceticism. Even that attempt at resolution, I think, is ultimately unsuccessful. First of all, what would it mean to teach yourself to value only those things? The other aspects of life—the enviable—are genuinely good things in a life. That includes joys of family, joys of community, joys of curiosity and play and self-expression. In speaking of a life of self-sacrifice, it is precisely these that we envisage being sacrificed. But because they are genuinely of value, a life of self-sacrifice [...] would be a life worse, in certain regards, than it could be. [...]

A second point is that even a life devoted to self-sacrifice might also not ultimately be as consistent as it looks. The ascetic goal is to value only the self-sacrificial virtues of the admirable life. But were one to pursue a life of self-sacrifice for others, precisely what would it be in others' lives that one was sacrificing for? There is a quote to this effect that may come from Evelyn Waugh, author of *Brideshead Revisited*. "I know that we are here for others; what I haven't figured out is what the others are for." In a life of a sacrifice, one is sacrificing oneself so that others can suffer less or enjoy more, can benefit the opportunities of self-development and self-fulfillment; can feel the warmth of the sun on their shoulders and glory in the joy of their children surrounding them. But those are the enviable aspects of life. So, despite the attempt then, one doesn't value only the self-sacrificial virtues in such a life. It is still the enviable aspects for which one is sacrificing. If those things are of such value in other people's lives, moreover, they must still be of potential value in one's own life. Even within the ideal of a life dedicated to the pursuit of the purely admirable, there is still this basic tension.

[...]

Questions

1. Explain Grim's distinction between an enviable life and an admirable life.
2. Grim talks about Plato's attempt to equate the enviable life and the admirable life. What does Grim think is right about this attempt? Why does Grim think the attempt ultimately fails?

Louis P. Pojman, Richard Joyce and Shaun Nichols give their views on what morality is

Louis P. Pojman

A central feature of morality is the moral principle. We have already noted that moral principles are practical action guides, but we must say more about the traits of such principles. Although there is no universal agreement on the traits a moral principle must have, there is a wide consensus about five traits:

1. Prescriptivity
2. Universalizability
3. Overridingness
4. Publicity
5. Practicability

Prescriptivity

Prescriptivity refers to the practical, or action-guiding, nature of morality. Moral principles are generally put forth as injunctions or imperatives (e.g., "Do not kill," "Do no unnecessary harm," and "Love your neighbor"). They are intended for use, to advise people and influence action. Prescriptivity shares this trait with all normative discourse. Retroactively, this trait is used to appraise behavior, assign praise and blame, and produce feelings of satisfaction or guilt. [...]

Universalizability

Moral principles must apply to all who are in the relevantly similar situation. If one judges that act X is right for a certain person P, then it is right for anyone relevantly similar to P. This trait is exemplified in the Golden Rule, "Do unto others what you would have them do unto you (if you were in their shoes)," and in the formal principle of justice:

> It cannot be right for A to treat B in a manner in which it would be wrong for B to treat A, merely on the

ground that they are two different individuals, and without there being any difference between the natures or circumstances of the two which can be stated as a reasonable ground for difference of treatment.[1]

Universalizability applies to all evaluative judgments. If I say that X is a good Y, then I am logically committed to judge that anything relevantly similar to X is a good Y. This trait is an extension of the principle of consistency: One ought to be consistent about one's value judgments, including one's moral judgments. [...]

Overridingness

Moral principles have hegemonic authority. They are not the only principles, but they take precedence over other considerations, including aesthetic, prudential, and legal ones. The artist Paul Gauguin may have been aesthetically justified in abandoning his family in order to devote his life to painting beautiful Pacific island pictures, but morally, or all things considered, he probably was not justified. It may be prudent to lie to save my reputation, but it probably is morally wrong to do so, in which case I should tell the truth. When the law becomes egregiously immoral, it may be my moral duty to exercise civil disobedience. There is a general moral duty to obey the law, since the law serves an overall moral purpose, and this overall purpose may give us moral reasons to obey laws that may not be moral or ideal. But there may come a time when the injustice of a bad law is intolerable and hence calls for illegal but moral defiance (such as the antebellum laws in the South requiring citizens to return slaves to their owners). Religion is a special case: Many philosophers argue that a religious person may be morally justified in following a perceived command from God that overrides a normal moral rule. John's pacifist religious beliefs may cause him to renege on an obligation to fight for his country. Religious morality is morality, and ethics recognizes its legitimacy. [...]

Publicity

Moral principles must be made public in order to guide our actions. Because we use principles to prescribe behavior, give advice, and assign praise and blame, it would be self-defeating to keep them a secret. [...]

Practicability

A moral theory must be workable; its rules must not lay a heavy burden on agents. Philosopher John Rawls speaks of the "strains of commitment"[2] that overly idealistic principles may cause in average moral agents. It might be desirable for morality to enjoin more altruism, but the result of such principles could be moral despair, deep or undue moral guilt, and ineffective action. Practicability may cause the difference between ethical standards over time and place. For instance, there is a discrepancy between Old Testament and New Testament ethics on such topics as divorce and the treatment of one's enemy. Jesus explained both these discrepancies. He said that, because of society's hardness of heart, God permitted divorce in pre-Christian times. Jesus also said that, in the future, it would be a valid principle to love one's enemies and pray for them, and he enjoined his disciples to begin living by this ideal morality. Most ethical systems take human limitations into consideration.

Since moral philosophers disagree somewhat about the above traits, discussing these traits fully would lead to a great deal of qualification. However, the present discussion should give you an idea of the general features of moral principles.

[...]

Richard Joyce

[...] What, then, *is* a moral judgment? [...]

- Moral judgments (as public utterances) are often ways of expressing conative attitudes, such as approval, contempt, or, more generally, subscription to standards; moral judgments nevertheless also express beliefs; i.e., they are assertions.
- Moral judgments pertaining to action purport to be deliberative considerations irrespective of the interests/ends of those to whom they are directed; thus they are not pieces of prudential advice.
- Moral judgments purport to be inescapable; there is no "opting out."

From *The Evolution of Morality,* by Richard Joyce. Cambridge, MA: MIT Press, 2006, pp. 70–2. © 2006 Massachusetts Institute of Technology, by permission of The MIT Press.

- Moral judgments purport to transcend human conventions.
- Moral judgments centrally govern interpersonal relations; they seem designed to combat rampant individualism in particular.
- Moral judgments imply notions of desert and justice (a system of "punishments and rewards").
- For creatures like us, the emotion of guilt (or "a moral conscience") is an important mechanism for regulating one's moral conduct.

Something to note about this list is that it includes two ways of thinking about morality: one in terms of a distinctive subject matter (concerning interpersonal relations), the other in terms of what might be called the "normative form" of morality (a particularly authoritative kind of evaluation). Both features deserve their place, and any hypothesis concerning the evolution of the human moral faculty is incomplete unless it can explain how natural selection would favor a kind of judgment with *both* these features.

Some of these features can be thought of merely as observations of features of human morality, whereas others very probably deserve the status of conceptual truths about the very nature of a moral judgment. But by and large this delicate philosophical distinction is something that doesn't need to be settled in this book, and so I am content to leave it be. Thus I am not claiming that this list succeeds in capturing the necessary and sufficient conditions for moral judgments. It is doubtful that our concept of *a moral judgment* is sufficiently determinate to allow of such an exposition. The sensibly cautious claim to make is that so long as a kind of value system satisfies *enough* of the above, then it counts as a moral system. A somewhat bolder claim would be that some of the items on the list (at least one but not all) are necessary features, and enough of the remainder must be satisfied in order to have a moral judgment. In either case, how much is "enough"? It would be pointless to stipulate. The fact of the matter is determined by how we, as a linguistic population, would actually respond if faced with such a decision concerning an unfamiliar community: If they had a distinctive value system satisfying, say, four of the above items, and for this system there was a word in their language (say, "woogle values"), would we translate "woogle" into "moral"?

It's not my place to guess with any confidence how that counterfactual decision would go. All I am claiming is that the above items would all be important considerations in that decision. [...]

It is possible that there are some important characteristics missing from the list. Some may simply not have occurred to me; others I have left out on purpose. It has been argued, for example, that one of the distinctive features of a moral judgment is that it is a *universal* prescription. [...] I have always found this a dubious assertion, both as a conceptual claim and as an empirical observation. Having our moral prescriptions be universalizable may well be a worthy goal, but saying this is very different from holding that they necessarily must be universalizable or else they don't even count as "moral." Many communities have value systems that we don't hesitate to call "moral," but which allow for *particular* judgments. For example, many (if not most) moral systems allow for strong distinctions to be made between community members and outsiders. Such distinctions *can* be supported by a universal judgment—e.g. "Anybody has special duties toward members of his or her community"—but it seems unlikely that they actually typically are derived from such a universal support. The Yanomamö people were once notorious for thinking nothing of killing any foreigners encountered. Who is to say that they conceived of "foreigner" as a universal category? Perhaps it just meant *anyone who is not a Yanomamö*, and perhaps this amounted to *anyone who is not descended from the blood of Periboriwa*. The fact that I don't know whether their understanding of "foreigner" was universal or ineliminably particular doesn't mean that I should remain correspondingly uncommitted about whether their rule "It is permissible to kill foreigners" counted as a *moral* liberty. [...]

Shaun Nichols

Many of the deepest issues concerning the nature of morality would be illuminated if we had an adequate account of the nature of moral judgment. [...] The

From *Sentimental Rules: On the Natural Foundations of Moral Judgment*, by Shaun Nichols. Oxford: Oxford University Press, 2004, pp. 4–7.

exploration of moral judgment in psychology stretches back for a century, through Kohlberg and Piaget. The philosophical lineage is much longer and enjoys an even more distinguished cast, including Kant, Hume, and Aristotle.

Throughout the twentieth century, philosophical work in metaethics largely ignored the psychological literature on moral judgment. Part of the explanation for this, I suspect, is simply that much of the best known psychological work seems not to intersect directly with the issues philosophers care about. Much of the psychological work on the nature of morality, for instance, charts developmental changes, gender differences, and cultural variations in moral cognition. But this kind of work seems not to address the core of morality—it does not tell us what is at the heart of moral judgment. As a result, it does not tell us what we want to know in metaethics. Over the last twenty years, a tradition in moral psychology has developed that really does, I will maintain, help us understand the nature of moral judgment. The research explores the ability to appreciate the distinctive status of morality, as reflected by the capacity to distinguish moral from conventional transgressions. [...]

In the psychological literature, the capacity for moral judgment has perhaps been most directly approached empirically by exploring the basic capacity to distinguish moral violations (e.g., pulling another person's hair) from conventional violations (e.g., chewing gum in class). This tradition in psychology began with the work of Elliott Turiel and has flourished over the last two decades (Turiel, Killen, and Helwig 1987; Dunn and Munn 1987; Smetana and Braeges 1990; Nucci 1986; Blair 1993). Turiel explicitly draws on the writings of several philosophers, including Searle, Brandt, and Rawls to draw the moral/conventional distinction. The distinction is characterized as follows: "Conventions are part of constitutive systems and are shared behaviors (uniformities, rules) whose meanings are defined by the constituted system in which they are embedded" (Turiel, Killen, and Helwig 1987, 169). Moral rules, on the other hand, are "unconditionally obligatory, generalizable, and impersonal insofar as they stem from concepts of welfare, justice, and rights" (Turiel, Killen, and Helwig 1987, 169–70). Although Turiel adverts to philosophical precedent for this distinction, the attempt to draw an analytic distinction between morality and convention is fraught with controversy. Fortunately, it is a controversy we can ignore. For we do not need to supply an analysis to see the significance of the data. The research program generated by Turiel's work indicates that people distinguish moral violations from conventional violations along several dimensions.

Rather than embark on an attempt to define the moral and conventional domains, the easiest way to see the import of the data on moral judgment is to consider how subjects distinguish canonical examples of moral violations from canonical examples of conventional violations. Hitting another person is a canonical example of a moral violation used in these studies. Other frequently used examples of moral violations are pulling hair, stealing, and pushing another child. The examples of conventional violations that have been studied are much more varied. Some of the examples are violations of school rules, such as not paying attention during story time or talking out of turn. Some of the examples are violations of etiquette, such as drinking soup out of a bowl. Other examples are violations of family rules, such as not clearing one's dishes. What is striking about this literature is that, from a young age, children distinguish the moral violations from the conventional violations on a number of dimensions. For instance, children tend to think that moral transgressions are generally less permissible and more serious than conventional transgressions. Children are also more likely to maintain that the moral violations are "generalizably" wrong, for example, that pulling hair is wrong in other countries too. And the explanations for why moral transgressions are wrong are given in terms of fairness and harm to victims. For example, children will say that pulling hair is wrong because it hurts the person. By contrast, the explanation for why conventional transgressions are wrong is given in terms of social acceptability—talking out of turn is wrong because it is rude or impolite, or because "you're not supposed to." Further, conventional rules, unlike moral rules, are viewed as dependent on authority. For instance, if at another school the teacher has no rule against chewing gum, children will judge that it is not wrong to chew gum at that school; but even if the teacher at another school has no rule against hitting, children claim that it is still wrong to hit. Indeed, a fascinating study on Amish teenagers indicates that moral judgments are not even regarded as dependent on God's authority. Nucci (1986) found that 100 percent of a group of Amish teenagers said that if God had made no rule against working on Sunday, it would not be wrong to work on Sunday. However, more than 80 percent of these subjects said that even if God had made no rule about hitting, it would still be wrong to hit.

These findings on the moral/conventional distinction are neither fragile nor superficial. On the contrary, the findings are quite robust. They have been replicated numerous times using a wide variety of stimuli (see Smetana 1993 and Tisak 1995 for reviews). Furthermore, the research apparently plumbs a fairly deep feature of moral judgment. For moral violations are treated as distinctive along several different dimensions. Moral violations attract high ratings on seriousness, they are regarded as having wide applicability, they have a status of authority independence, and they invite different kinds of justifications from conventional violations. Finally, this turns out to be a persistent feature of moral judgment. It is found in young and old alike. Thus, it seems that the capacity for drawing the moral/conventional distinction is part of basic moral psychology.

Most of the above research on the moral/conventional distinction has focused on moral violations that involve harming others, and that will be my main focus as well. However, it is clear that harm-centered violations do not exhaust the moral domain. To take one obvious example, we think it is wrong to cheat on one's taxes, but this has little direct bearing on harm. Furthermore, recent evidence indicates that the moral domain may not even be stable across cultures (e.g., Miller, Bersoff, and Harwood 1990; Haidt, Koller, and Diaz 1993). In a clever study by Jonathan Haidt and colleagues, they found that low socioeconomic status (SES) subjects were more likely than high SES subjects to maintain that people engaging in offensive or disrespectful actions (e.g., having sex with a dead chicken or cleaning the toilet with the national flag) should be stopped or punished (Haidt, Koller, and Diaz 1993). Haidt and colleagues conclude that it is parochial to think that harm is central to drawing the moral/conventional distinction (e.g., Haidt, Koller, and Diaz 1993, 625). Although there may be some relativity in the moral domain, the cross-cultural work also indicates that in all cultures, canonical examples of moral violations involve harming others (see, e.g., Hollos, Leis, and Turiel 1986; Nucci, Turiel, and Encarnacion-Gawrych 1983; Song, Smetana, and Kim 1987). Indeed, even Haidt and colleagues found that the subjects in different cultures and different SES groups made similar judgments about violations involving harm—for example, in all groups subjects tended to say that a girl who pushes a boy off a swing should be punished or stopped.

Thus, even though the moral domain is hardly exhausted by harm-based violations, it is plausible that judgments about harm-based violations constitute an important core of moral judgment. For the appreciation of harm-based violations shows up early ontogenetically [...], and it seems to be cross-culturally universal. Brian Scholl and Alan Leslie make a related point about "theory of mind," the capacity to understand other minds (Scholl and Leslie 1999). They note that, although there are cross-cultural differences in theory of mind, all cultures seem to share a core theory of mind that emerges early ontogenetically (140). Something similar might be said about the findings on moral judgment—despite the cross-cultural differences in moral judgment, the evidence indicates that all cultures share an important basic capacity, what I will call "core moral judgment." The capacity to recognize that harm-based violations have a special status (as compared to conventional violations) is an important indicator of the capacity for core moral judgment. As a first approximation, the capacity for core moral judgment can be thought of as the capacity to recognize that harm-based violations are very serious, authority independent, generalizable and that the actions are wrong because of welfare considerations.

[...]

Questions

1. Both Pojman and Joyce list various characteristics of morality. What characteristics are substantially the same on both lists? What characteristics are given by one but not the other?
2. Joyce is skeptical that universality is an essential characteristic of morality. What reasons does he give for his skepticism?
3. Nichols says that the psychological literature focuses on the distinction between the conventional and the moral. How does he characterize this distinction?

Notes (from Pojman)

1. Henry Sidgwick, *The Methods of Ethics,* 7th edn. (Macmillan, 1907), p. 380.
2. John Rawls, *A Theory of Justice* (Harvard University Press, 1971), pp. 176, 423.

References (from Nichols)

Blair, R. (1993). *The development of morality*. PhD diss. University of London.

Dunn, J., and P. Munn. (1987). Development of justification in disputes with mother and sibling. *Developmental Psychology* 23:791–8.

Haidt, J., S. Koller, and M. Dias. (1993). Affect, culture, and morality, or is it wrong to eat your dog? *Journal of Personality and Social Psychology* 65: 613–28.

Hollos, M., P. Leis, and E. Turiel. (1986). Social reasoning in Ijo children and adolescents in Nigerian communities. *Journal of Cross-Cultural Psychology* 17:352–74.

Miller, J., D. Bersoff, and L. Harwood. (1990). Perceptions of social responsibilities in India and the United States: Moral imperatives or personal decisions? *Journal of Personality and Social Psychology* 58:33–47.

Nucci, L. (1986). Children's conceptions of morality, social conventions and religious prescription. In *Moral dilemmas: Philosophical and psychological reconsiderations of the development of moral reasoning*, ed. C. Harding. Chicago: Precedent Press.

Nucci, L, E. Turiel, and G. Encarnacion-Gawrych. (1983). Children's social interactions and social concepts: Analyses of morality and convention in the Virgin Islands. *Journal of Cross-Cultural Psychology* 14:469–87.

Scholl, B., and A. Leslie. (1999). Modularity, development, and "theory of mind." *Mind and Language* 14:131–53.

Smetana, J. (1993). Understanding of social rules. In *The development of social cognition: The child as psychologist*, ed. M. Bennett, 111–41. New York: Guilford Press.

Smetana, J., and J. Braeges. (1990). The development of toddlers' moral and conventional judgements. *Merrill-Palmer Quarterly* 36:329–46.

Song, M., J. Smetana, and S. Kim. (1987). Korean children's conceptions of moral and conventional transgressions. *Developmental Psychology* 23: 577–82.

Tisak, M. (1995). Domains of social reasoning and beyond. In *Annals of child development*, vol. 11, ed. R. Vasta, 95–130. London: Jessica Kingsley.

Turiel, E., M. Killen, and C. Helwig. (1987). Morality: Its structure, functions, and vagaries. In *The emergence of morality in young children*, ed. J. Kagan and S. Lamb, 155–244. Chicago: University of Chicago Press.

Jonathan Haidt discusses biases in our moral reasoning

Why do you see the speck in your neighbour's eye, but do not notice the log in your own eye?

Matthew 7:3

[...] Scandal is great entertainment because it allows people to feel contempt, a moral emotion that gives feelings of moral superiority while asking nothing in return. With contempt you don't need to right the wrong (as with anger) or flee the scene (as with fear or disgust). And best of all, contempt, is made to share. Stories about the moral failings of others are among the most common kinds of gossip,[1] they are a staple of talk radio, and they offer a ready way for people to show that they share a common moral orientation. Tell an acquaintance a cynical story that ends with both of you smirking and shaking your heads and voila, you've got a bond.

Well, stop smirking. One of the most universal pieces of advice from across cultures and eras is that we are all hypocrites, and in our condemnation of others' hypocrisy we only compound our own. Social

psychologists have recently isolated the mechanisms that make us blind to the logs in our own eyes. The moral implications of these findings are disturbing; indeed, they challenge our greatest moral certainties. But the implications can be liberating, too, freeing you from destructive moralism and divisive self-righteousness.

[...]

The simplest way to cultivate a reputation for being fair is to really be fair, but life and psychology experiments sometimes force us to choose between appearance and reality. Dan Batson at the University of Kansas devised a clever way to make people choose, and his findings are not pretty. He brought students into his lab one at a time to take part in what they thought was a study of how unequal rewards affect teamwork.[2] The procedure was explained: One member of each team of two will be rewarded for correct responses to questions with a raffle ticket that could win a valuable prize. The other member will receive nothing. Subjects were also told that an additional part of the experiment concerned the effects of control: You, the subject, will decide which of you is rewarded, which of you is not. Your partner is already here, in another room, and the two of you will not meet. Your partner will be told that the decision was made by chance. You can make the decision in any way you like. Oh, and here is a coin: Most people in this study seem to think that flipping the coin is the fairest way to make the decision.

Subjects were then left alone to choose. About half of them used the coin. Batson knows this because the coin was wrapped in a plastic bag, and half the bags were ripped open. Of those who did not flip the coin, 90 percent chose the positive task for themselves. For those who did flip the coin, the laws of probability were suspended and 90 percent of them chose the positive task for themselves. Batson had given all the subjects a variety of questionnaires about morality weeks earlier (the subjects were students in psychology classes), so he was able to check how various measures of moral personality predicted behavior. His finding: People who reported being most concerned about caring for others and about issues of social responsibility were more likely to open the bag, but they were not more likely to give the other person the positive task. In other words, people who think they are particularly moral are in fact more likely to "do the right thing" and flip the coin, but when the coin flip comes out against them, they find a way to ignore it and follow their own self-interest. Batson called this tendency to value the appearance of morality over the reality "moral hypocrisy."

[...]

Proving that people are selfish, or that they'll sometimes cheat when they know they won't be caught, seems like a good way to get an article into the *Journal of Incredibly Obvious Results*. What's not so obvious is that, in nearly all these studies, people don't think they are doing anything wrong. It's the same in real life. From the person who cuts you off on the highway all the way to the Nazis who ran the concentration camps, most people think they are good people and that their actions are motivated by good reasons.

[...]

How do we get away with it?

One of the reasons people are often contemptuous of lawyers is that they fight for a client's interests, not for the truth. To be a good lawyer, it often helps to be a good liar. Although many lawyers won't tell a direct lie, most will do what they can to hide inconvenient facts while weaving a plausible alternative story for the judge and jury, a story that they sometimes know is

not true. Our inner lawyer works in the same way, but, somehow, we actually believe the stories he makes up.

[...]

When people are given difficult questions to think about—for example, whether the minimum wage should be raised—they generally lean one way or the other right away, and then put a call in to reasoning to see whether support for that position is forthcoming. For example, a person whose first instinct is that the minimum wage should be raised looks around for supporting evidence. If she thinks of her Aunt Flo who is working for the minimum wage and can't support her family on it then yes, that means the minimum wage should be raised.

[...]

People who are told that they have performed poorly on a test of social intelligence think extra hard to find reasons to discount the test; people who are asked to read a study showing that one of their habits—such as drinking coffee—is unhealthy think extra hard to find flaws in the study, flaws that people who don't drink coffee don't notice. Over and over again, studies show that people set out on a cognitive mission to bring back reasons to support their preferred belief or action. And because we are usually successful in this mission, we end up with the illusion of objectivity. We really believe that our position is rationally and objectively justified.

[...]

The rose-colored mirror

I don't want to blame everything on the lawyer. The lawyer is, after all, the rider—your conscious, reasoning self; and he is taking orders from the elephant—your automatic and unconscious self. The two are in cahoots to win at the game of life by playing Machiavellian tit for tat, and both are in denial about it.

To win at this game you must present your best possible self to others. You must appear virtuous, whether or not you are, and you must gain the benefits of cooperation whether or not you deserve them. But everyone else is playing the same game, so you must also play defense—you must be wary of others' self-presentations, and of their efforts to claim more for themselves than they deserve. Social life is therefore always a game of social comparison. We must compare ourselves to other people, and our actions to their actions, and we must somehow spin those comparisons in our favor. (In depression, part of the illness is that spin goes the other way, as described by Aaron Beck's cognitive triad: I'm bad, the world is terrible, and my future is bleak.) You can spin a comparison either by inflating your own claims or by disparaging the claims of others. You might expect, given what I've said so far, that we do both, but the consistent finding of psychological research is that we are fairly accurate in our perceptions of others. It's our self-perceptions that are distorted because we look at ourselves in a rose-colored mirror.

In Garrison Keillor's mythical town of Lake Wobegon, all the women are strong, all the men good looking, and all the children above average. But if the Wobegonians were real people, they would go further: Most of them would believe they were stronger, better looking, or smarter than the average Wobegonian. When Americans and Europeans are asked to rate themselves on virtues, skills, or other desirable traits (including intelligence, driving ability, sexual skills, and ethics), a large majority say they are above average.[3] (This effect is weaker in East Asian countries, and may not exist in Japan.)[4]

In a brilliant series of experiments,[5] Nick Epley and David Dunning figured out how we do it. They asked students at Cornell University to predict how many flowers they would buy in an upcoming charity event and how many the average Cornell student would buy. Then they looked at actual behavior. People had greatly overestimated their own virtue, but were pretty close on their guesses about others. In a second study, Epley and Dunning asked people to predict what they would do in a game that could be played for money either selfishly or cooperatively. Same findings: Eighty-four percent predicted that they'd cooperate, but the subjects expected (on average) that only 64 percent of others would cooperate. When they ran the real game, 61 percent cooperated. In a third study, Epley and Dunning paid people five dollars for participating in an experiment and then asked them to predict how much of the money they and others would donate, hypothetically, had they been given a particular charitable appeal after the study. People said (on average) they'd donate $2.44, and others would donate only $1.83. But when the study was rerun with a real request to give money, the average gift was $1.53.

In their cleverest study, the researchers described the details of the third study to a new group of subjects and asked them to predict how much money they would donate if they had been in the "real" condition, and how much money other Cornell students would donate. Once again, subjects predicted they'd be much more generous than others. But then subjects saw the actual amounts of money donated by real subjects from the third study, revealed to them one at a time (and averaging $1.53). After being given this new information, subjects were given a chance to revise their estimates, and they did. They lowered their estimates of what others would give, but they did not change their estimates of what they themselves would give. In other words, subjects used base rate information properly to revise their predictions of *others*, but they refused to apply it to their rosy self-assessments. We judge others by their behavior, but we think we have special information about ourselves— we know what we are "really like" inside, so we can easily find ways to explain away our selfish acts and cling to the illusion that we are better than others.

Ambiguity abets the illusion. For many traits, such as leadership, there are so many ways to define it that one is free to pick the criterion that will most flatter oneself. If I'm confident, I can define leadership as confidence. If I think I'm high on people skills, I can define leadership as the ability to understand and influence people. When comparing ourselves to others, the general process is this: Frame the question (unconsciously, automatically) so that the trait in question is related to a self-perceived strength, then go out and look for evidence that you have the strength. Once you find a piece of evidence, once you have a "makes-sense" story, you are done. You can stop thinking, and revel in your self-esteem. It's no wonder, then, that in a study of 1 million American high school students, 70 percent thought they were above average on leadership ability, but only 2 percent thought they were below average. Everyone can find *some* skill that might be construed as related to leadership, and then find *some* piece of evidence that one has that skill.[6] (College professors are less wise than high school students in this respect—94 percent of us think we do above-average work.)[7] But when there is little room for ambiguity—how tall are you? how good are you at juggling?—people tend to be much more modest.

If the only effect of these rampant esteem-inflating biases was to make people feel good about themselves, they would not be a problem. In fact, evidence shows that people who hold pervasive positive illusions about themselves, their abilities, and their future prospects are mentally healthier, happier, and better liked than people who lack such illusions.[8] But such biases can make people feel that they deserve more than they do, thereby setting the stage for endless disputes with other people who feel equally over-entitled.

[…]

Emily Pronin at Princeton and Lee Ross at Stanford have tried to help people overcome their self-serving biases by teaching them about biases and then asking, "OK, now that you know about these biases, do you want to change what you just said about yourself?" Across many studies, the results were the same:[9] People were quite happy to learn about the various forms of self-serving bias and then apply their newfound knowledge to predict others' responses. But their self-ratings were unaffected. Even when you grab people by the lapels, shake them, and say, "Listen to me! Most people have an inflated view of themselves. Be realistic!" they refuse, muttering to themselves, "Well, other people may be biased, but I *really am* above average on leadership."

Pronin and Ross trace this resistance to a phenomenon they call "naive realism": Each of us thinks we see the world directly, as it really is. We further believe that the facts as we see them are there for all to see, therefore others should agree with us. If they don't agree, it follows either that they have not yet been exposed to the relevant facts or else that they are blinded by their interests and ideologies. People acknowledge that their own backgrounds have shaped their views, but such experiences are invariably seen as deepening one's insights; for example, being a doctor gives a person special insight into the problems of the health-care industry. But the background of other people is used to explain their biases and covert motivations; for example, doctors think that lawyers disagree with them about tort reform not because they work with the victims of malpractice (and therefore have their own special insights) but because their self-interest biases their thinking. It just seems plain as day, to the naive realist, that everyone is influenced by ideology and self-interest. Except for me. I see things as they are.

If I could nominate one candidate for "biggest obstacle to world peace and social harmony," it would be naive realism because it is so easily ratcheted up from the individual to the group level: My group is right because we see things as they are. Those who disagree are obviously biased by their religion, their ideology, or their self-interest.

[…]

When you find a fault in yourself it will hurt, briefly, but if you keep going and acknowledge the fault, you are likely to be rewarded with a flash of pleasure that is mixed, oddly, with a hint of pride. It is the pleasure of taking responsibility for your own behavior. It is the feeling of honor.

[…]

The human mind may […] come equipped with cognitive processes that predispose us to hypocrisy, self-righteousness, and moralistic conflict. But sometimes, by knowing the mind's structure and strategies, we can step out of the ancient game of social manipulation and enter into a game of our choosing. By seeing the log in your own eye you can become less biased, less moralistic, and therefore less inclined toward argument and conflict […].

Questions

1. Summarize Dan Batson's coin-toss experiments What (in detail) do those experiments seem to show?

2. Summarize the Epley–Dunning experiments? What do those experiments seem to show?

3. People tend to have an inflated view of themselves and of the rationality of their own beliefs. What does Haidt think is good about this? What does he think is bad about this?

Notes

1. Hom, H. (2004). *Gossip as a vehicle for value comparison: The development of social norms and social bonding through moral judgment.* PhD diss., University of Virginia, Charlottesville.

2. Batson, C. D., Kobrynowicz, D., Dinnerstein, J. L., Kampf, H. C., & Wilson, A. D. (1997). In a very different voice: Unmasking moral hypocrisy. *Journal of Personality and Social Psychology*, 72, 1335–48; Batson, C. D., Thompson, E. R., Seuferling, G., Whitney, H., & Strongman, J. A. (1999). Moral hypocrisy: Appearing moral to oneself without being so. *Journal of Personality and Social Psychology,* 77, 525–37.

3. Alicke, M. D., Klotz, M. L., Breitenbecher, D. L., Yurak, T. J., & Vredenburg, D. S. (1995). Personal contact, individuation, and the better-than-average effect. *Journal of Personality and Social Psychology,* 68, 804–25; Hoorens, V. (1993). Self-enhancement and superiority biases in social comparisons. In vol. 4 of W. Strobe & M. Hewstone (Eds.), *European review of social psychology* (pp. 113–39). Chichester, UK: John Wiley.

4. Heine, S. J., & Lehman, D. R. (1999). Culture, self-discrepancies, and self-satisfaction. *Personality and Social Psychology Bulletin*, 25, 915–25; Markus, H. R., & Kitayama, S. (1991). Culture and the self: Implications for cognition, emotion, and motivation. *Psychological Review*, 98, 224–53.

5. Epley, N., & Dunning, D. (2000) Feeling "holier than thou": Are self-serving assessments produced by errors in self- or social prediction? *Journal of Personality and Social Psychology*, 79, 861–75.

6. This analysis of leadership, and the studies cited in the paragraph come from Dunning, D., Meverowitz, J. A., & Holzberg, A. D. (2002). *Ambiguity and self-evaluation: The role of idiosyncratic trait definitions in self-serving assessments of ability.* In *Heuristics and biases: The psychology of intuitive judgment* (pp. 324–33). Cambridge, UK: Cambridge University Press.

7. Cross, P. (1977). Not can but will college teaching be improved? *New Directions for Higher Education*, 17, 1–15.

8. Taylor S. E., Lerner. J. S., Sherman, D. K., Sage, R. M., & McDowell, N. K. (2003). Portrait of the self-enhancer: Well adjusted and well liked or maladjusted and friendless. *Journal of Personality and Social Psychology* 84, 165–76.

9. Pronin, E., Lin, D. Y., & Ross, L. (2002). The bias blind spot: Perceptions of bias in self versus others. *Personality and Social Psychology Bulletin*, 28, 369–81.

Part II

Moral Theory

4

Moral Theory
Fiction

Long Live the King

The land was ruled by a great King whose castle overlooked the town from a high hill. The towns-people told their children that the King was watching them from the castle, that if they were bad, the King would send His men down to punish them. It was a story for children, but not only that; even the towns-people had the feeling of being watched from on high.

The King was feared, but He was loved as well. The elders told stories of the magnificent processions they had once witnessed: How flower petals would be strewn over the main road; how grand lords and ladies in their finery would ride past in beautiful carriages; how at last the King would arrive in the most beautiful carriage of all. The lords and ladies would throw silver coins to the crowd; the coins the King threw were always of gold.

Sometimes the King's carriage would stop, and, to the obvious displeasure of His fierce guards, the King would descend and walk among the people. The King was so magnificent that people hardly dared look at Him, but it was said that those who did look witnessed the kindliest of smiles. Stories were told of the generous favors the King had bestowed, even on the lowliest of his subjects. Some of the stories seemed fantastical: Not everyone believed that the King had healed a crippled boy with His touch. But even the skeptics loved these accounts, for the stories spoke, however naively, of the King's goodness and the people's love for Him.

One day the King's visits ceased. Gradually, if uneasily, the townspeople accustomed themselves to His absence. Some said the King's absence was a test: He wanted to see if His people, like wayward children left to their own devices, would stray from the laws He had laid down for them. It was said that the people must be diligent in following all of the laws, so the King would not find them wanting when He returned.

One or two people wondered aloud if the King might be dead. But this thought was met with fierce resistance. If the King had died, wouldn't they have been told? Anyway, didn't the royal messengers still appear to deliver the King's edicts?

Still, perhaps a certain disquiet was the reason the townspeople kept pressing the elders to relate the old stories: Now, more than ever, people needed to feel the reality of their King.

One day *two* royal messengers appeared within the same hour in the town square to deliver royal edicts. This had never happened before. When the first edict was read, people were troubled to hear that the edict laid down important changes in the laws, changes that were bound to disrupt the listeners' lives. But their distress turned to alarm when the second edict was read: It also laid down changes, but these changes were at odds with those in the first edict!

When the messengers were questioned about these differences by the town council, each messenger replied—rather haughtily, it was said—that *his* edict

Contemporary Moral and Social Issues: An Introduction through Original Fiction, Discussion, and Readings, First Edition. Thomas D. Davis.
© 2014 John Wiley & Sons, Inc. Published 2014 by John Wiley & Sons, Inc.

represented the King's true wishes and that the other messenger and his false edict should be ignored.

The more the council members studied these two edicts, the greater seemed the disagreement between them. The council sent representatives to the Castle, hoping for a meeting with the King, only to be rebuffed by the fierce guards. The representatives were told that their visit was presumptuous; when and *if* the King wished to speak to them, He would send word.

The council fell into confusion—as did the rest of the town when it learned of these events. Some people wondered if the King had been overthrown. Yet who could possibly overthrow such a great King? In any event, if someone new was in charge, that personage would issue his orders through one messenger, not two.

Perhaps the King was away, and His absence had occasioned a jousting for power. Or He was here, but not yet aware of a struggle for power among His ministers. Whatever the situation, it appeared that some minister was trying to substitute his own orders for those of the King.

Or could this all be some sort of test of the King's devising? He might be saying: "You should know Me well enough by now to tell the true edict from the false ones."

But how were they to decide which edict was truly from the King—assuming that either of them was?

After much discussion, a strategy was devised: The council would study the King's past edicts and compare them to the two new "reform" edicts. Perhaps they would find subtle differences of style that would allow them to identify one or both of the new edicts as false.

The task of comparing the styles of the new edicts to the traditional ones was undertaken. Old scrolls were lifted out of the cabinets and cupboards where they had been stored; they were unfurled and examined and discussed. Lists were compiled, notes were made, details referenced. Scholars were brought in to confer.

After a month of such work, there was no agreement in the results. No oddities of style or appearance had been found that made it clear whether either of the reform edicts was legitimate or whether both were false. Unhappily, while there was no general

agreement, individual opinions were forming in ways that threatened to bring about serious dissension.

The situation looked grave. It was fortunate that neither of the reform edicts countermanded the most basic laws—such as those against killing the innocent and bearing false witness. But the reform edicts called for changes in council procedures and lines of authority—matters that could cause chaos if they weren't resolved. Changes demanded in the behavior of the townspeople were sometimes subtle, but since violations of the proposed laws often carried substantial penalties, the townspeople would be thrown into confusion unless the changes could be made clear and consistent.

Since studying the style of the edicts had brought no resolution, it was suggested that the council should look beyond the letter of the old edicts to determine what principles lay behind them. These principles might help determine which, if either, of the new edicts were true and provide a basis for ongoing legislation.

This task was undertaken and once more the results proved ambiguous. Again factions threatened to form around different suggested principles.

Someone said they must try to imagine themselves in the King's place, and ask what they, as King, would want for the people. This suggestion was met with scorn by some. How could the townspeople, with their limited minds, hope to fathom the wisdom of the King?

Others disagreed. If this were a test and they were given the task of determining the King's true wishes, how else could they proceed but to try to imagine, however humbly, what the King would want them to do?

One council member said he was sure that their good and great King would want His subjects to be happy. Of course, it wasn't in the power of even a great king to *make* the people happy, but the council could try to create laws that would help the people in their pursuit of happiness. Certainly the council could provide the means to keep the poorest of the subjects from the depths of misery.

But others vehemently objected to that idea. How could they, wretched creatures that they were, imagine that the King cared about their happiness? Didn't too much of their happiness depend on low pleasures like drunkenness and indecency? Just look at all the things that the King had forbidden in the earlier edicts. Obviously the King wanted to make his subjects worthy, not happy. True, some happiness might come from the knowledge that one had kept the King's commandments. But this was of secondary importance. They should feel content just to know they had avoided the King's wrath.

The debates continued without resolution, and confusion grew. But since people can tolerate uncertainty for only so long, opinions became fixed, and those with opinions in common began to solidify into factions.

The Traditionals were those who thought that only the old edicts could be relied upon, and that both new edicts were false. The First Reformers believed in the truth of the first new edict, and thought the second a fake; where there were conflicts between the First Reform Edict and the traditional ones, the first new edict would have priority. The Second Reformers held a similar position with regard to the Second Reform Edict.

There was a large faction that remained convinced that the King would want His subjects to be happy, would want the laws to promote the common weal or common good. This faction became known as the "Wealers."

(Actually there were some among the Wealers who doubted that the King was still alive, who thought that morality must now have a more commonplace basis—and what could be more common than happiness? But these individuals kept their suspicions about the death of the King to themselves.)

Even among the Wealers—already so different from the other factions—there arose a disagreement. What if laws proposed to further the common good would bring misery to a few individuals? Those who insisted such laws would not be justified broke off and became the "Individuals." They demanded that any set of laws give all individuals certain protections that could not be overridden for the common good.

These new divisions were disturbing: For as long as anyone could remember, the townspeople had lived in harmony, governed by the clear edicts of their King. To have so many factions—Traditionals, First Reformers, Second Reformers, Wealers, and Individuals—threw all of life into confusion. There

was enmity like none of them had experienced before—neighbor turning against neighbor—as the factions battled to have their way in the council. Positions hardened, compromise became more and more difficult. Sporadic violence broke out, and it looked as if there might be more.

Then one day a child was killed. It was quite by accident: A stone thrown in the general direction of an enemy just happened to catch a running child in the head. There was a day of stunned inaction, the whole town seemingly in shock from this terrible event. Feelings no doubt would have boiled up into greater violence if cooler heads in the council had not prevailed.

People could not agree, they said, but unless they could agree to disagree, any remnant of the old life and civility was bound to be destroyed.

The pressing question was, How could they keep their disagreements and still function as a town?

One level-headed member of the council proposed a solution: There must be a gathering of the leaders of all five factions. Their aim must be to settle on some minimum set of laws to which they could all agree, laws which would allow the town to function. They could not expect the town to be the close-knit community it had been in the past. Too much had happened for that. But at least they could keep the town from descending into chaos.

Though only the leaders of the factions would assemble, the leaders must be in constant contact with the townspeople they represented: No compromise would work were there not general agreement on the proposed laws.

Though everyone recognized the necessity of such a compromise, it was difficult for people to operate within its constraints. People kept wanting to point to their favored edict to prove what was true. "See what's written here," they would say. Yet, if this process were to succeed, it must be based on common agreement, not some other sort of "truth."

Gradually a set of laws—or procedures to determine laws—emerged. But no one was happy. Where there was lack of agreement, people had to be allowed to do as they please. To see so many things that were "obviously wrong" or "obviously bad" being permitted was almost unbearable to many of the townspeople.

Fear of violence, the sense that no faction was strong enough to overpower the others, and the need for the town to function in some manner kept the negotiations going. But there were few who did not daily glance with longing toward the Castle, dreaming of the day when the King would return and once again tell the townspeople what was true and good. Each faction continued to believe that it was right, and that the King, when He returned, would set the other factions on the one true path. How wonderful that day would be!

Questions

1. If we take this story as a parable, what or who could the King likely represent? Give evidence from the story to support your interpretation.
2. What happens to throw the townspeople into so much confusion? What unsuccessful attempts do they make to resolve the confusion?
3. Some townspeople try to imagine what the King would want them to do. What objection do others make to this approach?
4. Some townspeople say the King would want them to be happy. What objection do others make to this idea?
5. What similarities and differences are there between the Wealers and the Individuals?
6. The townspeople recognize the need for a minimal set of rules to which they could all agree. But what do they find so difficult and disappointing about the whole process?

5

Moral Theory
Discussion

Long Live the King

"Long Live the King" is a parable. Before we get to the meaning of the parable, let's make sure we're clear about the sequence of events it describes.

1. There was a time when the King regularly appeared to the townspeople. He also sent messengers to the town to convey His commands.
2. The King ceased to appear. The townspeople found this disquieting; however, since messengers continue to deliver the King's commands, life in town goes on as before.
3. One day two messengers appear with different sets of commands; each messenger claims his commands come from the King. The two new sets of edicts differ not only from each other, but from the older edicts. All three sets of edicts do agree on certain basic commands, such as those against murder and bearing false witness. But there are enough differences between the edicts to cause real trouble if the differences are not resolved.
4. No evidence is found that convinces everyone of the truth of any one set of edicts. Divisions begin to form among those who favor the old edicts or one of the two new sets of reform edicts. These factions take the names, the "Traditionals," the "First Reformers," and the "Second Reformers."
5. Some townspeople try to resolve the confusion by adopting the King's point of view, to decide what the King would want for them. Some decide the King would want them to be happy. These people form a faction called the "Wealers" (from the old English term "weal" for "well-being"). They believe laws should be based on what would lead to the happiness of the town as a whole.
6. A group splinters off from the Wealers, complaining that the laws should focus on the happiness of each individual, not just the group as a whole. This faction is called the "Individuals."
7. Each faction feels it should govern the town; the arguments between them become increasingly heated. Then an act of violence frightens everyone and leads people to seek a compromise.
8. The proposed compromise is that the five factions must come to an agreement on some minimal set of laws that will govern the town. These laws will leave out much that people want in the laws, but at least there will be enough law to allow the town to function.
9. An agreement is reached, but no one is happy with it. The people in each faction dream of the day when the King will return and confirm that *their* view is the true one.

With the basics of the parable in mind, let's think about how best to interpret it.

No doubt many of you have already concluded that the King symbolizes God. This equivalence could be

Contemporary Moral and Social Issues: An Introduction through Original Fiction, Discussion, and Readings, First Edition. Thomas D. Davis.
© 2014 John Wiley & Sons, Inc. Published 2014 by John Wiley & Sons, Inc.

inferred from the extraordinary powers attributed to the King—that He could observe the people from His high castle, that He might possibly have healed a crippled boy with his touch.

Actually, since the nature and even the existence of the King eventually come into doubt, it might be argued that the King would be better seen as symbolizing a *belief* in a God (who may or may not exist).

If we take the King as symbolizing (a belief in) God, the parable gives us a familiar picture of religion. The moral law is seen as issuing from the commands of God. Many religions imagine an earlier time when God revealed himself to a group of people, leaving them no doubt about His existence and His commands. Later, God is no longer so obviously manifest, and major religious divisions appear, with different groups following different commandments or interpreting some of the same commandments different ways. Some hold fast to the beliefs of their group. However, there is an increasing inclination among others to look for God behind all the religious divisions, to speculate as to what such a God might want. There is also an inclination—whether from disbelief in God or from frustration with religious disagreement—to construct morality on human terms, focusing on what people want. The Wealers decide that morality should be based on human happiness. But even with this premise, there is disagreement as to how much emphasis to put on the individual versus the common welfare.

The view of the Wealers bears some relation to the philosophy of utilitarianism, which says that an act or social system is right which leads to the greatest happiness of the greatest number. The Individuals sound like some of the critics of utilitarianism: these critics claim that utilitarianism puts too much emphasis on the general good and doesn't look out for the individual. Often critics of utilitarianism push for a human rights view of morality, either using rights to modify utilitarianism or as a substitute for it.

At the end of the parable, the townspeople reluctantly decide that, in the face of so much disagreement and the threat of violence, they had better compromise on some minimal agreement that will allow the town to function and the factions to coexist. As we shall see, this is analogous to a social contract view of morality, a view that became prominent in the seventeenth and eighteenth centuries, in part as a reaction to the European wars of religion.

In the next few sections we'll discuss these and other normative moral/ethical theories, along with metaethical perspectives used to justify the theories.

Religious ethics

God and the good

In "Long Live the King," the bulk of the fable is given over to the equivalent of religious morality: The people are looking to the King (God) to decide what they should and shouldn't do. As questions arise about what the King's true commandments are, the town is split into various religious factions believing in (somewhat) different moral codes. The relationship between morality and the King gets more tenuous as some begin to doubt that the commands are actually from the King or that the King is still alive. However, it seems as if all the townspeople agree on one thing: *If* people knew the King was there and knew what His commandments were, that would decide all questions of morality. The commands of God determine true morality.

Before we talk about that point directly, let's distinguish a number of different ways (not all mutually exclusive) that religion might be connected with morality:

1. *Religion might be crucial for motivating people to be moral*, by promising rewards for good behavior and punishment for bad. (Of course, religion can inspire as well, through its stories of saints and heroes.)

2. *Religion might be a crucial historical source of morality.* For instance, what we call the "Golden Rule" appeared in one form or another in several early religions. Monotheism has been credited with promoting (very slowly) the idea that all people are fundamentally equal as children of God. Christianity has been credited with holding up an ideal of love for all people.

3. *Religion might be crucial for determining moral truth.* That is, beyond being a motivator or source of morality, religion might provide the

logical underpinning of morality, a necessary condition of it. Without God, no morality. Without knowledge of God's will, no true knowledge of morality.

#1—that religion is crucial for motivating people to be moral—has passed as common sense throughout much of human history. Ruling classes—even when skeptics themselves—felt that only belief in divine reward and punishment could keep the common people in line; thus, it was important to support religion and put down any challenges to it.

One thing that makes *#1* seem so questionable today is that even as society has become more secular, people are still concerned with being moral. Or are they? One common theme of conservative preaching is that secular humanism has licensed immoral behavior. What's the truth here?

It's important to distinguish what sort of morality is being talked about. According to C. Daniel Batson and W. Larry Ventis in their book, *The Religious Experience,* studies of religion and morality have found a much stronger correlation between religious belief and avoidance of personal "sins" such as such as gambling, drinking and premarital sex, than between religion and the avoidance of social "sins" such as stealing, lying and cheating.

The correlation between religious belief and refraining from "personal sin" may have as much to do with how religion defines right and wrong as with religion motivating people to be good. Secular moralities tend to take a more relaxed attitude towards personal behavior, emphasizing the importance of social morality.

Regarding *#2*—that religion is a crucial historical source of morality—it is clear that much of our present-day morality arose in the context of religion. On the other hand, given that religion was the only context there was for most of human history—an amalgam of what would later be separated out as theology, philosophy, and science—this is hardly surprising. That morality arose from religion doesn't mean that it is now logically dependent on it. Mathematics also emerged from religious societies, was sometimes given a mystical flavor, and was said to reflect the mind of God. However, whatever its historical source, mathematical proofs require no religious premises. The same *might* be true of morality, despite its religious origins.

This brings us to *#3*—that religion is crucial for determining moral truth. The question is this: Is religion essential to the justification of moral beliefs or is such justification logically independent of religion?

There is a famous dilemma related to the connection between religion and morality that goes back to at least the ancient Greeks: (a) Is something good because God commands it or, (b) Does God command it because it is good?

a says that the mere act of God's commanding us to do (not do) something is enough to make that something right (wrong). "Mere act" means that it is the fact of God's commanding, not any reasons He might have for commanding, that makes something right/ wrong. This is often called the Divine Command theory of ethics.

b says that God commands things for reasons, and it is these reasons—not the mere fact of God's commanding—that makes things right or wrong.

a is the option that gives the closest tie between God and morality: It says that the only thing that makes something right/wrong is God's commanding it. The problem many people have with Divine Command theory is that it sets no prior limits on what God might have commanded. If God had commanded us to torture children, then torturing children would have been right.

If the Divine Command theory seems like a straw man—a position made up for purposes of easy attack—let me assure you it is not. It has played a prominent role in the history of Christian thought. According to theologian Jean Porter,

> The first theologian to defend a divine command theory of ethics appears to have been Duns Scotus (1266–1308). Scotus claimed that God's will is not bound by any considerations of order or justice, or any rational considerations save the law of non-contradiction.... God forbids (for example) murder and adultery, but absolutely speaking, God could have commanded otherwise, rendering such actions just and right.... Similar considerations led both Martin Luther (1483–1546) and John Calvin (1509–64) to affirm that God is the ultimate source of justice and morality. Not only does this mean that moral norms derive from God's will; it also implies the God's actions cannot be evaluated by our standards of justice and consistency....

The opposite of the Divine Command view is nicely illustrated by some anecdotes emerging from psychological studies of children's views of morality. An 11-year-old boy, a conservative Jew, was asked if it would be all right for Jews to steal if the Torah said that they should. He said, "Even if God says it, we know he [sic] can't mean it, because we know it is a very bad thing to steal...." As Eliot Turiel says of this child and others in this book, *The Culture of Morality*:

> The boy evaluated religious dictates in conjunction with an evaluation of the act, and did not solely presume that religion determines the good.... [A] 15-year-old female reasoned that God would not give such a command [to steal] "because...He's perfect, and if He's stealing He can't be perfect." These responses and the data more generally indicate that the relation between religion and morality entails an interweaving between moral judgments and what is given and should exist in religious precepts. Moral criteria of welfare, justice, and rights are applied to religion to at least the same extent as religious doctrine is seen to establish the good.

What follows if one rejects the Divine Command theory and accepts view *b*, that God commands something because it is good?

Sometimes it is said that *b* implies that God is no longer in a privileged position regarding morality. However, a believer can still claim that God's word should take precedence because God has much greater knowledge of those facets of the universe and human nature that impact moral judgments.

Still, *b* does seem to imply that morality is reasonable, not arbitrary, and that it makes sense for people to ask questions about the reasoning behind religiously based morality.

(It's important to note that we're talking here about what's moral, not what's prudential. You might decide to follow God's commands simply because He can enforce them, whether or not those commands are morally right. But, of course, most believers would say that God's commands are morally right.)

At one point in "Long Live the King," a contrast is made between two very different conceptions of what the King (God) wants from the townspeople:

> One council member said he was sure that their good and great King would want his subjects to be happy....

But others vehemently objected to that idea. How could they, wretched creatures that they were, imagine that the King cared about their happiness? Didn't too much of their happiness depend on low pleasures like drunkenness and indecency? Just look at all the things that the King had forbidden in the earlier edicts. Obviously the King wanted to make His subjects worthy, not happy. True, some happiness might come from the knowledge that one had kept the King's commandments. But this was of secondary importance. They should feel content just to know they had avoided the King's wrath.

The townspeople who emphasize the things the King has forbidden and the ways in which human beings have fallen short are conceiving the divinity as what might be called a "judgmental God." Such a God-type has a morality that is deontological and severely perfectionistic, with a heavy emphasis on desert. These terms need to be explained.

"Deontological ethics" (*deon* in Greek means "duty") are generally those that lay down rules with dos and don'ts, duties and obligations. (Such ethics are contrasted with "consequentialist ethics" that emphasize consequences rather than rules.) Most ethical systems are deontological.

The term "desert" signifies what people *deserve* in terms of blame or praise, punishment or reward. (Note that cakes and pies are "dessert" with a second "s.") Most moralities include some element of desert.

The term "perfectionism" in everyday life suggests a neurotic obsession with getting every little thing just right. However, the term as used in philosophy means something quite different. It has to do with setting standards of conduct and character that don't necessarily have anything to do with causing other people harm. One way to think about perfectionism is that it turns flourishing into a moral obligation. As we saw in the first chapter, flourishing is a word that covers the development of certain worthwhile human capacities such as intelligence, inquisitiveness, adventurousness, courage, sensitivity, freedom, love, and spirituality.

There we talked about flourishing in the context of non-moral personal values or ideals. Many value systems leave flourishing there—in the non-moral category. Compare maliciousness with laziness. If Louise were malicious, most of us would take that to be a serious moral failing, one that justifies moral pressure on Louise to change her behavior. On the other hand, if Louise were lazy, lots of people would take that to be a purely personal failing (at least insofar as it didn't relate to behaviors like failing to keep commitments). Some people might have less respect for Louise as a person, but they wouldn't see her being lazy as morally wrong. A perfectionist ethic, on the other hand, might see her laziness as morally wrong. I say "might" here because different perfectionist ethics elevate different characteristics to moral status. As we will see later, a perfectionist ethic need be neither severe nor associated with religion. The judgmental-God ethic is just one type of perfectionist ethic.

What is particular about the judgmental-God morality is that it combines severe perfectionism with a heavy emphasis on desert. That is, such a God-type sets difficult or nearly impossible standards and inflicts hard punishments on those who don't meet the standards. Even if such a God provides a way to escape punishment—the sacraments or being "born again"—the judgment remains that such harsh punishment would have been deserved.

It is also possible to imagine God as much more sympathetic toward human beings. Such a God would be more accepting of people as they are, would be more interested in helping them than changing them, and would primarily want humans to be happy. Such a God would emphasize the wrong of hurting other people and would likely reserve the most severe punishments for cruelty.

According to surveys, Americans are more inclined to believe in heaven (79%) than in hell (59%), though both are stressed in the Bible. The reasoning here may well be similar to the reasoning of the children discussed earlier by Turiel: The Americans who believe in heaven, but not hell, are thinking that a moral God wouldn't send people to hell.

While this "sympathetic God" tends to be the God of more liberal believers, a lot of liberalizing has taken place even among more conservative groups. Despite Jesus' stress on the virtues of poverty and charity, some conservative Christians are convinced that Jesus wants them to be rich. Observers have remarked how many of the evangelical mega-churches downplay Jesus' crucifixion and suffering and instead present a more upbeat Jesus. This may be a matter of marketing, but it reflects changes in doctrine as well.

Let's say that when we're imagining how God does, or would, want humans to behave, we're taking the "God perspective."

The God perspective

In the story, when the townspeople find no easy solution to which edicts are the true ones but nevertheless must decide what the King (God) would want them to do, someone suggests "they must try to imagine themselves in the King's place, and ask what they, as King, would want for the people."

If one believed in the Divine Command theory of ethics, the idea of imagining oneself in God's place would make absolutely no sense: Since, according to the theory, the commands of God are arbitrary by any human standard of reasoning, what could there be to imagine? However, if we know something of God's qualities (goodness) and know that God has fathomable reasons for what He does, asking ourselves what a moral God would want or do isn't so outlandish. According to Turiel (above), it's what a lot of us do in thinking about religious ethics.

Some thinkers have felt that this "God perspective" is a natural perspective from which to think about morality, *even if one isn't sure there is a God*. This makes sense under two conditions: (1) that morality isn't logically dependent on religion and (2) that a God's-eye perspective captures certain essential features of morality. We've already discussed *1*. As for *2*, some have argued that the essential features of morality include the following: That moral rules apply to all (at least all in some large group); that they shouldn't be biased in favor of any particular individual; that they should be concerned to some degree with the welfare of the whole; and, that they should reflect a general knowledge of the world and human behavior and not be based on ignorance.

The secular version of the God perspective is sometimes referred to as the "ideal observer theory." We are supposed to ask: What sort of ethic would an ideal observer endorse who was sympathetic to all human beings and their concerns, was not biased toward any particular individual or group, and had a general knowledge of the world? Obviously we can't really *be* the ideal observer, even in our imaginations, any more than we can *be* God. The idea is that trying to approximate this "moral point of view" gives us an appropriate imaginative standpoint from which to try to decide moral issues.

The first formulation of the ideal observer theory seems to have come from Adam Smith, who would later write the *Wealth of Nations*. In his *Theory of Moral Sentiments* (1759), Smith argued that the ground of morality was sympathy for other human beings.

Morality might develop through sympathy, according to Smith, but it also requires impartiality. This develops through our imaginative identification with others, but also through recognizing their imaginative identification with us. When a person can see and judge himself as one moral being among others, he develops within himself an "impartial spectator." From this perspective, the impartial approvals and disapprovals of human conduct will result in moral rules of thumb we can use to guide our conduct and urge on others.

Critics of sympathy as a grounding for morality have pointed out that sympathy can be episodic: Maybe I'm not feeling very sympathetic the day I have to decide how to vote on a bill to help the handicapped.

Smith and others have argued that we needn't—indeed shouldn't—rely on sympathy for our day-to-day decisions. The sympathetic impartial spectator in me decides the general rules, and it is those rules, plus a developed conscience urging me to follow the rules, that leads me to make morally justified decisions.

Some thinkers have argued, as did some of the townspeople in the story, that if we took a sympathetic God/ideal observer point of view, what we would want to see is as much happiness as possible in the world. This view suggests a utilitarian philosophy.

Let's discuss utilitarianism, consider some problems with it, and take a first look at human rights as a way to supplement or supplant utilitarianism.

Utilitarianism and rights

Utilitarianism

In his *Principles of Moral and Political Philosophy* (1789), Jeremy Bentham (see Readings), an early defender of utilitarianism, defined the doctrine as follows:

> By the principle of utility is meant that principle which approves or disapproves of every action whatsoever, according to the tendency which it appears to have to augment or diminish the happiness of the party whose interest is in question.... I say of every action whatsoever; and therefore not only of every action of a private individual, but of every measure of government.

The word "utility" (literally "usefulness") is employed by philosophers and economists to mean "happiness," "well-being" or "satisfaction."

According to utilitarianism, that act or set of policies is right which leads to the greatest happiness of the greatest number. Note that utilitarianism, as formulated here, has three different elements:

1. It is a *consequentialist ethic*: An act or policy is right or wrong solely in terms of its consequences.
2. It is *hedonistic*: The only consequences we need to consider are those relating to feelings of happiness and unhappiness.
3. It is *concerned with the sum total of happiness* created by any act or set of policies.

Utilitarianism can be formulated either as "act-utilitarianism" or "rule-utilitarianism." With act-utilitarianism, the utilitarian principle is to be applied by each agent to each decision she makes. With rule-utilitarianism, the utilitarian principle is used to decide a set of rules that would lead to the greatest happiness of the greatest number. Agents should then follow those rules, whether or not acting on them leads to the greatest happiness in each case,

Act-utilitarianism is open to some pretty convincing criticisms. Act-utilitarianism seems to give insufficient weight to promises and property; it also gives little, if any, weight to desert.

For example, act-utilitarianism seems to imply the following: If using the money I owe you to buy dinner for friends would create more happiness than paying you back, I ought to use the money to buy dinner; similar logic would apply if I'm thinking of stealing money from your wallet. As for desert, insofar as act-utilitarianism acknowledges any rules of reward and punishment, it seems to endorse breaking those rules whenever doing so would create more happiness than not. For instance, if others could benefit more from a reward you have earned, I ought to give them the reward.

There are rejoinders an act-utilitarian can make to these potential problems. If we take into account how a person's act will influence others, then the acts cited above (such as breaking promises and ignoring desert) would undermine promising and motivation to work—all practices beneficial to the long-term happiness of society. However, by the time this rejoinder is made, we are already close to rule-utilitarianism, where we apply the utilitarian principle not to individual acts but to general practices.

Since rule-utilitarianism has us follow rules rather than calculate consequences, it is a deontological ethic (though derived from a consequentialist first principle). Rule-utilitarianism will probably include notions of desert, that is, systems of reward and punishment: Deterring bad behavior and motivating good is likely to lead to good consequences. Once the system of desert is in place, I am obliged to give you any money you have earned; whether or not the money could be used elsewhere to create more happiness is irrelevant. The same logic applies to the rules of promising.

Though rule-utilitarianism seems a better theory than act-utilitarianism, it still faces some fairly powerful objections.

Objection a: Happiness and unhappiness are too subjective—too difficult to assess and compare between individuals—to be made the goal of public policy.

Even Bentham realized that to make utilitarian calculations on a large scale would require some objective (measurable) correlate of happiness. Bentham suggested wealth. Wealth, of course, is a terrific metric: You can determine objectively how much wealth an individual has; in many cases you can determine the degree to which she prefers A over B by how much she is willing to spend on A versus B; and you can make straightforward comparisons of wealth between persons. There certainly is some correlation between money and happiness: Some money allows you to satisfy some of your desires, more money allows you to satisfy more. Still, as we know from our discussion in the first chapter, the correlation between money and happiness isn't that strong. Further, any money–happiness correlation virtually vanishes when we're dealing with large amounts of money. For instance, it would make sense to imagine a king owning 80% of his country's wealth; it would make no sense to imagine him having 80% of his country's happiness.

Many utilitarians today talk in terms of satisfying preferences or interests rather than creating happiness.

This reflects a similar maneuver in economics. Preferences (whether stated or displayed in behavior) become a proxy for happiness. The idea is that if a person prefers A to B, we can stipulate that she's "better off" (or more "satisfied") with *A* than *B*; we don't have to talk about her subjective feelings. You get objectivity this way, but much more limited sorts of comparisons. You can only talk about people doing better or worse in terms of their own preference scales; there is no common measure. It's as if I could tell you that Sam has been gaining weight while Sheila is losing weight without ever being able to tell you how much they weigh in terms of some absolute measure (like pounds or kilograms).

We've seen how positive psychologists are working on trying to improve measures of, and collect data on, subjective well-being (SWB). However, this work is at an early stage and is still quite controversial. The best they're likely to get in the near future is solid data on the types of things that tend to make people happy. These data *might* be useful for some social policy decisions, but they're not likely to solve the interpersonal comparison problems.

None of this means that the utilitarian goal of the greatest happiness is a meaningless one. What it does mean is that the goal needs to be formulated more loosely with different correlates used in different contexts. For instance, in one context you might want to talk about basic goods, in another preferences, in another wealth.

Objection b: Utilitarianism treats all desires or preferences as equal, such as

i: the desire to improve one's mind or body versus the desire to goof off;

ii. the desire to treat all people equally versus the desire to discriminate on the basis of skin color.

i reflects the fact that utilitarianism sees no intrinsic value in flourishing. Utilitarianism is only interested in happiness or preference-satisfaction. Utilitarianism doesn't evaluate happiness or preferences as being higher or lower, better or worse: It can't do so, if happiness (SWB) is to be its sole value. Some utilitarians, like John Stuart Mill (see Readings), did try to distinguish between higher and lower pleasures, but such an attempt undermines what is unique about utilitarianism and turns it into the very sort of perfectionist ethic it was intended to replace.

For some critics of utilitarianism the lack of a perfectionist dimension is a weakness. (We'll talk more about perfectionism when we discuss "virtue ethics.")

ii creates a serious problem for utilitarianism as a moral theory. In a society of racists, the greatest happiness might be achieved by a system of discrimination against an ethnic minority: Such a possibility is one most people would expect a satisfactory moral theory to rule out. For one critic, philosopher Ronald Dworkin, this shows that, at the very least, utilitarianism needs to be supplemented by a system of basic rights. Rights would come first; then, in applying the utilitarian principle, any desire that amounted to a desire to violate someone else's rights could then be discounted.

Objection c: Utilitarianism seems to cater to the majority of individuals at the possible expense—maybe even very great expense—of the minority.

If the greatest overall happiness would be gained through a system that took serious advantage of a minority—even to the point of serfdom or slavery—it seems as if utilitarianism ought to endorse that system.

It's important to note the difference between objection *b-ii* and objection *c*. Objection *b-ii* complains that utilitarianism seems to include in its calculations preferences that most of us would consider immoral. Objection *c* isn't referring to the content of preferences but to the outcome of utilitarian calculations. Even in a society of well meaning people, it's possible that utilitarianism might approve a system in which the vast majority are very happy and a minority are very miserable.

For those who are attracted to the idea that morality ought to promote happiness but agree that utilitarianism doesn't afford enough protection to individuals, one way to go is to supplement utilitarianism with a rights view: Individuals have rights which afford them certain protections and guarantees; beyond that, social policy is decided according to the utilitarian principle.

We will talk about rights in the next section. However, it's important to stress that our discussion will be partial and provisional. We'll talk about rights only from the perspective of the sympathetic observer. Later on we'll talk about a narrower conception of rights from an altogether different metaethical perspective.

A first look at rights

A distinction is often made between "negative rights" and "positive rights." We want to make use of this distinction because it will connect with the distinction between "negative liberalism" and "positive liberalism" we'll discuss in the next chapter. However, the positive/negative labels can be misleading so it's important to clarify them.

"Negative rights" are related to a general right not to be interfered with or coerced—as, for instance, in the exercise of religion. However the label also covers basic democratic rights, such as the right to vote, that don't seem negative at all. Nonetheless, the label will work well enough for the moment if we think of negative rights as connected with *our right not to be interfered with without our consent*—and think of democratic rights as related to consent.

Positive rights are rights to resources that enable us to act in certain ways. The category of positive rights usually includes "welfare rights"—claims on society for resources or protections that give us a chance of having at least a minimally satisfying life. Welfare rights can include such things as the right to an education; the right to consumer protection regarding the quality of food and medicine; the right to safe working conditions; and the right to at least a minimal level of social insurance against unemployment, disability and ill health. Positive rights are more controversial than negative rights; also a society must attain a certain level of wealth before most such positive rights are affordable.

At a minimum, rights afford protections for the individual against the larger group or society. These protections aren't absolute: My right to freedom can be curtailed insofar as it interferes with others' right to freedom; my right to life is forfeited if I attempt to take your life. In extreme cases, such as war or massive famine, many rights might have to be suspended. But the point of rights is to give the individual a special weight against any decisions for the collective good—something, as we saw, that utilitarianism does not give.

One could modify rule-utilitarianism with a rights view as follows: That society ought to pursue the greatest happiness (or satisfaction of preferences) of the greatest number as long as certain positive and negative human rights are respected. Rights would come first, then the general happiness. In Ronald Dworkin's famous phrase, rights would "trump" any other considerations.

There are some rights views that seem to dispense with utilitarianism but end up in a similar place. These are views that emphasize negative and positive rights, then add in the free market as the way for society to proceed when basic rights are satisfied or not at issue. But free market theory developed hand in hand with utilitarianism: What you're looking at with the free market is, in a way, a system for the maximum satisfaction of preferences.

I do not mean to imply that any rights view is going to end up in the same place as rule-utilitarianism + rights. If you include enough entitlements into your basic positive rights (so that there is little left over to distribute by other means), you would end up with a morality that stresses economic equality, the kind of morality that could underlie socialism.

On the other hand, if you dispense with positive rights and only acknowledge the negative ones, you're likely to get a very individualist, very unequal society—the kind that could underlie laissez-faire capitalism. We'll talk about these possibilities later.

So far we've talked about assessing moral theories from a "God perspective," either from belief in a God or from seeing morality as that which would be chosen by an ideal observer. However, other philosophers have done their metaethics from what we'll call an "idealized human perspective." This is an attempt to ground ethics, not in religion or in a God-like perspective, but in an ideal of human nature or an idealized individual human perspective. Under this heading we'll discuss Aristotle and virtue ethics; Kant and universalizability; and John Rawls and ideal agent theories.

The idealized human perspective

Aristotle and virtue ethics

The ancient Greek philosophers, including Aristotle (see Readings), had a conception of morality that was very different from our own. As we noted in Part I,

> Historically, different moralities have had different emphases on acts, intentions, and character. For some of the ancient Greek philosophers, including Aristotle, the central emphasis of morality was on developing character traits that in today's terminology would be both moral (like being a just person) and non-moral (being a contemplative person).

One thing that confuses people reading the ancient Greek philosophers in English-language translations is the Greek philosophers' apparent claims about "happiness." We tend to read the word "happiness" as subjective well-being. Then we come up with a statement like the famous quote attributed to Solon: "Call no man happy until he is dead." "What?" we want to ask; "How can you be happy and dead?" But the statement makes sense if understand that the Greek word being translated as "happy" really means something like "successful"—"well lived." Then Solon's statement can be understood as saying, "Don't conclude that a person's life has been lived well until you've seen the whole if it." This does make sense. You wouldn't call the life of a wealthy, accomplished person successful if she ended up disgraced and in prison.

This point about happiness applies to Aristotle. As Patrick Grim said in the Readings in Part I:

> The core term in Aristotle, the core term throughout the *Nicomachean Ethics*, is "eudaimonia."...The term is standardly translated as "happiness." If you translate eudaimonia as happiness, since the *Nicomachean Ethics* is all about eudaimonia, what that would tell you is that one of Aristotle's central concerns is what happiness is and how we are to obtain it. But, as many translators of Aristotle will tell you, happiness is an extremely poor translation for the original Greek term, eudaimonia. A much better translation is "well-being." Some people suggest the term "human flourishing." If you translate eudaimonia as human flourishing, then the central concern of Aristotle's *Nicomachean Ethics* is what human flourishing is and how you obtain it.

Actually Grim is skipping a step here. Aristotle argues that the good life consists in *eudaimonia*—living well—and that *eudaimonia* consists in *arete*—which is more closely connected with flourishing.

Arete is another word that poses a translation problem. It is usually translated as "virtue"—a word that to modern ears suggests Victorian preachers urging us to be chaste. In our discussion we will use the word virtue for lack of anything better, but it must be taken in the broadest sense of flourishing, covering admirable character traits that include some we might not normally think of as moral. We must divest the term of any sexual, Victorian, or peculiarly feminine traits. In fact, for the Greeks and Romans *arete* included the "manly," warrior virtues.

Aristotle, like other ancient Greeks, thought that the way to find out what constituted a good character (*arete*, virtue) was through an analysis of human nature.

For Aristotle all things in the world had a function or activity that was peculiar to them; the good for each thing had to do with how well it performed its function. We won't follow Aristotle and other ancient philosophers in this because the idea that natural things and human beings have inherent purposes has been dispensed with in modern science.

Still many modern philosophers and psychologists are attracted by the "virtue ethics" of the Greeks; these thinkers like the way in which personal and moral values are combined in an overall sense of the good life, with an emphasis on individual flourishing. (This concern with flourishing makes virtue ethics a perfectionist ethic.) Below are some of the features of virtue ethics these modern thinkers find attractive:

1. To many people—and not only the familiar conservative critics—there is something poverty-stricken about the sort of lowest-common-denominator life promoted by commercial advertising. Whereas Bud Lite, rock and roll, ESPN, and celebrity gossip may be legitimate ingredients in a good life, humans are capable of so much more. It seems as if morality ought to put *some* pressure on us to develop our capabilities—to flourish.

2. The contrast between the pursuit of self-interest and the restraints of morality can make morality seem an alien thing—tending to provoke in us the little kid's whiny, "Do I *have* to?" Virtue ethics evokes a more attractive picture of morality as an aspect of flourishing, cultivated along with other good and strong aspects of our nature.

3. A number of female thinkers have argued that the dominant male-authored moralities have tended to stress autonomy and rationality, portraying society as isolated individuals reluctantly agreeing to certain constraints on their behavior. But what

about the caring for partners and children and other family members—the demands and pleasures of close relationships? All this gets ignored by modern morality as if it were something one could take for granted. Yet for most of us it is at the heart of morality. This "ethics of care" is not equivalent to virtue ethics, but a modified virtue ethics can accommodate these concerns better than the more theoretical, rule-based moralities we have discussed so far. (See the Jean Grimshaw selection in Readings for an extended discussion of the idea of a "female ethic.")

With so much going for it, one can see why some people might conclude that virtue ethics is superior to the rights and utilitarian views. However, virtue ethics by its very nature seems too limited to serve as the basis for ethics in modern society.

a. Virtue ethics has virtually nothing to say about the social morality of large-scale societies, such as what protections a society should afford its members and how wealth and other goods should be distributed.

b. Virtue ethics by itself is too vague to guide actions even on a smaller scale. It is a time-honored maxim that we learn virtue by emulating virtuous people. But how are we going to know a certain person is honest, for instance, unless we already know what honesty is? Suppose the person we think is honest flatters people with compliments they don't merit. Does this mean that honesty allows flattery? Or that the person isn't completely honest? It seems we have to answer this by looking at what honesty is/means, not by looking at what purportedly honest people do.

c. Which character traits are virtues—or, at least, which virtues are to be emphasized—depends on what ethics you are dealing with. Many virtue ethics from ancient times were directed to the few, rather than the many: They emphasized aristocratic or "heroic" virtues. In contrast, some religious thinkers saw the highest virtues as being almost the diametrical opposite of those aristocratic virtues: humility rather than pride, pacifism rather than warrior virtues, otherworldliness rather than success in this world. Commercial societies, at least in the beginning, have often emphasized "commercial virtues" like discipline, thrift, and hard work. It's difficult to see how one could debate which virtues are best without first discussing the relevant non-virtue ethics.

d. Elevating a particular conception of a flourishing life into something morally obligatory—as any perfectionist ethics does—is going to be enormously controversial in a society with different conceptions of the good life. Does the good life involve a scientific approach to the world or one based on revelation and faith? (If revelation and faith, which revelations, which faith?) Does it involve an acquisitive lifestyle or one devoted to service to others? Does it involve a life devoted to culture and higher learning or to popular enjoyments and technical skills? Due to these complications, there is a tendency to leave flourishing to the realm of personal values.

None of this is to say, however, that moral virtues shouldn't play a crucial role in any acceptable morality. For people to live moral lives, they need to develop the habits of morality—which is precisely what moral virtues are. And thinking in terms of virtues or good character is a way of integrating morality with your self and self-esteem. You can try to be kind as well as capable, fair as well as successful, and feel good about both.

Kant and universalizability

Another philosopher who does metaethics from what we're calling the idealized human perspective is Immanuel Kant (see Readings). We talked a bit about Kant in Part I; let's review some of what was said:

The eighteenth-century philosopher Immanuel Kant.... distinguished between hypothetical imperatives and categorical imperatives. A hypothetical imperative has the form, "If you want A, you ought to do B." "If you want to impress Mia, you ought to dress a little better." "If you want Lars to do you that favor, you ought to offer him something in return." With the hypothetical imperatives if you don't want to impress Mia or have Lars do you a favor, then the "oughts" don't apply. Kant thought that moral judgments were *not* hypothetical imperatives, but rather categorical imperatives. It wasn't that you weren't

supposed to kill if you wanted to be liked or to avoid jail: It was, Don't kill, period.

Kant claimed that moral rules were necessarily universal and could be recognized by subjecting them to a test we can think of as the ultimate Categorical Imperative: *Act only according to that maxim by which you can at the same time will that it should become a universal law.*

Kant argued that the only thing morally good in itself was a "good will," that is, doing what is morally right because it is right (our duty), not because we're inclined to do it anyway or because doing it is in our self-interest. (This fundamental emphasis on a single character trait would make Kant's a perfectionist ethic on our rough scheme.)

To do our duty is to act according to a moral law out of respect for that law; that's why moral laws are categorical, rather than hypothetical, imperatives.

Kant thought that reason could establish which laws qualify as moral laws; since reason was a common characteristic of all human beings, such moral laws must be apply to all human beings—be universal.

The Categorical Imperative is a test that is supposed to determine whether you are acting in accordance with a moral law. You ask yourself what is the maxim—or general principle—behind your intended action. You then ask whether or not you could will such a principle as a universal law. If not, it doesn't qualify as a moral law.

For example, Kant considers the following question: "May I when in distress make a promise with the intention not to keep it?" Kant says this question can be approached either as a prudential problem or a moral problem. If I consider the question prudentially—in terms of my own advantage—I *may* decide that it is better to keep my promises because my gain from breaking them will be more than offset by the bad reputation and lack of trust I will get from other people. This reasoning yields a principle—I should keep my promises—but, according to Kant, it would not be a *moral* principle. To approach the question as a moral question—to determine whether or not "a lying promise is consistent with duty"—I should ask myself:

...Should I be content that my maxim (to extricate myself from difficulty by a false promise) should hold good as a universal law, for myself as well as for others? and should I be able to say to myself, "Every one may make a deceitful promise when he finds himself in a difficulty from which he cannot otherwise extricate himself"? Then I presently become aware that while I can will the lie, I can by no means will that lying should be a universal law. For with such a law there would be no promises at all, since it would be in vain to allege my intention in regard to my future actions to those who would not believe this allegation, or if they over-hastily did so, would pay me back in my own coin. Hence my maxim, as soon as it should be made a universal law, would necessarily destroy itself....

As we saw in Part I, Kant believed that principles like "Do not lie" and "Do not break promises" derived from the Categorical Imperative were absolute in the sense of having no exceptions. To most of us that seems an unreasonably extreme position. For instance, what if a friend has come to your house to escape a would-be murderer who has threatened to kill him. And what if the would-be murderer appears at your door and asks if your friend is there? Aren't you allowed to lie in that case and say the friend isn't there?

Kant confronts this same hypothetical case in an essay entitled, "On a Supposed Right to Lie from Altruistic Motives." There he stands by his position that it is always wrong to lie, and he adds the following comments:

> After you have honestly answered the murderer's question as to whether his intended victim is at home, it may be that he has slipped out so that he does not come in the way of the murderer, and thus that the murder may not be committed. But if you had lied and said he was not at home when he had really gone out without your knowing it, and if the murderer had then met him as he went away and murdered him, you might justly be accused as the cause of his death, For if you had told the truth as far as you knew it, perhaps the murderer might have been apprehended by the neighbors while he searched the house and thus the deed might have been prevented. Therefore, whoever tells a lie, however well intentioned he might be, must answer for the consequences, however unforeseeable they were, and pay the penalty for them....

This looks like a dodge. We can easily imagine circumstances in which there is no reasonable doubt about what will happen if you tell the truth. Say you

have a studio apartment and your friend is hiding in the closet. If you give him away, he's dead. What Kant's position implies is that you must tell not tell a lie, even if you know that telling the truth will cost an innocent person his life.

It has seemed incredible to a number of critics that Kant should hold such an extreme view when it makes perfectly good sense to universalize rules with exceptions built into them. Exceptions are like sick days: As long as there are a limited number of them, the work will still get done. The practice of truth-telling can survive with exceptions allowing lies to save lives or to spare vulnerable people a lot of pain. The institution of promising can certainly survive even though your promise to meet me has exceptions for emergencies.

If we allow moral principles with exceptions, how does Kant's Categorical Imperative look as the ultimate test of whether or not a principle qualifies as a moral principle?

One thing that is initially attractive about the Categorical Imperative is its resemblance to the Golden Rule—a rule which can be found in many religions and has seemed to many people to be an essential ingredient of morality. The Rule can be stated positively—"Treat other people the way you would want them to treat you"—or negatively—"Don't treat others in ways you wouldn't want to be treated."

Note, however, that the Categorical Imperative is different from the Golden Rule in that what you would or wouldn't *want* is excluded from Kant's principle. Kant was after a foundational principle of ethics that would be derived from reason—not from human wants.

The Categorical Imperative seems to work best when applied to practices—like promising and respecting property—and this suggests that, like the rule-utilitarian, Kant's reasoning is concerned not to undercut practices that are socially beneficial. However, Kant isn't entitled to appeal to the general welfare.

So what then is supposed to go wrong when we imagine universalizing an action like that "lying promise"? That's not so clear.

Many critics have argued that the Categorical Imperative is too formal to generate all and only those principles we would generally consider true moral principles. It seems we could will without contradiction the principle, "Smile at your neighbors when you leave the house," but it would seem odd to think of that as a moral obligation. It seems we could universalize principles to the effect that women, like children, should be protected from making certain kinds of mistakes, but today most of us would consider such a principle to be morally wrong.

In spite of these difficulties, it has seemed to many thinkers that Kant is after something important—perhaps even crucial—with the Categorical Imperative. But what?

One idea connected with the Categorical Imperative is that morality involves general rules that must be impartial—at least in the formal sense discussed in Part I in connection with traffic laws.

> For the law to treat one driver differently than another driver, there must be general and relevant reasons for the differential treatment—that the one driver is driving under the influence or exceeding the posted speed limit. Moral rules would hardly be rules if they weren't impartial in this sense.

Moral reasoning also requires that in trying to formulate or identify moral laws, I should not bias them in my favor.

Kant's Categorical Imperative says that moral laws are universal—apply to all human beings. This is a view that has been shared by many thinkers throughout history. Before Kant, this view had been expressed by the ancient Greek stoics and several monotheistic religions; it is a belief shared today by certain forms of utilitarianism and by ethics based on human rights.

We've already noted that social contract theorists and cultural relativists deny that moral rules are universal. This is definite disagreement with Kant. However, within a societal context, such thinkers will look for laws that are general and impartial; in trying to identify such laws, many will use a type of Golden Rule. Thus their thinking will involve at least some resemblance to Kant's thinking.

Kant presented a second version of the Categorical Imperative he considered equivalent to the version we've been discussing.

> [A]ct as to treat humanity, whether in thine own person or in that of any other, in every case as an end withal, never as means only.

Most critics doubt that this version is actually equivalent to, "Act only according to that maxim by which you can at the same time will that it should become a universal law." Still the second formulation is clearly in line with Kant's view of human beings as rational beings able to perceive and adhere to the moral law. And this second formulation has inspired a number of thinkers, especially those who have emphasized human rights.

Let's turn now to our next philosopher, John Rawls, who takes an approach that has elements of Kantianism, social contract theory and ideal observer theory.

Rawls and the ideal agent

The most famous recent metaethical test for determining normative principles is one proposed by philosopher John Rawls, whose major work is *A Theory of Justice*. Rawls' test bears some resemblance to the ideal observer theory, except that we are to take the perspective, not of God, but of one of a number of idealized agents in an idealized social contract situation that forces them into Golden Rule thinking.

We have already glimpsed basic social contract theory at the end of "Long Live the King," where the townspeople, unable to agree on a religious morality, got together to try to settle on some minimal set of laws that would govern the town. We'll discuss basic contract theory later in this chapter.

Rawls' test involves an idealized social contract situation. As with the ideal observer theory, Rawls conceptualizes moral rules as those that would be chosen from an impartial, sympathetic, knowledgeable point of view. But Rawls substitutes for the detached ideal observer a series of ideal agents. We must choose principles as individuals in a hypothetical situation constructed in a such a way that much of our individuality is masked and selfishness and sympathy largely coincide.

Rawls asks us to imagine ourselves as people in an "original position of equality," choosing behind a "veil of ignorance" the general principles that will govern society. These people have general information about human wants as well as about economics, history and so on, but they cannot know what kind of social position they'll hold, what their natural talents will be, or what their life goals or life plan will be.

Rawls is a critic of utilitarianism. He argues that people in the original position would not choose to live according to the utilitarian principle, a principle which might allow a minority group in society to be sacrificed for the general happiness. He claims people in the original position wouldn't want to bet their one life on a society in which they might be sacrificed for the general welfare.

Instead, Rawls argues that people in the original position would choose the following two principles:

> ...the first requires equality in the assignment of basic rights and duties, while the second holds that social and economic inequalities, for example inequalities of wealth and authority, are just only if they result in compensating benefits for everyone, and in particular for the least advantaged members of society. These principles rule out justifying institutions on the grounds that the hardships of some are offset by a greater good in the aggregate....

Rawls argues that people in the original position would opt for basic rights and duties before any principle regarding the distribution of goods. He further argues that people would select as their principle of distribution what he calls the "difference principle." Rawls' difference principle is extremely egalitarian; it says that society should deviate from an equal distribution of goods only if, *and only to the extent that*, unequal distribution works to the greatest benefit of the least advantaged member of society.

How Rawls' difference principle would work out in practice requires some speculation, but it's likely it would yield a kind of democratic socialism—this in contrast to a pure utilitarian system which would be more likely to lead to our current system, or perhaps to one more extreme in terms of inequalities of wealth.

Some critics have argued that even granting Rawls' metaethical test, the utilitarian principle would be the most rational one to choose. If you're going to bet your life on a social system, it would make more sense to choose a utilitarian system, since a system promoting the greatest happiness of the greatest number would give you the best odds of being happy.

Rawls counters that people "betting" their one life on a social system would pick a more conservative strategy. The idea of losing out completely would be so awful that people would pick a society where the worst-off still did pretty well.

A third possibility—which would accord with people being cautious risk-takers—is that people would opt for a society with a substantial guaranteed minimum and the rest set up to give the best odds on wealth.

There is a risk of distortion in my calling Rawls' procedure a "metaethical test." Note that the kind of hypothetical social contract perspective that Rawls uses could be intended for one of several different purposes:

1. To capture *the* essence of morality;
2. To capture that part of morality that underlies social institutions; or,
3. To capture a fundamental justification for basic political institutions (without quite claiming that morality is involved).

Kant with his Categorical Imperative was clearly after 1—the essence of morality. Rawls started out more modestly, looking for something like 2—that part of morality that underlies social institutions. Eventually Rawls' claims became more modest yet—something like 3. Nonetheless, his work has been very important for metaethical theory and I want to interpret it in that light here.

Under our classification, Rawls' ethic is a sympathy ethic, focusing on human welfare. You could see it as a utilitarianism + rights view, but it is so heavily loaded with positive as well as negative rights that the greatest-welfare aspect is fairly minimal.

Rawls' metaethical test is set up in a way to assure that no perfectionist principles will govern society, including religious principles that don't focus on human welfare (such as those included in a judgmental-God morality). Rawls is unapologetic about this. He thinks that in pluralistic societies, no perfectionist ethic could command sufficient agreement to provide the basis for a stable society. Rawls assumes that people in the original position would demand religious freedom so that they could practice whatever religion they found themselves believing. (This freedom would presumably also allow them to strive for whatever perfectionist personal values they might hold.)

When we discuss Rawls in the context of morality and politics, we'll see that he argues against having desert/merit play any significant role in the distribution of social goods. However, that is a separate argument, not integral to his metaethical test. One could certainly make a case that people in the original position would want desert to play *some* role in the distribution of goods. (For example, if you choose a guaranteed minimum, you might make it conditional upon willingness to work.)

So far we've looked at various normative theories developed from one of two metaethical viewpoints: the God perspective and the idealized human perspective. Now we're going to bring in a third perspective—the unidealized human perspective. The phrase "unidealized" isn't meant to imply that these take an especially negative view of human nature. Some do, but that's not unique to them: No moralities outdo judgmental-God moralities in their dismal view of human beings. Rather, what the phrase "unidealized" is meant to convey is that these moralities don't ask much of people, don't aspire to much morally. They don't demand that people improve themselves; they don't view the needs of others with any special sympathy. What they emphasize is individual self-interest. Of course, as we discussed in Part I, if all they endorsed was self-interest, they wouldn't *be* moralities. Instead, what these theories demand (or reluctantly settle for) is allowing agents the maximum freedom to pursue their self-interest compatible with a like freedom for all. Here morality amounts to reciprocal arrangements among self-interested agents. (This would make them all what we're calling reciprocity ethics.)

It's important to stress that while self-interest can be equivalent to selfishness, it need not be. It could involve a focus on family. It could mean a focus on God. It could be a focus on science or art. Still, an ethics that licenses self-interest is going to minimize one's obligations to others.

All of the ethical views we cover in this chapter take it for granted that humans want the freedom to pursue their self-interest. Perfectionist ethics try to push people toward developing a higher self than they might be inclined to normally. Perfectionist ethics vary in how demanding they are. A judgmental-God ethic, if harsh enough, may demand a total renunciation of the self, while an Aristotelian virtue ethic simply urges the fulfillment of certain human potentials. Sympathy ethics try to push people beyond self-interest to a consideration of others, but they vary in how much consideration they say is owed to others. Some, like act-utilitarianism, insist that you must treat the interests of others as (virtually) equal to your own; others, like rule-utilitarianism and the rights views we've discussed, can leave you lots of room to pursue your own self-interest within the framework of your obligations to others. Still, all sympathy ethics insist on some ethical concern for the needs of others. The ethical views that emerge from the unidealized human perspective do not.

We will look at three types of theories emerging from the unidealized human perspective: evolutionary ethics, basic social contract theory and moral libertarianism.

The unidealized human perspective

Evolutionary ethics

The best-known evolutionary ethic is known as "social Darwinism." It originated in the nineteenth century with Herbert Spencer who took the ideas of evolution and developed them into a philosophy of human societies. Human life was portrayed as a struggle for existence among people, groups and races; it was Spencer, not Darwin, who coined the phrase "survival of the fittest."

Social Darwinists argued that humans should let this natural struggle happen rather than try to interfere with it: The result would be that strong humans would thrive and the weak perish. This idea was used to support laissez-faire (minimally regulated) capitalism and to argue against aid for the poor.

Later in the nineteenth century, Walter Bagehot extended social Darwinist ideas into an analysis of the evolution of societies: Stronger nations evolved by winning conflicts with weaker societies. His ideas were used by others to argue for imperialism by European nations.

Social Darwinism was also combined with the pseudo-scientific racial theories of the day to justify domination by the "white" race.

Social Darwinism lost respectability in the twentieth century. It was blamed in part for the imperialism and "master race" eugenics of the Nazis. It seemed to neglect culture as a crucial determinant of human development. It employed a popular concept of race that seemed to have little basis in genetics: Scientists found that of the small genetic variations that exist among humans, most occur within groups, rather than between them.

Still, for all the errors of social Darwinism, it did rely on one premise that many evolutionary theorists thought *ought* to be true: That all creatures always behave in self-interested ways. Self-interested behavior ought to promote one's survival; putting the interests of others ahead of one's own should diminish slightly one's prospects for survival; therefore, beings with "altruistic" tendencies ought to die out in any group.

Yet there is obvious altruism in nature—not conscious altruism, but behavioral altruism. Evolutionary biologist Richard Dawkins defines behavioral altruism as follows: "An entity, such as a baboon, is said to be altruistic if it behaves in such a way as to increase another such entity's welfare at the expense of its own. Selfish behavior has exactly the opposite effect."

Animals clearly exhibit behavior that is altruistic in this sense. As biologist Mary Midgley says,

> Animals do quite a number of things that can be called altruistic in the full natural sense, because they're actually aimed at serving others. Many creatures take great trouble over rearing their young, and also defend them vigorously, sometimes getting killed in the process. Many also defend and rescue young that are not their own; some will adopt orphans. Some (for example, dolphins and elephants) also help and rescue adults of their species in difficulties, and some, such as wild dogs, will also feed sick and injured adults. Many babysit, and some (such as wild dogs) will bring food to the babysitter.

How is this altruism compatible with the theory of evolution?

An essential part of the answer was developed in the 1960s by biologists George Williams and William Hamilton. Williams suggested that evolution worked fundamentally in terms of the survival of genes, not of the individuals possessing those genes. Often this came to the same thing, but not always. Particular genes survive if the individual survives; but those genes (or copies of them) also survive if the individual nurtures (or even gives up her life for) other individuals sharing those genes. Much of the altruism observed in nature is between genetically related individuals—whether members of the same hive or family. William Hamilton called this "kin selection" (also called "kin altruism"). A child shares half your genes; so does a brother or sister. A cousin shares an eighth of your genes. Hence J.B. Haldane's famous joke, "I will lay down my life for two brothers or eight cousins."

The revelation here was that while it made no sense to imagine evolution working at the level of individuals to produce individuals with some altruistic tendencies, it made perfect sense for evolution working at the level of genes to produce individuals with some altruistic tendencies. Thus evolution and (some) altruism were perfectly compatible.

There is another sort of altruism observed in nature among social species: reciprocal altruism. These are cases where creatures might take risks for, or share food with, other members of the social group who are not related. This works in small stable social groups where the members live long enough to benefit from their cooperation. It usually involves mechanisms for dealing with "cheaters," or "free riders," who try to take and not give back.

In trying to figure out how morality might have arisen from evolution—that is, large-scale human codes where following those codes didn't always coincide with obvious individual self-interest—some biologists argued that small group altruism and cooperation could have been extended to large human groups with the addition of a few other mechanisms. One of these is reputation: One might decide that cooperating (e.g., keeping promises) was the best prudential choice because if others know you cheat, they won't be inclined to cooperate with you in the future. Another mechanism is institutional punishment—a legal system that can penalize certain kinds of cheating.

Other biologists argue that prudential reciprocity is just too thin a basis for morality: For instance, for a large society to function morally, there must be a certain degree of mutual trust and group loyalty. However, once creatures exhibit kin altruism—and the emotions that go with it—such altruism can be extended beyond its original function. For instance, there is an emotional basis for seeing non-related fellow citizens as kin-like, as in "My fellow Americans." Some thinkers have even argued that living in cooperative groups has changed humans genetically so that they are now more cooperative by nature than they might have been in earlier stages of evolution.

These are ongoing debates we won't try to resolve. But one point to emphasize is that in terms of evolution and ethics, evolutionists are not arguing that humans by nature are necessarily self-interested or warlike. These days evolutionists acknowledge cooperative and altruistic human behavior and are trying to figure out how such behavior evolved.

This is not to say that evolutionary theorists are necessarily great optimists about the moral possibilities for human beings. While evolution may have produced a degree of behavioral (and sometimes cognitive) altruism, this altruism overlies a great deal of self-interested behavior. Also such altruism is likely to be strongest in terms of kin and in-groups and to be rather weak toward humans in general. As biologist Frans de Waal says, "evolutionary pressure responsible for our moral tendencies may not all have been nice and positive."

> After all, morality is very much an in-group phenomenon. Universally, humans treat outsiders far worse than members of their own community; in fact, moral rules hardly seem to apply to the outside. True, in modern times there is a movement to expand the circle of morality... but we all know how fragile an effort this is. Morality likely evolved as a within-group phenomenon in conjunction with other typical within-group capacities, such as conflict resolution, cooperation, and sharing....
>
> Obviously the most potent force to bring out a sense community is enmity toward outsiders.... And so the profound irony is that our noblest achievement—morality—has evolutionary ties to our basest behavior—warfare. The sense of community required by the former was provided by the latter....

All this may be of great interest from a scientific standpoint, but what, if anything, does it tell us about normative ethics or metaethics?

Social Darwinists tended to imply that "what is, is right," and this seems to many a blatantly fallacious premise. If certain people are "murderous," does that make their murdering right. If, as many conservative Christians believe, humans are born with original sin, would that make sinning "good"?

On the other hand, there is another familiar expression that seems more reasonable and might apply: "Ought implies can." This means that what can be demanded of people morally has to take account of what they are capable of being and doing. If people by nature are self-interested and favor their own kin and society, morality has to take account of that by not expecting too much of them. This in fact resembles a social conservative argument for free markets we'll see in the next chapter, based not on evolution but something closer to original sin: Given human self-interest and limited altruism, free markets will make of that the best for society; asking people to be selfless is bound to fail.

Of course, if these are directions in which our evolutionary past tends us, they are still only tendencies, and knowing those tendencies may help us overcome them to a degree. In *The Moral Animal*, author Robin Wright makes the following comment:

> We are potentially moral animals—which is more than any other animal can say—but we aren't naturally moral animals. To be moral animals, we must realize how thoroughly we aren't.

All this of course presupposes that pre-human evolutionary trends are still driving human culture. Some thinkers believe that with the advent of language, the ability to converse and reason, the ability to develop Smith's impartial spectator and the dynamics of life within large-scale societies, human life took on a new cultural dynamic that is now the primary driver of human morality.

Basic social contract theory

At the end of "Long Live the King," the townspeople arrive at a kind of social contract:

> People could not agree, they said, but unless they could agree to disagree, any remnant of the old life and civility was bound to be destroyed....

One level-headed member of the council proposed a solution: There must be a gathering of the leaders of all five factions. Their aim must be to settle on some minimum set of laws to which they could all agree, laws which would allow the town to function....

Though everyone recognized the necessity of such a compromise, it was difficult for people to operate within its constraints. People kept wanting to point to their favored edict to prove what was true. "See what's written here," they would say. Yet, if this process were to succeed, it must be based on common agreement, not some other sort of "truth."

An air of best-we-can-do hangs over much basic social contract theory. Certainly this is true of the negotiations at the end of the story. Many of the townspeople have religious moralities that overlap with, but include much more than is contained in, whatever minimal rules the town can agree to. People still believe their religions are true and wish that others could see the truth; they dream of the day the King/God will return and set the others straight. But given all the disagreements and threats of violence, they concede that some sort of common rules must be agreed upon.

There are also townspeople who doubt the existence of the King/God and want to look for morality in human terms—specifically in terms of happiness of society. But they too will have to settle for some minimal agreement made with those who believe morality should be based on the commandments of the King/God.

As in the story, the rise of social contract theory in the modern period was in reaction to religious disagreements and the fear of violence. The Reformation and subsequent wars of religion led some thinkers to doubt the existence of moral truth or to decide that even if such truth existed, people weren't going to agree on what it was. Something new was needed to justify the authority of those in power and the obligation of ordinary citizens to conform to the social order and follow its rules.

Thomas Hobbes (1588–1679) argued that prior to the institution of government, mankind had lived in a state of nature in which life was "solitary, poor, nasty, brutish, and short." Because people had equal needs and relatively equal strength and because they were capable of only limited altruism, the state of nature was bound to involve constant war. The only way to escape the state of nature was for people to agree to a set of rules by which they would be governed and to establish a government to enforce those rules. This agreement Hobbes called the "social contract." Hobbes thought the government had to be a monarchy in which the sovereign had absolute authority: Without such authority, society would fall back into a state of war.

No one today believes (if, indeed, Hobbes did) that historical societies were actually formed by social contracts. Instead, the social contract idea is conceived as a hypothetical test: What sorts of rules would we agree to if we had to draw up a social contract and how do these compare to the rules we have now?

With basic social contract theory, the contract situation is conceived of as hypothetical, but not idealized. In the idealized version we don't know our abilities and interests; in the basic (unidealized) version we do. What's forced upon us by this test isn't sympathy: instead we're to think about what sorts of basic social institutions we would arrive at if we were forced to work out some agreement based on self-interest.

Social contract theorists today assume that the contractors would choose democracy, not monarchy: The contractors would insist on a say in how their society is run. Knowing that there will be no universal agreement on religion, they would choose freedom of religion.

What about the economic system? It's probably safe to assume that the contractors would choose a relatively free market on grounds that this would generate wealth for the society as a whole. But it's not clear how unrestricted the market might be and what protections would be offered those at the bottom. Do we imagine that the powerful and talented would be better off than the others in the absence of society and so would dominate the negotiations? Or do we imagine the powerful and talented would be vulnerable against the greater number of others and so have to make many concessions? How much social insurance you think basic social contract theory is likely to yield depends on which group(s) you imagine would have to make the greatest concessions.

Basic social contract theory may provide a helpful background for thinking about social arrangements in an irreducibly pluralistic atmosphere. But no one would likely take it as capturing the whole of morality or even the essence of that part of morality that underlies social institutions. For one thing, social contract theory denies moral status to those who couldn't negotiate for themselves—for instance, children and people with mental disabilities.

Moral libertarianism

If basic social contract theory has an air of best-we-can-do, our next theory, moral libertarianism, has an air of pugnacious vitality.

Moral libertarianism is an ethical theory based on rights—not on positive rights, which it rejects, but on a very narrow version of negative human rights. The individual's right not to be interfered with becomes the most important—maybe the only—moral value. In the most famous defense of libertarianism, *Anarchy, State and Utopia*, the author, Robert Nozick, says this:

> Individuals have rights, and there are things no person or group may do to them (without violating their rights). So strong and far-reaching are these rights that they raise the question of what, if anything, the state and its officials may do.

Nozick is doing political philosophy, but he says that "Moral philosophy sets the background for, and the boundaries of, political philosophy." For Nozick, negative rights are primary and rule out treating people according to any calculation of the general good.

> ...There are only individual people, different individual people, with their own individual lives. Using one of these people for the benefit of others...does not sufficiently respect and take account of the fact that he is a separate person, that his is the only life he has. He does not get some overbalancing good from his sacrifice, and no one is entitled to force this on him—least of all a state or government that claims his allegiance (as other individuals do not) and that therefore scrupulously must be *neutral* between its citizens....

Nozick appeals to a concept of self-ownership in support of moral libertarianism. Nozick argues that if I own myself, then I own my labor, and if I own my labor, then I own the fruits of my labor. Taking away the fruits of my labor—by taxation, for instance—in order to help others violates my right of self-ownership.

> ...Seizing the results of someone's labor is equivalent to seizing hours from him and directing him to carry on various activities. If people force you to do certain work, or unrewarded work, for a certain period of time, they decide what you are to do and what purposes your work is to serve apart from your decisions. This process whereby they take this decision from you makes them a *part-owner* of you; it gives them a property right in you....

The self-ownership argument carries over into personal, as well as economic, life. Whether you choose to lead a flourishing life or not is your business. What sexual activities you choose, what drugs you take, what risks you take, what lifestyle you choose—none of this is anyone else's business, assuming your activities aren't directly threatening another person or violating some contract (marriage, employment) that you have voluntarily entered into. And assuming you are willing to take the consequences: No one else is obligated to help you out when things go bad.

In the next chapter we will discuss political libertarianism which is often, but not always, justified in terms of moral libertarianism. Here let's focus on moral libertarianism and ask ourselves what we are to think of it.

As the heirs of Western culture, we're likely to embrace the values of freedom and individuality. We are suspicious of people (or government) telling us how to live, and we often express a philosophy of live-and-let-live. Sometimes the moral claims made by one group or another seem so onerous and guilt-provoking that we'd like to shake ourselves free of those demands. On the other hand, can "You can't make me do what I don't want to do" be the final truth of morality? The culmination of centuries of saints and reformers, the fight against evil? The end-all of humans who have grown up in and had their identities forged by communities? Sometimes moral libertarianism seems only an anti-morality, insisting on self-interest as the ultimate good.

There's no doubt that negative rights are an enormously important aspect of morality. If enforced, they can protect individuals from all sorts of onslaughts and intrusions from other individuals or governments. Getting people and governments to respect such rights has been an enormous achievement in human history.

Still: What is the justification for seeing negative rights as the whole of morality? Certainly moral libertarianism isn't the morality reflected in most religions; it's hard to see it as the morality that would be approved by the sympathetic God/ideal observer or Rawls' ideal contractors. Of course, moral libertarians would reject those tests. But what test would yield their ethic? (One criticism of Nozick was that he provided no justification for his emphasis on strong negative rights.)

We'll be talking more about moral libertarianism when we discuss political libertarianism in Part III.

In this chapter we have discussed various moral theories divided into the categories of reciprocity, sympathy, and perfectionist ethics. This division is meant only to capture the main emphasis of each ethic. A judgmental-God ethic that allows for undeserved salvation under certain conditions is adding a sympathy element. Perfectionist ethics that include being charitable among the characteristics of a virtuous person includes a sympathy element. Sympathy ethics can make room for people to follow their personal ideals (which can include flourishing), but isn't likely to include substantial perfectionist moral elements.

It was noted earlier that most ethics include some elements of desert. As we'll see in the next chapter, desert is a central issue in political philosophy and a hotly contested one.

One final point before we move on. There's always the likelihood that any discussion of morality is going to get bogged down by the issue of moral relativism—with someone saying something like, "I don't see the point of talking about this stuff—it's all relative anyway." If this isn't a problem for you or your class, go ahead and move on to Part III. However, if it is a problem, I have appended to this chapter a discussion of moral relativism. I don't attempt to disprove the position as a whole—though certain popular versions of it are easy to disprove. The point of that discussion is to show what a sensible moral relativist position might look like and to show that holding such a position doesn't bar one from, or give one an excuse for not, participating in a discussion of moral issues.

Notes and selected sources

Religious ethics

SOURCES

C. Daniel Batson and W. Larry Ventis. *The Religious Experience: A Social-Psychological Perspective*. Oxford: Oxford University Press, 1982.

Jean Porter. "Trajectories in Christian Ethics." In *The Blackwell Companion to Religious Ethics*, ed. William Schweiker. Oxford: Blackwell Publishing, 2005, pp. 227–36.

Adam Smith. *Theory of Moral Sentiments* (1759).

Eliot Turiel. *The Culture of Morality: Social Development, Context, and Conflict*. Cambridge: Cambridge University Press. 2002.

NOTES

Personal sins vs. social sins: Batson/Ventis, pp. 282–9.

"Although the highly religious...." Batson/Ventis, p. 289.

"The first theologian to defend...." Porter, p. 228.

"Even if God said it...." Turiel, p. 114.

"The boy evaluated...." Turiel, pp. 114–15.

"According to surveys...." gallup.com/poll/27877

"Smith argued...." Smith, pt. III, ch. I

Utilitarianism and rights

SOURCES

Jeremy Bentham, *Principles of Moral and Political Philosophy* (1789).

Ronald Dworkin, *Taking Rights Seriously*. London: Duckworth, 1978.

John Stuart Mill, *Utilitarianism* (1861).

W. Stark (ed.) *Jeremy Bentham's Economic Writings*. London: George Allen & Unwin, 1954, vol 1.

NOTES

"By the principle of utility...." Bentham, ch. 1.

Bentham and wealth as metric: Stark (ed.), p. 117. Bentham says: "Money is the instrument of measuring the quantity of pain or pleasure. Those who are not satisfied with the accuracy of this instrument must find out some other that shall be more accurate, or bid adieu to politics and morals."

Mill on higher pleasures: Mill, II, "What Utilitarianism Is."

Dworkin on supplementing utilitarianism with rights: Dworkin, pp. xi–xii and 94–100.

Dworkin on rights as discounting certain desires: See article by Jeremy Waldron in Readings.

The idealized human perspective

SOURCES

Aristotle. *The Nicomachean Ethics*.

Immanuel Kant. *Fundamental Principles of the Metaphysic of Morals*. Trans. T. K. Abbott. Amherst, NY: Prometheus Books, 1988.

Immanuel Kant. "On the Supposed Right to Lie from Altruistic Motives." Trans. Lewis White Beck. *Immanuel Kant: Critique of Practical Reason and Other Writings in Moral Philosophy*. Chicago, IL: University of Chicago Press, 1949.

John Rawls, *A Theory of Justice*. Cambridge, MA: The Belknap Press of Harvard University Press, 1971.

NOTES

"...Should I be content that my maxim...?" Kant, Fundamentals. p. 28.

"After you have honestly answered...." Kant, "...Right to Lie...." p. 348.

"...the first requires equality in...." Rawls, pp. 14–15.

The unidealized human perspective

SOURCES

Richard Dawkins, *The Selfish Gene*. Oxford: Oxford University Press, 1976.

Frans de Waal. *Primates and Philosophers*. Princeton, NJ: Princeton University Press, 2006. (Edited and introduced by Josiah Ober and Stephen Macedo. Comments by Robert Wright, Christine M. Korsgaard, Phillip Kitcher and Peter Singer.)

Thomas Hobbes. *Leviathan* (1651).

Mary Midgley. *Beast and Man: The Roots of Human Nature*. Ithaca, NY: Cornell Univ. Press, 1978.

Robert Nozick. *Anarchy, State, and Utopia*. New York: Basic Books, 1974.

Matt Ridley. *The Origins of Virtue*. New York: Viking Penguin, 1996.

Robert Wright. *The Moral Animal: Why We Are the Way We Are: The New Science of Evolutionary Psychology*. New York: Pantheon Books, 1994.

NOTES

Dawkins def: Dawkins, p. 4.

"Animals do quite a number of things...." Midgley, p. 131.

Williams, Hamilton, etc. Ridley, pp. 17–24.

"After all, morality...." de Waal, pp. 53–4.

"We are potentially...." Wright, p. 344.

Re morality and culture, see Korsgaard and Kitcher in de Waal.

"solitary, nasty...." Hobbes, ch. 13.

"Individuals have rights...." Nozick, p. ix.

"Moral philosophy sets the background...." Nozick, p. 6.

"There are only individual people...." Nozick, p. 33.

"Seizing the results...." Nozick, p. 172.

Definitions

(Terms are defined in the order in which they appeared in the text.)

1. *Utilitarianism*: A view of morality which says that an act or social system is right which leads to the greatest happiness of the greatest number.
2. *Divine Command theory*. A metaethical theory that says that the only thing that makes something right/wrong is the mere fact of God's commanding it.
3. *Judgmental God* (as used here): A God-type with a morality that is deontological and severely perfectionistic, with a heavy emphasis on desert.
4. *Deontological ethics*: Ethics that deny right and wrong is simply a matter of consequences. (Deontological ethics are generally those that lay down rules with dos and don'ts, duties and obligations.)

5. *Desert*: What people *deserve* in terms of blame or praise, punishment or reward.
6. *Perfectionist ethics*: Those that set standards of conduct and character that don't necessarily have anything to do with causing other people harm.
7. *Sympathetic God* (as used here): A God-type who is more accepting (than a judgmental God would be) of people as they are and more interested in helping them than changing them.
8. *God perspective*: Imagining how a God would want humans to behave.
9. *Ideal observer theory*: A secular version of the God perspective in which one asks: What sort of ethic would an ideal observer endorse who was sympathetic to all human beings and their concerns, was

not biased toward any particular individual or group, and had a general knowledge of the world?

10. *Impartial spectator*: Adam Smith's term for a type of ideal observer.

11. *Utility*: Happiness, well-being, or "satisfaction.

12. *Consequentialist ethic*: An ethic which says that an act or policy is right or wrong solely in terms of its consequences.

13. *Hedonistic consequentialist ethic*: An ethic that says the only consequences we need to consider are those relating to feelings of happiness and unhappiness.

14. *Act-utilitarianism*: Each individual act is to be guided by the utilitarian principle.

15. *Rule-utilitarianism*: The utilitarian principle is used to determine the best set of rules; then those rules are to be followed irrespective of the consequences in particular cases.

16. *Negative rights*: Related to a general right not to be interfered with or coerced. (The label also covers basic democratic rights.)

17. *Positive rights*: Rights to resources that enable us to act in certain ways. (The category of positive rights usually includes "welfare rights.")

18. *Welfare rights*: Claims on society for resources or protections that give us a chance of having at least a minimally satisfying life.

19. *Idealized human perspective*: A metaethical perspective that attempts to ground ethics in an ideal of human nature or an idealized individual human perspective.

20. *Eudaimonia*: A Greek word for living well.

21. *Arete*: A Greek word for flourishing—good character.

22. *Virtue*: Admirable character trait

23. *The Categorical Imperative*: Kant's test supposed to determine whether or not you are acting in accordance with a moral law (whether you could will the principle behind your act as a universal law).

24. *Universalize*: To consider a rule as applying to all human beings.

25. *The Golden Rule*: A rule to treat others as you would want to be treated.

26. *Original position (of equality)*: Rawls' hypothetical position from which one would choose the general principles that will govern society.

27. *Veil of ignorance*: A condition Rawls' sets for those in the original position, that (among other things) they cannot know what kind of social position they'll hold, what their natural talents will be, or what their life goals will be.

28. *Difference principle*: One of Rawls' principles of justice, which says that society should deviate from an equal distribution of goods only if, *and only to the extent that*, unequal distribution works to the greatest benefit of the least advantaged member of society.

29. *Unidealized human perspective*: A metaethical perspective that minimizes the scope and demands of morality and allows maximum self-interest.

30. *Social Darwinism*: The view that evolution is a process that tends toward the survival of the fittest and that ethics should support this process.

31. *Altruism (biology)*: Behaviour that promotes the reproductive success of others ahead of its own.

32. *Kin altruism*: Altruism that promotes the reproductive success of genetically related individuals.

33. *Reciprocal altruism*: Helping another in a way that does not accord with your immediate self-interest but with the expectation of help being reciprocated later on.

34. *Social contract theory ("basic")*: It views morality as an actual or hypothetical contract among members of a society.

35. *State of nature*: The situation that humans did inhabit prior to the social contract (historical claim) or that they would inhabit without one (hypothetical claim).

36. *Moral libertarianism*: An ethical theory based on negative rights which views the individual's right not to be interfered with as the most basic right.

37. *Political libertarianism*: A political view (often based wholly or in part on moral libertarianism) which insists on minimal government interference in the economic and social realms. (To be discussed in Part III.)

Questions

(Please explain your answers, making specific reference to relevant passages in the discussion.)

1. The text gives three ways in which morality might be connected to religion. What are they?

2. *(a) Is something good because God commands it or, (b) Does God command it because it is good?*
   What answer does Divine Command theory give to this dilemma? What problems do some see with Divine Command theory?

3. The text characterizes a "judgmental God" type as one having a morality that is (i) deontological; (ii) severely perfectionistic; and, (iii) has a strong emphasis on desert. Explain these characteristics (i–iii).

4. What is the "God perspective"? What is the "ideal observer theory"?

5. What is utilitarianism? Why have some seen this as the morality a sympathetic ideal observer would choose?

6. Explain the difference between act-utilitarianism and rule-utilitarianism. Explain the difference between a deontological ethic and a consequentialist ethic. Is act-utilitarianism deontological or consequentialist? What about rule-utilitarianism?

7. Explain how rule-utilitarianism is supposed to solve some of the problems with act-utilitarianism?

8. What are some of the problems with rule-utilitarianism?

9. Explain why some want to supplement utilitarianism with a rights view.

10. Explain the distinction between positive and negative rights.

11. Aristotle said that all people seek *eudaimonia* and that *eudaimonia* consists in *arete*. What did he mean by this?

12. What is virtue ethics? What have some thinkers found so attractive about it?

13. What are some of the problems with virtue ethics?

14. Kant set a test—"the Categorical Imperative"—that we are supposed to use to decide if some rule counts as a moral law? Explain his test.

15. Explain how Kant applied his test to decide whether or not "a lying promise is consistent with duty."

16. What are some problems with Kant's Categorical Imperative as *the* method to determine what are, and aren't, moral laws?

17. Rawls asks us to imagine ourselves as people in an "original position of equality," choosing behind a "veil of ignorance" the general principles that will govern society. Explain this idea and say what we should hope to gain from such imaginings.

18. What are Rawls' complaints against utilitarianism?

19. Explain Rawls' difference principle. What are his arguments for that principle?

20. What is social Darwinism?

21. How do biologists reconcile altruism in nature with the theory of evolution?

22. Suppose we agree that evolution tends to promote certain human characteristics? What bearing would/should this have on our ethical views?

23. What is basic social contract theory? Explain the difference between its "real" and "hypothetical" forms.

24. Does social contract theory tend to take an optimistic view of ethics? Explain.

25. What is moral libertarianism? What arguments are given for it?

26. What bothers some people about moral libertarianism?

27. *You are taking a multiple choice test that you need to pass in order to get credit for a course you need to graduate. You can see just ahead of you the answers on the test sheet of a woman you know is doing well in the class. No one is monitoring you closely and you can see her answers without any obvious movements of your head. Do you copy some of her answers or not?*
   How would you go about deciding the morality of the situation if you were
   (a) an act-utilitarian;
   (b) a rule-utilitarian;
   (c) a Kantian;
   (d) traditionally religious (pick a particular tradition if you need to)?

28. *You've cheated on your partner and you feel awful about it. You're reading the newspaper together and come across a "Dear Amy" column about cheating. In the course of joking about the column, your partner asks you casually (at least it seems casual) if you've ever cheated in this relationship.*

    How would you go about deciding the morality of lying to your partner if you were

    (a) an act-utilitarian;
    (b) a rule-utilitarian;
    (c) a Kantian; and
    (d) traditionally religious?

29. *Your state has a proposition on the ballot that would legalize gay marriage in your state.*

    How would you go about deciding the morality of this proposition if you were:

    (a) a rule-utilitarian;
    (b) a libertarian;
    (c) John Rawls;
    (d) a believer in strong positive rights;
    (e) traditionally religious?

30. *Your state has a proposition on the ballot that would increase state income tax by half a percent on all those making over $250,000 in order to expand facilities for the increasing number of people who are homeless as a result of a bad economy.*

    How would you go about deciding the morality of this proposition if you were:

    (a) a rule-utilitarian;
    (b) John Rawls;
    (c) a libertarian;
    (d) a believer in strong positive rights?

Appendix: moral relativism

What's supposed to be relative?

If one asked the average student what relativism is, the answer might go something like this: Relativism says every belief is as good (or as true) as any other.

Or, since much relativism tends to focus on whole cultures, the answer might be this: Relativism says the beliefs of any culture are as good (or as true) as the beliefs of any other culture.

However, it's important that we not toss around the terms "good" and "true" interchangeably, as if they're synonyms. "True" is a property of statements, including belief-statements. To say a belief is true is to say something about its reflecting the way the world or our common experience is. To say a belief is good or bad (rather than true or false) is to say something very different.

Consider a patient in the hospital who has only a few days to live, but (not having seen the test results) believes she's going to recover. Her belief is false (let's say she would accept the test results if she saw them), but perhaps her false belief is good in that it spares her suffering during her last days. Whether her belief is good says nothing about whether it's true. We want to talk about relativism in the most challenging sense: Not that the beliefs of different cultures are equally good, but that they are equally true.

If we're talking about value judgments, of course, the judgments will use words like "good" or "right." But relativism still focuses on truth. For instance, with judgments like "X is good" and "X is bad," the question for relativism is whether all statements about something being good or bad are equally true.

When we consider relativism, we need to distinguish different kinds of belief. Consider the following two (totally imaginary) societies and some of their beliefs:

The Alphas are deists: They believe that there is one God who created the world and set it in motion and then remained totally uninvolved thereafter. This God created the world to be good.

The Betas are polytheists: They believe in a number of different gods, some benign, some malevolent.

The Alphas believe in the germ theory of disease. They believe disease is a totally natural phenomenon, though they recognize it has important psychological components.

The Betas believe that disease is purely a matter of warring spirits trying to hurt or heal human beings.

The Alphas consider the killing of children to be the worst offense there is. They have the death penalty for adults who intentionally kill children; they have the death penalty for other serious offenses as well.

The Betas allow the suffocation of deformed or unwanted infants, though they are very protective of, and affectionate toward, the infants they keep. They are horrified at the killing of an adult, and forbid killing in all instances but those of unavoidable self-defense. There is no death penalty.

Let's chart these differences:

Alphas	Betas
1. One benign but detached god	1. Warring benign and malevolent gods
2. Disease natural; germ theory	2. Disease caused by malevolent gods
3. Wrong to kill infants Death penalty for adults	3. Suffocation of certain infants OK Killing adults always wrong

We have what could be considered three types of beliefs here.

In the first line, we have *religious beliefs* (a subcategory of what are often called "metaphysical beliefs"). Each culture has a different belief in the type and nature of the gods and spirits that exist.

In the second line we have *factual* or *empirical beliefs*. If you'll remember from our discussion in the first chapter, "factual" doesn't mean "true." It relates more to questions of what the facts are. Facts here relates to matters covered by science and sense experience.

In the last line we have *value judgments*, in this case moral/ethical judgments having to do with the rightness or wrongness of killing.

The division of beliefs into metaphysical, empirical, and moral has a somewhat disreputable history. A group called the logical positivists tried to argue that only empirical beliefs, being tied in a certain way to sense experience, could be true or false. Metaphysical and normative judgments were literally meaningless, having at most a poetic or emotive significance.

I am not putting forward the distinction in order to disparage any particular type of statement. Nor do I claim that there are sharp dividing lines between the categories. But with those disclaimers, I think that the metaphysical/empirical/ethical distinction can be useful in sorting out types of relativism.

There are statements that fit into one category or another and must be approached with different kinds of evidence. Consider: Religious: "God exists";

Empirical: "HIV/AIDS is caused by a virus"; Moral: "Killing humans except in self-defense is always wrong."

Accordingly, we could have at least three kinds of relativism: Metaphysical (including religious) relativism; empirical relativism; and moral relativism. It's important to recognize the difference so we're not trying to prove, say, empirical relativism by bringing examples more appropriate to moral relativism.

A thoroughgoing relativist would believe in all three kinds. But to me the weakest form of relativism is empirical relativism. Regarding our fictional societies, I believe you would have an easier time proving the germ theory of disease versus the spirit theory of disease than you would resolving the religious or ethical controversies.

But wouldn't proving the germ theory of disease necessarily get you into religion/metaphysics since you'd have to prove either that the spirits don't exist or don't affect human health?

Not necessarily—not if we frame the issue more narrowly than that.

Think of how the germ theory and religion now co-exist in economically developed societies. The germ theory didn't disprove religion in general, but it did force religions to reformulate some beliefs about disease. Most religions eventually conceded that by and large diseases had natural causes. But they continued to believe that the spiritual also had an influence—continuing to believe, for instance, in the efficacy of prayer.

When I talk about proving the germ theory of disease I'm talking about proving that the germ theory is an important—perhaps the most important—explanation of disease and that spiritual explanations by themselves simply aren't adequate. I'm talking about proving, for instance, that a vaccine is better protection against disease than any religious rituals.

This is not to say that "proving" would be easy. In his book, *Cosmopolitanism*, philosopher Kwame Antony Appiah, whose father was from Ghana, has an amusing discussion of the difficulties that would be involved in trying to convince his father's Asante kinfolk of the germ theory of disease.

Take the simple-seeming question of whether you can be harmed by witchcraft. How would you go about persuading one of my Asante kinfolk that it could not be?....Akosua, your Asante interlocutor, has an aunt who fell ill last year and everyone knows it was caused by witchcraft by her daughter-in-law. The family went to a malaam and slaughtered a sheep. She got better. Akosua wants to know why her aunt got better, if the sheep had nothing to do with it; why she got ill, if there's no witchcraft. And, of course, while you think that these questions have answers, you don't know for sure what they are.

On the other hand, you have to persuade this Akosua of the existence of tiny, invisible atoms, strung together to make viruses, particles so small that you cannot see them with the most powerful magnifying lens, yet so potent that they can kill a healthy adult. Consider how long it took to persuade European scientists that this was so, how complex the chain of inferences that led first to the germ theory of disease and then to the identification of viruses. Why should anyone believe this story, just because you said so? And could you—and I mean you, not some biology professor—provide her with convincing evidence?...

Those of us who are given scientific educations have a significant advantage. It's not that we are individually more reasonable; it's that we have been given better materials with which to think about the world....The best traditional predictors of the weather in Asante—and that is something that matters for a farming civilization—are simply not as good as the ones that the National Meteorological Office now provides, using modern scientific models, Who knows where we would be with the HIV/AIDS pandemic in Africa if we did not have modern scientific tools: tests for the viruses, drugs for treatment, the understanding that predicts that condoms will prevent transmission of the disease? The advance of reason in the industrialized world is not the product of greater individual powers of reasoning. It is the result of the fact that we've developed institutions that can allow ordinary human beings to develop, test, and refine their ideas. What's wrong with the theory of witchcraft is not that it doesn't make sense but that it isn't true....

One might want to argue that even though a spirit-only theory of disease might be false, it could be more advantageous in other respects (promoting social cohesion or a more spiritual attitude toward life). This, however, would be to shift the argument. It would be to talk not about the *truth* of belief but about the *benefit* of belief. And relativism is supposed to be a thesis about truth.

Empirical relativism seems weak. What about metaphysical/religious relativism? Here we'll merely note the important distinction between religious *relativism* and religious *skepticism*. Both positions oppose the view that we can know a particular religious view is true, but the two positions are quite different:

Religious relativism: All religious beliefs are equally true.

Religious skepticism: Not all religious beliefs can be equally true (since they purport to describe different deities with different commands), but we can't know which, if any, is true.

For religious relativism to make any sense, you'd have to maintain that statements of different religions (or religious sects) don't conflict—that they are describing totally different phenomena or are merely symbolic. Some theologians have made that claim, though it strikes me as implausible as an analysis of all religious statements.

Religious skepticism would agree with believers that statements of belief are (usually) statements about something, but would argue that there is no strong evidence supporting one set of religious beliefs over against another. An agnostic would be a religious skeptic.

What we want to focus on is ethical (moral) relativism, which comes in several types. Here is a list covering the relativisms we've discussed so far plus the subtypes of ethical relativism we need to discuss:

1. Empirical relativism
2. Metaphysical (religious) relativism
3. Ethical/moral relativism
   a. Metaethical relativism
      i. Cultural relativism
      ii. Individual relativism (subjectivism)
   b. Normative relativism

Looking at the general category of ethical relativism, let's distinguish between metaethical and normative relativism.

Metaethical relativism says: *All moral beliefs (cultural or individual) are equally true.*

Normative relativism: *It's wrong (one ought not) to judge another (culture, individual).*

Metaethical relativism and normative relativism often get confused with one another, but they are very different. Normative relativism is a moral judgment about what's right and wrong. Metaethical relativism is a claim about the logic of moral judgments.

When the difference between metaethical relativism and normative relativism is recognized, it is often assumed that normative relativism follows from metaethical relativism. But that, too, is a confusion. For many people there does seem to be a *psychological connection* between the two. But there is no *logical connection*.

This should be simple to see once we're clear on the two concepts. Metaethical relativism says all moral judgments are equally true. Normative relativism says that "It's wrong to judge another person or culture." But according to metaethical relativism, "It's not wrong to judge another person or culture" must be equally true. Metaethical relativism implies no judgment about what's right or wrong.

It implies nothing about whether tolerance toward other beliefs is right or wrong.

We're not saying that tolerance may not be an important moral value; we're only saying tolerance has no logical connection to metaethical relativism.

It's important to note that you can see a lot of morality as relative without being a moral relativist. For instance, suppose you felt that the only objective moral wrong was to hurt another person (with the appropriate qualifications, like self-defense, written in). That wouldn't make you a relativist—just someone with a very stripped-down morality.

We're going to focus on the claim of metaethical relativism that all moral judgments are equally true. As indicated by the list above, there are two forms of metaethical relativism, one referring to cultures (the moral beliefs of all cultures are equally true), the other to individuals (the moral beliefs of different individuals are equally true). We will start with cultural relativism.

Cultural relativism

For ease of speaking, we'll simply say "cultural relativism," rather than "cultural moral relativism." However, it's important to remember that we are talking here only about moral beliefs, not empirical ones.

Cultural relativism seems to be making two claims:

CR1: The predominant moral beliefs of different cultures are equally true

CR2: Moral beliefs within a culture are true or false depending on whether they accord with the predominant beliefs of that culture.

CR2 is not always expressed by—perhaps not always believed by—people who would call themselves cultural relativists; the phrase "cultural relativism" is sometimes used rather loosely. Some cultural relativists have made *CR2* explicit, such as Ruth Benedict, a famous early twentieth-century anthropologist.

In any case, something like CR2 has to be part of cultural relativism or the position would reduce to individual relativism—that is, the idea that the beliefs of individuals are equally true. In order for cultural relativism to be distinct, it has to say that judgments within a culture are true or false depending on whether or not they are in accord with the predominant cultural morality.

There seem to be at least three reasons that tend people toward cultural relativism: The diversity of cultures; anthropological studies of native cultures that initially made them seem monolithic; and sympathy for native cultures against Western prejudice and imperialism.

The diversity of cultures.

The mere exposure to radically different moral beliefs has tended to shock people and challenge their beliefs. Morality seems to be helped by a certain provincialism, a sense that how we see and do things is how all humans see and do things. To find out that other humans see and do things very differently challenges the idea that our beliefs are "natural" and "self-evident." If they are not obviously true, what are they? Perhaps they are only the accidents of culture having no overriding truth.

Seeing each native culture as homogeneous, though different from other cultures.

Individual native cultures tend to be more traditional, with long-lasting customs and less diversity. Further, they tended to look more homogeneous than they really were to anthropologists who first began to study them, anthropologists struggling to form first impressions and learn the language. The contrasts that stood out were between different cultures as blocks of beliefs.

Sympathy for native cultures against Western prejudice and imperialism.

The late nineteenth and early twentieth centuries saw racism and imperialism given thorough scientific—that is, pseudo-scientific—support. Herbert Spencer took the idea of Darwinian evolution and (mis)applied it to human societies. Social Darwinists supported laissez-faire capitalism and argued that competition would give rise to the "fittest" human beings. Governments should not try to interfere in the process or try to help the weak in any way.

In the eighteenth century various systems arose for classifying humans and other living things and these systems often grouped humans in racial groups in a way that supported Western prejudice, with the peoples of Europe always designated as superior. In the nineteenth century these same prejudices attached to certain prejudice-confirming measurement schemes—such as measurements of the skull—that made the racism seem even more scientific.

The elevation of competition and the denigration of native peoples made a perfect justification for imperialism. Sometimes it was dressed up in a paternalistic guise—bringing civilization and Christianity to native peoples.

In the United States, Franz Boas (the teacher of Margaret Mead and Ruth Benedict) was one of the first anthropologists to reject the prevailing evolutionary anthropology of the time. He attacked pseudo-scientific claims about the differences between the races and pushed for an anthropological method that is used today—suspending judgment of a culture in order to understand that culture.

Many subsequent anthropologists argued that each culture made sense in its own terms and there was no justification for belief in the superiority of Western culture.

One can see how the position of cultural relativism arose. Still, as we have seen, moral relativism put in terms of cultures must include *CR2*. And *CR2* is obviously incorrect.

If *CR2* were true, we would resolve moral questions by looking to see what the majority of people in our society believes. That's not what we do.

Suppose I'm a conservative Catholic who believes that abortion is wrong in virtually every case. Suppose an opinion poll shows that the vast majority of Americans disagree with me. Must I conclude that my views on abortion are false? Of course not. Nobody thinks that right and wrong should be determined by opinion polls. But that's just what cultural relativism implies.

Cultural relativism could only make sense if cultures were monolithic. But they are not. Today it is clearer than ever how much disagreement there is within every culture.

If moral disagreement is to be used as evidence for relativism, it would have to be for individual relativism, not cultural relativism.

Individual relativism/moral subjectivism

It is important to note that individual relativism doesn't deny the evidence adduced for cultural relativism in terms of the vast differences between the moral beliefs of different cultures. It doesn't deny that many people adopt the beliefs of their cultures, that they are brought up to do so. It doesn't deny that many people may think in terms of their cultural mores when deciding ethical questions. What it does say, in effect, is that the relativity of morals doesn't stop at the level of culture; it goes all the way down to the individual.

I have used the term "individual relativism" to make obvious the contrast with cultural relativism. But individual relativism is more traditionally called "moral subjectivism," indicating that morality is relative because it reduces to the individual's subjective reactions to the world.

In the twentieth century, philosophers have tried to give careful analyses of our moral language to get at what we're saying when we make moral judgments. Moral subjectivists, believing that ethics is based more on feeling than fact, have offered analyses of moral language in terms of feelings and attitudes.

An early subjectivist claim was that in saying something is wrong, a person is saying she doesn't approve of it. "X is wrong"="I don't approve of X." You can see how, under this analysis, ethical judgments would all be equally true. If I say that second trimester abortion is always wrong and you say it isn't, I'm saying that I disapprove of it while you're saying you don't disapprove of it; assuming neither of us is lying, both statements can be equally true. Something can be both right and wrong at the same time, the same way something can be both liked and disliked at the same time.

The problem with this account is that it doesn't quite capture the sense of disagreement or clash that occurs in ethical discourse. Imperatives that express feelings seemed like a better model. Thus "abortion is wrong" might be better analyzed as "I disapprove of abortion—do so as well!" or "Let's not allow abortions!" Imperatives can convey the clashing of attitudes and intentions, but they aren't true or false. If someone says, "Let's go see that new slasher film tonight," you might say lots of things—"I hate that kind of movie—I won't go" or "I'd rather do something else tonight," but the one thing you wouldn't say was, "That's false."

Earlier we gave what amounted to an abbreviated definition of metaethical moral relativism in terms of beliefs being equally true or not. The full definition should read as follows: *Metaethical moral relativism says that all moral beliefs are equally true, or equal in being neither true nor false.* You can see now the reason for this expansion: Some subjectivists analyze moral judgments in terms of imperatives that are neither true nor false.

It would be implausible to argue that most people understand morality as a subjective activity. They may simply be referring to rules they've been taught to accept, perhaps rules prescribed by their religion. They may be projecting their feelings as if they were objective qualities of the world. The subjectivist argument is that if you look at *what is in common to the moral judgments* of various people, the only thing you will find is the emotive element, the generalized prescriptions of how people should treat each other.

What might incline one toward moral subjectivism? As we've already discussed at length, one factor would be the perceived diversity of moral beliefs—just not between whole cultures but between individuals within a culture.

Another push toward subjectivism is what strikes many philosophers as the oddness of moral predicates like "right" and "wrong." With empirical claims, we have a pretty good idea of what's being talked about—colors, shapes, sizes, times, distances. Where there are disagreements about matters of fact, we can

see what would be needed to resolve the disagreement—what facts we would need to search out or wait for to solve the disagreement. But what are we talking about when we use the terms "right" and "wrong"? What evidence would decide moral questions? (If your answer is, "knowing the will of God," remember that that response assumes a Divine Command theory of ethics—a theory that many believers reject.) Subjectivists say that the puzzling aspects of moral talk are resolved if we analyze such talk as being not about facts, but about feelings or attitudes toward those facts.

Before we discuss whether or not moral subjectivism is a reasonable position, let's get a little clearer on what it is and isn't, in part reviewing points already mentioned.

Again "moral subjectivism" is another name for individual metaethical moral relativism. Moral subjectivism does not say that all beliefs are relative or subjective—just moral ones. It does not say that different moral views are equally good—we're talking about truth here. It does not say it is wrong to judge other individuals (or cultures): That is a normative, not a metaethical judgment, and it does not follow from metaethical relativism.

Moral subjectivism/relativism is nothing like the caricature of it presented in the popular press—"Do whatever feels good, nothing is wrong." The statement in quotes is a normative judgment and moral subjectivism implies no normative judgment. (During World War II and afterwards there were existentialists who were moral relativists and who fought the Nazis, resisted torture, and were fiercely committed to social justice.)

Nor does moral subjectivism, at least in its modern philosophical forms, imply that morality is a completely irrational enterprise. We've already seen that even subjective value judgments will involve judgments of fact that can be true or false; even subjective value judgments can have an internal logic that can be more or less rational. By definition, moral rules apply to the larger group: They must be formulated in general terms and not refer to me and my interests. Of course people often do favor moral rules that would work out to their particular advantage, but at least they can't justify them in those terms. For instance, if I'm doing well and I support moral rules that favor the status quo, I have to argue for those rules without referring to my situation and my advantage. (E.g., "Economic rules that allow for considerable inequality are to the advantage of most people in the long run.")

If my principles refer to promoting human welfare (say, satisfying human preferences) then scientific evidence as to what people want and how best to satisfy those wants are relevant—getting us into empirical (not normative) disputes in economics, sociology, and so forth.

Certain rules of logic will apply. If I say, "Let's do X and Y," I have to be reasonably clear about what I mean by X and Y. And if it turns out that X and Y involve some subtle contradiction, the proposed principle will be unacceptable—at least in its present form.

One thing people lose sight of is that, whether moral judgments are subjective or not, we're all going to be making them anyway. If you're a subjectivist and your partner says, "It's not fair that you're doing so few household chores" or your child says, "It's not fair that I'm getting a smaller allowance than my friends get," what are you going to say, "Sorry, I'm a subjectivist, I can't discuss such irrational issues as fairness"? You might as well be a hermit if you're going to take that stance.

If you see someone bullying a weaker person or the government carrying out a policy that favors one group and severely harms another, are you going to say, "Well I may have my own subjective feelings here, but this is ethics and there's nothing rational to discuss"? Unlikely.

Ethics/morality is a communal enterprise and is how we attempt to get along with each other in some sort of ordered fashion. No morality = no order. Without morality, the social order would have to be based on nothing but force. Most people seem to share some sense of fairness and compassion and acknowledge perspective-taking as relevant to moral discussions. How far this might take us toward resolving moral disputes is an open question but at least there are some common lines of discussion in relation to moral issues. If nothing else, moral discussion can be seen as negotiation that must appeal to some good greater than the mere interests of the individual. Of course, some people may not be interested in being moral, but at least even those people feel they ought to *seem* moral—which at least forces them to engage in discussion on the moral level.

There's another strategy subjectivists can use to try to reduce moral conflict—the same strategy social contract theorists use to deal with pluralism: to try to get sufficient agreement for society to function satisfactorily and to leave the rest of morality to discussion and personal practice. In Western societies this is done in part by a separation of church and state: Letting people have the freedom to practice their religious values in a diverse society. This isn't always possible: The abortion and stem-cell controversies are examples of unavoidable conflict. Nonetheless, the more one can turn moral differences into personal lifestyle differences, the less clash there will be.

Notes and selected sources

(See further readings for additional source material.)

What's supposed to be relative?

NOTES

Kwame Anthony Appiah quote from his book, *Cosmopolitanism: Ethics in a World of Strangers*. New York: W. W. Norton, 2006, pp. 36–9.

Cultural relativism

SOURCES

Edward F. Fischer. *People and Cultures of the World*. Chantilly, VA: The Teaching Co., 2004, lectures 3 and 4.

Encyclopaedia Britannica. "Ethical Relativism." Encyclopaedia Britannica 2006. Ultimate Reference Suite DVD 12 July 2008.

James Rachels/Stuart Rachels. "The Challenge of Cultural Relativism," ch. 2 in *The Elements of Moral Philosophy*. 5th edn. Boston, MA: McGraw-Hill, 1999.

Definitions

(Terms are defined in the order in which they appeared in the text.)

1. *Relativism (loose definition)*: The view that every belief is as good (or as true) as any other.
2. *Metaphysical relativism*: All metaphysical (including religious) beliefs are equally true.
3. *Religious skepticism*: Only one set of religious beliefs is true, but we can't know which one is true.
4. *Empirical relativism*: All empirical beliefs (including scientific theories) are equally true.
5. *Moral relativism*: Two kinds:
   Metaethical relativism: The claim that all moral beliefs (cultural or individual) are equally true.

   Normative relativism: The claim that it's wrong (one ought not) to judge another (culture, individual).
6. *Cultural (metaethical) relativism*: The position that (a) The predominant moral beliefs of different cultures are equally true, and (b) Moral beliefs within a culture are true or false depending on whether they accord with the predominant beliefs of that culture.
7. *Individual (metaethical) relativism*: See moral subjectivism.
8. *Moral subjectivism*: The claim that all the moral beliefs of individuals are equally true (or equal in being neither true nor false).

Questions

(Please explain your answers, making specific reference to relevant passages in the discussion.)

1. Explain the difference between claiming a belief is true and claiming it is good.
2. Why might someone claim that all empirical/ scientific beliefs are equally true? What are some problems with that claim?
3. Explain the differences between the following three positions: (a) (traditional) religious believer; (b) religious skeptic; and (c) religious relativist.

4. What is (metaethical) cultural relativism? What has inclined people toward that view?
5. What is a crucial problem with (metaethical) cultural relativism?
6. What is moral subjectivism? Would a moral subjectivist necessarily believe that you should do whatever you like because nothing is wrong?
7. Does moral subjectivism commit one to the view that morality is a totally irrational enterprise? Explain.

6

Moral Theory
Readings

Jeremy Bentham presents a classic statement of the principle of utility

I. Nature has placed mankind under the governance of two sovereign masters, pain and pleasure. It is for them alone to point out what we ought to do, as well as to determine what we shall do. On the one hand the standard of right and wrong, on the other the chain of causes and effects, are fastened to their throne. They govern us in all we do, in all we say, in all we think: every effort we can make to throw off our subjection, will serve but to demonstrate and confirm it. In words a man may pretend to abjure their empire: but in reality he will remain subject to it all the while. The principle of utility recognizes this subjection, and assumes it for the foundation of that system, the object of which is to rear the fabric of felicity by the hands of reason and of law. Systems which attempt to question it, deal in sounds instead of sense, in caprice instead of reason, in darkness instead of light.

But enough of metaphor and declamation: it is not by such means that moral science is to be improved.

II. The principle of utility is the foundation of the present work: it will be proper therefore at the outset to give an explicit and determinate account of what is meant by it. By the principle of utility is meant

From *An Introduction to the Principles of Morals and Legislation* (1789), by Jeremy Bentham, ch. 1.

that principle which approves or disapproves of every action whatsoever, according to the tendency which it appears to have to augment or diminish the happiness of the party whose interest is in question: or, what is the same thing in other words, to promote or to oppose that happiness. I say of every action whatsoever; and therefore not only of every action of a private individual, but of every measure of government.

III. By utility is meant that property in any object, whereby it tends to produce benefit, advantage, pleasure, good, or happiness, (all this in the present case comes to the same thing) or (what comes again to the same thing) to prevent the happening of mischief, pain, evil, or unhappiness to the party whose interest is considered: if that party be the community in general, then the happiness of the community: if a particular individual, then the happiness of that individual.

IV. The interest of the community is one of the most general expressions that can occur in the phraseology of morals: no wonder that the meaning of it is often lost. When it has a meaning, it is this. The community is a fictitious body, composed of the individual persons who are considered as constituting as it were its members. The interest of the community then is, what? The sum of the interests of the several members who compose it.

V. It is in vain to talk of the interest of the community, without understanding what is the interest of the individual. A thing is said to promote the interest, or to be for the interest, of an individual, when it tends to add to the sum total of his pleasures: or, what comes to the same thing, to diminish the sum total of his pains. An action then may be said to be conformable to the principle of utility, or, for shortness sake, to utility, (meaning with respect to the community at large) when the tendency it has to augment the happiness of the community is greater than any it has to diminish it.

VII. A measure of government (which is but a particular kind of action, performed by a particular person or persons) may be said to be conformable to or dictated by the principle of utility when in like manner the tendency which it has to augment the happiness of the community is greater than any which it has to diminish it.

VIII. When an action, or in particular a measure of government, is supposed by a man to be conformable to the principle of utility, it may be convenient, for the purposes of discourse, to imagine a kind of law or dictate, called a law or dictate of utility: and to speak of the action in question, as being conformable to such law or dictate.

IX. A man may be said to be a partizan of the principle of utility, when the approbation or disapprobation he annexes to any action, or to any measure, is determined by and proportioned to the tendency which he conceives it to have to augment or to diminish the happiness of the community: or in other words, to its conformity or unconformity to the laws or dictates of utility.

X. Of an action that is conformable to the principle of utility one may always say either that it is one that ought to be done, or at least that it is not one that ought not to be done. One may say also, that it is right it should be done; at least that it is not wrong it should be done: that it is a right action; at least that it is not a wrong action. When thus interpreted, the words ought, and right and wrong, and others of that stamp, have a meaning: when otherwise, they have none.

XI. Has the rectitude of this principle been ever formally contested? It should seem that it had, by those who have not known what they have been meaning. Is it susceptible of any direct proof? It

should seem not: for that which is used to prove everything else, cannot itself be proved: a chain of proofs must have their commencement somewhere. To give such proof is as impossible as it is needless.

XII. Not that there is or ever has been that human creature breathing, however stupid or perverse, who has not on many, perhaps on most occasions of his life, deferred to it. By the natural constitution of the human frame, on most occasions of their lives men in general embrace this principle, without thinking of it: if not for the ordering of their own actions, yet for the trying of their own actions, as well as of those of other men. There have been, at the same time, not many, perhaps, even of the most intelligent, who have been disposed to embrace it purely and without reserve. There are even few who have not taken some occasion or other to quarrel with it, either on account of their not understanding always how to apply it, or on account of some prejudice or other which they were afraid to examine into, or could not bear to part with. For such is the stuff that man is made of in principle and in practice, in a right track and in a wrong one, the rarest of all human qualities is consistency.

XIII. When a man attempts to combat the principle of utility, it is with reasons drawn, without his being aware of it, from that very principle itself. His arguments, if they prove anything, prove not that the principle is wrong, but that, according to the applications he supposes to be made of it, it is misapplied. Is it possible for a man to move the earth? Yes; but he must first find out another earth to stand upon.

[…]

Admitting any other principle than the principle of utility to be a right principle, a principle that it is right for a man to pursue; admitting (what is not true) that the word right can have a meaning without reference to utility, let him say whether there is any such thing as a motive that a man can have to pursue the dictates of it: if there is, let him say what that motive is, and how it is to be distinguished from those which enforce the dictates of utility: if not, then lastly let him say what it is this other principle can be good for?

Questions

1. What, according to Bentham, motivates human beings?
2. What is the principle of utility?

3. What does Bentham say about those who disagree with the principle of utility?

John Stuart Mill argues that there are higher and lower forms of happiness

The creed which accepts as the foundation of morals "utility" or the "greatest happiness principle" holds that actions are right in proportion as they tend to promote happiness; wrong as they tend to produce the reverse of happiness. By happiness is intended pleasure and the absence of pain; by unhappiness, pain and the privation of pleasure. To give a clear view of the moral standard set up by the theory, much more requires to be said; in particular, what things it includes in the ideas of pain and pleasure, and to what extent this is left an open question. But these supplementary explanations do not affect the theory of life on which this theory of morality is grounded—namely, that pleasure and freedom from pain are the only things desirable as ends; and that all desirable things (which are as numerous in the utilitarian as in any other scheme) are desirable either for pleasure inherent in themselves or as means to the promotion of pleasure and the prevention of pain.

Now such a theory of life excites in many minds, and among them in some of the most estimable in feeling and purpose, inveterate dislike. To suppose that life has (as they express it) no higher end than pleasure—no better and nobler object of desire and pursuit—they designate as utterly mean and groveling, as a doctrine worthy only of swine, to whom the

From *Utilitarianism* (1861), by John Stuart Mill, ch. 2.

followers of Epicurus were, at a very early period, contemptuously likened [...].

When thus attacked, the Epicureans have always answered that it is not they, but their accusers, who represent human nature in a degrading light, since the accusation supposes human beings to be capable of no pleasures except those of which swine are capable. If this supposition were true, the charge could not be gainsaid, but would then be no longer an imputation; for if the sources of pleasure were precisely the same to human beings and to swine, the rule of life which is good enough for the one would be good enough for the other. The comparison of the Epicurean life to that of beasts is felt as degrading, precisely because a beast's pleasures do not satisfy a human being's conceptions of happiness. Human beings have faculties more elevated than the animal appetites and, when once made conscious of them, do not regard anything as happiness which does not include their gratification. I do not, indeed, consider the Epicureans to have been by any means faultless in drawing out their scheme of consequences from the utilitarian principle. To do this in any sufficient manner, many Stoic, as well as Christian, elements require to be included. But there is no known Epicurean theory of life which does not assign to the pleasures of the intellect, of the feelings and imagination, and of the moral sentiments a much higher value as pleasures than to those of mere sensation. It must be admitted, however, that utilitarian writers in general have placed the superiority of mental over bodily pleasures chiefly in the greater permanency, safety, uncostliness, etc., of the former—that is, in their circumstantial advantages rather than in their intrinsic nature. And on all these points utilitarians have fully proved their case; but they might have taken the other and, as it may be called, higher ground with entire consistency. It is quite compatible with the principle of utility to recognize the fact that some kinds of pleasure are more desirable and more valuable than others. It would be absurd that, while in estimating all other things quality is considered as well as quantity, the estimation of pleasure should be supposed to depend on quantity alone.

If I am asked what I mean by difference of quality in pleasures, or what makes one pleasure more valuable than another, merely as a pleasure, except its being greater in amount, there is but one possible answer. Of two pleasures, if there be one to which all or almost all who have experience of both give a decided preference, irrespective of any feeling of moral obligation to prefer it, that is the more desirable pleasure. If one of the two is, by those who are competently acquainted with both, placed so far above the other that they prefer it, even though knowing it to be attended with a greater amount of discontent, and would not resign it for any quantity of the other pleasure which their nature is capable of, we are justified in ascribing to the preferred enjoyment a superiority in quality so far outweighing quantity as to render it, in comparison, of small account.

Now it is an unquestionable fact that those who are equally acquainted with and equally capable of appreciating and enjoying both do give a most marked preference to the manner of existence which employs their higher faculties. Few human creatures would consent to be changed into any of the lower animals for a promise of the fullest allowance of a beast's pleasures; no intelligent human being would consent to be a fool, no instructed person would be an ignoramus, no person of feeling and conscience would be selfish and base, even though they should be persuaded that the fool, the dunce, or the rascal is better satisfied with his lot than they are with theirs. They would not resign what they possess more than he for the most complete satisfaction of all the desires which they have in common with him. If they ever fancy they would, it is only in cases of unhappiness so extreme that to escape from it they would exchange their lot for almost any other, however undesirable in their own eyes. A being of higher faculties requires more to make him happy, is capable probably of more acute suffering, and certainly accessible to it at more points, than one of an inferior type; but in spite of these liabilities, he can never really wish to sink into what he feels to be a lower grade of existence. We may give what explanation we please of this unwillingness; we may attribute it to pride, a name which is given indiscriminately to some of the most and to some of the least estimable feelings of which mankind are capable; we may refer it to the love of liberty and personal independence, an appeal to which was with the Stoics one of the most effective means for the inculcation of it; to the love of power or to the love of excitement, both of which do really enter into and contribute to it; but its most appropriate appellation is a sense of dignity, which all human beings possess in one form or other, and in some, though by no means in exact, proportion to their higher faculties, and which is so essential a part of the happiness of those in whom it is strong that nothing which conflicts with it could be otherwise than momentarily an object of desire to them. Whoever supposes that this preference takes place at a sacrifice of happiness—that the superior being, in anything like equal circumstances, is not happier than the inferior—confounds the two very different ideas of happiness and content. It is indisputable that the being whose capacities of enjoyment are low has the greatest chance of having them fully satisfied; and a highly endowed being will always feel that any happiness which he can look for, as the world is constituted, is imperfect. But he can learn to bear its imperfections, if they are at all bearable; and they will not make him envy the being who is indeed unconscious of the imperfections, but only because he feels not at all the good which those imperfections qualify. It is better to be a human being dissatisfied than a pig satisfied; better to be Socrates dissatisfied than a fool satisfied. And if the fool, or the pig, are of a different opinion, it is because they only know their own side of the question. The other party to the comparison knows both sides.

Questions

1. According to Mill: What did the Epicureans believe? Why did their critics call them swine? In what way did those critics misinterpret the Epicurean philosophy?
2. What does Mill mean by the higher and lower qualities of pleasure?

3. "It is better to be a human being dissatisfied than a pig satisfied." Is this statement consistent with Mill's claim that "pleasure and freedom from pain are the only things desirable as ends"? Explain.

Peter Singer discusses what ethics is and offers a justification for a utilitarian ethic

[…]

What is it to make a moral judgment, or to argue about an ethical issue, or to live according to ethical standards? How do moral judgments differ from other practical judgments? Why do we regard a woman's decision to have an abortion as raising an ethical issue, but not her decision to change her job? What is the difference between a person who lives by ethical standards and one who doesn't?

All these questions are related, so we need to consider only one of them; but to do this we need to say something about the nature of ethics. Suppose that we have studied the lives of a number of different people, and we know a lot about what they do, what they believe, and so on. Can we then decide which of them are living by ethical standards and which are not?

We might think that the way to proceed here is to find out who believes it wrong to lie, cheat, steal, and so on and does not do any of these things, and who has no such beliefs and shows no such restraint in his actions. Then those in the first group would be living according to ethical standards and those in the second group would not be. But this procedure

From *Practical Ethics*, by Peter Singer. Cambridge: Cambridge University Press, 1979 © 1980 Cambridge University Press, reproduced with permission.

mistakenly assimilates two distinctions: the first is the distinction between living according to (what we judge to be) the right ethical standards and living according to (what we judge to be) mistaken ethical standards; the second is the distinction between living according to some ethical standards and living according to no ethical standards at all. Those who lie and cheat but do not believe what they are doing to be wrong may be living according to ethical standards. They may believe, for any of a number of possible reasons, that it is right to lie, cheat, steal, and so on. They are not living according to conventional ethical standards, but they may be living according to some other ethical standards.

This first attempt to distinguish the ethical from the nonethical was mistaken, but we can learn from our mistakes. We found that we must concede that those who hold unconventional ethical beliefs are still living according to ethical standards, *if they believe, for any reason, that it is right to do as they are doing*. The italicized condition gives us a clue to the answer we are seeking. The notion of living according to ethical standards is tied up with the notion of defending the way one is living, of giving a reason for it, of justifying it. Thus people may do all kinds of things we regard as wrong yet still be living according to ethical standards, if they are prepared to defend and justify what they do. We may find the justification inadequate, and may hold that the actions are wrong, but the attempt at justification, whether successful or not, is sufficient to bring the person's conduct within the domain of the ethical as opposed to the nonethical. When, on the other hand, people cannot put forward any justification for what they do, we may reject their claim to be living according to ethical standards, even if what they do is in accordance with conventional moral principles.

We can go further. If we are to accept that a person is living according to ethical standards, the justification must be of a certain kind. For instance, a justification in terms of self-interest alone will not do. When Macbeth, contemplating the murder of Duncan, admits that only "vaulting ambition" drives him to do it, he is admitting that the act cannot be justified ethically. "So that I can be king in his place" is not a weak attempt at an ethical justification for assassination; it is not the sort of reason that counts as an ethical justification at all. Self-interested acts must be shown to be compatible with more broadly based ethical principles if they are to be ethically defensible, for the notion of ethics carries with it the idea of something bigger than the individual. If I am to defend my conduct on ethical grounds, I cannot point only to the benefits it brings me. I must address myself to a larger audience.

From ancient times, philosophers and moralists have expressed the idea that ethical conduct is acceptable from a point of view that is somehow universal. The "Golden Rule" attributed to Moses, to be found in the book of Leviticus and subsequently repeated by Jesus, tells us to go beyond our own personal interests and "love thy neighbor as thyself"—in other words, give the same weight to the interests of others as one gives to one's own interests. The same idea of putting oneself in the position of another is involved in the other Christian formulation of the commandment, that we do to others as we would have them do to us. The Stoics held that ethics derives from a universal natural law. Kant developed this idea into his famous formula: "Act only on that maxim through which you can at the same time will that it should become a universal law." Kant's theory has itself been modified and developed by R. M. Hare, who sees universalizability as a logical feature of moral judgments. The eighteenth-century British philosophers Hutcheson, Hume, and Adam Smith appealed to an imaginary "impartial spectator" as the test of a moral judgment, and this theory has its modern version in the Ideal Observer theory. Utilitarians, from Jeremy Bentham to J.J.C. Smart,

take it as axiomatic that in deciding moral issues "each counts for one and none for more than one"; while John Rawls, a leading contemporary critic of utilitarianism, incorporates essentially the same axiom into his own theory by deriving basic ethical principles from an imaginary choice in which those choosing do not know whether they will be the ones who gain or lose by the principles they select. Even continental European philosophers like the existentialist Jean-Paul Sartre and the critical theorist Jürgen Habermas, who differ in many ways from their English-speaking colleagues—and from each other—agree that ethics is in some sense universal.

One could argue endlessly about the merits of each of these characterizations of the ethical; but what they have in common is more important than their differences. They agree that an ethical principle cannot be justified in relation to any partial or sectional group. Ethics takes a universal point of view. This does not mean that a particular ethical judgment must be universally applicable. Circumstances alter cases, as we have seen. What it does mean is that in making ethical judgments we go beyond our own likes and dislikes. From an ethical point of view, the fact that it is I who benefit from, say, a more equal distribution of income, and you who lose by it, is irrelevant. Ethics requires us to go beyond "I" and "you" to the universal law, the universalizable judgment, the standpoint of the impartial spectator or ideal observer, or whatever we choose to call it.

Can we use this universal aspect of ethics to derive an ethical theory that will give us guidance about right and wrong? Philosophers from the Stoics to Hare and Rawls have attempted this. No attempt has met with general acceptance. The problem is that if we describe the universal aspect of ethics in bare, formal terms, a wide range of ethical theories, including quite irreconcilable ones, are compatible with this notion of universality; if, on the other hand, we build up our description of the universal aspect of ethics so that it leads us ineluctably to one particular ethical theory, we shall be accused of smuggling our own ethical beliefs into our definition of the ethical—and this definition was supposed to be broad enough, and neutral enough, to encompass all serious candidates for the status of "ethical theory." Since so many others have failed to overcome this obstacle to deducing an ethical theory from the universal aspect of ethics, it would be foolhardy to attempt to do so in a brief introduction to a work with a quite different aim. Nevertheless I shall propose something only a little less ambitious. The universal aspect of ethics, I suggest, does provide a persuasive, although not conclusive, reason for taking a broadly utilitarian position.

My reason for suggesting this is as follows. In accepting that ethical judgments must be made from a universal point of view, I am accepting that my own interests cannot, simply because they are my interests, count more than the interests of anyone else. Thus my very natural concern that my own interests be looked after must, when I think ethically, be extended to the interests of others. Now, imagine that I am trying to decide between two possible courses of action—perhaps whether to eat all the fruits I have collected myself, or to share them with others. Imagine, too, that I am deciding in a complete ethical vacuum, that I know nothing of any ethical considerations—I am, we might say, in a pre-ethical stage of thinking. How would I make up my mind? One thing that would be still relevant would be how the possible courses of action will affect my interests. Indeed, if we define "interests" broadly enough, so that we count anything people desire as in their interests (unless it is incompatible with another desire or desires), then it would seem that at this pre-ethical stage, *only* one's own interests can be relevant to the decision.

Suppose I then begin to think ethically, to the extent of recognizing that my own interests cannot count for more, simply because they are my own, than the interests of others. In place of my own interests, I now have to take into account the interests of all those affected by my decision. This requires me to weigh up all these interests and adopt the course of action most likely to maximize the interests of those affected. Thus at least at some level in my moral reasoning I must choose the course of action that has the best consequences, on balance, for all affected. (I say "at some level in my moral reasoning" because as we shall see later, there are utilitarian reasons for believing that we ought to try to calculate these consequences not for every ethical decision we make in our daily lives, but only in very unusual circumstances, or perhaps when we are reflecting on our choice of general principles

to guide us in future. In other words, in the specific example given, at first glance one might think it obvious that sharing the fruits that I have gathered has better consequences for all affected than not sharing them. This may in the end also be the best general principle for us all to adopt, but before we can have grounds for believing this to be the case, we must also consider whether the effect of a general practice of sharing gathered fruits will benefit all those affected, by bringing about a more equal distribution, or whether it will reduce the amount of food gathered, because some will cease to gather anything if they know that they will get sufficient from their share of what others gather.)

The way of thinking I have outlined is a form of utilitarianism. It differs from classical utilitarianism in that "best consequences" is understood as meaning what, on balance, furthers the interests of those affected, rather than merely what increases pleasure and reduces pain. (It has, however, been suggested that classical utilitarians like Bentham and John Stuart Mill used "pleasure" and "pain" in a broad sense that allowed them to include achieving what one desired as a "pleasure" and the reverse as a "pain." If this interpretation is correct, the difference between classical utilitarianism and utilitarianism based on interests disappears.)

What does this show? It does not show that utilitarianism can be deduced from the universal aspect of ethics. There are other ethical ideals—like individual rights, the sanctity of life, justice, purity, and so on—that are universal in the required sense, and are, at least in some versions, incompatible with utilitarianism. It does show that we very swiftly arrive at an initially utilitarian position once we apply the universal aspect of ethics to simple, pre-ethical decision making. This, I believe, places the onus of proof on those who seek to go beyond utilitarianism. The utilitarian position is a minimal one, a first base that we reach by universalizing self-interested decision making. We cannot, if we are to think ethically, refuse to take this step. If we are to be persuaded that we should go beyond utilitarianism and accept nonutilitarian moral rules or ideals, we need to be provided with good reasons for taking this further step. Until such reasons are produced, we have some grounds for remaining utilitarians.

Questions

1. According to Singer, what is it for a person to live according to ethical standards?
2. Singer argues that "the universal aspect of ethics" provides "a persuasive, although not conclusive, reason for taking a broadly utilitarian position." What is his argument?

Immanuel Kant argues that ethics is based on "the categorical imperative"

Nothing can possibly be conceived in the world, or even out of it, which can be called good, without qualification, except a Good Will. Intelligence, wit, judgment, and the other talents of the mind, however they may be named, or courage, resolution, perseverance, as qualities of temperament, are undoubtedly good and desirable in many respects; but these gifts of nature may also become extremely bad and mischievous if the will which is to make use of them, and which, therefore, constitutes what is called character, is not good. [...]

A good will is good not because of what it performs or effects, not by its aptness for the attainment of some proposed end, but simply by virtue of the volition, that is, it is good in itself, and considered by itself is to be esteemed much higher than all that can be brought about by it in favour of any inclination, nay, even of the sum-total of all inclinations. Even if it should happen that, owing to special disfavour of fortune, or the niggardly provision of a step-motherly nature, this will should wholly lack power to accomplish its purpose, if with its greatest efforts it should yet achieve nothing, and there should remain only the good will (not, to be sure, a mere wish, but the summoning of all means in our power), then, like a jewel, it would still shine by its own light, as a thing which has its whole value in

itself. Its usefulness or fruitlessness can neither add to nor take away anything from this value. It would be, as it were, only the setting to enable us to handle it the more conveniently in common commerce, or to attract to it the attention of those who are not yet connoisseurs, but not to recommend it to true connoisseurs, or to determine its value.

[...]

We have then to develop the notion of a will which deserves to be highly esteemed for itself, and is good without a view to anything further, a notion which exists already in the sound natural understanding, requiring rather to be cleared up than to be taught, and which in estimating the value of our actions always takes the first place, and constitutes the condition of all the rest. In order to do this, we will take the notion of duty, which includes that of a good will, although implying certain subjective restrictions and hindrances. These, however, far from concealing it, or rendering it unrecognizable, rather bring it out by contrast, and make it shine forth so much the brighter.

I omit here all actions which are already recognized as inconsistent with duty, although they may be useful for this or that purpose, for with these the question whether they are done from duty cannot arise at all, since they even conflict with it. I also set aside those actions which really conform to duty, but to which men have no direct inclination, performing them because they are impelled thereto by some other inclination. For in this case we can readily distinguish whether the action which agrees with duty is done from duty, or from a selfish view. It is much harder to make this distinction when the action accords with duty, and the subject has besides a direct inclination to it. [...]

From Kant, *Critique of Practical Reason* (originally published 1788), trans. Thomas Kingswill Abbott (1909).

[…] it is a duty to maintain one's life; and, in addition, everyone has also a direct inclination to do so. But on this account the often anxious care which most men take for it has no intrinsic worth, and their maxim has no moral import. They preserve their life as duty requires, no doubt, but not because duty requires. On the other hand, if adversity and hopeless sorrow have completely taken away the relish for life; if the unfortunate one, strong in mind, indignant at his fate rather than desponding or dejected, wishes for death, and yet preserves his life without loving it—not from inclination or fear, but from duty—then his maxim has a moral worth.

To be beneficent when we can is a duty; and besides this, there are many minds so sympathetically constituted that, without any other motive of vanity or self-interest, they find a pleasure in spreading joy around them, and can take delight in the satisfaction of others so far as it is their own work. But I maintain that in such a case an action of this kind, however proper, however amiable it may be, has nevertheless no true moral worth, but is on a level with other inclinations, e.g. the inclination to honour which, if it is happily directed to that which is in fact of public utility and accordant with duty, and consequently honourable, deserves praise and encouragement, but not esteem. For the maxim lacks the moral import, namely, that such actions be done from duty, not from inclination. Put the case that the mind of that philanthropist was clouded by sorrow of his own, extinguishing all sympathy with the lot of others, and that while he still has the power to benefit others in distress, he is not touched by their trouble because he is absorbed with his own; and now suppose that he tears himself out of this dead insensibility, and performs the action without any inclination to it, but simply from duty, then first has his action its genuine moral worth […]

The second proposition is: That an action done from duty derives its moral worth, not from the purpose which is to be attained by it, but from the maxim by which it is determined, and therefore does not depend on the realization of the object of the action, but merely on the principle of volition by which the action has taken place, without regard to any object of desire. […]

The third proposition, which is a consequence of the two preceding, I would express thus: Duty is the necessity of acting from respect for the law. I may have inclination for an object as the effect of my proposed action, but I cannot have respect for it, just for this reason, that it is an effect and not an energy of will […].

Thus the moral worth of an action does not lie in the effect expected from it, nor in any principle of action which requires to borrow its motive from this expected effect. For all these effects—agreeableness of one's condition, and even the promotion of the happiness of others—could have been also brought about by other causes, so that for this there would have been no need of the will of a rational being; whereas it is in this alone that the supreme and unconditional good can be found. The preeminent good which we call moral can therefore consist in nothing else than the conception of law in itself, which certainly is only possible in a rational being, in so far as this conception, and not the expected effect, determines the will. This is a good which is already present in the person who acts accordingly, and we have not to wait for it to appear first in the result.

But what sort of law can that be, the conception of which must determine the will, even without paying any regard to the effect expected from it, in order that this will may be called good absolutely and without qualification? As I have deprived the will of every impulse which could arise to it from obedience to any law, there remains nothing but the universal conformity of its actions to law in general, which alone is to serve the will as a principle, i.e. I am never to act otherwise than so that I could also will that my maxim should become a universal law. Here, now, it is the simple conformity to law in general, without assuming any particular law applicable to certain actions, that serves the will as its principle, and must so serve it, if duty is not to be a vain delusion and a chimerical notion. The common reason of men in its practical judgments perfectly coincides with this, and always has in view the principle here suggested.

Let the question be, for example: May I when in distress make a promise with the intention not to keep it? I readily distinguish here between the two significations which the question may have: Whether it is prudent, or whether it is right, to make a false promise? The former may undoubtedly often be the case. I see clearly indeed that it is not enough to extricate myself from a present difficulty by means of this subterfuge, but it must be well considered whether there may not hereafter spring from this lie much greater inconvenience than that from which I now free myself, and as, with all my supposed cunning, the consequences cannot be so easily foreseen but that credit once lost may be much more injurious to me than any mischief which I seek to avoid at present, it should be considered whether it would not be more prudent to act herein according to a universal maxim, and to make it a habit to promise nothing except with the intention of keeping it. But it is soon clear to me that such a maxim will still only be based on the fear of consequences. Now it is a wholly different thing to be truthful from duty, and to be so from apprehension of injurious consequences. In the first case, the very notion of the action already implies a law for me; in the second case, I must first look about elsewhere to see what results maybe combined with it which would affect myself. For to deviate from the principle of duty is beyond all doubt wicked; but to be unfaithful to my maxim of prudence may often be very advantageous to me, although to abide by it is certainly safer. The shortest way, however, and an unerring one, to discover the answer to this question whether a lying promise is consistent with duty, is to ask myself, Should I be content that my maxim (to extricate myself from difficulty by a false promise) should hold good as a universal law, for myself as well as for others? and should I be able to say to myself, "Every one may make a deceitful promise when he finds himself in a difficulty from which he cannot otherwise extricate himself"? Then I presently become aware that while I can will the lie, I can by no means will that lying should be a universal law. For with such a law there would be no promises at all, since it would be in vain to allege my intention in regard to my future actions to those who would not believe this allegation, or if they over-hastily did so, would pay me back in my own coin. Hence my maxim, as soon as it should be made a universal law, would necessarily destroy itself.

[…]

There is therefore but one categorical imperative, namely this, *Act only on that maxim whereby thou canst at the same time will that it should become a universal law.*

[…]

We will now enumerate a few duties […]

1. A man reduced to despair by a series of misfortunes feels wearied of life, but is still so far in possession of his reason that he can ask himself whether it would not be contrary to his duty to himself to take his own life. Now he inquires whether the maxim of his action could become a universal law of nature. His maxim is: From self-love I adopt it as a principle to shorten my life when its longer duration is likely to bring more evil than satisfaction. It is asked then simply whether this principle founded on self-love can become a universal law of nature. Now we see at once that a system of nature of which it should be a law to destroy life by means of the very feeling whose special nature it is to impel to the improvement of life would contradict itself, and therefore could not exist as a system of nature; hence that maxim cannot possibly exist as a universal law of nature, and consequently would be wholly inconsistent with the supreme principle of all duty.

2. Another finds himself forced by necessity to borrow money. He knows that he will not be able to repay it, but sees also that nothing will be lent to him, unless he promises stoutly to repay it in a definite time. He desires to make this promise, but he has still so much conscience as to ask himself: Is it not unlawful and inconsistent with duty to get out of a difficulty in this way? Suppose, however, that he resolves to do so, then the maxim of his action would be expressed thus: When I think myself in want of money, I will borrow money and promise to repay it, although I know that I never can do so. Now this principle of self-love or of one's own advantage may perhaps be consistent with my whole future welfare; but the question now is, Is it right? I change then the suggestion of self-love into a universal law, and state the question thus: How would it be if my maxim were a universal law? Then I see at once that it could never hold as a universal law of nature, but would necessarily contradict itself. For supposing it to be a universal law that everyone when he thinks himself in a difficulty should be able to promise whatever he pleases, with the purpose of not keeping his promise, the promise itself would become impossible, as well as the end that one might have in view in it, since no

one would consider that anything was promised to him, but would ridicule all such statements as vain pretences.

3. A third finds in himself a talent which with the help of some culture might make him a useful man in many respects. But he finds himself in comfortable circumstances, and prefers to indulge in pleasure rather than to take pains in enlarging and improving his happy natural capacities. He asks, however, whether his maxim of neglect of his natural gifts, besides agreeing with his inclination to indulgence, agrees also with what is called duty. He sees then that a system of nature could indeed subsist with such a universal law although men (like the South Sea islanders) should let their talents rest, and resolve to devote their lives merely to idleness, amusement, and propagation of their species—in a word, to enjoyment; but he cannot possibly will that this should be a universal law of nature, or be implanted in us as such by a natural instinct. For, as a rational being, he necessarily wills that his faculties be developed, since they serve him, and have been given him, for all sorts of possible purposes.

4. A fourth, who is in prosperity, while he sees that others have to contend with great wretchedness and that he could help them, thinks: What concern is it of mine? Let everyone be as happy as Heaven pleases, or as he can make himself; I will take nothing from him nor even envy him, only I do not wish to contribute anything to his welfare or to his assistance in distress! Now no doubt if such a mode of thinking were a universal law, the human race might very well subsist, and doubtless even better than in a state in which everyone talks of sympathy and good-will, or even takes care occasionally to put it into practice, but, on the other side, also cheats when he can, betrays the rights of men, or otherwise violates them. But although it is possible that a universal law of nature might exist in accordance with that maxim, it is impossible to will that such a principle should have the universal validity of a law of nature. For a will which resolved this would contradict itself, inasmuch as many cases might occur in which one would have need of the love and sympathy of others, and in which, by such a law of nature,

sprung from his own will, he would deprive himself of all hope of the aid he desires.

[…]

[…] man and generally any rational being exists as an end in himself, *not merely as a means* to be arbitrarily used by this or that will, but in all his actions, whether they concern himself or other rational beings, must be always regarded at the same time as an end. All objects of the inclinations have only a conditional worth, for if the inclinations and the wants founded on them did not exist, then their object would be without value. But the inclinations themselves being sources of want, are so far from having an absolute worth for which they should be desired, that on the contrary it must be the universal wish of every rational being to be wholly free from them. Thus the worth of any object which is *to be acquired* by our action is always conditional. Beings whose existence depends not on our will but on nature's, have nevertheless, if they are irrational beings, only a relative value as means, and are therefore called *things*; rational beings, on the contrary, are called *persons*, because their very nature points them out as ends in themselves, that is as something which must not be used merely as means, and so far therefore restricts freedom of action (and is an object of respect). These, therefore, are not merely subjective ends whose existence has a worth for us as an effect of our action but *objective ends*, that is things whose existence is an end in itself: an end moreover for which no other can be substituted, which they should subserve *merely* as means, for otherwise nothing whatever would possess *absolute worth*; but if all worth were conditioned and therefore contingent, then there would be no supreme practical principle of reason whatever.

If then there is a supreme practical principle or, in respect of the human will, a categorical imperative, it must be one which, being drawn from the conception of that which is necessarily an end for every one because it is *an end in itself*, constitutes an *objective* principle of will, and can therefore serve as a universal practical law. The foundation of this principle is: *rational nature exists as an end in itself.* Man necessarily conceives his own existence as being so; so far then this is a *subjective* principle of human actions. But every other rational being regards its existence similarly, just on the same rational principle that holds for me: so that it is at the same time an objective principle, from which as a supreme practical law all laws of the will must be capable of being deduced.

Accordingly the practical imperative will be as follows: *So act as to treat humanity, whether in thine own person or in that of any other, in every case as an end withal, never as means only*. [...]

Questions

1. Kant claims that there is nothing that "can be called good, without qualification, except a Good Will." What does he mean by this?
2. Compare two persons: The first helps the poor out of sympathy for their condition; the second has no sympathy for the poor but gives out of a sense of obligation. Which person does Kant consider to be the most moral? Why? Do you agree?
3. If I'm trying to determine whether lying is wrong, how should I reason, according to Kant?

John Rawls argues that from an original position of equality we would reject utilitarianism in favor of his two principles of justice

[...]

The main idea of the theory of justice

My aim is to present a conception of justice which generalizes and carries to a higher level of abstraction the familiar theory of the social contract as found, say, in Locke, Rousseau, and Kant.[1] In order to do this we are not to think of the original contract as one to enter a particular society or to set up a particular form of government. Rather, the guiding idea is that the principles of justice for the basic structure of society are the object of the original agreement. They are the principles that free and rational persons concerned to further their own interests would accept in an initial position of equality as defining the fundamental terms of their association. These principles are to regulate all further

Reprinted by permission of the publisher from *A Theory of Justice*, by John Rawls, pp. 11–15, 60–1, Cambridge, MA: The Belknap Press of Harvard University Press, Copyright © 1971 by the President and Fellows of Harvard College.

agreements; they specify the kinds of social cooperation that can be entered into and the forms of government that can be established. This way of regarding the principles of justice I shall call justice as fairness.

Thus we are to imagine that those who engage in social cooperation choose together, in one joint act, the principles which are to assign basic rights and duties and to determine the division of social benefits. Men are to decide in advance how they are to regulate their claims against one another and what is to be the foundation charter of their society. Just as each person must decide by rational reflection what constitutes his good, that is, the system of ends which it is rational for him to pursue, so a group of persons must decide once and for all what is to count among them as just and unjust. The choice which rational men would make in this hypothetical situation of equal liberty, assuming for the present that this choice problem has a solution, determines the principles of justice.

In justice as fairness the original position of equality corresponds to the state of nature in the traditional theory of the social contract. This original position is not, of course, thought of as an actual historical state of affairs, much less as a primitive condition of culture. It is understood as a purely hypothetical situation characterized so as to lead to a certain conception of justice.[2] Among the essential features of this situation is that no one knows his place in society, his class position or social status, nor does any one know his fortune in the distribution of natural assets and abilities, his intelligence, strength, and the like. I shall even assume that the parties do not know their conceptions of the good or their special psychological propensities. The principles of justice are chosen behind a veil of ignorance. This ensures that no one is advantaged or disadvantaged in the choice of principles by the outcome of natural chance or the contingency of social circumstances. Since all are similarly situated and no one is able to design principles to favor his particular condition, the principles of justice are the result of a fair agreement or bargain. For given the circumstances of the original position, the symmetry of everyone's relations to each other, this initial situation is fair between individuals as moral persons, that is, as rational beings with their own ends and capable, I shall assume, of a sense of justice. The original position is, one might say, the appropriate initial status quo, and thus the fundamental agreements reached in it are fair. This explains the propriety of the name "justice as fairness": it conveys the idea that the principles of justice are agreed to in an initial situation that is fair. The name does not mean that the concepts of justice and fairness are the same, any more than the phrase "poetry as metaphor" means that the concepts of poetry and metaphor are the same.

Justice as fairness begins, as I have said, with one of the most general of all choices which persons might make together, namely, with the choice of the first principles of a conception of justice which is to regulate all subsequent criticism and reform of institutions. Then, having chosen a conception of justice, we can suppose that they are to choose a constitution and a legislature to enact laws, and so on, all in accordance with the principles of justice initially agreed upon. Our social situation is just if it is such that by this sequence of hypothetical agreements we would have contracted into the general system of rules which defines it. Moreover, assuming that the original position does determine a set of principles (that is, that a particular conception of justice would be chosen), it will then be true that whenever social institutions satisfy these principles those engaged in them can say to one another that they are cooperating on terms to which they would agree if they were free and equal persons whose relations with respect to one another were fair. They could all view their arrangements as meeting the stipulations which they would acknowledge in an initial

situation that embodies widely accepted and reasonable constraints on the choice of principles. The general recognition of this fact would provide the basis for a public acceptance of the corresponding principles of justice. No society can, of course, be a scheme of cooperation which men enter voluntarily in a literal sense; each person finds himself placed at birth in some particular position in some particular society, and the nature of this position materially affects his life prospects. Yet a society satisfying the principles of justice as fairness comes as close as a society can to being a voluntary scheme, for it meets the principles which free and equal persons would assent to under circumstances that are fair. In this sense its members are autonomous and the obligations they recognize self-imposed.

One feature of justice as fairness is to think of the parties in the initial situation as rational and mutually disinterested. This does not mean that the parties are egoists, that is, individuals with only certain kinds of interests, say in wealth, prestige, and domination. But they are conceived as not taking an interest in one another's interests. They are to presume that even their spiritual aims may be opposed, in the way that the aims of those of different religions may be opposed. [...]

In working out the conception of justice as fairness one main task clearly is to determine which principles of justice would be chosen in the original position. To do this we must describe this situation in some detail and formulate with care the problem of choice which it presents. These matters I shall take up in the immediately succeeding chapters. It may be observed, however, that once the principles of justice are thought of as arising from an original agreement in a situation of equality, it is an open question whether the principle of utility would be acknowledged. Offhand it hardly seems likely that persons who view themselves as equals, entitled to press their claims upon one another, would agree to a principle which may require lesser life prospects for some simply for the sake of a greater sum of advantages enjoyed by others. Since each desires to protect his interests, his capacity to advance his conception of the good, no one has a reason to acquiesce in an enduring loss for himself in order to bring about a greater net balance of satisfaction. In the absence of strong and lasting benevolent impulses, a rational man would not accept a basic structure merely because it maximized the algebraic sum of advantages irrespective of its permanent effects on his own basic rights and interests. Thus it seems that the principle of utility is incompatible with the conception of social cooperation among equals for mutual advantage. It appears to be inconsistent with the idea of reciprocity implicit in the notion of a well-ordered society. Or, at any rate, so I shall argue.

I shall maintain instead that the persons in the initial situation, would choose two rather different principles: the first requires equality in the assignment of basic rights and duties, while the second holds that social and economic inequalities, for example inequalities of wealth and authority, are just only if they result in compensating benefits for everyone, and in particular for the least advantaged members of society. These principles rule out justifying institutions on the grounds that the hardships of some are offset by a greater good in the aggregate. It may be expedient but it is not just that some should have less in order that others may prosper. But there is no injustice in the greater benefits earned by a few provided that the situation of persons not so fortunate is thereby improved. The intuitive idea is that since everyone's well-being depends upon a scheme of cooperation without which no one could have a satisfactory life, the division of advantages should be such as to draw forth the willing cooperation of everyone taking part in it, including those less well situated. Yet this can be expected only if reasonable terms are proposed. The two principles mentioned seem to be a fair agreement on the basis of which those better endowed, or more fortunate in their social position, neither of which we can be said to deserve, could expect the willing cooperation of others when some workable scheme is a necessary condition of the welfare of all.[3] Once we decide to look for a conception of justice that nullifies the accidents of natural endowment and the contingencies of social circumstance as counters in quest for political and economic advantage, we are led to these principles. They express the result of leaving aside those aspects of the social world that seem arbitrary from a moral point of view

[...]

Two principles of justice

I shall now state in a provisional form the two principles of justice that I believe would be chosen in the original position. [...]

The first statement of the two principles reads as follows.

First: each person is to have an equal right to the most extensive basic liberty compatible with a similar liberty for others.

Second: social and economic inequalities are to be arranged so that they are both (a) reasonably expected to be to everyone's advantage, and (b) attached to positions and offices open to all. [...]

By way of general comment, these principles primarily apply, as I have said, to the basic structure of society. They are to govern the assignment of rights and duties and to regulate the distribution of social and economic advantages. As their formulation suggests, these principles presuppose that the social structure can be divided into two more or less distinct parts, the first principle applying to the one, the second to the other. They distinguish between those aspects of the social system that define and secure the equal liberties of citizenship and those that specify and establish social and economic inequalities. The basic liberties of citizens are, roughly speaking, political liberty (the right to vote and to be eligible for public office) together with freedom of speech and assembly; liberty of conscience and freedom of thought; freedom of the person along with the right to hold (personal) property; and freedom from arbitrary arrest and seizure as defined by the concept of the rule of law. These liberties are all required to be equal by the first principle, since citizens of a just society are to have the same basic rights.

The second principle applies, in the first approximation, to the distribution of income and wealth and to the design of organizations that make use of differences in authority and responsibility, or chains of command. While the distribution of wealth and income need not be equal, it must be to everyone's advantage, and at the same time, positions of authority and offices of command must be accessible to all. One applies the second principle by holding positions open, and then, subject to this constraint, arranges social and economic inequalities so that everyone benefits.

These principles are to be arranged in a serial order with the first principle prior to the second. This ordering means that a departure from the institutions of equal liberty required by the first principle cannot be justified by, or compensated for, by greater social and economic advantages. [...]

Questions

1. Explain Rawls' concepts of "the original posi-
    tion" and the "veil of ignorance." In what sense is
    Rawls basing his theory on the idea of the "social
    contract"?

2. Why does Rawls think people in the original
    position would not choose the utilitarian principle?

3. What principles does Rawls suggest such people
    would choose?

Notes

1. As the text suggests, I shall regard Locke's *Second Treatise
    of Government*, Rousseau's *The Social Contract*, and Kant's
    ethical works beginning with *The Foundations of the
    Metaphysics of Morals* as definitive of the contract
    tradition. For all of its greatness, Hobbes's *Leviathan*
    raises special problems. A general historical survey is
    provided by J. W. Gough, *The Social Contract*, 2nd ed.
    (Oxford, The Clarendon Press, 1957), and Otto Gierke,
    Natural Law and the Theory of Society, trans. with an
    introduction by Ernest Barker (Cambridge, The
    University Press, 1934). A presentation of the contract
    view as primarily an ethical theory is to be found in G.
    R. Grice, *The Grounds of Moral Judgment* (Cambridge,
    The University Press, 1967). See also §19, note 30.

2. Kant is clear that the original agreement is hypothetical.
    See *The Metaphysics of Morals*, pt. I (*Rechtslehre*), especially
    §§47, 52; and pt. II of the essay "Concerning the
    Common Saying: This May Be True in Theory but It
    Does Not Apply in Practice," in *Kant's Political Writings*,
    ed. Hans Reiss and trans, by H. B. Nisbet (Cambridge,
    The University Press, 1970), pp. 73–87. See Georges
    Vlachos, *La Pensée politique de Kant* (Paris, Presses
    Universitaires de France, 1962), pp. 326–35; and J. G.
    Murphy, *Kant: The Philosophy of Right* (London,
    Macmillan, 1970), pp. 109–12, 133–6, for a further
    discussion.

3. For the formulation of this intuitive idea I am indebted
    to Alan Gibbard.

Robert Nozick discusses the moral principles behind his political libertarianism

Individuals have rights, and there are things no person
or group may do to them (without violating their
rights). So strong and far-reaching are these rights that
they raise the question of what, if anything, the state
and its officials may do.

[...]

Moral philosophy sets the background for, and
boundaries of, political philosophy. What persons may
and may not do to one another limits what they may
do through the apparatus of a state, or do to establish
such an apparatus.

From *Anarchy, State and Utopia*, by Robert Nozick. New York: Basic
Books, 1974, pp. ix, 6, 28–33, 150–163.

[...]

It may, indeed, seem to be a necessary truth that
"right," "ought," "should," and so on, are to be
explained in terms of what is, or is intended to be,
productive of the greatest good, with all goals built
into the good. Thus it is often thought that what is
wrong with utilitarianism (which *is* of this form) is
its too narrow conception of good. Utilitarianism
doesn't, it is said, properly take rights and their nonviolation into account; it instead leaves them a deriv-
ative status. Many of the counterexample cases to
utilitarianism fit under this objection, for example,
punishing an innocent man to save a neighborhood
from a vengeful rampage. But a theory may include in
a primary way the nonviolation of rights, yet include
it in the wrong place and the wrong manner. For suppose some condition about minimizing the total
(weighted) amount of violations of rights is built into
the desirable end state to be achieved. We then would

have something like a "utilitarianism of rights"; violations of rights (to be *minimized*) merely would replace the total happiness as the relevant end state in the utilitarian structure. [...] This still would require us to violate someone's rights when doing so minimizes the total (weighted) amount of the violation of rights in the society. For example, violating someone's rights might deflect others from *their* intended action of gravely violating rights, or might remove their motive for doing so, or might divert their attention, and so on. A mob rampaging through a part of town killing and burning *will* violate the rights of those living there. Therefore, someone might try to justify his punishing another *he* knows to be innocent of a crime that enraged a mob, on the grounds that punishing this innocent person would help to avoid even greater violations of rights by others, and so would lead to a minimum weighted score for rights violations in the society.

In contrast to incorporating rights into the end state to be achieved, one might place them as side constraints upon the actions to be done: don't violate constraints *C*. The rights of others determine the constraints upon your actions.

[...]

Side constraints express the inviolability of other persons. But why may not one violate persons for the greater social good? Individually, we each sometimes choose to undergo some pain or sacrifice for a greater benefit or to avoid a greater harm: we go to the dentist to avoid worse suffering later; we do some unpleasant work for its results; some persons diet to improve their health or looks; some save money to support themselves when they are older. In each case, some cost is borne for the sake of the greater overall good. Why not, *similarly*, hold that some persons have to bear some costs that benefit other persons more, for the sake of the overall social good? But there is no *social entity* with a good that undergoes some sacrifice for its own good. There are only individual people, different individual people, with their own individual lives. Using one of these people for the benefit of others, uses him and benefits the others. Nothing more. What happens is that something is done to him for the sake of others. Talk of an overall social good covers this up. (Intentionally?) To use a person in this way does not sufficiently respect and take account of

the fact that he is a separate person, that his is the only life he has. *He* does not get some overbalancing good from his sacrifice, and no one is entitled to force this upon him—least of all a state or government that claims his allegiance (as other individuals do not) and that therefore scrupulously must be *neutral* between its citizens.

[...]

The moral side constraints upon what we may do, I claim, reflect the fact of our separate existences. They reflect the fact that no moral balancing act can take place among us; there is no moral outweighing of one of our lives by others so as to lead to a greater overall *social* good. There is no justified sacrifice of some of us for others.

[...]

The minimal state is the most extensive state that can be justified. Any state more extensive violates people's rights. Yet many persons have put forth reasons purporting to justify a more extensive state. [...] [Here] we consider the claim that a more extensive state is justified, because necessary (or the best instrument) to achieve distributive justice. [...]

The term "distributive justice" is not a neutral one. Hearing the term "distribution," most people presume that some thing or mechanism uses some principle or criterion to give out a supply of things. Into this process of distributing shares some error may have crept. So it is an open question, at least, whether redistribution should take place; whether we should do again what has already been done once, though poorly. However, we are not in the position of children who have been given portions of pie by someone who now makes last minute adjustments to rectify careless cutting. There is no *central* distribution, no person or group entitled to control all the resources, jointly deciding how they are to be doled out. What each person gets, he gets from others who give to him in exchange for something, or as a gift. In a free society, diverse persons control different resources, and new holdings arise out of the voluntary exchanges and actions of persons. There is no more a distributing or distribution of shares than there is a distributing of mates in a society in which persons choose whom they shall marry. The total result is the product of many individual decisions which the different individuals involved are entitled to make. [...]

The subject of justice in holdings consists of three major topics. The first is the *original acquisition of holdings*, the appropriation of unheld things. This includes the issues of how unheld things may come to be held, the process, or processes, by which unheld things may come to be held, the things that may come to be held by these processes, the extent of what comes to be held by a particular process, and so on. We shall refer to the complicated truth about this topic, which we shall not formulate here, as the principle of justice in acquisition. The second topic concerns the *transfer of holdings* from one person to another. By what processes may a person transfer holdings to another? How may a person acquire a holding from another who holds it? Under this topic come general descriptions of voluntary exchange, and gift and (on the other hand) fraud, as well as reference to particular conventional details fixed upon in a given society. The complicated truth about this subject (with placeholders for conventional details) we shall call the principle of justice in transfer. (And we shall suppose it also includes principles governing how a person may divest himself of a holding, passing it into an unheld state.)

If the world were wholly just, the following inductive definition would exhaustively cover the subject of justice in holdings.

1. A person who acquires a holding in accordance with the principle of justice in acquisition is entitled to that holding.
2. A person who acquires a holding in accordance with the principle of justice in transfer, from someone else entitled to the holding, is entitled to the holding.
3. No one is entitled to a holding except by (repeated) applications of 1 and 2.

The complete principle of distributive justice would say simply that a distribution is just if everyone is entitled to the holdings they possess under the distribution.

A distribution is just if it arises from another just distribution by legitimate means. The legitimate means of moving from one distribution to another are specified by the principle of justice in transfer. The legitimate first "moves" are specified by the principle of justice in acquisition.[1] Whatever arises from a just situation by just steps is itself just. The means of change specified by the principle of justice in transfer preserve justice. [...]

Not all actual situations are generated in accordance with the two principles of justice in holdings: the principle of justice in acquisition and the principle of justice in transfer. Some people steal from others, or defraud them, or enslave them, seizing their product and preventing them from living as they choose, or forcibly exclude others from competing in exchanges. None of these are permissible modes of transition from one situation to another. And some persons acquire holdings by means not sanctioned by the principle of justice in acquisition. The existence of past injustice (previous violations of the first two principles of justice in holdings) raises the third major topic under justice in holdings: the rectification of injustice in holdings. If past injustice has shaped present holdings in various ways, some identifiable and some not, what now, if anything, ought to be done to rectify these injustices? What obligations do the performers of injustice have toward those whose position is worse than it would have been had the injustice not been done?

[...]

The general outlines of the entitlement theory illuminate the nature and defects of other conceptions of distributive justice. The entitlement theory of justice in distribution is *historical*; whether a distribution is just depends upon how it came about. In contrast, *current time-slice principles* of justice hold that the justice of a distribution is determined by how things are distributed (who has what) as judged by some *structural* principle(s) of just distribution. A utilitarian who judges between any two distributions by seeing which has the greater sum of utility and, if the sums tie, applies some fixed equality criterion to choose the more equal distribution, would hold a current time-slice principle of justice. [...]

Most persons do not accept current time-slice principles as constituting the whole story about distributive shares. They think it relevant in assessing the justice of a situation to consider not only the distribution it embodies, but also how that distribution came about. If some persons are in prison for murder or war crimes, we do not say that to assess the justice of the distribution in the society we must look only at what this person has, and that person has, and that person has, … at the current time. We think it relevant to ask whether someone did something so that he *deserved* to be punished, deserved to have a lower share.

[…]

It is not clear how those holding alternative conceptions of distributive justice can reject the entitlement conception of justice in holdings. For suppose a distribution favored by one of these non-entitlement conceptions is realized. Let us suppose it is your favorite one and let us call this distribution D_1; perhaps everyone has an equal share, perhaps shares vary in accordance with some dimension you treasure. Now suppose that Wilt Chamberlain is greatly in demand by basketball teams, being a great gate attraction. (Also suppose contracts run only for a year, with players being free agents.) He signs the following sort of contract with a team: In each home game, twenty-five cents from the price of each ticket of admission goes to him. (We ignore the question of whether he is "gouging" the owners, letting them look out for themselves.) The season starts, and people cheerfully attend his team's games; they buy their tickets, each time dropping a separate twenty-five cents of their admission price into a special box with Chamberlain's name on it. They are excited about seeing him play; it is worth the total admission price to them. Let us suppose that in one season one million persons attend his home games, and Wilt Chamberlain winds up with $250,000, a much larger sum than the average income and larger even than anyone else has. Is he entitled to this income? Is this new distribution D_2, unjust? If so, why? There is *no* question about whether each of the people was entitled to the control over the resources they held in D_1; because that was the distribution (your favorite) that (for the purposes of argument) we assumed was acceptable. Each of these persons *chose* to give twenty-five cents of their money

to Chamberlain. They could have spent it on going to the movies, or on candy bars, or on copies of *Dissent* magazine, or of *Monthly Review*. But they all, at least one million of them, converged on giving it to Wilt Chamberlain in exchange for watching him play basketball. If D_1 was a just distribution, and people voluntarily moved from it to D_2, transferring parts of their shares they were given under D_1 (what was it for if not to do something with?), isn't D_2 also just? If the people were entitled to dispose of the resources to which they were entitled (under D_1), didn't this include their being entitled to give it to, or exchange it with, Wilt Chamberlain? Can anyone else complain on grounds of justice? Each other person already has his legitimate share under D_1. Under D_1, there is nothing that anyone has that anyone else has a claim of justice against. After someone transfers something to Wilt Chamberlain, third parties *still* have their legitimate shares; *their* shares are not changed. By what process could such a transfer among two persons give rise to a legitimate claim of distributive justice on a portion of what was transferred, by a third party who had no claim of justice on any holding of the others *before* the transfer? To cut off objections irrelevant here, we might imagine the exchanges occurring in a socialist society, after hours. After playing whatever basketball he does in his daily work, or doing whatever other daily work he does, Wilt Chamberlain decides to put in *overtime* to earn additional money. (First his work quota is set; he works time over that.)

[…]

The general point illustrated by the Wilt Chamberlain example and the example of the entrepreneur in a socialist society is that no end-state principle or distributional patterned principle of justice can be continuously realized without continuous interference with people's lives. […]

Questions

1. What does Nozick mean by the conception of rights as "side constraints." What does he contrast this conception with?
2. What is Nozick's complaint about the term "distributive justice"?
3. Contrast "historical principles of justice" with "time-slice principles of justice." Which type does Nozick favor?
4. Review Nozick's Wilt Chamberlain example and explain the point of it.

Note

1. Applications of the principle of justice in acquisition may also occur as part of the move from one distribution to another. You may find an unheld thing now and appropriate it. Acquistions also are to be understood as included when, to simplify, I speak only of transitions by transfers.

Jeremy Waldron discusses the concept of human rights and gives an argument for "welfare rights"

That individuals have *rights* and that these rights mark important limits on what may be done to them by the state, or in the name of other moral conceptions – this is now a familiar position in modern political philosophy.

Of course, the idea is familiar in non-philosophical contexts too. Many countries embody a list of rights in their constitution, proclaiming, for example, that the government will not interfere with the free speech of its citizens, or with their freedom of travel, their sexual privacy, their religious liberty, or their equal access to the law. These Bills of Rights also reflect the importance in the international community of the idea of *human* rights—the conviction that there are liberties and interests so basic that *every* society should secure them irrespective of its traditions, history or level of economic development.

[…]

In international human rights circles, diplomats talk about 'first-', 'second-' and 'third-generation' rights (see Alston, 1987, p. 307). First-generation rights are the traditional liberties and privileges of citizenship: religious toleration, freedom from arbitrary arrest, free speech, the right to vote, and so on. Second-generation rights are socio-economic claims: the right to education, housing, health care, employment and an adequate standard of living. Though these are thought to be more radical claims requiring a more

Reproduced with permission from "Rights" by Jeremy Waldron in *A Companion to Contemporary Political Philosophy*. Oxford: Blackwell Publishers, 1993, ch. 33.

interventionist state, they remain essentially individualistic in their content, inasmuch as it is the material welfare of each man, woman, and child that is supposed to be secured by these provisions. Third-generation rights, by contrast, have to do with communities or whole peoples, rather than individual persons.

[…]

What about second-generation rights? Do people have rights to social and economic welfare? There are three lines of argument, which lead to the conclusion that they do. The first argues that recognition of second-generation rights is necessary if we are to be serious in our commitment to any rights at all. No one can fully enjoy or exercise *any* right that she is supposed to have if she lacks the essentials for a healthy and active life. Even if most rights are oriented towards the exercise of agency and freedom, still we know that things like malnutrition and epidemic disease can debilitate and finally destroy all the human faculties that individual autonomy involves (Shue, 1980, pp. 24–5).

[…]

The second argument for welfare rights is more direct. Instead of saying that economic security is necessary if *other* rights are to be taken seriously, it states bluntly that socio-economic needs are as important as any other interests, and that a moral theory of individual dignity and well-being is plainly inadequate if it does not take them into account. The advantage of this approach is that it concedes nothing in the way of priority to first-generation rights.

[…]

However, arguments along these lines must meet the challenge posed by Robert Nozick: it is all very well to base human rights on material need, but other people may already have property rights over the resources that would have to be used to satisfy these needs. Particular private entitlements might, as he put it, 'fill the space of rights, leaving no room for general rights to be in a certain material condition' (Nozick, 1974, p. 238).

This critique assumes that rights based on need occupy a relatively superficial role in a general theory of economic entitlement—as though we *first* determine who owns what, and *then* determine what to do about the needs that are left unsatisfied. Perhaps needs should play a more fundamental role, governing the initial allocation of property rights themselves. This is the third of the arguments I mentioned. Instead of making socioeconomic rights the basis of a duty of compulsory charity incumbent upon existing property-holders, we use them instead to call existing property arrangements into question. We reverse Nozick's order of priorities, and insist that no system of ownership is justified if it leaves large numbers of people destitute and hungry (Waldron, 1986, pp. 475–82). On this account, welfare provision is seen as a first step towards a complete overhaul of a property distribution whose failure to respect fundamental rights is indicated by the fact that many people continue to be without access to the resources they need in order to live.

This third line of argument can also be used to respond to another common criticism of second-generation claims—that they are impracticable or too expensive. Some critics argue that putative welfare rights violate the logical principle 'Ought implies can': many states do not have the resources to provide even minimal economic security for masses of their citizens. Moreover, since states differ considerably in this regard, it hardly makes sense to regard economic provision as matter of universal human entitlement (Cranston, 1967, pp. 50–1). However, the alleged impossibility in many of these cases stems from an assumption that the existing distribution of resources (local and global) is to remain largely undisturbed. When a conservative government in the West says, for example, in response to some plea for welfare provision or overseas aid, 'The money simply isn't there', what is usually meant is that it would be impolitic to try to raise it by taxation. The more radical challenge posed to the underlying distribution of wealth is simply ignored. once matters are put in this way, it becomes clear that the 'ought' of human rights is being

frustrated less by the 'can't' of impracticability, than by the 'won't' of selfishness and greed.

Still, someone might insist, aren't these rights awfully demanding? At least first-generation rights require only that we and our governments refrain from various acts of tyranny and violence. They are 'negative' rights correlative to duties of omission, whereas socioeconomic rights are correlated with positive duties of assistance. One advantage of negative rights is that they never conflict with one another, for one can perform an infinite number of omissions at any given time. With positive rights, by contrast, we always have to consider the scarcity of the resources and services that are called for (Cranston, 1967, p. 50).

Unfortunately, this correlation of first- and second-generation claims with duties of omission and duties of positive assistance will not stand up. Many first-generation rights (for example, the right to vote) require a considerable effort to establish and maintain political frameworks, and all such rights make costly calls upon scarce police and forensic resources. As for second-generation rights, they may be correlated with duties that are positive or negative, depending on the context. If people are actually starving, their rights make a call on our active assistance. But if they are living satisfactorily in a traditional subsistence economy, all the right may require is that we refrain from economic initiatives that might disturb that situation (Shue, 1980, pp. 35–64).

In general, where resources are scarce relative to human wants, *any* system of rights or entitlements will seem demanding to those who are constrained by it. If an economic system includes provision for welfare assistance, it may seem overly demanding to taxpayers. But if it does not include such provision, then the system of *property rights* in such an economy will seem overly demanding to the poor, requiring as it does that they refrain from making use of resources (belonging to others) that they need in order to survive. As usual, the question is not whether we are to have a system of demanding rights, but how the costs of these demands are to be distributed.

All the same, thinking about scarcity does have the advantage of forcing rights theorists to take seriously the issue of justice. It is an unhappy feature of rights that they express moral claims in a sort of 'line item' way, presenting each individual's case peremptorily as though it brooked no denial or compromise. If we want to say (as I have argued) that people have rights that may conflict, then rights have got to be linked to a theory of social justice that takes seriously the distributive issues that they raise. But once that link is established, we may find it harder than we thought to insist on a determinate content for either property rights or welfare rights (or, for that matter, civil rights). John Rawls' work on social justice suggests that problems of fair distribution are better approached by articulating general principles for the evaluation of social structures than by laying down particular rights which allocate to individuals as a matter of entitlement a certain share of social wealth (Rawls, 1971, pp. 64 and 88–90).

Justification

Since the time of Jeremy Bentham, it has been a common complaint against rights that they are nothing but question-begging assertions. Reasoned social reform, Bentham argued, requires detailed attention to empirical circumstances, and that in turn requires 'strength of mind to weigh, and patience to investigate'. The language of natural rights, by contrast, 'is from beginning to end so much flat assertion: it lays down as a fundamental and inviolable principle whatever is in dispute' (Bentham [1794] 1987, p. 74).

This concern continues to resonate 200 years later. Though rights sound nice, most students of public policy prefer the idiom of utilitarian analysis—calculating the effects of a given reform proposal on the well-being of each individual, and choosing the course of action which will produce the greatest balance of satisfaction over suffering, taking everything into account.

In considering this critique, we must take care that our admiration for the painstaking complexity of policy analysis does not blind us to some of its real moral difficulties. Since utilitarians aggregate all consequences on the same scale, they must figure that any loss to an individual can always be offset by a sufficiently widespread gain to others, even if that gain is just a marginal increment of convenience for each of a large number of people. The maximizing logic of their position requires them to accept with equanimity the neglect or sacrifice of some for the sake of the

greater good of others. Often what sounds like 'so much flat assertion', on the part of rights theorists, is simply an adamant insistence that that is not satisfactory as a moral basis for public policy.

[…]

Theorists of rights also have difficulty with the utilitarian assumption that every human preference has a claim to satisfaction. Ronald Dworkin (1978, pp. 232–8; 1984, pp. 155–67) has argued that racist preferences, for example, should not be counted when we are calculating costs and benefits since their content is incompatible with the egalitarian assumption that everyone is entitled to the same concern and respect. Now in practice it is impossible to disentangle such 'external' preferences from people's desires for their own well-being. However, Dworkin suggests that it is the role of rights to correct for the distortions introduced into utilitarian calculations by the entangled presence of external preferences. This explains why rights are to be conceived, in his famous phrase, as 'trumps' over utility (Dworkin, 1978, p. xi) – that is, why rights have moral priority over any cost/benefit calculation in which racist or other inegalitarian preferences may be present.

[…]

It is because each of us wants a life governed in large part by her own thinking, feeling and decision-making that the idea of individual rights seems so attractive.

Certainly this is the sense that modern theories give to the old Kantian precept that we are to treat humanity in each person as an end in itself, never merely as a means to others' ends (Kant, [1785] 1969, pp. 52–4). Morally the most important fact about our humanity is the ability each of us has to exercise agency in accordance with practical reason. We know that this capacity can be exploited in some people for the benefit of others: slavery and the domestic subordination of women remain the most striking examples of people living lives on others' terms, not their own. In the final analysis, the idea of rights commits its proponent to oppose all such subordination, and in general to do what she can (individually and collectively through the state) to secure the benefits of each person's own rational agency, fully developed, for the life that person has chosen to lead.

Questions

1. What according to Waldron are "first-generation rights"? What are "second-generation rights"? Which are also called "welfare rights"?
2. Waldron gives three arguments for welfare rights. What are these?

3. What, according to Waldron, is the utilitarian argument against rights? What counter-arguments does Waldron give against the utilitarian argument?

References

Alston, P.: 'A third generation of solidarity rights: progressive development or obfuscation of international human rights law?', *Netherlands International Law Review*, 29 (1987), 307–65.

Bentham, J.: *Anarchical Fallacies; being an examination of the Declarations of Rights issued during the French Revolution* (1796), excerpted in Waldron (1987a, pp. 46–76).

Cranston, M.: 'Human rights, real and supposed', in *Political Theory and the Rights of Man*, ed. D. D. Raphael (London: Macmillan, 1967).

Dworkin, R.: *Taking Rights Seriously* (London: Duckworth, 1978).

————: 'Rights as trumps', in Waldron (1984), pp. 153–67.

Nozick, R.: *Anarchy, State and Utopia* (Oxford: Blackwell, 1974).

Rawls, J.: *A Theory of Justice* (Cambridge, MA: Harvard University Press, 1971).

Shue, H.: *Basic Rights: Subsistence, Affluence, and US Foreign Policy* (Princeton, NJ: Princeton University Press, 1980).

Waldron, J., ed.: *Theories of Rights* (Oxford: Oxford University Press, 1984).

————: 'Welfare and the images of charity', *Philosophical Quarterly*, 36 (1986), 463–82.

Aristotle analyzes happiness as a life lived according to virtue

As every science and undertaking aims at some good, what is in our view the good at which political science aims, and what is the highest of all practical goods? As to its name there is, I may say, a general agreement. The masses and the cultured classes agree in calling it happiness, and conceive that "to live well" or "to do well" is the same thing as "to be happy."

[…]

Perhaps, however, it seems a commonplace to say that happiness is the supreme good; what is wanted is to define its nature a little more clearly. The way

of arriving at such a definition will probably be to ascertain the function of man. For, as with a flute player, a sculptor, or any artist, or in fact anybody who has a special function or activity, his goodness and excellence seem to lie in his function, so it would seem to be with man, if indeed he has a special function. Can it be said that, while a carpenter and a cobbler have special functions and activities, man, unlike them, is naturally functionless? Or, as the eye, the hand, the foot, and similarly each part of the body has a special function, so may man be regarded as having a special function apart from all these? What, then, can this function be? It is not life; for life is apparently something that man shares with plants; and we are looking for something peculiar to him. We must exclude therefore the life of nutrition and growth. There is next what may be called the life of sensation. But this too, apparently, is shared by man with horses, cattle, and all other animals. There remains what I may

From *The Nicomachean Ethics*, by Aristotle, trans. James E. C. Weldon (Macmillan, 1897), Books I and II.

call the active life of the rational part of man's being. Now this rational part is twofold; one part is rational in the sense of being obedient to reason, and the other in the sense of possessing and exercising reason and intelligence.

The function of man then is activity of soul in accordance with reason, or not apart from reason. Now, the function of a man of a certain kind, and of a man who is good of that kind—for example, of a harpist and a good harpist—are in our view the same in kind. This is true of all people of all kinds without exception, the superior excellence being only an addition to the function; for it is the function of a harpist to play the harp, and of a good harpist to play the harp well. This being so, if we define the function of man as a kind of life, and this life as an activity of the soul or a course of action in accordance with reason, and if the function of a good man is such activity of a good and noble kind, and if everything is well done when it is done in accordance with its proper excellence, it follows that the good of man is activity of soul in accordance with virtue.

[...]

Virtue [...] is twofold, partly intellectual and partly moral, and intellectual virtue is originated and fostered mainly by teaching; it therefore demands experience and time. Moral virtue on the other hand is the outcome of habit. From this fact it is clear that moral virtue is not implanted in us by nature, for a law of nature cannot be altered by habituation. Thus a stone, that naturally tends to fall downwards, cannot be habituated or trained to rise upwards. It is neither by nature then nor in defiance of nature that virtues are implanted in us. Nature gives us the capacity of receiving them, and that capacity is perfected by habit.

Again, if we take the various natural powers which belong to us, we first possess the proper faculties and afterwards display the activities. It is obviously so with the senses. Not by seeing frequently or hearing frequently do we acquire the sense of seeing or hearing; on the contrary, because we have the senses we make use of them; we do not get them by making use of them. But the virtues we get by first practicing them, as we do in the arts. For it is by doing what we ought to do when we study the arts that we learn the arts themselves; we become builders by building

and harpists by playing the harp. Similarly, it is by doing just acts that we become just, by doing temperate acts that we become temperate, by doing brave acts that we become brave. The experience of states confirms this statement, for it is by training in good habits that lawmakers make the citizens good. This is the object all lawmakers have at heart; if they do not succeed in it, they fail of their purpose; and it makes the distinction between a good constitution and a bad one.

Again, the causes and means by which any virtue is produced and destroyed are the same. It is by our actions in dealing between man and man that we become either just or unjust. It is by our actions in the face of danger and by our training ourselves to fear or to courage that we become either cowardly or courageous. It is much the same with our appetite and angry passions. People become temperate and gentle, others licentious and passionate, by behaving in one or the other way in particular circumstances. In a word, moral states are the results of activities like the states themselves. It is our duty therefore to keep a certain character in our activities, since our moral states depend on the differences in our activities. So the difference between one and another training in habits in our childhood is not a light matter, but important, or rather, all-important.

Our present study is not, like other studies, purely theoretical in intention; for the object of our inquiry is not to know what virtue is but how to become good, and that is the sole benefit of it. We must, therefore, consider the right way of performing actions, for it is acts that determine the character of the resulting moral states.

That we should act in accordance with right reason is a common general principle, which may here be taken for granted. [...]

The first point to be observed is that in matters we are now considering deficiency and excess are both fatal. It is so, we see, in questions of health and strength. Too much or too little gymnastic exercise is fatal to strength. Similarly, too much or too little meat and drink is fatal to health, whereas a suitable amount produces, increases, and sustains it. It is the same with temperance, courage, and other moral virtues. A person who avoids and is afraid of everything and faces nothing becomes a coward; a person who is not afraid of anything but is ready to face everything becomes foolhardy. Similarly, he who enjoys every pleasure and abstains from none is licentious; he who refuses all pleasures, like a boor, is an insensible sort of person. For temperance and courage are destroyed by excess and deficiency but preserved by the mean. […]

Every art then performs its function well, if it regards the mean and refers the works which it produces to the mean. This is the reason why it is usually said of successful works that it is impossible to take anything from them or to add anything to them, which implies that excess or deficiency is fatal to excellence but that the mean state ensures it. Good artists too, as we say, have an eye to the mean in their works. But virtue, like Nature herself, is more accurate and better than any art; virtue therefore will aim at the mean; I speak of moral virtue, as it is moral virtue which is concerned with emotions and actions, and it is these which admit of excess and deficiency and the mean. Thus it is possible to go too far, or not to go far enough, in respect of fear, courage, desire, anger, pity, and pleasure and pain generally, and the excess and the deficiency are alike wrong; but to experience these emotions at the right times and on the right occasions and towards the right persons and for the right causes and in the right manner is the mean or the supreme good, which is characteristic of virtue. Similarly there may be excess, deficiency, or the mean, in regard to actions. But virtue is concerned with emotions and actions, and here excess is an error and deficiency a fault, whereas the mean is successful and laudable, and success and merit are both characteristics of virtue.

It appears then that virtue is a mean state, so far at least as it aims at the mean […].

But not every action or every emotion admits of a mean. There are some whose very name implies wickedness, as, for example, malice, shamelessness, and envy among the emotions, and adultery, theft, and murder among the actions. All these and others like them are marked as intrinsically wicked, not merely excesses or deficiencies of them. It is never possible then to be right in them; they are always sinful. Right or wrong in such acts as adultery does not depend on our committing it with the right woman, at the right time, or in the right manner; on the contrary it is wrong to do it at all. It would be equally false to suppose that there can be a mean or excess of deficiency in unjust, cowardly, or licentious conduct […].

There are then three dispositions, two being vices, namely, excess and deficiency, and one virtue, which is the mean between them; and they are all in a sense morally opposed. Thus the brave man appears foolhardy compared with the coward, but cowardly compared with the foolhardy. Similarly, the temperate man appears licentious compared with the insensible man but insensible compared with the licentious; and the liberal man appears extravagant compared with the stingy man but stingy compared with the spendthrift. The result is that the extremes each denounce the mean as belonging to the other extreme; the coward calls the brave man foolhardy, and the foolhardy man calls him cowardly; and so on in other cases. […]

That is why it is so hard to be good; for it is always hard to find the mean in anything; anybody can get angry—that is easy—and anybody can give or spend money, but to give it to the right person, to give the right amount of it, at the right time, for the right cause and in the right way, this is not what anybody can do, nor is it easy. That is why goodness is rare, praiseworthy, and noble […].

Questions

1. Why does Aristotle think human beings have a "function"? What does he believe that function to be?

2. Explain Aristotle's theory of virtue.

Jonathan Haidt discusses virtue ethics in the context of positive psychology

[...] The philosopher Edmund Pincoffs[1] has argued that consequentialists and deontologists worked together to convince Westerners in the twentieth century that morality is the study of moral quandaries and dilemmas. Where the Greeks focused on the *character* of a person and asked what kind of person we should each aim to become, modern ethics focuses on *actions*, asking when a particular action is right or wrong. Philosophers wrestle with life-and-death dilemmas: Kill one to save five? Allow aborted fetuses to be used as a source of stem cells? Remove the feeding tube from a woman who has been unconscious for fifteen years? Nonphilosophers wrestle with smaller quandaries: Pay my taxes when others are cheating? Turn in a wallet full of money that appears to belong to a drug dealer? Tell my spouse about a sexual indiscretion?

This turn from character ethics to quandary ethics has turned moral education away from virtues and toward moral reasoning. If morality is about dilemmas, then moral education is training in problem solving. Children must be taught how to think about moral problems, especially how to overcome their natural egoism and take into their calculations the needs of others. As the United States became more ethnically diverse in the 1970s and 1980s, and also more averse to authoritarian methods of education, the idea of teaching specific moral facts and values went out of fashion. Instead, the rationalist legacy of quandary ethics gave us teachers and many parents who would enthusiastically endorse this line, from a recent child-rearing handbook: "My approach does not teach children what and what not to do and why, but rather, it teaches them how to think so they can decide for themselves what and what not to do, and why."[2]

I believe that this turn from character to quandary was a profound mistake, for two reasons. First, it weakens morality and limits its scope. Where the ancients saw virtue and character at work in everything a person does, our modern conception confines morality to a set of situations that arise for each person only a few times in any given week: tradeoffs between self-interest and the interests of others.

[...]

The second problem with the turn to moral reasoning is that it relies on bad psychology. Many moral education efforts since the 1970s take the rider off of the elephant and train him to solve problems on his own. After being exposed to hours of case studies, classroom discussions about moral dilemmas, and videos about people who faced dilemmas and made the right choices, the child learns how (not what) to think. Then class ends, the rider gets back on the elephant, and nothing changes at recess.

[...]

The cry that, we've lost our way is heard from some quarter in every country and era, but it has been particularly loud in the United States since the social turmoil of the 1960s and the economic malaise and rising crime of the 1970s. Political conservatives, particularly those who have strong religious beliefs, bridled at the "value-free" approach to moral education and the "empowering" of children to think for themselves instead of teaching them facts and values to think about. [...]

Also in the 1980s, several philosophers helped to revive virtue theories. Most notably, Alasdair MacIntyre argued in *After Virtue*[3] that the "enlightenment project" of creating a universal, context-tree morality was doomed from the beginning. Cultures that have shared values and rich traditions invariably generate a framework in which people can value and evaluate each other. [...] MacIntyre says that the loss of a language of virtue, grounded in a particular tradition, makes it difficult for us to find meaning, coherence, and purpose in life.[4]

In recent years, even psychology has become involved. In 1998, Martin Seligman founded positive psychology when he asserted that psychology had lost its way. Psychology had become obsessed with pathology and the dark side of human nature, blind to all that was good and noble in people. Seligman noted that psychologists had created an enormous manual, known as the "DSM" (the *Diagnostic and Statistical Manual of Mental Disorders*), to diagnose every possible mental illness and behavioral annoyance, but psychology didn't even have a language with which to talk about the upper reaches of human health, talent, and possibility. When Seligman launched

From *The Happiness Hypothesis: Finding Modern Truth in Ancient Wisdom*, by Jonathan Haidt. New York: Basic Books, 2006, pp. 163–70.

positive psychology, one of his first goals was to create a diagnostic manual for the strengths and virtues. He and another psychologist, Chris Peterson of the University of Michigan, set out to construct a list of the strengths and virtues, one that might be valid for any human culture. I argued with them that the list did *not* have to be valid for all cultures to be useful; they should focus just on large-scale industrial societies. Several anthropologists told them that a universal list could never be created. Fortunately, however, they persevered.

As a first step, Peterson and Seligman surveyed every list of virtues they could find, from the holy books of major religions down to the Boy Scout Oath ("trustworthy, loyal, helpful, friendly..."). They made large tables of virtues and tried to see which ones were common across lists. Although no specific virtue made every list, six broad virtues, or families of related virtues, appeared on nearly all lists: wisdom, courage, humanity, justice, temperance, and transcendence (the ability to forge connections to something larger than the self). These virtues are widely endorsed because they are abstract: There are many ways to be wise, or courageous, or humane, and it is impossible to find a human culture that rejects all forms of any of these virtues. (Can we even imagine a culture in which parents hope that their children will grow up to be foolish, cowardly, and cruel?) But the real value of the list of six is that it serves as an organizing framework for more specific *strengths of character*. Peterson and Seligman define character strengths as specific ways of displaying, practicing, and cultivating the virtues. Several paths lead to each virtue. People, as well as cultures, vary in the degree to which they value each path. This is the real power of the classification: It points to specific means of growth toward widely valued ends without insisting that any one way is mandatory for all people at all times. The classification is a tool for diagnosing people's diverse strengths and for helping them find ways to cultivate excellence.

Peterson and Seligman suggest that there are twenty-four principle [*sic*] character strengths, each leading to one of the six higher-level virtues.[5] You can diagnose yourself by looking at the list below or by taking the strengths test (at www.authentichappiness.org).

1. Wisdom:
   - Curiosity
   - Love of learning
   - Judgment
   - Ingenuity
   - Emotional intelligence
   - Perspective
2. Courage:
   - Valor
   - Perseverance
   - Integrity
3. Humanity:
   - Kindness
   - Loving
4. Justice:
   - Citizenship
   - Fairness
   - Leadership
5. Temperance:
   - Self-control
   - Prudence
   - Humility
6. Transcendence:
   - Appreciation of beauty and excellence
   - Gratitude
   - Hope
   - Spirituality
   - Forgiveness
   - Humor
   - Zest

Odds are that you don't have much trouble with the list of six virtue families, but you do have objections to the longer list of strengths. Why is humor a means to transcendence? Why is leadership on the list, but not the virtues of followers and subordinates—duty, respect, and obedience? Please, go ahead and argue. The genius of Peterson and Seligman's classification is to get the conversation going, to propose a specific list of strengths and virtues and then let the scientific and therapeutic communities work out the details.[...]

This classification is already generating exciting research and liberating ideas. Here's my favorite idea: Work on your strengths, not your weaknesses. How many of your New Year's resolutions have been about fixing a flaw? And how many of those resolutions have you made several years in a row? It's difficult to change any aspect of your personality by sheer force of will, and if it is a weakness you choose to work on, you probably won't enjoy the process. If you don't find pleasure or reinforcement along the way, then—unless you have the willpower of Ben Franklin—you'll soon give up. But you don't really have to be good at everything. Life offers so many chances to use one tool in-stead of another, and often you can use a strength to get around a weakness.

In the positive psychology class I teach at the University of Virginia, the final project is to make yourself a better person, using all the tools of psychology, and then prove that you have done so. About half the students each year succeed, and the most successful ones usually either use cognitive behavioral therapy on themselves (it really does work!) or employ a strength, or both. For example, one student lamented her inability to forgive. Her mental life was dominated by ruminations about how those to whom she was closest had hurt her. For her project, she drew on her strength of loving: Each time she found herself spiraling down into thoughts about victimhood, she brought to mind a positive memory about the person in question, which triggered a flash of affection. Each flash cut off her anger and freed her, temporarily, from rumination. In time, this effortful mental process became habitual and she became more forgiving (as she demonstrated using the reports she had filled out each day to chart her progress).[...]

Another outstanding project was done by a woman who had just undergone surgery for brain cancer. At the age of twenty-one, Julia faced no better than even odds of surviving. To deal with her fears, she cultivated one of her strengths—zest. She made lists of the activities going on at the university and of the beautiful hikes and parks in the nearby Blue Ridge Mountains. She shared these lists with the rest of the class, she took time away from her studies to go on these hikes, and she invited friends and classmates to join her. People often say that adversity makes them want to live each day to the fullest, and when Julia made a conscious effort to cultivate her natural strength of zest, she really did it. (She is still full of zest today.)

Virtue sounds like hard work, and often is. But when virtues are re-conceived as excellences, each of which can be achieved by the practice of several strengths of character, and when the practice of these strengths is often intrinsically rewarding, suddenly the work [...] engages you fully, draws on your strengths, and allows you to lose self-consciousness and immerse yourself in what you are doing.

[...]

Questions

1. Explain the distinction Haidt discusses between quandary ethics and character or virtue ethics? Which approach to ethics does Haidt prefer? Why?

2. What were the reasons Peterson and Seligman created their list of virtues?

3. If you were in Haidt's class, what strength would you want to work on? How would you go about it?

Notes

1. Pincoffs, E. L. (1986). Quandaries and virtues: Against reductivism in ethics. Lawrence, KS: University of Kansas.

2. Sure, M. B. "Raising a Thinking Child Workbook," retrieved on April 15, 2005, from www.thinkingchild.com

3. MacIntyre, A. (1981). After virtue. Notre Dame, IN: University of Notre Dame Press.

4. See also Taylor, C. (1989). Sources of the self: The making of the modern identity. Cambridge, MA: Harvard University Press.

5. Peterson, C., & Seligman, M. E. P. (2004). Character strengths and virtues: A handbook and classification. Washington, DC: American Psychological Association and Oxford University Press.

Jean Grimshaw discusses the idea of a female ethic, reviewing some contemporary writers on the subject

Questions about gender have scarcely been central to mainstream moral philosophy this century. But the idea that virtue is in some way *gendered*, that the standards and criteria of morality are different for women and men, is one that has been central to the ethical thinking of a great many philosophers. It is to the eighteenth century that we can trace the beginnings of those ideas of a 'female ethic', of 'feminine' nature and specifically female forms of virtue, which have formed the essential background to a great deal of feminist thinking about ethics.

[…]

Many women in the nineteenth century, including a large number who were concerned with the question of women's emancipation, remained attracted to the idea, not merely that there were specifically female virtues, but sometimes that women were morally superior to men, and to the belief that society could be morally transformed through the influence of women. What many women envisaged was, as it were, an *extension* throughout society of the 'female values' of the private sphere of home and family. But, unlike many male writers, they used the idea of female virtue as a reason for women's entry into the 'public' sphere rather than as a reason for their being restricted to the 'private' one. And in a context where any sort of female independence was so immensely difficult to achieve, it is easy to see the attraction of any view which sought to re-evaluate and affirm those strengths and virtues conventionally seen as 'feminine'.

The context of contemporary feminist thought is of course very different. Most of the formal barriers to the entry of women into spheres other than the domestic have been removed, and a constant theme of feminist writing in the last twenty years has been a critique of women's restriction to the domestic role or the 'private' sphere. Despite this, however, the idea

Reproduced with permission from "The Idea of a Female Ethic." In *A Companion to Ethics*, ed. Peter Singer. Oxford: Blackwell, 1993, pp. 491–6.

of 'a female ethic' has remained very important within feminist thinking. A number of concerns underlie the continued interest within feminism in the idea of a 'female ethic'. Perhaps most important is concern about the violent and destructive consequences to human life and to the planet of those fields of activity which have been largely male-dominated, such as war, politics, and capitalist economic domination. The view that the frequently destructive nature of these things is at least in part *due* to the fact that they are male-dominated is not of course new; it was common enough in many arguments for female suffrage at the beginning of the twentieth century. In some contemporary feminist thinking this has been linked to a view that many forms of aggression and destruction are closely linked to the nature of 'masculinity' and the male psyche.

Such beliefs about the nature of masculinity and about the destructive nature of male spheres of activity are sometimes linked to 'essentialist' beliefs about male and female nature. [...]

Such essentialist views of male and female nature are of course a problem if one believes that the 'nature' of men and women is not something that is monolithic or unchanging, but is, rather, socially and historically constructed. And a great deal of feminist thinking has rejected any form of essentialism. [...]

The second sort of approach to the idea of a 'female ethic' results [...] from an attempt to see whether an alternative approach to questions about moral reasoning and ethical priorities can be derived from a consideration of those spheres of life and activity which have been regarded as paradigmatically female. Two things, in particular, have been suggested. The first is that there *are* in fact common or typical differences in the ways in which women and men think on reason about moral issues. [...]

The second important suggestion can be summarized as follows. It starts from the assumption that specific social practices generate their own vision of what is 'good' or what is to be especially valued, their own concerns and priorities, and their own criteria for what is to be seen as a 'virtue'. Perhaps, then, the social practices, especially those of mothering and caring for others, which have traditionally been regarded as female, can be seen as generating ethical priorities and conceptions of 'virtue' which should not only not be devalued but which can also provide a corrective to the more destructive values and priorities of those spheres of activity which have been dominated by men.

In her influential book *In A Different Voice: Psychological Theory and Women's Development* (1982) Carol Gilligan argued that those who have suggested that women typically reason differently from men about moral issues are right; what is wrong is their assumption of the inferiority or deficiency of female moral reasoning. The starting point for Gilligan's work was an examination of the work of Lawrence Kohlberg on moral development in children. Kohlberg attempted to identify 'stages' in moral development, which could be analysed by a consideration of the responses children gave to questions about how they would resolve a moral dilemma. The 'highest' stage, the stage at which, in fact, Kohlberg wanted to say that a specifically *moral* framework of reasoning was being used, was that at which moral dilemmas were resolved by an appeal to rules and principles, a logical decision about priorities, in the light of the prior acceptance of such rules or principles.

A much quoted example of Kohlberg's method, discussed in detail by Gilligan, is the case of two eleven-year-old children, 'Jake' and 'Amy'. Jake and Amy were asked to respond to the following dilemma; a man called Heinz has a wife who is dying, but he cannot afford the drug she needs. Should he steal the drug in order to save his wife's life? Jake is clear that Heinz *should* steal the drug; and his answer revolves around a resolution of the rules governing life and property. Amy, however, responded very differently. She suggested that Heinz should go and talk to the druggist and see if they could not find some solution to the problem. Whereas Jake sees the situation as needing mediation through systems of logic or law, Amy, Gilligan suggests, sees a need for mediation through communication in relationships.

It is clear that Kohlberg's understanding of morality is based on the tradition that derives from Kant and moves through the work of such contemporary philosophers as John Rawls and R. M. Hare. The emphasis in this tradition is indeed on rules and principles, and Gilligan is by no means the only critic to suggest that any such understanding of morality will be bound to misrepresent women's moral reasoning

and set up a typically male pattern of moral reasoning as a standard against which to judge women to be deficient. Nel Noddings, for example, in her book *Caring: A Feminine Approach to Ethics and Moral Education* (1984), argues that a morality based on rules or principles is in itself inadequate, and that it does not capture what is distinctive or typical about female moral thinking. She points out how, in a great deal of moral philosophy, it has been supposed that the moral task is, as it were, to abstract the 'local detail' from a situation and see it as falling under a rule or principle. Beyond that, it is a question of deciding or choosing, in a case of conflict, how to order or rank one's principles in a hierarchy. And to rank as a *moral* one, a principle must be universalizable; that is to say, of the form 'Whenever X, then do Y'. Noddings argues that the posing of moral dilemmas in such a way misrepresents the nature of moral decision-making. Posing moral issues in the 'desert-island dilemma' form, in which only the 'bare bones' of a situation are described, usually serves to conceal rather than to reveal the sorts of questions to which only situational and contextual knowledge can provide an answer, and which are essential to moral judgement in the specific context.

[...]

Gilligan and Noddings suggest, therefore, that there are, as a matter of fact, differences in the ways in which women and men reason about moral issues. But such views of difference always pose great difficulties. The nature of the evidence involved is inevitably problematic; it would not be difficult to find two eleven-year-old children who reacted quite differently to Heinz's dilemma; and appeals to 'common experience' of how women and men reason about moral issues can always be challenged by pointing to exceptions or by appealing to different experience.

The question, however, is not just one of empirical difficulty. Even if there *were* some common or typical differences between women and men, there is always a problem about how such differences are to be described. [...] It might, for example, be the case, not so much that women and men *reason differently* about moral issues, but that their ethical priorities differ, as that what is regarded as an important principle by women (such as maintaining relationships) is commonly seen by men as a *failure* of principle.

At best then, I think that the view that women 'reason differently' over moral issues is difficult to spell out clearly or substantiate [...]. But perhaps there is some truth in the view that women's ethical *priorities* may commonly differ from those of men? [...]

There have been a number of attempts in recent feminist philosophy to suggest that the practices in which women engage, in particular the practices of childcare and the physical and emotional maintenance of other human beings, might be seen as generating social priorities and conceptions of virtue which are different from those which inform other aspects of social life. Sara Ruddick, for example, in an article entitled 'Maternal thinking' (1980) argues that the task of mothering generates a conception of virtue which might provide a resource for a critique of those values and priorities which underpin much contemporary social life including those of militarism. [...]

There are, however, great problems in the idea that female practices can generate an autonomous or coherent set of 'alternative' values. Female practices are always socially situated and inflected by things such as class, race, material poverty or well-being, which have divided women and which they do not all share. Furthermore, practices such as childbirth and the education and rearing of children have been the focus of constant ideological concern and struggle; they have not just been developed by women in isolation from other aspects of the culture. The history of childcare this century, for example, has constantly been shaped by the (frequently contradictory) interventions both of 'experts' in childcare (who have often been male) and by the state. Norms of motherhood have also been used in ways that have reinforced classist and racist assumptions about the 'pathology' of working-class or black families. They have been used, too, by women themselves, in the service of such things as devotion to Hitler's 'Fatherland' or the bitter opposition to feminism and equal rights in the USA. For all these reasons, if there is any usefulness at all in the idea of a 'female ethic', I do not think it can consist in appealing to a supposedly autonomous realm of female values which can provide a simple corrective or alternative to the values of male-dominated spheres of activity.

[...]

Questions

1. According to Grimshaw, what are some of the motivations behind the search for a "female ethic"?
2. What are some of the difficulties behind linking a "female ethic" to essential differences between men and women?
3. What are some of the difficulties behind linking a "female ethic" to what is special about traditional female activities?
4. Do you think there are certain qualities or outlooks traditionally associated with women that ought to be stressed in ethics? If so, which ones?

References

Gilligan, C.: In a *Different Voice: Psychological Theory and Women's Development* (Cambridge, MA: Harvard University Press, 1982).

Kohlberg, L.: *The Philosophy of Moral Development* (San Francisco: Harper and Row, 1984).

Noddings, N.: *Caring: A Feminine Approach to Ethics and Education* (Berkeley: University of California Press, 1978).

Ruddick, S.: 'Maternal thinking', *Feminist Studies*, 6, (Summer 1980).

Simon Blackburn warns against confusions we should avoid if we read popular literature on ethics and evolution

There exists a vague belief that some combination of evolutionary theory, biology, and neuroscience will support a Grand Unifying Pessimism. Indeed, most of the popular books on ethics in the bookstores fall into one of two camps. There are those that provide chicken soup for the soul: soggy confections of consolation and uplift. Or, there are those that are written by one or another life scientist: a neuroscientist or biologist or animal behaviourist or evolutionary theorist, anxious to tell that 'science' has shown that we are all one thing or another. Once more we stand unmasked: human beings are 'programmed'. We are egoists, altruism doesn't exist, ethics is only a fig-leaf for selfish strategies, we are all conditioned, women are nurturing, men are rapists, we care above all for our genes.[…]

We should only venture into this literature if we are armed against three confusions. The first is this. It is one thing to explain how we come to be as we are. It is a different thing to say that we are different from what we think we are. Yet these are fatally easy to confuse with each other. Suppose, for instance, evolutionary theory tells us that mother-love is an adaptation. This means that it has been 'selected for', because animals in which it exists reproduce and spread their genetic material more successfully than ones in which it does not. We could, if we like, imagine a 'gene for mother-love'. Then the claim would be that animals with this gene are and have been more successful than animals having only a variant (an allele) that does not code for mother-love (this is likely to be grossly oversimplified, but it's a model that will make the point). The confusion would be to infer that *therefore* there is not really any such thing as mother-love: thus we unmask it! The confusion is to infer that underneath the mask we are only concerned to spread genetic material more successfully.

From *Being Good: A Short Introduction to Ethics*, by Simon Blackburn. Oxford: Oxford University Press, 2001, pp. 37–43.

Not only does this not follow, but it actually contradicts the starting point. The starting point is 'Mother-love exists, and this is why'; the conclusion is that mother-love doesn't exist.

In other words, an evolutionary story, plausible or not, about the genetic function of a trait such as mother-love must not be confused with a psychological story unmasking a mother's 'real concern'. […] [C]onsider the idea of 'reciprocal altruism'. Game theorists and biologists noticed that animals frequently help each other when it would seem to be to their advantage not to do so. They asked the perfectly good question of how such behaviour could have evolved, when it looks set to lose out to a more selfish strategy. The answer is (or may be) that it is adaptive insofar as it triggers reciprocal helping behaviour from the animal helped, or from others witnessing the original event. In other words, we have a version of 'You scratch my back and I'll scratch yours'.

The explanation may be perfectly correct. It may provide the reason why we ourselves have inherited altruistic tendencies. The confusion strikes again, however, when it is inferred that altruism doesn't *really* exist, or that we don't *really* care disinterestedly for one another—we only care to maximize our chance of getting a return on our investments of helping behaviour. The mistake is just the same—inferring that the psychology is not what it seems because of its functional explanation—but it seems more seductive here, probably because we fear that the conclusion is true more often in this case than in the case of mother-love. There are indeed cases of seeming altruism disguising hope for future benefits. But there are of course cases in which it is not like this […]. The driver gives the penniless hitch-hiker a lift; the diner tips the waiter he knows he will never see again; they each do it when there are no bystanders to watch the action.

[…]

The second confusion is to infer the impossibility that such-and-such a concern should exist, from the fact that we have no evolutionary explanation for it. This is unwarranted, for it may well be that there is no evolutionary explanation for all kinds of quirks: no explanation for why we enjoy birdsong, or like the taste of cinnamon, or have ticklish feet.

[…]

The third confusion to guard against is to read psychology into nature, and in particular into the gene, and then read it back into the person whose gene it is. The most notorious example of this mistake is in *The Selfish Gene*, by Richard Dawkins. Here the fact that genes replicate and have a different chance of replicating in different environments is presented metaphorically in terms of their being 'selfish' and indulging a kind of ruthless competition to beat out other genes. It is then inferred that the human animal must itself be selfish, since somehow this is the only appropriate psychology for the vehicle in which these little monsters are carried. Or at least, if we are not selfish, it is because by some strange miracle we can transcend and fight off the genetic pressure to be so. Dawkins has since repudiated this idea, but it maintains a life of its own.

To state this train of thought is to expose its silliness. Genes are not selfish—they just have different chances of replicating themselves in different environments. Not only may they do better if the person carrying them is unselfish, altruistic, and principled, but it is easy to see why this should be so. A society of unselfish, altruistic, and principled persons is obviously set to do better than a group in which there are none of these traits, but only a 'war of all against all'. [...]

Questions

1. What is Blackburn's general worry about the sorts of "explanations" evolutionary ethics gives for various human traits?
2. "Mother-love doesn't really exist because mothers are really only concerned to spread their genes." What would Blackburn say to this?
3. What is Blackburn's complaint about the idea of genes being "selfish"?

George Lakoff describes two forms of Christianity that parallel two different models of the family

[...] The God As Father metaphor attributes to God both authority and nurturance. But there are various possibilities for how authority and nurturance can go together. In the Nurturant Parent model, the child's obedience to the parents' authority is a consequence of the parents' proper nurturance. In the Strict Father model, the reverse is true: authority comes first. First and foremost, the child must obey and not challenge the strict father's authority; to the obedient child, nurturance then comes as a proper reward [...].

Reproduced with permission from George Lakoff, *Moral Politics: What Conservatives Know that Liberals Don't*, University of Chicago Press, 1996, pp. 248, 260–1.

One's relation to God can be interpreted in either way. On the Nurturant Parent interpretation, you accept God's authority because of his original and continuing nurturance. On the Strict Father interpretation, God is seen as setting the rules and demanding authority; if you obey, you get nurturance. The difference is one of priorities, and, as we have seen, that is an all-important difference.

[...]

The Nurturant Parent interpretation of Christianity has very different consequences than the Strict Father model. First, it presents a completely different view of the proper relationship between human beings and God.

In Strict Parent Christianity, God is a moral authority, and the role of human beings is to obey his strict commandments. The way you learn to obey is by being punished for not obeying and by developing the self-discipline to obey through self-denial.

In Nurturant Parent Christianity, God is a nurturer and the proper relationship to God is to accept his nurturance (Grace) and follow Christ's example of how to act nurturantly to others. There are no strict rules; rather one must develop empathy and learn to act compassionately for the benefit of others, whatever that might require. You learn to become nurturant through receiving nurturance, through accepting the pleasures of nurturance, developing, growing, and following the example of the ultimate nurturer (Christ).

The two forms of Christianity assume very different views of human nature. Strict Father Christianity assumes folk behaviorism, that people function to get rewards and avoid punishments, and that discipline and denial build character. Nurturant Parent Christianity, on the other hand, does not assume folk behaviorism nor the need for discipline and denial to build character. Instead, it assumes that being nurtured builds the right kind of character (nurturant character) and that those who are nurtured will thereby incorporate nurturant instincts into them.

The two forms of Christianity assume different ideas of what a good person is. Strict Father Christianity assumes that a good person is one who is self-disciplined and self-reliant and who can function well in a hierarchy, someone who can obey strict orders from those above and give strict orders to those below—and enforce those orders with pain. Nurturant Parent Christianity sees a good person as one who is nurturant, one who can function well in interdependent situations, where social ties, communication, cooperation, kindness, and trust are essential.

Finally, the two forms of Christianity have very different understandings of what the world should be like so that such ideal persons can be produced. Strict Father Christianity requires that the world be competitive and survival difficult if the right kind of people (strong people) are to be produced and rewarded. Nurturant Parent Christianity requires that the world be as interdependent, nurturant and benign as possible, if the right kind of people—nurturant people—are to be produced.

[…]

Questions

1. Compare and contrast what Lakoff calls the "two forms of Christianity."
2. How do these two forms relate to the distinction made in the text between the judgmental and sympathetic God-types?

3. Are you aware of similarly contrasting views of God within other religious traditions? Judaism, for instance? Or Islam? Explain.

James Rachels discusses "the challenge of cultural relativism"

[There is] a recurring theme in the literature of social science: Different cultures have different moral codes. What is thought right within one group may be utterly abhorrent to the members of another group, and vice versa. […]

Reproduced with permission from "The Challenge of Cultural Relativism," in *The Elements of Moral Philosophy*, 5th ed., by James Rachels/Stuart Rachels. Boston, MA: McGraw-Hill, 1999, ch. 2.

Consider the Eskimos. The Eskimos are the indigenous peoples of Alaska, northern Canada, Greenland, and northeastern Siberia. (Today, none of these groups call themselves "Eskimos"; however, I'll use that term because it's the only one that refers to this scattered Arctic population.) Traditionally, Eskimos have lived in small settlements, separated by great distances. Prior to the 20th century, the outside world knew little about them. Then explorers began to bring back strange tales.

Eskimo customs turned out to be very different from our own. The men often had more than one wife, and they would share their wives with guests, lending them out for the night as a sign of hospitality.

[…]

The Eskimos also seemed to have less regard for human life. Infanticide, for example, was common. Knud Rasmussen, one of the most famous early explorers, reported that he met one woman who had borne 20 children but had killed 10 of them at birth. Female babies, he found, were especially liable to be killed, and this was permitted simply at the parents' discretion, with no social stigma attached to it. Old people as well, when they became too feeble to contribute to the family, were left out in the snow to die. So, in Eskimo society, there seemed to be remarkably little respect for life.

[…]

To many thinkers, this observation—"Different cultures have different moral codes"—has seemed to be the key to understanding morality. The idea of universal truth in ethics, that say, is a myth. The customs of different societies are all that exist. These customs cannot be said to be "correct" or "incorrect," for that implies that we have an independent standard of right and wrong by which they may be judged. But no such independent standard exists; every standard is culture-bound. […]

This line of thought, more than any other, has persuaded people to be skeptical about ethics. Cultural Relativism, as it has been called, challenges our belief in the objectivity and universality of moral truth. It says, in effect, that there is no such thing as universal truth in ethics; there are only the various cultural codes, and nothing more. Moreover, our own code has no special status; it is merely one among many.

[…]

Cultural Relativism is a theory about the nature of morality. At first blush, it seems quite plausible. However, like all such theories, it may be subjected to rational analysis; and when we analyze Cultural Relativism, we find that it is not as plausible as it initially appears to be.

The first thing to notice is that at the heart of Cultural Relativism is a certain *form of argument*. Cultural relativists argue from facts about the differences between cultural outlooks to a conclusion about the status of morality. Thus, we are invited to accept this reasoning:

[…]

1. Different cultures have different moral codes.
2. Therefore, there is no objective "truth" in morality. Right and wrong are only matters of opinion, and opinions vary from culture to culture.

We may call this the Cultural Differences Argument. To many people, it is persuasive. But from a logical point of view, is it sound?

It is not sound. The problem is that the conclusion does not follow from the premise—that is, even if the premise is true, the conclusion still might be false. The premise concerns what people *believe*—in some societies, people believe one thing; in other societies, people believe something else. The conclusion, however, concerns what *really is the case*. The trouble is that this sort of conclusion does not follow logically from this sort of premise.

[…]

In some societies, people believe the earth is flat. In other societies, such as our own, people believe the earth is spherical. Does it follow, from the mere fact that people disagree, that there is no "objective truth" in geography? Of course not

[…]

The original impetus for Cultural Relativism comes from the observation that cultures differ dramatically in their views of right and wrong. But how much do they actually differ? It is true that there are differences. However, it is easy to overestimate the extent of those differences. Often, when we examine what seems to be a dramatic difference, we find that the cultures do not differ nearly as much as it appears.

[…]

Consider again the Eskimos, who killed perfectly healthy infants, especially girls. We do not approve of such things; in our society, a parent who kills a baby will be locked up. Thus, there appears to be a great difference in the values of our two cultures. But suppose we ask why the Eskimos did this. The explanation is not that they had no affection for their children or lacked respect for human life. An Eskimo family would always protect its babies if conditions permitted. But the Eskimos lived in a harsh environment, where food was in short supply. A fundamental postulate of Eskimo thought was this: "Life is hard, and the margin of safety small." A family may want to nourish its babies but be unable to do so.

As in many traditional societies, Eskimo mothers would nurse their infants over a much longer period than mothers in our culture—for four years, and perhaps even longer. So, even in the best of times, there were limits to the number of infants one mother could sustain. Moreover, the Eskimos were nomadic; unable to farm in the harsh northern climate, they had to move about in search of food. Infants had to be carried, and a mother could carry only one baby in her parka as she traveled and went about her outdoor work.

Infant girls were more readily disposed of for two reasons. First, in Eskimo society, the males were the primary food providers—they were the hunters—and it is obviously important to maintain a sufficient number of food providers. But there was an important second reason as well. Because the hunters suffered a high casualty rate, the adult men who died prematurely far outnumbered the women who died early. If male and female infants had survived in equal numbers, the female adult population would have greatly outnumbered the male adult population. [...]

So among the Eskimos, infanticide did not signal a fundamentally different attitude toward children. Instead, it arose from the recognition that drastic measures are sometimes needed to ensure the family's survival. Even then, however, killing the baby was not the first option considered. Adoption was common; childless couples were especially happy to take a more fertile couple's "surplus." Killing was the last resort. I emphasize this in order to show that the raw data of anthropologists can be misleading; it can make the differences in values between cultures appear greater than they are. The Eskimos' values were not all that different from our own. It is only that life forced choices upon them that we do not have to make.

[...]

It should not be surprising that, despite appearances, the Eskimos were protective of their children. How could it be otherwise? How could a group survive that did not value its young? [...]

Similar reasoning shows that other values must be more or less universal. Imagine what it would be like for a society to place no value on truth telling. When one person spoke to another, there would be no presumption that she was telling the truth, for she could just as easily be lying. Within that society, there would be no reason to pay attention to what anyone says. [...] Communication would be extremely difficult, if not impossible. And because complex societies cannot exist without communication among their members, society would become impossible. It follows that in any complex society there must be a presumption in favor of truthfulness. There may, of course, be exceptions to this rule; that is, there may be situations in which it is thought to be permissible to lie. Nevertheless, these will be exceptions to a rule that *is* in force in the society.

[...]

There is a general theoretical point here, namely, that *there are some moral rules that all societies must have in common, because those rules are necessary for society to exist*. The rules against lying and murder are two examples. And, in fact, we do find these rules in force in all viable cultures. Cultures may differ in what they regard as legitimate exceptions to the rules, but this disagreement exists against a broad background of agreement. Therefore, it is a mistake to overestimate the amount of difference between cultures. Not every moral rule can vary from society to society.

[...] Excision is a permanently disfiguring procedure that is sometimes called "female circumcision," although it bears little resemblance to the Jewish practice. More commonly, at least in Western media, it is referred to as "female genital mutilation."

According to the World Health Organization, the practice is widespread in 26 African nations, and 2 million girls each year are painfully excised. In some instances, excision is part of an elaborate tribal ritual, performed in small villages, and girls look forward to it because it signals their acceptance into the adult world. In other instances, the practice is carried out in cities on young women who desperately resist.

[...]

Although they are personally horrified by excision, many thoughtful people are reluctant to say it is wrong, for at least three reasons. First, there is an understandable nervousness about interfering in the social customs of other peoples. Europeans and their cultural descendants in America have a shabby history of destroying native cultures in the name of Christianity and enlightenment. Recoiling from this shameful record, some people refuse to criticize other cultures, especially cultures that resemble those that have been wronged in the past. There is a difference, however, between (a) judging a cultural practice to be deficient and (b) thinking that we should announce that fact, conduct a campaign, apply diplomatic pressure, and send in the troops. The first is just a matter of trying to see the world clearly, from a moral point of view. The second is something else entirely. Sometimes it may be right to "do something about it," but often it will not be.

Second, people may feel, rightly enough, that they should be tolerant of other cultures. Tolerance is, no doubt, a virtue—a tolerant person is willing to live in peaceful cooperation with those who see things differently. But there is nothing in the nature of tolerance that requires us to say that all beliefs, all religions, and all social practices are equally admirable. On the contrary, if we did not think that some were better than others, there would be nothing for us to tolerate.

Finally, people may be reluctant to judge because they do not want to express contempt for the society being criticized. But again, this is misguided: To condemn a particular practice is not to say that the culture on the whole is contemptible or that it is generally inferior to any other culture, including one's own. It could have many admirable features. In fact, we should expect this to be true of most human societies—they are mixtures of good and bad practices. Excision happens to be one of the bad ones.

[…]

Questions

1. *(1) Different cultures have different moral codes.*
   (2) Therefore, there is no objective "truth" in morality. Right and wrong are only matters of opinion, and opinions vary from culture to culture.

   What, in detail, does Rachels say is wrong with this argument?

2. Rachels claims that all societies will have some moral rules in common. What is his reasoning here?

3. Why, according to Rachels, are many people reluctant to say that "genital mutilation" is wrong? Why does Rachels think this reluctance is a mistake?

Part III

Morality and Politics

7

Morality and Politics
Fiction

The Divided States of America

Images flickered at her from monitors lining the walls: Conservative troop maneuvers along the border near St Louis; the Coast Guard turning back a boatload of people trying to cross the Potomac into the Liberal District; Federal forces quelling a small riot at a refugee camp in the border zone near Reno.

Images like these poured into the Agency 24 hours a day. Much of the time Sheila was aware of them only as background. She had people assigned to keep an eye on the various feeds; they would alert her to any significant developments.

Sheila Eldred was the head of the Federal Internal Borders Monitoring Agency (FIBMA). She was doing her daily stroll through the Agency offices, nodding to employees, letting herself be seen. Today she couldn't shake the feeling she was engaged in a farewell tour. This wasn't farewell—not yet: It was still months before the Agency would close. Still, it felt like farewell, with the sight of movers clearing furniture from two offices vacated earlier in the week.

The sense of things ending gave her a depressed feeling. Sheila wasn't depressed for herself and the loss of her job. What depressed her was the massive failure the closing of the Agency represented. At least, that's what it represented to her. Apparently most people in the "United States" disagreed. People had already divided the USA into four political districts; those districts would soon become four separate countries.

As Sheila turned a corner, she got a straight-on view of one of the major monitoring rooms, long rows of stacked screens facing other long rows of stacked screens, as in the TV section of some gigantic department store. Maybe it was just as well she'd be getting away from this job: She was beginning to see these endless images in her dreams.

There was just so much to monitor along the hundreds of miles of federally controlled border zones that separated the country's four political districts.

The border zones were ten-mile wide ribbons of land dotted with army bases, border patrol stations and refugee camps. The Agency had a system of satellites that could be focused on any stretch of border; Agency personnel could also access any of the hundreds of surveillance cameras the Federal Border Police used to augment their patrols. Beyond that, the Agency had the responsibility of monitoring all television signals broadcast within any of the districts. Several of the districts jammed radio and television signals coming from other districts, but the Temporary Secession Agreement (TSA) had given FIBMA the right to monitor such signals. It was important for the Agency to get each district's news and commentary in order to anticipate developments that might lead to trouble between the districts.

For the last few days there'd been an air of excitement in the office, talk of a potential crisis. Agency personnel had been paying particular attention to increased troop movements within the Conservative

Contemporary Moral and Social Issues: An Introduction through Original Fiction, Discussion, and Readings, First Edition. Thomas D. Davis.
© 2014 John Wiley & Sons, Inc. Published 2014 by John Wiley & Sons, Inc.

District. Pessimists had been predicting clashes—even war—between Conservative and Federal forces. Sheila couldn't afford to ignore the possibility, but she didn't take it seriously. Why would the Conservatives take a chance on attacking the still superior Federal forces when all Federal forces would be dissolved within a year—along with what was left of the Federal government?

Sheila's theory was that the Conservative troop movements near the border amounted to nothing more than an elaborate recruiting campaign aimed at the soon-to-be-discharged Federal soldiers. The Conservatives had taken steps to develop the largest and best trained military of any district—and had outfitted their troops in impressive looking uniforms. What the soldiers liked especially was the shoulder insignia—the head of a ferocious eagle, with blazing red eyes, set against a dark blue background covered with small white crosses. The same image was on the Conservative flag.

Sheila believed the Conservative troop movements were intended to impress the Federal troops; she was sure recruiting flyers would soon follow. The Conservative District would be in a good position to recruit: If past politics was any indication, the majority of Federal soldiers would find the authoritarian and religious values of the Conservative District the most compatible with their own approach to the world.

The other districts had been slow to develop their own military units and to recognize that there would be a recruiting battle over the soon-to-be-disbanded Federal troops. Aware now of their vulnerabilities, those districts were asking the Federal government for help. But there would be no help: The Federal government was on its way out.

Without quite realizing it, Sheila had stopped before a large map with the heading, "United States of America."

The name "United States of America" was an anachronism, of course. The country hadn't been united for years. Nor were there states any more. True, this map still contained faint lines marking what had once been states, but that was little more than nostalgia. The real divisions in the country now were the districts—four of them, of unequal size: Libertarian, Conservative, Liberal, and Socialist.

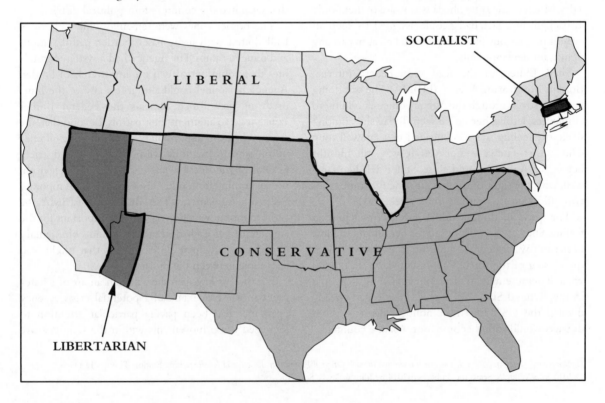

"United Districts of America" had been proposed as an alternate name for the country, but it had never caught on, and now was itself an anachronism: In a year the districts would become separate countries. There was talk of an "American Union" modeled after the "European Union" but given the animosity between districts, that amount of cooperation was unlikely. The districts would be lucky if they weren't at war with one another in a couple of years.

It was hard to believe that sixty years ago—at the turn of the twenty-first century—there'd actually been a "United States." True, the political divisiveness that would rip the country apart between 2032 and 2040 was already visible in 2000, but there'd been little inkling of just how angry the various factions would become. It was more than a little ironic that such divisiveness had accelerated in spite of foreign threats that should have brought the country together.

There had been moments of unity after the terror- ist attacks of 2001, 2025, and that devastating attack of 2031, but those moments hadn't lasted. Even when the USA had closed its borders in 2036 and had become the armed citadel against the world it was today, that hadn't unified the country. Instead it had only magnified the antagonisms.

There had been a point where many were predict- ing a second Civil War, but the analogy had never been good: There were too many groups trying to tear the country into too many pieces. Of course there'd been the usual liberal and conservative blocks continuing their ever angrier fights over social pro- grams, taxation, government regulation of business, and the place of religion in public life. But there had also been militant splinter groups moving farther right or left or into some other dimension altogether. Violence by environmental, animal rights, anti-tax, anti-abortion, and Christian Reconstructionist groups had dramatically increased, as well as acts of violence by individuals who seemed inspired by nothing more than the violence of the times. Certain regions of the country were closing up against others, and several were talking of secession. There had been talk of mar- tial law—even a military coup—though it had never gone farther than talk.

Negotiation had prevented civil strife by bringing about what amounted to a trial separation. It had been decided that after a transitional period of ten years, the country would divide into districts. Each district would have a status somewhere between that of a super-state and a separate country—with its own constitution and central government. The Federal government would be charged with national defense and enforcing the district borders and little else: All other functions would be subsumed by the districts.

That ten-year transitional period had been unbe- lievably complicated, but those complications had provided just the distraction the country needed. People were excited about the upcoming political divisions, feeling relieved that they could finally have political units with people sharing their own views. They could almost be kind to their opponents, know- ing they wouldn't have to deal with them much longer. And there had been so many details that needed seeing to, so many adjustments that needed to be made. Who had time to worry about political antagonisms if one had, say, to move one's family from Texas to California to seek a new life? Or to help rela- tives who were moving into Texas from California? And to do this while adjusting to new changes in everything from tax policies to schooling?

From the beginning, it was taken for granted that the country would divide into at least a liberal and a conservative district. The big question was whether the smaller divisions could be accommodated within these general rubrics. Surveys had been developed, given, refined, and given again. There'd been inter- views with representative members of smaller groups and negotiations with the likely leaders of the liberal and conservative factions as to what kind of accom- modation could be made with those groups.

The problem with the general category of "conservative" was that the US version had been composed of an uneasy alliance of economic conserv- atives, who wanted minimal government and the freest possible markets, and religious conservatives, who wanted anti-abortion laws, tougher laws against drug use and pornography, and general government support of Judeo-Christian beliefs and values.

The existence of a common enemy, liberalism, had given economic and religious conservatives an incen- tive to compromise. But without that common enemy, their differences had come to the fore. Religious conservatives had insisted on what amounted to a free-market theocracy: There would be minimal regulation of the general conduct of business, but all society would be subject to regulations necessary to bring it in line with Judeo-Christian morality.

Those economic conservatives who had no desire to live under a theocracy but couldn't stomach liberalism had insisted there be a libertarian district with minimal government and freedom of both economic activity *and* lifestyles.

The Libertarian District now occupied what had once been Nevada and half of Arizona; its capital was Las Vegas. There was a limited trade agreement between the Libertarian and Conservative districts—limited because the conservatives were determined to avoid any cultural pollution from the free-wheeling Libertarian District, and the libertarians had no desire to be preached to by the conservatives.

On the far left there were a number of democratic socialists who had refused to be satisfied with the proposed Liberal District. Conservatives couldn't understand this since to them the proposed Liberal District already seemed thoroughly socialistic: Tax rates on the highest earnings were raised fifty percent and the social safety net substantially enlarged; unions in most areas of the economy were to be strengthened and encouraged; worker safety and product safety laws were to be toughened; health care was to be thoroughly nationalized; there was to be tough regulation of banks and other financial institutions; the equality of women, the right to abortion, and the right to same-sex marriage were to be included in the new constitution; and, finally, there were likely to be stronger laws restricting hate speech as well as speech that denigrated various ethnic and other cultural groups.

Still, socialists insisted that they wanted even greater economic equality, a number of state-run and worker-run enterprises, government pressure toward greater social equality and solidarity, and government efforts to promote a cultural life consistent with socialist ideals.

Finally it had been agreed that there would be a Socialist District. It had been formed out of a portion of Massachusetts; its capital was Cambridge. A limited trade agreement was signed with the Liberal District—limited, in this case, not in terms of culture but economics: The Socialist District needed to protect its enterprises (primarily textbook publishing to start) while it developed its alternate economic institutions.

Sheila glanced at the line representing the northern border of the USA. Interestingly, Canada had played a significant role in the negotiations for the Temporary Secession Agreement (TSA), supplying mediators when it seemed impossible to find neutral parties within the USA, even providing meeting sites for some of the more intense discussions. Of course, mediating the dispute had been in the Canadians' interest: They weren't anxious to see their southern neighbor descend into violent chaos, and they were hoping to persuade the USA to loosen what the Canadians saw as the paranoid border restrictions in place since 2036. (In fact, liberals were already negotiating a special relationship with Canada that would take place once the Liberal District became a separate country.)

However, whatever their motives, the Canadians had been generous and helpful, sharing from their long-term experiences in negotiating with Quebec and various ethnic groups. To help facilitate the TSA, Canada had offered residence—with the possibility of citizenship—to former Federal officials wishing to move to Canada after the districts became separate nations. The offer had been meant to soothe the fears of Federal officials who worried they might suffer repercussions for their work after the dissolution of the Federal government. Whatever the intent of the offer, it had been written loosely, with few real conditions. Sheila knew a couple of colleagues who had no reason to fear for their safety but were still thinking of making the move.

Sheila turned away from the map and checked the monitors again. The riot near Reno seemed to have been subdued, but the situation would bear watching. The rioters were all refugees from the Libertarian District, most of them drug-addicts in various stages of withdrawal: It was bound to be a volatile group. Since the Libertarian District had no anti-drug laws, it had seemed a paradise to heavy drug users from other areas of the country. Most of the users had lacked the foresight or caution to worry about what might happen if their lives turned sour. Since the Libertarian District had no social safety net and had the toughest police policies of any of the districts when it came to protecting property rights against squatters and thieves, the down-and-out addict who didn't want to die in the streets had little choice but to leave the

Libertarian District and seek the free medical services available from the Federal government in the Border Zones (BZs).

However, the addict, having received food and medical treatment, wouldn't be anxious to stay in the BZ. By agreement with the Districts which funded them, BZs housed the refugees in camps that were bare-bones: The camps provided food, used clothes, shelter and medical treatment—but that was pretty much it. BZs were needed as a temporary safety valve for those people who discovered they had made a terrible mistake in their choice of district, but the cost of choosing refugee status was designed to be high: Districts didn't want people trying to switch back and forth between districts in order to juggle social services and economic opportunities. Anyone choosing refugee status had a minimum stay of twelve months at the camp and had to apply for admission to another district. No drugs or alcohol were allowed in the refugee camps and, given their isolated locations, the rules were pretty easy to enforce. Thus addicts of any kind would soon be feeling pretty cranky. Yes, it would be a volatile group.

The Libertarian District had been a puzzle from the beginning. The guiding libertarian image seemed to be that of people moving into a wilderness, settling on plots of land, and gaining rights to the land and what it produced by working it. The only legitimate role of government was to keep those people from impinging on each other's rights to life, liberty and property. Taxes were allowed only to the extent necessary to carry on those functions in the most cost-effective way possible.

Since it was impossible to go back to the wilderness and start over, modern-day libertarians had once talked about gradually cutting back government until only its protective functions were left. But the division of the country into districts hadn't allowed for anything gradual; how then was one to create an instant Libertarian District out of a fully developed and functioning state (or state and a half, since the district was comprised of Nevada plus half of Arizona)? What had been decided on was economic shock therapy analogous to what had once been tried in Eastern Europe after the fall of Communism: Change the system all at once in the faith that the right sort of order would emerge out of the immediate chaos.

It had been decided that any Nevada/eastern Arizona residents who wanted to stay could keep their property—with the understanding that they would now live under a new political system. Everything else was put up for sale, not only private property, but all public property as well—roads, prisons, schools. Government officials then in charge were given transition contracts to orient the new owners to the running of these public functions; after the transition, the officials would be gone. The promise of virtually unregulated business drew in plenty of money, and it wasn't long before most of the state was sold.

But labor would be a big potential problem: How was one going to attract workers to a district where there were no unions, no worker safety laws, no workman's compensation, no unemployment insurance, no safety net at all? Further, the worker-as-consumer would be functioning in a world where there were virtually no regulatory guarantees of product reliability and safety, with few restrictions on what advertisers or salespeople could say when pushing those products.

The only way for business to attract workers was to offer them contracts guaranteeing them much higher salaries or wages than they could get elsewhere—pay which, under the new system, would be virtually tax free. This meant a lot of upfront money, but those who ran the businesses had a number of long-term advantages. They knew that many workers, dazzled by quick money, wouldn't think very far down the road. Nor would they read and/or understand the complicated employment contracts. The Libertarian District would have fraud laws which would be vigorously enforced. However, in the spirit of laissez-faire—or "let the buyer beware"—fraud would be defined so narrowly that little but a blatant lie would count. Once the fine print in the contract was enforced, the worker would have no recourse but to sue, since there would be no government regulatory agencies to interfere. Suing would be protracted and expensive. Eventually workers would have to accept whatever wage was offered.

What hadn't been anticipated was the degree to which the non-regulation of social and personal life would draw so many drug users. It was made clear from the beginning that there would be no free social services for those who fell on hard times, but this news did little to deter a group prone to risk-taking. Or maybe it hadn't seemed like such a gamble; maybe some people were misled by the sometime libertarian claim that in a libertarian society private charities would take up the slack from the lack of public welfare. The problem was that charitable people just weren't attracted to a libertarian society. It's true there were a few religious charities (they saw themselves as missionaries to Sodom and Gomorrah) but these charities were in no position to cope with the mass of problems. Hence the exodus of addicts and the riots near Reno.

Suddenly needing a cup of coffee, Sheila headed for the nearest break room. Even here there were more monitors, though often these were tuned to enter- tainment programs recorded from the various district broadcasts. Someone was watching what Sheila knew to be the top-rated show in the Liberal District— *Where's Fred?* Each week the main character, Fred, a white male, would find himself in the midst of some disadvantaged group. Fred would good-naturedly, if nervously, try to fit in; he would make politically incorrect gaffs, suffer a torrent of abuse, but, finally, toward the end of the show, begin to "get it." However, since there was always some other disadvantaged group to go to, Fred was in for a long and painful—if ultimately redeeming—education.

In a sense the show mirrored the hottest issue in the Liberal District—"oppression points." Sheila didn't know who had first raised the issue; she just knew it had suddenly caught fire. The idea was that disadvantaged groups would be ranked to create an oppression hierarchy. Oppression points would earn the "oppressed" reparations in terms of tax breaks and direct payments, as well as priority in hiring and school admissions—even, on one proposal, places in line. The debate was getting pretty hot, and even a bit medieval in its intricacies—how many different oppressed categories one could occupy and whether if one were oppressed in one respect (say, ethnic group) but also an oppressor in another (say, male, or supervisor), plus and minus points should be considered.

Some people—mostly white males—complained that the whole idea of the Liberal District had been to *stop* oppression and, anyway, most of the oppressors were now in the Conservative and Libertarian districts. With a bit of eye-rolling, others explained to them that oppression didn't require an *oppressor*, that it was built into the very systems of society.

Sheila saw that another television was tuned to the top-rated show in the Conservative District, *Pastor Bob*. Bob had a large family—no doubt a symbolic reflection of the fact that abortion was illegal and contraception highly restricted. Pastor Bob's children were in business and doing very well: They were constantly urging their old-fashioned father to apply modern business methods to his church and ministry. But the unmarried daughter had just had a pregnancy scare, and here Bob had a lesson to teach: Free-market capitalism might be a God-given gift, but Christians had to be careful not to let too much materialism corrupt their basic Christian principles.

Remarks made here and there in *Pastor Bob* were indicative of some of the divisions that were showing up in the Conservative District. (Sheila was begin- ning to think that once one started dividing up the United States, the divisions could continue *ad infinitum*.)

It had always been a conservative fantasy to revert to nineteenth-century America when markets had been at their freest and Protestant Christianity had domi- nated the cultural—or at least religious—landscape. In recent times, the great enemy, liberalism, had brought together conservatives of various religious persuasions. But now that liberalism had been banished from the District, old divisions were showing up again—not only strains of anti-Semitism and anti-Catholicism, but divisions within conservative Protestantism between fundamentalists, evangelicals, and charismatics, between pre-millennialists, mid-Tribulation Rapture pre-mil- lennialists, post-Tribulation Rapture pre-millennialists, and post-millennialists.

The official culture of the Conservative District consisted of Judeo-Christian values and the Western "canon" of literature. In reality, "Judeo-Christian" was slanted heavily toward Evangelical Protestantism (with the "Judeo" part interpreted through the New Testament). As for the Western "canon" of literature, it was so heavily edited to eliminate anything that might conflict with Christian doctrine and morals that the resulting "great works" were beginning to resemble a series of Reader's Digest Condensed Books. "Young people's editions"—those that could be used in schools or sold to people under eighteen years of age—were edited down even further.

Such editing was a reflection of the "values committees" the government was setting up to oversee various aspects of life. Public education had been radically affected: Prayers opened and closed the school day, some schools were experimenting with (so far non-sectarian) "chapel," and all science and literature that might undercut the religious faith of the students had been eliminated from the curriculum. Not everyone in the Conservative District was happy about these developments. Parents who wanted their children exposed to the theory of evolution and a less censored version of Western art and literature were doing home schooling or trying to establish small private academies. However, a voucher movement to help fund these academies was going nowhere.

Pastor Bob took a commercial break. Like most of the Conservative commercials, these were upbeat and wholesome; almost all sexual suggestiveness was edited out by the Judeo-Christian Media Advisory Board. The religious censorship of commercials had seemed to crimp business in the beginning, but with government so pro-business, the consumers as materialistic as ever, and consumers having much more cash due to lowered tax rates, business soon began to boom again.

The only TV network the financially strapped Socialist District had managed so far was a kind of low-budget PBS showing mostly old documentaries on such subjects as the oppression of workers, white-collar crime, global warming, and endangered species. There was cable coverage of endless meetings as the socialists tried to talk their way haltingly toward a classless society. One new socialist show called *They Didn't Deserve It!* attempted to lay some groundwork for this. The narrator would relate some individual success story. Then a panel of sociologists and psychologists would analyze the combination of factors—looks, character traits (including motivation), mental abilities, family connections, education—that had led to that person's success and then show how all those particular factors could be traced back to other factors—family environment,

fetal environment, genetics—over which the person had had no control. The moral of these anti-success narratives was always the same: What we come to be and what we accomplish are in the end "just a matter of luck"; thus, we do not deserve differential rewards as a result. It was heavy stuff—and more than a little depressing.

Still, skimming TV shows and commercials was a fascinating exercise in cross-cultural comparisons. The Libertarians had a no-holds-barred approach: Sheila still couldn't get over the idea of heroin dealers advertising their stuff on cable television. The uncensored porn movies were also a bit of a shock. It was such a contrast with the Conservative District, where even the classic Disney movies were edited to remove vaguely suggestive remarks and scenes.

Not that the Conservative District had managed to banish sin, or even expected to. Prostitution, bootleg liquor, and gambling still could be found in back alleys, but it was strictly contained. Nothing like organized crime had been able to get started: The Conservative District had a strong police force much less inhibited by "civil rights" than police had been in the old days.

The Liberal District didn't censor for sexual content per se, but the PC Media Advisory Board imposed so much political censorship—nothing nonconsensual, nothing degrading to women, minorities or animals, nothing remotely violent— that the sexual acts in films had such an upbeat, gymnastic quality that they had lost almost all of their pornographic appeal. Apparently an underground porn market was developing, but law enforcement in this area was very strict, and the porn market wasn't making much headway.

The socialists were like the liberals, only more so: With the socialists' constant emphasis on education intended to mold better citizens, the only thing resembling porn films on their public-run channel was sex instruction tapes, the sexual act accompanied by academic voice-overs describing the various techniques and referring the viewer to supplementary reading material.

Sheila noticed a Liberal District ad for a "Darwin Day sale" on a nearby screen: "Fashion has evolved," the announcer was saying, "maybe you should too." One day historians would have a field day doing cross-cultural studies of the different holidays in the four districts.

The Liberal District had fulfilled one of the conservatives' worst fears by finally getting the "Christ" out of Christmas. It had been jarring the previous year to hear stores touting so many shopping days "'til X-mas." There was supposed to be a new name by the coming holiday season, but given the cultural and ethnic wrangling that went on constantly, Sheila doubted the liberals would manage to agree on a name.

There was a similar sort of wrangling over the Pledge of Allegiance. There had been near universal agreement in the Liberal District that the word "God" should be removed from the Pledge (as well as from coins and bills). The controversy concerned whether there should be a Pledge at all, or even ceremonies of respect for the new Liberal flag. To many liberals, all such gestures seemed vaguely "fascistic."

Holiday names in the Socialist District were an entirely serious affair—"Equality Day," "Solidarity Day," as well "Robert Owens Day," "Friedrich Engels Day," and "Karl Marx Day" (the latter having taken the place of Christmas in the Socialist calendar).

Holidays in the Conservative District were almost as serious, given the theocratic tendency to give most of them religious significance. In addition to Christmas and Easter (the Easter bunny had been banished as sacrilegious), there were such holidays as "St Paul's Day," "Jerry Falwell Day," and so on. (Christian fundamentalists were still blocking the proposal to make "Blessed Virgin Day" a national holiday, but it was celebrated in Catholic communities.) The conservatives did have a few "fun" holidays, such as "NRA Day" (celebrated with fireworks and other explosives) and the not-quite-official but widely celebrated "Red Meat Day" (which filled the air with even more smoke than did NRA day.)

The libertarians didn't have any official holidays since "official" meant government, and they didn't want government telling people what they should and shouldn't celebrate. More importantly, why would businesses want to give workers paid days off? However, the business community soon realized that if workers didn't get *any* time off, they couldn't do

their job as consumers; businesses would suffer as a result. Gradually there developed a loose agreement among companies to give workers Sunday and half of Wednesday off.

If the contrast in holiday ads was strange enough, the contrast in documentaries was bizarre. In the last two weeks, Sheila had seen a conservative documentary on drilling in the Grand Canyon and another on the opening of "Spotted Owl hunting season" (dreamed up as a "lark," but still real). She'd seen one liberal documentary proposing full citizenship for the Great Apes, and another....

Sheila's attention was drawn to some images from a documentary that she had seen last week and wasn't remotely tempted to smile about. It discussed the heartbreak of families split apart by differing political and religious loyalties. Sheila knew all about that, though in her case such loyalties were not the prime cause. Sheila and her husband had begun drifting apart soon after the death of their teenage son in a riot in the violent years just preceding the TSA. Her husband had found his consolation in religion, and Sheila hadn't been willing to follow him there—nor to the Conservative District where he was now determined to live. The break-up of her marriage was inevitable, she supposed, but it added an extra aura of sadness to the break-up of the country.

She shook her head. She had been so sure that the rifts between the districts would be temporary, that once people had had a chance to separate and cool off, they'd feel the impact of what they were losing— the greatness that had once been the United States of America, despite its various failings. People would put aside their petty disagreements and angry ideologies and find a way to put their country back together again.

But it was not to be and the failure of it saddened her deeply. The United States was gone: Soon it would be four separate countries. Maybe those four would keep on sub-dividing—at least until some unified enemy picked up the pieces for itself.

Sheila didn't want to watch it happen. Her husband could join the conservatives and others could join the socialists, liberals, or libertarians. As for her, she was going to Canada.

Questions

1. According to the story, how did the United States come to be divided into four political districts?

2. What is the current role of the Federal Government under this arrangement? What are the border zones? What is their purpose?

3. Describe in some detail the political arrangements in each of the four districts: (a) Libertarian (b) Conservative; (c) Liberal, and (d) Socialist.

4. Describe the following television shows mentioned in the story and say how those shows connect with the philosophy of the district in which they are shown: (i) *Where's Fred?*; (ii) *Pastor Bob*; and (iii) *They Didn't Deserve It!*

5. If you had to choose one of the districts to live in, which one would it be? In what ways would that district be a good fit for your ideas and preferred lifestyle? In what ways not?

8

Morality and Politics
Discussion

The Divided States of America

The story, "Divided States," imagines a time in the future when the political and moral divisions within the United States of America had become so extreme that a trial separation became necessary. As a result, the USA was divided into four different "districts," with each devoted to a particular moral/political philosophy. Each district is like a country within the larger United States, having its own set of district laws. The Federal Government exists but in an extremely stripped-down form: Besides defending the USA. from foreign enemies, it is responsible for enforcing the borders between the different districts and managing refugee camps for those who decide too late that they have chosen the wrong district to live in.

The two largest districts are the Liberal District and the Conservative District. The Liberal district emphasizes freedom of lifestyle, a strict separation of church and state, a strong social safety net for the disadvantaged, and government support for multiculturalism. The Conservative district promotes a freer market with much less government regulation, government support of conservative Judeo-Christian values, and a much smaller tax-based government safety net for the less fortunate.

There is the Libertarian District which insists on minimal government interference in the market and in the lifestyles of its citizens; it does not have any kind of social safety net. Finally, there is a tiny Socialist District which, while democratic, insists on much greater economic and social equality among its citizens.

"Divided States" is intended to emphasize by satirical exaggeration the main political and moral divisions that now exist in the United States. We will be discussing the four major political philosophies that are caricatured in the story—emphasizing the American versions of these views.

The exaggeration in the story, while useful for satire, is something we'll want to undo in the course of our more serious discussion. Politics in the USA is rife with simplifications and distortions. Most people in the USA are not knowledgeable about government, economics or the world situation, nor are they especially interested in politics: Slogans are much easier to deal with than position papers. The Democratic and Republican parties run advertising campaigns seeking votes; like most advertising campaigns, these political ones are going to be blunt instruments, creating a falsely attractive picture of its side and a falsely unattractive picture of the other side. Further, the passion in politics often comes from ideologues who promote simplified views of the world; they, in turn, are aided by media that thrive on the simple and dramatic.

I'm using the word "ideology" in its familiar negative sense. An ideology starts with a few simple beliefs (e.g., capitalism is all good or all bad, government is all good or all bad) and spins a world view around these simple starting points. An ideology divides possible positions into just two or three: Its own view plus one or two others that are exaggerated and vilified. Ideological speech is filled with the kinds of basic fallacies discussed in any book on informal logic, fallacies such as *false dilemma* (speaking as if there are only two possible positions on an issue when there are many more); *straw man* (exaggerating the opponent's position to make it less attractive); *ad hominem* (attacking the person rather than the argument); and so on.

One crucial characteristic of ideologies is that they are not susceptible to reason in the scientific sense of being ready to change one's views if contrary evidence arises. For ideologues, the only evidence taken seriously is evidence for, and all possible evidence against is dismissed out of hand without serious evaluation.

The inherent biases in our reasoning discussed in Part I make us all susceptible to ideological thinking. On the other hand, ideology is one of the enemies of philosophy, which seeks to encourage reason, open-mindedness, and a fair evaluation of evidence. In what follows, I hope we can get beyond political slogans and deal with the various issues in greater complexity. We will focus on the four political philosophies in the story—libertarianism, conservativism, liberalism, and socialism. It's important to note that we're using the terms "conservativism" and "liberalism" in their contemporary American political sense. (Those terms mean something quite different in contemporary British politics, for example.)

Before we get to the four philosophies, however, let's do some preliminary work involving morality and free markets, democracy, and the relationship between religion and the state.

Preliminary issues

Morality and free markets

All four of the political philosophies we'll discuss accept the necessity of free markets. This acceptance ranges from the grudging to the euphoric, from markets that are partially free to almost completely free, but it is acceptance nonetheless. This is true even

of the form of socialism we will consider: Versions of socialism that do away with markets altogether in favor of a planned economy are generally considered to be unworkable.

When economists refer to "markets" they are referring to a system in which buyers and sellers interact to exchange goods and services and determine prices. "Capitalism" refers to an economic system in which there is private property *and* in which people interact through the market both in their roles as buyers and sellers and as owners and workers. The word "capitalism" was coined in the nineteenth century by socialists as a term of abuse, but by the twentieth century had become a more neutral technical term in the social sciences.

We need to distinguish between laissez-faire capitalism and welfare capitalism. "Laissez-faire" (French, meaning "let alone") refers to capitalism with the minimum of government interference. Laissez-faire capitalism is pretty much dead, existing only in the fantasies of some libertarians and extreme economic conservatives. It has been replaced by one version or another of what's called "welfare capitalism," where the government does not simply facilitate the market but modifies it or redistributes its benefits in the name of promoting the welfare of some—or in some cases, all—of its citizens.

Since the word "welfare" is an explosive one in politics, we need to take care about how it is being used. The word has at least three different meanings. We'll move from the narrowest to the broadest meaning.

Welfare (1): "Means-tested welfare" or "welfare assistance," that is, government subsidies to people whose economic means fall below a certain level.

Such programs in the USA include Temporary Assistance to Needy Families (TANF), Aid to Families with Dependent Children (AFDC), and Medicaid.

Welfare (2): Government modification of the market and/or redistribution of its benefits in the name of promoting the well-being of most or all of its citizens.

This broader definition includes means-tested welfare, but much else besides. The modern welfare state subsidizes a whole range of activities that have nothing do with the "poor" per se: Building roads, providing money for schools, offering assistance for communities struck by catastrophes, licensing doctors and other health-care providers, trying to ensure that only safe food and medicines are available through the market, ensuring safe conditions in the workplace, and so forth.

Welfare (3): Personal well-being.

We talked about personal well-being in the first chapter when we discussed happiness and flourishing.

When we talk about welfare capitalism we're talking of "welfare (2)." The current political arguments between liberals and conservatives have to do with how much of a welfare dimension capitalism should have, not whether it should have one. Only the most extreme libertarian would want to get rid of the welfare state altogether in the sense of no public education, no degree of government-supervised drug and food testing, and no sort of social security program. Debates about means-tested welfare—whether it ought to be "workfare," whether its benefits should be lessened and its eligibility requirements tightened—are all debates *within* the broad framework of welfare capitalism.

We've already noted that versions of socialism that do away with markets altogether in favor of government planning are generally considered to be unworkable. This is so not only because of the collapse of the communist experiments, but because of our increased knowledge of how markets work.

As writer John Cassidy says:

> Market systems have proved durable for several reasons. In allowing individuals, firms, and countries to specialize in what they are best at, they expand the economy's productive capacity. In providing incentives for investment and innovation, they facilitate a gradual rise in productivity and wages, which, over decades and centuries, compound and greatly improve living standards. And in relying on self-interest rather than administrative fiat to guide the decisions of consumers, investors, and business executives, markets obviate the need for a feudal overlord or omniscient central planner to organize everything.

The superiority of capitalism and markets to produce wealth is pretty much taken for granted these days; in any case, we shall take it for granted. One of the main questions we shall consider concerns the degree to which capitalism should be modified to alter some of its effects, even if those modifications lessen the total wealth produced at a given time or even in the long run. How much welfare should there be in welfare capitalism? To what degree should the general wealth creation (efficiency) of the market be overridden by other considerations, such as protecting workers and consumers?

Democracy

One thing our four philosophies have in common is a belief in democratic government and the political equality of all citizens as expressed in certain fundamental legal rights. A belief in political equality was arrived at slowly over the centuries, with opponents kicking and screaming the whole way. However, acceptance of democracy and political equality is now a reality—at least equality in a formal sense. What is controversial is what form democracy should take and how much equality there should be in fact.

"Democracy" literally means "rule by the people" and is generally taken to mean any society in which governments are produced by open, free and fair elections. It is important to distinguish between "direct democracy" in which the major policy decisions are decided by popular vote and "representative democracy" in which major policy decisions are made by representatives chosen by popular vote. It is also important to distinguish between democracy as pure majority rule and "constitutional democracy" in which there are constitutional protections for individuals and minorities. Such constitutional protections are likely to cover the right to vote and hold public office; the right to own at least some property; freedom of speech and of the press; freedom of association and religion; and freedom from arbitrary arrest and seizure.

The United States is a constitutional, representative democracy.

"Democracy" is a partially descriptive, partially normative term—what philosophers call an "essentially contested concept." If we get to arguing about what an ideal democracy would look like or whether some society is *really* democratic, we're most likely arguing values rather than straightforward definitions.

Ironically, if there is a universal theme among people who favor democracy, it is something like, "Democracy—Yes!—but not too much." We've already noted that no one wants legally unrestrained majority rule. However, even when it comes to constitutional representative democracies, lots of people would like to see that much democracy held in check. To those concerned with social and political equality, there is the worry that democracy will lead to racist and sexist policies. To those concerned with education and higher culture, there is the worry that democracy will lead to superstition and to a culture geared to the lowest common denominator. To enthusiasts of capitalism, there is the worry that democracy will result in limiting markets and redistribution of income.

A concern about democracy leading to redistribution of wealth has been a fear of capitalists since the start of democratic movements. According to historian Jerry Z. Muller,

> ...it's important to keep in mind that most western European societies became capitalist societies before they became democratic societies. In fact, there was a great deal of concern among 19th-century European intellectuals, including liberals such as John Stuart Mill, that with the coming of democracy, the newly enfranchised working class would use its political power in a way that would destroy capitalism....

According to Muller, some of what Mill feared was that "those who didn't possess property might impose an undue burden of taxation on those who did possess property"; that voters "might decide to tax away inheritances or they might decide to expand government spending for their own benefit"; that "working-class voters would use legislation to try to raise wages, to try to limit competition in the labor market, or even to discourage labor-saving devices."

From the standpoint of someone who favors unrestricted capitalism, most of Mill's fears have come true. From the standpoint of those who feel welfare capitalism is a kinder or more just system, these consequences of democracy have been a good thing.

Religion in the public square

"Divided States" embodies the negative fantasies of both liberals and conservatives as to how the other views the ideal relationship between religion and the state.

> Religious conservatives had insisted on what amounted to a free-market theocracy: There would be minimal regulation of the general conduct of business, but all society would be subject to regulations necessary to bring it in line with Judeo-Christian morality.
>
> The Liberal District had fulfilled one of the conservatives' worst fears by finally getting the "Christ" out of Christmas. It had been jarring the previous year to hear stores touting so many shopping days "till X-mas."...
>
> ...There had been near universal agreement in the Liberal District that the word "God" should be removed from the Pledge [of Allegiance] (as well as from coins and bills)....

Of course the fantasies in the story do have grains of truth. Let's examine those grains more closely.

Of our four political philosophies, only conservativism approves of religion as an active ingredient of political life. More specifically, much American conservativism favors the promotion of Christian (Judeo-Christian) values as part of the nation's heritage (though nowhere near to the degree indicated in the story).

The other three political philosophies endorse freedom of religion, but they want government to be neutral in terms of favoring any particular religion.

The constitutional status of religion in the United States has been in dispute since the country's founding. The First Amendment to the Constitution of the United States says, in part: "Congress shall make no law respecting an establishment of religion, or prohibiting the free exercise thereof...." (These two prohibitions are referred to by legal scholars as the "Establishment Clause" and the "Free Exercise Clause.")

A central question is this: Would it be constitutional for the Federal Government, as well as local governments, to openly promote Christian (Judeo-Christian) beliefs and values? One side says, no, that the Constitution requires a strict separation of church and state. The other side says, yes, that the United States was founded as a Christian nation and that favoring Christianity wouldn't amount to "establishing" a church or prohibiting the exercise of other religions.

Those against the Christian-nation view of the United States cite the fact that there is no mention of God or Christ in the Constitution; quote President Jefferson's phrase (from an official letter) about a "wall of separation between church and state"; and, point to the Treaty of Tripoli, signed during the presidency of George Washington, that said the United States "was in no way founded upon the Christian religion." Those in favor of the Christian-nation view cite the religious history of the colonies with their established churches. They point out that the Founders were faced with different versions of Christianity, not different religions, when they wrote the Bill of Rights; that the Founders seemed to have little problem with religious symbolism in public life; and that the Constitution was not originally intended to apply to state governments (that changed with the Fourteenth Amendment in 1868).

The current view of US courts regarding the relationship between church and state is complex, not always clear, and constantly evolving. The issue came to the forefront after World War II in a series of cases that often involved public schooling—either in terms of instruction or potential government funding.

In a 1947 case the Supreme Court made it official that the Establishment Clause in the Federal Constitution applied to state governments. The opinion, written by Justice Hugo Black, quoted Jefferson's comment about a wall of separation between church and state and said that the purpose of that wall was to protect religious minorities from persecution.

In a subsequent case, Justice Felix Frankfurter spoke about public schools as a force for national unity. He thought that religious instruction in the schools would put minorities in the difficult position of either conforming against conscience from peer pressure or of opting out and thus emphasizing their differences with others.

In the 1960s, on similar grounds, the Supreme Court declared school-sponsored prayer and Bible-reading to be unconstitutional. The Court set a two-part test that any law must meet to withstand a challenge under the Establishment Clause: It must have "a secular purpose and a primary effect that neither advances nor inhibits religion." In the case of *Lemon v. Kurtzman*, the Court added a third part to the test, that it not entangle government with religion. This three-part test has become known as the "Lemon test."

The "secular" test has slowly given way to a "neutrality" test as the Court has allowed public displays of religious symbols when secular symbols are also present—a Nativity scene along with Santa Claus and reindeer in a Christmas display. The Court has also allowed public funds to be used for voucher programs that could be used for religious schools if they could be used for non-religious schools as well.

A third test that the Court has employed is the "coercion test": whether a given state action has coerced citizens into supporting or participating in religious activities. What's made this test confusing is that the Court has included in the test indirect coercion that subjects students to peer pressure. Critics have wondered in what sense peer pressure is state coercion, but the test does echo Frankfurter's concerns about state activities emphasizing religious differences.

Let's move on now to discuss the four political philosophies we listed earlier: libertarianism, conservativism, liberalism, and socialism. Before we deal with them individually, let's do a general comparison. This comparison treats the four political philosophies as they are normally defined, not as they are caricatured in "Divided States." We'll deal with the caricatures—and the criticisms suggested by the caricatures—when we deal with the philosophies individually.

Four political philosophies

Of the terms we will use to describe the four political philosophies, the most troublesome is "liberal." You'll sometimes hear it said that American conservativism is in the Western liberal tradition. How can conservativism be in a liberal tradition? The answer is that "liberal" is being used in two different senses: (1) "classical liberalism" (sometimes called "negative liberalism") and (2) "modern liberalism" (sometimes called "positive liberalism").

It would be useful here to review a distinction made in Part II between negative and positive rights:

"Negative rights" are those rights related to a general right not to be interfered with or coerced—as, for instance, in the exercise of religion. However the label also covers basic democratic rights, such as the right to vote, that don't seem negative at all....

Positive rights are rights to resources that enable us to act in certain ways. The category of positive rights usually includes "welfare rights"—claims on society for resources or protections that give us a chance of having at least a minimally satisfying life. Welfare rights can include such things as the right to an education; the right to consumer protection regarding the quality of food and medicine; the right to safe working conditions; and the right to at least a minimal level of social insurance against unemployment, disability and ill health.

We can tighten up the idea of negative rights if we separate out basic democratic rights and leave negative rights to mean the right not to be interfered with by government (or anyone else). In contrast to negative rights, positive rights justify government intervention (govt>) to promote those rights (rights to safe working conditions, to a basic education, and so forth).

Both classical liberalism and modern liberalism embrace democratic rights (in one form of another). They differ in part in their view of rights in the economic sphere, with classical liberals promoting mostly negative rights and modern-day liberals also promoting positive (welfare) rights. We can start to chart the differences as follows:

Philosophy	Political Sphere	Economic Sphere	Social Sphere
CLASSICAL LIBERALISM	democratic rights	mostly negative rights	
MODERN LIBERALISM	democratic rights	+positive rights (*govt* > welfare)	

You should see now why conservatives are in the classical liberal tradition: They emphasize negative rights in the economic sphere.

The similarity between conservativism and classical liberalism becomes even stronger if we bring in the social sphere. Classical liberals, like conservatives today, assumed it was necessary and desirable for government to support religion and traditional morals; in contrast, modern liberals are more inclined to push for negative rights in the social sphere, wanting no government promotion of religion, as well as moral rules tied to particular religious views. Thus:

Philosophy	Political Sphere	Economic Sphere	Social Sphere
CONSERVATIVISM	democratic rights	mostly negative rights	*govt* > traditional values
LIBERALISM (MODERN)	democratic rights	+positive rights (*govt* > welfare)	mostly negative rights

It's important to keep in mind that we are talking in comparative terms here. As mentioned earlier, most conservatives today accept some sort of welfare state, some sort of government intervention to help the poorest and most vulnerable members of society; what they want is a much more limited welfare state (and with it, less government intervention in the workings of the market). Modern liberals agree with conservatives in generally supporting a free market with market interactions left up to businesses, workers, and consumers. However, modern liberals support an enlarged welfare state and greater government intervention to support that state. Similarly, conservatives, like liberals, support an overall freedom of lifestyle, but do want government to promote traditional religious values and traditional religious morality—as in allowing prayers in school, promoting abstinence education and discouraging (if not banning) abortion.

Classical liberalism is sometimes called "negative liberalism," even though it doesn't support negative rights in the social sphere. However, if we took the term "negative liberalism" literally—and out of historical context—it would be equivalent to libertarianism, which endorses strong negative rights in both the economic and social spheres. If we add in libertarianism, our chart will look like this:

Philosophy	Political Sphere	Economic Sphere	Social Sphere
LIBERTARIANISM	democratic rights	strong negative rights	strong negative rights
CONSERVATIVISM	democratic rights	mostly negative rights	*govt* > traditional values
LIBERALISM	democratic rights	+positive rights (*govt* > welfare)	mostly negative rights

As for socialism, the forms of it we'll consider are both democratic and market-oriented (either in the sense of employing markets or trying to mimic markets in state- or worker-run enterprises). Socialists differ from liberals in wanting a much more equal distribution of income and are willing to tolerate greater government intervention and markets that are less free in order to accomplish this.

Socialists are like conservatives in the sense of wanting government intervention in the social sphere to promote certain aims. However, the aims of socialists are much different than those of conservatives. Instead of supporting traditional values, socialists are after a kind of secular social equality—a sense of community that diminishes or eliminates distinctions of class, race or power. Adding in socialism, we have a chart of the four philosophies:

Philosophy	Political Sphere	Economic Sphere	Social Sphere
LIBERTARIANISM	democratic rights	strong negative rights	strong negative rights
CONSERVATIVISM	democratic rights	mostly negative rights	*govt*>traditional values
LIBERALISM	democratic rights	+positive rights (*govt*>welfare)	mostly negative rights
SOCIALISM (Democratic)	democratic rights	++*positive* rights (*govt*>equality)	*govt*>social equality

One last modification: To say that all four political philosophies support democratic rights is true but a bit misleading. Liberals and socialists want to go beyond formal democratic rights to give citizens more equal influence; they accept government intervention to accomplish this. (Socialists push this farther than do liberals.) For example, while conservatives insist on an equal right to vote, they are fine with corporations and wealthy individuals having unequal influence in the political process. Liberals and socialists are more likely to want interventions (like limiting campaign contributions) that create more equal political influence.

With that said, our full chart looks like this:

Philosophy	Political Sphere	Economic Sphere	Social Sphere
LIBERTARIANISM	democratic rights	strong negative rights	strong negative rights
CONSERVATIVISM	democratic rights	mostly negative rights	*govt*>traditional values
LIBERALISM	dem. rights (*govt*> more-equal influence)	+positive rights (*govt*>welfare)	mostly negative rights
SOCIALISM (Democratic)	dem. rights (*govt*> equal influence)	++*positive* rights *govt*>equality	*govt*>social equality

Now that we've done a general comparison, let's examine the four philosophies individually—both in themselves and as portrayed by "Divided States."

Libertarianism

The political philosophy of libertarianism, as we'll discuss it, accords with the tenets of the American Libertarian Party and the views of many of the intellectuals who explicitly defend libertarianism. Later on we'll discuss a more informal use of the "libertarian" label which designates a more moderate political outlook—an outlook that often isn't thought of as libertarian by those who hold it.

Political libertarianism is often based on moral libertarianism. As we've seen, moral libertarianism is a moral theory that consists entirely of negative rights. According to moral libertarianism, as long as you do not violate the negative rights of others, you are entitled to do as you please; the only claim anyone else has on you is that you respect their negative rights.

(This assumes that you haven't voluntarily assumed other obligations by entering into a contract—anything from a loan agreement to a marriage.)

Moral libertarianism underlies much political libertarianism, but also extends beyond it. We'll see this in Part IV when we discuss world poverty.

Political libertarianism is often given other justifications. One argument—also pressed by conservatives—is that markets will bring about the greatest overall welfare (wealth) if they are not restricted by government regulation. Another argument is that government in general is so dangerous or incompetent that it should be kept to a minimum. However, unlike the argument from moral libertarianism, these other arguments are "contingent" in the sense that they depend on empirical as well as moral claims. (For instance, showing that greater overall welfare was promoted by some redistribution of income or showing that some forms of government are less dangerous than no government would undercut the argument.)

According to libertarianism, the one legitimate role for government (other than providing national defense) is to protect our negative rights—that is, to protect each of us from interference by others.

The negative right of non-interference has a complex structure. I have the right

(a) not to be interfered with by others (assuming I am not interfering with them);
(b) not to be interfered with by government; and,
(c) to have the government discourage others from interfering with me.

For libertarians, *c* is the only justification for there being a government. This conception of minimal government guarding negative rights is sometimes referred to as the "nightwatchman state." (Someone who believed there was no such thing as legitimate government would be termed an "anarchist.")

Taxation is allowed only to the extent necessary for the government to provide a military to protect us against interference by other countries), a legal system to defend us against interference by our fellow citizens and whatever minimum mechanism is necessary to enable a free market. Any additional taxation—especially taxation to help the needy—is considered a violation of our negative rights.

Along the same lines, there is no justification for government trying to save people from themselves—to be a "nanny state," in the current political vernacular. Not only should there be no laws forcing us to wear seat belts or motorcycle helmets, there should be no laws requiring safe working conditions or safe products.

All these elements of libertarianism are satirized in "The Divided States of America." In the Libertarian District, government has been cut to a minimum. Most government functions have been privatized, most government officials fired.

There is no problem attracting business to the District: Business is virtually unregulated and taxes minimal. But there is a potential problem attracting labor:

> How was one going to attract workers to a district where there were no unions, no worker safety laws, no workman's compensation, no unemployment insurance, no safety net at all? Further, the worker-as-consumer would be functioning in a world where there were virtually no regulatory guarantees of product reliability and safety, with few restrictions on what advertisers or salespeople could say when pushing those products.

According to the story, the workers are attracted by quick money and low taxes, but are soon taken advantage of by businesses which give the workers complicated contracts they aren't equipped to understand. Businesses can use the fine print in contracts to their advantage without violating consumer protection laws (there are none). Workers can try to sue, but even if they have a case, suing "would be protracted and expensive."

Libertarians would argue that the story's portrayal of life under libertarianism is the opposite of what would actually happen. Here is the rosy picture painted by John Hospers (see Readings), a philosopher who was one of the founders of the Libertarian Party:

> "But then you'd let the people go hungry!" comes the rejoinder. This, the libertarian insists, is precisely what would not happen; with the restrictions removed, the economy would flourish as never before. With the

controls taken off business, existing enterprises would expand, new ones spring into existence, satisfying more and more consumer needs; millions more people would be gainfully employed instead of subsisting on welfare, and all kinds of research and production, released from the stranglehold of government, would proliferate, fulfilling man's needs and desires as never before....

Maybe, maybe not. The thing is that, if the economics didn't work out as Hospers envisions, there would be no moral pressure on such a society to help those in trouble. This point comes up in the story in connection with the problems of drug users.

The Libertarian District puts no restrictions on drug use (this would be to act as a nanny state) and at the same time offers no help to those who get in trouble from their drug use (this would involve taxing people to help others). Drug users are warned that they will be without help if things go bad, but being prone to high-risk behavior, they pay no attention. However, the story mentions another possible source of confusion:

> ...maybe it hadn't seemed like such a gamble; maybe some people were misled by the some time libertarian claim that in a libertarian society private charities would take up the slack from the lack of public welfare. The problem was that charitable people just weren't attracted to a libertarian society. It's true there were a few religious charities (they saw themselves as missionaries to Sodom and Gomorrah) but these charities were in no position to cope with the mass of problems.

Moral libertarianism works against the idea of private charities for the down-and-out: There simply is no obligation to help others. Giving to charity has at most the status of a hobby, like collecting stamps or joining a bowling league. It's hard to imagine much charitable giving coming out of that sort of atmosphere.

What would life be like for the average person in a libertarian society in which there were no worker-safety or product-safety laws? Libertarians argue that a combination of law suits and market pressures would provide comparable protections without government interference. Employers with safer working conditions would attract more workers; injured workers could sue for redress. A host of private consumer-protection agencies would arise to advise consumers

on the safest products. Yet it was the absence of, or the inefficiency of, such mechanisms that brought about government protections in the first place.

Libertarians do say they would have no laws giving businesses special advantages. But what would this mean? Are they going to do away with corporations? To do so would be to deprive society of one of the most successful engines of wealth-creation. Yet if there are corporations, then their limited liability makes dangerous products much less risky for them than for consumers. The idea that safer work places would attract more workers only works if there are many more jobs than workers: In tough economic times, workers have to take what they can get. And it's hard to see how any set of laws could offset the advantage that money would play in politics and in the courts. It's hard to see how a libertarian society could be other than a really tough place to live for most people.

As noted, libertarians are against laws that protect people from themselves—such as the requirement that motorcyclists wear helmets. Libertarians do acknowledge that it's all right to have a law against driving under the influence; driving in such a condition threatens the safety of others. What about the fact that helmet laws arose in part to protect a society that guarantees emergency medical care to those who can't afford medical care (including those hurt by their own risky behavior)? According to libertarians, we shouldn't be guaranteeing emergency medical care. However, to follow through on that, society would have to be willing to let medically uninsured cyclists die by the side of the road. That's just not a society most people would be willing to live in.

Libertarianism faces a real problem as to how to substitute for the coordination functions that government now handles. A frequently mentioned example is that of roads. Under libertarianism, all roads would be privately owned. Presumably, then, these roads would be toll roads (perhaps with the costs partially offset by lots and lots of billboards). Paying the tolls per se shouldn't be a problem: With lower taxes, people would have more money. But what happens if my local road company raises tolls to an exorbitant amount? Do I walk to work—assuming the same company doesn't own the sidewalks and charge exorbitant tolls for those as well? I'd certainly better not try cutting through the yards of my neighbors in a society that has fierce private property rights. Do we have companies building duplicate roads and sidewalks to provide competition? And that's assuming they could even get the land: There won't be any right of eminent domain in a libertarian society.

Americans aren't especially attracted to doctrinaire libertarianism: The American Libertarian Party candidate for President gets about 400,000 votes. However, the word "libertarian" is often used in a looser sense that encompasses many more Americans. "Libertarian" in this looser sense is a *tendency* to favor less government interference in the economic sphere (letting the market generally do its thing) and less government interference in the social sphere (letting people generally do their thing). That is, the term covers those who tend to be conservative in their economic views and liberal in their social views. According to *The Economist*, 10-20% of Americans are libertarians in this sense. (In fact, *The Economist*, which is often described as conservative, likes to describe itself as libertarian.) In this looser sense—freer markets and freer lifestyle—libertarianism is a vital force in American politics and life.

Conservatism

There are various strands of conservativism in the United States. A 2005 *Economist* article contrasted business conservatives with religious conservatives; small government conservatives with big government conservatives; and neo-conservatives with traditional conservatives. In a 2010 *Newsweek* opinion piece, Jacob Weisberg contrasted different regional conservative views:

> Northeastern conservativism is moderate, accepts the modern welfare state, and dislikes mixing religion with politics. Western conservativism is hawkish, hates government, and embraces individual freedom. Southern conservativism is populist [and] draws on evangelical Christianity....

The best we can do is to define American conservativism as we already have—as promoting negative economic rights and social traditionalism. Conservatives want government (a) out of the economic sphere

(though not to the degree that libertarians do) but (b) supporting traditional values in the social sphere.

Political philosophies are usually a combination of moral and empirical claims. For instance, we've already seen how political libertarianism often combines a moral thesis about the primacy of certain negative rights with empirical theses about the efficiency of the market and the inefficiency of government.

Social traditionalism isn't something we've discussed before. What is it? A moral position? An empirical one?

The answer is that it can be either or both. The earliest versions of conservativism saw God's providential hand in human history, implying that that the existing institutions and religious/moral traditions were those He had willed. Theologically this can be a bit troublesome: If God is doing so much in the world (rather than leaving events to people's free-will choices), it makes it harder to separate God from the evil in the world. Nonetheless, the God's-hand-in-history view seems to have been the dominant one in the history of Christianity. You can see this today in the way some Christian conservatives view the founding documents of the United States much as they do the Bible: God's hand guided the writing of the American Constitution and Americans are supposed to follow it to the letter.

There is an empirical, as well as moral, approach to social traditionalism: If you have a sufficiently pessimistic view of human nature and feel that any sort of social stability is a hard-won victory, you might claim that change is likely to lead to something worse and so should be undertaken only very slowly and cautiously. In fact, conservatives, on average, have a much more negative view of human nature than do liberals and socialists.

One form of traditionalism involves a focus on Western civilization and a generalized version of Judeo-Christian religious/moral tradition. Under this traditionalism, education might focus on the "Great Books"—the Bible, Shakespeare and Milton, the writers of ancient Greece and Rome. Conservativism to a much greater degree than any of the other political philosophies sees such writers as the source of enduring truths.

A different traditionalism, often at odds with the first, is that of the Christian right: This traditionalist view sees truth only in the Bible (or, for Roman Catholics, in Church tradition) and sees much of Western civilization as being at odds with this Christian view.

"Divided States of America" imagines conservative Christianity as culturally dominant in the Conservative District. This characterization is meant less as a reflection of conservativism than a reflection of liberal fears of conservativism (though it is true that *some* members of today's Christian right would approve of the way the Conservative District is run).

> The official culture of the Conservative District consisted of Judeo-Christian values and the Western "canon" of literature.
>
> In reality, "Judeo-Christian" was slanted heavily toward Evangelical Protestantism (with the "Judeo" part interpreted through the New Testament). As for the Western "canon" of literature, it was so heavily edited to eliminate anything that might conflict with Christian doctrine and morals that the resulting "great works" were beginning to resemble a series of Reader's Digest Condensed Books....
>
> Such editing was a reflection of the "values committees" the government was setting up to oversee various aspects of life. Public education had been radically affected: Prayers opened and closed the school day, some schools were experimenting with (so far non-sectarian) "chapel," and all science and literature that might undercut the religious faith of the students had been eliminated from the curriculum....

The Conservative District embraces a free market within a conservative Christian outlook:

> Religious conservatives had insisted on what amounted to a free-market theocracy: There would be minimal regulation of the general conduct of business, but all society would be subject to regulations necessary to bring it in line with Judeo-Christian morality.

It is important to stress that all four of our political philosophies would agree that the free market must be subject to *some* moral constraints: No one would endorse a free market for hit men or child pornographers. What moral constraints are endorsed will depend in part on what moral views are held. Conservativism, which often includes a heavy dose of what we've called judgmental-God morality, tends to have more of an emphasis on non-harm based "personal sins" than liberalism. Not only does this incline

conservativism to greater intervention in the social sphere, it also creates an oft-noted tension between conservative morality and its push for free markets. The marketing intended to convince the public to buy will often involve appeals to what traditionalists of whatever stripe consider "lower," less moral tastes. (Think of the general conservative disapproval of so many Hollywood films.)

Of course, many conservatives are much more interested in free markets than they are in social traditionalism. Let's look at some of the arguments conservatives, as well as libertarians, give for the claim that we should have the freest possible markets. (We'll consider the counter-arguments later.)

Argument 1. Free markets lead to greater overall well-being than any other system.

According to this argument, free markets create more overall wealth than any other system—with wealth being an indicator of well-being. This looks like an argument with special appeal to utilitarians, but it could be supplemented by arguments to the effect that even the poor are better off in the long run with free markets than they would have been with a planned economy.

Argument 2. Freedom is a great good and free markets allow greater freedom than any other economic system.

One crucial question here is why we should consider economic freedom so important relative to other values. Libertarians would link economic freedom to what they see as our general right not to be interfered with. It's not clear conservatives could consistently make this argument since they don't recognize a general right not to be interfered with. (Think of the social sphere.)

Argument 3. Free markets distribute rewards according to desert/merit to a greater degree than any other distributive system.

This argument has to be put carefully to be plausible. The idea that you get what you deserve in a free market system has a certain popular appeal—as in the familiar contrast between the "working guy" and the "welfare loafer." But anyone with even a little knowledge of economics knows that the market distributes according to supply and demand, not desert. It's hard to imagine anyone claiming that a fashion model, teen heartthrob or wealthy heir "deserves" more money than a heart surgeon or fighter pilot; certainly the traditional values espoused by conservativism wouldn't support such a claim.

(It's important to distinguish between someone deserving something and being entitled to it. Within the framework of the market, whatever money you earn within the law is money you are entitled to. In this sense the fashion model is entitled to more money that the fighter pilot. The question here is whether or not such entitlements can be said to reflect what people deserve.)

To make argument 3 plausible, you'd have to say that desert is an important moral value and any system that distributed equally would be ignoring desert altogether. The common-sense notion is that if Grace and Gideon have comparable jobs and comparable skills and if Grace works longer hours than Gideon, then Grace should be paid more; if Grace also goes to night school and improves her skills, whereas Gideon spends his nights bowling, then, other things being equal, Grace ought to earn more money. Even that much doesn't always work in reality, but sometimes it does; with enforced equal pay, it never would.

Liberalism

As we saw in our introduction to the four political philosophies, liberalism emphasizes negative rights in the social sphere but adds positive rights in the economic one. According to liberals, people are entitled to certain things from society/government not necessarily provided for by the free market: social insurance (such things as a guaranteed minimum income if unable to work or medical treatment, if unable to pay), safe products (especially food and drugs) and safe working conditions. (As noted, conservatives have come to accept at least some sort of welfare state as inevitable but try to keep it to a minimum.)

Classical liberals promoted negative rights in the economic sphere in part as protection for individuals against government. Those who later became modern-day liberals came to believe that in some circumstances the accumulation of wealth and power made possible by the market could be as oppressive to the individual as government could. Let's consider these claims as we discuss counters to the free-market arguments outlined earlier.

Reply to Argument 1 that free markets lead to greater overall well-being than any other system.

Many liberals would concede that markets create the greatest overall well-being—at least under some measures. However, they would argue—much as rights theorists did against utilitarianism—that the greatest overall well-being isn't the proper moral standard, that the best system should at least guarantee everyone some minimum level of well-being.

Reply to Argument 2 that free markets allow greater freedom than any other economic system.

As in the reply to argument 1, liberals would respond that economic freedom is good but isn't the only morally relevant good. Protection for the less fortunate—those who lose out in a market-driven society—is also morally important.

Conservatives like to say that they are for freedom, while liberals are for equality. In fact, as we know from our earlier discussion, it is much more correct to say that libertarians are for freedom and socialists for equality. Instead, conservatives are for a mix of freedom and traditionalism, while liberals are for a mix of freedom and protection.

Still, there is a distinction to be made between moderate liberals, who fit the definition of modern-day liberals given in the initial comparison of the four philosophies, and egalitarian liberals, who are much closer to socialists. Egalitarian liberals, like socialists, do favor (a high degree of) economic equality. (More on these two types of liberals below.)

Reply to Argument 3 that free markets distribute rewards according to desert/merit to a greater degree than any other distributive system.

Moderate liberals, who leave much of the distribution of wealth to the free market, would agree with argument 3 and applaud the fact that markets reward merit in a way that equal distribution would not. However, they would emphasize how much market activity has nothing to do with merit. If I have family money and she doesn't, if I have educational opportunities that he doesn't have, if I'm more attractive than she is, or if I'm healthy and he's handicapped, my doing better in the market (which, statistically, I will) doesn't have anything to do with comparative merit in any reasonable sense. Giving those with disadvantages some extra help (not a free ride) would seem fairer (under conventional ideas of fairness) than simply letting the market determine the distribution of all wealth.

Egalitarian liberals and many socialists have a very different take on the supposed market–merit connection: They argue that there is no such thing as merit, that what we are (and therefore what we earn as a result of what we are) is just a matter of "luck." One label given to those holding this view is "luck egalitarians."

The topic of luck versus merit is a difficult one. Conservatives and libertarians sometimes seem to hold a superficial view of freedom and merit, talking of freedom in a way that ignores a century of psychological and sociological research into the causes of people's actions. On the other hand, egalitarian liberals and socialists often seem to be denying freedom altogether, pushing a deterministic view according to which no one ever deserves anything. This deterministic view is presented in one of the television programs described in "Divided States."

> One new socialist show called *They Didn't Deserve It!* attempted to lay some groundwork for this [a classless society]. The narrator would relate some individual success story. Then a panel of sociologists and psychologists would analyze the combination of factors—looks, character traits (including motivation), mental abilities, family connections, education—that had led to that person's success and then show how all those particular factors could be traced back to other factors—family environment, fetal environment, genetics—over which the person had had no control. The moral of these anti-success narratives was always the same: What we come to be and what we accomplish are in the end "just a matter of luck"; thus, we do not deserve differential rewards as a result. It was heavy stuff—and more than a little depressing.

Think back to John Rawls and his ideal agents choosing principles from behind a veil of ignorance. Not only would these agents not know their eventual positions in society, they would not know what talents, personalities and motivations they would possess. The situation is set up to minimize merit as a consideration. Rawls claims that his ideal agents would choose a principle that would allow inequalities only to the degree that such inequalities benefit the worst-off. Benefit, not merit, is the ultimate criterion.

Rawls said his view could be characterized either as left-liberal (what we're calling egalitarian liberal) or democratic socialist.

In "Divided States," the Liberal District reflects the more extreme—that is to say, egalitarian—forms of liberalism. In fact, the conservatives in the story can't see much difference between liberalism and socialism.

> On the far left there were a number of democratic socialists who had refused to be satisfied with the proposed Liberal District. Conservatives couldn't understand this since to them the proposed Liberal District already seemed thoroughly socialistic: Tax rates on the highest earnings were to be tripled and the social safety net substantially enlarged; unions in most areas of the economy were to be strengthened and encouraged; worker safety and product safety laws were to be toughened; health care was to be thoroughly nationalized; there was to be tough regulation of banks and other financial institutions....

Liberalism is often based on a sympathy ethic that emphasizes harm-based wrongs. In the economic sphere, liberalism wants society to protect the worst-off from the harms of the market. In the social sphere, liberalism isn't interested in regulating behavior that doesn't cause harm—whether or not such behavior is considered "bad" by religion or tradition. In contrast, conservatives are more inclined to have the state enforce non-harm-based traditional moral standards. Think of the differences between liberals and conservatives in terms of how they would regulate sexual activity.

A general characteristic of liberalism (and libertarianism) is the belief in what has been called "liberal neutrality": This is the idea that the state shouldn't promote a particular conception of the "good life," but rather enforce the right of people to pursue their own conception of the good. The state should not support a particular religious view or any religious view at all; it should not favor traditional lifestyles or traditional ways of looking at things; it should allow people to pursue their own cultural practices, at least assuming that these practices do not involve harm and are not imposed by the group on its members.

However, there is an apparent discrepancy between liberalism as characterized in our initial discussion and liberalism as portrayed in the story. If liberalism emphasizes "liberal neutrality, if it promotes negative rights in the social sphere, why is the government of the Liberal District so intrusive?

> ...there were likely to be stronger laws restricting hate speech as well as speech that denigrated various ethnic and other cultural groups.

> ...the show mirrored the hottest issue in the Liberal District—"oppression points." Sheila didn't know who had first raised the issue; she just knew it had suddenly caught fire. The idea was that disadvantaged groups would be ranked to create an oppression hierarchy. Oppression points would earn the "oppressed" reparations in terms of tax breaks and direct payments, as well as priority in hiring and school admissions—even, on one proposal, places in line.

> The Liberal District didn't censor for sexual content per se, but the PC Media Advisory Board imposed so much political censorship—nothing nonconsensual, nothing degrading to women, minorities or animals, nothing remotely violent—that the sexual acts in films had such an upbeat, gymnastic quality that they had lost almost all of their pornographic appeal.

The main reason for this discrepancy is that the liberalism of the Liberal District is egalitarian liberalism, which is much closer to socialism than is moderate liberalism. Let's look again at how our chart set out the comparisons between the four philosophies regarding the political and social spheres.

Philosophy	Political Sphere	Social Sphere
LIBERTARIANISM	democratic rights	strong negative rights
CONSERVATIVISM	democratic rights	*govt>* traditional values
LIBERALISM	dem. rights *govt>* more-equal influence	mostly negative rights
SOCIALISM (*Democratic*)	dem. rights *govt>* equal influence	*govt>* social equality

It's important to remind ourselves again that liberalism (like socialism) is much more willing than either conservatism or libertarianism to have government try to bring about a greater equality of influence in the political sphere. But what the above quotes from the story really portray is an attempt by government to bring about greater social equality and this is more a characteristic of socialism than moderate liberalism.

Liberalism can shade into socialism (in much the same way that conservativism can shade into theocracy or libertarianism, depending on whether the emphasis is on social traditionalism or economic negative rights). How close liberalism gets to socialism will depend on how much of an economic guarantee it affords those at the bottom, how much government intervention to promote equality of influence is endorsed, and whether it is willing to use government to promote social equality.

Socialism

Many Americans still have a stereotype of socialism as a totalitarian system in which government owns the means of production and forces equality on the population. This version of socialism is dead, certainly in Western societies. There have been too many horrors connected with totalitarianism and too many economic disasters associated with planned economies. Socialists today support democracy and assume that *some* use of market mechanisms is necessary to produce a desirable level of wealth.

Of the four political philosophies caricatured in "Divided States," socialism gets off the easiest. Partly this is because a number of socialist ideas are already reflected in the Liberal District; partly it is because there has never been a serious socialist movement in the United States. (That there were communist sympathizers before and after World War II doesn't count as a socialist political movement.) Still, because liberalism can shade into socialism and because socialism is a vital force in parts of Europe, it's important to know something about it.

Behind socialism is a belief that all human beings are morally equal and that such equality should be the guiding principle behind the way humans treat one another. In some sense all our political philosophies are premised on human equality, but the other three view this equality in a more formal sense—the right to vote; the right to a public education; the right to make what you can of your life, given whatever advantages or disadvantages you begin with.

Socialists, at a minimum, want a system that promotes much greater economic and political equality and that discourages great concentrations of economic and political power. What, if any, inequalities would be allowed are debated among socialists, but the essential impulse is plain enough. As Peter Self (see Readings) puts it:

> Economic inequalities are so enormous in the modern capitalist world that substantial progress over reducing them should be practicable without running into the sands of detailed judgements about differential claims. In allegedly affluent countries, such as the United States or the United Kingdom, the top 10 per cent command over nine times the income (even after tax) of the bottom group, and completely dominate the ownership of wealth. Increasing numbers of millionaires or billionaires coexist with a sixth of the population living below the official poverty line....The contrast between rich and poor countries is still more glaring with two-thirds of the world still locked in hunger (and increasingly so in many countries), while the affluent are titillated with ever more sophisticated—and often environmentally destructive—consumer goods. Thus the pursuit of equality can be seen as essentially an onslaught upon gross inequalities which contradict the very idea of the dignity and worth of the individual....

We might see socialism as an extreme sympathy ethic, where sympathy trumps self-interest to a greater degree than in other moral/political theories.

Today the religion of most Protestants, Catholics and Jews has embraced the free market and materialism. But socialism is very much in the spirit of the early Christian communities which preached caring and sharing. One English writer commented that British socialism was more Methodist than Marxist.

Of course there are secular approaches to socialism as well. We've already discussed how John Rawls imagines his ideal contractors choosing a system that could be described as democratic socialist.

We've also discussed how socialists are likely to be "luck egalitarians," tracing accomplishments back to traits over which the individual ultimately had no control. Thus they would treat the concept of merit/desert with suspicion. If what we do is all or mostly

a matter of luck, then differential rewards can only make sense insofar as they are absolutely necessary to motivate people to produce.

Still, as we've said, socialists today assume that some use of market mechanisms is necessary to produce a desirable level of wealth. The two forms of socialism that seem to be the most discussed these days are "democratic socialism" and "market socialism." These names are a bit unfortunate because both versions of socialism are democratic and both use markets. Nonetheless, these are the names used.

"Democratic socialism" is the version of socialism reflected in our chart of the four political philosophies. Economically it supports a relatively free market while using the welfare state to effect a much greater equality of income. "Market socialism" comes in different versions but the idea is that worker- or state-owned enterprises would mimic the competitive free market in producing wealth, without creating disparities in the resulting possession of wealth. One version of market socialism has individual firms competing and has managers and workers gaining financial rewards for success; however, all the investment in larger firms is done by the government which then collects the profits and uses them to support social services.

The Socialist District in "Divided States" seems to exemplify democratic socialism, while also experimenting with market socialism.

> On the far left there were a number of democratic socialists who had refused to be satisfied with the liberal proposal for a much enlarged social safety net underlying an otherwise free market. These socialists wanted much greater economic equality and a combination of state-run and worker-run enterprises…

One of the more successful societies with heavily socialist leanings is Sweden. In the "Swedish model," most of Swedish industry (90%) is privately owned and most workers (80%) are unionized. Negotiations over wages and working conditions are conducted by boards of manufacturers and unions with government as a third party. Such labor negotiations plus one of the highest tax rates in Europe has provided Swedish workers with a high level of social services, including health care, child care for working parents, and high unemployment compensation.

Sweden has been cutting back its welfare state, partly as result of severe recessions in the early 1990s and the later 2000s, partly as a result of changes in the workforce which have diluted the size and power of the unions, and partly as a result of changing attitudes. Nonetheless, what results is still a much more expansive welfare state and much greater economic equality than in a country like the USA.

Capitalism assumes that people are self-interested. Critics complain that this assumption is self-fulfilling: Self-interest is promoted as well as assumed; the spirit of competitive self-interest seeps from the economic into the political and social spheres of life; too much emphasis is put on the individual versus the group. In addition, critics claim that capitalist mass marketing promotes lowest-common-denominator tastes.

Socialists are looking for what they see as something better than that—more cooperation and less competition, more community and less isolation, more civic participation and less apathy, more education and less indulgence. Instead of accepting people as essentially self-interested and working around that, socialists think we should promote people's better sides. Socialism would use education to try to make citizens capable of a little higher level of culture. This perfectionist strain in socialism is analogous to the perfectionist strain in conservativism, though what counts as "perfection" is much different. Conservatives are for individuals who will compete ferociously in the market while also adhering to traditional religious values. Socialists are looking for secular citizens who care for each other and can work together in a spirit of cooperation.

Of course, the criticisms of socialism are familiar enough: that such an optimistic view of human beings is unrealistic; that the selection of a particular cultural view is arrogant in the face of so much pluralism; that the emphasis on a secular culture is prejudiced against those holding religious views; that most people (Americans anyway) resist the impulse toward enforced equality, wanting the opportunity to compete and accumulate; that too extensive government restriction and redistribution will interfere with essential wealth-creating aspects of the market; and that the large-scale bureaucracies necessary to run a socialist state are bound to intrude into people's life in unacceptable ways and generally slow down the pace at which people can get things done.

The danger is that in reacting against socialism, we end up rejecting sympathy altogether and adopting the kind of indignant selfishness that characterizes much libertarian thinking.

We're going to move on now to five topics in applied ethics—world poverty, abortion, animals, the environment, and genetic engineering. Since the ethical dimensions of the next five topics get tangled up with empirical issues, each of the coming chapters contains a section called "Facts and Factual Issues" to help give us a common empirical basis for our discussions.

Notes and selected sources

Morality and free markets

SOURCES

John Cassidy. *How Markets Fail: The Logic of Economic Calamities*. New York: Farrar, Straus and Giroux, 2009.

James Fulcher. *Capitalism: A Very Short Introduction*. Oxford: Oxford University Press, 2004.

Daniel M. Hausman and Michael S. McPherson. *Economic Analysis, Moral Philosophy, and Public Policy*. 2nd edn. Cambridge: Cambridge University Press, 2006.

Jerry Z. Muller. *Thinking About Capitalism*. Chantilly, VA: The Teaching Company, 2008.

NOTES

"Market systems have proved durable…." Cassidy, p. 25.

Democracy

SOURCES

Bernard Crick. *Democracy: A Very Short Introduction*. Oxford: Oxford University Press, 2002.

Robert A. Dahl. *On Democracy*. New Haven, CN: Yale University Press, 1998.

Muller, *Capitalism* (above)

Fareed Zakaria. *The Future of Freedom: Illiberal Democracy at Home and Abroad*. New York: W. W. Norton & Company, 2003.

NOTES

"…it's important to keep in mind…" and following paragraph: Muller, pt. 3, lecture 32, pp. 112–13.

Religion in the public square

SOURCES

Noah Feldman. *Divided by God: America's Church–State Problem and What We Should Do about It*. New York: Farrar, Straus and Giroux, 2005.

Frank Lambert. *The Founding Fathers and the Place of Religion in America*. Princeton, NJ: Princeton University Press, 2003.

NOTES

On Christian nation controversy, see Feldman, ch. 1.

On court cases, see Feldman, chs. 5 & 6.

Libertarianism

SOURCES

American Libertarian Party Platform: lp.org/platform

John Hospers. "What Libertarianism Is." In *The Libertarian Alternative*, ed. Tibor Machan. Chicago: Nelson-Hall, 1974.

Will Kymlicka. *Contemporary Political Philosophy*. 2nd edn. Oxford: Oxford University Press, 2002. ch. 4.

Jan Narveson. *The Libertarian Idea*. Philadelphia: Temple University Press, 1988.

Robert Nozick. *Anarchy, State, and Utopia*. New York: Basic Books, 1974.

NOTES

"But then you'd let the people…." Hospers, p. 566.

Looser libertarianism: "Lexington: Raising the Barr." *Economist*, May 31, 2008.

Conservatism

SOURCES

Patrick N. Allitt. *The Conservative Tradition*. Chantilly, VA: The Teaching Company, 2009, lecture 1.

Philip Norton. "Conservativism." In *Ideas that Shape Politics*, ed. Michael Foley. Manchester, UK: Manchester University Press, 1994.

Anthony Quinton. "Conservativism." In *A Companion to Contemporary Political Philosophy*. Eds. Robert E. Goodin and Phillip Petit. Oxford: Blackwell Publishers, 1993.

NOTES

"A 2005 *Economist* article…." "A Hammer Blow: The Conservative Movement." *Economist*, Oct. 1, 2005.

"In a 2010 *Newsweek* opinion piece…." Jacob Weisberg. "The GOP Looks West." *Newsweek*, May 28, 2010.

Liberalism

SOURCES

Kymlicka, *Contemporary Political Philosophy* (above), ch. 3.

John Rawls. *A Theory of Justice*. Cambridge, MA: The Belknap Press of Harvard University Press, 1971.

Alan Ryan. "Liberalism." In *A Companion to Contemporary Political Philosophy* (above).

Amartya Sen. "The Moral Standing of the Market." In *Ethics and Economics*. Eds. Ellen Frankel Paul, Fred D. Miller, Jr., Jeffrey Paul. Oxford: Blackwell, 1985.

Paul Starr. *Freedom's Power: The True Force of Liberalism*. New York: Basic Books, 2007.

NOTES

On arguments for and against the freedom of the market, see Sen.

On liberal neutrality, see Kymlicka, pp. 217–19.

On liberal equality and undeserved natural endowments, see Kymlicka, pp. 70–91.

Rawls' view as left-liberal or democratic socialist, see Kymlicka, pp. 195–6.

Socialism

SOURCES

Pranab Bardhan and John Roemer (eds.) *Market Socialism: The Current Debate*. Oxford: Oxford University Press, 1993.

James Fulcher, *Capitalism* (above).

Brian Gould. "Social Democracy." In *Ideas that Shape Politics* (above).

Kymlicka, *Political Philosophy* (above), ch. 5.

Peter Self. "Socialism." In *A Companion to Contemporary Political Philosophy* (above).

NOTES

"Economic inequalities are so enormous…." Self, p. 339.

On Sweden, Fulcher, pp. 58–64.

Definitions

(Terms are defined in the order in which they appeared in the text.)

1. *Markets*: A system in which buyers and sellers interact to exchange goods and services and determine prices.

2. *Capitalism*: An economic system in which there is private property *and* in which people interact through the market both in their roles as buyers and sellers and as owners and workers.

3. *Laissez-faire capitalism*: Capitalism with a minimum of government interference.

4. *Welfare capitalism*: A version of capitalism in which government does not simply facilitate the market but modifies it or redistributes its benefits in the name of promoting the welfare of some or all of its citizens.

5. *Welfare*: Different meanings:
   (a) "Means-tested welfare" or "welfare assistance," that is, government subsidies to people whose economic means fall below a certain level.
   (b) Government modification of the market and/or redistribution of its benefits in the name of promoting the well-being of most or all of its citizens. (As in "welfare capitalism" above.)
   (c) Personal well-being.

6. *Democracy*: Rule by the people; it is generally taken to mean any society in which governments are produced by open, free and fair elections.

7. *Direct democracy*: Democracy in which major policy decisions are decided by popular vote.

8. *Representative democracy*: Democracy in which major policy decisions are made by representatives chosen by popular vote.

9. *Constitutional democracy*: Democracy in which there are constitutional protections for individuals and minorities (contrasted with pure majority-rule democracy).

10. *Establishment Clause* of the First Amendment to the (US) Constitution: "Congress shall make no law respecting an establishment of religion...."

11. *Free Exercise Clause* of the First Amendment to the (US) Constitution: "Congress shall make no law... prohibiting the free exercise [of religion]...."

12. *Tests the Supreme Court has set at one time or another that a law or practice must meet to withstand a challenge under the Establishment Clause*:
   (a) *Lemon test*: The law must (i) have a secular purpose; (ii) have a primary effect that neither advances nor inhibits religion; and (iii) not entangle government with religion.
   (b) *Neutrality test*: Public displays of religious symbols are acceptable when secular symbols are also present.

   (c) *Coercion test*: A state action must not coerce citizens into supporting or participating in religious activities.

13. *Classical liberalism* (sometimes called "negative liberalism"): Pushed for restrictions on government power and great individual rights. It is the precursor of both conservatism and modern liberalism, though in its original form it was closer to today's conservativism.

14. *Liberalism* (also called "modern" or "positive" liberalism): Stands for government promotion of more equal political power and substantial economic guarantees for all, but strong negative rights in social sphere.

15. *Socialism* (democratic): Stands for government promotion of equal political power, strong democratic rights, (at least) strong economic guarantees for all, and general social equality.

16. *Conservativism*: Stands for a combination of democratic rights, negative rights in the economic sphere, and government promotion of traditional values.

17. *Libertarianism* (political): Stands for democratic rights, and strong negative rights in both the economic and social spheres. (Often supported by moral libertarianism.)

18. *Nightwatchman state*: A minimal government doing little more than guarding negative rights.

19. *Anarchism*: The belief that there is no such thing as legitimate government.

20. *Nanny state*: Pejorative term for the welfare state.

21. *Egalitarian liberalism*: Liberalism with so much stress on equality as to be close to forms of socialism.

22. *Luck egalitarianism*: The belief that what we are, and what we get as a result, is just the matter of luck; nothing is "deserved."

23. *Liberal neutrality*: The belief—held by some liberals and libertarians—that the state shouldn't promote a particular conception of the "good life," but rather enforce the right of people to pursue their own conception of the good.

24. *Market socialism*: A version of socialism that would have worker- or state-owned enterprises mimic the competitive free market in producing wealth, without creating disparities in the resulting possession of wealth.

Questions

(Please explain your answers, making specific reference to relevant passages in the discussion.)

1. What is capitalism? Explain the differences between laissez-faire capitalism and welfare capitalism.
2. Give three meanings of the word "welfare".
3. What is democracy? Explain the differences between direct and representative democracy and between pure majority rule and constitutional democracy.
4. Give examples of why people of all political persuasions want to put some limits on democracy.
5. Of our four political philosophies (liberalism, conservativism, libertarianism and socialism), which one is more likely to have the government promoting religious views/values? Explain.
6. "The United States was founded as a Christian nation." What can be said for and against this view?
7. What is the Establishment Clause of the First Amendment? What are the tests that the Supreme Court has put forward to determine if a law or practice can withstand a challenge under the Establishment Clause.
8. Compare our four political philosophies in terms of how they think the political system should operate in (a) the political sphere; (b) the economic sphere; and (c) the social sphere?
9. What would supporters of libertarianism say in favor of that political philosophy? What would critics say against it?
10. What would supporters of liberalism say in favor of that political philosophy? What would critics say against it?
11. What would supporters of conservatism say in favor of that political philosophy? What would critics say against it?
12. What would supporters of socialism say in favor of that political philosophy? What would critics say against it?

9

Morality and Politics
Readings

Jerry Z. Muller defines capitalism and talks about some of the tensions between capitalism and democracy

What is capitalism? How should we define it? Before we try to come up with a working definition, let's turn our attention for a moment to the history of the word. The term "capitalism" is relatively new, though as often happens in the history of ideas, the phenomenon existed long before the term. It existed under a variety of other labels. Originally, "capitalism," the term, was really a political slogan, a term coined by socialists who sought to stigmatize the phenomenon. Karl Marx never used the noun "capitalism," but he did write about the "capitalist system of production," and though others had made use of it before Marx, it was really Marx who gave the term wider currency. And for Marx, the term "the capitalist system" had a clearly polemical meaning. It was made to indicate that the system worked on behalf of those who had money and who invested that money, at the expense of everyone else.

The term came into a more neutral, social scientific usage at the beginning of the 20th century, when the German sociologist Werner Sombart entitled his book

Modern Capitalism in 1902. Two years later, another German sociologist, Max Weber, published the first part of his famous essay, "The Protestant Ethic and the 'Spirit' of Capitalism." After that, people started to use the term "capitalism" in a more value-neutral sense; that is to say, the term was used both by people who approved of capitalism and those who didn't.

But well before the word "capitalism" was in use, people were using a variety of other words to designate more or less the same phenomenon. Adam Smith, for example, writing in 1776, spoke of "commercial society," by which he meant something very close to capitalism. Like most concepts in the social sciences, capitalism is an ideal type. It's a kind of model. It's an abstraction from experience that helps us grasp key elements and their relationship to one another. So what are the key elements of capitalism?

The first is private property. That is by no means a simple concept. It actually implies a lot. You might think, isn't all property private, or at least isn't that the default position for property? The answer is no. In the real world, things belong to whoever has the power to take them unless there's a power that guarantees that other people won't take them. And so usually, private property depends on the existence of government power, that is to say, a power that is able to protect property from those who would like to steal it.

The second element of our model is that capitalism involves exchange between legally free individuals.

From *Thinking About Capitalism*, by Jerry Z. Muller, Chantilly, VA: The Teaching Company, 2008, lecture 1 and lecture 32. © 2008 The Teaching Company. Reproduced with permission of The Teaching Company, www.thegreatcourses.com.

That means that in a capitalist society when one person works for another, it's for wages, and when he exchanges something of value with someone else, it's for money. Well, you might say, what's the alternative? The historical alternative before the rise of modern capitalism was often a situation in which you worked for someone else because he was your political superior, or because he owned you.

[…]

The third element of capitalism is that it's a system in which the production and distribution of goods operate primarily through the market mechanism. When we say that production and distribution operate through the market mechanism, we mean that prices are not set by custom, they're not set by government decision, they're not set by those who produce the goods; they're set by supply and demand. In other words, prices are not determined by anybody in particular. So our working definition of capitalism involves private property, exchange between legally free individuals, where production and distribution of goods occurs [sic] primarily through the market. But this is a sort of model from which in historical fact there have been many variations and divergences.

[…]

Capitalism and Democracy

While there have been many historical instances of capitalism without liberal democracy, there are no known cases of liberal democracy without capitalism. It's important to keep that in mind. Democracy, in the sense of universal suffrage for all adult men, came to most European societies in the last third of the 19th century. Until then, the right to vote and to hold office was based on property qualifications that excluded most men and, of course, all women. So it's important to keep in mind that most western European societies became capitalist societies before they became democratic societies. In fact, there was a great deal of concern among 19th-century European intellectuals, including liberals such as John Stuart Mill, that with the coming of democracy, the newly enfranchised working class would use its political power in a way that would destroy capitalism.

In a book he published in 1861, called *Considerations on Representative Government*, Mill worried that a democracy with a majority of working-class voters, people who didn't own property, might be inclined to enact policies that would damage or even destroy the capitalist market. He said that those who didn't possess property might impose an undue burden of taxation on those who did possess property, and that would diminish the savings that were available for investment as capital, and that would lead to a slowdown of the capitalist economy. Or he thought that voters might strike at the basis of private property in other ways. They might, for example, decide to repudiate the national debt. They might decide to tax away inheritances or they might decide to expand government spending for their own benefit, without considering the negative consequences of doing so.

Mill also feared that perhaps these new working-class voters would use legislation to try to raise wages, to try to limit competition in the labor market, or even to discourage labor-saving innovations—all of which might help them in the short run but would slow down capitalist development in the long run. Or he was afraid that they might try to enact tariffs to protect local producers from foreign competition. Well, not all of those fears turned out to be justified, but it's useful to keep them in mind when we turn to the situation in the 1970s. In theory, and sometimes in practice, democracy has a number of advantages when it comes to sustaining capitalist economic growth.

First of all, the fact that people have a voice in government, through elections, makes them more accepting of government. And in that sense, a functioning democracy helps to legitimate government actions that are the prerequisites for ongoing capitalist growth, like the protection of private property, or the enforcement of contracts. If enough people think that government is not legitimate, then it leads to revolution. And in that sense, democracy is an important method of creating government legitimacy, and government legitimacy, in turn, is important for ongoing capitalist development.

Second, over time, democracy tends to bring about the development of policies that blunt the rough edges of capitalism, policies like insurance schemes that protect people against accidents, against illness, and against old age. In short, to put it in a nutshell, welfare-state policies further add to capitalist legitimacy. And third, democracy can provide an informational feedback mechanism. That's particularly important in dealing with the negative externalities of enterprises. What do I mean by that? By negative externalities, I mean effects of market transactions that aren't paid for by the buyer or the seller, like pollution.

Let me give you an example. If I build a plastics factory, and that factory emits chemicals that pollute the air, and that air makes Jack sick, and Jack has to pay to get medical care, then it's a negative externality. I, as the seller, don't pay for it, nor do you, as the customer who buys my plastic. The person who pays is an uninvolved third party, namely Jack. Now, it's possible to create a law that would make me, the owner, pay the costs of that negative externality—and as a good capitalist, I'll try to pass on the costs to you, the customer. That's a good thing because it creates incentives for me to create less pollution, and it creates incentives for you to buy things that involve less pollution in their manufacture.

These kinds of corrective laws are what economists call "internalizing the externalities"—that is to say, making you and I [sic] pay for the damage we're doing, and giving us incentives to correct it. But without a democratic system to let the government know about the fact that Jack is distressed by the pollution, there'll be no corrective laws. Indeed, one of the greatest costs of communism was the degradation of the environment that came about precisely because those kinds of democratic mechanisms were missing. And as a result, at the end of the Soviet era, much of the former Soviet Union was heavily polluted, with terrible consequences in terms of sickness and premature death, leading to what one major student of the subject has called ecocide: ecologically caused death.

Forcing companies to pay for the pollution they cause may seem like a brake on economic growth—and in the short run it may be—but since this forces consumers to pay for the real costs of the goods they consume, it leads to a more efficient use of resources. It leads to a healthier population, and it leads to a more sustainable environment.

[...]

In 1975, a widely quoted report called "The Crisis of Democracy" was published by the Trilateral Commission. It was written by three leading social scientists, Samuel Huntington from the United States, Michel Crozier from France, and Joji Watanuki from Japan. That report coined the terms "ungovernability" and "democratic overload" to describe what was happening not just in American society but in Europe and Japan as well.

Under these circumstances, a number of thinkers—above all, in the United States—turned to the issue of the relationship between capitalism and political representation. The notion that political processes might inhibit economic growth wasn't an entirely new theme. Let me remind you that it was actually one of the main themes of Adam Smith's *Wealth of Nations*. You'll remember that most of the first half of Smith's book explains how the capitalist economy, under conditions of competitive capitalism, can lead to an ongoing rise in the standard of living for the vast majority of the population. But much of the second half of Smith's book examined the forces that stood in the way of a competitive market, and those were above all, various political lobbies that managed to convince politicians to restrict the market in a way that served their narrower interests at the public's expense. Now, in Smith's day, with a highly limited franchise (very small number of voters), it was merchants and manufacturers who were especially well-positioned to influence politicians to adopt policies that favored their interests at the expense of the general good. What changed between 1776 and 1976 was that the right to vote had become universal. That meant that now everyone had a chance to organize in order to influence politicians to adopt policies that protect one group or another at the expense of the common good.

One school of thought that was devoted to this issue was the school called "public choice." It was centered on James M. Buchanan, an American economist who was later awarded the Nobel Prize in Economics in 1986 for his work. Buchanan was born in 1919. He grew up on a farm in Tennessee. He received his PhD in Economics from the University of Chicago in 1948. [...] [A]s a southerner who was suspicious of government, and as an economist influenced by the market-oriented ideas of his teachers at the University of Chicago, James Buchanan was skeptical of federal government power. And a lot of his work was motivated by the urge to deromanticize government—that is to say, in an age when many people considered that the market was based on self-interest, but that government action was based on the pursuit of the public interest, Buchanan devoted himself to calling those views into question.

While much of liberal thought in those years was focused on the dysfunctions of the market, what are called market failures, Buchanan and his school focused on government failure—that is to say, why governments enact policies that fail to deliver what they promise, or that are actually at odds with the public good. His key assumption was that politicians running for office also pursued their self-interest, not in the sense of getting rich, but their interest was to get votes, and they often appealed to the voter's sense of the voter's own self-interest in order to get those votes. So politicians enacted policies that satisfied the narrow or short-term self-interest of their voters. But the net effect was often to bring about government policies that were harmful to the public as a whole.

[...]

Another influential analysis of the tensions between democracy and capitalism came from another American economist, Mancur Olson. His theory is often referred to by a key term that he coined, "the logic of collective action." [...]

Now, what Olson pointed out was that in political life, well-organized small groups actually have an advantage in getting politicians to adopt policies that will help people in that small group at the expense of everyone else. Here's what he pointed out: An individual, who is part of a large group with a common interest, that individual is unlikely to devote his time and money to trying to influence politicians because his gains from attaining the goal of the group are tiny. But in a small group, where each individual stands to gain a great deal from attaining the group's goal, each individual in that small group has a far greater incentive to exert himself to try to influence politicians on behalf of the group's interest.

[...]

Questions

1. According to Muller, what are the essential elements of capitalism?
2. What were some fears of early capitalists regarding the expansion of democracy?

3. Muller argues that there are certain advantages democracy brings to a capitalist system. What are these?

Fareed Zakaria analyzes the two strands of "liberal democracy"—democracy and constitutional liberalism

[...]

"Suppose elections are free and fair and those elected are racists, fascists, separatists," said the American diplomat Richard Holbrooke about Yugoslavia in the 1990s.

From *The Future of Freedom: Illiberal Democracy at Home and Abroad*, by Fareed Zakaria, pp. 17–22. Copyright © 2003 by Fareed Zakaria. Used by permission of W. W. Norton & Company, Inc. and the author.

"That is the dilemma." Indeed it is, and not merely in Yugoslavia's past but in the world's present. [...] Across the globe, democratically elected regimes, often ones that have been re-elected or reaffirmed through referenda, are routinely ignoring constitutional limits on their power and depriving their citizens of basic rights. This disturbing phenomenon—visible from Peru to the Palestinian territories, from Ghana to Venezuela—could be called "illiberal democracy."

For people in the West, democracy means "liberal democracy" a political system marked not only by free and fair elections but also the rule of law, a separation of powers, and the protection of basic liberties of speech, assembly, religion, and property. But this bundle of freedoms—what might be termed "constitutional liberalism"—has nothing intrinsically to do with democracy and the two have not always gone together, even in the West. After all, Adolf Hitler became chancellor of Germany via free elections. Over the last half-century in the West, democracy and liberty have merged. But today the two strands of liberal democracy, interwoven in the Western political fabric, are coming apart across the globe. Democracy is flourishing; liberty is not.

[…]

First, let's be clear what we mean by political democracy. From the time of Herodotus it has been defined, first and foremost, as the rule of the people. This definition of democracy as a process of selecting governments is now widely used by scholars. In *The Third Wave*, the eminent political scientist Samuel P. Huntington explains why:

> Elections, open, free and fair, are the essence of democracy, the inescapable sine qua non. Governments produced by elections may be inefficient, corrupt, shortsighted, irresponsible, dominated by special interests, and incapable of adopting policies demanded by the public good. These qualities make such governments undesirable but they do not make them undemocratic. Democracy is one public virtue, not the only one, and the relation of democracy to other public virtues and vices can only be understood if democracy is clearly distinguished from the other characteristics of political systems.

This definition also accords with the commonsense view of the term. If a country holds competitive, multiparty elections, we call it "democratic." When public participation in a country's politics is increased—for example, through the enfranchisement of women—that country is seen as having become more democratic. Of course elections must be open and fair, and this requires some protections for the freedom of speech and assembly. But to go beyond this minimal requirement and label a country democratic only if it guarantees a particular catalog of social, political, economic, and religious rights—which will vary with every observer—makes the word "democracy" meaningless. After all, Sweden has an economic system that many argue curtails

individual property rights, France until recently had a state monopoly on television, and Britain has a state religion. But they are all clearly and identifiably democracies. To have "democracy" mean, subjectively, "a good government" makes it analytically useless.

Constitutional liberalism, on the other hand, is not about the procedures for selecting government but, rather, government's goals. It refers to the tradition, deep in Western history, that seeks to protect an individual's autonomy and dignity against coercion, whatever the source—state, church, or society. The term marries two closely connected ideas. It is liberal[1] because it draws on the philosophical strain, beginning with the Greeks and Romans, that emphasizes individual liberty. It is constitutional because it places the rule of law at the center of politics. Constitutional liberalism developed in Western Europe and the United States as a defense of an individual's right to life and property and the freedoms of religion and speech. To secure these rights, it emphasized checks on the power of government, equality under the law, impartial courts and tribunals, and the separation of church and state. In almost all of its variants, constitutional liberalism argues that human beings have certain natural (or "inalienable") rights and that governments must accept a basic law, limiting its own powers, to secure them. […]

Since 1945 Western governments have, for the most part, embodied both democracy and constitutional liberalism. Thus it is difficult to imagine the two apart, in the form of either illiberal democracy or liberal autocracy. In fact both have existed in the past and persist in the present. Until the twentieth century, most countries in western Europe were liberal autocracies or, at best, semidemocracies. The franchise was tightly restricted, and elected legislatures had limited power. In 1830 Great Britain, one of the most democratic European countries, allowed barely 2 percent of its population to vote for one house of Parliament. Only in the late 1940s did most Western countries become full-fledged democracies, with universal adult suffrage. But one hundred years earlier, by the late 1840s, most of them had adopted important aspects of constitutional liberalism—the rule of law, private property rights, and increasingly, separated powers and free speech and assembly. For much of modern history, what characterized governments in Europe and

North America, and differentiated them from those around the world, was not democracy but constitutional liberalism. The "Western model of government" is best symbolized not by the mass plebiscite but the impartial judge.

[...]

It is odd that the United States is so often the advocate of unrestrained democracy abroad. What is distinctive about the American system is not how democratic it is but rather how undemocratic it is, placing as it does multiple constraints on electoral majorities. The Bill of Rights, after all, is a list of things that the government may not do, regardless of the wishes of the majority. Of America's three branches of government, the Supreme Court—arguably the paramount branch—is headed by nine unelected men and women with life tenure. The US Senate is the most unrepresentative upper house in the world, with the lone exception of the House of Lords, which is powerless and in any event on the verge of transformation. Each American state sends two senators to Washington, DC, regardless of its population. Thus California's 30 million people have as many votes in the Senate as Arizona's 3.7 million—hardly one man, one vote.

[...]

Questions

1. Can democracy lead to bad things? Explain.
2. What is constitutional liberalism and how does it differ from simple democracy?
3. According to Zakaria, how democratic is the United States? Explain.

Note

1. I use the term "liberal" in the nineteenth-century sense, meaning concerned with individual economic, political, and religious liberty, which is sometimes called "classical liberalism," not in the modern, American sense, which associates it with the welfare state, affirmative action, and other policies.

Noah Feldman discusses the origins of the Free Exercise and Establishment Clauses of the First Amendment

For ten days in August 2003, with an insurgency brewing and soldiers dying in newly conquered Iraq, the nation's attention suddenly became riveted on sleepy Montgomery, Alabama. Late one night the previous winter, Judge Roy

From *Divided by God: America's Church–State Problem and What We Should Do about It*, by Noah Feldman. New York: Farrar, Straus and Giroux, 2005, pp. 3–53. Copyright © 2005 by Noah Feldman. Reprinted by permission of Farrar, Straus and Giroux, LLC.

Moore, the elected chief justice of the Alabama Supreme Court, had arranged for a two-and-a-half-ton block of granite to be erected in the rotunda of his courthouse. The enormous rock, which took a team of men and machinery to move, was inscribed with the Ten Commandments. A federal district court found the monument to be an unconstitutional infringement on the separation of church and state, and ordered its removal; in late summer, a federal court of appeals agreed.[1]

What happened next grabbed the public eye: Moore refused. This extraordinary act of civil disobedience by a judge sworn to uphold the law brought out spokespeople and activists for both of the two most prominent schools of thought about church and state in the contemporary United States. On the front steps of the courthouse and on live television, their arguments began with the framers of the Constitution. The evangelicals declared that our entire system was built on Judeo-Christian values, and that the founding fathers, whose moral sense was based on the Bible, would have been astonished and horrified to see the Ten Commandments proscribed by court order. The secularists invoked Thomas Jefferson and James Madison to support their view that the symbols of religion ought to be kept out of the governmental sphere altogether. Both sides shared the assumption that they could win the argument if they could prove that history was on their side.

The Montgomery controversy mattered for reasons greater than the specter of a politically ambitious Alabama judge refusing to follow a federal court's order, or the constitutional question of whether the Ten Commandments may lawfully be displayed in public places, which the Supreme Court had yet to resolve. With a presidential election looming, the evangelicals and the secularists were enacting in microcosm the national debate about the right relationship between religion and government in the United States. The stakes of that debate extend beyond statues to billions of dollars in government funding, basic moral questions of life, death, and family, and the recurrent challenge of what it means for Americans to belong to a nation. The Ten Commandments were just a symbolic stand-in. Judge Moore had struck a vein of division that runs deep in America's history and its psyche.

In the darkest days of the Civil War, the absolute low point of division in American history, Abraham Lincoln could still imagine religion as a potentially unifying force. North and South, he observed in his second inaugural address, prayed to the same God and read the same Bible, even if they interpreted it differently. Through a shared faith, the American people could someday bind up the nation's wounds, inflicted by a just God as punishment for the original sin of slavery.

Today, the overwhelming majority of Americans still say they believe in God, but a common understanding of how faith should inform nationhood can no longer bring Americans together. To the contrary, no question divides Americans more fundamentally than that of the relation between religion and government. For many, moral values derived from religion are the lodestar of political judgment. Almost a quarter of the electorate in the 2004 presidential election described values as the most important issue to them, and of these, some four-fifths voted for President George W. Bush.[2] Yet many Americans believe with equal commitment that

religion is a private matter that should not figure in the sphere of politics—a view expressly adopted by Senator John Kerry in the presidential debates, where he explained his pro-choice stance by asserting that his personal beliefs as a Catholic must not be imposed on women who held different beliefs about abortion.[3] Although church membership did not predict which candidate a voter would choose, one statistic stood out sharply: the more often you attended church, the more likely you were to vote for President Bush.

The deep divide in American life, then, is not primarily over religious belief or affiliation—it is over the role that belief should play in the business of politics and government.[4] Consider same-sex marriage, which appeared on ballots in eleven states in 2004 and shows no sign of disappearing from public debate. Many Americans insist that marriage is "between one man and one woman" but say they have no objection to civil unions that give gay couples the same rights as married people. If there is no legal difference between civil union and marriage, why object to the word "marriage"? What's in a name? The obvious answer is that even though marriage is a state institution, it has a traditional religious definition, which opponents of same-sex marriage do not want to change. The reason so many people oppose same-sex "marriage" is that they believe the state's sanction of marriage should take account of a moral value derived from religion.

Religious values also figure prominently in the debates about stem-cell research, abortion, euthanasia, and the death penalty. On each of these life-and-death issues, one school of thought insists that citizens' private religious values should not decide government policy, while an equally vociferous alternative view maintains that the right answers to such ultimate questions must come from the wisdom of religious tradition. In each case, the debate is as much about whether faith should inform political debate as about the rights or wrongs of the issue. "We are a religious people," the Supreme Court said in 1952, "whose institutions presuppose a Supreme Being."[5] Clearly, not everyone agrees. Is the Court's dictum true today? Was it ever true in our history?

The essential question of how religion and government should interact becomes most salient when we confront the controversial constitutional problems that arise under the heading of church and state: Should the government be able to fund religious schools or social programs through the model of charitable choice? May courthouses display the Ten Commandments? Do the words "under God" in the Pledge of Allegiance amount to an establishment of religion? No one lives or dies as the result of our resolution of these hard questions on which the Supreme Court inevitably opines, but they are nevertheless lightning rods for debate, because they go to the very heart of who we are as a nation. They raise the central challenges of citizenship and peoplehood: who belongs here? To what kind of nation do we belong?

[...] Two sides dominate the church–state debate in contemporary American life, corresponding to what today are the two most prominent approaches to the proper relation of religion and government. In this book, I call those who insist on the direct relevance of religious values to political life "values evangelicals." Not every values evangelical is, technically speaking, an evangelical or born-again Christian, although many are. Values evangelicals can include Jews, Catholics, Muslims, and even people who do not focus on a particular religious tradition but care primarily about identifying traditional moral values that can in theory be shared by everyone. What all values evangelicals have in common is the goal of evangelizing *for* values: promoting a strong set of ideas about the best way to live one's life and urging the government to adopt those values and encourage them wherever possible. To them, the best way to hold the United States together as a nation, not just a country, is for us to know what values we really hold and to stand up for them. Convergence on true, traditional values is the key to unity and strength.

On the other side of the debate are those who see religion as a matter of personal belief and choice largely irrelevant to government, and who are concerned that values derived from religion will divide us, not unite us. I call those who hold this view "legal secularists," not because they are necessarily strongly secular in their personal worldviews—though many are—but because they believe that government should be secular and that the laws should make it so. To the legal secularists, full citizenship means fully sharing in the core legal and political commitments of the nation. If the nation defines itself in terms of values drawn from religion, they worry, then it will inevitably tend to adopt the religious values of the majority, excluding religious minorities and nonreligious people from full citizenship.

Despite their differences, both approaches, values evangelicalism and legal secularism, are trying to come to terms with the same fundamental tension in American life. The United States has always been home to striking religious diversity—diversity that has by fits and starts expanded over the last 230 years. At the same time, we strive to be a nation with a common identity and a common project. Religious division threatens that unity, as we can see today more clearly than at any time in a century, yet almost all Americans want to make sure that we do not let our religious diversity pull us apart.[6] Values evangelicals think that the solution lies in finding and embracing traditional values we can all share and without which we will never hold together. Legal secularists think that we can maintain our national unity only if we treat religion as a personal, private matter, separate from concerns of citizenship. The goal of reconciling national unity with religious diversity is the same, but the methods for doing it are deeply opposed.

[…]

Both evangelicals and secularists like to claim that our constitutional past and tradition support their approach. Both are wrong.

[…]

Why *do* we have a First Amendment prohibiting the establishment of religion and protecting the free exercise thereof? The answer combines principle and politics. The principled reason behind the religion clauses of the First Amendment was to protect the liberty of conscience of religious dissenters—and everybody involved in the process understood that fact. The political reason for the clauses was that no one in the new United States opposed the idea of religious liberty, and given the religious diversity among Americans, no one denomination seriously believed it could establish a national religion of its own.

[…]

[James] Madison had the political sense to realize that ratification of the Constitution could not ultimately succeed without a Bill of Rights attached. He then took up the cause of a constitutional amendment guaranteeing religious liberty, pursuing it with characteristic vigor in the first Congress.

[…]

The draft language that Madison proposed in the House of Representatives once he had joined the cause of seeking a constitutional amendment guaranteed that no one's civil rights would be "abridged on account of religious belief or worship"; it said that no national religion could be established; and it protected "the full and equal rights of conscience" from being infringed "in any manner, or on any pretext."[7] This language grew from the proposals of the state ratifying conventions, all of which mentioned conscience or religious liberty. A House committee changed the draft language to "no religion shall be established by law, nor shall the equal rights of conscience be infringed."[8]

Congressman Benjamin Huntington of Connecticut immediately objected, expressing his concern that if this ban on established religion were understood to apply to the states, his own New England practice of requiring taxpayers to support their own churches "might be construed into a religious establishment" and therefore prohibited or at least not be enforced in the federal courts.[9] Madison did not assuage Huntington's concern by saying that the New England arrangement was not an establishment—Madison no doubt believed that the Connecticut system was indeed an establishment, unjust to New England dissenters. Instead, Madison told Huntington that the Constitution was talking only about the federal government, not the states.

[…]

This exchange between Madison and the New Englander Huntington shows definitively that, despite what is sometimes claimed, the framers understood perfectly well that nonpreferential support for religion could and probably would be understood as an establishment of religion. At the same time, it is absolutely correct to say that the First Amendment to the federal Constitution was drafted so that it would not apply to the states when it was enacted. The Bill of Rights, as initially ratified, did not stop the states from abridging the freedom of speech or from inflicting cruel and unusual punishments. It was not until the post-Civil War passage of the Fourteenth Amendment, and its subsequent interpretation in the twentieth century by the Supreme Court, that the Bill of Rights came to apply to the states as well.

But that does not mean that the Establishment Clause (as it is now called) of the Constitution was actually intended to protect state establishments of religion from congressional interference by specifying that Congress could make no law "respecting an establishment of religion." The framers would never have imagined that *Congress* would possess the power to change state arrangements with respect to religion. Moreover, in

1791, no state was prepared to acknowledge that its church–state arrangements counted as an establishment, because "establishment" was a term of condemnation. Even Congressman Huntington did not admit that his home state of Connecticut actually had an establishment of religion; he just acknowledged that the New England Way could be "construed into an establishment" by its opponents. At the time that the First Amendment came into being, Americans were almost universally prepared to say that establishment of religion was a bad thing. They understood perfectly well that the federal Constitution prohibited Congress from creating arrangements like those in New England. It is therefore historically incorrect to claim that the Constitution, by banning an establishment of religion, allowed the government to support religion generally or nonpreferentially.

The new constitutional amendment, then, guaranteed two things. The Establishment Clause guaranteed that the government would not compel anybody to support any religious teaching or worship with which he conscientiously disagreed. The Free Exercise Clause guaranteed that the government would not stop anybody from worshipping or practicing his religion as he chose. Both clauses were necessary because the framers understood that there was a difference between making somebody do something against his will and stopping him from doing something he wanted to do. Prohibiting establishment protected citizens from being placed in the position where they must act against conscience in the realm of religion. Guaranteed free exercise protected their right to worship in the way their consciences told them they must.[10] These guarantees still apply to us today—but their interpretation has been much contested, and some of their contemporary applications would seem very strange indeed to those who framed them.

If the Establishment Clause protected against compulsory support of organized religion, and the Free Exercise Clause protected worship, what did the Constitution say about religious symbols and their use in the public realm? Such symbolic questions are, after all, often the focus of our contemporary church–state debates. The framers are invoked on both sides of the debate about religious symbolism. What, for instance, would the framers' Constitution have had to say about the fifty-two-hundred-pound block of granite, inscribed with the Ten Commandments, that Judge Roy Moore erected in the rotunda of the Alabama Supreme Court in the summer of 2003?

The answer is that the framers were not especially concerned with public religious symbolism one way or the other. They would certainly not have approved of the use of federal public funds to erect churches or support religious teaching, because they would have understood the taxes involved to be obtained through coercion of conscience. But they were supremely untroubled by norms like the opening of legislative sessions with symbolic prayers. The framers would no doubt have thought it odd to erect a monument to the Ten Commandments in a government building, since government had no authority in religious affairs. But the framers would also probably have been perplexed by the legal secularists' vociferous opposition to the monument, so long as its presence did not expend government funds and therefore coerced no one to act in contravention of his own beliefs.

The main reason the framers did not react with horror to public symbols of religion is that they were not secularists in the modern sense. They did not think that the state needed to be protected from the dangers of religious influence, nor were they particularly concerned with keeping religious symbolism out of the public sphere. For that matter, American religion, too, was very different than it is today. Church attendance was low, at least by today's standards. There was no national movement devoted to promoting the role of religion in public life. A monument like Judge Moore's, if anyone had been able to imagine it, would have had an entirely different meaning than it did in 2003, when it was erected in large part as a symbolic rejection of legal secularism. At the same time, there was no great danger that government would give offense to religious minorities when public prayers were offered or God's name invoked as a symbol of the fledgling republic. In

the framers' America, almost everybody was a Protestant of some kind, and atheism as a publicly acknowledged stance was essentially unknown. The remaining orthodox Calvinists still adhered to the doctrine of the predestined salvation of only a small elect, while more liberal Protestants increasingly opened the doors of possible salvation much wider, and deists like Jefferson rejected the very idea of a personal God. But these different ideas swam in a sea of Protestant assumptions, and the framers' generation argued politics in the light of ideals connected to their common Protestant legacy. Rather than insisting anachronistically on "Judeo-Christian values," it would be more accurate to say that the framers assumed a whole set of principles that grew out of Protestant Christianity as interpreted by English liberals such as John Locke.

Where contemporary values evangelicals go wrong historically is in assuming that those Protestant-originated principles required that Christian values infuse all the activities of the state. Rather, the framers' Protestant-inflected worldview included a crucial distinction between the religious realm and the civil. As Locke bluntly put it, "there is absolutely no such thing, *under the Gospel*, as a Christian Commonwealth."[11] Locke, in this formulation and elsewhere in his writings, offered a religiously grounded explanation for why government lacked authority in religious matters. According to Locke and the overwhelming majority of Americans who accepted some version of his views, there was no basis either in religion or in reason for allowing government to exercise coercive power in affairs of religion. The individual's conscience must be left free in order for religious faith to have any meaning at all.

[…]

Questions

1. Explain Feldman's distinction between "values evangelicals" and "legal secularists."
2. What did the Establishment Clause of the First Amendment guarantee? To whom did it apply originally? What extended its application?
3. According to Feldman, how would the framers of the Constitution have reacted to public symbols of religion?
4. Does Feldman think the framers believed that "Christian values should infuse all the activities of the state"? Explain.

Notes

1. Glassroth v. Moore, 242 F. Supp.2d 1067 (M.D.Ala. 2002), aff'ch 335 F.3d 1282 (11th Cir. July 1, 2003), cert den., 124 S. Ct. 497 (Nov. 3, 2003).
2. For these and other exit polling statistics, see CNN's exit polls, available at www.cnn.com/ELECTION/2004/pages/results/states/US/P/00/epolls.0. html. The question that produced the answer regarding moral values has been criticized on the ground that the limited number of options produced a skew in favor of "moral values" for Bush voters. Without entering the debate, one may note that all such limited-option questions are liable to distortion, and that the important fact is that 18 percent of Kerry voters chose moral values as opposed to 80 percent of Bush voters.
3. Debate transcript at www.debates.org/pages/trans 2004c.html.
4. I am therefore not taking issue with sociologist Alan Wolfe, who has argued that Americans' religious faith is not in itself a source of deep division. See Alan Wolfe, *The Transformation of American Religion: How We Actually Live Our Faith* (New York: Free Press, 2003); Alan Wolfe, *One Nation, After All* (New York: Penguin, 1998). My aim is that the division is over the role religious values should play in political choices.
5. Zorach v. Clauson, 343 U.S. 306, 313 (1952). The Court cited the statement approvingly as recently as 1984. See Lynch v. Donnelly, 465 U.S. 668, 675 (1984).
6. On the recurrent tension between religious diversity and national unity, see William R. Hutchison, *Religious Pluralism in America: The Contentious History of a Founding Ideal* (New Haven, CT: Yale University Press, 2003), 8, 10; Martin Marty, *The One and the Many: America's Struggle for the Common Good* (Cambridge, MA: Harvard University Press, 1997). An important work on the broader question of unity and values diversity is Stephen Macedo, *Diversity and Distrust* (Cambridge, MA: Harvard University Press, 2000). The most thoughtful recent work on the relation between different religious and liberal conceptions of politics and the good is Jeffrey Stout, *Democracy and Tradition* (Princeton, NJ: Princeton University Press, 2004).
7. Joseph Gales, ed., Annals of Congress (1789), 796. This change was proposed by Fisher Ames of Massachusetts. For one view of Ames's ideology on the question and place in the debate, see Marc M. Arkin, "Regionalism and the Religion Clauses: The Contribution of Fisher Ames," *Buffalo Law Review* 47 (1999): 763, 786–90.
8. Annals of Congress, 757.
9. Ibid., 758.
10. Ibid., 759 (emphasis added).
11. Locke, *Letter Concerning Toleration*, 40 (emphasis added).

John Hospers discusses libertarianism

[…]

The political philosophy that is called libertarianism (from the Latin *libertas*, liberty) is the doctrine that every person is the owner of his own life, and that no one is the owner of anyone else's life: and that consequently every human being has the right to act in accordance with his own choices, unless those actions infringe on the equal liberty of other human beings to act in accordance with their choices.

Reproduced from "What Libertarianism Is." In *The Libertarian Alternative*, ed. Tibor Machan. Chicago: Nelson-Hall, 1974.

There are several other ways of stating the same libertarian thesis:

1. *No one is anyone else's master, and no one is anyone else's slave.* Since I am the one to decide how my life is to be conducted just as you decide about yours, I have no right (even if I had the power) to make you my slave and be your master, nor have you the right to become the master by enslaving me. Slavery is *forced* servitude, and since no one owns the life of anyone else, no one has the right to enslave another. Political theories past and present have traditionally been concerned with who should be the master (usually the king, the dictator, or government bureaucracy) and who should be the slaves, and what the extent of the

slavery should be. Libertarianism holds that no one has the right to use force to enslave the life of another, or any portion or aspect of that life.

2. *Other men's lives are not yours to dispose of.* I enjoy seeing operas; but operas are expensive to produce. Opera-lovers often say, "The state (or the city, etc.) should subsidize opera, so that we can all see it. Also it would be for people's betterment, cultural benefit, etc." But what they are advocating is nothing more or less than legalized plunder. They can't pay for the productions themselves, and yet they want to see opera, which involves a large number of people and their labor; so what they are saying in effect is, "Get the money through legalized force. Take a little bit more out of every worker's paycheck every week to pay for the operas we want to see." But I have no right to take by force from the workers' pockets to pay for what I want.

Perhaps it would be better if he *did*, go to see opera—then I should try to convince him to go voluntarily. But to take the money from him forcibly, because in my opinion it would be good for *him*, is still seizure of his earnings, which is plunder.

Besides, if I have the right to force him to help pay for my pet projects, hasn't he equally the right to force me to help pay for his? Perhaps he in turn wants the government to subsidize rock-and-roll, or his new car, or a house in the country? If I have the right to milk him, why hasn't he the right to milk me? If I can be a moral cannibal, why can't, he too?

We should beware of the inventors of utopias. They would remake the world according to their vision—with the lives and fruits of the labor of *other* human beings. Is it someone's utopian vision that others should build pyramids to beautify the landscape? Very well, then other men should provide the labor; and if he is in a position of political power, and he can't get men to do it voluntarily, then he must *compel* them to "cooperate"—i.e., he must enslave them.

[...]

3. *No human being should be a nonvoluntary mortgage on the life of another.* I cannot claim your life, your work, or the products of your effort as mine. The fruit of one man's labor should not be fair game for every freeloader who comes along and demands it as his own. The orchard that has been carefully grown, nurtured, and harvested by its owner should not be ripe

for the plucking for any bypasser who has a yen for the ripe fruit. The wealth that some men have produced should not be fair game for looting by government, to be used for whatever purposes its representatives determine, no matter what their motives in so doing may be. The theft of your money by a robber is not justified by the fact that he used it to help his injured mother.

It will already be evident that libertarian doctrine is embedded in a view of the rights of man. Each human being has the right to live his life as he chooses, compatibly with the equal right of all other human beings to live their lives as they choose.

All man's rights are implicit in the above statement. Each man has the right to life: any attempt by others to take it away from him, or even to injure him, violates this right, through the use of coercion against him. Each man has the right to liberty: to conduct his life in accordance with the alternatives open to him without coercive action by others. And every man has the right to property: to work to sustain his life (and the lives of whichever others he chooses to sustain, such as his family) and to retain the fruits of his labor.

People often defend the rights of life and liberty but denigrate property rights, and yet the right to property is as basic as the other two: indeed, without property rights no other rights are possible. Depriving you of property is depriving you of the means by which you live.

[...]

When I claim a right, I carve out a niche, as it were, in my life, saying in effect. "This activity I must be able to perform without interference from others. For you and everyone else, this is off limits." And so I put up a "no trespassing" sign, which marks off the area of my right. Each individual's right is his "no trespassing" sign in relation to me and others. I may not encroach upon his domain any more than he upon mine, without my consent. Every right entails a duty, true—but the duty is only that of *forbearance*—that is, of *refraining* from violating the other person's right. If you have a life, I have no right to take your life; if you have a right to the products of your labor (property), I have no right to take it from you without your consent. The nonviolation of these rights will not guarantee you protection against natural catastrophes such as floods and earthquakes, but it will protect you against the aggressive activities *of other men*. And rights, after all, have to do with one's relations to other human beings, not with one's relations to physical nature.

Nor were these rights created by government; governments—some governments, obviously not all—*recognize* and *protect* the rights that individuals already have. Governments regularly forbid homicide and theft; and, at a more advanced stage, protect individuals against such things as libel and breach of contract....

The *right to property* is the most misunderstood and unappreciated of human rights, and it is one most constantly violated by governments. "Property" of course does not mean only real estate; it includes anything you can call your own—your clothing, your car, your jewelry, your books and papers.

[...]

Government is the most dangerous institution known to man. Throughout history it has violated the rights of men more than any individual or group of individuals could do: it has killed people, enslaved them, sent them to forced labor and concentration camps, and regularly robbed and pillaged them of the fruits of their expended labor. Unlike individual criminals, government has the power to arrest and try; unlike individual criminals, it can surround and encompass a person totally, dominating every aspect of one's life, so that one has no recourse from it but to leave the country (and in totalitarian nations even that is prohibited). Government throughout history has a much sorrier record than any individual, even that of a ruthless mass murderer. The signs we see on bumper stickers are chillingly accurate: "Beware: the Government Is Armed and Dangerous."

The only proper role of government, according to libertarians, is that of the protector of the citizen against aggression by other individuals.

[...]

Laws may be classified into three types: (1) laws protecting individuals against themselves, such as laws against fornication and other sexual behavior, alcohol, and drugs; (2) laws protecting individuals against aggressions by other individuals, such as laws against murder, robbery, and fraud; (3) laws requiring people to help one another; for example all laws which rob Peter to pay Paul, such as welfare

Libertarians reject the first class of laws totally. Behavior which harms no one else is strictly the individual's own affair. Thus, there should be no law: against becoming intoxicated, since whether or not to become intoxicated is the individual's own decision: but there should be laws against driving while intoxicated, since the drunken driver is a threat to every other motorist on the highway (drunken driving falls into type 2). Similarly, there should be no laws against drugs (except the prohibition of sale of drugs to minors) as long as the taking of these drugs poses no threat to anyone else.

[...]

Laws should be limited to the second class only: aggression by individuals against other individuals. These are laws whose function is to protect human beings against encroachment by others; and this, as we have seen, is (according to libertarianism) the sole function of government.

Libertarians also reject the third class of laws totally: no one should be forced by law to help others, not even to tell them the time of day if requested, and certainly not to give them a portion of one's weekly paycheck. Governments, in the guise of humanitarianism, have given to some by taking from others (charging a "handling fee" in the process, which, because of the government's waste and inefficiency, sometimes is several hundred percent). And in so doing they have decreased incentive, violated the rights of individuals and lowered the standard of living of almost everyone.

All such laws constitute what libertarians call *moral cannibalism*. A cannibal in the physical sense is a person who lives off the flesh of other human beings. A *moral* cannibal is one who believes he has a right to live off the "spirit" of other human beings—who believes that he has a moral claim on the productive capacity, time, and effort expended by others.

It has become fashionable to claim virtually everything that one needs or desires as one's *right*. Thus, many people claim that they have a right to a job, the right to free medical care, to free food and clothing, to a decent home, and so on. Now if one asks, apart from any specific context, whether it would be desirable if everyone had these things, one might well say yes. But there is a gimmick attached to each of them: *At whose expense?* Jobs, medical care, education, and so on, don't grow on trees. These are goods and services *produced only by men.* Who then is to provide them, and under what conditions?

If you have a right to a job, who is to supply it? Must an employer supply it even if he doesn't want to hire you? What if you are unemployable, or incurably lazy? (If you say "the government must supply it," does that mean that a job must be created for you which no employer needs done, and that you must be kept in it regardless of how much or little you work?) If the employer is forced to supply it at his expense even if he doesn't need you, then isn't *he* being enslaved to that extent? What ever happened to *his* right to conduct his life and his affairs in accordance with his choices?

If you have a right to free medical care, then, since medical care doesn't exist in nature as wild apples do, some people will have to supply it to you for free: that is, they will have to spend their time and money and energy taking care of you whether they want to or not. What ever happened to *their* right to conduct their lives as they see fit? Or do you have a right to violate theirs? Can there be a right to violate rights?

All those who demand this or that as a "free service" are consciously or unconsciously evading the fact that there is in reality no such thing as free services. All man-made goods and services are the result of human expenditure of time and effort. There is no such thing as "something for nothing" in this world. If you demand something free, you are demanding that other men give their time and effort to you without compensation. If they voluntarily choose to do this, there is no problem; but if you demand that they be

forced to do it, you are interfering with their right not to do it if they so choose. "Swimming in this pool ought to be free!" says the indignant passerby. What he means is that others should build a pool, others should provide the material, and still others should run it and keep it in functioning order, so that *he* can use it without fee. But what right has he to the expenditure of *their* time and effort? To expect something "for free" is to expect it *to be paid for by others* whether they choose to or not.

Many questions, particularly about economic matters, will be generated by the libertarian account of human rights and the role of government. Should government, have a role in assisting the needy, in providing social security, in legislating minimum wages, in fixing prices and putting a ceiling on rents, in curbing monopolies, in erecting tariffs, in guaranteeing jobs, in managing the money supply? To these and all similar questions the libertarian answers with an unequivocal no.

"But then you'd let people go hungry!" comes the rejoinder. This, the libertarian insists, is precisely what would not happen; with the restrictions removed, the economy would flourish as never before. With the controls taken off business, existing enterprises would expand and new ones would spring into existence satisfying more and more consumer needs; millions more people would be gainfully employed instead of subsisting on welfare, and all kinds of research and production, released from the stranglehold of government, would proliferate, fulfilling man's needs and desires as never before. It has always been so whenever government has permitted men to be free traders on a free market.

[…]

Questions

1. What, according to Hospers, is the essence of libertarianism?
2. Why does Hospers say that property rights are essential under a libertarian view?
3. Hospers talks about three types of laws. What are they? How do libertarians view each of those types?

Patrick N. Allitt discusses conservativism

[…]

Now, in politics, the world is always changing. Conservatism in politics is an attitude towards change. It favors cautious and prudential changes rather than opposing them at all costs. Conservatism is skeptical about radical changes and much prefers to stay with what is familiar and what has withstood the test of time. Conservatives tend to take this view: If the world is the way it is, that must be because we intended it to be this way or because we found that in practice, it works. Now, of course, the obvious rebuttal to a claim like that is: The world does work very well for some people, but unfortunately, it lets them prosper at the expense of others, who are victimized by the world as it is.

Conservatism can't simply turn its back against all possible forms of change. It tends to be accepting of moderate changes and sympathetic to the idea of redressing obvious injustices, but it always counsels patience rather than perfectionism. Built into conservatism is the idea that the world is never going to be made perfect and that unfortunately, the attempt to make the world perfect can sometimes do more harm than good.

In particular, conservatives have always been skeptical about the idea that you can make a blueprint, a plan, for creating a new society right from first principles. Conservatives say it's not possible to create a new society from scratch because planners can't possibly encompass the full complexity of the world as it is. And they say the attempt to make a planned society is likely to be coercive in practice. They can certainly quote as example the Soviet experiment [...].

And, say conservatives, it's very difficult indeed, in a planned society, to accommodate the fact of social change. Because history is always moving on, if a new society starts in one way, what's going to happen when new technologies, or new problems, or new diseases, or new opportunities develop? How, then, can things like that be written into the plan themselves since at the time the plan was made, these new

From *The Conservative Tradition*, by Patrick N. Allitt, Chantilly, VA: The Teaching Company, 2009, lecture 1. © 2009 The Teaching Company. Reproduced with permission of The Teaching Company, www.thegreatcourses.com.

possibilities didn't exist? Conservatives say planned societies are coercive and repressive because they resist the reality of human variability. After all, isn't it true that different people want different things? We actually love cultural variety. We like the fact that at different times in our lives, different things appeal to us. Some people want to work very, very hard to make great gains. People want to become wealthy. Others, particularly in many societies outside of the English-speaking world, have valued leisure, perhaps more highly than we do. Ideas about what we want differ, not only from person to person but even within particular individuals at different times in the life cycle. Trying to plan all these infinite complexities would surely be impossible.

Another strong, strong characteristic of conservatism is the belief that human nature is the way it is and it's not going to be changed or transformed. I think a useful way of thinking about this is to pick up on the religious idea of original sin, one of the foundational concepts of the Judeo-Christian tradition—this idea that there's a deep-seated human propensity to go wrong. This doesn't have to be thought of explicitly in religious terms. You can think of it in purely secular ways. We know what we ought to do, but we don't always do it. We rationalize our actions to suit our interests. We never consider the effect of our actions on people we don't know with the same attention we give to their effects for ourselves. This, again, is consonant with the idea that planning a society is impossible because the planners themselves are going to be more attentive to their own ideas about what's good and right than everyone else.

Just think about the way in which our sinfulness affects our everyday conduct. Even people who know that there is starvation in the world can enjoy restaurants. Why? Because they live far enough away from the victims not to confront their suffering directly. Probably when people are out celebrating in restaurants, the very last thing they want to be reminded of is the way in which they're wasting resources which could actually be used to save the lives of suffering people elsewhere. In the same way, we know that driving fast endangers the lives of other people, but we break the speed limits anyway.

These are all little forms of our imperfection. Now, conservatives take the view [that] since people are like that, we've got to plan society, we've got to organize society in a way which makes full recognition of these imperfections rather than hoping that somehow people will become better.

Another classic example of the conflict between conservatives and their adversaries is the conservative belief that war is a permanent part of the human condition. As far back as we look in history, there have always been wars, and therefore, it's very, very reasonable to think—sadly but truly—that war will continue to be an integral part of the human condition for the indefinite future. There have always been wars and there have always been lesser forms of conflict because of human egotism. Egotism persists, ambition persists, and it will generate new conflicts. They often come up in ways which haven't been anticipated, but nevertheless, they're very powerful in each new generation.

So, say the conservatives, the sensible approach is to assume that warfare will continue and then to prepare to meet the contingency, while doing whatever possible to avert it since we also know that war is not necessarily a chronic condition. In practical terms, this often means, for example, that when liberals take the view "Perhaps we should undertake a phase of disarmament," conservatives tend to answer—you can see this, for example, in the America of the 1980s—"No, no, warfare will continue; therefore, it's much more sensible for us to prevent war by being terrifyingly strong than by being even potentially vulnerable. You stave off war by threatening potential adversaries with your overwhelming strength." It is not a pleasing view, but it's a realistic one.

[...]

Now, think about economics for a second. When conservatives think about economic questions, they again accept the principle that people are going to be overwhelmingly self-interested, and therefore—even if it's sad, even if it's regrettable, it's nonetheless true—and therefore, the economy has got to be organized around this truth. How can we find ways to manage a society, most of whose members are deeply economically self-interested? It may not be inspiring or elevating, but since it's true, there are ways of making private gain contribute to public welfare. In fact, this is really the single great insight of capitalism, which has been the prevailing economic system over the last 250 years

in the English-speaking countries of the world. It's self-interest linked to the idea of social and political stability.

Another characteristic of the conservative frame of mind is the assumption that all the really important questions facing humanity have already been asked and answered. Now, that has important educational implications because it implies that the insights of ancient writers, like Plato, and Aristotle, and the authors of the Hebrew Bible, are likely to be able to give us relevant answers to the questions which continue to confront us, even though we're living thousands of years later. So you could take the view that our world is so different from that of the ancients that they no longer have much to teach us, but conservatives are much more likely to take the view that the similarities outweigh the differences, and therefore, the wisdom of the classics is still relevant to us today.

More generally, thinking about historical study, every generation has to think about this problem: Are we essentially the same as our ancestors, or are we essentially different from them? Now, on the whole—this is a generalization, but that's what I'm doing in this lecture; [I'm] generalizing—conservatives tend to minimize the differences. They tend to say if we were to encounter people from any period in the history of the world, we'd recognize our essential sameness with those people and we'd be able to find close analogs from our problems with their problems.

[...]

[A]nother paradox of conservative history is that at different times, the same set of ideas can seem either radical or conservative. Let me give you the example of capitalism [...]. Supporters of the free-market economy were radicals in the late 18th and early 19th centuries in Britain. But yet, supporters of the market economy in America in the 20th century and in Britain are conservatives. Now, to believe in capitalism is a very conservative thing. Adam Smith, the great theorist of capitalism, who wrote his book *The Inquiry into the Wealth of Nations* in 1776, had the radical idea—as it then was—of sweeping away government interference with the economy. But in the 20th century, the threat of communism made defense of the free market a conservative idea, even though capitalism has probably done more than anything else in world history to transform the world. [...]

Conservatism has usually been elitist and hierarchical, but more recently, particularly in the 20th century, universal democracy has also given rise to populist forms of conservatism. [...]

In the 20th century, I could give you the example of McCarthyism in the 1950s—this sort of populist belief that the ordinary American people are immune from communism and that the people who are most tempted by it are elitists. [...]

More recently, in our own times, the new Christian right of the 1980s, and '90s, and the first decade of the 21st century also has the idea that we're the ordinary conservative folks, and we're protesting against the ideas of an overeducated elite on issues like creation science, for example.

[...]

In the United States, there was no self-conscious and self-declared conservative movement really until the 1950s. That came about when William Buckley, Jr., founded the *National Review* in 1955 and helped to create the Barry Goldwater movement, which came to power inside the Republican Party in 1964 and led to his presidential candidacy. It was unsuccessful, but then the later candidacy of Reagan in 1980 succeeded. But, of course, even though the conservative movement was something new in America in the post–Second World War era, the impulse was there earlier in certain parties and certain individuals, and they are people whose lives we'll be investigating.

The fact that Britain and America have been politically separated since 1776 also means that the particulars of conservatism in each country differ widely, even when the impulse is similar. I'll give you an example from ideas about hunting. In America, it's common for a conservative candidate to claim that he or she is a hunter because it carries the implication of strength, and vigor, and resilience. But it's a claim that a British candidate would never make. It would ruin a British conservative candidate's chances of being elected because in Britain, hunting is perceived as cruel and it's perceived as haughty—the preserve of the old aristocracy. So, again, the symbolic meaning of hunting in the two countries is very different. Britain and America differ widely in the political uses of religion by conservatives. Britain is a far more secularized country than the United States by now. So to avow religion in public light in Britain would seem like a slightly crackpot notion, whereas in America, for a conservative candidate, it's almost indispensable to claim to be religiously active, and it's certainly an issue that has to be addressed.

There is also, of course, a great array of religion-related issues in American politics, of which abortion is probably the most salient—very much an issue which every American conservative has to come to terms with but not at all in the United Kingdom, where only a tiny, tiny handful of Catholic politicians ever even mentions the question.

So we have this paradox: that conservatives in each country favor policies that would be anathema in the other. British conservatives, for example, are staunchly against the idea that ordinary citizens should be allowed to own guns and are steadily supportive of the idea of the national health service, whereas American conservatives almost overwhelmingly tend to be in favor of the idea of gun ownership but against the idea of a nationalized health service—profound differences for us to understand, which in each case flow out of the preceding political traditions of the particular country.

[...]

Questions

1. According to Allitt, what is the conservative attitude toward change?
2. What is the conservative view of human nature and how does that affect the conservative view of human institutions?
3. "A paradox of conservative history is that at different times, the same set of ideas can seem either radical or conservative." Give some examples of this.

Paul Starr discusses liberalism

[...]

Liberalism is notoriously difficult to define. The term has been used to describe a sprawling profusion of ideas, practices, movements, and parties in different societies and historical periods. Often emerging as a philosophy of opposition, whether to feudal privilege, absolute monarchy, colonialism, theocracy, communism, or fascism, liberalism has served, as the word suggests, as a force for liberation, or at least liberalization— for the opening up of channels of free initiative. But liberalism in its oppositional and even revolutionary moments has not necessarily been the same as the liberalism of established parties and governments. In different countries, depending on their particular histories, parties bearing the name "Liberal" have variously ended up on the right or left and thereby colored the understanding of what liberalism means as a political philosophy. This book primarily reflects the understanding of liberalism in Britain and the United States, though it has been conceived in substantially different ways even in the Anglo-American world.

Two conceptions of liberalism chiefly concern us, as they help organize the argument in this book. In its broader meaning, liberalism refers to the fundamental principles of constitutional government and individual rights shared by modern liberals and conservatives alike, though often differently interpreted by them. This tradition of *constitutional liberalism*—classical political liberalism—emerged in the seventeenth and eighteenth centuries, culminated in the American and French Revolutions, and continues to provide the foundation of the modern liberal state. The classical liberals themselves were a diverse group, but they generally stood for freedom of conscience and religious liberty, freedom of thought and speech, the division of governmental powers, an independent civil society, and rights of private property and economic freedom that evolved in the nineteenth century into the doctrine of laissez-faire. [...] The second [is] to *modern democratic liberalism*, which has developed out of the more egalitarian

aspects of the broader tradition and serves as the basis of contemporary liberal politics. The relationship between liberalism in these two phases has been predominantly cumulative: while rejecting laissez-faire economic policy, modern democratic liberalism continues to take the broader tradition of constitutional liberalism as its foundation. That is why it is possible to speak not only of the two separately, but also of an overarching set of ideas that unites them.

In everyday language, "liberal" also has a meaning that predates but still bears on its political use. "Liberal" often refers to such qualities as a tolerant and open frame of mind, generosity of spirit, breadth of education, lack of prejudice, willingness to acknowledge others' rights, acceptance of disagreement and diversity, and receptiveness to innovation. These are exemplary liberal virtues, and a liberal society will promote them if it is true to its ideals. As a political doctrine, however, liberalism means something more particular—or rather, it has come to refer to a series of things, all of which, taken together, make up a design of power in support of freedom.

A great deal about that design, including its theoretical foundation, has been subject to dispute. Philosophically, liberals have started from different premises—some, for example, from a belief in natural law and natural rights; others from a utilitarian commitment to the greatest good for the greatest number; still others from a theory of history; yet others from moral principles based on equality of respect and concern for individuals and an acceptance of diverse values. Some liberals believe in the possibility of identifying a few rational and consistent principles for a just society, while others hold that politics and moral life are inherently tragic and pose choices between rival values that no philosophical system can resolve. No matter—at least for the purpose of determining what counts as liberalism. Liberals are defined more by their shared political principles than by agreement on the ultimate grounds on which those principles rest.[1]

One of those political principles, as I earlier suggested, is an equal right to freedom, where freedom has been successively understood in a more expansive way: first, as a right to civil liberty and freedom from arbitrary power; then, as a right to political liberty and a share in the government; and finally, as a right to basic requirements of human development and security necessary to assure equal opportunity and personal dignity.

Although I have described these ideas as a series of rights, they imply corresponding responsibilities that a liberal society expects of its members, individually and collectively. Inasmuch as individuals enjoy rights to civil liberty and freedom from arbitrary power, they are responsible for their own actions and what they make of their lives. Inasmuch as citizens enjoy a right to political liberty and a share of their government, they have the responsibilities of citizenship to make democracy work. And inasmuch as the members of a liberal society have a right to basic requirements of human development such as education and a minimum standard of security, they have obligations to each other, mutually and through their government, to ensure that conditions exist enabling every person to have the opportunity for success in life.[2]

[…]

A series of changes during the nineteenth and early twentieth centuries pushed liberal politics and thought toward their modern form. At the heart of this shift was the democratization of liberalism. A few eighteenth-century liberals were genuine democrats, but early liberal thought typically justified limiting political participation only to men with property on the grounds that they alone had both an independent will and a stake in a well-ordered society. Liberalism without democracy, however, proved an unstable combination in the face of the social and economic changes and popular movements accompanying industrialization and economic growth, and by the early twentieth century liberals generally stood for the political equality of all citizens, men and women. Democracy was workable, liberals believed, only through the extension of education and the creation of civic organizations that would promote responsible citizenship and political cooperation across class lines. Political inclusion, in this view, involved not just extending the right to vote but integrating new voters into the traditions of constitutional government and social reform.

A second development was the emergence of a positive conception of freedom based on the idea of self-determination. Liberalism would never have been as attractive a set of ideas if it had consisted only of a negative conception of freedom or a purely rational understanding of the self. Influenced particularly by German idealism and the romantic movement, liberals during the nineteenth century came increasingly to view freedom as self-realization and to emphasize the claims of individual expression and the cultivation of the aesthetic and moral faculties. Liberalism was already identified with the idea that the young, rather than following a course prescribed by tradition and their elders, ought to be free to choose their occupation, spouse, and path in life. […]

Both the democratization of liberalization and the growing emphasis on freedom as self-determination worked in favor of a third movement—the liberal advocacy of more positive government. As the right to vote was extended, liberals had to appeal to wider constituencies among the working class and the poor in competition with socialists and others to their left, and this competition led them to become more sympathetic to demands for substantive as well as formal equality, to endorse the rights of labor unions, and to support more active intervention in the economy. The conception of freedom as self-determination favored universal public education and other means of achieving equal opportunity. In Britain during the nineteenth century, support for much of the early regulation of factories and working hours cut across the Conservative and Liberal Parties, and an administrative revolution inspired greater confidence in the capacity of government to undertake new functions. Doctrinaire laissez-faire was already outside of the mainstream of British liberalism by the 1880s; by the turn of the century, the dominant New Liberalism called for state intervention to achieve greater social equality and to protect individuals against downturns in the economy and other adverse turns in life that could destroy their independence. The older liberals, including the classical economists, had supported a limited role for government in advancing social equality, primarily through education. What was new was liberal support for such policies as workers' compensation, unemployment insurance, national health insurance, and old-age pensions, which in continental Europe originated with conservative, Catholic, and social democratic parties. Britain's New Liberals saw that these pillars of the welfare state could be constructed on liberal lines; contributory insurance programs, for example, preserved the concept of individually earned benefits. Progressives in the United States began to adopt these ideas in the early 1900s, while calling for new measures such as antitrust legislation and financial regulation to control the growing power of private corporations and concentrated wealth. Liberals also increasingly favored progressive taxation and, still later, government spending to manage the business cycle and reduce unemployment. The almost continuous crisis of the twentieth century from World War I through the Depression, World War II, and the Cold War played a crucial role in consolidating liberal support for an enlarged state.

Yet that long crisis also had the effect of strengthening liberal commitments to individual freedom. The creation of a governmental propaganda machine and the suppression of dissent during World War I and its aftermath proved a turning point in the liberal view of the state and led to the establishment of organizations to protect civil liberties. In the United States, those who had earlier called themselves "progressives" now began describing themselves as "liberals," partly to emphasize continuities with the philosophical traditions of liberalism and an affinity with Britain's New Liberals. [...]

Through the mid-twentieth century, liberalism occupied the political center, offering a middle way between communism and socialism, on the left, and conservatism and authoritarianism, on the right. [...] Socialists often said liberals were objectively no different from conservatives because they both supported capitalism, while conservatives often said liberals were tantamount to socialists because, they both supported collectivism. But socialists wanted to replace capitalism with collective ownership of industry and finance, whereas liberals wanted to reform capitalism while preserving private ownership. And whereas conservatives generally defended the inequalities produced in the market and the interests of corporations and private wealth, liberals wanted to limit the extreme disparities of wealth and power that threatened to make a mockery of the ideals of democratic government and equal opportunity.

As liberalism has evolved, so has conservatism—and the grounds of conflict between them have changed. The classical opposition in the eighteenth century was between a liberalism that upheld the principles of individual freedom and equality against a conservatism that defended a more hierarchical, paternalistic, and tradition-minded society. Beginning with the embrace of laissez-faire in the early nineteenth century, however, conservatives in the Anglo-American world underwent their own liberalization, even as they continued to uphold the values of tradition, authority, and social hierarchy. The conversion of conservatives to universal suffrage came more slowly in Britain than in America. But in both countries, especially the United States, modern democratic conservatism has become a combination, in varying degrees, of devotion to the free market and social traditionalism. [...] In struggles over rights and equality, conservatives have generally opposed the liberal enlargement of freedom of expression and other civil liberties and the extension of rights to subordinate social groups, though they have usually assented at least to formal rights after the fact.

By the mid-twentieth century, most conservatives had also accommodated themselves to the public provision of education and social and economic security. The liberal consensus of the post–World War II era extended considerably beyond the foundations of constitutionalism and democracy. It encompassed public education, most elements of the welfare state, progressive taxation of income and estates, Keynesian management of the business cycle, and the regulation of finance and such industries as communications where, it was generally agreed, unregulated markets suffered from endemic problems of inefficiency, inequity, or instability.

[...]

The conservative reaction began with a backlash against the liberalism of the 1960s but turned into a wholesale repudiation of the mid-twentieth-century liberal consensus. In domestic affairs, conservatives sought to undo the progressive taxation of incomes and estates; to privatize government services, including Social Security and schools; to deregulate markets, including finance, communications, and energy; and to reverse the framework of constitutional interpretation dating to the 1930s and covering such issues as federal powers and relations of church and state. In foreign policy, conservatives rejected liberal internationalism in favor of a unilateralist foreign policy with more emphasis on military force. In the collapse of the Soviet Union, conservatives saw a vindication of these policies, and in the aftermath of September 11, 2001, they saw grounds for renewing them. The collapse of Soviet communism and socialism generally also contributed to a triumphalist belief in free markets and the unrestrained exercise of American power. And the same triumphalist spirit encouraged some conservatives to bring the Cold War home in a war on liberalism.

[...]

Questions

1. According to Starr, what are the similarities and differences between "constitutional liberalism" and "modern democratic liberalism"?
2. How, on Starr's view, have modern liberals expanded the idea of freedom?

3. "As liberalism has evolved, so has conservatism—and the grounds of conflict between them have changed." Explain this statement.

Notes

1. In saying that liberals share political principles while disagreeing about their foundations, I mean only to bracket the foundational questions for purposes of defining liberalism. The idea that a liberal polity does not require comprehensive moral agreement is itself a particular position within liberalism, associated with John Rawls. See his *Political Liberalism*, expanded ed. (New York: Columbia University Press, 2005); and for discussion, see the essays in Shaun P. Young, ed., *Political*

Liberalism: Variations on a Theme (Albany: State University of New York Press, 2004).

2. My formulation of the first and third of these responsibilities reflects the influence of Ronald Dworkin's conception of two principles of human dignity—the principles of "personal responsibility" and of "intrinsic value." See Ronald Dworkin, Is Democracy Possible Here? *Principles for a New Political Debate* (Princeton, NJ: Princeton University Press, 2006), ch. 1.

Peter Self discusses socialism

[…]

Any account of modern socialist ideology has to come to terms with the legacy of Marxism, even though much (but by no means all) that Marx and Engels proclaimed in the second half of the last century has now to be discarded as false or no longer relevant.

[…]

Marxism did much to provide the emerging socialist parties of Western Europe with a general philosophy and a final goal in the shape of the 'common ownership of all means of production and distribution'. This goal could incorporate the various socialist beliefs in workers' co-operation and self-management without specifying clearly how a socialist society would actually operate. […]

Reproduced with permission from "Socialism," by Peter Self in *A Companion to Contemporary Political Philosophy*. Oxford: Blackwell Publishers Ltd, 1993, pp. 334–51.

Socialism, however, remained too diffuse and varied a creed to be confined within any one political doctrine or interpretation. British and still more American labour movements were unresponsive to the dogmatic and revolutionary elements in Marxism, preferring peaceful democratic evolution towards a vaguely defined goal. […]

The First World War and the Russian Revolution transformed socialism and created an enduring split between its communist and democratic forms.

[…]

Democratic socialism took a long while to recover from the frequent association of socialism with authoritarian communist regimes. Indeed, thanks to the critics of socialism, this disengagement is still not complete. Yet while communism deteriorated and eventually foundered on the rocks, democratic socialist parties managed gradually to win power in Scandinavia and Western Europe.

[…]

What remains distinctively socialist? Marxism remains relevent for its critique of capitalism but the economic fate of the communist states has given a sharp warning of the bureaucratic and other problems that are inherent in comprehensive state management of economic resources. The goal of 'public ownership of the means of production and distribution' was always for democratic Labour parties a final aspiration, and was only very partially and unsatisfactorily implemented when they gained power. Now it has largely dropped out of the vocabulary of party politics. This does not mean that this goal has become irrelevant, but that socialists must give it a more limited and acceptable meaning and relate it to other elements of a coherent philosophy.

At least the 1980s witnessed a revival of socialist thought. Democratic socialism has trod a long hard road, lessons have been learned (especially over the limits of Marxism and the fate of Communism) and its emerging philosophy is groping for a new synthesis of principles and their possible applications.

First we are now dealing with 'socialisms' (Wright, 1986). The rich heritage of socialist thought, submerged for a time by simple-minded panaceas, is being rediscovered. The idea that there are different possible forms of socialism, suitable for different times and places, is congruent with a new belief in freedom, diversity and experiment, but in itself would be thin and muddled were it not for a second return to traditional beliefs.

This is the rediscovery of 'ethical socialism', the belief that socialism must be founded upon and reflect the acceptable moral principles of a good society. Marxism had rejected and ridiculed this belief, despite drawing freely in practice on moral indignation about the evils of capitalism, but now it is the Marxist vision of a classless society—not the appeal to moral principles—which can be seen as utopian. Moral purpose is an essential ingredient of all successful causes, including the world religions.

Abstract moral principles are also inadequate. They must be capable of realization, which implies the need for an effective theory of social transformation. Socialists are still struggling to meet this need by developing theories of the economy, the state and social change, which draw on the socialist heritage but which recognize how much the world has changed from the one known to their predecessors. The remainder of this essay will outline

these efforts and some of the puzzles which they present.

Socialism has a more optimistic and positive view of human nature than does conservatism or liberalism. One guiding belief is in the equal moral worth of each individual. This idea reflects a long Christian and humanist tradition, notably expressed in the moral philosophy of Immanuel Kant ([1785] 1948). Kant held that every person should be treated as an end in him or herself [...].

The belief in 'equal moral worth', 'equal moral capacity' and consequently 'equal entitlement to consideration' is not, of course, confined to socialists. The difference is that socialists take its implications seriously. Conservatives accept a hierarchical order of privilege or talent. Liberals accept the gross inequalities of the market system. Socialism is nothing if it does not struggle to carry the implications of 'equal worth' into the social and economic realms.

[...]

What then is the socialist goal? One approach is to start with a strong presumption in favour of equality, and to insist upon cogent reasons being given for treating individuals differentially. The problem is that defenders of inequality can give reasons for their position, even for a system such as apartheid. Thus one must further require that the reasons are acceptable moral ones which recognize that most basic individual wants and aspirations are common to all (Rees, 1971, pp. 91–125). But this is no more than to return to the socialist's starting point; either the factor of our common humanity is seen or it is not. One cannot make the blind see.

For practical purposes the socialist has an answer to these problems. Economic inequalities are so enormous in the modern capitalist world that substantial progress over reducing them should be practicable without running into the sands of detailed judgements about differential claims. In allegedly affluent countries, such as the United States or the United Kingdom, the top 10 per cent command over nine times the income (even after tax) of the bottom group, and completely dominate the ownership of wealth. Increasing numbers of millionaires or billionaires coexist with a sixth of the population living below the official poverty line (for a survey, see Hoover and Plant, 1989). The contrast between rich and poor countries is still more glaring with two-thirds of the world still locked in hunger (and increasingly so in many countries), while the affluent are titillated with ever more sophisticated—and often environmentally destructive—consumer goods (Harrington, 1989, ch. 6). Thus the pursuit of equality can be seen as essentially an onslaught upon gross inequalities which contradict the very idea of the dignity and worth of the individual.

[...]

Restrictive coercions upon individual freedom will always exist and come variously from the state, the economic system and, as J. S. Mill stressed, the sanctions of public opinion, but these sources can also provide beneficent opportunities. The critical questions are how to trade off the diverse pattern of restrictions and opportunities which surround the individual. Libertarians insist on regarding the state as the sole agent of coercion, and it is true enough that the state has a unique power of direct coercion which has produced the worst tyrannies. Vigilance against excessive state power is as necessary for a socialist as anyone else. Yet it is surely perverse to ignore the enormous indirect power of the capitalist system over individual lives and opportunities, exercised with the necessary support of the state over the making and enforcement of laws of property and contract, and supported by the substantial political influence of wealth.

[...]

Thus it is natural for socialists to bring in the state, not only to combat gross inequalities but to diffuse and modify economic power and to enlarge the opportunities open to individuals, more particularly the poor and disadvantaged. Free men and women cannot accept the Hayekian thesis that an admittedly amoral (or immoral) economic system must not be interfered with because of the latent danger of an unacceptable degree of state coercion. That is an appeal to Hobbesian fears, not this time of anarchy but of its opposite. In considering the balances of coercion and freedom one has to ask the old question: is the rich man more restricted by having to pay a high tax rate or the poor family by being unable to keep their children healthy or send them to a decent school?

T. H. Green, a liberal before the great split between liberals who believed in welfare (and often became socialists) and those who stuck with *laissez-faire*, described the role of the state as 'removing obstacles to the good life' (Green, 1890). Ethical socialism has an Aristotelian belief in the promotion of individual capacities for self-development and personal fulfilment. There is a difference here from the agnostic liberal view that the 'good life' is a wholly subjective matter of personal opinion and choice (Dworkin, 1978), or that alternatively, as Bentham put it 'quantity of pleasure being equal, pushpin is as good as poetry'.

The belief of earlier socialists in the great value of education and cultural development generally, exemplified by such bodies as the Workers' Educational Association, seems to have faded away in the modern world of the mass media and capitalist 'bread and circuses', yet this belief in the capacity of individuals to pursue 'higher goals', according to their special capacities and tastes, still needs to remain basic to socialist goals. It is a necessary condition of responsible citizenship, without which a socialist world can never be democratically created. It extends not only to the enrichment of leisure, but to the transformation of the work system so that William Morris's ideal of 'honourable and fitting work' for all in 'decent surroundings' should become a possibility, not (as in the capitalist society) an irrelevance. Within this context, monopoly ownership and trivialization of the mass media, and the perversion of education to meet solely market demands not personal development, are especially offensive to socialists.

[...]

Socialism is basically about human welfare. Socialists have always wanted to put 'first things first', to attend to the basic requirements of a good or at least decent life for all before satisfying the luxuries of the affluent. Today this concern necessarily extends (in view of environmental crises) to the basic needs of future generations and to the general quality of life for all (the affluent included). Moreover *democratic* socialism is dedicated to the promotion of individual autonomy and responsible participation in social and political life. Socialism seeks to broaden the political concepts of both social welfare and democratic procedures.

[...]

[B]ureaucracy represents a formidable challenge for socialism. The dangers of 'technocracy' are now widely understood and feared, not least by many socialists.

However if socialism is to strive for a society which places much more stress upon basic needs and less upon profit-making, and which enlists technology positively to overcome pressing environmental dangers and to design a more creative system of work, skilled advice and support has to be assembled for these purposes and given the encouragement to produce fertile ideas. [...] [T]he dehumanizing secrecy of bureaucratic opinion needs to be ended, and open, creative debate encouraged among official experts and advisers, while leaving final decisions to the politicians. Conversely, impartiality and incorruptibility are more necessary than ever in the actual administration of the laws, given the many obstructions and financial temptations which capitalist institutions can use to block socialist reforms. However much decentralization is introduced, the revival of a distinctive sense of public service and the 'public interest' is an essential step forward for democratic socialism.

[...]

The 'responsible citizen' that socialism needs is far removed from the apathetic individual absorbed in private consumption and pleasure who is so willingly tolerated and indeed preferred by dominant interests in Western societies; he or she is a long way too from the calculating egoist assumed and even admired by much liberal thought. The responsible citizen actually takes politics seriously and has social ideals. Socialists therefore have to give priority, not just afterthoughts, to educational goals and to the reform of the media so as to achieve greater diversity of opinion, more and more reliable information and fuller treatment of social issues.

[...]

Questions

1. According to Self, what is the essence of socialism? What does he mean when he says that socialism wants to put "first things first"?
2. Why is bureaucracy a "formidable challenge" for socialism? How does Self think the challenge needs to be met?
3. What kind of citizen does socialism aspire to? How would such a citizen differ from the kind we would find in, say, the United States today? What would socialism do to create that kind of citizen?

References

Dworkin, R.: 'Liberalism', in *Public and Private Morality*, ed. S. Hampshire (Cambridge: Cambridge University Press, 1978).

Green, T. H.: *Lectures on the Principles of Political Obligation* (1879); reprinted in *Collected Works*, ed. R. Nettleship (London: Longmans Green, 1890), vol. 2.

Harrington, M.: *Socialism Past and Future* (New York: Arcade Publishing, 1989).

Hoover, K. and Plant, R.: *Conservative Capitalism in Britain and the US* (London: Routledge, 1989).

Kant, I.: *The Moral Law* (1785); ed. H. J. Paton (London: Hutchinson, 1948).

Rees, J.: *Equality* (London: Macmillan, 1971).

Wright, A.: *Socialisms: Theories and Practices* (Oxford: Oxford University Press, 1986).

Part IV

World Poverty

_____

10

World Poverty
Fiction

The River

It wasn't a life most Westerners would have tolerated, let alone embraced.

Rennert was living in the African country of Ajapa, one of the "LDCs," or "least developed countries," according to the developmental jargon, though "god-forsaken" would have been a better label. Ajapa was a sub-Saharan hell-hole, ranked at the bottom in almost every quality-of-life indicator; it excelled only in disease, corruption and cruelty.

Rennert was the sole resident of a small hydrologic station situated at the edge of a river that separated Ajapa from the country of Sungura. The river was so turbulent it could be crossed only by powerboats like his own. Around him was nothing but thick forest, forest that turned to jungle farther downstream.

Rennert rarely saw people, and then almost always on the river. He might see a soldier staring out from a noisy patrol boat, or glimpse others, moving more quietly—smugglers, he'd been told. The faces, when he could make them out, seemed passive, incurious.

In the beginning Rennert had wondered about his own safety. He needn't have worried. He was a small part of a large aid package lining the pockets of the thugs who ran Ajapa. Attacking him might jeopardize too much. Apparently the word was out that he was to be left alone. And he was.

His solitude was almost total. Still, Rennert had taken to it with a bitter passion, caressing it the way a suicide might caress a silken rope he had just slipped over his neck. Being here was a kind of self-imposed death. Though a comfortable one. He had once been a part of the world. He wanted no more of it.

Not the human world—at least, not the present one. He loved the beauty of the river and the forest. He loved the beauty of the books and music he lived in at night. He ate well. Food supplies were delivered by land every four months, supplies he supplemented with local fruit and fish. He always had plenty of alcohol.

This hydrologic station was called "scientific," though what he was doing was more technician's work, taking tedious measurements of the river. Those who'd interviewed him had told him he was over-qualified. Yet the real qualification was being able to stand the loneliness. In the end, they'd realized, he was perfect for the job.

He'd been different once—young and absurdly idealistic. He remembered dreaming of how science might help the hungry people of the world. And it could help—creating genetically altered high-yield crops that could feed the poor. But science, if paid well enough by business, could develop a gene to make the seeds of those crops sterile, forcing the poor to keep buying seeds at prices they could hardly afford.

And even science could do nothing about the Western politicians who put up trade barriers to keep the crops grown by those desperate people from being sold in Europe and the United States. Science could do nothing about the world financial agencies that

Contemporary Moral and Social Issues: An Introduction through Original Fiction, Discussion, and Readings, First Edition. Thomas D. Davis.
© 2014 John Wiley & Sons, Inc. Published 2014 by John Wiley & Sons, Inc.

gave aid only to projects that would pay back Western loans and favor Western agribusiness—all while the poor continued to go hungry.

He'd had enough of all that. Enough of believing.

He'd wanted this place as an escape. He later realized he'd sought it as a punishment as well, punishment meted out by that part of himself that condemned him for running away. He'd managed the escape, but not much of the punishment: He'd taken to this life only too well.

Three times a year Bjornson, his immediate supervisor, paid him a visit to deliver supplies. At first Rennert had been starved for company and conversation. He'd kept Bjornson up most of the night, plying him with drinks, coaxing him for news of everything. But now, though Rennert tried to be a good host, he could hardly wait for Bjornson's visits to be over. It was a kind of madness, he supposed, this love of loneliness. He'd made a life out of his solitary routine—days of mindless technical work in the midst of this natural splendor, nights lost in books and music. He could no longer imagine any other kind of life for himself. He had no doubt that when he had to leave here he would take his small pension and find some other place, equally remote, in which to duplicate this life.

★★★★★

He was more curious than startled when he glimpsed the two figures on the far bank of the river. They posed no threat, not even a potential imposition. The river was at least fifty meters wide, the water too dangerous to swim across. Anyway it was only a woman and a boy. They were sitting on a grassy stretch of bank above the rocks.

He'd been on that stretch of bank once or twice. At first he'd thought it an island, with its rounded shape, set farther into the river than the rest of the bank. In fact, it was a small peninsula, attached to the main bank by a narrow strip of land, like a child's balloon straining to float away.

Bjornson had told him it was a sacred place, that there'd once been a temple there. Now the place looked barren: If there were any artifacts left, it would take an anthropologist's eyes and tools to find them.

The Anansi, who'd once worshiped there, had been decimated by the Sunguran majority in one of those paroxysms of ethnic cleansing the human race was given to, especially among peoples whose countries had been invented for them by others during periods of imperialism or in the aftermath of war. The Anansi who were still alive lived in Sungura as virtual slaves. For years the United Nations—as well as private organizations like Amnesty International and Human Rights Watch—had protested their plight, but the Sungura had oil—lots of oil. No one in the West wanted to cede the oil to Russia or China by pushing human rights too hard.

It was mid-morning when Rennert had first noticed the woman and child on the far bank; it was now noon and they were still there. It was a bit unnerving the way they sat so still, making no sound, their faces toward him as if they were staring. He didn't know if they were staring—their faces were too vague at this distance to be sure. It would have been natural enough for them to stare: He and his station were the only logical thing to look at.

However, there had been no waving or other gestures; they just sat. What were they waiting for? A boat, perhaps?

Whatever they were doing, he wasn't going to get involved. He forced himself to ignore them and focus on his work. But in the mid-afternoon something must have caught his attention—a movement, a voice—because he looked across the river and a third person was there—a man. The boy's father, perhaps?

The man showed none of the passivity of the woman and the boy. He talked animatedly, pointed toward Rennert's station, then seemingly beyond. The man paced the bank for a minute or two, said something to the woman, climbed down onto the rocks and then dove into the water.

"You fool," said Rennert softly, disbelieving. As Rennert knew would happen, the man took a few strokes, began to be pulled downstream, then stroked harder, to no avail. The man gave a cry, disappeared under the water, emerged briefly thirty meters downstream, then disappeared again.

Rennert knew it was already too late to help. But some sense of decency—along with the feeling that the woman and child were watching him—made him run to his boat, start it up, and head off in a token rescue mission.

As he'd expected, he found no sign of the man— even after exploring a kilometer downstream. As he headed back, he saw the woman and child still sitting in the same spot, the woman now hugging the boy.

Without quite making a decision, Rennert turned his boat toward the bank where the woman and child were. He did have the presence to look beyond them as he approached, to make sure there weren't others who might pose a danger to him. He could see they were alone.

The woman looked vaguely apprehensive as Rennert climbed the bank toward her. But she remained where she was, her arms around the boy.

Communication would have been impossible if Rennert had been without language and context. However, he'd taken a crash course in Swahili before coming to Africa—little dreaming how few conversations he'd have with any Africans—and he knew enough of the language to muddle through a rudimentary conversation. From Bjornson he knew the general background of the situation with the Anansi and Sungurans.

Even so it took him close to an hour to get some sense of their situation. Apparently there'd been another wave of Sunguran violence against the Anansi. Rennert knew he'd be aware of those events if he'd bothered listening to the BBC news on his radio. But over the last year he'd found himself taking less and less interest in what was going on in the larger world.

The woman told him she and the child had managed to escape and come here to the nearest sacred Anansi site. She seemed to think that the Sungurans wouldn't dare follow them here. Rennert didn't know if she was right, but it made some sense. Many polytheists conceded some reality and power to their enemies' gods.

Rennert asked how the two of them were planning to live here on this barren peninsula. The woman had given a shrug. Perhaps the two of them would die, she said. But that was better than being hacked to death by Sunguran machetes.

There was nothing dramatic in the way the woman expressed this. But Rennert felt the drama. Were these two really going to sit here and slowly starve to death while he worked his trivial chores on the far bank?

Rennert asked about the man who'd jumped in the river. The woman only knew he'd been another Anansi trying to escape. The man had told the woman there was a United Nations refugee camp across the river, two days' walk. He'd been determined to swim to the other shore and try to reach the camp.

Rennert knew vaguely about the camp, just across the border in Esana. He was sure there were no roads in that direction from his outpost. He asked if she and the boy could make it to the camp if he took them across the river. The woman said they would try.

Her reply made his decision easy. A boat ride, two guests for the evening, a few provisions from his store—and life would be back to normal. There was little imposition in that. Anyway, the alternative was too terrible to think about.

It turned out the woman and the boy didn't even wait until the next day. They wanted to be on their way. A few provisions and they disappeared into the forest.

Rennert found himself strangely restless that night—he, who usually had no trouble sleeping. He couldn't imagine he was worried about the woman and the boy, though he wished them well: In spite of the brief contact he'd had with them, they were still strangers in the most profound sense. He certainly wasn't congratulating himself on what he had done— it had been little more than a reflex. If he had saved their lives, it had been as much to avoid his own discomfort at watching them die. What he finally realized was bothering him was the deep sense of having been intruded on—not by the woman and child per se—but something else—human contact. No, *human need*—that was it. He didn't want to have anyone need him.

Well, it's over, he told himself. He could get back to his life.

*****

Except it wasn't over. At noon the next day more people appeared on the far bank. There seemed to be at least eight of them, including a couple of men. His first thought was that these people knew Rennert had helped the woman and child. But that made no sense. No one had been around the other day, and the woman and child were now far away in the opposite direction. It must simply be that other Anansi— assuming they were Anansi—were making the same decision the woman had made—preferring death by starvation in an ancient religious site to being hacked to death by the Sungurans.

It didn't matter, he decided. He wasn't going to do any more—wasn't going to get involved in this. Besides, the woman and child had obviously posed no

threat. This time there were males in the group and
who knew how aggressive they might get? It would
be very tempting for desperate people to kill Rennert
and steal his stores of food. Rennert had a handgun
and knew how to use it, but he'd never shot at a
human being; anyway, he could hardly help people
while holding a gun on them.

He went about his normal routine, forcing his mind
to focus on the tasks at hand rather than on those
people across the river. However, an occasional glance
was an all-but-unstoppable reflex. Sometimes he
would see one or two of them looking in his direction.
But they never yelled or even gestured. Still, it was hard
not to feel as if their eyes were on him. In his dreams
that night he seemed to hear them crying for help.

The next morning, the group on the far bank
seemed to have grown. Rennert called Bjornson for
news. What the Anansi woman had told Rennert was
correct. News agencies were reporting more genocide in Sungura. There were the usual protests, the
usual overtures from the UN. So far there'd been
nothing but denials from the Sunguran government.

Rennert told Bjornson about the woman and child
and the new group of refugees on the peninsula. He
asked Bjornson to see if some agency would provide
boats to get the Anansi across the river and perhaps
trucks to take them to the refugee camp. Bjornson
said he would.

When Rennert went outside again, he wished he
could tell the people across the river he was trying to
get help for them. But he wasn't going to go near that
bank. Anyway he knew the urge to tell them was
mostly a sop to his own self-consciousness. He had no
positive news for them; he wasn't sure that any would
be forthcoming. But it was hard to seem to be ignoring them completely, as if he had no conscience at all.

That day and the next he tried to go about his
normal routine, though he found himself staying
inside more, away from the view of the Anansi; he was
starting his "evenings" of books and music in the
mid-afternoon. He called Bjornson again, but the
man had nothing new to tell him.

At noon the following day Rennert heard a woman's wrenching cry. He jerked his head up and looked
across the river. A woman was cradling a child, while
others gathered around her, making agitated sounds.
Was the child dead? Dying?

It was the children who had always gotten to
Rennert. The adults, no matter how desperate their
lives and limited their options, had always had *some*
choices. But not the children.

Oh hell, he thought. *Hell.*

Rennert ran into the station, grabbed cans of
condensed milk and put them in a satchel, slipped his
gun into his belt, then raced back outside and took off
in the boat. He slowed the boat as he approached the
far bank, making sure there weren't other Anansi he
hadn't noticed. But there were only the fifteen or so
he'd estimated with his last count—four men, maybe
six women, and the rest children ranging in age from
perhaps ten to two. It was the youngest child that the
woman was cradling.

The men got to their feet as the boat reached their
shore. They didn't seem to be armed, and up close
they didn't seem threatening, just uncertain. Still,
Rennert warned himself he needed to be on guard.

He called out "Maiziwa"—what he knew to be the
general Swahili word for milk—hoping it covered
the canned stuff he had with him. He maneuvered the
boat to a safe spot between two rocks, tied it up, and
got out with his satchel. He climbed the rocks
carefully keeping his eyes on the Anansi. They, in turn,
backed away, keeping their eyes on him. Their eyes
seemed to take in the gun at his belt.

Rennert put down the satchel, removed the cans
and opened several, then backed away, repeating
"Maiziwa" again. It was the women who came, taking
the cans and rushing them over to the children.
Rennert noticed, to his relief, that the very small child
the woman had been cradling wasn't dead, though it
did look ill.

Once the milk was consumed, Rennert struggled
through another conversation in Swahili, made more
complicated this time by too many Anansi trying to
talk too fast. Still he finally seemed to get his information across. He told them he'd asked for help from the
UN but had to admit he wasn't sure when, or even if,
it would be coming. He told them about the UN
camp in Esana, a difficult two days' walk from his side
of the river. He told them he could spare them a few
days' worth of provisions and could take them across
the river if they wanted to try for the camp.

After holding a conference, the Anansi decided to
try for the camp. Rennert ferried them across the

river in three trips, keeping each group to an unthreatening number, making sure never to completely turn his back on the men. The operation went without a hitch.

Unlike the woman and child, these Anansi decided to camp near the station for the night, eating and preparing food to take with them. Rennert gave them rice and beans to cook and some cans of vegetable stew. That night, alone in the station, Rennert carefully locked the windows and bolted the doors. He felt vaguely guilty about this, but you never knew. By eight the next morning, his visitors were gone.

By eight the following morning, more Anansi had appeared.

★★★★★

Rennert was yelling into the phone.

"Damn it, Bjornson, somebody's got to do something!"

"Calm down. People are trying. You know the logistics of these things are never easy. The politics are even worse."

Bjornson had contacted the appropriate UN agencies, but it turned out that what had seemed a simple operation wasn't so simple after all. The boats, the food and the trucks could be managed—though just how soon was still a question. But the Esana refugee camp was already dangerously overcrowded; it wasn't clear where the refugees could be taken. Setting up an another camp could be a complicated process. The Sunguran government was still denying the situation and certainly wouldn't allow any "rescue operations" for a situation they claimed didn't exist. The Ajapan government was worried about cooperating in anything that would embarrass their larger and more powerful neighbor.

"Somebody's got to do something," said Rennert.

"I'm sure they will," said Bjornson. "You just have to be patient. Meanwhile, stay out of it. What you're doing could be dangerous. Leave it to the people whose job it is to help. You just stick to your own job."

Rennert wanted to stay out of it—he hated being thrust into this situation—but after a half-hearted attempt to do what Bjornson had told him, he knew he couldn't let it alone.

He told himself to approach the situation rationally. He went down to the store room and assessed his provisions. Fortunately, Bjornson had always brought much more than Rennert actually needed—mostly as insurance against any delivery delays in the future. Rennert calculated what supplies he needed for his own safety and comfort over the next few months and set aside what was left over. With those extras, he could afford to help the Anansi for a couple more days—assuming their numbers stayed about the same.

He needed to do at least the minimum required by his job. He owed it to his employers and, anyway, he didn't want to jeopardize his position here. But mornings should take care of that in the short-term. He didn't see any reason he should have to give up his evenings: He lived for his dinners, his books and music; in any case, trying to do rescue work in the dark would be too tricky.

That would leave him several hours each afternoon he could spend helping the Anansi. How many more could be coming, after all? Either outside pressure would ease the situation in Sungura—and there'd be no need for the remaining Anansi to escape—or the slaughter would run its course and there wouldn't be that many left to escape. It was unlikely that the pressures on Rennert could last that much longer.

He spent the next two afternoons transporting Anansi across the river, giving them provisions, and sending them on their way to the camp. Once two Anansi men who'd just arrived on the peninsula became pushy, insisting that they be taken in the next boatload. Fortunately the other Anansi managed to resolve the situation and the men grudgingly backed off. But the incident reminded Rennert once again that he'd better be alert. He told himself if anything like it happened again, he'd stop trying to help. He needed to protect himself. Still, he could sense he was looking for some excuse to stop and so refused to rest his case on that one incident.

On the following two days the arrival of Anansi seemed to increase. He couldn't understand it. Why weren't the Sungurans preventing this small exodus? Even if the Sungurans didn't dare intrude on the holy site of an Anansi god, it would have been an easy matter to block access to the peninsula. Could the Sungurans be easing up due to international pressure and the Anansi didn't know it yet? Or were the Sungurans focusing on other sites where larger numbers of Anansi might be escaping? Rennert didn't know and nothing the Anansi were able to tell him answered the puzzle.

He kept calling Bjornson, pleading for help. He felt himself getting angrier and angrier as nothing got done. He was feeling bad for the Anansi, but for himself, too, he knew. He hated this—the loss of his solitude and routine and some of his comfort—but more than that he hated being confronted with so much need, feeling so much responsibility. He wanted to go back to his old life.

He was now starting his trips in mid-morning. He worried about the supplies, cutting the rations he gave each Anansi. He kept revisiting his own stores, taking out a little extra here and there, deciding he would do with less for himself. As for his evenings, those were becoming things of the past. He was so exhausted by nightfall that he fixed the simplest meal his energy allowed, and either fell asleep quickly over a book or dispensed with the reading altogether.

★★★★★

The phone call from Bjornson came while he was asleep. Rennert tried to clear his head. He couldn't believe the clock read ten AM. How had he slept so long? Rennert realized he wasn't feeling well: He was exhausted and maybe running a fever.

Rennert tried to focus on what Bjornson was saying, but he was still too sleepy. Then something caught his attention and he felt adrenaline kicking in.

"Wait a minute," said Rennert. "You're telling me they're going to let them die?"

"That's not what I'm saying," said Bjornson. "People are doing what they can. They're trying to keep up the pressure on Sungura. There are some indications that the killing has decreased."

"But they're not sending boats or trucks?"

"I told you the UN can't do anything without the permission of the Ajapans and the Ajapans still won't give it. Ajapa is afraid of Sungura. And, truth be told, Ajapa has done some ethnic cleansing of its own: I'm sure they're not that anxious to bring the whole issue into the open."

"But the Anansi: We can't just let them die."

"Look, I'm sorry, Rennert. I know the situation's hell, but you've got to get some perspective. You know Africa: It keeps on making its own hell."

"The Anansi didn't make this situation."

"Maybe not this one," said Bjornson. "But don't be naive. Victims always look innocent until they're back on top: Then they turn out to be as nasty as everyone else. The Anansi have had their own violent history. They're not innocent. The oppressed are just oppressors down on their luck."

"Cynicism's too easy an excuse for not helping."

"You really think you're helping?" said Bjornson, his voice angry now. "I was talking to the UN people the other day. The camp at Esana is dangerously overcrowded: If they have to handle any more refugees, it's going to make the situation worse."

"But they did take in the Anansi I helped. You told me they did."

"That's right: They did. But they might not be able to squeeze in the next group or the one after that. Even if they do, it will just screw up things for the refugees who are already there. And the UN people told me something else: The area the Anansi have to cross is inhabited by violent tribes. The Anansi are just as likely to get killed or enslaved as to make it to the camp."

"But you told me some Anansi got through. That's better than all of them dying."

"Not much," said Bjornson. "Anyway, there's another thing. What you've done so far is too small to attract attention. But if the Ajapans learn what you're doing, we'll have to pull you out of there. We can't afford to let you jeopardize the project—not just the hydrologic work—that's minor—but all the work we're doing to fight hunger and disease. We've got to pick our battles, and this is one we're going to lose. You've got to stop helping, Rennert."

"I think this whole thing stinks."

"Yeah, well, welcome to the real world."

Depressed, Rennert went back to sleep. When he woke it was evening. He felt disoriented and a little light-headed. He fixed himself a meal, but discovered he didn't have the appetite for it. He tried to read, but had trouble concentrating. He dozed a little, but fitfully. He paced some, but mostly he just sat, staring at nothing.

He was grateful for the sign of first light, but when he stepped outside, the first thing he saw was the group of Anansi across the river. They would have arrived yesterday, while he had confined himself to the house.

Rennert knew he must ignore them now. He spent the morning trying to catch up on his work, picking only the simplest tasks since he knew his mind wasn't functioning well.

He had trouble focusing on his work. His mind was crammed with images of Anansi filling up the far bank, images confirmed by the occasional glances he couldn't resist.

He thought he heard a child's cry. He glanced across the river but the best he could tell, the cry had come from his own mind. When it came again, and later again, he knew it was only his imagination. But he sensed the cry wasn't going to stop.

He let out a long sigh and began walking to his boat. He knew he had to try to do what he could, for as long as he could. Maybe the situation was hopeless, maybe most of his efforts would be wasted. But all that seemed an abstraction compared to the desperate people he could see across the river. He had to try to help these people. Really, he had no choice.

Questions

1. Rennert lives in relative isolation at the hydrologic station of Ajapa because he feels disillusioned with the world. What are the particular reasons for his disillusionment?

2. What is the status of the Anansi people in the country of Sungura? Why are the Anansi refugees apparently safe from attack on the peninsula across the river? What will likely happen to them if they stay where they are?

3. Why is the UN unable to help the Anansi cross the river and settle in a refugee camp? What are the problems Rennert faces in trying to help the Anansi himself?

4. What is Bjornson's advice to Rennert? Why doesn't Rennert take that advice? Do you agree with Rennert's decision?

5. What might you have done in Rennert's place?

11

World Poverty
Discussion

The River

In "The River," a man, Rennert, who is disillusioned with the West, has isolated himself in a small hydrologic station on a river in the sub-Saharan country of Ajapa. He lives and works alone at the station, taking measurements of the river by day, and immersing himself in books and music at night. He sees his supervisor, Bjornson, once every three months when the man brings supplies; the only Africans he sees are figures passing in boats on the river, soldiers or smugglers.

Rennert's disillusionment with the West reflects familiar criticisms of Western aid efforts:

> He'd been different once—young and absurdly idealistic. He remembered dreaming of how science might help the hungry people of the world. And it could help—creating genetically altered high-yield crops that could feed the poor. But science, if paid well enough by business, could develop a gene to make the seeds of those crops sterile, forcing the poor to keep buying seeds at prices they could hardly afford.
>
> And even science could do nothing about the Western politicians who put up trade barriers to keep the crops grown by those desperate people from being sold in Europe and the United States. Science could do nothing about the world financial agencies that gave aid only to projects that would pay back Western loans and favor Western agribusiness—all while the poor continued to go hungry.

It isn't only the West that comes in for criticism. The hydrologic station is part of an aid package "lining the pockets of the thugs who ran Ajapa," a country that excels "only in disease, corruption and cruelty." Across the river is the country of Sungura, which has engaged in ethnic cleansing of a minority group, the Anansi.

> The Anansi who were still alive lived in Sungura as virtual slaves. For years the United Nations—as well as private organizations like Amnesty International and Human Rights Watch—had protested their plight, but the Sungura had oil—lots of oil. No one in the West wanted to cede the oil to Russia or China by pushing human rights too hard.

Anansi appear on a small peninsula across the river, fleeing a surge of Sunguran violence. Since the peninsula is a sacred site, the Anansi are safe from attack there; however they will starve unless they are helped across the river, which is too treacherous for swimming.

Rennert begins taking small groups of Anansi across the river, giving them a few provisions, and sending them on toward a UN refugee camp in Esana, a two-day walk from there. Rennert becomes exhausted from helping and hates the disruption of his life. However his ordeal should soon be over. Bjornson has promised to try to get the UN and other agencies to help the refugees.

Contemporary Moral and Social Issues: An Introduction through Original Fiction, Discussion, and Readings, First Edition. Thomas D. Davis.
© 2014 John Wiley & Sons, Inc. Published 2014 by John Wiley & Sons, Inc.

Bjornson's subsequent reports aren't hopeful. Sungura is denying the charge of ethnic cleansing. Ajapa is afraid of antagonizing its more powerful neighbor by enabling the UN to mount a rescue effort from its side of the river. International agencies are trying to put political pressure on Sungura but so far it's done little good. Another problem is that the refugee camp at Esana is dangerously overcrowded and can't handle many more refugees.

Finally Bjornson tells Rennert that help won't be coming. Sungura and Ajapa won't cooperate with the proposed UN efforts. It's a terrible situation, but Rennert has to accept it. He must stop trying to help. The UN camp in Esana simply can't take more people. The UN people have told Bjornson the area the Anansi must travel through to get to the camp is inhabited by violent tribes likely to kill or enslave any Anansi they catch. It's true that a few Anansi have gotten through and have been taken in at the camp, but it's likely that anything else Rennert does will be for nothing.

When Rennert expresses his despair, Bjornson tells him that's the way Africa is. Anyway, Rennert has no real choice. To date Rennert's efforts have been too little to attract much attention, but if the Ajapan government notices and protests, Bjornson will have to pull Rennert out of there to avoid jeopardizing the whole aid package.

Depressed and exhausted, Rennert sleeps around the clock. When he gets up and goes outside, he sees the peninsula teeming with Anansi. He tells himself he can't do any more and must focus on his work. But even as he avoids looking across the river, he feels the weight of their distress.

Toward evening, he sighs and heads for his boat.

> He knew he had to try to do what he could, for as long as he could. Maybe the situation was hopeless, maybe most of his efforts would be wasted. But all that seemed an abstraction compared to the desperate people he could see across the river. He had to try to help these people. Really, he had no choice.

"The River" touches on the plight of the world's poor and oppressed, along with the practical and political difficulties of helping them. Sungura is unwilling to admit what it is doing to the Anansi, let alone cooperate in their rescue. Sungura seems to be exempt from serious international pressure because it has oil everyone wants. Ajapa refuses to assist in a rescue from its side of the river because it is afraid of Sungura. Rennert's attempt to help some Anansi get to an UN camp is threatened by the fact that the camp is so overcrowded it can't handle more refugees. Also the territory the Anansi must get through to get to the camp is inhabited by people who will try to kill or enslave the them. Then there is Bjornson's cynical take as well:

> "Look, I'm sorry, Rennert. I know the situation's hell, but you've got to get some perspective. You know Africa: It keeps on making its own hell."
>
> "The Anansi didn't make this situation."
>
> "Maybe not this one," said Bjornson. "But don't be naive. Victims always look innocent until they're back on top: Then they turn out to be as nasty as everyone else. The Anansi have had their own violent history. They're not innocent. The oppressed are just oppressors down on their luck."

In Rennert we see the predicament of the person who is confronted with the suffering of the world's poor and oppressed, the person who feels responsible for doing something in spite of the obstacles and in spite of the fact that others are doing so little. What is required of him morally, if anything? Should he ruin his own life to do what little he can? Or does it make more sense to try to ignore the suffering and go on with his life?

We will go into these moral dilemmas later in the chapter. First let's discuss basic facts about global poverty, review various aid efforts, and discuss debates about what, if anything, aid programs are successfully doing to reduce poverty and relieve suffering.

Facts and factual issues

World poverty: basic facts

It is customary to distinguish between absolute poverty and relative poverty. The poorest of the poor in the United States may be suffering relative to the rest of the country, but they can get enough food to survive, have or can find shelter, are sufficiently clothed against the weather, and can get emergency medical treatment: Even this much makes them much better off than those in other parts of the world who are in absolute poverty—those whose minimal needs for food, shelter and clothing are not met.

Absolute poverty is divided into "poverty" and "extreme poverty." In this chapter we will focus primarily on extreme poverty, that is, the poorest people (often in the poorest countries) in the world, people who can't afford the minimum necessities, including food that will supply a minimum calorie requirement.

Extreme poverty can be described in a number of ways, but the best known is the dollar-a-day standard set by the World Bank in a 1990 report. Extreme poverty was defined as living on $1 a day or less—$1 a day being the amount of money that would buy a person the minimum needed for bare survival.

The dollar-a-day standard is not quite as simple as it seems. A "dollar a day" refers to what could have been purchased *in* the US in 1985 for $1. (Remember, the standard was first set in 1990). The dollar-a-day standard always has to be translated into the 1985 equivalent—what is called "purchasing power parity" or "PPP." Adjusting for inflation, the dollar-a-day equivalent in 2005 would have been $1.45.

Until recently, the most frequently repeated statistic regarding global poverty was that 1 billion people lived on less than a dollar a day.

However, in 2008, the World Bank revised its poverty standards. Researchers felt that the current dollar-a-day equivalent of $1.45 was a little too high to capture the original intention of the standard, which was to designate the poorest of the poor. The researchers wanted a standard that would translate into poverty so dire that no one would doubt it was true poverty.

The new line for extreme poverty was set according to the mean of the national poverty lines for the 15 poorest nations. (These national poverty lines are set in consultation with the World Bank.) The mean of those poverty lines—and hence the new worldwide standard for extreme poverty—is $1.25 a day or less.

At the same time, the World Bank updated its worldwide surveys of households and found that it had underestimated living costs in certain regions, including China. According to this new research, 1.4 billion people live on less than $1.25 a day and so count as suffering "extreme poverty." This is just under a fourth of the world's population.

Using the new World Bank standard, the numbers of extreme poor have fallen from 1.9 billion in 1981 to the current figure of 1.4 billion. (Whether or not this decrease had much to do with aid is a matter we will take up later.)

It's important to note that these monetary definitions of poverty, while convenient for compiling global numbers and making international comparisons, capture at most very limited dimensions of poverty. In addition to a lack of basic food, clothing and shelter, other aspects of poverty include a greater threat of preventable illness, a lack of sanitation and clean drinking water, and a lack of health care, including care for pregnant women and for infants.

Global-development researchers tend to divide countries into three categories: "developed," referring to the richer, industrialized nations; "developing," referring to nations with expanding economies; and, "underdeveloped," referring to nations that are poor and lack large-scale industry and technology. A subset of the underdeveloped countries are the "least developed countries" or "LDCs," of which our fictional country of Ajapa is one. LDCs are almost totally lacking in infrastructure, industry and technology.

You will hear different terms meant to contrast the developed countries with all the others: "the Core" versus "the Periphery"; "the North" versus "the South" (not very accurate, but many of the poorest countries do tend to be in warmer regions of the globe); and "the West" versus "the Rest" (the "West" would have to include Japan here to make any sort of sense). These references tend to be more catchy than accurate, but are okay if you read in the proper qualifications. (Where necessary, as in the story, we will use "the West" as shorthand for the developed nations.)

In the next section we'll talk about the history of foreign aid given by developed countries, including the US, but first some cautions are in order.

It is important to recognize that there are different kinds of foreign aid. There is country-to-country aid; there is aid given by international organizations like the UN and the World Bank to which wealthier countries contribute; and there is aid delivered by non-governmental organizations (NGOs) like Save the Children to which foundations, individuals, and sometimes governments contribute.

Aid might be in the form of money, food, or technological aid. It might be intended to promote a country's overall development, say, infrastructure, or it might be earmarked for specific interventions, such as vaccinations. The aid might come with conditions, such as requiring that the recipient purchase goods, or use consultants, from the donor country, or it might not. It might be emergency relief for famine or some natural disaster—or it might be for the longer term.

In talking about aid numbers and aid effectiveness, it will be important to distinguish the various types of aid, rather than lumping them all together.

As has often been noted, people in the US vastly overestimate the amount of foreign aid given by their country. Surveys have shown that Americans tend to judge foreign aid to be about 20% of the total federal budget; they then complain it is far too high. In fact, US foreign aid is less than 1% of the total budget. Some researchers wondered whether this overestimation might be a result of Americans confusing foreign aid with military expenditures. Apparently it isn't. Even when questionnaires make clear the distinction between foreign aid and military expenditures, Americans still overestimate foreign aid by 15 to 20 times.

Financial aid and economic growth

During the Cold War, much US aid had little to do with alleviating poverty. It was intended to buy the friendship of countries considered of strategic importance to the US in order to keep those countries from allying with the Soviet Union. The money was intended to be used for general infrastructure, as well as for health care and education. However, many of the governments receiving the aid were corrupt and used the money to enrich themselves and their cronies. For instance, hundreds of millions of dollars went into the Swiss bank accounts of the Congolese dictator Mobutu Sese Seko.

In the 1970s, loans were made to developing countries that were rich in natural resources, especially oil. These too were often mismanaged. In the 1980s when the prices of natural materials went down and interest rates on loans went up, these countries were unable to repay the loans.

At that point the World Bank and the International Monetary Fund (IMF) stepped in to renegotiate the loans. The World Bank is an international organization of member nations, established in 1944, which provides loans to poor countries to help with development and the reduction of poverty. The IMF, a related organization, is a United Nations agency designed to promote international monetary cooperation.

The renegotiated loans had two purposes: to help the countries repay their loans and emerge from debt; and, to help turn them into free market economies which would enrich those countries financially and provide markets for Western nations.

As a condition for more loans, the World Bank and the IMF required what were called "structural adjustment programs" (SAPs). These programs required donor countries to cut expenses by limiting social spending, cutting jobs and lowering wages. They also stressed developing agriculture that would lead to profitable exports, while deemphasizing agriculture that would feed the population within the country.

Much of this was done under conservative governments in the US and Britain, governments that were against welfare and that preached "trickle-down" economics where the benefits of development would filter down to the poor.

One reason the SAPs have gotten such a bad name is that they didn't work. If they had worked, if they had led to development, they would have led to poverty reduction in the long run, whatever the initial suffering caused to the poor.

There's no doubt that the greatest force for general poverty reduction is economic growth. Many would argue that you need growth plus social programs to reach the poorest of the poor, but growth can provide the money to pay for such programs.

There have been great reductions in extreme poverty over the last three decades: We've already seen that, using the $1.25-a-day standard, the number of extreme poor has fallen from 1.9 billion in 1981 to the current figure of 1.4 billion. However, this reduction has occurred primarily in China and India and was not the result of Western aid. It was the result of home-initiated development involving freeing up of markets, better government, and basic health care and education.

There's very little evidence that Western aid has led to overall macroeconomic growth. Neither pure investment nor the SAPs have done it. More recently, developmental economists have stressed the importance of political, legal and social institutions, but such institutions are difficult to get into place.

Some critics of developmental aid claim it is useless. Others claim that bigger and better approaches can succeed. We'll discuss this issue later, but first let's talk more specifically about attempts to reduce hunger—namely, food aid and the Green Revolution.

Food aid and the "Green Revolution"

In the late eighteenth century, Thomas Malthus argued against the Enlightenment hope that science would eventually lead to universal well-being. Malthus theorized that any rate of growth in the food supply would stimulate an even higher rate of population growth until the population growth was finally checked by famine, war and disease. According to his theory, poverty and hunger were inevitable. Malthus's arguments were often used to support the view that it was pointless to try to help the poor.

As late as the 1960s, Paul Ehrlich (*The Population Bomb*) was using Malthus-like arguments to claim a billion would starve to death by 1990. Garrett Hardin ("The Tragedy of the Commons") argued that Westerners were in a lifeboat of prosperity in a sea of hardship and that trying to save others would simply sink the boat. Malthusian arguments against helping the poor are still heard today in popular conversation.

However, we now know that while there are still, and will continue to be, overpopulation problems, Malthus's view about the inevitability of population outstripping food supply is false. For one thing, the Green Revolution, with its genetically modified crops such as wheat and rice, has increased food on a scale Malthus could scarcely have imagined. Further, it turns out that as societies become more affluent, population growth slows. The United Nations predicts that the world's population will increase from the current 7+ billion human beings to 9+ billion in 2050, but will eventually stabilize at 11 billion in 2200. We produce enough food right now to feed everyone on the planet and another few million more, though not on a Western diet.

Our thinking about world hunger has radically changed. Due to the work of economist Amartya Sen and others, we realize that famines occur not because of shortages of food per se but because of how food is distributed. During the terrible potato famine in Ireland in the mid-nineteenth century, England was importing Irish potatoes. During a twentieth-century Ethiopian famine, the country was exporting green beans to Europe. Food wasn't available to the famine-stricken areas because the people couldn't afford to buy it.

In the mid-twentieth century, one response to world poverty was food aid. The US government had accumulated huge stores of surplus grain as a result of subsidies to US farmers, and the cost of such storage was high. Why not send the surplus food to help the world's poor? By and large, food aid was less than successful. Some governments receiving the food aid simply sold the supplies to other countries to get cash; when the food was offered to the poor, it was often at a price they couldn't afford.

More importantly, we now know that food aid depresses local food prices and so undercuts the local agriculture needed to provide income and food to the local population on a regular basis. Further, Western trade barriers prevent local agriculture from taking advantage of trade opportunities. Most economists agree it would help world poverty if Western trade barriers were lowered, but powerful agricultural interests have so far stymied such proposals in Europe and the US.

The Green Revolution has failed to reach certain parts of the world, especially Africa. Often poorer farmers have been unable to supply the water and chemicals necessary to make the new crop strains successful and so have done worse with the new strains. Further, in order to recoup their investments, companies that developed the grain sold it to the poor on condition that the seeds wouldn't be replanted—so those receiving the seeds had to buy them again the next year—something the poor couldn't afford. In the story, Rennert expresses some of his disillusionment as follows:

He remembered dreaming how science might help the hungry people of the world. And it could help—creating genetically altered high-yield crops that could feed the poor. But science, if paid well enough by business, could develop a gene to make the seeds of those crops sterile, forcing the poor to keep buying seeds at prices they could hardly afford.

In fact, a gene that would keep genetically altered plants from producing fertile seeds was developed. It was called the Technological Protection System (TPS), but dubbed "The Terminator" by its opponents. When word of the gene was leaked out, there was such an outcry against it that so far it has not been implemented. Still, the restrictions on using seeds are still in place.

Of course, many argue that it is not the responsibility of companies involved in the Green Revolution to lose profits by discounting seeds—a practice that would discourage research in the long term. It's rather the responsibility of the countries and agencies involved in poverty-reduction to help the poor pay for the seeds.

In any case, while the Green Revolution has been tremendously successful in reducing hunger in developing nations able to engage in agriculture on a large scale, it has done little to help the poorest of the world.

If hunger is to be reduced in the poorest areas, different approaches need to be taken. We need to find out what, if anything, might work.

Trying to find out what works

In September 2000, the United Nations issued a declaration that included eight human development goals—the Millennium Development Goals (MDGs)—to be reached by 2015. The goals were as follows:

1. *Eradicate extreme poverty and hunger*
2. *Achieve universal primary education*
3. *Promote gender equality and empower women*
4. *Reduce child mortality*
5. *Improve maternal health*
6. *Combat HIV/AIDS, malaria, and other diseases*
7. *Ensure environmental sustainability*
8. *Develop a global partnership for development*

The director of the UN Millennium Project is economist Jeffrey Sachs of Columbia University. In speeches, as well as in his book, *The End of Poverty*, Sachs has been the main spokesperson for the MDGs, along with offering his own plan for ending extreme poverty by 2025.

The MDGs are supposed to represent a change from early approaches to poverty. It is Sachs' contention that the poorest countries are caught in a "poverty trap" where combinations of conditions work against attempts to improve just one or two. For instance, it is hopeless to try to improve employment or education if the people are too sick to work or study. It is important to have a coordinated approach that works on the whole problem at once.

The UN isn't on track to meet its goals. Where progress has been made it has often been in countries like China where economic development hasn't been the result of aid. Places like sub-Saharan Africa are falling behind. There are critics who have challenged the whole Millennium Development Project as hopelessly misguided.

One of the most prominent critics is economist William Easterly, author of *The White Man's Burden: Why the West's Efforts to Aid the Rest Have Done So Much Ill and So Little Good* (2006).

Easterly says that a lot of compassionate people have spoken about "the tragedy of extreme poverty afflicting billions of people, with millions of children dying from easily preventable diseases." But he says there is not enough talk about the "other tragedy of the world's poor":

> This is the tragedy in which the West spent $2.3 trillion on foreign aid over the last five decades and still had not managed to get twelve-cent medicines to children to prevent half of all malaria deaths. The West spent $2.3 trillion and still had not managed to get four-dollar bed nets to poor families....

Easterly criticizes the top-down, big-plan approach of the foreign-aid establishment, "the Planners." According to Easterly, the Planners "raise expectations but take no responsibility for meeting them." The Planners think they already know the answers, think the problems can be solved with "global blueprints." He contrasts the Planners with "Searchers" who "find out what reality is at the bottom," adapt interventions to local conditions, and engage in trial and error to find out what works.

For Easterly, the mentality of Searchers is epitomized by those working in free markets, but, unlike some critics of foreign aid, Easterly doesn't think free markets are the solution to world poverty.

> The poorest people in the world have no money to motivate market Searchers to meet their desperate needs. However, the mentality of Searchers in markets is a guide to a constructive approach to foreign aid.

Easterly has no "big plan" to offer. Rather his claim is that no big plan is going to work, that only small-scale aid successes are possible.

Those who continue to support the big-plan approach argue that big plans to help the extreme poor have never really been tried. The big-money plans in the past had different purposes: political goals, such as buying the loyalty of some dictator; opening up markets for the donor countries; dumping food that was costing the developed nations millions of dollars to store; catering to the farm lobby; and, simply perpetuating the existence of aid organizations.

Still, even those with big plans agree that smarter approaches need to be taken. Jeffrey Sachs is leading the Millennium Villages Project, which intervenes directly in the lives of African villages, bypassing the larger government bureaucracies. The programs work on improving agriculture, education, and health; villagers work with experts to determine priorities and it is a condition of the grants that women must be involved in the decision-making.

The project began in 2005 with ten villages with 60,000 inhabitants; it has now grown to eighty villages with 400,000 people. It will be another year or two before we will know whether or not the Millennium Villages Project is succeeding.

As we've seen, one complaint about the big plans is that the agencies involved have made no serious attempts to determine which approaches are effective and which ones are not. They throw money at problems, publicize the instances where interventions seem to work and downplay instances where they don't—all the while having no idea of cause and effect. If we're going to have any chance of reducing extreme poverty, we need hard information about what works and doesn't.

The gold standard here would be the kind of methodology used in testing the safety and effectiveness of drugs. Trials are run where participants are randomly divided into a treatment group (those getting the drug in question) and a control group (those not getting the drug); efforts are made to keep both groups and those in contact with the groups from knowing whether or not they're getting the drug to avoid increasing the placebo effect.

One organization that has been a leader in doing, and pushing others to do, randomized tests of anti-poverty programs is the Abdul Latif Jameel Poverty Action Lab (J-PAL) at MIT. One of their projects was to do trials regarding absentee teachers in India. A big problem with attempts to achieve better education by building new schools is teacher absenteeism—teachers who collect their pay but don't show up (and perhaps give the students answers to the final tests so it looks as if there has been some teaching going on). J-PAL tested an intervention that required teachers to film themselves with students using a time-coded camera that could not be tampered with. J-PAL found that use of the camera led to less absenteeism and better student scores.

One area of agreement between aid advocates and their critics is that there have been successes in the area of health. Projects involving limited interventions—like child immunization campaigns—are the simplest to run and have often shown great effectiveness. Between 1967 and 1979, smallpox deaths fell from 2 million people a year to virtually none. In 1988 1000 children a day contracted polio; by 2008 the number was down to five. Between 2000 and 2007, deaths from measles fell by 75 percent worldwide and by 89 percent in Africa.

Another great and ongoing success has been a campaign against river blindness in sub-Saharan Africa. In 1974, in eleven west African countries, nearly a tenth of the 20 million inhabitants were infected with the disease and 200,000 were blind. Through a combination of aerial spraying against the blackflies that spread the disease and the distribution of medications donated by Merck & Co, transmission of the disease had been halted by 2002. The program is now expanding to the rest of sub-Saharan Africa.

Recently it was announced that malaria deaths had been cut in half in Rwanda and Ethiopia, the two countries that have been most affected by that disease. The result was achieved through the use of insecticide-treated bed nets, insecticide spraying and new drugs. The fight is complicated by getting people to understand and cooperate with the program, but that has been helped by the use of nationwide campaigns. The programs have to be ongoing because if they lapse, malaria soon comes back in full force.

Campaigns against tuberculosis and HIV/AIDS are continuing and showing progress.

Thus, while there are complex debates about the effectiveness of various kinds of aid, it is indisputable that certain kinds of aid related to health have saved lives.

What, if anything, can individuals do to help?

In the next part of the chapter we'll be discussing the question of what obligations, if any, we have as a nation and/or as individuals to help the world's poor. If the United States, for instance, isn't doing enough to help, it's important that concerned citizens speak up and put some pressure on elected representatives to change the country's foreign-aid policies. However, there's also the question of responsibilities individuals might have to act directly, either as citizens doing their fair share of what their countries should be doing or as individuals with direct humanitarian obligations to the poor. Such individual responsibilities depend in part on whether or not we could actually help through donations to, or involvement in, NGOs

that are trying to ease world poverty. We need to know: What NGOs are carrying out effective programs, how effective are they, and how much effect, if any, would one's own donations make?

Unfortunately, this is not an easy question to answer with as much clarity as we'd like. Charity rankings tend to be based on data submitted to the IRS and deal with such matters as the percentage of donations spent on administration expenses (including fund raising) rather than on actual programs. A respectable figure here is 30% or less devoted to administrative expenses. On the other hand, few charities can produce convincing data on the effectiveness of their programs because they do not have those data; as indicated above, it is only recently that pressure has been put on charities to provide such data.

GiveWell is a new organization devoted to evaluating charities based on evidence of effectiveness, cost-effectiveness, transparency, and the ability to use further donations effectively (called the "funding gap"). Below are their top-rated international charities (see givewell.org for the complete chart and further information).

It's important not to make too much of the lack of effectiveness data. Pressure on organizations to show effectiveness in a quasi-scientific way is fairly recent; also, the more varied and complex an organization's activities are, the more difficult and expensive it would be to provide data of effectiveness. It seems reasonable to assume that prominent charities (Save the Children, Doctors Without Borders, Oxfam, etc.) with publicized activities and a good ratio of administrative expenses to helping outlays are doing good work—especially if they are working in the area of health.

Charity name	Focus	Evidence effective	Cost-effective	Funding gap	Transparency
Village Reach	Immunizations	Strong	Excellent	Significant	Excellent
Stop TB Partnership	Tuberculosis	Strong	Excellent	Significant	Strong
Against Malaria Foundation	Malaria	Moderate	Excellent	Significant	Excellent
Population Services International	HIV/AIDS; malaria	Moderate	Excellent	Probable	Excellent
Partners in Health	Health Clinics	Moderate	Moderate	Probable	Above average
Small Enterprise Foundation	Microfinance	Limited	Moderate	Moderate	Excellent
Village Enterprise Fund	Small business support	Limited	Moderate	Moderate	Excellent

Consulting sources such as the American Institute of Philanthropy (AIP) will give you the names of charities within such categories as "International Relief and Development" and will tell you how such charities are doing in terms of percentage spent on program services and how much they have to spend to raise $100. However, the push for more program-effectiveness data is important. To anyone skeptical about the effectiveness of aid, such data can provide both an antidote to skepticism and a proven channel for effective donations.

As we'll see, some famous ethical arguments regarding our responsibilities towards the world's poor revolve around the cost of saving a life. Thus it's important to have up-to-date information about this.

Both Village Reach and Stop Tuberculosis (on the GiveWell chart above) provide evidence that they can save a life for between $200 and $1000. This is in line with other responsible estimates of what it costs to save a life through some of the international health programs. For instance, William Easterly, the big-plan skeptic, estimates that the program against malaria, diarrhea, and other diseases run by the World Health Organization costs about $300 per life saved. If you see a figure under $200, it's probably not reliable. One organization claims that each $10 bed net saves a child's life from malaria—but this ignores the fact that not every net is used and that most children who get nets wouldn't have died of malaria without them. More reliable estimates of the cost of saving a life through bed nets range from $200 (Jeffrey Sachs) to over $800 (Population Services International) per life saved.

Having reviewed some of the facts and factual issues related to world poverty, let's turn now to the moral question concerning what, if anything, are our obligations to the world's poor. We'll start with a prominent philosopher, Peter Singer, who argues for the most demanding of standards.

Peter Singer: we owe much to the world's poor

Singer's Shallow Pond argument

In 1972 Philosopher Peter Singer published a now-classic article on our obligations to the world's poor, entitled "Famine, Affluence and Morality" (see Readings). The article, which referred to a terrible famine in Bengal, presents a powerful argument on behalf of the claim that each of us is obligated to give away a large percentage—maybe even most—of our money to help the poor peoples of the world. Given Singer's startling conclusion, it isn't surprising that his article has been much commented on, and criticized. (As we'll see in a later chapter, Singer has made equally powerful and startling arguments about our "speciesist" treatment of animals.)

In 1996, another philosopher, Peter Unger, published a book called *Living High and Letting Die* in which he tried to support and deepen Singer's arguments on poverty with elaborate analogies and arguments. Singer, in a 1999 article in the *New York Times Magazine*, entitled "The Singer Solution to World Poverty," used some of Unger's analogies in his overall argument. We will focus on those works here. Later on we'll touch on Singer's 2009 book, *The Life You Can Save*.

Singer's argument in "Famine" presents the following two premises.

Premise 1. "[S]uffering and death from lack of food, shelter, and medical care are bad." (He believes this is a premise with which virtually everyone would agree.)

Premise 2. "[I]f it is in our power to prevent something bad from happening, without thereby sacrificing anything of comparable moral importance, we ought, morally, to do it."

(Singer offers an alternate version of Premise 2, which substitutes "without sacrificing anything morally significant" for "without sacrificing anything of comparable moral importance." As we shall see, this softens the premise—but only a little.)

He then gives an analogy in support of Premise 2 which has led to the entire argument being labeled the "Shallow Pond argument":

> if I am walking past a shallow pond and see a child drowning in it, I ought to wade in and pull the child out. This will mean getting my clothes muddy, but this is insignificant, while the death of the child will presumably be a very bad thing.

Note that the pond is a shallow one: I don't have to swim; I'm in no danger of drowning. All I have to do is wade in and pull the child out. It costs me only some time and effort—plus the cost of cleaning the suit (at worst the cost of buying a new one).

Singer argues that wading in to save the child isn't just a generous, charitable thing to do: It is morally obligatory—that is, something required by morality.

Singer argues that Premise 2 takes "no account of proximity or distance": If I can do something that will save a child's life, it doesn't matter whether the child is someone in my neighborhood or a Bengali child starving to death. It might have made a difference in earlier times, but today

> Expert observers and supervisors, sent out by famine relief organizations or permanently stationed in famine-prone areas, can direct our aid to a refugee in Bengali almost as effectively as we could get it to someone in our own block.

Further, Premise 2 doesn't depend on whether others are, or aren't, helping. If there were other people who saw the child drowning in the pond and didn't do anything, it would still be my obligation to wade in and save her.

In "Singer Solution," Singer refers to some of Peter Unger's specific arguments. Unger imagines a case of a man who has invested his savings in a valuable vintage car which he has parked at the end of an old railroad siding while he goes for a walk. Coming back he sees a runaway train racing toward a small child playing on the tracks, a child too far away to reach or warn. The man can throw a switch that will divert the train and save the child, but throwing the switch will send the train crashing into his (uninsured) car. The man doesn't throw the switch, the child dies, and the man continues to enjoy his car for many years, eventually selling it to pay for his retirement.

Presumably most people would say the man's conduct was wrong. But, says Singer, Unger "reminds us that we, too have opportunities to save the lives of children." Unger had called up some experts and calculated that "$200 in donations would help transform a sickly 2-year-old into a healthy 6-year-old, offering safe passage through childhood's most dangerous years"; Unger had given his readers toll-free numbers they could call to donate to UNICEF or Oxfam America. Singer tells us, "Now you, too, have the information you need to save a child's life."

Let's say you were thinking of spending the $200 (or $500) on some new clothes. Moved by the Singer/Unger argument, you decide instead to donate that money to UNICEF. Singer says,

> Now that you have distinguished yourself morally from the people who put their vintage cars ahead of a child's life, how about treating yourself and your partner to a dinner at your favorite restaurant? But wait. The money you will spend at the restaurant could also help save the lives of children overseas!

Sorry, no fancy dinner celebration—not now, not ever. No fancy new clothes—not ever. There will always be a child drowning (starving, threatened by deadly illness) somewhere that you can save for the cost of a new suit or fancy dinner. Until you have made yourself substantially poorer (how poor we'll take up in a moment), dying children will have a stronger claim on that next $200 than you and your family do.

"The River" is a kind of extension of the Shallow Pond with many real-world complications added in. Rennert finds himself in a situation where he can save the lives of the Anansi who have taken refuge at the religious site across the river from his hydrologic station. To do so, he must spend time ferrying them across the river and providing them provisions for a trek to the UN refugee camp at Esana.

Rennert isn't responsible for the plight of the Anansi: The country of Sungura is. Large nations which might be able to put pressure on Sungura aren't doing so, in part because they want Sunguran oil. Ajapa could help, but is afraid of Sungura and has some secrets of its own. International agencies are helpless to act without the cooperation of Sungura and Ajapa.

It's left to Rennert to do what he can. He's anything but a saint. He wants to be left alone by the world, to do his solitary work and enjoy his food, books, and music. But his conscience won't let him be. He spends more and more time helping the Anansi, giving them more and more of the food he has stored up for himself. He helps out to the point where he is too exhausted to enjoy his own life. Was he morally obligated to do so much? Is he obligated to keep going?

Singer wouldn't argue that someone is morally obligated to do what's pointless. Singer is after results, not gestures. If it got to the point where nothing Rennert could do would do any good—if the refugee camp was shut tight or the tribes in the area between the hydrologic station and the camps were capturing and killing all the Anansi who entered those lands— then Rennert would be off the hook. But is Rennert justified in stopping anywhere short of that?

This is where the two versions of Singer's second premise come in. According to the first version, you must keep giving until you reach the level where giving any more would lead you to sacrifice something of comparable moral importance—or, as Singer says, "the level at which, by giving more, I would cause as much suffering to myself or my dependents as I would relieve by my gift." (He calls this the "level of marginal utility.") In other words, you would have to keep giving until you and your family were at the same level as the very poor who needed your help.

The second demands less, with the vaguer phrase, "without sacrificing anything morally significant." As interpreted by Singer, this version would seem to allow you a very modest Western lifestyle: adequate clothes, food, and shelter and furnishings (no big TV or entertainment center), an inexpensive car or public transportation, education at a state college rather than a private one, and so forth. Most of us would view someone who had a large income but kept her life modest in order to give to the poor as a rather saintly person. However, according to Singer's argument in "Famine," *this would be your minimum obligation.* He really thinks the tougher version of Premise 2 is the correct one.

In the first chapter we mentioned a distinction between acts that are obligatory and those that are "above duty" (supererogatory), including acts of charity. For Singer, in situations where lives are at stake or people are suffering extreme poverty, the extent of our obligations becomes enormous and there are very few sorts of acts left that could be described as above duty (supererogatory) or even charitable. We're not being charitable if we are giving what we owe.

Singer is a utilitarian. He says he has purposely tried to present an argument for our obligations to the poor that does not depend on utilitarianism; his argument must be dealt with on its own terms. However,

it's worth pointing out that a similar argument could be made on act-utilitarian grounds, if we allow what seem like common-sense interpersonal comparisons. Is $10 worth more to a starving woman than to a millionaire? Some economists might hem and haw here because it is difficult to verify and quantify vast interpersonal comparisons in a way that allows for the mathematics which economists want in their theory. But no one else would have any problem answering, "Yes, that $10 is worth more to a starving woman." There would no point at all in ever giving to charity if we didn't believe this. As long there are enough starving people in the world, the money for almost any purchase we can think of for ourselves would do more good in terms of increasing pleasure or diminishing pain if given to the sick and hungry. Since an act-utilitarian must do that act which creates the greatest balance of happiness over pain and since there are always opportunities to give to charities for the worse-off, the act-utilitarian would be entitled to keep little for herself.

We will be dealing directly with Singer's Shallow Pond argument. However, the larger considerations brought up by Singer's argument will apply to the act-utilitarian argument as well.

Singer is an extremely challenging philosopher— both in the sense that he often attacks comfortable moral positions and in the sense that he presents arguments for his views that aren't easy to counter. Too often the immediate reaction to Singer is an angry dismissal that masks a discomfort at his conclusions and inability to counter his arguments at his level of sophistication. However, he is worth paying attention to, both because of the quality of his arguments and because, after all, he is arguing on behalf of beings in pain, whether human or animal. If you engage him, even if you don't accept his conclusions, you will find that he has forced you to revise and deepen your thinking and perhaps change some of your behaviors as well.

Many of you will have read the story of Kevin and Joan Salwen of Atlanta who, at the suggestion of their 14-year-old daughter, Hannah, sold their house for $1,600,000 and donated half the money to villagers in Ghana. Though many people were supportive, other people reacted with puzzlement or anger.

Friends had been baffled or worse. One close friend of Joan's had started to cry and said, "This is not my family's reality."…

Whether or not Singer's "reality" turns out to be yours, it's important to engage his arguments.

There have been lots of criticisms of Singer's position on what we owe to the poor. We'll begin by considering some of the more sympathetic critiques—those which agree with the claim that we as individuals and as citizens of wealthy countries have obligations to help the world's poor. Some of these critiques have been accompanied by more modest alternate proposals as to what we owe to the poor.

Following that, we will then talk about Singer's 2009 book, *The Life You Can Save*. In that book Singer gives vigorous counter-arguments against his critics, but finally makes a rather large concession to the claim that his principles are so demanding that they actually turn people off to giving.

Then we will review the libertarian position on our obligations to the poor—they say we have none—followed by an interesting contention by Thomas Pogge that even on libertarian premises, an argument can be made that the West does owe help to the world's poor. Finally we will discuss religious views of our obligations toward the poor.

Sympathetic critiques and alternate proposals

One criticism of Singer's Shallow Pond argument is this: The argument breaks down when Singer tries to apply our intuitions in the case of a single child to an endless series of such cases. That is, these critics argue that even if the Shallow Pond analogy shows that we're obligated to rescue one child in a particular situation, it doesn't show that we're obligated to keep on repeating rescues to the point where rescuing consumes our lives. As Garrett Cullity puts it:

A potential contributor to aid agencies is more closely analogous to someone confronted by a great many drowning people than to someone confronted by one. So why not simply examine our intuitions concerning the more closely analogous case? Suppose, then, that what I come across is not a pond containing one or two drowning children, but the nightmarish scene of a lake, or even a sea, teeming with them. And suppose (to complete the analogy) that many other people could help to save them, but relatively few are doing so. But now, it is surely far from intuitively obvious that it would be wrong of me not to spend practically every waking moment saving lives….

Let's condense and exaggerate the kind of elements found in "The River" to create a nightmarish scene along the lines of Cullity's. We'll call this Deep River and later contrast it to Singer's Shallow Pond.

You interrupt your Sunday drive at the sight of people holding up signs begging you to help save drowning people. Pulling off the highway, you come across this surreal scene:

There's a violent river full of people being swept downstream. A glance upriver shows you that these people are victims of various ongoing catastrophes. Cliffs have collapsed, along with the flimsy dwellings built on them. A raging forest fire is compelling people to leap in the water to escape burning. Elsewhere trucks are hauling people to the riverbank where soldiers are forcing the people into the river at gunpoint—an ongoing act of genocide, you hear someone say.

Just in front of you, rescue efforts are being attempted. Some rescuers are holding long poles out over the river, hoping some of the victims get close enough to the bank to grab the poles; few do. Other rescuers are hurling life preservers out into the river. Many of the preservers simply hit the water and skip away unused in the quick current. Some are grabbed by those attempting to swim, but you soon realize that grabbing a preserver only assures the people in the water a chance at survival: They still face a waterfall and some rapids beyond.

You demand to know why nothing is being done beyond these pathetic rescue efforts. Why isn't someone trying to stop the genocide? Why is no one helping fight the forest fire with heavy equipment?

The explanations you get are long and difficult to follow, but the gist is that the powers-that-be claim there is little that can be done at a cost people are willing to bear. Some of those trying to help are writing letters and arranging protests, but so far these efforts have produced only modest results. Meanwhile there is little that can be done beyond holding out poles and throwing preservers.

You want to leave, but conscience holds you: At least you should do something. You spend two hours throwing preservers. Two of these are caught and even though you can't be sure those people will make it, it feels good to have given them a chance. You decide to come back for a couple of hours next Sunday—no, you can't Sunday, you have a family gathering—but the Sunday after that. Maybe you'll bring a couple of friends. You'll also do some research into what's happening and see if you can find some way to help bring pressure on the powers-that-be.

The good feeling you have as you walk away is soon squelched by other rescuers who abuse you for leaving. How can you walk away from this emergency, leaving people to die? You should be spending all your time here. Or, if you must work, come back whenever you're not working and contribute most of what you earn to the rescue efforts. That's what a moral person would do, they say.

Now, instead of walking away, you're running.

And thinking:

1. *Why are you getting abused when you at least did something and so many others are doing nothing?*
2. *What's happening here isn't your fault. In some cases, it's the fault of others—in some cases the fault of no one. But it's not your fault: Why should it be your responsibility?*
3. *If anyone should be doing something it is those with the power and money to make a real difference. Why aren't they doing more?*
4. *What can you alone accomplish anyway? You could stand there all day throwing preservers: There's no guarantee anyone would catch one you threw; even if they did, there's no guarantee they would survive very long.*
5. *Even if common decency requires you do something, it's ludicrous to demand you should do more than your fair share.*
6. *Someone used the word "emergency," but emergencies are temporary. It looks like these disasters have been going on for a long time and will continue indefinitely.*

The Deep River looks more like the real situation we face than does the Shallow Pond, though Deep River is undoubtedly exaggerated in the other direction.

Singer can argue reasonably vis-à-vis the Shallow Pond that if there were two children in the pond, you're obligated to try to save both, not just one, and you have that obligation even if no one else is helping. But when the Shallow Pond turns into Cullity's crowded pond or our Deep River, it's not clear that such arguments retain their force. At least, such has been argued by some of Singer's critics.

As we said, some of Singer's critics who are sympathetic to the idea that we owe something to the world's poor have offered alternate principles that are less demanding.

One principle dubbed "the emergency principle" or "the principle of easy rescue" is phrased by philosopher Kwame Anthony Appiah (see Readings) as follows: "If you are the person in the best position to prevent something really awful, and it won't cost you much to do it, do it."

Such a principle is compatible with the intuition that we really are responsible for saving that one child in the pond, but doesn't lead us to anything like the obligations that Singer argues we have. The problem may be that it is far too undemanding. It terms of world poverty, "It won't cost you much," sounds as if all you need to do to comply is to toss a couple of bucks into the cup of someone collecting for relief efforts once in a while. That's doing virtually nothing.

A more demanding principle is one proposed by philosopher Liam Murphey, among others. Murphey argues that we are obligated to help but are only obligated to do our fair share—our share of what it would take to substantially improve the condition of the world's poor. He argues that our obligations of beneficence have a "compliance condition"—that is, our obligations are restricted to the amount we would need to pay if everyone were helping.

Singer's argument and the responses to it bring up a number of fundamental issues of morality that were mentioned in Part I. Let's take a moment to remind ourselves what they were.

> …what about my feeling that it is morally acceptable for me to be partial to the welfare of myself, my family, and my friends as against the welfare of strangers—whether people in my society or in other parts of the world? Some philosophers will argue that such partiality—at least to the extent most of us practice it—is morally wrong.…
>
> This question of impartiality relates to a larger question of moral theory, namely how demanding morality is or should be. Some moralists claim that morality demands almost everything of us—our total devotion to God or to the poor. Others argue that morality demands almost nothing of us—just that we follow some basic rules and otherwise leave each other alone. Still others argue that while morality allows us

considerable freedom to live our lives our way, it still demands more than most of us seem willing to give.

There's a related issue here of obligation and motivation. If morality demands too much, too few people will follow it: Morality becomes like a general marching into battle with no force behind him, his troops all having deserted. On the other hand, if what passes as morality fights no battles and demands almost nothing, one has to wonder if it really *is* morality: Humans are far from perfect; isn't the point of morality to at least push us to be better?

Singer's Shallow Pond argument assumes that morality is impartial in the extreme. That is, my interests as well as those of my friends and my family, can have no priority in my moral calculations—at least on the strong version of Singer's argument: As long as others are leading painful lives, my first responsibilities are to relieve their suffering: Bringing pleasure to myself or my family has no weight. Under the weaker version of his principle, I can favor myself and my family up to the level of a certain modest lifestyle, but thereafter the misery of the poor takes priority. In contrast, most people would feel they have a right, even an obligation, to devote most of their resources to themselves and their family.

In this sense, Singer envisions morality as extremely demanding: The claims of others create great moral obligations for you.

The debate over Singer's argument also brings up the tricky issue of morality and motivation. What if someone looks over Singer's argument, decides Singer is essentially correct, then shrugs and says, "I guess I'm just not interested in being that moral." What then? Some philosophers even argued that pushing such heavy moral demands on people might have a negative effect, making them less inclined to give anything. Like the person in Deep River who gets abused for helping too little, people might just give up helping at all.

Philosophers Hugh LaFollette and Larry May have some interesting remarks to make about this issue in an article they wrote about world poverty.

Although it may be intellectually satisfying to determine whether children have a right to be fed or whether we have an obligation to assist them, if those arguments do not move us to action, then it is of little use—at least to the children in need. So we are especially interested in philosophical arguments which are more likely to motivate people to act. We think arguments that keep the spotlight on starving children are more likely to have that effect.

Moreover, by thinking about hunger in these ways we can better understand and respond to those who claim we have no obligation to assist the starving. We suspect that when all the rhetoric of rights, obligations, and population control are swept away, what most objectors fear is that asking people to assist the starving and undernourished is to ask too much. Morality or no, people are unlikely to act in ways they think require them to substantially sacrifice their personal interests. Thus, as long as most people think helping others demands too much, they are unlikely to provide help....

At bottom, we suspect that what is at issue is the proper conception and scope of morality. Some philosophers have argued that morality should not be exceedingly demanding; indeed, one of the stock criticisms of utilitarianism is that it is far too demanding. On the other hand, some theorists, including more than a few utilitarians, have bitten the proverbial bullet and claimed that morality is indeed demanding, and that its demandingness in no way counts against its cogency. On the former view, morality should set expectations which all but the most weak-willed and self-centered person can satisfy; on the latter view, morality makes demands that are beyond the reach of most, if not all, of us.

We wish to take the middle ground and suggest that morality is a delicate balancing act between Milquetoast expectations which merely sanctify what people already do, and expectations which are excessively demanding and, thus, are psychologically impossible—or at least highly improbable. Our view is that the purpose of morality is not to establish an edifice that people fear, but to set expectations that are likely to improve us, and—more relevant to the current issue—to improve the lot of those we might assist. Morality would thus be like any goal which enables us to grow and mature: they must be within reach, yet not easily reachable. Of course, what is within reach changes over time; and what is psychologically probable depends, in no small measure, on our beliefs about what is morally expected of us. So by expecting ourselves to do more and to be more than we currently do and are, we effectively stimulate ourselves to grow and improve. But all that is part of the balancing act of which we speak....

Singer seems to have acknowledged that the stringency of the demands put forth by his argument can be counter-productive. In his 2009 book, *The Life You Can Save*, Singer emphasizes that he still thinks his original argument is correct and spends some time countering objections to that argument. Still he acknowledges the problem of morality and motivation. He says that pushing a high moral standard will motivate some people to do more, but with others it can have the opposite effect.

> Asking people to give more than almost anyone else gives risks turning them off, and at some level might cause them to question the point of striving to live an ethical life at all. Daunted by what it takes to do the right thing, they may ask themselves why they are bothering to try. To avoid that danger, we should advocate a level of giving that will lead to a positive response....

Asked how he can consistently push a less than optimal moral standard, Singer makes an analogy with rule-utilitarianism—how having people follow rules that don't necessarily produce the greatest happiness in a particular case might lead to the greatest happiness overall. (That is, even if lying might lead to the greatest overall happiness in an individual, lying in general is likely to have less than beneficial effects—undermining trust, for example.)

Singer asks what a "fair share" contribution might look like—which first requires asking, "Share of what?" He thinks we should take what it would cost to achieve the Millennium Development Goals, subtract whatever money has already been pledged, and divide that up among the income earners of the "twenty-two rich OECD countries." Eliminating those citizens whose income is below a certain level, he introduces a sliding scale, starting at 5% for those earning over $105,000 and moving up from there.

Singer's particular figures as to our "fair share" aren't important here for our purposes: Debating such figures already puts you in the camp of those who believe we have obligations to the world's poor. Let's move on for the moment to those who say we have no such obligation, including the libertarians and social contract theorists.

Libertarians: we owe nothing to the world's poor

Arguments of libertarians and social contract theorists

You can already anticipate the response of the moral libertarians, for whom the whole of morality consists of negative rights. They would say that we have no obligation to help anyone in need (at least anyone for whom we've not assumed some sort of contractual responsibility). We would have no moral obligation to save the drowning child, or help the poor in our own society, or help the world's poor.

Libertarians—and others as well—have claimed that a crucial weakness with Singer's argument is that he equates letting people die with killing them (causing them to die). Libertarians agree it would be wrong to kill people; it is not wrong to let people die. Other people have no moral claim on us other than for us not to interfere with their negative rights. (Again this assumes that we are not responsible for their predicament in the first place).

Social contract theorists would likely agree with the libertarians that we have no obligation to help the world's poor, but their reasoning would be different. They would argue that moral obligations only arise in a situation of common social institutions to which we can apply a contractualist test. Social contract theorists differ in their views of our obligations to the poor in our own society. Some basic social contract theorists argue for a political libertarianism with little or no social safety net. Some ideal social contract theorists like Rawls argue for a social democratic society with a high degree of equality. But all agree that whatever obligations, if any, we have to the less well off do not extend beyond our own society.

Taken strictly, social contract theory would seem to imply that no morality whatsoever would apply to interactions between people in different societies—at least insofar as those interactions didn't involve specific treaties, agreements, or contracts. However, it's unlikely that many social contract theorists today would actually take such a position. More likely, they would acknowledge some bare-bones universal morality, agree that it is morally wrong to kill, rob, or rape any human being from any society. Like the libertarian, they would agree that all human beings have some minimal negative rights. Unlike the libertarian, they might acknowledge a more complex series of negative and positive rights within one's society.

In that sense we can take the libertarian and social contract theorist positions as basically equivalent when it comes to the world's poor—that the poor have some minimal negative rights but no positive right to be helped by us.

The social contract theorist might further argue that we have a positive obligation to favor the interests of people in our society over those in other parts of the world. This view would be shared by nationalists (whether conservative or liberal) who claim that the interests of one's own country and one's own citizens should take precedence over the interests of other countries and peoples.

As mentioned earlier, philosopher Thomas Pogge has argued that even on libertarian and social contract principles, we (as a Western nation) have an obligation to help the world's poor.

Pogge: obligations even on libertarian principles

Pogge agrees with the libertarians against Singer that the distinction between killing and letting die is morally significant: We do not have a general obligation to keep people from dying. He agrees with those who argue that we have a right or responsibility to favor those in our own society. But he thinks we have a responsibility to help the world's poor because (a) they have a right not to be harmed and because (b) we are harming them through unfair international practices.

Pogge doesn't argue (as some would) that we have responsibility towards the world's poor because they are being harmed by the present effects of past colonial practices. He thinks the current generation can't be held responsible for colonialism. Instead, Pogge's argument goes something like this:

Fair competition is within a framework of rules. We recognize that the rules can be bent or distorted by the strong so that the competition becomes unfair.

> Implicit in our moral thinking and practice, there is then an important distinction…between matters legitimately subject to change through competing group interests, on

the one hand, and certain basic features of the institutional order requisite to preserve the fairness of the competition, on the other. I extend and apply this fundamental distinction to the global plane, arguing that *any* coercive institutional order must meet certain minimal conditions.… The existing global institutional order falls short of meeting these conditions, on account of the excessive inequalities in bargaining power and the immense poverty and economic inequality it avoidably produces.

Pogge says that most researchers search for the causes of world poverty among national and local factors. Pogge grants that if those were the only relevant causal factors, that would undercut his argument. However, Pogge argues that the claim is implausible: Too much of the world economy depends on international trade agreements that favor the strong. Speaking of the World Trade Organization (WTO) regime, Pogge notes that, unlike some of its critics, he is not an opponent of free trade.

> I do not complain that the WTO regime opens markets too much, but that it has opened *our* markets *too little* and has thereby gained for us the benefits of free trade while withholding these benefits from the global poor. Poor populations continue to face great barriers to exporting their products, and even greater barriers to offering their services where these would fetch a decent income. And some competitive markets of vital importance to them—markets in generic versions of advanced medicines, for instance—have been shut down under WTO rules designed to facilitate global monopolies.…

Pogge considers the objection that he's omitted the most important cause of poverty: "the incompetence, corruption, and tyranny entrenched in the governments, social institutions, and cultures of many poor countries."

Pogge says that if we told the world's poor that the fault for world poverty lies not with us but with their governments, the poor could reply to us as follows:

- Those governments were installed by force (sometimes with our connivance); they do not express the will of the people as expressed in free and open elections;

- In buying the natural resources from those governments, we are cooperating in the survival of those governments and in taking away resources that belong in part to the poor
- By giving those governments international borrowing privileges, we are also contributing to their survival
- We make trade treaties with those governments that profit us, those governments and the elites of those countries—treaties that offer nothing to the poor.

Pogge emphasizes that his is not a socialist critique, but one made on premises that libertarians and others on the political right should acknowledge.

> Those on the political right, too, condemn poverty caused by an unjust coercive international order—for instance, severe poverty and dependence engendered by feudal regimes or by the collectivist agriculture imposed by Stalin in 1928. They agree that such poverty is unjust and that those who brought it about are responsible for it and also have the responsibility to eradicate it. Their moral and political outlook is thus quite consistent with my claim that we have the duty to help eradicate severe poverty in the less developed countries. If they deny this claim it is because they—along with most Westerners anywhere on the political spectrum—assume too easily that we, and the global order we impose, do not substantially contribute to severe poverty abroad.

Opponents of Pogge would claim that ultimately those international treaties he criticizes will facilitate the development of the less developed countries—which, in the long run, will help the severe poor. Much of Pogge's book is devoted to arguing against those opponents. That debate is far too complex to take up within the scope of this text. Instead let's consider some other possible reactions to Pogge's general argument:

One objection is that unless we're planning to invade all those countries with oppressive governments—which we're not—we have to deal with those countries as they are. Their resources are going to get sold to somebody: If we refuse, someone else will buy their resources and we, as a nation, will lose out.

As I read Pogge, he is not arguing that we must refrain from buying resources from oppressive governments. But what we must do is two things: (a) keep working toward more just international arrangements and (b) do what we can directly to help the severe poor. A number of people would agree with *a* (think of pressure on China to improve human rights), though how seriously we take this imperative is another matter. But few of us think much about *b* on Pogge's terms: That we, as a nation, should make a serious commitment to relieve the plight of the severe poor as compensation for the money we make off of them.

Another objection would be that even if we are to some degree responsible for the severe poor, there are too many other factors to hold us primarily responsible.

However, note Pogge is arguing that *we are obligated to help the world's poor only to the degree that we are responsible for their plight.* How responsible would be a complex issue, but at least it would move us away from the position that we have no responsibility for and no obligations toward the world's poor.

For many people responsibilities to the poor are tied up with their religious views. We'll now talk about different religious views.

Religion and aiding the poor

Most religions impose some obligation on believers to aid the poor. Often this religious obligation is phased in terms of "charity." Singer likes to avoid the word "charity" since, he believes, quite correctly, that it often implies something optional; however, in religious contexts, charity is sometimes seen as an obligation. In this section we will use the word "charity" in such a way that there is nothing contradictory about referring to charity as an obligation.

Of course, the subject of religion and charity is an enormous and complex one, given the number of religions and the number of divisions within religions, as well as individual interpretations of religious doctrine. Further, it often seems that, when it comes to money, religious views get modified, or interpreted, according to one's economic views rather than vice-versa. One example was given in our first story, "Too Much."

The Burkes were conservative Catholics. Charles, a successful stockbroker, seemed to take the Church's line on everything—except for its suspicion of laissez-faire capitalism. Charles dismissed that suspicion as the bias of the "dear, old men" who were better at theology than economics, who were too removed from the world to know how things really worked. Charles said that the Church talked about dividing goods as if those goods fell like manna from heaven, rather than having to be created by a system that needed incentives to function and was bound to lead to inequalities.

Still, there are certain general things we can say. If we contrast religious and secular giving (using "secular" to refer to giving not directly motivated by religious injunctions), we often find that religion has a special emphasis on the dimensions of giving other than giving material help to the poor. Both the religious and the secular aspire to giving that is effective in improving the material conditions of the poor (1 below). However with religious giving, two other dimensions of giving are often emphasized (2 and 3 below):

1. Giving so the recipient is helped materially
2. Giving so the recipient is helped spiritually
3. Giving in the right spirit

As for 3, most traditional religions have a heavy perfectionist element that emphasizes the importance of virtue; thus the motives of the giver become as important, if not more important, than the benefit of the recipient.

In Matthew 6:1, Jesus warns against giving to charity out of the desire to impress others.

> Take heed that you do not your alms before men, to be seen of them: otherwise ye have no reward of your Father which is in heaven....

In the Hindu tradition, according to religious scholar Werner Menski,

> Charitable giving ranks high among good deeds the Hindu may do.... The utterly selfless act of giving produces unseen merit, though acting with a view to acquiring that merit clearly defeats the purpose. The mental state of the giver is important and there's a danger of hypocrisy.

Where achieving merit is important (where, say, it is supposed to affect one's future destiny), one can see how easy it would be for the religiously sensitive to become obsessed over whether they had just the right attitude. Imagine how tied in knots a Hindu Martin Luther could become trying to give selflessly without acting out of a desire for the rewards that come from acting selflessly. Concern for the poor could get lost in all that self-absorption.

I remember a country song about a driver who stops at a light, ignores a homeless man asking for change, then drives away. The word "change" sticks in the driver's head, connecting with thoughts he's been having about how he should change his life. He pulls off the road, overcome with regret, then later drives on, determined to be a better person—especially a better husband and father. I kept waiting for the driver to go back and give the homeless man some money or make a resolution to help the needy in the future—but there was none of that. The homeless man seemed to have lost all reality except as a symbol of the man's spiritual journey.

On the other hand, the emphasis on the state of the giver can be a powerful motivation for giving. If helping the poor is a crucial part of my (spiritual) self-esteem, that could be a stronger, more consistent motive for helping others than episodic feelings of sympathy.

It's important not to make too much of 3 as something unique to religious giving. Most secular ethics have some virtue dimension. People are seen as more admirable if they give from the right motives. You want people to develop the habit of giving and that's much the same as wanting people to be charitable. But with a secular ethic, helping the poor is the main thing. For the religious the motives are likely to be at least as important as the giving.

The idea of 2—giving so the recipient is helped spiritually—is a familiar theme in Christian missionary efforts to help people materially and convert them to the Christian faith. Buddhism is emphatic that the best help goes beyond curing poverty and disease to promoting spiritual health.

Let's consider what Hinduism, Buddhism, Judaism, Christianity and Islam have to say about our obligations to the poor—and about wealth in general.

It's interesting to note that, of those five traditions, Christianity expresses the most negative attitude toward wealth: Jesus frequently criticizes wealth, describing it as an obstacle to salvation. He famously said that it was harder for a rich man to enter heaven than for a camel to go through the eye of a needle. And when a young rich man came to Jesus to ask what he should do, Jesus told him to sell all he owned and give it to the poor. Of course Christians—even Christian literalists—have managed to reinterpret that: They argue that it isn't money but the (excessive) love of money that Jesus was condemning or they simply ignore those portions of the Bible.

The other four traditions are much less hostile to wealth. In Hinduism, though there is often an emphasis on renunciation, seeking wealth and power (*artha*) can be a legitimate aim of life.

For Buddhists, it is proper to seek wealth as long as it is done honestly, as long as excessive concern for wealth is avoided. Such concern can plague both rich and poor, depriving them of the quiet spirit that is one of the goals of Buddhism. Both Judaism and Islam consider wealth a blessing, though such wealth makes one subject to certain community obligations.

Hinduism, Buddhism, Judaism, Christianity and Islam all stress strong obligations to give to the poor. We've already noted that charitable giving ranks high among the good deeds a Hindu may do and (if done with the proper attitude) brings spiritual merit. Buddhism stresses generosity as an important virtue. As religious scholar Peggy Morgan says,

> A central part of all Buddhist practice is the cultivation of a heart that is loving and compassionate towards all beings. People who are loving and kind feel the sufferings of others as much as their own and have a strong sense of interdependence or interbeing....

Charity as obligation becomes particularly clear in Judaism, where the Hebrew word for charity— *Tzedaka*—is also the word for justice. In Judaism wealth is considered a blessing, but that wealth is to be used for the good of the community as well as for oneself and one's family. This is also true of Islam. The Qur'an talks frequently of an obligation toward the poor; in addition to voluntary charity, it talks about the *zakat*, an obligatory religious tax. It seems analogous to the tithe—paying a tenth of one's income for religious purposes—a practice that dates from the Old Testament and was mandatory for many Christians (through church and/or secular law) from the sixth century into the seventeenth. It is still encouraged by some Christian groups today.

There are a number of religiously oriented organizations targeting world poverty. We'll conclude by naming a few (from the list of those rated highly by AIP) and quoting their mission statements:

WORLD VISION INTERNATIONAL:
We seek to follow Jesus—in his identification with the poor, the powerless, the afflicted, the oppressed, and the marginalised; in his special concern for children; in his respect for the dignity bestowed equally on women and men; in his challenge to unjust attitudes and systems; in his call to share resources with each other; in his love for all people without discrimination or conditions; his offer of new life through faith in him....

We are called to serve the neediest people of the earth; relieve their suffering and to promote the transformation of their well-being. We stand in solidarity and a common search for justice. We seek to understand the situation the poor and work alongside them....

AMERICAN JEWISH WORLD SERVICE:
American Jewish World Service (AJWS) is an international development organization motivated by Judaism's imperative to pursue justice. AJWS is dedicated to alleviating poverty, hunger and disease among the people of the developing world regardless of race, religion or nationality....

CATHOLIC RELIEF SERVICES:
Our mission is to assist impoverished and disadvantaged people overseas, working in the spirit of Catholic Social Teaching about the sacredness of human life and dignity of the human person. Although our mission is rooted in the Catholic faith, our operations serve people based solely on need, regardless of their race, religion or ethnicity....

The fundamental motivating force in all activities of CRS is the Gospel of Jesus Christ as it pertains to the alleviation of human suffering, the development of people and the fostering of charity and justice.

Notes and selected sources

Facts and factual issues

SOURCES

Sandra Alters, *World Poverty*. Information Plus® Reference Series. (Detroit MI: Gale Cengage Learning, 2008.)

Abhijit V. Banerjee and Esther Duflo. *Poor Economics: A Radical Rethinking of the Way to Fight Global Poverty*. New York: Public Affairs, 2011.

William Easterly. *The White Man's Burden*. New York: The Penguin Press, 2006.

Ruth Levine et. al. *Case Studies in Global Health: Millions Saved*. Boston: Jones and Bartlett Publishers, 2007.

Richard H. Robbins (ed). *Global Problems and the Culture of Capitalism*. 4th Ed. Boston, MA: Pearson, 2008.

Jeffrey Sachs. *The End of Poverty*. New York. The Penguin Press, 2005.

Jeffrey Sachs. *Common Wealth*: New York. The Penguin Press, 2008.

Peter Singer, *The Life You Can Save*. New York: Random House, 2009.

Timothy Taylor. *America and the New Global Economy*. Chantilly, VA: The Teaching Company, 2008, lectures 27, 28 and 33.

Robert Whaples. *Modern Economic Issues*. Chantilly, VA: The Teaching Co., 2007, lecture 32.

NOTES

Re poverty definitions: Alters, Info Plus, ch. 1.

Re $1.25 a day: "A Dollar a Day Revisited." World Bank Research Digest, vol. 2, no. 4. Summer 2008; "New Data Show 1.4 Billion Live on Less than US$1.25 a Day, but Progress against Poverty Remains Strong." World Bank press release, Aug. 26, 2008.

Re American beliefs about foreign aid: Taylor, lecture 33; "Americans on Foreign Aid and World Hunger: A Study of US Public Attitudes (Feb. 2, 2001). Program on International Policy Attitudes (PIPA).

Re US aid, World Bank and IMF: Alters, Info Plus, ch. 2; Whaples, lecture 32.

Re aid and economic growth: Taylor, lecture 33.

Re Malthus, population growth and "Green Revolution": Taylor, lecture 27; Robbins, chs. 5 & 6.

Re Millennium Development Goals: Alters, Info Plus, ch. 10.

Easterly summary and quotes: Easterly, pp. 3–5.

Re Millennium Villages: Singer, pp. 117–20; Sachs, *Common Wealth*, ch. 3.

Re J-PAL: Ian Parker. "The Poverty Lab." *New Yorker*, May 17, 2010.

Re successes in the area of health: Taylor, lecture 33; Levine, esp. "Cases" 1, 3, 5 and 7.

Peter Singer: We owe much to the world's poor

SOURCES

William Aiken and Hugh LaFollette eds. *World Hunger and Morality*, 2nd edn. Upper Saddle River, NJ: Prentice-Hall, 1986:
  –John Arthur, "Rights and the Duty to Bring Aid," pp. 39–50.
  –Garrett Cullity, "The Life-Saving Analogy," pp. 51–69.
  –Hugh LaFollette and Larry May, "Suffer the Little Children," pp. 70–84.

Kwame Anthony Appiah. *Cosmopolitanism: Ethics in a World of Strangers*. New York: W. W. Norton, 2006.

Liam B. Murphey. *Moral Demands in Nonideal Theory*. Oxford: Oxford University Press, 2000.

Peter Singer. *The Life You Can Save* (above).

Peter Singer. *Writings on an Ethical Life*. New York: Harper Collins, 2000:
  –"Famine, Affluence, and Morality."
  –"The Singer Solution to World Poverty."

Peter Unger. *Living High and Letting Die: Our Illusion of Innocence*. New York: Oxford, 1996.

NOTES

Shallow Pond argument in Singer, "Famine" and *Life You Can Save*.

"No account of proximity…" Singer, "Famine," p. 107.

"Expert observers...." Singer, "Famine," p. 108.

Singer's and Unger's arguments: Singer, "Singer Solution" and Unger, *Living High*.

"…reminds us that we, too...." Singer, "Singer Solution," p. 120.

"Now that you have distinguished...." Singer, "Singer Solution," pp. 121–2.

Story of Kevin and Joan Salwen. *New Yorker*, March 15, 2010, pp. 22–3.

Garret Cullity and "A potential contributor...." Cullity in Aiken, pp. 51–69.

"the emergency principle" See Appiah, pp. 160–6.

Principle of Liam Murphey: Murphey, *Moral Demands*.

Philosophers Hugh LaFollette....: See LaFollette and May, in Aiken, pp. 70–84.

"Asking people to give more…" Singer, *Life You Can Save*, p. 151.

Singer's suggested "level of giving": Singer, *Life You Can Save*, ch. 10: "A Realistic Approach."

Libertarians: We owe nothing to the world's poor

SOURCES

Jan Narveson. "Feeding the Hungry," pp. 143–56 in Narveson, *Moral Matters*. Peterborough, Ontario, Canada: Broadview Press Ltd., 1999.

Thomas Pogge. *World Poverty and Human Rights*. 2nd edn. Cambridge, UK: Polity Press, 2008. General Introduction.

NOTES

Pogge agrees with the libertarians, Pogge, p. 15.

"Implicit in our moral thinking...." Pogge, pp. 15–16.

"I do not complain that the WTO...." Pogge, pp. 18–19.

Counter-arguments to objection that fault lies with local governments, Pogge, pp. 28–30.

"Those on the political right...." Pogge, p. 31.

Pogge on obligations to compensate the global poor, Pogge, p. 26.

Religion and aiding the poor

SOURCES

Peggy Morgan and Clive A. Lawton (Eds). *Ethical Issues in Six Religious Traditions*. Edinburgh: Edinburgh University Press, 2007.

– Werner Menski: "Hinduism"

– Peggy Morgan: "Buddhism"

– Clive A. Lawton: "Judaism"

– Alan Brown: "Christianity"

– Azim Nanji: "Islam"

Jim Wallis, *God's Politics*. New York, HarperCollins, 2005.

NOTES

"Charitable giving ranks...." Menskin in Morgan/Lawton, p. 28.

"A central part of all Buddhist...." Morgan in Morgan/Lawton, p. 86.

On charitable giving in Judaism and Islam, see Lawton and Nanji articles in Morgan/Lawton.

World Vision International: wvi.org (See "Core Values.")

American Jewish World Service: ajws.org/who_we_are/

Catholic Relief Services: crs.org/about/

Definitions

(Terms are defined in the order in which they appeared in the text.)

1. *Relative poverty*: Poverty in relation to standards of living within a particular society.
2. *Absolute poverty*: Poverty in relation to global standards of living.
3. *Extreme poverty*: The poorest of the poor within the category of absolute poverty. (The World Bank's standard for extreme poverty is $1.25 a day.)
4. *Purchasing power parity* (*PPP*): An equivalence measure of what it would take to purchase certain items at different times and places.
5. *Developed nations*: The richer, industrialized nations.
6. *Developing nations*: Those with expanding economies.
7. *Underdeveloped nations*: Those that are poor and lack large-scale industry and technology.
8. *Least developed countries* (*LDCs*): The poorest subset of the underdeveloped countries.
9. *NGOs*: Non-governmental organizations
10. *World Bank*: An international organization of member nations, which provides loans to poor countries to help with development and the reduction of poverty.
11. *International Monetary Fund* (IMF): A United Nations agency designed to promote international monetary cooperation.
12. *Structural adjustment programs* (*SAPs*): Programs made a prerequisite for receiving World Bank/IMF loans that required those nations receiving loans to cut expenses by limiting social spending, cutting jobs and lowering wages.
13. *The Green Revolution*: Technological advances (including genetic modifications of crops) that led to a huge increase in the world's food supply.
14. *Millennium Development Goals* (*MDGs*): Eight development goals set by the United Nations in 2000.
15. *Poverty trap*: A complex of factors that work against any attempt to improve one or two dimensions of poverty.
16. *Millennium Villages Project*: A UN project, under the leadership of Jeffrey Sachs, which attempts to lift selected African villages out of poverty by treating various dimensions of poverty simultaneously.
17. *The Shallow Pond argument*: A name given to the argument of Singer's that moves from our obligation to save one drowning child to the conclusion that we are obligated to contribute most of what we have to save the world's poor.

18. *Emergency principle*: The principle that "If you are the person in the best position to prevent something really awful, and it won't cost you much to do it, do it."

19. *Compliance condition* (*of our obligation of beneficence*): The idea that we are obligated to give our part (but only our part) of what it would take to alleviate poverty if everyone who was able contributed.

20. *World Trade Organization* (*WTO*): A multi-national organization involved in the making and enforcing of free trade agreements.

21. *Charity*: Giving to people in need. (The word can be used both of giving considered optional and giving considered obligatory.)

22. *Artha*: The pursuit of wealth and power (Hinduism).

23. *Tzedaka*: The Hebrew word for charity (also for justice).

Questions

(Please explain your answers, making specific reference to relevant passages in the discussion.)

1. Explain the World Bank's most recent standard for "extreme poverty" and how it was arrived at.

2. What are some different types of foreign aid?

3. What was Thomas Malthus' theory about food and population growth? Why does his theory (at least in its most pessimistic forms) seem wrong today?

4. Summarize the debate between Jeffrey Sachs and William Easterly regarding large-scale aid programs.

5. How are some aid organizations trying to answer questions about whether or not aid works?

6. Present Peter Singer's "Shallow Pond argument." He presents two versions of this argument: What is the difference between them?

7. Critics who agree we have obligations to help the poor have suggested alternate principles of giving. What are two of those?

8. Why is Singer now promoting a fair-share principle of giving? Has he rejected his earlier Shallow Pond argument?

9. What is the libertarian case against any obligation to help the world's poor?

10. Summarize Pogge's argument to the effect that even under libertarian principles, we still have some obligation toward the world's poor.

11. What are the three dimensions often stressed in a religious view of helping the poor?

12. How would you say that Peter Singer compares to the world's great religions in his view of our obligation toward the poor?

12

World Poverty
Readings

Nicholas D. Kristof discusses the failures and successes of foreign aid

The number of bleeding hearts has soared exponentially over the last decade. Celebrities embraced Africa, while conservatives went from showing disdain for humanitarian aid ("money down a rat hole") to displaying leadership in the fight against AIDS and malaria. Compassion became contagious and then it became consensus.

Yet all the wringing hands never quite clasped. Just as the bleeding hearts seemed victorious, they divided in a ferocious intellectual debate about how best to help poor people around the world. One group, led by Bono and the indefatigable Jeffrey Sachs of Columbia University, argues that the crucial need is for more money. After all, aid for development is quite modest: for every $100 in national income, we Americans donate just 18 cents in "official development assistance" to poor countries. Sweden donates five times as much. Sachs's book "The End of Poverty" is the bible of this camp.

The rival camp, led by William Easterly of New York University, argues that more money doesn't necessarily help, and may hurt. Easterly, whose powerful and provocative book "The White Man's Burden: Why the West's Efforts to Aid the Rest Have Done So Much Ill and So Little Good" appeared in 2006, is still

rocking the world of do-gooders. His book was a direct assault on Sachs's, and it has been influential because, frankly, much of his critique rings true, even among aid workers.

Easterly has been joined this year by Dambisa Moyo, a Zambian economist who wrote "Dead Aid: Why Aid Is Not Working and How There Is a Better Way for Africa."[…]

The Easterly/Moyo camp notes that anybody who has traveled in Africa has seen aid projects that have failed, undermined self-reliance and entrepreneur-ship, even harmed people. Economists find no correlation between countries that received aid and those that grew quickly. Indeed, the great economic successes in modern times (mostly in Asia) often received little aid.

It's also clear that doing good is harder than it looks. For example, abundant evidence suggests that education can be transformative in a poor country, so donors often pay for schools. But building a school is expensive and can line the pockets of corrupt officials. And in my reporting I've found that the big truancy problem in poor countries typically involves not students but teachers: I remember one rural Indian school where the teachers appeared only once or twice a year to administer standardized tests. To make sure that the students didn't do embarrassingly badly on those exams, the teachers wrote all the answers on the blackboard. The critics can cite similar unexpected difficulties in almost every nook of the aid universe.

Reproduced with permission from "How Can We Help?" by Nicholas Kristof. *NY Times Book Review*, Mar. 22, 2009, p. 27.

If Sachs represents the Hegelian thesis and Easterly the antithesis, we now have hope of seeing an emerging synthesis. It would acknowledge the shortcomings of aid, but also note some grand successes. For example, the number of children dying each year before the age of 5 has dropped by three million worldwide since 1990, largely because of foreign aid. Yes, aid often fails— but more than balancing the failures is quite a triumph: one child's life saved every 11 seconds (according to my calculations from United Nations statistics).

Moreover, pragmatic donors are figuring out creative ways to overcome the obstacles. Take education. Given the problems with school-building programs, donors have turned to other strategies to increase the number of students, and these are often much more cost-effective: (1) Deworm children. This costs about 50 cents per child per year and reduces absenteeism from anemia, sickness and malnutrition. A Kenya study found, in effect, that it is only one twenty-fifth as expensive to increase school attendance by deworming students as by constructing schools. (2) Bribe parents. One of the most successful antipoverty initiatives is Oportunidades in Mexico, which pays impoverished mothers a monthly stipend if their kids attend school regularly. Oportunidades has raised high school enrollment in some rural areas by 85 percent.

I don't mean to imply that building brick-and-mortar schools is an outmoded idea. [...] The point is to be relentlessly empirical.

One of the challenges with the empirical approach is that aid organizations typically claim that every project succeeds. Failures are buried so as not to discourage donors, and evaluations are often done by the organizations themselves—ensuring that every intervention is above average. Yet recently there has been a revolution in evaluation, led by economists at the Poverty Action Lab at MIT. They have designed rigorous studies to see what actually works. The idea is to introduce new aid initiatives randomly in some areas and not in others, and to measure how much change occurred and at what cost. This approach is expensive but gives a much clearer sense of which interventions are most cost-effective.

The upshot is that we can now see that there are many aid programs that work very well. We don't need to distract ourselves with theoretical questions about aid, so long as we can focus on deworming children and bribing parents. The new synthesis should embrace specific interventions that all sides agree have merit, while also borrowing from an important insight of the aid critics: trade is usually preferable to aid.

I was recently in Liberia, a fragile African democracy struggling to rebuild. It is chock-full of aid groups rushing around in white SUVs doing wonderful work. But it also needs factories to employ people, build skills and pay salaries and taxes. Americans are horrified by sweatshops, but nothing would help Liberia more than if China moved some of its sweatshops there, so that Liberians could make sandals and T-shirts.

[...]

As these ideas spread, we're seeing more aid organizations that blur the boundary with business, pursuing what's called a double bottom line: profits but also a social return. For example, the New York-based Acumen Fund is a cross between a venture capital operation and an aid group: it invests "patient capital," accepting below-market returns and offering management help in a Tanzanian company that makes antimalaria bed nets, for instance, and in a hospital company in India that offers a for-profit model to fight maternal mortality. [...]

In the 1960s, there were grand intellectual debates about whether capitalism was heroic or evil; today we simply worry about how to make it work. At last, we may be doing the same with foreign aid.

Questions

1. According to Kristof, what's the debate between Jeffrey Sachs and William Easterly about?

2. What is the "synthesis" of these ideas that Kristof thinks we're now seeing?

Abhijit V. Banerjee and Esther Duflo discuss the debate on world poverty and the need for controlled trials to see what interventions work

Every year, 9 million children die before their fifth birthday.[1] A woman in sub-Saharan Africa has a one-in-thirty chance of dying while giving birth—in the developed world, the chance is one in 5,600. There are at least twenty-five countries, most of them in sub-Saharan Africa, where the average person is expected to live no more than fifty-five years. In India alone, more than 50 million school-going children cannot read a very simple text.[2]

This is the kind of paragraph that might make you want to shut this book and, ideally, forget about this whole business of world poverty: The problem seems too big, too intractable. Our goal with this book is to persuade you not to.

A recent experiment at the University of Pennsylvania illustrates well how easily we can feel overwhelmed by the magnitude of the problem.[3] Researchers gave students $5 to fill out a short survey. They then showed them a flyer and asked them to make a donation to Save the Children, one of the world's leading charities. There were two different flyers. Some (randomly selected) students were shown this:

> Food shortages in Malawi are affecting more than 3 million children; In Zambia, severe rainfall deficits have resulted in a 42% drop in maize production from 2000. As a result, an estimated 3 million Zambians face hunger; Four million Angolans—one third of the population— have been forced to flee their homes; More than 11 million people in Ethiopia need immediate food assistance.

Other students were shown a flyer featuring a picture of a young girl and these words:

> Rokia, a 7-year-old girl from Mali, Africa, is desperately poor and faces a threat of severe hunger or even starvation.

Her life will be changed for the better as a result of your financial gift. With your support, and the support of other caring sponsors, Save the Children will work with Rokia's family and other members of the community to help feed her, provide her with education, as well as basic medical care and hygiene education.

The first flyer raised an average of $1.16 from each student. The second flyer, in which the plight of millions became the plight of one, raised $2.83. The students, it seems, were willing to take some responsibility for helping Rokia, but when faced with the scale of the global problem, they felt discouraged.

Some other students, also chosen at random, were shown the same two flyers after being told that people are more likely to donate money to an identifiable victim than when presented with general information. Those shown the first flyer, for Zambia, Angola, and Mali, gave more or less what that flyer had raised without the warning—$1.26. Those shown the second flyer, for Rokia, after this warning gave only $1.36, less than half of what their colleagues had committed without it. Encouraging students to think again prompted them to be less generous to Rokia, but not more generous to everyone else in Mali.

The students' reaction is typical of how most of us feel when we are confronted with problems like poverty. Our first instinct is to be generous, especially when facing an imperiled seven-year-old girl. But, like the Penn students, our second thought is often that there is really no point: Our contribution would be a drop in the bucket, and the bucket probably leaks. This book is an invitation to think again, *again*: to turn away from the feeling that the fight against poverty is too overwhelming, and to start to think of the challenge as a set of concrete problems that, once properly identified and understood, can be solved one at a time.

Unfortunately, this is not how the debates on poverty are usually framed. Instead of discussing how best to fight diarrhea or dengue, many of the most vocal experts tend to be fixated on the "big questions": What is the ultimate cause of poverty? How much faith should we place in free markets? Is democracy good for the poor? Does foreign aid have a role to play? And so on.

Jeffrey Sachs, adviser to the United Nations, director of the Earth Institute at Columbia University in New York City, and one such expert, has an answer to all these questions: Poor countries are poor because they are hot, infertile, malaria infested, often landlocked; this makes it hard for them to be productive without an initial large investment to help them deal with these endemic problems. But they cannot pay for the investments precisely because they are poor—they are in what economists call a "poverty trap." Until something is done about these problems, neither free markets nor democracy will do very much for them. This is why foreign aid is key: It can kick-start a virtuous cycle by helping poor countries invest in these critical areas and make them more productive. The resulting higher incomes will generate further investments; the beneficial spiral will continue. In his best-selling 2005 book, *The End of Poverty*,[4] Sachs argues that if the rich world had committed $195 billion in foreign aid per year between 2005 and 2025, poverty could have been entirely eliminated by the end of this period.

But then there are others, equally vocal, who believe that all of Sachs's answers are wrong. William Easterly, who battles Sachs from New York University at the other end of Manhattan, has become one of the most influential anti-aid public figures, following the publication of two books, *The Elusive Quest for Growth* and *The White Man's Burden*.[5] Dambisa Moyo, an economist who previously worked at Goldman Sachs and at the World Bank, has joined her voice to Easterly's with her recent book, *Dead Aid*.[6] Both argue that aid does more bad than good: It prevents people from searching for their own solutions, while corrupting and undermining local institutions and creating a self-perpetuating lobby of aid agencies. The best bet for poor countries is to rely on one simple idea: When markets are free and the incentives are right, people can find ways to solve their problems. They do not need handouts, from foreigners or from their own governments. In this sense, the aid pessimists are actually quite optimistic about the way the world works. According to Easterly, there are no such things as poverty traps.

Whom should we believe? Those who tell us that aid can solve the problem? Or those who say that it makes things worse? The debate cannot be solved in the abstract: We need evidence. But unfortunately, the kind of data usually used to answer the big questions does not inspire confidence. There is never a shortage of compelling anecdotes, and it is always possible to find at least one to support any position. Rwanda, for example, received a lot of aid money in the years immediately after the genocide, and prospered. Now that the economy is thriving, President Paul Kagame has started to wean the country off aid. Should we count Rwanda as an example of the good that aid can do (as Sachs suggests), or as a poster child for self-reliance (as Moyo presents it)? Or both?

Because individual examples like Rwanda cannot be pinned down, most researchers trying to answer the big philosophical questions prefer multicountry comparisons. For example, the data on a couple of hundred countries in the world show that those that received more aid did not grow faster than the rest. This is often interpreted as evidence that aid does not work, but in fact, it could also mean the opposite. Perhaps the aid helped them avoid a major disaster, and things would have been much worse without it. We simply do not know; we are just speculating on a grand scale.

But if there is really no evidence for or against aid, what are we supposed to do—give up on the poor? Fortunately, we don't need to be quite so defeatist. There are in fact answers—indeed, this whole book is in the form of an extended answer—it is just that they are not the kind of sweeping answers that Sachs and Easterly favor. This book will not tell you whether aid is good or bad, but it will say whether particular instances of aid did some good or not. We cannot pronounce on the efficacy of democracy, but we do have something to say about whether democracy could be made more effective in rural Indonesia by changing the way it is organized on the ground and so on.

In any case, it is not clear that answering some of these big questions, like whether foreign aid works, is as important as we are sometimes led to believe. Aid looms large for those in London, Paris, or Washington, DC, who are passionate about helping the poor (and those less passionate, who resent paying for it). But in truth, aid is only a very small part of the money that is spent on the poor every year. Most programs targeted at the world's poor are funded out of their country's own resources. India, for example, receives essentially no aid. In 2004–2005, it spent half a trillion rupees ($31 billion USD PPP)[7] just on primary-education programs for the poor. Even in Africa, where foreign aid has a much more important role, it represented only 5.7 percent of total government budgets in 2003

(12 percent if we exclude Nigeria and South Africa, two big countries that receive very little aid).[8]

More important, the endless debates about the rights and wrongs of aid often obscure what really matters: not so much where the money comes from, but where it goes. This is a matter of choosing the right kind of project to fund—should it be food for the indigent, pensions for the elderly, or clinics for the ailing?—and then figuring out how best to run it. Clinics, for example, can be run and staffed in many different ways.

No one in the aid debate really disagrees with the basic premise that we should help the poor when we can. This is no surprise. The philosopher Peter Singer has written about the moral imperative to save the lives of those we don't know. He observes that most people would willingly sacrifice a $1,000 suit to rescue a child seen drowning in a pond[9] and argues that there should be no difference between that drowning child and the 9 million children who, every year, die before their fifth birthday. Many people would also agree with Amartya Sen, the economist-philosopher and Nobel Prize Laureate, that poverty leads to an intolerable waste of talent. As he puts it, poverty is not just a lack of money; it is not having the capability to realize one's full potential as a human being.[10] A poor girl from Africa will probably go to school for at most a few years even if she is brilliant, and most likely won't get the nutrition to be the world-class athlete she might have been, or the funds to start a business if she has a great idea.

It is true that this wasted life probably does not directly affect people in the developed world, but it is not impossible that it might: She might end up as an HIV-positive prostitute who infects a traveling American who then brings the disease home, or she might develop a strain of antibiotic-resistant TB that will eventually find its way to Europe. Had she gone to school, she might have turned out to be the person who invented the cure for Alzheimer's. Or perhaps, like Dai Manju, a Chinese teenager who got to go to school because of a clerical error at a bank, she would end up as a business tycoon employing thousands of others (Nicholas Kristof and Sheryl WuDunn tell her story in their book *Half the Sky*).[11] And even if she doesn't, what could justify not giving her a chance?

The main disagreement shows up when we turn to the question, "Do we know of effective ways to help the poor?" Implicit in Singer's argument for helping others is the idea that you know how to do it: The

moral imperative to ruin your suit is much less compelling if you do not know how to swim. This is why, in *The Life You Can Save*, Singer takes the trouble to offer his readers a list of concrete examples of things that they should support, regularly updated on his Web site.[12] Kristof and WuDunn do the same. The point is simple: Talking about the problems of the world without talking about some accessible solutions is the way to paralysis rather than progress.

This is why it is really helpful to think in terms of concrete problems which can have specific answers, rather than foreign assistance in general: "aid" rather than "Aid." To take an example, according to the World Health Organization (WHO), malaria caused almost 1 million deaths in 2008, mostly among African children.[13] One thing we know is that sleeping under insecticide-treated bed nets can help save many of these lives. Studies have shown that in areas where malaria infection is common, sleeping under an insecticide-treated bed net reduces the incidence of malaria by half.[14] What, then, is the *best* way to make sure that children sleep under bed nets?

For approximately $10, you can deliver an insecticide-treated net to a family and teach the household how to use it. Should the government or an NGO give parents free bed nets, or ask them to buy their own, perhaps at a subsidized price? Or should we let them buy it in the market at full price? These questions can be answered, but the answers are by no means obvious. Yet many "experts" take strong positions on them that have little to do with evidence.

Because malaria is contagious, if Mary sleeps under a bed net, John is less likely to get malaria—if at least half the population sleeps under a net, then even those who do not have much less risk of getting infected.[15] The problem is that fewer than one-fourth of kids at risk sleep under a net:[16] It looks like the $10 cost is too much for many families in Mali or Kenya. Given the benefits both to the user and others in the neighborhood, selling the nets at a discount or even giving them away would seem to be a good idea. Indeed, free bed-net distribution is one thing that Jeffrey Sachs advocates. Easterly and Moyo object, arguing that people will not value (and hence will not use) the nets if they get them for free. And even if they do, they may become used to handouts and refuse to buy more nets in the future, when they are not free, or refuse to buy other things that they need unless these are also subsidized. This could wreck well-functioning markets. Moyo tells the story of how a bed-net supplier was ruined by a free bed-net distribution program. When free distribution stopped, there was no one to supply bed nets at any price.

To shed light on this debate, we need to answer three questions. First, if people must pay full price (or at least a significant fraction of the price) for a bed net, will they prefer to go without? Second, if bed nets are given to them free or at some subsidized price, will people use them, or will they be wasted? Third, after getting the net at subsidized price once, will they become more or less willing to pay for the next one if the subsidies are reduced in the future?

To answer these questions, we would need to observe the behavior of comparable groups of people facing different levels of subsidy. The key word here is "comparable." People who pay for bed nets and people who get them for free are usually not going to be alike: It is possible that those who paid for their nets will be richer and better educated, and have a better understanding of why they need a bed net; those who got them for free might have been chosen by an NGO precisely because they were poor. But there could also be the opposite pattern: Those who got them for free are the well connected, whereas the poor and isolated had to pay full price. Either way, we cannot draw any conclusion from the way they used their net.

For this reason, the cleanest way to answer such questions is to mimic the randomized trials that are used in medicine to evaluate the effectiveness of new drugs. Pascaline Dupas, of the University of California at Los Angeles, carried out such an experiment in Kenya, and others followed suit with similar experiments in Uganda and Madagascar.[17] In Dupas's experiment, individuals were randomly selected to receive different levels of subsidy to purchase bed nets. By comparing the behavior of randomly selected equivalent groups that were offered a net at different prices, she was able to answer all three of our questions, at least in the context in which the experiment was carried out.

In Chapter 3 of this book, we will have a lot to say about what she found. [Ed.: The studies referred to indicate that the poor are more likely to obtain bed nets when they are subsidized or free and no less likely to use nets that were provided free. The puzzle was that there was such low demand for nets among the poor at any price—a puzzle that chapter attempts to analyze.]

Although open questions remain (the experiments do not yet tell us about whether the distribution of subsidized imported bed nets hurt local producers, for example), these findings did a lot to move this debate and influenced both the discourse and the direction of policy.

The shift from broad general questions to much narrower ones has another advantage. When we learn about whether poor people are willing to pay money for bed nets, and whether they use them if they get them for free, we learn about much more than the best way to distribute bed nets: We start to understand how poor people make decisions. For example, what stands in the way of more widespread bed net adoption? It could be a lack of information about their benefits, or the fact that poor people cannot afford them. It could also be that the poor are so absorbed by the problems of the present that they don't have the mental space to worry about the future, or there could be something entirely different going on. Answering these questions, we get to understand what, if anything, is special about the poor: Do they just live like everyone else, except with less money, or is there something fundamentally different about life under extreme poverty?

[…]

This radical shift in perspective, away from the universal answers, required us to step out of the office and look more carefully at the world. In doing so, we were following a long tradition of development economists who have emphasized the importance of collecting the right data to be able to say anything useful about the world. However, we had two advantages over the previous generations: First, there are now high-quality data from a number of poor countries that were not available before. Second, we have a new, powerful tool: randomized control trials (RCTs), which give researchers, working with a local partner, a chance to implement large-scale experiments designed to test their theories. In an RCT, as in the studies on bed nets, individuals or communities are randomly assigned to different "treatments"— different programs or different versions of the same program. Since the individuals assigned to different treatments are exactly comparable (because they were chosen at random), any difference between them is the effect of the treatment.

A single experiment does not provide a final answer on whether a program would universally "work." But we can conduct a series of experiments, differing in either the kind of location in which they are conducted or the exact intervention being tested (or both). Together, this allows us to both verify the robustness of our conclusions (Does what works in Kenya also work in Madagascar?) and narrow the set of possible theories that can explain the data. [...]

In 2003, we founded the Poverty Action Lab (which later became the Abdul Latif Jameel Poverty Action Lab, or J-PAL) to encourage and support other researchers, governments, and nongovernmental organizations to work together on this new way of doing economics, and to help diffuse what they have learned among policy makers. The response has been overwhelming. By 2010, J-PAL researchers had completed or were engaged in over 240 experiments in forty countries around the world, and very large numbers of organizations, researchers, and policy makers have embraced the idea of randomized trials.

The response to J-PAL's work suggests that there are many who share our basic premise—that it is possible to make very significant progress against the biggest problem in the world through the accumulation of a set of small steps, each well thought out, carefully tested, and judiciously implemented.

This might seem self-evident, but as we will argue throughout the book, it is not how policy usually gets made. The practice of development policy, as well as the accompanying debates, seems to be premised on the impossibility of relying on evidence: Verifiable evidence is a chimera, at best a distant fantasy, at worst a distraction. "We have to get on with the work, while you indulge yourselves in the pursuit of evidence," is what hardheaded policy makers and their even harder-headed advisers often told us when we started down this path. Even today, there are many who hold this view. But there are also many people who have always felt disempowered by this unreasoned urgency. They feel, as we do, that the best anyone can do is to understand deeply the specific problems that afflict the poor and to try to identify the most effective ways to intervene. In some instances, no doubt, the best option will be to do nothing, but there is no general rule here, just as there is no general principle that spending money always works. It is the body of knowledge that grows out of each specific answer and the understanding that goes into those answers that give us the best shot at, one day, ending poverty.

[...]

Questions

1. Banerjee and Duflo talk about an experiment that reflects on our responses to appeals to help the poor. What was this experiment and what did it seem to show?

2. How do Banerjee and Duflo think we ought to approach questions about helping the poor?

3. Why do these questions concern more than foreign aid?

Notes

1. United Nations, Department of Economic and Social Affairs, *The Millennium Development Goals Report* (2010).
2. Pratham Annual Status of Education Report 2005: Final Edition, available at http://scripts.mit.edu/—varun_ag/readinggroup/images/1/14/ASER.pdf.
3. Deborah Small, George Loewenstein, and Paul Slovic, "Sympathy and Callousness: The Impact of Deliberative Thought on Donations to Identifiable and Statistical Victims," *Organizational Behavior and Human Decision Processes* 102 (2007): 143–53.

4. Jeffrey Sachs, *The End of Poverty: Economic Possibilities for Our Time* (New York: Penguin Press, 2005).
5. William Easterly, *The White Man's Burden: Why the West's Efforts to Aid the Rest Have Done So Much Ill and So Little Good* (Oxford: Oxford University Press, 2006); and William Easterly, *The Elusive Quest for Growth: Economists' Adventures and Misadventures in the Tropics* (Cambridge: MIT Press, 2001).
6. Dambisa Moyo, *Dead Aid: Why Aid Is Not Working and How There Is a Better Way for Africa* (London: Allen Lane, 2009).

7. Everywhere in the book, whenever we present an amount in a country's local currency, we give the equivalent amount in dollars, adjusted for the cost of living [...]. This is denoted by USD PPP (USD at purchasing power parity).

8. Todd Moss, Gunilla Pettersson, and Nicolas van de Walle, "An Aid-Institutions Paradox? A Review Essay on Aid Dependency and State Building in Sub-Saharan Africa," Working Paper No. 74, Center for Global Development (January 2006). Still, eleven countries out of forty-six received more than 10 percent of their budget in aid, and eleven got more than 20 percent.

9. Peter Singer, "Famine, Affluence, and Morality," *Philosophy and Public Affairs* 1 (3) (1972): 229–43.

10. Amartya Sen, *Development as Freedom* (New York: Knopf, 1999).

11. Nicholas D. Kristof and Sheryl WuDunn, *Half the Sky: Turning Oppression into Opportunity for Women Worldwide* (New York: Knopf, 2009).

12. Peter Singer, The Life You Can Save (New York: Random House, 2009), available at http://wvvw.thelifeyoucansave.com.

13. See the WHO fact sheet on malaria, available at http://www.who.int/mediacentre/factsheets/fs094/en/index.html. Note that here, as in many other places in the book, we cite the official international statistics. It is good to keep in mind that the numbers are not always accurate: On many issues, the data these numbers are based on are incomplete or of doubtful quality.

14. C. Lengeler, "Insecticide-Treated Bed Nets and Curtains for Preventing Malaria," *Cochrane Database of Systematic Reviews* 2 (2004), Art. No. CD000363.

15. William A. Hawley, Penelope A. Phillips-Howard, Feiko O. Ter Kuile, Dianne J. Terlouw, John M. Vulule, Maurice Ombok, Bernard L. Nahlen, John E. Gimnig, Simon K. Kariuki, Margarette S. Kolczak, and Allen W. Hightower, "Community-Wide Effects of Permethrin-Treated Bed Nets on Child Mortality and Malaria Morbidity in Western Kenya," *American Journal of Tropical Medicine and Hygiene* 68 (2003): 121–7.

16. World Malaria report, available at http://www.whoint/malaria/ world_malaria_report_2009/factsheet/en/index.html.

17. Pascaline Dupas, "Short-Run Subsidies and Long-Run Adoption of New Health Products: Evidence from a Field Experiment," draft (2010); Jessica Cohen and Pascaline Dupas, "Free Distribution or Cost-Sharing? Evidence from a Randomized Malaria Prevention Experiment," *Quarterly Journal of Economics* 125 (1) (February 2010): 1–45; V Hoffmann, "Demand, Retention, and Intra-Household Allocation of Free and Purchased Mosquito Nets," *American Economic Review: Papers and Proceedings* (May 2009); Paul Krezanoski, Alison Comfort, and Davidson Hamer, "Effect of Incentives on Insecticide-Treated Bed Net Use in Sub-Saharan Africa: A Cluster Randomized Trial in Madagascar," *Malaria Journal* 9 (186) (June 27, 2010).

Peter Singer argues that to live a morally decent life, the well-off would have to give most of what they have to the world's poor

As I write this, in November 1971 people are dying in East Bengal from lack of food, shelter, and medical care. The suffering and death that are occurring there now are not inevitable, not unavoidable in any fatalistic sense

From "Famine, Affluence, and Morality," by Peter Singer, *Philosophy and Public Affairs*, 1:3, 1972, 229–43. Copyright © 1972 by Princeton University Press. This material is reproduced with permission of John Wiley & Sons, Inc.

of the term. Constant poverty, a cyclone, and a civil war have turned at least nine million people into destitute refugees, nevertheless, it is not beyond the capacity of the richer nations to give enough assistance to reduce any further suffering to very small proportions.

[...]

I begin with the assumption that suffering and death from lack of food, shelter, and medical care are bad. I think most people will agree. [...]

My next point is this: if it is in our power to prevent something bad from happening, without thereby sacrificing anything of comparable moral importance, we ought, morally, to do it. By "without sacrificing anything of comparable moral importance" I mean without causing anything else comparably bad to happen, or doing something that is wrong in itself, or failing to promote some moral good, comparable in significance to the bad thing that we can prevent. This principle seems almost as uncontroversial as the last one. It requires us only to prevent what is bad, and not to promote what is good, and it requires this of us only when we can do it without sacrificing anything that is form the moral point of view, comparably important. I could even, as far as the application of my argument to the Bengal emergency is concerned, qualify the point so as to make it: if it is in our power to prevent something very bad from happening without thereby sacrificing anything morally significant, we ought, morally, to do it. An application of this principle would be as follows: if I am walking past a shallow pond and see a child drowning in it, I ought to wade in and pull the child out This will mean getting my clothes muddy, but this is insignificant, while the death of the child would presumably be a very bad thing.

The uncontroversial appearance of the principle just stated is deceptive. If it were acted upon, even in its qualified from, our lives, our society, and our world would be fundamentally changed. For the principle takes, first, no account of proximity or distance. It makes no moral difference whether the person I can help is a neighbor's child ten yards from me or a Bengali whose name I shall never know, ten thousand miles away. Second, the principle makes no distinction between cases in which I am the only person who could possibly do anything and cases in which I am just one among millions in the same position.

I do not think I need to say much in defense of the refusal to take proximity and distance into account. The fact that a person is physically near to us, so that we have personal contact with him, may make it more likely that we *shall* assist him, but this does not show that we *ought* to help him rather than another who happens to be further away. If we accept any principle of impartiality, universalizability, equality, or whatever, we cannot discriminate against someone merely because he is far away from us (or we are far away from him). Admittedly, it is possible that we are in a better position to judge what needs to be done to help a person near to us than one far away, and perhaps also to provide the assistance we judge to be necessary. If this were the case, it would be a reason for helping those near to us first. This may once have been a justification for being more concerned with the poor in one's own town than with famine victims in India. Unfortunately for those who like to keep their moral responsibilities limited, instant communication and swift transportation have changed the situation. From the moral point of view, the development of the world into a "global village" has made an important, though still unrecognized, difference to our moral situation. Expert observers and supervisors, sent out by famine relief organizations or permanently stationed in famine-prone areas, can direct our aid to a refugee in Bengal almost as effectively as we could get it to someone in our own block. There would seem, therefore, to be no possible justification for discriminating on geographical grounds.

There may be a greater need to defend the second implication of my principle—that the fact that there are millions of other people in the same position, in respect to the Bengali refugees, as I am, does not make the situation significantly different from a situation in which I am the only person who can prevent something very bad from occurring. Again, of course, I admit that there is a psychological difference between the cases: one feels less guilty about doing nothing if one can point to others, similarly placed, who have also done nothing. Yet this can make no real difference to our moral obligations. Should I consider that I am less obliged to pull the drowning child out of the pond if on looking around I see other people, no further away than I am, who have also noticed the child but are doing nothing? One has only to ask this question to see the absurdity of the view that numbers lessen obligation. It is a view that is an ideal excuse for inactivity; unfortunately most of the major evils—poverty, overpopulation, pollution—are problems in which everyone is almost equally involved.

[…]

The outcome of this argument is that our traditional moral categories are upset. The traditional distinction between duty and charity cannot be drawn, or at least cannot be drawn in the place we normally draw it. Giving money to the Bengal Relief Fund is regarded as an act of charity in our society. The bodies which collect money are known as "charities." These organizations see themselves in this way—if you send them a check, you will be thanked for your "generosity." Because giving money is regarded as an act of charity, it is not thought that there is anything wrong with not giving. The charitable man may be praised, but the man who is not charitable is not condemned. People do not feel in any way ashamed or guilty about spending money on new clothes or a new car instead of giving it to famine relief. (Indeed, the altenative does not occur to them.) This way of looking at the matter cannot be justified. When we buy new clothes not to keep ourselves warm but to look "well-dressed," we are not providing for any important need. We would not be sacrificing anything significant if we were to continue to wear our old clothes and give the money to famine relief. By doing so, we would be preventing another person from starving. It follows from what I have said earlier that we ought to give money away, rather than spend it on clothes which we do not need to keep us warm.

[…]

I do not, of course, want to dispute the contention that governments of affluent nations should be giving many times the amount of genuine, no-strings-attached aid that they are giving now. I agree, too, that giving privately is not enough, and that we ought to be campaigning actively for entirely new standards for both public and private contributions to famine relief.

[…]

A […] point raised by the conclusion reached earlier relates to the question of just how much we all ought to be giving away. One possibility, which has already been mentioned, is that we ought to give until we reach the level of marginal utility—that is, the level at which, by giving more, I would cause as much suffering to myself or my dependents as I would relieve by my gift. This would mean, of course, that one would reduce oneself to very near the material circumstances of a Bengali refugee. It will be recalled that earlier I put forward both a strong and a moderate version of the principle of preventing bad occurrences. The strong version, which required us to prevent bad things from happening unless in doing so we would be sacrificing something of comparable moral significance, does seem to require reducing ourselves to the level of marginal utility. I should also say that the strong version seems to

me to be the correct one. I proposed the more moderate version—that we should prevent bad occurrences unless, to do so, we had to sacrifice something morally significant—only in order to show that even on this surely undeniable principle a great change in our way of life is required. On the more moderate principle, it may not follow that we ought to reduce ourselves to the level of marginal utility, for one might hold that to reduce oneself and one's family to this level is to cause something significantly bad to happen. Whether this is so I shall not discuss, since, as I have said, I can see no good reason for holding the moderate version of the principle rather than the strong version. Even if we accepted the principle only in its moderate form, however, it should be clear that we would have to give away enough to ensure that the consumer society, dependent as it is on people spending on trivia rather than giving to famine relief, would slow down and perhaps disappear entirely. […] Yet looking at the matter purely from the point of view of overseas aid, there must be a limit to the extent to which we should deliberately slow down our economy, for it might be the case that if we gave away, say, forty percent of our gross national product, we would slow down the economy so much that in absolute terms we would he giving less than if we gave twenty-five percent of the much larger GNP that we would have if we limited our contribution to this smaller percentage.

I mention this only as an indication of the sort of factor that one would have to take into account in working out an ideal. Since Western societies generally consider one percent of the GNP an acceptable level for overseas aid, the matter is entirely academic. Nor does it affect the question of how much an individual should give in a society in which very few are giving substantial amounts.

[…]

Questions

1. What does Singer believe is our moral obligation to those people in the world who are dying from famine and disease? What is his argument for this moral obligation and how does that argument connect to his imagined case of the drowning child?

2. "I can't be expected to give so much when so few others are giving anything." What is Singer's argument against this sort of claim?

Kwame Anthony Appiah argues that we do not owe so much to strangers as Singer claims

[…]

The Singer principle requires you to prevent bad things from happening if the cost is something less awful. Upon reflection, however, it's not so clear that the principle even gets the drowning case right. Saving the child may be preventing something bad; but *not* saving the child might, for all we know, prevent something worse. After all, shouldn't I be busy about saving those hundreds of thousands of starving children? And wouldn't selling my suit raise a few hundred dollars? And wouldn't ruining it mean I couldn't raise those dollars? The principle says that, if this kid right here has to drown for me to save my suit for sale so I can save, say, ninety other children, so be it; though it also leaves me free to let the ninety die if I can find something worse to prevent.[…]

The larger point, of course, is that our conviction that we should save the drowning child doesn't by itself tell us *why* we should do so. I have already argued that our moral intuitions are often more secure than the principles we appeal to in explaining them. There are countless principles that would get you to save the drowning child without justifying your own immiseration. Here's one:

> If you are the person in the best position to prevent something really awful, and it won't cost you much to do so, do it.

Now this principle—which I am inclined, for the moment, to think may be right—simply doesn't have the radical consequences of the Singer principle. I'm not especially well placed to save the children that UNICEF has told me about. And even if I were, giving away most of my means would radically reduce my quality of life. […]

This principle—I'll call it the emergency principle—is a low-level one that I think is pretty

plausible. I wouldn't be surprised, though, if some philosopher came up with a case where the emergency principle gave what I thought was the wrong answer. That's because figuring out moral principles, as an idle glance at the history of moral philosophy will show you, is *hard*. […]

On the other hand, many decisions *aren't* so hard, because some of our firmest moral knowledge is about particular cases. I have no doubt at all that I should save the drowning child and ruin my suit. (Oddly, American states differ as to whether this requirement is a legal one.) There are many arguments that I might make in defense of this view, especially to someone who was seriously convinced that he was free to let the child drown. But I am less certain of most of those arguments than I am that I should save the child.

The emergency principle may or may not be sound, but it tells me nothing about what I should do when UNICEF sends me a request for money. I think that a cosmopolitan who believes that every human being matters cannot be satisfied with that. So let's start with the sort of core moral ideas increasingly articulated in our conception of basic human rights. People have needs—health, food, shelter, education—that must be met if they are to lead decent lives. There are certain options that they ought to have: to seek sexual satisfaction with consenting partners; to have children if they wish to; to move from place to place; to express and share ideas; to help manage their societies; to exercise their imaginations. (These are options. People should also be free not to exercise them.) And there are certain obstacles to a good life that ought not to be imposed upon them: needless pain, unwarranted contempt, the mutilation of their bodies. To recognize that everybody is entitled, where possible, to have their basic needs met, to exercise certain human capabilities, and to be protected from certain harms, is not yet to say how all these things are to be assured. But if you accept that these basic needs ought to be met, what obligations have you incurred? I want to offer some constraints on an acceptable answer.

First, the primary mechanism for ensuring these entitlements remains the nation-state. […] Accepting the nation-state means accepting that we have a special responsibility for the life and the justice of our own;

but we still have to play our part in ensuring that all states respect the rights and meet the needs of their citizens. If they cannot, then all of us—through our nations, if they will do it, and in spite of them, if they won't—share the collective obligation to change them; and if the reason they fail their citizens is that they lack resources, providing resources can be part of that collective obligation. That is an equally fundamental cosmopolitan commitment.

But, second, our obligation is not to carry the whole burden alone. Each of us should do our fair share; but we cannot be required to do more. This is a constraint, however inchoate, that the Shallow Pond theorists do not respect. The Singer principle just doesn't begin to capture the subtlety of our actual moral thought. A different philosopher's story, this one offered by Richard W. Miller, makes the point. An adult is plummeting from a tenth-story window, and you, on the sidewalk below, know that you can save that person's life by cushioning his fall. If you did so, however, you would very likely suffer broken bones, which would heal, perhaps painfully and imperfectly, over a period of months. (Suppose you know all this because you're an orthopedic surgeon.) To Miller it's clear that you can do your "fair share in making the world a better place while turning down this chance for world-improvement."[1] Since the death you failed to prevent is worse than a few months of suffering, the Singer principle, of course, says otherwise. Our ordinary moral thinking makes distinctions the principle doesn't capture.

Now, I agree that it's not easy to specify what our fair share might be, and especially how it might be affected by the derelictions of others. Suppose we had a plan for guaranteeing everyone his or her basic entitlements. Let's call the share that I owe—suppose it would be paid as a development tax—my basic obligation. Even if we could get everyone to agree on the virtues of the plan; and even if we could determine how each of us, depending on our resources, should contribute his or her fair share, we can be pretty confident that some people would not give their fair share. That means there would still be some unmet entitlements. What is the obligation of those who have already met their basic obligation? Is it enough simply to say, "I know there are unmet entitlements, but I have done my part"? After all, the unmet entitlements are still unmet, and they're still entitlements.

Third, whatever our basic obligations, they must be consistent with our being, as I said at the beginning, partial to those closest to us: to our families, our friends, our nations; to the many groups that call upon us through our identities, chosen and unchosen; and, of course, to ourselves. Whatever my basic obligations are to the poor far away, they cannot be enough, I believe, to trump my concerns for my family, my friends, my country; nor can an argument that every life matters require me to be indifferent to the fact that one of those lives is mine. This constraint is another that the Shallow Pond theorists are indifferent toward. They think that it is so important to avoid the bad things in other lives that we should be willing to accept for ourselves, our families and friends, lives that are barely worth living. This third constraint interacts, I think, with the worry that I expressed about the second. For if so many people in the world are not doing their share—and they clearly are not—it seems to me I cannot be required to derail my life to take up the slack.

Let me add one final, general constraint. Any plausible answer to the question of what we owe to others will have to take account of many values; no sensible story of our obligations to strangers can ignore the diversity of the things that matter in human life. Cosmopolitans, more than anyone else, know this. Imagine a drab totalitarian regime with excellent pre-natal healthcare. After a "velvet revolution," a vibrant democracy emerges and freedom reigns. But perhaps because the health care system is a little wobblier (or perhaps because some pregnant mothers exercise their newly won right to smoke and drink), the rates of infant mortality are a little higher. Most people would still plump for the velvet revolution. We think the death of a child is a very bad thing; but clearly we don't think it's the only thing that matters. This is part of why the child in the pond isn't adequate to the real complexity of our thinking.

What would the world look like if people always spent their money to alleviate diarrhea in the Third World and never on a ticket to the opera (or a donation to a local theater company, gallery, symphony orchestra, library, or what have you)? Well, it would probably be a flat and dreary place.

[…]

Questions

1. Appiah gives an alternate principle he claims is compatible with Singer's drowning child case. What is it?

2. Appiah presents four constraints he believes must be met by any "acceptable answer" to the question of what we owe the very poor. What are these constraints?

Note

1. Richard W. Miller, "Cosmopolitan Respect and Patriotic Concern," *Philosophy and Public Affairs* 27 (1998): 209.

Jan Narveson, a Libertarian, argues that feeding the hungry is not an obligation

Throughout history it has been the lot of most people to know of others worse off than they, and often enough of others who face starvation. In the contemporary world, television and other mass media enable all of us in the better-off areas to hear about starvation in even the most remote places. What, if any, are our obligations toward victims of starvation?

This can be a rather complex subject in real-world situations. We must begin by distinguishing importantly different cases. For *starve* functions both as a passive verb, indicating something that happens to one, and as an active verb, designating something inflicted by one person on another. In the latter case, starvation is a form of killing, and of course comes under the same strictures that any other method of killing is liable to. But when the problem is plague, crop-failure due to drought, or sheer lack of know-how, there is no obviously guilty party. Then the question is whether we, the amply fed, are guilty parties if we fail to come to the rescue of those victims.

From "Feeding the Hungry," in *Moral Matters* by Jan Narveson. Peterborough, Ontario, Canada: Broadview Press Ltd., 1999, pp. 143–56. Copyright © 1999, Jan Narveson. Reprinted with the permission of Broadview Press.

If I lock you in a room with no food and don't let you out, I have murdered you. If group A burns the crops of group B, it has slaughtered the Bs. There is, surely, no genuine *issue* about such cases. It is wrong to kill innocent people, and one way of killing them is as eligible for condemnation by this principle as any other, so far as killing goes. Such cases are happily unusual, and we need say no more about them.

Our interest, then, is in the cases where this is not so, or at least not obviously so. But some writers, such as James Rachels, hold that letting someone die is morally equivalent to killing them. Or "basically" equivalent. Is this so? Most people do not think so; it takes a subtle philosophical argument to persuade them of this. The difference between a bad thing which I intentionally or at least foreseeably brought about, and one which just happened, through no fault of my own, matters to most of us in practice. Is our view sustainable in principle, too? Suppose the case is one I could do something about, as when you are starving and my granary is burgeoning. Does that make a difference?

[...]

What about the claim that killing and letting die are "morally equivalent"? Here [...] there is a danger of begging the question. *If* we have a duty to feed the hungry and we don't, then not doing so might be morally equivalent to killing them, perhaps—though I doubt that any proponent would seriously propose life imprisonment for failing to contribute to the cause of feeding the hungry! But again, the consequence clearly doesn't follow if we don't have that duty, which is in question. Those who think we do not have fundamental duties to take care of each other, but only duties to refrain from killing and the like will deny that they are morally equivalent.

The liberty proponent will thus insist that when Beethoven wrote symphonies instead of using his talents to grow food for the starving like the peasants he depicted in his Pastorale [*sic*] symphony, he was doing what he had a perfect right to do. A connoisseur of music might go further and hold that he was also *doing the right thing*: that someone with the talents of a Beethoven does more for people by composing great music than by trying to save lives—even if he would have been *successful* in saving those lives, which is not terribly likely anyway!

How do we settle this issue? If we were all connoisseurs, it would be easy: if you know and love great music, you will find it easy to believe that a symphony by Beethoven or Mahler is worth more than prolonging the lives of a few hundred starvelings for another few miserable years. If you are one of those starving persons, your view might be different. (But it might not. Consider the starving artist in his garret, famed in Romantic novels and operas: they lived *voluntarily* in squalor, believing that what they were doing was worth the sacrifice.)

We are not all connoisseurs, nor are most of us starving. Advocates of welfare duties talk glibly as though there were a single point of view ("welfare") that dominates everything else. But it's not true. There are all kinds of points of view, diverse, and to a large extent incommensurable. Uniting them is not as simple as the welfarist or utilitarian may think. It is *not* certain, not obvious, that we "add more to the sum of human happiness" by supporting Oxfam than by supporting the opera. How are we to unite diverse people on these evaluative matters? The most plausible answer, I think, is the point of view that allows different people to live their various lives, by forbidding interference with them. Rather than insisting, with threats to back it up, that I help someone for whose projects and purposes I have no sympathy whatever, let us all agree to respect each other's pursuits. We'll agree to let each person live as that person sees fit, with only our bumpings into each

other being subject to public control. To do this, we need to draw a sort of line around each person, and insist that others not cross that line without the permission of the occupant. The rule will be not to forcibly intervene in the lives of others, thus requiring that our relations be mutually agreeable. Enforced feeding of the starving, however, does cross the line, invading the farmer or the merchant, forcing him to part with some of his hard-earned produce and give it without compensation to others. That, says the advocate of liberty, is theft, not charity.

So if someone is starving, we may pity him or we may be indifferent, but the question so far as our *obligations* are concerned is only this: how did he *get* that way? If it was not the result of my previous activities, then I have no obligation to him, and may help him out or not, as I choose. If it was such a result, then of course I must do something. If you live and have long lived downstream from me, and I decide to dam up the river and divert the water elsewhere, then I have deprived you of your water and must compensate you, by supplying you with the equivalent, or else desist. But if you live in the middle of a parched desert and it does not rain, so that you are faced with death from thirst, that is not my doing and I have no compensating to do.

This liberty-respecting idea avoids, by and large, the need to make the sort of utility comparisons essential to the utility or welfare view. If we have no general obligation to manufacture as much utility for others as possible, then we don't have to concern ourselves about measuring that utility. Being free to pursue our own projects, we will evaluate our results as best we may, each in our own way. There is no need to keep a constant check on others to see whether we ought to be doing more for them and less for ourselves.

In stark contrast to the liberty-respecting view stands the idea that we are to count the satisfactions of others as equal in value to our own. If I can create a little more pleasure for some stranger by spending my dollar on him than I would create for myself by spending it on an ice cream cone, I then have a putative *obligation* to spend it on him. Thus I am to continually defer to others in the organization of my activities, and shall be assailed by guilt whenever I am not bending my energies to the relief of those allegedly less fortunate than I. Benefit others, at the expense of yourself—and keep doing it until you are as poor and miserable as those whose poverty and misery you are supposed to be relieving! That is the ethics of the hair shirt.

How should we react to this idea? Negatively, in my view—and, I think, in yours. Doesn't that view really make us the slaves of the (supposedly) less well off? Surely a rule of conduct that permits people to be themselves and to try to live the best and most interesting lives they can is better than one which makes us all, in effect, functionaries in a welfare state? The rule that neither the rich nor the poor ought to be enslaved by the others is surely the better rule. Some, of course, think that the poor are, inherently, the "slaves" of rich, and the rich inherently their masters. Such is the Marxist line, for instance. It's an important argument, but it's important also to realize that it's simply wrong. The wealthy do not have the right to hold a gun to the head of the nonwealthy and tell them what to do. On the contrary, the wealthy, in countries with reasonably free economies, become wealthy by selling things to others, things that those others voluntarily purchase. This makes the purchaser better off as well as the seller; and of course the employees of the latter become better off in the process of making those things, via their wages. The result of this activity is that there are more goods in the world than there would otherwise be.

This is precisely the opposite of the way the thief makes his money. He expends time and energy depriving someone else, involuntarily, of what his victims worked to produce, rather than devoting his own energies to productive activities. He in consequence leaves the world poorer than it was before he set out on his exploitative ways. The Marxist assimilates the honest accumulator to the thief. Rather than being, as so many seem to think, a profound contribution to social theory, that is a first-rank conceptual error, a failure to appreciate that wealth comes about precisely because of the prohibition of theft, rather than by its wholesale exercise.

But the anti-welfarist idea can be taken too far as well. Should people be disposed to assist each other in time of need? Certainly! But the appropriate rule for this is not that each person is duty-bound to minister to the poor until he himself is a pauper or near-pauper as well. Rather, the appropriate rule is what

the characterization, "in time of need" more nearly suggests. There are indeed emergencies in life when a modest effort by someone will do a great deal for someone else. People who aren't ready to help others are people who deserve to be avoided when they themselves turn to others in time of need.

But this all assumes that these occasions are, in the first place, relatively unusual, and in the second, that the help offered is genuinely of modest cost to the provider. If a stranger on the street asks for directions, a trifling expenditure of time and effort saves him great frustration, and perhaps also makes for a pleasant encounter with another human (which that other human should try to make so, by being polite and saying "thanks!" for example). But if as I walk down the street I am accosted on all sides by similar requests, then I shall never get my day's work done if I can't just say, "Sorry, I've got to be going!" or merely ignore the questioners and walk right on. If instead I must minister to each, then soon there will be nothing to give, since its existence depends entirely on the activities of people who produce it. If the stranger asks me to drive him around town all day looking for a long-lost friend, for instance, then that's going too far. Though of course we should be free to help him out even to that extent, if we are so inclined.

What about parting with the means for making your sweet little daughter's birthday party a memorable one, in order to keep a dozen strangers alive on the other side of the world? Is this something you are morally required to do? Indeed not. She may well *matter* to you more than they. This illustrates again the fact that people do *not* "count equally" for most of us. Normal people care more about some people than others, and build their very lives around those carings. It is both absurd and very arrogant for theorists, talking airily about the equality of all people, to insist on cramming it down our throats—which is how ordinary people do see it.

It is reasonable, then, to arrive at a general understanding that we shall be ready to help when help is urgent and when giving it is not very onerous to us. But a general understanding that we shall help everyone as if they were our spouses or dearest friends is quite another matter. Only a thinker whose heart has been replaced by a calculating machine could suppose that to be reasonable.

[…]

Questions

1. Pick out from Narveson's essay some of the libertarian ideas and arguments we've encountered before.
2. Unlike some libertarians, Narveson does seem willing to embrace a modest obligation to help others. What is this obligation? How does it compare to Appiah's "emergency principle" in the previous essay?

Thomas Pogge argues that even on libertarian principles the West has some responsibility for alleviating world poverty

[…]

There are sophisticated thinkers [... who] know of the massive deprivations caused by global poverty, understand that this catastrophe is not already disappearing, acknowledge that our Western countries could do much to solve the problem at little cost to ourselves—and nonetheless argue that we have no strong obligations to do so. [...]

Such a defense concedes that we could prevent much desperate poverty through more foreign aid or other redistributive mechanisms. But it takes such preventability to indicate not that we are actively causing poverty, but that we fail to contribute as much as we might to poverty eradication. This distinction is thought to have great moral significance: As individuals, we could do more to protect foreigners from life-threatening poverty than we are doing in fact. But failing to save lives is not morally on a par with killing. [...] The same holds for the conduct of our governments. And the point is thought to apply also to the influence we exert on the design of the global economic order: we affluent Western states could design this order to be more poverty avoiding. [...]

Reproduced with permission from *World Poverty and Human Rights*, by Thomas Pogge, 2nd edn. Cambridge, UK: Polity Press, 2008, General Introduction.

Skillful defenses of our acquiescence in world poverty typically also draw on the common belief that people may give priority to their compatriots, especially in the context of a system of competing states: it is permissible for us and our political representatives vigorously to pursue our interests within an adversarial system in which others and their representatives can vigorously pursue their interests. [...]

This defense combines two claims. First, while it may be seriously wrong to harm foreigners by actively causing their severe poverty, it is not seriously wrong to fail to benefit foreigners by not preventing as much severe poverty abroad as we might. Second, as regards severe poverty abroad, we are not actively causing it but merely failing to prevent as much of it as we might.

Disputing the first claim, one might argue that the distinction between actively causing poverty and failing to prevent it has little or no moral importance. Allowing hunger to kill people whom one could easily save, even mere foreigners, is morally on a par with killing them, or at any rate little better.[1] But I agree, on this point, with libertarians and defenders of the second prejudice that the distinction between actively causing poverty and merely failing to prevent it is morally significant in regard to both conduct and institutional design. [...]

My response to the skillful defense challenges its second claim—specifically in regard to the global institutional order for which our governments, hence we, bear primary responsibility. I deny that our imposition of the existing global order is not actively causing poverty, not harming the poor. [...] I argue that the existence of an adversarial system can justify prioritizing fellow-members and group interests only if the institutional framework structuring the competition is minimally fair.

When groups competitively pursue their interests within a framework of rules, these rules themselves and their adjudication typically become objects of the competition and may then be deformed by stronger parties to the point where the framework becomes manifestly unfair. Such cases are familiar from domestic contexts: powerful corporations lobby for rules that stifle emergent competitors, incumbent political parties revise the electoral laws or districts to perpetuate their rule, wealthy litigants vastly outspend their opponents on jury specialists, expert witnesses, and complicated motions. Although they emerge from the competitive pursuit of group interests within an adversarial system, some such outcomes, and efforts to achieve and perpetuate them, are nonetheless morally condemned.

Implicit in our moral thinking and practice, there is then an important distinction—albeit not precisely formulated or well justified—between matters legitimately subject to change through competing group interests, on the one hand, and certain basic features of the institutional order requisite to preserve the fairness of the competition, on the other. I extend and apply this fundamental distinction to the global plane, arguing that *any* coercive institutional order must meet certain minimal conditions [...]. The existing global institutional order falls short of meeting these conditions, on account of the excessive inequalities in bargaining power and the immense poverty and economic inequality it avoidably reproduces.

Even in a competitive context, the priority we may give to our compatriots is then limited in scope. We may not shape the rules framing this competition in our favor to the point where these rules violate basic standards of justice or fairness. Inflicting seriously unjust rules upon others is harming them. And when it comes to harming, the priority for the near and dear gives out. We may well have less reason to benefit foreigners than to confer equivalent benefits on our compatriots. But this asymmetry does not carry over from cases of assistance to duties not to harm: driving when drunk, for instance, is not morally more acceptable abroad, where one is endangering only foreigners. [...]

My challenge to the skillful defense hinges then on whether the global institutional order in its present design is unjust and our imposition of it a harm done to the global poor. [...]

Many critics of the World Trade Organization (WTO) regime are, and many more are dismissed as, opponents of open markets, free trade, or globalization. It is worth stressing that my critique involves no such opposition. I do not complain that the WTO regime opens markets too much, but that it has opened *our* markets *too little* and has thereby gained for us the benefits of free trade while withholding these benefits from the global poor. Poor populations continue to face great barriers to exporting their products, and even greater barriers to offering their services where these would fetch a decent income. And some competitive markets of vital importance to them—markets in generic versions of advanced medicines, for instance—have been shut down under WTO rules designed to facilitate global monopolies.

[...]

One piece of evidence [...] can be gleaned from *The Economist*, a magazine that, laboring to outdo all other news media in its defense of the WTO and in its vilification of protesters against it as enemies of the poor,[2] can certainly not be accused of anti-WTO bias:

> Rich countries cut their tariffs by less in the Uruguay Round than poor ones did. Since then, they have found new ways to close their markets, notably by imposing anti-dumping duties on imports they deem "unfairly cheap." Rich countries are particularly protectionist in many of the sectors where developing countries are best able to compete, such as agriculture, textiles, and clothing. As a result, according to a new study by Thomas Hertel, of Purdue University, and Will Martin, of the World Bank, rich countries' average tariffs on manufacturing imports from poor countries are four times higher than those on imports from other rich countries. This imposes a big burden on poor countries. The United Nations Conference on Trade and Development (UNCTAD) estimates that they could export $700 billion more a year by 2005 if rich countries did more to open their markets. Poor countries are also hobbled by a lack of know-how. Many had little understanding of what they signed up to in the Uruguay Round. That ignorance is now costing them dear. Michael Finger of

the World Bank and Philip Schuler of the University of Maryland estimate that implementing commitments to improve trade procedures and establish technical and intellectual-property standards can cost more than a year's development budget for the poorest countries. Moreover, in those areas where poor countries could benefit from world trade rules, they are often unable to do so.... Of the WTO's 134 members, 29 do not even have missions at its headquarters in Geneva. Many more can barely afford to bring cases to the WTO.[3]

This report makes clear that some of the rules negotiated in the Uruguay Round are very costly for the poor countries and their people. These rules exacerbate poverty and bring about additional deaths and suffering from poverty-related causes.

[...]

Some hold (and I have been accused of holding) that we are harming the global poor insofar as we choose to treat them worse than we might—that only the best feasible treatment qualifies as non-harmful.[4] My view [...] defines a notion of harm that is much more restrictive in six distinct respects. First, we are harming the global poor only if our conduct sets back their most basic interests—the standard of social justice I employ is sensitive only to *human rights deficits*. Second, I am focusing exclusively on human rights deficits that are *causally traceable to social institutions*. Third, I am assigning moral responsibility for such a human rights deficit only to those who *actively cooperate* in designing or imposing the relevant social institutions—and only to them am I then ascribing compensatory obligations to do their share toward reforming these social institutions or toward protecting its victims. Fourth, I allow that our active cooperation is harming the global poor only if it is *foreseeable* that this order gives rise to substantial human rights deficits. Fifth, I require that these human rights deficits be *reasonably avoidable* in the sense that a feasible alternative design of the relevant institutional order would not produce comparable human rights deficits or other ills of comparable magnitude. Sixth, this avoidability must be *knowable*: we must be able to be confident that the alternative institutional design would do much better in giving participants secure access to the objects of their human rights.

I believe that we are involved in harming—and, more specifically, in massively violating the human rights of—the global poor in this quite restrictive sense. This does not mean that we must become hermits or emigrants. We can compensate for our contribution to collective harm also by contributing to efforts toward institutional reform or toward protecting the victims of present institutional injustice. Focusing on negative duties alone, I limit such compensatory duties to the amount of harm one is responsible for by cooperating in the imposition of an unjust institutional order. Setting aside any open-ended positive duty to help the badly off, my appeal to a negative duty generates then compensatory obligations that are tightly limited in *range* (to persons subject to an institutional order one cooperates in imposing), in *subject matter* (to the avoidance of human rights deficits), and in *demandingness* (to compensation for one's share of that part of the human rights deficit that foreseeably is reasonably avoidable through a feasible alternative institutional design).

[...]

As sketched thus far, my position on world poverty can be charged with leaving out the most important factor: the incompetence, corruption, and tyranny entrenched in the governments, social institutions, and cultures of many poor countries. This factor [...] may seem to undercut much of my argument: if the vital interests of the global poor are neglected in international negotiations, it is because their own governments do not vigorously represent these interests. And even if our governments had nonetheless agreed to reduce protectionist barriers against exports from the poor countries, this would have done far more toward enriching their corrupt elites than toward improving conditions for the poor. The main responsibility for the persistence of world poverty rests then with the leaders and elites of the poor countries rather than with our governments and ourselves.

This objection is right about the responsibilities of poor-country rulers and elites. Many of them are autocratic, corrupt, brutal, and unresponsive to the interests of the poor majority. They are greatly at fault for not representing the interests of the poor in international negotiations and for consenting to treaties that benefit themselves and foreigners at the expense of their impoverished populations. But can we plausibly tell the poor that, insofar as the global economic order is unjust to them, they only have their own leaders to blame for this? They can surely point out in response that they did not authorize the clique that rules them in anything resembling free and fair elections and that their interests can be sold out by this clique only because we treat it as entitled to consent on behalf of the people it manages to subjugate. Just think of who made the decision to join the WTO, for example: Myanmar/Burma was signed on by its notorious SLORC junta (the State Law and Order Restoration Council), Nigeria by its military dictator Sani Abacha, Indonesia by Suharto, Zimbabwe by Robert Mugabe, Zaire/Congo by dictator Mobuto Sese Seko, and so on.

This response can be extended to show that we share responsibility not only for the damage authoritarian rulers can do to the interests of "their" people in international negotiations, but also for authoritarianism and corruption being so widespread in the less developed countries. In this vein it is often mentioned that our governments have instigated the violent installation of many oppressive rulers in poor countries, are selling juntas and autocrats the weapons they need to stay in power, and have fostered a culture of corruption by permitting our firms to bribe foreign officials, by blessing such bribes with tax deductibility, and by providing safe havens for such illicit wealth.[5] Still more significant, in my view, are the resource and borrowing privileges that our global order confers upon those who manage to bring a country under their control. Such rulers are internationally recognized as entitled to sell natural resources and to borrow money in the name of the country and its people. These international privileges facilitate oppressive rule and greatly encourage coup attempts and civil wars in the less developed countries.

[…]

Questions

1. Consider the following quote from the Narveson essay:

    So if someone is starving, we may pity him or we may be indifferent, but the question so far as our *obligations* are concerned is this: how did he get that way? If it was not the result of my previous activities, then I have no obligation to him and may help him out or not, as I choose. If it was such a result, then of course I must do something.

    Would Pogge agree with this point? What would Pogge say to Narveson about our obligations to the global poor?

2. What does Pogge say about the argument that corrupt leaders, not we Westerners, are responsible for the plight of the extreme poor?

Notes

1. This critique is exemplified in Singer, "Famine, Affluence, and Morality," and [Peter] Unger, *Living High and Letting Die*. (Oxford: Oxford University Press, 1996).

2. See, for instance, *The Economist*'s cover of December 11, 1999, showing an Indian child in rags with the heading "The Real Losers of Seattle." See also its editorial in the same issue (ibid., p. 15), its flimsy "The Case for Globalization" (*The Economist*, September 23, 2000, pp. 19–20 and 85–7), and its remarkable lead editorial "A Question of Justice?" (*The Economist*, March 13, 2004).

3. "White Man's Shame," *The Economist*, September 25, 1999, p. 89.

4. [Alan] Patten, "Should We Stop Thinking [About Poverty in Terms of Helping the Poor?" *Ethics and International Affairs*," 19 (2005)] pp. 26–7.

5. Cf. [Raymond W.] Baker, *Capitalism's Achilles Heel* [: *Dirty Money and How to Renew the Free-Market System*. Hoboken, NJ: John Wiley & Sons (2005)].

Jim Wallis talks about biblical injunctions to help the poor

[…]

It's time to reassert and reclaim the gospel faith—especially in our public life. When we do, we discover that faith challenges the powers that be to do justice for the poor, instead of preaching a "prosperity gospel" and supporting politicians who further enrich the wealthy. We remember that faith hates violence and tries to reduce it and exerts a fundamental presumption against war, instead of justifying it in God's name. We see that faith creates community from racial, class, and gender divisions and prefers international community over nationalist religion, and we see that "God bless America" is found nowhere in the Bible. And we are reminded that faith regards matters such as the sacredness of life and family bonds as so important that they should never be used as ideological symbols or mere political pawns in partisan warfare.

The media like to say, "Oh, then you must be the religious Left." No, not at all, and the very question is the problem. Just because a religious Right has fashioned itself for political power in one utterly predictable ideological guise does not mean that those who question this political seduction must be their opposite political counterpart. The best public contribution of religion is precisely *not* to be ideologically predictable or a loyal partisan. To always raise the moral issues of human rights, for example, will challenge both left- and right-wing governments that put power above principles. Religious action is rooted in a much deeper place than "rights"—that place being the image of God in every human being.

Similarly, when the poor are defended on moral or religious grounds, it is certainly not "class warfare," as the rich often charge, but rather a direct response to the overwhelming focus on the poor in the Scriptures, which claim they are regularly neglected, exploited, and oppressed by wealthy elites, political rulers, and indifferent affluent populations. Those Scriptures don't simply endorse the social programs of the liberals or the conservatives, but they make it clear that poverty is indeed a religious issue, and the failure of political leaders to help uplift the poor will be judged a moral failing.

[…]

All that came home to me dramatically during my first year of seminary. I was freshly converted out of the student movements of the 1960s and I wanted to go to a theological school where they took the Bible seriously. So I chose Trinity Evangelical Divinity School, outside of Chicago, instead of one of the more "liberal" seminaries in the country. Almost immediately upon our arrival, a small group of activist evangelical seminarians began to form, and we quickly turned our attention to the Bible.

I've told the story many times about how we discovered a "Bible full of holes," when it came to the question of the poor. Here's what we did. Our band of eager young first-year seminary students did a thorough study to find *every* verse in the Bible that dealt with the poor. We scoured the Old and New Testaments for every single reference to poor people, to wealth and poverty, to injustice and oppression, and to what the response to all those subjects was to be for the people of God.

We found *several thousand* verses in the Bible on the poor and God's response to injustice. We found it to be the second most prominent theme in the Hebrew Scriptures Old Testament—the first was idolatry, and the two often were related. One of every sixteen verses in the New Testament is about the poor or the subject of money (Mammon, as the gospels call it). In the first three (Synoptic) gospels it is one out of ten verses, and in the book of Luke, it is one in seven!

After we completed our study, we all sat in a circle to discuss how the subject had been treated in the various churches in which we had grown up. Astoundingly, but also tellingly, not one of us could remember even one sermon on the poor from the pulpit of our home churches. In the Bible, the poor were everywhere; yet the subject was not to be found in our churches.

Then we decided to try what became a famous experiment. One member of our group took an old

Reproduced from *God's Politics: Why the Right Gets It Wrong and the Left Doesn't Get It*, by Jim Wallis. New York: HarperSanFrancisco, 2005, pp. 4–5, 212–14.

Bible and a new pair of scissors and began the long process of literally cutting out every single biblical text about the poor. It took him a very long time.

The prophets were simply decimated. When he got to the resounding command of Amos to "let justice roll down like waters, and righteousness like an ever-flowing stream," he just cut it out. When he found God speaking through Isaiah to say, "Is not this the fast that I choose: to loose the bonds of injustice, to undo the thongs of the yoke, and let the oppressed go free?" he just cut it out. When he discovered the summation of God's call in Micah to "do justice, love kindness, and walk humbly with your God," he just cut it out.

He cut out almost everything that the Hebrew prophets had to say about how nations, rulers, and all of us are instructed to treat the poor. Much of the Psalms also disappeared, where God is seen as the defender and deliverer of the oppressed. And all references to the Hebrew tradition of Jubilee had to be cut where, from Leviticus onward, the practice of a periodic "leveling" was lifted up as crucial to the health of a society—slaves were to be set free, debts canceled, and land redistributed to its rightful owners. It was all too dangerous to remain in the bible.

When he got to the New Testament, the seminarian with the scissors had a lot of work to do. He began with the thankful prayer of a simple peasant woman who would bear the new messiah. Mary's famous Magnificat prophesied the meaning of the coming of Jesus: "He has brought down the powerful from their thrones, and lifted up the lowly; he has filled the hungry with good things, and sent the rich empty away." Because Mary didn't sound like a religious service provider with a faith-based federal grant, but instead like a social revolutionary; her prayer had to be cut. Then there was Jesus's first sermon at Nazareth, his "Nazareth manifesto," where he announced his messianic vocation. Hearkening back to Isaiah, Jesus proclaimed his own mission statement by saying, "The Spirit of the Lord is upon me, because he has anointed me to bring good news to the poor. He has sent me to proclaim release to the captives and recovery of sight to the blind, to let the oppressed go free, to proclaim the year of the Lord's favor." Because all the biblical scholars agree Jesus is talking about that

Jubilee thing again, this was a mission statement that had to be cut before it reached committee. His Sermon on the Mount, and especially the Beatitudes, threatened to turn the world (as we know it) upside down by saying, in his kingdom, the blessed ones are the poor, the meek, the merciful, the peacemakers, the persecuted, and the ones who are hungry and thirsty for justice. It clearly had to go.

That account of how the early church began to practice economic sharing, after the Spirit landed on them, would be pretty incredulous to churches today. And so would the totally unrealistic assertion that "there was not a needy person among them," even if Paul was encouraging economic redistribution as a sign of fellowship wherever he went. Snip, snip, snip. All the stuff from John about not having the love of God in you unless you open your heart to the needy just doesn't apply to some of our most important and pious church leaders, not to mention our television evangelists. And the idea from James that "faith without works is dead" was dangerously close to the "social gospel." So some more cuts were in order.

When the zealous seminarian was done with all his editorial cuts, that old Bible would hardly hold together, it was so sliced up. It was literally falling apart in our hands. What we had done was to create a Bible full of holes.

I began taking that damaged and fragile Bible out with me when I preached. I'd hold it up high above American congregations and say, "Brothers and sisters, this *is* our American Bible; it is full of holes." Each one of us might as well take our Bibles, a pair of scissors, and begin cutting out all the Scriptures we pay no attention to, all the biblical texts that we just ignore.

We still have that old Bible full of holes. It serves as a constant reminder to me of how you can miss so much, even when it is right in front of your eyes. I learned in my little home church that people can really love the Bible, believe they are basing their lives upon it, and yet completely miss some of its most central themes. We don't see what would most challenge us and perhaps change our lives.

Yet, down deep in our souls, we do know the poor are there: in the heart of God, in the compassion of Christ, and in our own communities—if we would just open our eyes. Revealing the poor in the Scriptures and in our own world is always the prophetic task of faith. To discover the forgotten poor is more than the work of "social action," as some would call it. It is rather to put our Bibles back together again. Indeed, it is nothing less than to restore the integrity of the Word of God—in our lives, our congregations, our communities, and our world. What could be more important?

[...]

Questions

1. What is Wallis' account of the "Bible full of holes" and what does he think it shows?

2. From what Wallis says, does it seem as if the Bible promotes "class warfare"?

Part V

Abortion

13

Abortion

Fiction

The Blessing of the Blastocysts

Elizabeth was excited as she got into the visitor's line. She knew from her textbook that the group of buildings in front of her had once been called "Fetal Factory IV," with an industrial look as drab as the name. Now the place was called the Boston Birth Haven, was painted in soft pastels, and had landscaped grounds full of spring flowers.

A visit here was required of all students taking Reproductive Technologies. Elizabeth was excited, but also a little nervous: She still tended to be a bit squeamish about some of the details of reproduction. Not about sex, of course: Sex was good fun, and if you happened to stay with a guy for a while, it could even be sort of meaningful. But reproduction and sex had nothing to do with each other anymore. In the past, of course, reproduction had been connected with sex: Elizabeth knew about this not only from her textbook, but from talks she'd had with her great-grand-mother, before Nana had died. Back then, a woman was supposed to get married, have sex with one man, and have children. Elizabeth knew it hadn't really worked that way—Nana had been divorced twice and had had a boyfriend at the time of her death. Still the idea that you would have sex with only one person seemed weird. And what seemed beyond weird—what seemed incredibly yucky—was the idea of a woman actually having a baby—having to carry a living thing inside her for nine months and then have it squeeze out of her—like in some horror movie. It must have been so painful—dangerous too.

All that had changed with what later became known as the "Europan flu." Though it had looked like a disaster for the human race, now that science had found a way to cope, it was hard, as a young woman, not to be grateful it had happened.

Though, as Elizabeth knew from her readings, it had been awfully frightening at the time. Not the initial "flu," which had seemed innocent enough, but the malformed births that happened soon afterwards. The malformations had continued into the next year, even among women who hadn't been pregnant during the flu season. Public health officials, going into crisis mode, eventually figured out there'd been severe chromosomal damage to most of the human race; they traced the problem, not to any actual flu, but to micro-organisms that had somehow slipped through all the screening done after the return of the manned mission to Europa, one of the moons of Jupiter. Doctors discovered that only three percent of the human race could produce normal sperm and eggs. There was no way the human race was going to survive without massive social engineering: Plans were drawn up to forcibly sterilize the defective ninety-seven percent of the population in order to prevent more malformed infants. The healthy three percent would be confined in government facilities where compulsory sperm and egg donations would be taken and combined in the laboratory; fertilized

Contemporary Moral and Social Issues: An Introduction through Original Fiction, Discussion, and Readings, First Edition. Thomas D. Davis.
© 2014 John Wiley & Sons, Inc. Published 2014 by John Wiley & Sons, Inc.

eggs would then be implanted in the females (whether or not they were willing).

This had seemed so awful to so many people—especially the idea of women being forced to bear children year after year—that public protests might have doomed that attempt to save the race. But maybe the fear and confusion had been all to the good. When the scientists did come up with a solution to the problem, their radical solution seemed so mild in terms of what people had been afraid of, that enough of the population accepted it to make it workable.

It was lucky that reproductive technologies had already made great strides at the time of the crisis. For more than half a century it had been routine to combine sperm and eggs in the laboratory, screen the resulting embryos for defects, then plant the healthy embryos in women's wombs. The obvious next step—though many people at the time considered it to be impossible—was to create an artificial womb with a placenta in which an embryo could develop into a baby. This "impossible" breakthrough had perhaps saved the human race.

So: No women had ever been forced to become "baby-bearing slaves." At puberty the sperm of all males and the eggs of all females were examined for defects: Those young people with healthy sperm and eggs were drafted for two years to be donors; after their two years of service, they were sterilized and released, taking their place among all the others who had been sterilized at puberty. Not that many people complained about their service: They were made more than comfortable during their stay, were given whatever schooling or training they wanted, and were released with honors and a nice cash bonus.

Even with the general relief at not having to force some women to have all the babies, it had still taken society a while to adjust to the idea of the fetus developing outside the womb. In a global publicity campaign, world leaders had put forward scientists to assure the public that ectogenesis—the development of the embryo outside the mother's body—was quite normal in nature: The embryonic development of fish, for example, took place in water, that of birds in eggs. Eventually even the Roman Catholic Church, perhaps bowing to the inevitable, declared ectogenesis "natural" and acceptable. Popular opinion adjusted as well, and within a generation, the idea of a woman carrying a fetus inside her began to seem very strange.

It was assumed at first that the babies would be adopted out to couples who would then raise them in a traditional family and neighborhood setting. That did happen to some degree during the first five years, but decreasingly after that. With the process of pregnancy gone—along with the idea that the child would be a biological continuation of oneself—the motivation for parenting seemed to disappear. Raising a child began to seem like far too much work—too much voluntary work at that. Better to pay the higher taxes and let the state do it. Today the vast majority of children were raised in communal nurseries and schools.

★★★★★★

Elizabeth had almost made it to the front of the line. When the line moved again, she was able to slip in at the end of a group of twenty or so people who would be given the next tour. As people shuffled for position in the foyer, Elizabeth got a look at the guide, a thirty-something woman with short brown hair, who was dressed in gray slacks, a white blouse, and a black jacket with a baby blue *BBH* logo on the pocket. The woman was moving her hands excitedly, alternately waving the tour group toward her and pressing her open hands downward in a signal for them to quiet down. The instinct of the group was to form a circle around the guide, but she gestured them into a half-circle, pointing, in explanation, toward a huge blank screen set against the far wall.

After a few welcoming remarks, the guide removed a remote control device from her pocket and pointed it at a machine beneath the screen; a three-dimensional color photograph appeared—of a sperm. Elizabeth gave an inward groan. It looked like they were about to get a lecture on the basics of reproduction—the kind of information any student would get in fifth or sixth grade. Then Elizabeth realized she was looking at this the wrong way around. As a would-be professional in the field of reproductive technologies, she might some day need to give such a presentation, and this was a good opportunity to learn how it was done. And she realized she was making a silly assumption—that the others in the group (all adults) would also find this information boringly basic because they'd had it all in school. There were so many things she'd been taught in primary and secondary school that she'd already forgotten, and she was only twenty years old; how much more would the older adults in the group have forgotten. Besides, she'd been keeping up on the subject in college and so she knew the latest information; much of the information these people had been given would be long out of date.

Elizabeth supposed that back in the days when men and women had had babies together, people had been anxious to learn all they could about the details of reproduction and to keep their information up to date. But these days, what would be the motivation? People didn't have children or raise children anymore. One saw children, of course, but they weren't ever-present the way they must have been in the old days, when they lived in houses with their parents and accompanied them much of the time in public. Today children were much more on the margins of everyday life—in their nurseries and schools, tended to by professionals. One didn't see all that much of them until they became adults and took their place in society.

As the guide discussed in vitro fertilization, or IVF, the images on the screen switched from gowned and masked technicians working in laboratories to enlargements of microscopic images of a sperm fertilizing an egg to produce an embryo.

When the guide discussed how the embryos were screened for defects prior to implantation in the artificial womb, one of the tour group voiced concern that they were "designing humans." The guide responded with an emphatic, "No, we're not," and began talking about the strictness of the laws and the review of the processes by the legal/medical/ethics committees set up for that purpose. Elizabeth knew from discussions at school that the issue was not that cut and dried. Not implanting embryos that were likely to develop Parkinson's disease was a way of "designing" humanity to be without that disease. But the spirit of the guide's answer was correct. The country had been firmly against any procedure biased in favor of particular skin, hair, or eye color, or that would promote such characteristics as superior physical strength, musical ability, or intelligence.

Elizabeth had read one interesting book—sharply criticized by her professor—which had speculated, approvingly, that humanity was on a road that would lead it toward "redesigning" humans. The writer had said that once certain obvious disabilities (like the tendency toward Parkinson's) had been removed from the population, another category, previously viewed as untouchable (as, for instance, tendencies toward alcoholism or obesity), would take their place and the same process would start up again. Further, if the state of humanity ever became more perilous than at present, there would be strong pressure to redesign humans in a way that would allow them to survive, and even flourish. Now that the old religious notion of what was "natural" had taken such a hit, now that there was no longer an identification of adults with a particular child, now that science had so successfully handled a catastrophe that had threatened to destroy humanity or else turn it into a science fiction nightmare of forced "labor" (literally), many of the old human fears and prejudices against "perfecting" mankind were disappearing.

Someone else asked the guide's opinion about a question that popped up in the media from time to time—whether, if science ever managed to stamp out the "Europan flu" (something science had not come close to doing), humans would again begin to reproduce in the "natural" way. During the Europan-flu crisis, people had been so panicked about the monster births, so caught up with the desperate "forced labor" schemes, and so grateful for the "salvation" afforded by science, that most of the romanticism about natural reproduction had gone by the wayside. Now that things had stabilized, there were certain people—in particular those with conservative religious beliefs—who spoke nostalgically about the "old ways." However, the guide said, it was unlikely that those old ways would ever be reinstated. Too many attitudes and mores had changed. Women, no longer the natural bearers and caretakers of children, had gained a greater equality with men and were expected to have careers just as men did. Perhaps more important than any other factor, the younger women had come to find the thought of going through the painful and dangerous process of childbearing so distressing—even disgusting—that a change of policy or fashion necessary to reinstate the old ways seemed nearly unthinkable.

The guide returned to the video presentation, which showed the fertilized egg growing into a blastocyst, with several hundred cells. At this point, as in natural reproduction, the technicians implanted the blastocyst into the endometrium, or lining, of the womb. There were microscopic images of the blastocyst sinking slightly into the uterine lining, like a ball landing in mud.

The artificial womb itself rested within a large jar-like enclosure of darkened plastic, which itself was placed on a sturdy metal rack with wheels. Tubes attached to the jar allowed delivery of the proper nutrients and hormones and removal of metabolic wastes. Also attached to the jar were all sorts of wires and dials and lights. According to the guide, one of the greatest challenges to building an artificial womb was to understand and then mimic the complex molecular signals that passed back and forth between the natural mother and fetus. The temperature inside each jar was kept at a constant 37 °C.

Most of the tour group were surprised to learn that the birth havens were divided into rooms according to months, with the jars containing womb and embryo moved to a new room each month—a process culminating in the ninth month room. The division into months was perhaps an unnecessary nod to tradition, but the assembly-line style movement allowed for rooms with specialized equipment and personnel devoted to a particular stage in the fetal development.

With the video presentation done, the guide answered two more questions, then quieted the group. Giving them a stern look, she told the group that they would have to be especially quiet as they moved into and through the Blessing Room. They were very fortunate to be taking this tour at just the moment a sacred ceremony was taking place; the condition of their witnessing the ceremony was that they must be quiet and on their most respectful behavior. The tour guide would be able to speak softly to the group, but the group members must refrain from speaking to each other or asking questions until the group reached the Month 1 room. There they could talk freely.

With a last silencing finger to her lips, the guide turned and led them through large doors that opened and closed with barely a whisper.

Elizabeth could tell the group was surprised by the room. Though she herself had known in general what to expect, the reality of it had a more dramatic impact than she'd anticipated.

Unlike the antiseptic rooms shown in the video, this room was very dimly lit. The womb jars that had

appeared black in the brighter video glowed a faint green and seemed vaguely transparent, though not enough so one could make out anything inside. The monitor lights that had been barely noticeable in the video blinked vividly in the vicinity of each jar. Soft music played within the room—not muzak, Elizabeth realized—but something churchy, hymn-like.

There were one or two of the expected technicians, but they seemed to hang back, deferring to the other figures moving throughout the room. These men—no, Elizabeth now saw that there were a few women among them—were dressed in heavy robes with hoods. The robes were identical—a dark maroon color, with black velvety trim at the wrists and hem. Elizabeth watched the robed figures move about among the womb jars, pausing in front of one, then moving on to another. Some figures made the sign of the cross, others held up a hand, others simply stood, slightly bowed, in an attitude of prayer.

Several in the tour group started buzzing, in spite of the guide's injunction, but were quickly hushed. The guide, moving the members of the group in close together, whispered that they were witnessing the "Blessing of the Blastocysts." The recently implanted blastocysts were being blessed by various religious personages—priests, ministers, rabbis among them—each in his or her own way. The uniform robes were a way of emphasizing the non-denominational aspect of the blessing, as well as giving it a suitably grave and ceremonial air.

Years before, the guide explained, there'd been theologians who were convinced that the soul appeared at the very moment the sperm fertilized the egg. Since they thought of each embryo as a person, the disposal of embryos screened out for deformities or simply not needed had seemed equivalent to murder; thus those theologians had been against any and all in vitro fertilization. However, after the Europan flu, when it had become obvious that the human race would not survive without in vitro fertilization, the theologians had reconsidered their positions. Edging back toward earlier church traditions that had ensoulment taking place some time after conception, theologians and church leaders, meeting at a world-wide conference, had eventually agreed that ensoulment took place at about the moment the blastocyst became attached to the uterus. Political leaders had worried that resistance to the new policies by church leaders might lead to general public resistance. Relieved by the theological agreement, politicians had been more than happy to incorporate this non-denominational religious ceremony into the state-run birthing process.

After the guide finished speaking, the group stood in silence for a few minutes observing the ceremony; then they moved to the next room.

★★★★★

There was much about the Month 1 room that the group could have anticipated from the guide's opening lecture: The room seemed part lab, part hospital, but brightened by colors more appropriate to a nursery. BBH personnel in lab coats moved among the womb jars that were perched atop their equipment-laden frames.

There was one element of the room that was obviously a surprise to the group—something that had not been anticipated in the lecture. It was something fairly new. Elizabeth had heard a little about it in her classes, but had not gotten any details, let alone seen photographs. So, in a way, it was a surprise for her as well. Certainly it was a delight.

Each equipment-laden frame holding up a womb jar was covered on three sides by a conical shield. Attached to the shield were what looked like color photographs, though they weren't actually photographs, Elizabeth knew, just computer-generated images. Each shield had what looked like a series of photos taken every couple of years from the birth of the child until it reached the age of eighteen. For instance, on the frame nearest her—below a plaque giving the name "Jules" along with some fine print—a cute—and eventually handsome—dark-haired boy stared out. One of Elizabeth's first thoughts on seeing the face of the eighteen-year-old was that he was someone she wouldn't mind asking out. Except that this eighteen-year-old hadn't even been *born* yet. How strange.

The guide was talking now, explaining that the "photos" were actually computer predictions as to what each fetus would look like at various ages.

Several in the tour group balked at this idea. How could scientists possibly make such predictions. The fetuses still didn't look anything like people, did they?

The guide admitted they didn't. In this, the first month, the fetus was considerably less than a quarter inch long. As for what it looked like, they could be the judge. The guide pointed to a series of small photos mounted on a short wooden stand nearby, photos no one had noticed, focused as they'd been on the pictures mounted on the womb jars.

These were photos of fetuses ranging from a week to four weeks in age. Such photos were all too familiar to Elizabeth but she leaned in anyway, imagining how she might describe the fetuses, if pressed. At the end of the first week, the fetus looked like a small gooey ball with strings. At four weeks it looked like a fish with gills. No, it certainly didn't resemble any of the computer pictures of babies.

The guide said to remember that the scientists making the predictions did know what the parents looked like. More than that, scientists were getting very good at reading genes. There had been a thorough genetic examination of the sperm and egg prior to fertilization and of the fertilized egg afterwards. And the fact that these fetuses would grow in carefully controlled uterine conditions also reduced the variables. It wasn't just looks that the scientists were predicting. If we'd been able to see the small print under each name, said the guide, we would see likely tendencies in terms of such things as temperament, as well as musical, intellectual and/or athletic ability.

Several people said it sounded as if they were programming the fetuses.

The guide replied that the scientists were not involved in programming in any way. They were just noting likely tendencies.

Elizabeth asked if such information wouldn't bias those who supervised the children in nursery school and beyond. Wouldn't there be a natural inclination to nudge the children in the directions indicated by the tendencies?

The guide said that every effort would be made to see that didn't happen. The data were here for two purposes: The first was to inspire the workers by personalizing the fetuses; the administration wanted the workers at BBH to feel they were caregivers and not just lab assistants. The second was that the full data—most of which was not available to the workers—would be used for a long-term study of genetics. None of the data would leave BBH; none of the personnel at the nurseries or schools, nor the subjects themselves, would ever see the data. The scientists didn't want the data turned into self-fulfilling prophecies. Since tendencies and inclinations were only that, they might or might not be fulfilled according to circumstances. To push students in the directions of their "tendencies" would artificially limit the possibilities and in some cases cause anguish to the young people. Fear of possible programming was leading society to a much more flexible and sensitive educational system than in the old days, a system more open to students finding their own way in deciding what they wanted to do. Of course, there was a real world out there that required students to have certain skills and schools did have a licensing function; however, within those parameters, the schools were trying to be as flexible as possible.

"The hell with him! And with you too...."

Elizabeth jumped, though she realized a moment later that the voice had been more gruff than loud. What was startling was the suddenness of it, how out of place the words seemed. She recovered to see an angry-looking man—some sort of lab assistant, from the look of his clothes—striding across her field of vision toward the Month 2 room where they were about to go. Elizabeth caught a whiff of alcohol as the man passed. In his wake was a woman—an administrator, Elizabeth guessed, given that she had a badge but wore normal clothes. The administrator glanced apologetically at the group, then followed the man.

Elizabeth noticed the guide move her chin toward one shoulder and speak into what was obviously a mike. The guide paused, evidently listening, then nodded and spoke again. She looked up at the group, apologized, said something about a "personnel problem." She said they should move on.

The Month 2 room looked much like the Month 1 room, with more womb jars. There was no impression of "growth" from Month 1, since, again, each womb jar had its own set of pictures showing the predicted stages from birth to age 18. The only visual images of growth were in the small photos on another wooden stand, showing Month 2 fetal development. In these, the fetus progressed from the fish-like creature, to something resembling a tiny pre-historic monster, to a half-inch long alien, to something which, at an inch plus in length, though still alien, was beginning to take on a vague resemblance to a baby.

Two security guards rushed by the group, probably going after the "personnel problem" with the whiskey breath. Elizabeth stared after them, but then something arrested her gaze. It was a photo of a girl, perhaps eight years old, on the nearest of the womb-jar frames. The girl had short dark hair, beautiful eyes, and a mischievous smile. She reminded Elizabeth of a girl Elizabeth had known in second grade, a bit of a scamp, who hadn't been intimidated by any of the boys and could best them at almost anything. Elizabeth had always looked up to her. Elizabeth couldn't remember her name: The girl and her family had moved away about fourth grade. Occasionally Elizabeth would remember her and wonder what had become of her. If the pictures on the frame in front of her were any indication, that girl had grown up to be beautiful.

Elizabeth leaned toward the frame and read the name on the plate: "Rachel." Elizabeth was squinting to try to read the finer print on the plate when she noticed a lab worker looking at her. Elizabeth pulled back, wondering if she'd violated some rule, like getting too close to the equipment.

But then she saw that the lab worker's look wasn't admonishing. The worker—a middle-aged woman—was giving Elizabeth what looked like a proud, proprietorial smile.

"She's darling, isn't she," said the worker, whose name tag read, "Joan Hansen."

"Yes, she is," Elizabeth agreed.

"I think Rachel's going to be special," said Ms Hansen. "We're not supposed to play favorites—and we don't—but you can't help...." Ms Hansen smiled and shrugged. "She's going to be a beautiful, talented woman. Musical talent. I imagine her sometimes becoming a concert violinist. On the other hand, she's likely to be strong and outgoing. Maybe she'll...." Ms Hansen stopped and blushed. "Just listen to me going on."

There was a sudden loud commotion off to Elizabeth's right, shouts, the sounds of metal objects clattering to the floor. One voice sounded above the others, though Elizabeth could only catch some of the words, "...sick of this job...the way you're treating me...."

The commotion got louder and suddenly the man with the whiskey breath came into the room, pursued by the two security men.

"...leave me alone..." the man was yelling.

He bumped into a technician, carrying a tray. Several small vials went smashing to the floor.

"...be careful..." the security man was calling. "Just stop!"

But the man didn't stop. He was coming toward Elizabeth and the group, apparently heading for the door just behind them. Elizabeth tried to step out of the way, but guessed wrong, stepped where the man was stepping, moving into his path. He bounced off Elizabeth and into something heavy. He pushed at the obstacle violently, trying to get it out of his way.

With all her attention focused on keeping her balance, Elizabeth wasn't aware of what was happening overhead. What alerted her was someone whispering, "No," in a tone of horror. Almost too late, Elizabeth glanced up and saw something heavy toppling toward her. She stepped back in time to avoid being hit directly, but the crashing sound was followed by a spray of warm liquid and broken glass over her legs. She started to slip, but an arm caught her, keeping her from falling.

The horrified "No," came again, and Elizabeth realized the voice was Ms Hansen's.

The faces around Elizabeth were looking down toward the floor. The man who'd caused the commotion was also staring. He looked sick with fear.

"Murderer," said Ms Hansen, her voice edging toward hysteria.

Elizabeth looked down again and suddenly understood. Soaking in the liquid were pictures of Rachel. Her womb jar had fallen and smashed; the pictures were soaked with the amniotic fluid. Elizabeth felt an intake of breath, felt tears rush to her eyes.

"Murderer," cried Ms Hansen.

Elizabeth noticed something else. It was something on the top of her shoe, something gross, something that looked like a misshapen fish. Startled, she gave her shoe a shake, to get rid of the thing. It seemed to slither off her shoe, though its motion was only the flow of amniotic fluid.

"No! Don't move."

Ms Hansen was suddenly kneeling on the floor by Elizabeth's feet, her hands scooping at the fluid on the floor. The woman raised her hands toward her face, and Elizabeth saw the small piece of fish-like flesh in the woman's hands.

"Oh, Rachel, Rachel," the woman moaned. "That man killed you. My God, he killed you!"

Questions

(Please explain your answers, making specific reference to relevant passages in the story.)

1. According to "Blessing of the Blastocysts," what was the "Europan flu" and what were its immediate effects on people?

2a. Why did it seem as if certain women would have to become "baby-bearing slaves"?

b. What technology averted this possibility?

c. What is now required of those young people who produce healthy sperm and eggs?

3. In the birth havens, how does "conception" take place?

4a. What do the images on the cones below the womb jars represent?

b. Does the birth-haven process program the fetuses to be certain kinds of children?

5. Contrast the images on the womb-jar cones with the images of fetuses shown in a separate display.

6a. What is the ceremony called "the blessing of the blastocysts"?

b. What change of religious doctrine lay behind the "blessing" ceremony? How was this change justified?

7a. At the end of the story, why does Joan Hansen call the inebriated employee a "murderer"?

b. What confusion does a tearful Elizabeth experience in that moment?

8. What charge do you think should be brought against the employee who knocked over the womb jar? Murder? Manslaughter? Property damage? Explain.

14

Abortion

Discussion

The Blessing of the Blastocysts

"Blessing of the Blastocysts" imagines a time in the future when human beings have accomplished the *ectogenesis* of the human being—the full development of a human embryo/fetus outside the human body. Ectogenesis occurs in nature, for instance with the eggs of birds and fish. However, in "Blessing," the process is artificial.

The scientists begin with in vitro fertilization: sperm and egg are combined in an artificial environment (in vitro) rather than in the woman's body (in utero). Instead of reintroducing the fertilized egg (embryo) into the woman's body, the embryo is put into an artificial placenta/womb where it will continue to develop until it is ready to be "born."

"Blessing" imagines that human beings were pushed to develop ectogenesis as a result of a catastrophe. A microorganism brought back to earth from space ended up infecting the reproductive cells of human beings, making most humans incapable of producing healthy children. At first it was thought that those young people able to produce healthy children would have to be conscripted to bear children for the rest of the human race. This prospect was avoided through the development of ectogenesis.

In the story, young people at puberty are required to be tested. Those unable to produce healthy reproductive cells must submit to sterilization. The others are separated from society for two years and required to make donations of sperm and eggs. After those two years are up, they too are sterilized.

"Blessing" supposes that in the absence of normal reproduction, couples have lost the motivation to raise children. Instead children are raised in communal nurseries and schools. There is a continuation of "recreational" or "meaningful" sex and presumably the possibility of long-term relationships; but no one is interested in marriage anymore.

Though the average citizen has little personal interest in children, the birthing and child-rearing institutions of society are devoted to being the best they can be.

After in vitro fertilization, the embryos are put in womb jars inside special facilities called "birth havens." These early-stage embryos ("blastocysts") are blessed in a non-denominational religious ceremony. Thereafter, each fetus is named. Predictions have been made about its likely looks and dispositions. The predictions for each fetus—along with computer-generated images of how the fetus is predicted to look as it grows from child- to adulthood—are attached to each womb jar. These predictions are primarily generated as scientific data for the field of genetics. The reason they are posted on the womb jars is to give the birth-haven workers a sense of the reality and importance of each fetus. The workers are aware of the actual state of the fetus at any given point in the nine-month gestation. But the greater emphasis is on the children these fetuses will become.

Elizabeth, a student of reproductive technology, is touring the Boston Birth Haven. She finds herself feeling an emotional attachment to a particular embryo, named Rachel, because the computer images

Contemporary Moral and Social Issues: An Introduction through Original Fiction, Discussion, and Readings, First Edition. Thomas D. Davis.
© 2014 John Wiley & Sons, Inc. Published 2014 by John Wiley & Sons, Inc.

of the future Rachel remind Elizabeth of a friend she had in elementary school. Ms Hansen, a worker with whom Elizabeth talks, has also formed a special emotional attachment to Rachel.

At the end of the story an inebriated worker knocks over the womb jar containing Rachel. Ms Hansen becomes hysterical, yelling "Murderer." Elizabeth feels her eyes fill with tears as she stares down at the sodden pictures of Rachel covered with fluid from the womb jar. But then she's confused by her other glimpse of Rachel, the quarter-inch piece of fish-like goo slithering over her shoe.

Of course the story is intended to dramatize two very different ways of conceptualizing the fetus—as a small particle of cells versus the person it could become. Imagining ectogenesis also lets us distinguish questions about the moral status of the fetus from those about the moral rights of the woman carrying the fetus. We'll take up both those sorts of questions after we discuss some abortion-related facts and factual issues.

Facts and factual issues

Abortion: definition and statistics

We will use the term "abortion" to mean induced abortion—the intentional termination of pregnancy, causing the death of the embryo or fetus. (Medicine tends to use the word "embryo" before the eighth week, the word "fetus" thereafter.)

The two main sources for abortion statistics are the US government's Centers for Disease Control and Prevention (CDC) and the private Alan Guttmacher Institute (AGI). The CDC gets its abortion statistics by compiling information from state health departments and hospitals, as well as other medical facilities. The AGI compiles its abortion statistics by directly contacting all abortion providers. The total number of abortions reported by the AGI tends to be higher than the number reported by the CDC. The reason for this seems to be that early abortions are usually done in physicians' offices and this type of abortion is underreported to the CDC.

According to the 2007 CDC figures: The *abortion ratio* was 231 legal abortions for every 1000 live births; the *abortion rate* was 16 legal abortions performed for every 1000 women (ages 15–44).

The AGI figures were higher: For instance, their calculated abortion rate for 2008 was 19.6 legal abortions performed for every 1000 women (ages 15–44).

The following table gives the CDC figures for the timing of abortion in weeks for 2007:

Timing of Abortion	% of Abortions
8 weeks or less	63.6%
9–13 weeks	28.0%
14–15 weeks	3.3%
16–17 weeks	1.8%
18–20 weeks	2.0%
21 weeks or more	1.3%

Adding the first two rows, we see that 91.6% of abortions occur within the first 12 weeks.

As for why women seek abortions,

> The Guttmacher Institute…notes that each year almost half of all pregnancies in the United States are unplanned. Four out of ten women with unplanned pregnancies obtain an abortion. On average, women give at least three reasons for choosing abortion:
>
> - Three-quarters say that having a baby would interfere with their work, school, or other responsibilities.
> - Two-thirds say they cannot afford a child.
> - Half say they do not want to be a single parent or are having problems with their husband or partner.

According to the Guttmacher Institute, 46% of women who have abortions had not used contraception in the month they became pregnant. Among those who had used contraception, "76% of pill users and 49% of condom users report having used their method inconsistently."

Abortion methods

Drug-based methods of abortion: These are sometimes referred to as "medical abortion" as opposed to "surgical abortion." One combination of drugs is mifepristone (formerly known as RU-486) and misoprostol: Used within the first seven weeks of pregnancy, the method can be up to 95% effective.

Surgical abortion procedures include the following:

Suction cutterage: This method is used for over 95% of surgical abortions. The cervix is dilated and a small tube inserted into the uterus. A suction device empties the contents of the uterus through the tube. It is a fairly quick procedure and can be done under local anesthetic.

Dilation and evacuation (D&E): In a way, this is a more complex version of suction cutterage, used after the 13th week of pregnancy. Because the procedure involves a larger fetus, the cervix must be dilated more—a procedure that can require the woman to stay in the clinic overnight. After the cervix is dilated, suction cutterage is used. Then the physician uses forceps to make sure the fetus has been totally removed, and finally scrapes the uterus to remove any remaining fetal tissue.

"Partial-birth abortion": This term (which is political, not medical) covers what might be considered a late-gestation extension of dilation and evacuation. Methods called "intact dilation and evacuation" or "dilation and extraction" (D&X) are used after the 20th week of pregnancy: They involve the partial delivery of the fetus, legs first, then collapsing the skull to allow full removal of the fetus.

Induction method: This method is used late in the second trimester. The physician injects the patient with a solution designed to induce contractions. Depending on the solution used, labor should result after 12 or 24 hours.

Development of the embryo/fetus

The embryo is given different names at different early stages: For instance, it is called a "zygote" when it is a single fertilized cell and a "blastocyst" (as in the story) when, a week after fertilization, having grown to close to a hundred cells, it implants itself in the wall of the uterus.

From the moment of fertilization, the full genetic code is in place. Up to about 14 or 15 days after fertilization, "twinning" may occur which will result in multiple births. Beyond that point, the individuality of the embryo is assured.

About this same time, the primitive brain and the first nerve cells begin to form.

At about 3 weeks after fertilization, the embryo is less than a tenth of an inch long. It looks roughly like a tiny tube cleft at both ends. Over the next few weeks, the embryo grows to half an inch long, going through a fascinating metamorphosis in which it looks like a tadpole, a seahorse, then something prehistoric with a grotesquely large head and tail, then a fish. "Rachel" was at this latter stage in the story.

By the 8th week after fertilization, the "fetus," as it's now called, is perhaps an inch long and weighs a third to half an ounce. All of its organs are in place. To the affectionate eye, the fetus will now look human, through it would be more correct to say it looks "mammalian": At this point, human and monkey fetuses look very much alike. The human fetus will look more human-baby-like in the coming weeks.

At about 10 weeks after fertilization, the first demonstrable connections occur between neural cells in an area where the brain cortex will develop. At about 12 weeks, an electroencephalograph (EEG) can detect the first signs of electrical activity in the brain.

We need to note here a confusing matter of usage. Technical references to the early stages of embryonic/fetal development tend to refer to the days or weeks after the actual fertilization of the egg. However, later on, reflecting popular usage, much talk is about not weeks after fertilization but "weeks pregnant." When people say that a woman is "12 weeks pregnant," that is roughly equivalent to "10 weeks after fertilization." The reason for this is that pregnancy is traditionally dated, not from the moment of fertilization, but from the first day of the woman's last menstrual period—*about* two weeks earlier. Since much of our current talk about abortion reflects the pregnancy dating, we can't avoid it. But we will clarify which reference is being used by referring either to "weeks(fert)" or "weeks(preg)."

Between 16 and 20 weeks (preg), the mother will experience sensations she can identify as the fetus moving inside her. Historically, this moment has been called "quickening."

The "viability" of the fetus (when it can survive outside the womb) depends on the state of medical technology: Very premature babies need extensive and sophisticated medical care to survive. Survival rates vary from 40% at week 23 (preg) to 90 % at week 28 (preg).

To some, 23 weeks (preg) looks like something of a natural lower limit to viability because of the immature state of the lungs. Even then, many very premature infants suffer severe permanent disabilities.

Constant, well organized brain activity seems to occur sometime after the 22nd week (preg); at about 32 weeks (preg) permanent electroencephalographic activity is detectable. During this period the fetus can respond to light and sound.

Legal status of abortion

The following are some of the major court cases and laws regarding abortion:

In the 1972 case, *Roe v. Wade*, the Supreme Court declared unconstitutional a Texas law that banned abortion except when the mother's life was at stake. The Court ruled that the law violated the "due process" law of the Fourteenth Amendment. The Fourteenth Amendment had declared that state governments are covered by the Fifth Amendment's guarantee that government cannot arbitrarily or unfairly deprive individuals of their right to life, liberty, and property. The majority on the Court invoked a "right to privacy" not mentioned in the Constitution but previously invoked by the Court in connection with the Fourteenth Amendment and applied to personal privacy in marriage, family relationships, and contraception, among others.

The Court said the "right to privacy" wasn't absolute and did allow the states to interfere with privacy rights during the later stages of pregnancy.

Citing the increasing risks in the later stages of pregnancy and the viability of the fetus in the third trimester, the Court set up the following schedule:

During the first trimester (three months), the state must leave the decision to abort to the woman and her physician.

During the second trimester, the state may regulate abortion as necessary to protect the woman's health.

During the third trimester, the state may regulate or forbid abortion to protect the potential life of the fetus, except where necessary to preserve the life or health of the mother.

Since *Roe v. Wade*, however, further decisions by the Court have increasingly allowed government to impose various restrictions related to abortion:

• States are not required to fund abortions or to provide public abortion facilities.

• The federal government may ban federally funded clinics from counseling about abortion as an option.

• States may require parental notification in cases where the woman is unmarried and under the age of 18.

In a 1989 case, *Webster v. Reproductive Health Services*, even though the court narrowly upheld *Roe v. Wade*, a majority of the judges indicated they were generally opposed to abortion. They also indicated that they no longer supported the rigid trimester system set down in *Roe*.

By the time of *Planned Parenthood of Southeastern Pennsylvania v. Casey* (1992), many were predicting that the Court would reverse *Roe v. Wade*. However, by a split decision of 5 to 4, the Court upheld *Roe*. The Court referred to the "liberty" mentioned in the Fourteenth Amendment and said:

> Though abortion is conduct, it does not follow that the state is entitled to proscribe it in all cases. That is, because the liberty of the woman is at stake in a sense unique to the human condition, and so, unique to the law. The mother who carries a child to full term is subject to anxieties, to physical constraints, to pain that only she must bear.... Her suffering is too intimate and personal for the State to insist, without more, upon its own vision of the woman's role, however dominant that vision has been in the course of our history and our culture. The destiny of the woman must be shaped to a large extent on her own conception of her spiritual imperatives and her place in society.

The Court rejected the trimester framework of *Roe* and allowed that states may put restrictions on the abortion process, as long as the restrictions did not place an "undue burden" in the path of a woman seeking abortion.

Crucially, *Casey* upheld the life-and-health exception during the third trimester of pregnancy. States can forbid abortion after viability only if they provide exceptions for pregnancies that may endanger the woman's life or health.

The life-and-health exception, established by *Roe* and upheld in other cases, extended the freedom to have an abortion far beyond what even the pro-choice advocates originally expected. In an early case, *Beal, Secretary, Department of Public Welfare of Pennsylvania v. Doe* (1977), the Court said that doctors, in deciding what was necessary for health, should consider "all factors—physical, emotional, psychological, familial, and the woman's age—relevant to the well-being of the patient." In effect, the Court makes the doctor the final judge of whether or not a woman may have an abortion, even if the fetus is viable.

As Cynthia Gorney puts it in her article, "Gambling with Abortion":

> The late abortion language about the definition of "health" was left intact in Casey. That means the Supreme Court doctrine still requires states to permit any abortion, even if the fetus is developed enough to survive on its own, once the doctor pronounces the abortion necessary to protect the woman's physical or psychological health…. From time to time, for rhetorical purposes, the prom dress girl is invoked—a fictional teenager who has suddenly decided she's too pregnant for her formal and walks into a clinic at twenty-eight weeks demanding to have it taken care of. Nobody has ever produced an actual prom dress girl; the point about the prom dress girl is theoretical, and in a theoretical way is true: under *Roe*, and under *Casey*, in the unlikely event that the prom girl were able to find a suitably cooperative doctor, she could theoretically be able to claim a legal right to abortion—a constitutionally protected "right to choose."…

In 2007, by a 5–4 decision, the Court upheld the Partial-Birth Abortion Ban Act of 2003 in which Congress made the procedure a crime. The law allows exceptions where it is necessary to save the woman's life but none where it is necessary to preserve her health. The Court agreed that the health of the woman is not grounds for allowing any particular method of abortion, so long as other methods are available. (The induction method, referred to above, would be such an alternative.)

Religious positions

Summarizing religious positions is tricky because so much depends on whether we're talking about conservative or liberal versions of the religion—not to mention individual opinion. But here are some of the "official views":

ROMAN CATHOLICISM: During much of Church history, theologians debated the point of "hominization" or "ensoulment"—the point at which a fetus becomes a human being by acquiring a soul. Some theologians felt that ensoulment didn't happen until birth. Others taught that it happened early in pregnancy—at forty days for males and eighty days for females. In the mid-19th century, the Church declared that hominization occurred at conception and pronounced abortion homicide.

The Roman Catholic Church has the toughest life-of-the-mother condition for allowing abortion. Only when the loss of the fetus is a *direct* result of an operation necessary to save the mother's life (from, say, cancer of the uterus) is an operation that would kill the fetus acceptable. Abortion would not be allowed, for instance, in a case where evidence indicated that a woman with cardiac disease would likely die as a result of carrying a child to term. It's important to emphasize that this is *the official position* of the Roman Catholic Church. Many Catholics disagree with that official position; there is, after all, an organization called Catholics for a Free Choice. And, according to the AGI, of the woman obtaining abortions in 2003, 27% identified themselves as Catholics (43% as Protestant).

PROTESTANTISM: From its beginnings, Protestantism has tended to espouse the idea that hominization begins at conception. Through the years, Protestantism has tended to discourage abortion, but unlike the Catholic Church, has tended to place less value on the life of the fetus than on the life of the mother—allowing abortion in a much greater range of cases when the "life and health of the mother" is at stake and also in cases of rape.

In recent years, however, many conservative Protestants have narrowed the allowable grounds for abortion. One reason for this is that political circumstances have forced conservative Protestants to frame their anti-abortion arguments in secular terms to appeal to a broader range of society: Thus appeals to religious prohibition and anti-promiscuity arguments have been put aside in favor of abortion as homicide. However, if you conceptualize abortion as murder, certain excusing conditions such as rape cease to make as much sense.

JUDAISM: Aníbal Faúnes and José S. Barzeleto, authors of *The Human Drama of Abortion*, say this of the Jewish tradition:

> The moral status of the fetus, according to Jewish tradition, progresses with gestational age and proximity

to viability, but the fetus is not considered to become a full person until birth (traditionally when the head of the newborn emerges from the birth canal).

With respect to abortion, the discussion and commentary take one of two courses: Either (1) the fetus is part of the body of a woman and does not, therefore, have an equal moral claim or (2) according to a later understanding put forward by Maimonides in the 12th century, in cases where pregnancy is endangering the life or health of the woman, the fetus can be considered…an aggressor…which may be killed as a permitted act of self defense….

However, among Orthodox Jews only saving the life of the woman is a justification of abortion.

ISLAM: The Koran teaches that the fetus receives a soul after 120 days. Some Muslims believe abortion is permissible before ensoulment, some do not. Most agree that abortion is acceptable whenever necessary to save the mother's life.

Public opinion

According to a 2011 Gallup poll, 51% of the respondents said that in general abortion was morally wrong, while 39% said that in general it was morally acceptable. At the same time, 50% said it should be legal under certain circumstances, 27% said it should be legal under all circumstances and 22% said it should be illegal under all circumstances.

According to a 2009 Harris poll, 51% favored *Roe v. Wade* and 44% opposed it.

The General Social Survey (2002) queried, "Please tell me whether or not you think it should be possible for a pregnant woman to obtain a legal abortion if…"

	Yes	No	Don't know
If the woman's own health is seriously endangered by the pregnancy?	89%	9%	2%
If she becomes pregnant as a result of rape?	76%	22%	2%
If there is a strong chance of serious defect in the baby?	75%	22%	3%
If she is not married and does not want to marry the man?	39%	58%	3%
If the family has a very low income and cannot afford any more children?	41%	56%	3%
If she is married and does not want any more children?	41%	56%	3%
If the woman wants it for any reason?	40%	57%	3%

The complexity of the abortion issue

A range of positions

The politically driven labels "pro-life" and "pro-choice" tend to blur the fact that there are a continuum of positions one can take on abortion. Most Americans don't fit comfortably in either category: Polls consistently show that Americans take a middle or moderate position on abortion. Obviously there would be no middle position on an either/or issue.

We might think of moral positions on abortion as forming a spectrum as follows:

PRO-CHOICE		MODERATE	PRO-LIFE	
Always permissible	Usually permissible	Often/often not permissible	Rarely permissible	Never permissible

Reflecting their use in political debate, we'll use the label "pro-choice" for those who think abortion is always or usually permissible and "pro-life" for those who think abortion is rarely or never permissible. Obviously these two extremes will shade into the moderate position—that abortion is in many cases permissible and in many cases not.

I don't know of any pro-life groups which claim abortion is always impermissible, though the official Roman Catholic position discussed earlier comes close.

There are many possible moderate positions: You might think abortion is morally permissible in the first trimester, morally wrong in the third trimester, and morally ambiguous in the second. Or you might think abortion is morally permissible in the first trimester, but morally impermissible thereafter except for certain exceptions that become narrower as the pregnancy advances.

It is important to stress that one's position on the morality of abortion need not be the same as one's position on the legality of abortion. Often it is the case that those holding a pro-life position want most or all abortions to be illegal, while those hold pro-choice views want few, if any, laws against abortion. But there are pro-life people who think a legal ban on abortion would be a disaster—difficult to enforce, undercutting respect for law, and leading to too many deaths through incompetent abortions. They believe in trying to use moral persuasion to reduce abortions. Some pro-choice people agree that certain cases of abortion—like that of the hypothetical prom-queen—would be immoral, but foresee too many complications if such abortions were made illegal.

Let's talk about the moral/legal distinction and some of the complications that would be involved in formulating an abortion law.

The moral versus the legal

Most of us have moral views that are specific in some respects and quite vague and incomplete in others. We come across cases we haven't anticipated and have to decide what's right or wrong on the spot.

The law is different. It can't decide after the fact that what you did was illegal. It must try to anticipate and be specific. Laws must be published in ways that are comprehensible to the general public (or at least

to their attorneys.) These factors make writing laws a difficult project. In addition, lawmakers must consider how the law is to be administered effectively, what the costs of administration will be, and what impact the law may have on the general conduct of life.

Sometimes these complications lead lawmakers to formulate laws that are much simpler and less satisfactory than what was originally conceived.

Obviously the simplest abortion laws would be ones that either banned or allowed all abortions. The problem with these simple laws is that they wouldn't reflect the views of the majority of Americans: There would probably be an enormous political backlash and problems of lack of enforcement and compliance.

Suppose lawmakers tried to formulate an abortion law that matched what seem to be the predominant moral views of the American people: Allowing abortions in the first trimester, banning them in the third trimester (with a few strict exceptions), and restricting abortions in the second trimester. (This would be generally in line with *Roe v. Wade*, but would not leave all decisions to the woman and her physician.)

What exceptions would you allow during the second trimester and how would you determine whether a particular case qualified?

Reflecting the majority view, you'd want exceptions for risk to the mother's life and health, as well as exceptions for rape, incest, and fetal deformity. What about an exception for someone who had difficulty getting funds for an abortion or difficulty getting to an abortion provider on time (some states have no providers)? Or for someone—perhaps a very young woman—who didn't know she was pregnant (perhaps being in denial)? Or for someone who had been subjected to intense family pressure not to have an abortion? Or for a woman abandoned by a partner on whom she depended for financial support?

Whatever exceptions you allowed, you'd need to establish an administrative/judicial system to rule on cases where exceptions were claimed. Perhaps you'd need to set up a system of medical boards to rule on claims of physical/mental risk and fetal deformity. What about the rape exception? Would you only consider rape claims if the rapes had been reported at the time they allegedly occurred? Or would you allow for later claims of rape if they were then reported to the police? (Obviously you can't require rape convictions because the pregnancies would have come to term.)

How would you determine the validity of claimed exceptions for undue pressure, financial hardship, and partner abandonment? Unless you're going to accept the woman's word (which would likely make that part of the law a farce), you will need rules of evidence and perhaps some investigations by expanded social service or law enforcement agencies. All this is going to require a considerable expansion of the government bureaucracy and cost quite a bit of money.

Maybe you think it worth the expanded bureaucracy and consequent costs to have a law setting restrictions on second trimester abortions. Or maybe you just throw up your hands and decide to save the restrictions for the third trimester.

As for the third trimester, you'd like to limit your exceptions to cases where there is substantial risk to the woman's life or health. However, if you want the law generally in line with American public opinion, you'll also have an exception for fetal deformity. It turns out that due to the medically appropriate timing of certain tests and the timing of the normal lab and notification procedures, many woman don't find out their fetuses have serious deformities until the third trimester. Still you should be able to handle that with hospital boards (overseen by some federal agency) that review the case for abortion being made by the woman and her personal physician.

What about women who violate the law and obtain an illegal abortion? Do you send them to jail? Fine them? What about the women who are unable to pay the fines?

Many pro-life groups have decided that pushing for penalties against the women who get illegal abortions would be politically risky. Instead the proposals have been to direct legal penalties against the abortion providers.

There could be complications here, however. Unless you set this up just right, you could find that those potentially involved in abortions—hospital boards and doctors (along with their insurance carriers)—are so frightened by the huge fines or threat of jail, that, in practice, no doctor or hospital is going to be willing to perform many of those abortions you intend to permit. It is also possible that doctors are going to be reluctant to perform various legitimate procedures on pregnant women for risk of an inadvertent abortion. Or perhaps they'll feel the need to get permission in advance of doing any procedure on pregnant women in the third trimester. Again, you will need more medical review.

What is likely to be the net gain in fetal lives saved by having no restrictions on abortions in the first and second trimester and reasonably strict legal restrictions on third trimester abortions?

Estimates of the number of yearly third trimester abortions are in the 750 to 1000 range. Pro-choice groups claim that virtually all of third trimester abortions take place because the woman's life or health is seriously endangered or because of a strong chance of a serious defect in the baby. Pro-life groups dispute this—though there seems little doubt that many third trimester abortions would fall into the mother's life/health and fetal deformity categories.

Let's suppose—*and this is just supposition*—that there were a 1000 third trimester abortions a year and the breakdown of that number came out as follows:

400 due to a life/serious health risk to the mother;
400 due to serious fetal deformity;
200 other.

The legal apparatus you are setting up to ban third trimester abortions is aimed at those 200 Americans per year. Who are they? We know that a disproportionate number of third trimester abortions are obtained by teenagers who, through denial or fear, manage to hide their pregnancies until late term. Many are the younger teenagers. Let's suppose that of those 200, 133 are teenagers (of whom 100 are 16 or under).

That's a lot of law and a lot of money to combat 200 (mostly teenage) abortions. And while deterring 200 abortions would not be inconsequential, 200 is a long way down from what has been called the "national tragedy" of 1.3 million abortions a year. Is there a more practical, non-legal approach to the problem?

I don't mean to slant this so as to imply that there is no feasible way to put legal limits on abortions. If you hold a staunch pro-life view, your object is to make as many abortions as possible illegal; whatever subsidiary suffering and injustice results will pale beside the goal of stopping abortion (which you see as murder). I just wish to point out how complicated the issue of legal restrictions becomes if you hold a moderate view of abortion.

The obvious non-legal approach to reducing abortions would be the promotion of contraception. But, as we all know, this is another contentious issue in the United States.

Practical means to reducing abortion

In theory, it seems that *substantially reducing* abortions in general would be a relatively simple matter. We would need to institute programs that would do the following:

1. *Provide increased sex education through schools and run public awareness campaigns that emphasize contraception.*
2. *Make contraception easily available.*
3. *Along with 1 and 2, frame contraception as hip and smart, and abortion-as-contraception as stupid.*
4. *Institute or improve social services that provide financial and other support for pregnant women (single and otherwise) who wish to have the child but are deterred by lack of financial and other support.*
5. *Intensify efforts to identify the biological father of the child and mandate child support.*

The mouth-dropping difficulty of imagining such a program getting through the American political process demonstrates how much more complicated the whole issue of abortion is than just the morality of killing the fetus.

Many religious conservatives consider sex education that emphasizes contraception to be an invitation to pre-marital sex. Preventing pre-marital sex often seems as important to these conservatives as preventing abortion. On the face of it, this seems incredible, if abortion is supposed to be equivalent to murder. However, the religious conservatives would argue that immoral means (means that would at least indirectly promote pre-marital sex) should not be employed to achieve the (even greater) moral goal of preventing abortion. Many conservative Roman Catholics are against contraception quite apart from its effect in promoting pre-marital sex and would be against using this means to avoid abortion even among married women.

The other huge obstacle is the idea of increased social services for pregnant women who are deterred by financial and other problems from carrying the child to term (with the intention either of keeping it or putting it up for adoption). Many of the pro-life forces are against (or at least allied politically with those who are against) increased social services. Further, these particular social services could be seen as promoting pre-marital sex by diminishing the "cost" to the woman of getting pregnant.

So much for the factual issues and the various legal and practical complications related to abortion. We'll turn now to the various moral positions and arguments. First, a few preliminaries about the relevant moral issues.

Two central moral issues

Any ethical position on abortion (whether pro-life, moderate, or pro-choice) needs to take a position on the following two major issues:

1. The moral status of the fetus; and
2. How the claims of the mother are to be weighed against whatever moral status the fetus has.

Considering *1—the moral status of the fetus*—requires us to confront questions like these:

- Is the fetus a "person," a "potential person," or something else? Does being a "person" matter? Why? Why not?
- Does the fetus have rights, especially the right to life? At what point, if any, does the fetus gain the right to life? At conception? If the fetus gains a right to life sometime after conception, what moral significance, if any, does the fetus have prior to that point?
- Given the above and other considerations, is it morally wrong to end the life of a fetus? Why? Why not? At what stage of fetal development is it wrong. At viability? At some earlier stage? At conception?

Considering *2—the claims of the mother vis-à-vis the fetus*—requires us to confront questions like these:

- If at any point the fetus has the right to life, how should the mother's rights be weighed as against those of the fetus?
- If at any point, the fetus has a moral significance short of actually having rights, how should the

mother's rights and concerns be weighed against the moral significance of the fetus?

(If the fetus has no moral status at all, then there is no question of weighing claims. Morally the mother can abort or not at any point as she chooses.)

In the course of analyzing the claims of the mother versus the fetus, philosophers have come up with some rather wild analogies (some of which we'll examine). One philosopher has claimed that in the course of all this logical argument, the reality of abortion gets lost. In *The Family on Trial*, philosopher Philip Abbott writes:

> Sixteen examples (and there are variations) are used to analyze the morality of abortion. What examples! The world of the philosopher is filled with people seeds, child missile launchers, Martians, talking robots, dogs, kittens, chimps, jigsaw cells that form human beings, transparent wombs, and cool hands—everything in fact but fetuses growing in wombs and infants cradled in parents' arms.

Obviously abortion can be a very emotional issue, both for women facing abortion and for those with extremely strong pro-life and pro-choice views.

But emotional moral views like any moral views are subject to evaluation and criticism. Some pro-life people talk as if the four-week-old embryo, about to be aborted, is like an innocent prisoner facing execution, crying out for help. Others on the pro-choice side are thinking, "Are you nuts? You're talking about something less than half an inch long, with a tail, no less, and with no thoughts or feelings. What 'prisoner'? The embryo is more like a tumor you're free to remove." To the pro-life side, this response, at a minimum, seems "unfeeling."

However, the central question isn't who is more emotional or sensitive. The central question is, Which of these emotional responses, if either, is appropriate?

Clearly emotional responses have their judgmental components and can be critiqued. Think of a man who *feels sure* his partner is cheating on him. One doesn't say, "Well, those are just his feelings; no one has the right to criticize them." Inside we ask: Are his feelings correct? Is the partner cheating or is the man mistaken?

Or take the case of a woman who feels her partner doesn't really love her, even though the partner behaves and talks consistently in a loving way. You don't think: Well, that's just the way she feels. Instead you're likely to think that she's very insecure and should consider counseling.

Take an example related to a different moral issue. A friend who attended an animal rights conference told me about a woman who was affectionately dubbed "The Chicken Lady" for her crusade on behalf of factory-farmed chickens. One can imagine the "Chicken Lady" making her pitch to some of the pro-life people and having the pro-life people think: "Is she nuts? Chickens?! *We* are talking about human beings!"

The Chicken Lady might respond indignantly that her chickens, unlike their embryos, have independent lives and can feel pain. (We'll discuss chickens, as a matter of fact, in the chapter on animals.)

The point is that, though feelings do play a legitimate and important role in our moral judgments, what we want to know is whether those feelings are reasonable. In the Abbott quote above, the phrase "fetuses growing in wombs" is juxtaposed with "infants cradled in parents' arms" as if the two are somehow comparable. But are they? Emotion isn't sufficient to decide the issue. We need reason as well.

The moral status of the fetus

Fetal development and moral status

On the following page is a crude chart of the nine months of pregnancy. The chart includes points in fetal development that people have found important with respect to the abortion issue.

At conception the zygote—the fused cell that has not yet divided to become an embryo—has the full genetic code (*DNA*) and might be considered a "potential person" (*PtPer*). At about 15 days after fertilization the primitive nerve cells and brain (*PrimNerv*) begin to form.

In the third month, the fetus has what some would think of as a recognizable human form (*HumFrm?*). Toward the end of the third month, the first signs of brain waves appear as measured by an electroencephalograph (*EEG*).

During the fifth month, "quickening" (*Quick*) occurs, when the fetus' movements are first felt by the mother.

Month 1	2	3	4	5	6	7	8	Month 9+	Later
CONCEPTION								BIRTH	
DNA		HumFrm?		Quick		Viable		Baby	Person?
PtPer		EEG				OrgBr			
PrimNerv									

During the seventh month, there is well organized brain activity (*OrgBr*) and the fetus reacts to external stimuli, such as sound. About that time, too, the fetus becomes *viable*, meaning it could survive outside the womb (with extensive medical care).

Birth, of course, occurs after nine months, but, as we shall see, some will argue that the individual does not become a *person* in the full-blown moral sense until much later.

In deciding on the moral status of the fetus, we need to decide at what point(s) in the process of gestation we would consider the fetus to have:

- a right to life (RtL),
- moral significance (M-Sig), and/or
- no moral significance (No M-Sig)

To attribute to the fetus a "right to life" (RtL) is to say that in any life-and-death decision, the life of the fetus is to have (*almost*?) the same weight as the life of a child or an adult. The fudge factor *almost* is there because one might be able to reconcile saying the fetus has a right to life, while allowing that the right to life of the mother would take precedence. However, it would make no sense to say that the fetus has a "right to life" that could be outweighed by the mother's feeling of stress, her not wanting the baby, or her feeling financial hardship. If the moral weight the fetus has can be overridden so easily, that weight doesn't amount to a "right to life."

To say that the fetus has "moral significance" (M-Sig) would be to say that its life has a certain degree of moral weight, but that this weight doesn't have the force of a right. For instance, if you thought that it was all right for a mother to abort a five-month-old fetus if the continued pregnancy was likely to cause her life-long health problems, but not if she'd simply changed her mind about wanting a baby, you'd be attributing to the five-month-old fetus a certain degree of moral significance, but not a right to life.

Of course, to decide that the fetus has moral significance is not in itself to say how *much* weight to give the life of the fetus. That would have to be made more specific in anyone's moral thinking. Also note that, unlike a right to life, moral significance doesn't have to be an either/or matter. You could give the fetus a growing moral significance so that, for instance, it might figure more heavily in moral calculations in the fourth month than the second month.

At this point, you might make yourself a crude chart like the one above and mark down the points, if any, where you think the fetus takes on a right to

Month 1	2	3	4	5	6	7	8	Month 9+	Later
CONCEPTION								BIRTH	
DNA		HumFrm?		Quick		Viable		Baby	Person?
PtPer		EEG				OrgBr			
PrimNerv									
No M-Sig		M-Sig		M-Sig+		RtL			

life (RtL), when it takes on moral significance (M–Sig), and/or where it has no moral significance (No M–Sig). If you think at a certain point its moral significance increases, you could mark that point as M–Sig+. As an illustration, the chart at the bottom of p. 246 has been filled in to indicate one of the moderate positions.

The bottom row indicates the belief that the fetus has no moral significance for the first couple of months; it takes on and gains significance from months 3 through 6; and it has a full-fledged right to life starting the seventh month.

A person holding a strong pro-life position would likely put "RtL" in the Month 1 column and that would be that. A person holding a strong pro-choice position might put "No M–Sig" in the Month 1 column and nothing else until "RtL" at Month 9+.

Why don't you mark your own chart and save it. See if your views change at all as you discuss these issues.

Before going on to discuss the pro-life, moderate, and pro-choice positions, let's take a closer look at the interim development points on the chart and see why one or another might seem morally important to someone holding a moderate view of abortion. (Pro-choice and pro-life advocates reject the moral importance of these points of development; we will discuss their arguments later.)

a. Brain development (EEG & OrgBr)

At the end of the third, and beginning of the fourth, month, the first demonstrable connections occur between neural cells in an area where the brain cortex will develop, and an electroencephalograph (EEG) can detect the first signs of electrical activity in the brain.

Some philosophers and theologians, noting that we take "brain death" as the termination of the human being, think it makes sense to mark the beginning of the human being with the beginning of brain waves ("brain life").

On the other hand, there is a different way to construe a "brain life" criterion. Though there are some brain waves from the third month on, it is not until the sixth month that there is well organized brain activity (*OrgBr*) and ongoing brain waves; this is when the fetus begins to respond to external stimuli. Many medical researchers believe that it is not until this point—22 to 24 weeks (preg)—that the neural pathways are sufficiently developed to transmit pain messages to the fetal cortex.

Some philosophers have argued that if we were to mark the beginning of "brain life" in the fetus, the sixth month, rather than the third, would be the most reasonable point.

b. Human form (HumFrm?)

It's natural enough that images of the fetus would have some effect on our feelings about abortion. Some years ago, when the first good photographs of the fetuses in utero appeared, some people who viewed the pictures found themselves less comfortable than they had been previously with a blanket acceptance of abortion.

Certainly pictures of aborted fetuses have been influential in converting people to the pro-life movement. For a long time it was a tactic of pro-life organizations to carry pictures of aborted fetuses at pro-life rallies. Many have stopped this practice: Apparently the bloody pictures simply repulsed passersby, rather than provoking sympathy for a pro-life view. But even when photos are effective, their use by pro-life people carries a danger—namely, the possible implication that abortion doesn't matter when the fetus doesn't look human. Pro-life protesters would hardly be inclined to carry photos of fetuses aborted when they still looked like snails or fish.

Whether the look of the fetus *should* influence our feelings on abortion is a matter of debate.

c. Quickening (Quick)

In less medically sophisticated times, "quickening" (when the mother first feels the fetus move) was taken as a significant stage of fetal development and the point at which abortion was no longer allowed. Quickening is an emotionally important point for the mother (and partner), but we now know that it doesn't mean much in terms of fetal development. It tends to occur between the fourth and six months, but the movements the mother feels are simply the result of fetal movements that have been going on since the sixth week. We also know that mothers who have previously given birth tend to "feel" the movements earlier than those who have not.

d. Viability (Viable)

This is the point at which the fetus can survive outside the womb (though only with sophisticated and extensive medical care). To many (including the Supreme Court in *Roe v. Wade*), viability is a crucial point regarding the moral standing of the fetus. The fact that the fetus could survive outside the womb seems to give the fetus an independent baby-like moral status it might not have had before.

At the time of *Roe v. Wade*, viability was thought to be at about 28 weeks of pregnancy. Though medical science has since improved on that, it looks as if 23 weeks is a natural limit, since before then the fetus' lungs are too immature to survive, even with respirators. Right now only 10% of babies born at 23 weeks survive even with the best medical care.

Pro-life arguments re fetal status

As we discussed earlier, a number of religions tie a prohibition against abortion to a theological belief about when the fetus gains a soul. Having a soul makes a creature a human being and brings the homicide prohibition into play. Since the Roman Catholic Church and many conservative Protestant groups believe the embryo gains a soul at conception, they consider abortion (in the absence of limited excusing conditions) to be murder.

However, even within Christianity, the case against abortion isn't as clear as it might be.

Two of the most revered Roman Catholic theologians in history, St Augustine and St Thomas Aquinas, declared that abortion was not homicide. From the twelfth through the thirteenth century, the Church's position varied according to the popes' personal beliefs about when ensoulment took place. It was not until the nineteenth century that the Roman Catholic Church adopted its current position, and that adoption was at least partially influenced by other religious doctrines, like that of the Immaculate Conception.

It's true that from the Reformation on, Protestants have held the view that the fetus was fully human from conception. But for a religion that is said to be Bible-based, it's difficult to find firm Biblical support for a pro-life position. Abortion has been practiced since ancient times, yet the Bible has no direct prohibition against it. The best that anti-abortion Protestants can do

is quote verses like Jeremiah 1.4 ("Before you were in the womb, I knew you....") that seem to imply that the fetus is something God knows and values.

Whatever the justifications for an anti-abortion position within religions, when believers operate in the political realm and push for an anti-abortion law within a religiously diverse and often secular country like the United States, they need to present arguments that will make a prohibition against abortion seem reasonable to secularists or those with very different beliefs.

These days, one of the main non-religious arguments put forward on behalf of a pro-life view has two parts:

Argument 1a. If you are born of human parents, you are a human being, and the prohibition against killing human beings immediately applies.

This is bolstered by pointing out what we now know, that the zygote/embryo has the full genetic code from which the individual human being will develop.

Argument 1b. Any doubts about the embryo being human from the beginning should be set to rest when you see that there is no point during pregnancy when it would be reasonable to say that just there *the fetus is human and* just there *it is not.*

Arguments are then given against each possible starting point for attributing humanity to the fetus. Some of the arguments are as follows:

Against birth as the point at which the fetus becomes human: How can the mere location of a being affect its moral status? The one-day-old newborn is no different from the fetus it was the day before; it could have been born the day, a week, a month earlier. How could the moment of birth make such a difference?

(Note that we are now talking only about the status of the fetus itself, not the conflicting claims of mother and fetus. Obviously birth can make a difference from the conflicting-claims perspective. We'll get to that later.)

Against viability as the point at which the fetus becomes human: It makes no sense to think that the humanity of the *fetus* should be dependent on *our* technological ability, yet that is just what the viability of the fetus does depend on. Further, it makes no sense to think of viability as the point at which the fetus can stay alive on its own because fetuses delivered at the early stages of viability can't stay alive without serious medical assistance. Not even babies can stay alive on their own.

Against the ability to have experiences as the point at which the fetus becomes human: Though the full nervous system may not be in place until about 24 weeks, there are signs of brain activity as early as 10 weeks. Even before then the zygote is alive and responding to its environment. Anyway, we wouldn't say that a human in a coma is less human because she is temporarily deprived of experience.

Against the look of the fetus as the point at which the fetus becomes human: How can we properly predicate humanity on how a being looks, when that is exactly what is wrong with racial discrimination and discrimination of people with severe disabilities?

A second pro-life argument goes like this.

2. From the beginning, the zygote/embryo has the potential to become a full human being; thus it is entitled to the same rights as other humans.

This argument is usually adjusted to take care of an obvious problem: If abortion is murder on grounds of potentiality, why isn't contraception—or even abstinence—murder as well? After all, the sperm and egg also have the potentiality to become human beings.

One attempt to take care of this problem redefines potentiality in terms of probability. Judge John Noonan (see Readings), who writes in support of a pro-life position, points out that a spermatozoa in a normal ejaculate has a one in two hundred millionth of a chance of developing into a zygote, whereas the zygote has an 80% chance of becoming a human infant. (It has been claimed that 50% is a truer figure, but the difference is still enormous.) Thus the zygote has a degree of potentiality vastly greater than that of a spermatozoa.

Pro-choice arguments re fetal status

Philosopher Mary Anne Warren (see Readings) asks:

> How are we to define the moral community, the set of beings with full and equal moral rights, such that we can decide whether a human fetus is a member of this community or not? What sort of entity, exactly, has the inalienable rights to life, liberty, and the pursuit of happiness?

Her suggestion is that what qualifies one for inclusion in the moral community is being a *person*, rather than being a genetic human being. Personhood involves those characteristics we would look for to decide if some extra-terrestrial creature deserved to be treated morally. What we would look for, she suggests, would be some combination of characteristics like the following: consciousness (especially the capacity to feel pain), reasoning, self-motivated activity, the capacity to communicate, and the presence of self-concepts and self-awareness.

She argues that since fetuses don't have these characteristics, they don't qualify as persons; thus, the fetus doesn't have the kind of moral weight that would count against the mother's desire to have an abortion.

One huge problem with this position is that it seems to license not only abortion, but also infanticide; judging by Warren's criteria, infants don't qualify as persons either. Warren doesn't believe that infanticide is justified: She argues that while infants don't get rights by being persons, we have other reasons to extend rights to them, or at least some analogous protections. We care about them and feel a special connection to them. Also, if we don't treat them *as if* they had strong moral rights, they won't grow up to become autonomous, morally responsible adults.

Philosopher Michael Tooley also holds that only persons have rights, but, unlike Warren, he accepts the implication of a personhood-view regarding the permissibility of infanticide. He believes our opposition to infanticide isn't rational; it is only a taboo, based on revulsion.

Unlike Warren and Tooley, most pro-choice thinkers wouldn't rest their arguments so heavily on the status of the fetus. These others would emphasize the mother's "right to control her own body." We'll discuss those arguments in our conflicting-claims section.

Moderate-position arguments re fetal status

We have defined the moderate positions as holding that abortion is often permissible, but often not. One philosopher who develops such a position is L. W. Sumner.

Sumner suggests that instead of analyzing the status of the fetus in terms of personhood, we use the more general concept of "moral standing" (close to what we have been calling "moral significance"). According to Sumner, the minimum condition for moral standing is sentience. Moral standing will increase as a being approaches what Sumner considers the qualifications for full moral standing: Being rational, capable of being a moral agent, capable of participating in the moral life of the community.

Sumner believes that the moral issues "raised by early abortion are precisely those raised by contraception" while those "raised by late abortion are similar to those raised by infanticide." In terms of the status of the fetus, early abortions are morally permissible, late abortions are not (though the rights of the mother will have to be weighed against the rights of the fetus).

What about the middle period of pregnancy? Sumner says,

> The status of the borderline cases in the middle weeks of the second trimester is simply indeterminate. We cannot say of them with certainty either that the fetus has a right to life or that it does not…. What we can say is that, from the moral point of view, the earlier an abortion is performed the better.…

Sumner seems to favor a social policy on abortion that permits all abortions in the first trimester, begins restrictions on those in the second trimester, and puts tough restrictions on those in the third trimester.

Writer Gregg Easterbrook (see Readings) holds a different moderate position. Instead of viewing fetal sentience as developing slowly, he marshals evidence supporting the view that the fetus becomes conscious at about 26 weeks. He thinks abortion is morally wrong from that point on. He also believes abortion should be illegal after the 26th week: There should be a life/health exception, but it should be more narrowly defined.

What might moderates say about the arguments of the pro-choice and pro-life ends of the spectrum? Here are some likely moderate counter-arguments:

- *Against the pro-choice argument that fetuses don't have rights because they are not "persons" in the sense of being able to reason, able to communicate and so on.*

The moderate might say that what's wrong with the personhood view is analogous to what's wrong with contractualism: Too much of our morality is left out. What counts most strongly against this view is its implications for infanticide. It's true that Warren argues that we have consequentialist grounds for extending rights and analogous protections to children. But this makes protections for children too tenuous: It implies that if circumstances changed, we would be justified in putting those protections aside.

- *Against the pro-life argument that fetuses are human beings by virtue of having the full genetic code.*

The moderate might argue here that the genetic code is analogous to the blueprint, not the building. It is part of what will go into making a human being, but having a human genetic code isn't sufficient to make one a human being. It is only human in the most general sense in which a sample of tissue can be analyzed as human: We wouldn't say a tissue sample is a human being. At best, having the genetic code marks the embryo as a potential human being. (See below).

- *Against the pro-life argument that as a potential human being, the fetus deserves the same right to life as an actual human being.*

If "potential" here means "having the full genetic code" then the above response applies. But if we borrow Noonan's odds argument above, we might substitute for "potential" the idea that the fetus "is highly likely to become a human being in the natural course of things." Then the argument would turn on whether such probability implies a right to life or simply some degree of moral significance.

- *Against the pro-life argument that since no sensible dividing line can be found during fetal development, such that on one side the fetus is human and on the other side, not, you must say the embryo/fetus is human from the beginning embryo.*

The principle behind this argument seems to be that unless you can find a sharp and sensible dividing line within a continuum, you can't make a distinction between the two extremes. A familiar counter to this involves the example of baldness: Just because you can't find the definitive point in hair loss where a man becomes bald, doesn't mean that "bald" doesn't mark a real distinction. We say a man is bald when most of his hair is gone, even though we can't give a definition of "most" in terms of percentage of hairs.

If, like Easterbrook, we decide a right-to-life should be tied to consciousness and the evidence is ambiguous as to whether the brain states necessary for consciousness are developed by the 22nd rather than 26th week, we could take a cautious approach and assume a right-to-life at week 22. If, in addition, we think a fetus has increasing moral significance during the 2nd trimester, we could progressively narrow the morally acceptable reasons for abortion during that trimester.

The sensible-dividing-line objection only works if we assume in advance that there must be a hard-and-fast answer to the question of when, if ever, abortion is morally permissible. However, perhaps the answer itself must be complex and, in some cases, a bit ambiguous.

So far we have discussed the morality of abortion in terms of questions about the moral status of the fetus—questions that were at the heart of the "Blessing" story. Joan Hansen, a worker at BBH, developed a maternal love for "Rachel," the name given to one of the embryos. Because the science of genetics is so advanced in that society, sophisticated predictive images and descriptions of the fetuses give their future selves a vivid reality. Actually, "reality" isn't quite the right word, since the specifics of the predictions could be wrong (they are predictions, after all). Nonetheless, vividness of the predictions make us feel vividly the potentialities of each fetus.

On the other hand, along with the sense of what the embryo will be, we are given a sense of what that embryo is now—a fish-like piece of goo. Faced with this reality, Ms Hansen maintains her focus on what that embryo will become. Elizabeth's reaction is more uncertain. She, too, has been captivated by the computer-generated images of Rachel and feels shock at the loss that the smashed womb jar and soaking images represent. Still, Elizabeth has a much different reaction when confronted with the actual "Rachel."

> Elizabeth noticed something else. It was something on the top of her shoe, something gross, something that looked like a misshapen fish. Startled, she gave her shoe

a shake, to get rid of the thing. It seemed to slither off her shoe, though its motion was only the flow of amniotic fluid.

Can the destruction of that tiny piece of flesh be considered murder? Can it even be considered killing? Those are some of the central questions of the abortion debate.

So far we have focused only on the moral status of the fetus, neglecting another crucial dimension of the abortion issue: the claims and rights of the mother. The pro-choice movement emphasizes the woman's "right to choose" and some such right (even if more limited) would almost certainly figure in any moderate position. Even the pro-life positions give at least some weight to the life of the mother.

Let us turn now to the issue of the claims of the mother versus the "claims of the fetus"—the latter phrase being a metaphor for whatever moral protections the fetus is entitled to.

Conflicting claims of the mother versus the fetus

We have talked about three types of moral status one might accord the fetus: A right to life, moral significance (possibly in varying degrees), and no moral significance. How does the status of the fetus impact on the mother's claims to life, health, and freedom?

At first glance it would seem to be the case that:

- If the fetus has no moral significance (as in the personhood analysis), the fetus need have no moral weight in the mother's decision to abort.
- If the fetus has moral significance, then the degree of significance at any point would have to be weighed against the seriousness of the mother's claims.
- If the fetus has a full right to life, only a threat to the mother's life could justify abortion (since she also has a right to life).

However, this last point was disputed in a famous article by Judith Jarvis Thomson, entitled "A Defense of Abortion" (see Readings). Thomson argues that even if we grant that the fetus is a person with a right to life, abortion would still be justified in a wide range of cases.

To illustrate this point, Thomson asks us to imagine the following case:

> You wake up in the morning and find yourself back to back in bed with an unconscious violinist. He's been found to have a fatal kidney ailment, and the Society of Music Lovers has canvassed all the available medical records and found that you alone have the right blood type to help. They have therefore kidnapped you, and last night the violinist's circulatory system was plugged into yours, so that your kidneys can be used to extract poisons from his blood as well as your own. The director of the hospital now tells you, "Look, we're sorry the Society of Music Lovers did this to you—we would never have permitted it if we had known. But still, they did it, and the violinist now is plugged into you. To unplug you would be to kill him. But never mind, it's only for nine months. By then he will have recovered from his ailment and can safely be unplugged from you"....

Thomson thinks most of us would find the director's reasoning outrageous. She claims this hypothetical case shows that there is something wrong with the argument that the fetus' right to life outweighs the mother's right to decide what happens in and to her body.

She claims that having a right to life doesn't imply the right to get whatever you need to live. To update one of Thomson's examples, suppose a feverish (and, let's say, highly neurotic) woman lying on her death bed needed the cool touch of Brad Pitt's hand on her forehead to pull her through. Does she have the right to have Brad Pitt brought to her? Does Brad have a moral obligation to fly across the country to her bedside? Of course not. It would be nice if Brad did make the effort, but he certainly isn't obliged to do so. In the same way, Thomson thinks, the right to life of the fetus doesn't oblige the mother to continue the pregnancy.

Thomson recognizes an obvious limitation to the violinist example: the fact that you have been forced into the position where the violinist is dependent on you. Certainly the violinist case would seem to justify abortion in the case of rape—something the

pro-life arguments can't consistently allow. But what about cases where the mother has voluntarily engaged in intercourse, knowing she might get pregnant?

Thomson argues that abortion is justified in cases of voluntary intercourse if the woman has taken reasonable precautions: She's then not responsible for the existence of the fetus inside her. The fetus becomes more like a burglar who had gotten in the house despite the fact that the occupant had locked the doors and windows.

Even if we granted Thomson's whole argument—and many people would not—the argument does not justify abortion in many cases where abortion seems legitimate to those holding pro-choice and even moderate views: For instance, it wouldn't seem to justify even the earliest abortions in cases where the couple failed to take precautions. And it doesn't touch on cases of fetal deformity.

Philosopher Joel Feinberg (see Readings) has done a particularly detailed analysis of the arguments and analogies used with regard to the conflict of claims between the mother and fetus.

Feinberg starts by making the point that the claimed right to abortion is a discretionary right—like the right to liberty—and is subject to limits. For instance, my right to move around is limited by the boundaries of your property. He says that

> ...the alleged right to an abortion cannot be understood in a vacuum; it is a right that can only be understood by reference to the other, more fundamental rights from which it has often been claimed to be derived. Three of these rights are... (1)...property right; (2) the right to self-defense, and (3) the right to bodily autonomy....

According to Feinberg, if we start from Thomson's stipulated premise that the fetus has a right to life (or, in Feinberg's phrasing, "is a moral person"), it is impossible to think of the fetus as mere property.

A more plausible analogy, says Feinberg is not that the woman owns the fetus, but that she "shelters" it—that she owns her body (womb) "the way an innkeeper owns a hotel or a homeowner her house and garden."

However, he says, there are a number of problems with this analogy. Above all

...one is not *morally* entitled, in virtue of one's property rights, to expel a weak and helpless person from one's shelter when that is tantamount to consigning the person to a certain death, and surely one is not entitled to shoot and kill a trespasser who will not, or cannot, leave one's property. In no department of human life does the vindication of property rights justify homicide....

Having found the analogy to property rights unsatisfactory, Feinberg considers the analogy of self-defense. He says there are two aspects of the right of self-defense:

The first is proportionality. To protect ourselves, we are entitled to use force proportional to (or slightly greater than) the harm we are likely to suffer. We're entitled to kill to save ourselves from being killed or very seriously injured; we're not entitled to kill to avoid getting a black eye. Feinberg says it's not clear that a woman who aborts to avoid some months of inconvenience and discomfort is using proportional force. Not all abortion can be justified this way.

The second aspect he considers is the problem of the fetus as aggressor. If the fetus is an aggressor, it is an innocent, not a responsible one. One may sometimes kill an innocent aggressor—suppose someone with paranoid delusions tries to kill you and you can't run away—but the person must be an assailant. It's not clear that the fetus could be considered an assailant—except possibly in a case like rape.

Feinberg thinks the most interesting argument has to do with bodily autonomy, the right to exercise control over your own body. But he thinks what is crucial here is how responsible you are for what is attached to your body, whether the violinist or the baby. He thinks Thomson's violist analogy justifies you detaching the fetus if you can't be held responsible for it being there. He agrees that Thomson's analogy works for rape and actual contraceptive failure. But he thinks it is weak where the woman didn't want to be pregnant but was negligent about contraception or where she wanted to be pregnant but then changed her mind.

Summary

We said that the ethical arguments regarding abortion tend to revolve around two issues: The moral status of the fetus, and how the claims of the mother are to be weighed against whatever status the fetus has.

We said that at any point from conception through birth one could imagine the fetus having a right to life, moral significance, or no moral significance.

If and while the fetus has no moral significance, it need have no moral weight in the mother's decision to abort. This seems uncontroversial (perhaps it's even tautological).

If the fetus has moral significance, but not a right to life, then the degree of significance at any point would have to be weighed against the seriousness of the mother's claims. This general point seems uncontroversial. (However, how much moral significance the fetus has and how heavily it should be weighed against the mother's concerns would be controversial.)

If the fetus has a full right to life...what? Provisionally, it looked as if abortion would only be justified where the pregnancy threatened the mother's life or threatened serious harm to her health. However, if we agree with Feinberg, we might say that killing a fetus with a full right to life would be justified in all cases where killing an innocent aggressor would be justified—as in cases of rape.

So, does the fetus have a right to life? And if so, at what point in its development?

We reviewed religious and other arguments claiming that the fetus has a right to life from the moment of conception. We examined arguments claiming that the fetus has a right to life only during (roughly) the third trimester. We reviewed arguments for the claim that the fetus *never* has a right to life.

We discussed claims that the fetus gains moral significance (rather than a right to life) at some point during the pregnancy. Perhaps this significance grows during the course of the pregnancy: If so, the justifications for abortion must become more and more substantial.

After you work out your view of the morality of abortion—what you think is the moral status of the fetus and how you think the claims of mother and fetus should be weighed against each other—you should formulate your view of what the law should be. What abortions, if any, would you make illegal? What legal mechanisms would you put in place to enforce

the law? What might be the problems with those mechanisms and how might you avoid them? As we've seen, any law that doesn't simply ban or allow all abortions is going to take a lot of ingenuity to get right.

Notes and selected sources

Facts and factual issues

SOURCES

For factual information I have relied most heavily on:

Sandra M. Alters. *Abortion: An Eternal Social and Moral Question*. Information Plus® Reference Series. (Detroit, MI: Thomson Gale, 2008, 2010 & 2012).

Some other sources regarding factual information:

Ed. Fritz K. Beller and Robert F. Weir. *The Beginning of Human Life*. © 1994 Kluwer Academic Publishers. Printed in the Netherlands. Part I.

Aníbal Faúnes and José S. Barzeleto. *The Human Drama of Abortion: A Global Search for Consensus*. Nashville, TN: Vanderbilt University Press, 2006.

Cynthia Gorney. "Gambling with Abortion: Why both sides think they have everything to lose." *Harpers*. Nov. 2004, pp. 33–46.

Guttmacher Institute: "Facts on Induced Abortion in the United States," Aug. 2011, www.guttmacher.org.

Rodridgo O. Kuljis. "Development of the Human Brain: The Emergence of the Neural Substrate for Pain Perception and Conscious Experience." In Beller/Weir, pp. 49–56.

Jane Maienschein, *Whose View of Life? Embryos, Cloning, and Stem Cells*. Cambridge, MA: Harvard University 2003.

NOTES

CDC & AGI figures, Alters/Info Plus, 2012, pp. 47–9.

"The Guttmacher Institute notes…" Alters/Info Plus, 2008. p. 50.

"According to the Guttmacher institute…." Guttmacher.

"…The late abortion language about…." Gorney, pp. 39–40.

"The moral status of the fetus…." Faúnes/Barzeleto, pp. 84–5.

The complexity of the abortion issue

NOTES

"Sixteen examples (and there are variations)…" from Philip Abbott, *The Family on Trial: Special Relationships in Modern Political Thought*, University Park, PA: Pennsylvania State University Press, p. 138.

The moral status of the fetus

SOURCES

Fritz K. Beller and Robert F. Weir (Eds.) *The Beginning of Human Life* (above).

Jane English. "Abortion: Beyond the Personhood Argument" In Pojman, pp. 315–24.

Gregg Easterbrook. "What Neither Side Wants You to Know. Abortion and Brain Waves." *New Republic*, Jan. 24, 2000.

Don Marquis. "Why Abortion is Immoral," pp. 275–90 in Pojman/Beckwith (see below).

John T. Noonan, Jr. "Abortion is Morally Wrong," pp. 203–8 in Pojman/Beckwith.

Gregory E. Pence (ed.), *Classic Works in Medical Ethics*. Boston: McGraw-Hill, 1998. pp. 1–18.

Gregory E. Pence. "Ethical Theories and Medical Ethics." Introduction in Pence (ed.).

Louis P. Pojman and Francis J. Beckwith (eds.). *The Abortion Controversy: 25 Years After Roe v. Wade: A Reader*. 2nd edn. Belmont, CA: Wadsworth, 1998.

L. W. Sumner. "A Defense of the Moderate Position," pp. 299–312 in Pojman/Beckwith.

Judith Jarvis Thompson. "A Defense of Abortion," pp. 117–31 in Pojman/Beckwith.

Barbara Steinbock. *Life Before Birth: The Moral and Legal Status of Embryos and Fetuses*. Oxford: Oxford University Press, 1992.

Michael Tooley, "In Defense of Abortion and Infanticide," pp. 209–33 in Pojman/Beckwith.

Mary Anne Warren. "On the Moral and Legal Status of Abortion," pp. 169–99 in Pence (ed.)

NOTES

"How are we to define the moral community…." Warren in Pence, p. 176.

Tooley on infanticide, see Tooley above.

Sumner on moderate position, see Sumner above.

"raised by early abortion…." Sumner, pp. 308–9.

"…The status of the borderline cases…." Sumner, p. 309.

Sumner seems to favor, Sumner, p. 309.

Writer Gregg Easterbrook, see Easterbrook.

Conflicting claims of the mother versus the fetus

SOURCES

Joel Feinberg. "Abortion," in Tom Regan (ed.), *Matters of Life and Death: New Introductory Essays in Moral Philosophy*, 3rd edn. New York: McGraw-Hill, 1980.

Also: All readings already listed under the heading "Moral status of the fetus" above.

NOTES

"…You wake up in the morning…."Thomson, pp. 118–19.
"…the alleged right to an abortion…." Feinberg, pp. 214–15.
"shelters…the way an innkeeper…." Feinberg, p. 215.
"…one is not *morally entitled*…." Feinberg, p. 216.

Definitions

(Terms are defined in the order in which they appeared in the text.)

1. *Ectogenesis*: The full development of an embryo/fetus outside the body
2. *In vitro fertilization (IVF)*: The combining of sperm and egg in an artificial environment (in vitro) rather than in the female body (in utero).
3. *Embryo*: The fertilized egg up to the eighth week of development.
4. *Fetus*: What the embryo becomes at the eighth week until birth. (Some prefer to use the term "fetus" from conception to birth.)
5. *Abortion ratio*: Number of legal abortions per 1000 live births.
6. *Abortion rate*: Number of legal abortions for every 1000 women.
7. *Medical abortion*: Refers to drug-based methods of abortion used in the first few weeks of pregnancy. (Contrast with "surgical abortion.")
8. *Suction cutterage*: A surgical abortion procedure in which the cervix is dilated and a small tube inserted into the uterus. A suction device empties the contents of the uterus through the tube.
9. *Dilation and evacuation (D&E)*: A more complex version of suction cutterage, used after the 13th week of pregnancy. The cervix is dilated more before suction cutterage is used. Then the physician uses forceps to make sure the fetus has been totally removed, and finally scrapes the uterus to remove any remaining fetal tissue.
10. *Dilation and extraction (D&X)*: A late-gestation extension of dilation and evacuation. It involves the partial delivery of the fetus, legs first, then collapsing the skull to allow full removal of the fetus. ("Intact dilation and evacuation" is similar.)
11. *"Partial-birth abortion"*: A political, not medical, name for late gestation abortion; it covers dilation and extraction as well as intact dilation and evacuation.
12. *Induction method*: This method of abortion is used late in the second trimester. The physician injects the patient with a solution designed to induce contractions, then labor.
13. *Zygote*: A single fertilized cell.
14. *Blastocyst*: The embryo at the stage when it is implanted in the wall of the uterus.
15. *Viability*: The stage when the fetus can survive outside the womb.
16. *Ensoulment*: The point at which, according to religious doctrine, the embryo/fetus gains a soul.
17. *Pro-choice*: The position of those who think abortion is always or usually permissible.
18. *Pro-life*: The position of those for those who think abortion is rarely or never permissible.
19. *Moderate*: The position of those who think abortion is in many cases permissible and in many cases not.
20. *Quickening*: The point at which the mother first feels the fetus move.
21. *Moral significance*: Having some moral standing short of a right to life.
22. *Brain life*: A phrase sometimes used to indicate that there is electrical activity in the brain as detected by an electroencephalograph (EEG). (It is meant to contrast with "brain death"—the end of such activity.)
23. *Person*: A term sometimes used to indicate only those humans capable of such qualities as self-consciousness and rationality. (In this latter sense a newborn human would not be a "person.")

Questions

(Please explain your answers, making specific reference to relevant passages in the discussion.)

1. Do you hold a "pro-life," "pro-choice," or moderate position on abortion (according to the particular definitions of these labels used in the text)? Under what circumstances, if any, do you think abortion is permissible?

2. What do you think the law should be regarding a woman's right to have an abortion? Would this law exactly correspond to what you think is morally right or wrong regarding a woman having an abortion? If there are differences, what are they? How do you justify them?

3. What are some questions regarding the moral status of the fetus? What are some of the questions regarding the moral status of the mother versus the moral status of the fetus?

4. What does it mean, according to the text, if the fetus has a "right to life"? "Moral significance"? "No moral significance"?

5. Describe the points during fetal development that have been thought, by one person or another, to be important in terms of the embryo/fetus gaining a right to life.
   In terms of its gaining moral significance.

6. Present some pro-life arguments re fetal status.

7. Present some pro-choice arguments re fetal status.

8. Present some moderate arguments re fetal status.

9. What is Judith Jarvis Thomson's violinist analogy supposed to illustrate?

10. What limitations does Thomson see in her own analogy?

11. Joel Feinberg imagines a woman's right to an abortion being justified on the basis of three different "defenses": (a) that the fetus is merely the woman's property that she is free to destroy if she wishes; (b) that the fetus can be considered an aggressor that the woman can kill in self-defense; (c) that the woman has a right to bodily autonomy that justifies her killing the fetus. What strengths and/or weaknesses does he find with these defenses?

15

Abortion

Readings

Roger A. Paynter discusses different interpretations of what the Bible has to say about abortion

[…]

Now, let me paint the issue in its most extreme ideological perspectives and then muddy the water a bit. […]

On one extreme is the position that sees the fetus as a piece of human tissue, no more, and the abortion decision as no more a moral choice than removing any other item of mere tissue. This position would say that a woman's right to abortion is absolute. I have read expressions of this position a couple of times, and I have seen it posed in television debates, but I have never known anyone to claim it as *their* position. Each writer or speaker qualifies his or her position in some manner.

The other extreme, the "Right to Life" position, says that from conception the life begun is a human person and to abort a fetus is murder. The fetus's right to life is *absolute*.

Now let me begin to "muddy the waters" by saying that an absolute right—that is, *one* right taken out of the framework of *all other rights*—is often what gets us into trouble. As Abraham Heschel said, "The opposite

Reproduced with permission from "Life in the Tragic Dimension: A Sermon on Abortion," by Roger A. Paynter, in *The Ethics of Abortion*, 3rd edn., ed. Robert M. Baird and Stuart E. Rosenbaum. Amherst, NY: Prometheus Books, 2003, pp. 233–6. Courtesy of R. Paynter.

of a profound truth is another profound truth and the opposite of a human right is another human right."[1]

The first point I would make is that the worlds of medicine, philosophy, and the law have been unable to determine a "magic moment" when personhood begins. Life begins at conception, but when does human personhood begin? A variety of positions have been taken:

1. *conception*, the point at which the new genotype is set.
2. *implantation*, when the conceptus implants in the mother's womb (fourteen days). (By the way, the IUD contraceptive device comes into consideration here, for it works not by preventing conception, but by keeping implantation from occurring.)
3. *eight weeks*, when the cerebral cortex begins to form and all internal organs are formed. Both Aristotle and Augustine believed that a male fetus obtained its soul at forty days and a female fetus was ensouled at eighty to ninety days. Augustine called this homonization—the point at which a developing embryo experiences "ensoulment." Before this point (eight weeks), Augustine allowed for the possibility of abortion. Arguing about the possible resurrection of aborted fetuses, "which are fully formed," he says about those not fully formed: "Who is not disposed to think that unformed fetuses perish like seeds which have been fructified." There is a whole history of important

positions that the early church fathers held with respect to this issue, a history that the Roman Church would rather not admit into consideration.[2]

4. *quickening*, (sixteen to eighteen weeks) when the mother feels the fetus move.

5. *viability*, when the unborn child can survive outside the mother's body (around twenty-six weeks). This is the point when the Supreme Court protects the life of the unborn. A woman can have an abortion in the last "trimester" only if her life is at stake.

6. *birth*, when the baby draws its first breath.

Thousands of years of debate are represented in these positions, and still there is no consensus about when human life becomes a human person. Despite the efforts of movies like *The Silent Scream*, no scientific information can yet determine when unborn life becomes a human person. Just as medical science has never absolutely, clearly, and without an ounce of reservation been able to determine when a dying person loses personhood, science cannot tell us with absolute clarity when personhood begins.

But neither has the church formed a consensus on the question, "When does personhood begin?" One of the reasons for this lack of consensus is that the Bible has no clear word. In the absence of such a clear mandate, a number of interpretations have arisen. Let me share some with you. I repeat, there is no place in the Bible where it is said: "Thou shalt not have an abortion."

The primary Jewish position is that human personhood begins when the baby is born and draws breath. Gen. 2:7 declares that "God breathed into his nostrils the breath of life and man became a living soul." Elsewhere, there is a place in Old Testament law (Exod. 21:22–25) that makes a value distinction between the life of the mother and the life of the unborn:

> When men strive together and hurt a woman with child, so that this is miscarriage, and yet no harm follows, the one who hurt her shall be fined, according as the woman's husband shall lay upon him ... if any harm follows then you shall give life for life, eye for eye, tooth for tooth, hand for hand....

That is, if the being in utero is harmed, a fine is imposed; if the mother dies, then the life of the injurer is demanded. While this is not the noblest form of jurisprudence, it is the only passage in the Bible directly applicable to the abortion issue. The New Testament, by the way, is completely and strangely silent.[3]

Now, the "Right to Life" people have, as you well know, a number of biblical passages at their disposal—the prominent ones being from Jeremiah, Job, and the Psalmist:

> Before I formed you in the womb, I knew you. (Jer. 1:4–5)
>
> Your own hands shaped me, molded me. (Job 10:8)
>
> For thou didst form my inward parts—Thou didst knit me together in my mother's womb. (Ps. 139:13)

These passages are all poetic expressions of the truth that God is the Creator and the source of all creative processes. They should instill in us a reverence toward all life, unborn as well as born. However, I do not think we should use them as proof of when, in the complex physical, spiritual process of creation, fetal life becomes human personhood. Poetry and "legal or scientific" arguments do not mix well. When a man says he has a broken heart, the physician does not do "open-heart" surgery. [...]

The Bible does not prohibit abortion, but it always encourages a respect for life. Left with this ambiguity, believers have through the years taken very different positions. The Jewish community, for the most part, has valued the life and health of the mother above that of the unborn.[4] The Roman Catholic Church has held its very clear position only since 1869 and Pope Pius IX. It has always been against the abortion of a human being—don't get me wrong—but thinkers in the Catholic Church have held diverse opinions about when the fetus becomes an ensouled being. A diversity of opinions is still held, but no longer formally. The issue is now covered by the legislative function of the church. Abortions can get you excommunicated. You cannot have an abortion, even to save the life of the mother. You may try to save the mother's life and *indirectly* end the life of the fetus. This is to be contrasted, in Catholic reasoning, from directly aborting the fetus.[5] By the way, the legislative function of the Catholic Church is different from the teaching office, the Magisterium. The pope is infallible only in the teaching, not in the legislative area.

Therefore, the prohibition of abortion is not governed by papal infallibility.

Protestant groups have taken a whole range of positions. Southern Baptists have repeatedly gone on record as opposing abortion, except in the case of rape, incest, severe fetal deformity, or danger to the mother's health. Thus, we must invoke the Protestant principle which says that in cases where Scripture is not clear, final interpretation should be left to each individual person, given guidance within his or her community of faith. The Roman Catholic position, of course, is that the church interprets Scripture for all its people on all issues.

[…]

Questions

1. According to Paynter, what are the "most extreme ideological perspectives on abortion"?
2. Why does Paynter think scientific evidence is ambiguous in supporting either extreme position?
3. According to Paynter, where does it say in the Old Testament that abortion is wrong? Where in the New Testament?
4. Some people say that Bible verses like, "Before I formed you in the womb, I knew you" show that abortion is wrong. What does Paynter say?

Notes

1. Abraham Joshua Heschel, from the original version of his sermon on abortion.
2. Jan Hurst, *The History of Abortion in the Catholic Church: The Untold Story* (Washington, DC: Catholics for a Free Choice, 1981), p. 7.
3. H. Stephen Shoemaker, "The Moral Crisis of Abortion," unpublished sermon.
4. Rabbi David Feldman as quoted by Paul Simmons, *Birth and Death: Bioethical Decisionmaking* (Philadelphia: Westminster Press, 1983), p. 94.
5. Hurst, *The History of Abortion in the Catholic Church*, p. 17.

John T. Noonan, Jr. argues that abortion is morally wrong

The most fundamental question involved in the long history of thought on abortion is: How do you determine the humanity of a being? To phrase the question that way is to put in comprehensive humanistic terms

Reprinted by permission of the publisher from "An Almost Absolute Value in History," by John T. Noonan, Jr. in *The Morality of Abortion: Legal and Historical Perspectives*, ed. John T. Noonan, Jr., pp. 51–9, Cambridge, MA: Harvard University Press. Copyright © 1970 by the President and Fellows of Harvard College.

what the theologians either dealt with as an explicitly theological question under the heading of "ensoulment" or dealt with implicitly in their treatment of abortion. […] But the theological notion of ensoulment could easily be translated into humanistic language by substituting "human" for "rational soul"; the problem of knowing when a man is a man is common to theology and humanism.

If one steps outside the specific categories used by the theologians, the answer they gave can be analyzed as a refusal to discriminate among human beings on the basis of their varying potentialities. Once conceived, the being was recognized as man because he had man's potential. The criterion for humanity, thus, was simple and all-embracing: if you are conceived by human parents, you are human.

The strength of this position may be tested by a review of some of the other distinctions offered in the contemporary controversy over legalizing abortion. Perhaps the most popular distinction is in terms of viability. Before an age of so many months, the fetus is not viable, that is, it cannot be removed from the mother's womb and live apart from her. To that extent, the life of the fetus is absolutely dependent on the life of the mother. This dependence is made the basis of denying recognition to its humanity.

[…]

The most important objection to this approach is that dependence is not ended by viability. The fetus is still absolutely dependent on someone's care in order to continue existence; indeed a child of one or three or even five years of age is absolutely dependent on another's care for existence; uncared for, the older fetus or the younger child will die as surely as the early fetus detached from the mother. The unsubstantial lessening in dependence at viability does not seem to signify any special acquisition of humanity.

A second distinction has been attempted in terms of experience. A being who has had experience, has lived and suffered, who possesses memories, is more human than one who has not. Humanity depends on formation by experience. The fetus is thus "unformed" in the most basic human sense.

This distinction is not serviceable for the embryo which is already experiencing and reacting. The embryo is responsive to touch after eight weeks and at least at that point is experiencing. At an earlier stage the zygote is certainly alive and responding to its environment. [ature…]

A third distinction is made by appeal to the sentiments of adults. If a fetus dies, the grief of the parents is not the grief they would have for a living child. The fetus is an unnamed "it" till birth, and is not perceived as personality until at least the fourth month of existence when movements in the womb manifest a vigorous presence demanding joyful recognition by the parents.

Yet feeling is notoriously an unsure guide to the humanity of others. Many groups of humans have had difficulty in feeling that persons of another tongue, color, religion, sex, are as human as they. Apart from reactions to alien groups, we mourn the loss of a ten-year-old boy more than the loss of his one-day-old brother or his 90-year-old grandfather. The difference felt and the grief expressed vary with the potentialities extinguished, or the experience wiped out; they do not seem to point to any substantial difference in the humanity of baby, boy, or grandfather.

Distinctions are also made in terms of sensation by the parents. The embryo is felt within the womb only after about the fourth month. The embryo is seen only at birth. What can be neither seen nor felt is different from what is tangible. If the fetus cannot be seen or touched at all, it cannot be perceived as man.

Yet experience shows that sight is even more untrustworthy than feeling in determining humanity. By sight, color became an appropriate index for saying who was a man, and the evil of racial discrimination was given foundation. Nor can touch provide the test; a being confined by sickness, "out of touch" with others, does not thereby seem to lose his humanity. To the extent that touch still has appeal as a criterion, it appears to be a survival of the old English idea of "quickening"— a possible mistranslation of the Latin *animatus* used in the canon law. To that extent touch as a criterion seems to be dependent on the Aristotelian notion of ensoulment, and to fall when this notion is discarded.

[…]

The rejection of the attempted distinctions based on viability and visibility, experience and feeling, may be buttressed by the following considerations: Moral judgments often rest on distinctions, but if the distinctions are not to appear arbitrary fiat, they should relate to some real difference in probabilities. There is a kind of continuity in all life, but the earlier stages of the elements of human life possess tiny probabilities of development. Consider for example, the spermatozoa in any normal ejaculate: There are about 200,000,000 in any single ejaculate, of which one has a chance of developing into a zygote. Consider the oocytes which may become ova: there are 100,000 to 1,000,000 oocytes in a female infant, of which a maximum of 390 are ovulated. But once spermatozoon and ovum meet and the conceptus is formed, such studies as have been made show that roughly in only 20 percent of the cases will spontaneous abortion occur. In other words, the chances are about 4 out of 5 that this new being will develop. At this stage in the life of the being there is a sharp shift in probabilities, an immense jump in potentialities. To make a distinction between the rights of spermatozoa and the rights of the fertilized ovum is to respond to an enormous shift in possibilities. For about twenty days after conception the egg may split to form twins or combine with another egg to form a chimera, but the probability of either event happening is very small.

It may be asked, What does a change in biological probabilities have to do with establishing humanity? The argument from probabilities is not aimed at establishing humanity but at establishing an objective discontinuity which may be taken into account in moral discourse. As life itself is a matter of probabilities, as most moral reasoning is an estimate of probabilities, so it seems in accord with the structure of reality and the nature of moral thought to found a moral judgment on the change in probabilities at conception. The appeal to probabilities is the most commonsensical of arguments, to a greater or smaller degree all of us base our actions on probabilities, and in morals, as in law, prudence and negligence are often measured by the account one has taken of the probabilities. If the chance is 200,000,000 to 1 that the movement in the bushes into which you shoot is a man's, I doubt if many persons would hold you careless in shooting; but if the chances are 4 out of 5 that the movement is a human being's, few would acquit you of blame. Would the argument be different if only one out of ten children conceived came to term? Of course this argument would be different. This argument is an appeal to probabilities that actually exist, not to any and all states of affairs which may be imagined.

The probabilities as they do exist do not show the humanity of the embryo in the sense of a demonstration in logic any more than the probabilities of the movement in the bush being a man demonstrate beyond all doubt that the being is a man. The appeal is a "buttressing" consideration, showing the plausibility of the standard adopted. The argument focuses on the decisional factor in any moral judgment and assumes that part of the business of a moralist is drawing lines. One evidence of the nonarbitrary character of the line drawn is the difference of probabilities on either side of it. If a spermatozoon is destroyed, one destroys a being which had a chance of far less than 1 in 200 million of developing into a reasoning being,

possessed of the genetic code, a heart and other organs, and capable of pain. If a fetus is destroyed, one destroys a being already possessed of the genetic code, organs, and sensitivity to pain, and one which had an 80 percent chance of developing further into a baby outside the womb who, in time, would reason.

The positive argument for conception as the decisive moment of humanization is that at conception the new being receives the genetic code. It is this genetic information which determines his characteristics, which is the biological carrier of the possibility of human wisdom, which makes him a self-evolving being. A being with a human genetic code is man.

[…]

Even with the fetus weighed as human, one interest could be weighed as equal or superior: that of the mother in her own life. The casuists between 1450 and 1895 were willing to weigh this interest as superior. Since 1895, that interest was given decisive weight only in the two special cases of the cancerous uterus and the ectopic pregnancy. In both of these cases the fetus itself had little chance of survival even if the abortion were not performed. As the balance was once struck in favor of the mother whenever her life was endangered, it could be so struck again. The balance reached between 1895 and 1930 attempted prudentially and pastorally to forestall a multitude of exceptions for interests less than life.

The perception of the humanity of the fetus and the weighing of fetal rights against other human rights constituted the work of the moral analysts. But what spirit animated their abstract judgments? For the Christian community it was the injunction of Scripture to love your neighbor as yourself. The fetus as human was a neighbor; his life had parity with one's own. The commandment gave life to what otherwise would have been only rational calculation.

The commandment could be put in humanistic as well as theological terms: Do not injure your fellow man without reason. In these terms, once the humanity of the fetus is perceived, abortion is never right except in self-defense. When life must be taken to save life, reason alone cannot say that a mother must prefer a child's life to her own. With this exception, now of great rarity, abortion violates the rational humanist tenet of the equality of human lives.

[…]

Questions

1. At what point, according to Noonan, does the embryo or fetus become a human being? What makes it human?

2. What does Noonan say to those who argue that the humanity of the fetus starts when it has experience? When it is viable?

3. What role does the discussion of probabilities play in Noonan's argument?

4. Is Noonan approaching abortion from a religious perspective? A humanistic perspective? Both? Explain.

Mary Ann Warren argues that fetuses don't qualify as persons with a right to life

[...]

The question which we must answer in order to produce a satisfactory solution to the problem of the moral status of abortion is this: How are we to define the moral community, the set of beings with full and equal moral rights, such that we can decide whether a human fetus is a member of this community or not? What sort of entity, exactly, has the inalienable rights to life, liberty, and the pursuit of happiness? Jefferson attributed these rights to all *men*, and it may or may not be fair to suggest that he intended to attribute them *only* to men. Perhaps he ought to have attributed them to all human beings. If so, then we arrive, first at [John] Noonan's problem of defining what makes a being human, and, second, at the equally vital question which Noonan does not consider, namely: What reason is there for identifying the moral community with the set of all human beings, in whatever way we have chosen to define that term?

On the definition of "human"

One reason why this vital second question is so frequently overlooked in the debate over the moral

From "On the Moral and Legal Status of Abortion," by Mary Anne Warren, *Monist* 57 (Jan. 1973), 43–61. Copyright © *The Monist: An International Quarterly Journal of General Philosophical Inquiry*, The Hegeler Institute, Peru, IL. Reprinted by permission.

status of abortion is that the term "human" has two distinct, but not often distinguished, senses. This fact results in a slide of meaning, which serves to conceal the fallaciousness of the traditional argument that since (1) it is wrong to kill innocent human beings, and (2) fetuses are innocent human beings, then (3) it is wrong to kill fetuses. For if "human" is used in the same sense in both (1) and (2) then, whichever of the two senses is meant, one of these premises is question-begging. And if it is used in two different senses then of course the conclusion doesn't follow.

Thus, (1) is a self-evident moral truth, and avoids begging the question about abortion, only if "human being" is used to mean something like "a full-fledged member of the moral community." (It may or may not also be meant to refer exclusively to members of the species *Homo sapiens*.) We may call this the *moral* sense of "human." It is not to be confused with what we will call the *genetic* sense, i.e., the sense in which any member of the species is a human being, and no member of any other species could be. If (1) is acceptable only if the moral sense is intended, (2) is non-question-begging only if what is intended is the genetic sense.

In "Deciding Who is Human," Noonan argues for the classification of fetuses with human beings by pointing to the presence of the full genetic code, and the potential capacity for rational thought.[1] It is clear that what he needs to show, for his version of the traditional argument to be valid, is that fetuses are human in the moral sense, the sense in which it is analytically true that all human beings have full moral rights. But, in the absence of any argument showing that whatever is genetically human is also morally human, and he gives none, nothing more than genetic humanity can be demonstrated by the presence of the human genetic code. And, as we will see, the *potential* capacity for rational thought can at most show that an entity has the potential for *becoming* human in the moral sense.

Defining the moral community

Can it be established that genetic humanity is sufficient for moral humanity? I think that there are very good reasons for not defining the moral community in this way. I would like to suggest an alternative way of defining the moral community, which I will argue for only to the extent of explaining why it is, or should be, self-evident. The suggestion is simply that the moral community consists of all and only *people*, rather than all and only human beings; and probably the best way of demonstrating its self-evidence is by considering the concept of personhood, to see what sorts of entity are and are not persons, and what the decision that a being is or is not a person implies about its moral rights.

What characteristics entitle an entity to be considered a person?

[...]

I suggest that the traits which are most central to the concept of personhood, or humanity in the moral sense, are, very roughly, the following:

1. consciousness (of objects and events external and/or internal to the being), and in particular the capacity to feel pain;
2. reasoning (the *developed* capacity to solve new and relatively complex problems);
3. self-motivated activity (activity which is relatively independent of either genetic or direct external control);
4. the capacity to communicate, by whatever means, messages of an indefinite variety of types, that is, not just with an indefinite number of possible contents, but on indefinitely many possible topics;
5. the presence of self-concepts, and self-awareness, either individual or racial, or both.

[...]

All we need to claim, to demonstrate that a fetus is not a person is that any being which satisfies *none* of (1)–(5) is certainly not a person. I consider this claim to be so obvious that I think anyone who denied it, and claimed that a being which satisfied none of (1)–(5) was a person all the same, would thereby demonstrate that he had no notion at all of what a person is.

[...]

Now if (1)–(5) are indeed the primary criteria of personhood, then it is clear that genetic humanity is neither necessary nor sufficient for establishing that an entity is a person. Some human beings are not people, and there may well be people who are not human beings. A man or woman whose consciousness has been permanently obliterated but who remains alive is a human being which is no longer a person; defective human beings with no appreciable mental capacity, are not and presumably never will be people; and a fetus is a human being which is not yet a person, and which therefore cannot coherently be said to have full moral rights. Citizens of the next century should be prepared to recognize highly advanced, self-aware robots or computers, should be such [*sic*] developed, and intelligent inhabitants of other worlds, should such be found, as people in the fullest sense, and to respect their moral rights. But to ascribe full moral rights to an entity which is not a person is as absurd as to ascribe moral obligations and responsibilities to such an entity.

Fetal development and the right to life

Two problems arise in the application of these suggestions for the definition of the moral community to the determination of the precise moral status of a human fetus. Given that the paradigm example of a person is a normal adult human being, then (1) How like this paradigm, in particular how far advanced since conception, does a human being need to be before it begins to have a right to life by virtue, not of being fully a person as of yet, but of being *like* a person? and (2) To what extent, if any, does the fact that a fetus has the *potential* for becoming a person endow it with some of the same rights? Each of these questions requires some comment.

In answering the first question, we need not attempt a detailed consideration of the moral rights of organisms which are not developed enough, aware enough, intelligent enough, etc., to be considered people, but which resemble people in some respects. It does seem reasonable to suggest that the more like a person, in the relevant respects, a being is, the stronger is the case for regarding it as having a right to life, and indeed the stronger its right to life is. Thus we ought to take seriously the suggestion that, insofar as "the human individual develops biologically in a continuous fashion... the rights of a human person might develop in the same way."[2] But we must keep in mind that the attributes which are relevant in determining whether or not an entity is enough like a person to be regarded as having some of the same moral rights are no different from those which are relevant to determining whether or not it is fully a person—i.e., are no different from (1)-(5)— and that being genetically human, or having recognizably human facial and other physical features, or detectable brain activity, or the capacity to survive outside the uterus, are simply not among these relevant attributes.

Thus it is clear that though a seven- or eight-month fetus has features which make it apt to arouse in us almost the same powerful protective instinct as is commonly aroused by a small infant, nevertheless it is not significantly more personlike than is a very small embryo. It is *somewhat* more personlike; it can apparently feel and respond to pain, and it may even have a rudimentary form of consciousness, insofar as its brain is quite active. Nevertheless, it seems safe to say that it is not fully conscious, in the way that an infant of a few months is, and that it cannot reason, or communicate messages of indefinitely many sorts, does not engage in self-motivated activity, and has no self-awareness. Thus, in the *relevant* respects, a fetus, even a fully developed one, is considerably less personlike than is the average mature mammal, indeed the average fish. And I think that a rational person must conclude that if the right to life of a fetus is to be based upon its resemblance to a person, then it cannot be said to have any more right to life than, let us say, a newborn guppy (which also seems to be capable of feeling pain), and that a right of that magnitude

could never override a woman's right to obtain an abortion, at any stage of her pregnancy.

[...]

Thus, since the fact that even a fully developed fetus is not personlike enough to have any significant right to life on the basis of its personlikeness shows that no legal restrictions upon the stage of pregnancy in which an abortion may be performed can be justified on the grounds that we should protect the rights of the older fetus; and since there is no other apparent justification for such restrictions, we may conclude that they are entirely unjustified. Whether or not it would be *indecent* (whatever that means) for a woman in her seventh month to obtain an abortion just to avoid having to postpone a trip to Europe, it would not, in itself, be *immoral*, and therefore it ought to be permitted.

Potential personhood and the right to life

We have seen that a fetus does not resemble a person in any way which can support the claim that it has even some of the same rights. But what about its *potential*, the fact that if nurtured and allowed to develop naturally it will very probably become a person? Doesn't that alone give it at least some right to life? It is hard to deny that the fact that an entity is a potential person is a strong prima facie reason for not destroying it; but we need not conclude from this that a potential person has a right to life by virtue of that potential. It may be that our feeling that it is better, other things being equal, not to destroy a potential person is better explained by the fact that potential people are still (felt to be) an invaluable resource, not to be lightly squandered. Surely, if every speck of dust were a potential person, we would be much less apt to conclude that every potential person has a right to become actual.

Still, we do not need to insist that a potential person has no right to life whatever. There may well be something immoral, and not just imprudent, about wantonly destroying potential people, when doing so isn't necessary to protect anyone's rights. But even if a potential person does have some prima facie right to life, such a right could not possibly outweigh the right of a woman to obtain an abortion, since the rights of any actual person invariably outweigh those of any potential person, whenever the two conflict. Since this may not be immediately obvious in the case of a human fetus, let us look at another case.

Suppose that our space explorer falls into the hands of an alien culture, whose scientists decide to create a few hundred thousand or more human beings, by breaking his body into its component cells, and using these to create fully developed human beings, with, of course, his genetic code. We may imagine that each of these newly created men will have all of the original man's abilities, skills, knowledge, and so on, and also have an individual self-concept, in short that each of them will be a bona fide (though hardly unique) person. Imagine that the whole project will take only seconds, and that its chances of success are extremely high, and that our explorer knows all of this, and also knows that these people will be treated fairly. I maintain that in such a situation he would have every right to escape if he could, and thus to deprive all of these potential people of their potential lives; for his right to life outweighs all of theirs together, in spite of the fact that they are all genetically human, all innocent, and all have a very high probability of becoming people very soon, if only he refrains from acting.

Indeed, I think he would have a right to escape even if it were not his life which the alien scientists planned to take, but only a year of his freedom, or, indeed, only a day. Nor would he be obligated to stay if he had gotten captured (thus bringing all these people-potentials into existence) because of his own carelessness, or even if he had done so deliberately, knowing the consequences. Regardless of how he got captured, he is not morally obligated to remain in captivity for *any* period of time for the sake of permitting any number of potential people to come into actuality, so great is the margin by which one actual person's right to liberty outweighs whatever right to life even a hundred thousand potential people have. And it seems reasonable to conclude that the rights of a woman will outweigh by a similar margin whatever right to life a fetus may have by virtue of its potential personhood.

Thus, neither a fetus's resemblance to a person, nor its potential for becoming a person provides any basis whatever for the claim that it has any significant right to life. Consequently, a woman's right to protect her health, happiness, freedom, and even her life, by terminating an unwanted pregnancy, will always override whatever right to life it may be appropriate to ascribe to a fetus, even a fully developed one. And thus, in the absence of any overwhelming social need for every possible child, the laws which restrict the right to obtain an abortion, or limit the period of pregnancy during which an abortion may be performed, are a wholly unjustified violation of a woman's most basic moral and constitutional rights.

Questions

1. Warren thinks the distinction between being "human" and being a "person" is crucial to the abortion debate. According to her, what is this distinction and why is it crucial?
2. Does Warren think it would be immoral for a woman to have an abortion in the seventh month so she could travel abroad? Explain Warren's reasoning.
3. Warren tells us a story of a space explorer who is captured by an alien culture. What happens in the story and how is it relevant to her argument?
4. How would Noonan argue against Warren?

Notes

1. John Noonan, "Deciding Who Is Human," *National Law Forum*, 13 (1968): 135.

2. Thomas L. Hayes, "A Biological View," *Commonwealth* 85 (March 17, 1967): 677-78.

Gregg Easterbrook argues that third-trimester abortions—but those only—should be tightly restricted

No other issue in American politics stands at such an impasse. Decades after *Roe* v. *Wade*, the abortion debate remains a clash of absolutes: one side insists that all abortions be permitted, the other that all be prohibited. The stalemate has many and familiar causes, but a critical and little-noticed one is this: Public understanding has not kept pace with scientific discovery. When *Roe* was decided in 1973, medical knowledge of the physiology and neurology of the fetus was surprisingly scant. Law and religion defined our understanding, because science had little to say. That is now changing, and it is time for the abortion debate to change in response.

[...]

EEGs show that third-trimester babies display complex brain activity, similar to that found in full-term newborns. The legal and moral implications of this new evidence are enormous. After all, society increasingly uses cessation of brain activity to define when life ends. Why not use the onset of brain activity to define when life begins?

[...] [A]round the sixth week, faint electrical activity can be detected from the fetal nervous system. Some pro-life commentators say this means that brain activity begins during the sixth week, but, according to Dr Martha Herbert, a neurologist at Massachusetts General Hospital, there is little research to support that claim. Most neurologists assume that electrical activity in the first trimester represents random neuron firings as nerves connect—basically, tiny spasms.

The fetus's heart begins to beat, and by about the twentieth week the fetus can kick. Kicking is probably a spasm, too, at least initially, because the fetal cerebral cortex, the center of voluntary brain function, is not yet "wired," its neurons still nonfunctional. (Readings from twenty- to twenty-two-week-old premature babies who died at birth show only very feeble EEG signals.) From the twenty-second week to the twenty-fourth week, connections start to be established

Reproduced with permission from "What Neither Side Wants You to Know: Abortion and Brain Waves," by Gregg Easterbrook. *The New Republic*, Jan. 24, 2000.

between the cortex and the thalamus, the part of the brain that translates thoughts into nervous-system commands. Fetal consciousness seems physically "impossible" before these connections form, says Fisk, of the Imperial College School of Medicine.

At about the twenty-third week the lungs become able to function, and, as a result, twenty-three weeks is the earliest date at which premature babies have survived. At twenty-four weeks the third trimester begins, and at about this time, as the cerebral cortex becomes "wired," fetal EEG readings begin to look more and more like those of a newborn. It may be a logical consequence, either of natural selection or of divine creation, that fetal higher brain activity begins at about the time when life outside the mother becomes possible. After all, without brain function, prematurely born fetuses would lack elementary survival skills, such as the ability to root for nourishment.

At about twenty-six weeks the cell structure of the fetal brain begins to resemble a newborn's, though many changes remain in store. By the twenty-seventh week, according to Dr Phillip Pearl, a pediatric neurologist at Children's Hospital in Washington, DC, the fetal EEG reading shows well-organized activity that partly overlaps with the brain activity of adults, although the patterns are far from mature and will continue to change for many weeks. By the thirty-second week, the fetal brain pattern is close to identical to that of a full-term baby.

[...]

In 1997, the Royal College of Obstetricians and Gynecologists, Britain's equivalent to a panel of the National Academy of Sciences, found that, because new research shows that the fetus has complex brain activity from the third trimester on, "we recommend that practitioners who undertake termination of pregnancy at 24 weeks or later should consider the requirements for feticide or fetal analgesia and sedation." In this usage, "feticide" means killing the fetus the day before the abortion with an injection of potassium that stops the fetus's heart, so that death comes within the womb. Otherwise, the Royal College suggests that doctors anesthetize the fetus before a third-trimester termination—because the fetus will feel the pain of death and may even, in some sense, be aware that it is being killed.

If a woman's life is imperiled, sacrificing a third-trimester fetus may be unavoidable. But the American

Medical Association (AMA) says late-term abortions to save the mother's life are required only under "extraordinary circumstances"; almost all late-term abortions are elective. In turn the best estimates suggest that about 750 late-term abortions occur annually in the United States, less than one percent of total abortions. (An estimated 89 percent of US abortions occur in the first trimester, ethically the least perilous time.) Pro-choice advocates sometimes claim that, because less than 1 percent of abortions are late-term, the issue doesn't matter. But moral dilemmas are not attenuated by percentages: no one would claim that 750 avoidable deaths of adults did not matter.

On paper the whole issue would seem moot, because Supreme Court decisions appear to outlaw late-term abortion except when the woman's life is imperiled. But in practice the current legal regime allows almost any abortion at anytime, which turns out to be a corruption of *Roe*.

[...]

It is time to admit what everyone knows and what the new science makes clear: that third-trimester abortion should be very tightly restricted. The hopelessly confusing viability standard should be dropped in favor of a bright line drawn at the start of the third trimester, when complex fetal brain activity begins. Restricting abortion after that point would not undermine the rights granted by *Roe*, because there is no complex brain activity before the third trimester and thus no slippery slope to start down. Scientifically based late-term abortion restrictions would not enter into law poignant but unprovable spiritual assumptions about the spark of life but would simply protect lives whose humanity is now known.

To be sure, restrictions on late-term abortion would harm the rights of American women, but the harm would be small, while the moral foundation of abortion choice overall would be strengthened by removing the taint of late-term abortion.

[...]

Questions

1. In the first reading, Roger A. Paynter says that "no scientific evidence can yet determine when unborn life becomes a human person." What would Easterbrook likely say to this?

2. Would it be fair to say that Easterbrook supports a tough version of *Roe v. Wade*? Explain.

3. Would Easterbrook allow any third-trimester abortions? Explain.

Judith Jarvis Thomson argues that even if it were granted that the fetus is a person, many abortions can still be justified in terms of the rights of the mother

Most opposition to abortion relies on the premise that the fetus is a human being, a person, from the moment of conception. The premise is argued for,

Reproduced with permission from "A Defense of Abortion," by Judith Jarvis Thomson, *Philosophy and Public Affairs*, 1, Fall 1971, 47–56.

but, as I think, not well. Take, for example, the most common argument. We are asked to notice that the development of a human being from conception through birth into childhood is continuous; then it is said that to draw a line, to choose a point in this development and say "before this point the thing is not a person, after this point it is a person" is to make an arbitrary choice, a choice for which in the nature of things no good reason can be given. It is concluded that the fetus is, or anyway that we had better say it is, a person from the moment of conception. But this conclusion does not follow. Similar things might be said about the development of an acorn into an oak tree, and it does not follow that acorns are oak trees, or that we had better say they are. Arguments of this form are sometimes called "slippery slope arguments"—the phrase is perhaps self-explanatory—and it is dismaying that opponents of abortion rely on them so heavily and uncritically.

I am inclined to agree, however, that the prospects for "drawing a line" in the development of the fetus look dim. I am inclined to think also that we shall probably have to agree that the fetus has already become a human person well before birth. Indeed, it comes as a surprise when one first learns how early in its life it begins to acquire human characteristics. By the tenth week, for example, it already has a face, arms and legs, fingers and toes; it has internal organs, and brain activity is detectable. On the other hand, I think that the premise is false, that the fetus is not a person from the moment of conception. A newly fertilized ovum, a newly implanted clump of cells, is no more a person than an acorn is an oak tree. But I shall not discuss any of this. For it seems to me to be of great interest to ask what happens if, for the sake of argument, we allow the premise. How, precisely, are we supposed to get from there to the conclusion that abortion is morally impermissible? Opponents of abortion commonly spend most of their time establishing that the fetus is a person, and hardly any time explaining the step from there to the impermissibility of abortion. Perhaps they think the step too simple and obvious to require much comment. Or perhaps instead they are simply being economical in argument. Many of those who defend abortion rely on the premise that the fetus is not a person, but only a bit of tissue that will become a person at birth; and why pay out more arguments than you have to? Whatever the explanation, I suggest that the step they take is neither easy nor obvious, that it calls for closer examination than it is commonly given, and that when we do give it this closer examination we shall feel inclined to reject it.

I propose, then, that we grant that the fetus is a person from the moment of conception. How does the argument go from here? Something like this, I take it. Every person has a right to life. So the fetus has a right to life. No doubt the mother has a right to decide what shall happen in and to her body; everyone

would grant that. But surely a person's right to life is stronger and more stringent than the mother's right to decide what happens in and to her body, and so outweighs it. So the fetus may not be killed; an abortion may not be performed.

It sounds plausible. But now let me ask you to imagine this. You wake up in the morning and find yourself back to back in bed with an unconscious violinist. A famous unconscious violinist. He has been found to have a fatal kidney ailment, and the Society of Music Lovers has canvassed all the available medical records and found that you alone have the right blood type to help. They have therefore kidnapped you, and last night the violinist's circulatory system was plugged into yours, so that your kidneys can be used to extract poisons from his blood as well as your own. The director of the hospital now tells you, "Look, we're sorry the Society of Music Lovers did this to you—we would never have permitted it if we had known. But still, they did it, and the violinist now is plugged into you. To unplug you would be to kill him. But never mind, it's only for nine months. By then he will have recovered from his ailment, and can safely be unplugged from you." Is it morally incumbent on you to accede to this situation? No doubt it would be very nice of you if you did, a great kindness. But do you *have* to accede to it? What if it were not nine months, but nine years? Or longer still? What if the director of the hospital says, "Tough luck, I agree, but you've now got to stay in bed, with the violinist plugged into you, for the rest of your life. Because remember this. All persons have a right to life, and violinists are persons. Granted you have a right to decide what happens in and to your body, but a person's right to life outweighs your right to decide what happens in and to your body. So you cannot ever be unplugged from him." I imagine you would regard this as outrageous, which suggests that something really is wrong with that plausible-sounding argument I mentioned a moment ago.

In this case, of course, you were kidnapped; you didn't volunteer for the operation that plugged the violinist into your kidneys. Can those who oppose abortion on the ground I mentioned make an exception for a pregnancy due to rape? Certainly. They can say that persons have a right to life only if they didn't come into existence because of rape; or they can say that all persons have a right to life, but that some have less of a right to life than others, in particular, that those who came into existence because of rape have less. But these statements have a rather unpleasant sound. Surely the question of whether you have a right to life at all, or how much of it you have, shouldn't turn on the question of whether or not you are the product of a rape. And in fact the people who oppose abortion on the ground I mentioned do not make this distinction, and hence do not make an exception in case of rape.

[…]

[We should now] ask what it comes to, to have a right to life. In some views having a right to life includes having a right to be given at least the bare minimum one needs for continued life. But suppose that what in fact *is* the bare minimum a man needs for continued life is something he has no right at all to be given? If I am sick unto death, and the only thing that will save my life is the touch of Henry Fonda's cool hand on my fevered brow, then all the same, I have no right to be given the touch of Henry Fonda's cool hand on my fevered brow. It would be frightfully nice of him to fly in from the West Coast to provide it. It would be less nice, though no doubt well meant, if my friends flew out to the West Coast and carried Henry Fonda back with them. But I have no right at all against anybody that he should do this for me. Or again, to return to the story I told earlier, the fact that for continued life that violinist needs the continued use of your kidneys does not establish that he has a right to be given the continued use of your kidneys. He certainly has no right against you that *you* should give him continued use of your kidneys. For nobody has any right to use your kidneys unless you give him such a right; and nobody has the right against you that you shall give him this right—if you do allow him to go on using your kidneys, this is a kindness on your part, and not something he can claim from you as his due. Nor has he any right against anybody else that *they* should give him continued use of your kidneys. Certainly he had no right against the Society of Music Lovers that they should plug him into you in the first place. And if you now start to unplug yourself, having learned that you will otherwise have to spend nine years in bed with him,

there is nobody in the world who must try to prevent you, in order to see to it that he is given something he has a right to be given

[…]

The emendation which may be made at this point is this: the right to life consists not in the right not to be killed, but rather in the right not to be killed unjustly. This runs a risk of circularity, but never mind: it would enable us to square the fact that the violinist has a right to life with the fact that you do not act unjustly toward him in unplugging yourself, thereby killing him. For if you do not kill him unjustly, you do not violate his right to life, and so it is no wonder you do him no injustice.

But if this emendation is accepted, the gap in the argument against abortion stares us plainly in the face: it is by no means enough to show that the fetus is a person, and to remind us that all persons have a right to life—we need to be shown also that killing the fetus violates its right to life, i.e., that abortion is unjust killing. And is it?

I suppose we may take it as a datum that in a case of pregnancy due to rape the mother has not given the unborn person a right to the use of her body for food and shelter. Indeed, in what pregnancy could it be supposed that the mother has given the unborn person such a right? It is not as if there were unborn persons drifting about the world, to whom a woman who wants a child says "I invite you in."

But it might be argued that there are other ways one can have acquired a right to the use of another person's body than by having been invited to use it by that person. Suppose a woman voluntarily indulges in intercourse, knowing of the chance it will issue in pregnancy, and then she does become pregnant; is she not in part responsible for the presence, in fact the very existence, of the unborn person inside her? No doubt she did not invite it in. But doesn't her partial responsibility for its being there itself give it a right to the use of her body? […]

And then, too, it might be asked whether or not she can kill it even to save her own life: If she voluntarily called it into existence, how can she now kill it, even in self-defense?

The first thing to be said about this is that, it is something new. Opponents of abortion have been so concerned to make out the independence of the fetus, in order to establish that, it has a right to life, just as its mother does, that they have tended to overlook the possible support they might gain from making out that the fetus is *dependent* on the mother, in order to establish that she has a special kind of responsibility for it, a responsibility that gives it rights against her which are not possessed by any independent person—such as an ailing violinist, who is a stranger to her.

On the other hand, this argument would give the unborn person a right to its mother's body only if her pregnancy resulted, from a voluntary act, undertaken in full knowledge of the chance a pregnancy might result from it. It would leave out entirely the unborn person whose existence is due to rape. Pending the availability of some further argument, then, we would be left with the conclusion that unborn persons whose existence is due to rape have no right to the use of their mothers' bodies, and thus that aborting them is not depriving them of anything they have a right to and hence is not unjust killing.

And we should also notice that it is not at all plain that this argument really does go even as far as it purports to. For there are cases and cases, and the details make a difference. If the room is stuffy, and I therefore open a window to air it, and a burglar climbs in, it would be absurd to say, "Ah, now he can stay, she's given him a right to the use of her house—for she is partially responsible for his presence there, having voluntarily done what enabled him to get in, in full knowledge that there are such things as burglars, and that burglars burgle." It would be still more absurd to say this if I had had bars installed outside my windows, precisely to prevent burglars from getting in, and a burglar got in only because of a defect in the bars. It remains equally absurd if we imagine it is not a burglar who climbs in, but an innocent person who blunders or falls in. Again, suppose it were like this: people-seeds drift about in the air like pollen, and if you open your windows, one may drift in and take root in your carpets or upholstery. You don't want children, so you fix up your windows with fine mesh screens, the very best you can buy. As can happen, however, and on very, very rare occasions does happen, one of the screens is defective; and a seed drifts in and takes root. Does the person-plant who now develops have a right to the use of your house? Surely not—despite the fact that you voluntarily opened your windows, you knowingly kept carpets and upholstered furniture, and you knew that screens were sometimes defective. Someone may argue that you are responsible for its rooting, that it does have a right to your house, because after all you *could* have lived out your life with bare floors and furniture, or with sealed windows and doors. But this won't do— for by the same token anyone can avoid a pregnancy due to rape by having a hysterectomy, or anyway by never leaving home without a (reliable!) army.

It seems to me that the argument we are looking at can establish at most that there are *some* cases in which the unborn person has a right to the use of its mother's body, and therefore *some* cases in which abortion is unjust killing. There is room for much discussion and argument as to precisely which, if any. But I think we should sidestep this issue and leave it open, for at any rate the argument certainly does not establish that all abortion is unjust killing.

There is room for yet another argument here, however. We surely must all grant that there may be cases in which it would be morally indecent to detach a person from your body at the cost of his life. Suppose you learn that what the violinist needs is not nine years of your life, but only one hour: all you need do to save his life is to spend one hour in that bed with him. Suppose also that letting him use your kidneys for that one hour would not affect your health in the slightest. Admittedly you were kidnapped. Admittedly you did not give anyone permission to plug him into you. Nevertheless it seems to me plain you *ought* to allow him to use your kidneys for that hour—it would be indecent to refuse.

Again, suppose pregnancy lasted only an hour, and constituted no threat to life or health. And suppose that a woman becomes pregnant as a result of rape. Admittedly she did not voluntarily do anything to bring about the existence of a child. Admittedly she did nothing at all which would give the unborn person a right to the use of her body. All the same it might well be said, as in the newly emended violinist story, that she *ought* to allow it to remain for that hour—that it would be indecent in her to refuse.

[...]

My argument will be found unsatisfactory on two counts by many of those who want to regard abortion as morally permissible. First, while I do argue that abortion is not impermissible, I do not argue that it is always permissible. There may well be cases in which carrying the child to term requires only Minimally Decent Samaritanism of the mother, and this is a standard we must not fall below. I am inclined to think it a merit of my account precisely that it does *not* give a general yes or a general no. It allows for and supports our sense that, for example, a sick and desperately frightened fourteen-year-old schoolgirl, pregnant due to rape, may *of course* choose abortion, and that any law which rules this out is an insane law. And it also allows for and supports our sense that in other cases resort to abortion is even positively indecent. It would be indecent in the woman to request an abortion, and indecent in a doctor to perform it, if she is in her seventh month, and wants the abortion just to avoid the nuisance of postponing a trip abroad. The very fact that the arguments I have been drawing attention to treat all cases of abortion, or even all cases of abortion in which the mother's life is not at stake, as morally on a par ought to have made them suspect at the outset.

Secondly, while I am arguing for the permissibility of abortion in some cases, I am not arguing for the right to secure the death of the unborn child. It is easy to confuse these two things in that up to a certain point in the life of the fetus it is not able to survive outside the mother's body; hence removing it from her body guarantees its death. But they are importantly different. I have argued that you are not morally required to spend nine months in bed, sustaining the life of that violinist; but to say this is by no means to say that if, when you unplug yourself, there is a miracle and he survives, you then have a right to turn round and slit his throat. You may detach yourself even if this costs him his life; you have no right to be guaranteed his death, by some other means, if unplugging yourself does not kill him. There are some people who will feel dissatisfied by this feature of my argument. A woman may be utterly devastated by the thought of a child, a bit of herself, put out for adoption and never seen or heard of again. She may therefore want not merely that the child be detached from her, but more, that it die. Some opponents of abortion are inclined to regard this as beneath contempt—thereby showing insensitivity to what is surely a powerful source of despair. All the same, I agree that the desire for the child's death is not one which anybody may gratify, should it turn out to be possible to detach the child alive.

At this place, however, it should be remembered that we have only been pretending throughout that the fetus is a human being from the moment of conception. A very early abortion is surely not the killing of a person, and so is not dealt with by anything I have said here.

[...]

Questions

1. Does Thomson believe the fetus is a person from the moment of conception? Justify your answer by citing relevant passages in her essay.

2. What is Thomson's main argument in this essay? Discuss her "unconscious violinist" analogy and how it is used to support her main argument.

3. Thomson realizes that her main argument would justify at most a limited right to abortion. She discusses this point in terms of a house, people-seeds, screens and burglars. Outline that particular discussion.

Joel Feinberg and Barbara Baum Levenbook consider the claim that even if the fetus is a person, the interests of the mother justify abortion in many cases

[...]

The problem of the status of the fetus is the first and perhaps the most difficult of the questions that must be settled before we can come to a considered view about the moral justifiability of abortion, but its solution does not necessarily resolve all moral perplexities about abortion. Even if we were to grant that the fetus is a moral person and thus has a valid claim to life, it would not follow that abortion is always wrong. For there are other moral persons, in addition to the fetus, whose interests are involved. The woman in whose uterus the fetus abides, in particular, has needs and interests that may well conflict with bringing the fetus to term. Do any of these needs and interests of the woman provide grounds for her having a genuine claim to an abortion and, if they do, which of the two conflicting claims—the woman's claim to an abortion or the fetus's claim to life—ought to be respected if they happen to conflict?

[...]

What we must realize [...] is that the alleged right to an abortion cannot be understood in a vacuum; it is a right that can only be understood by reference to the other, more fundamental rights from which it has often been claimed to be derived. Three of these rights and their possible association with the right to an abortion deserve our closest scrutiny. These are (1) [...] property rights, (2) the right to self-defense, and (3) the right to bodily autonomy. We shall consider each in its turn.

[...]

Within very wide limits any person has a right to control the uses of his or her own body. [...] It is highly implausible, however, to think of a human fetus, even if it does fall short of moral personhood, as no more than a temporary organ or a parasitic growth. A fetus is not a constituent organ of the mother, like her vermiform appendix, but rather an entity which, while presently dependent, will become independent.

It would be still less plausible to derive a maternal right to an abortion from a characterization of the fetus as the property of the pregnant woman and thus in the same category as her wristwatch, clothing, or jewelry. [...]

It is more plausible at first sight to claim that the pregnant woman owns not the fetus but the body in which she shelters the fetus. On this analogy, she owns her body (and particularly her womb) in roughly the way an innkeeper owns a hotel or a homeowner her house and garden. These analogies, however, are also defective. [...] One cannot conceive of what it would be like for a fetus to enter into a contract with a woman for the use of her womb for nine months or to fall in arrears in its payments and thus forfeit its right of occupancy. [...] Besides, [...] one is not *morally* entitled, in virtue of one's property rights, to expel a weak and helpless person from one's shelter when that is tantamount to consigning the person to a certain death, and surely one is not entitled to shoot and kill a trespasser who will not, or cannot, leave one's property.

[...]

The trouble with the use of self-defense as a model for abortion right is that none of the examples of self-defense makes an *exact* analogy to the abortion situation. The examples that come closest to providing models for justified abortion are the "innocent aggressor cases" and these would apply [...] only to abortions that are necessary to prevent death to the pregnant woman. Even these examples do not fit the abortion case exactly, since the fetus is in no way itself an aggressor, culpable or innocent, but is at most a "nonaggressive, nonculpable threat," in some respects like an innocent shield. And the more we change the examples to bring them closer to the situation of the fetus, the less clear is their resemblance to the central models of self-defense. Once we are allowed to protect ourselves (and

From "Abortion." By Joel Feinberg & Barbara Baum Levenbook. Reproduced with permission from *Matters of Life and Death: New Introductory Essays in Moral Philosophy*, 3rd ed., edn. Tom Regan. New York: McGraw-Hill, 1980, pp. 213–16, 220–6.

especially to protect interests less weighty than self-preservation) at the expense of nonaggressive innocents, it becomes difficult to distinguish the latter from innocent bystanders whom we kill as means to our own good, and that, in turn, begins to look like unvarnished murder. The killing of an innocent person simply because his continued existence in the circumstances would make the killer's life miserable is a homicide that cannot be justified. It is not self-defense to kill your boss because he makes your work life intolerable and you are unable to find another job. [...]

Partly because of deficiencies in the hypothetical examples of self-defense, Thomson invented a different sort of example intended at once to be a much closer analogy to the abortion situation and also such that the killing can be seen to be morally justified for reasons less compelling than defense of the killer's very life:

> You wake up in the morning and find yourself back to back in bed with an unconscious violinist. A famous unconscious violinist. He has been found to have a fatal kidney ailment, and the Society of Music Lovers has canvassed all the available medical records and found that you alone have the right blood type to help. They have therefore kidnapped you, and last night the violinist's circulatory system was plugged into yours, so that your kidneys can be used to extract poisons from his blood as well as your own. The director of the hospital now tells you, "Look, we're sorry the Society of Music Lovers did this to you—we would never have permitted it if we had known. But still they did it, and the violinist now is plugged into you. To unplug you would be to kill him. But never mind, it's only for nine months. By then he will have recovered from his ailment, and can safely be unplugged from you." Is it morally incumbent on you to accede to this situation? No doubt it would be very nice of you if you did, a great kindness. But do you have to accede to it? ... What if the director ... says ... "Granted you have a right to decide what happens in and to your body, but a person's right to life outweighs your right to decide what happens in and to your body. So you cannot ... be unplugged from him." I imagine you would regard this as outrageous....[1]

Suppose that you defy the director on your own, and exercise your control over your own body by

unplugging the unconscious violinist, thereby causing his death. This would be to kill in defense of an interest far less important than self-preservation or the prevention of serious injury to oneself. And it would be to kill an innocent nonaggressor, indeed a victim who remains unconscious throughout the entire period during which he is a threat. We have, therefore, an example that—if it works—offers far more encouragement to the proabortion position than the model of self-defense does. We must now pose two questions: (1) Would you in fact be morally justified in unplugging the violinist? and (2) How close an analogy does this bizarre example make to the abortion situation?

[...]

There is good reason to grant Thomson her claim that a stranger would have a right to unplug the violinist from herself.

But how close an analogy after all is this to the normal case of pregnancy? [...]

The most important difference [...] between the violinist case and the normal pregnancy is that in the former the woman had absolutely nothing to do with creating the situation from which she wishes to escape. She bears no responsibility whatever for being in a state of "plugged-in-ness" with the violinist. As many commentators have pointed out, this makes Thomson's analogy fit at most one very special class of pregnancies, namely, those imposed upon a woman entirely against her will, as in rape. In the normal case of pregnancy, the voluntary action of the woman herself (knowingly consenting to sexual intercourse) has something to do with her becoming pregnant. [...]

Voluntariness and Responsibility If we continue the line of reasoning suggested by our criticism of the violinist example, we will soon reach a general principle, namely, that whether or not a woman has a duty to continue her pregnancy depends, at least in part, on how responsible she is for being pregnant in the first place, that is, on the extent to which her pregnancy is the consequence of her own voluntary actions. [...]

Since the voluntariness of an action or omission is a matter of degree, so is the responsibility that stems from it, as is the stringency of the duty that derives from that responsibility. The duty to continue a pregnancy, then, will be stronger (other things being equal) in the case where the pregnancy was entered into in a fully voluntary way than it will be in the case that fits the violinist model, where the pregnancy is totally involuntary. But in between these two extremes is a whole range of cases where moral judgments are more difficult to make. We can sketch the whole spectrum as follows:

1. Pregnancy caused by rape (totally involuntary).
2. Pregnancy caused by contraceptive failure, where the fault is entirely that of the manufacturer or pharmaceutical company.
3. Pregnancy caused by contraceptive failure within the advertised 1 percent margin of error (no one's fault).
4. Pregnancy caused by the negligence of the woman (or the man, or both). They are careless in the use of the contraceptive or else fail to use it at all, being unaware of a large risk that they *ought* to have been aware of.
5. Pregnancy caused by the recklessness of the woman (or the man, or both). They think of the risk but get swept along by passion and consciously disregard it.
6. Pregnancy caused by intercourse between partners who are genuinely indifferent at the time whether or not pregnancy results.
7. Pregnancy caused by the deliberate decision of the parties to produce it (completely voluntary).

There would be a somewhat hollow ring to the claim in case 7 that one has no obligation to continue one's bodily support for a moral person whose dependence on that support one has deliberately caused. That would be like denying that one has a duty to save the drowning swimmer that one has just pushed out of the boat. The case for cessation of bodily support is hardly any stronger in 6 and 5 than in 7. Perhaps it is misleading to say of the negligence case (4) that the pregnancy is only partially involuntary, or involuntary "to a degree," since the couple did not *intentionally* produce or run the risk of producing a fetus. But there is no need to haggle over that terminological question.

Whether wholly or partially involuntary, the actions of the couple in the circumstances were faulty and the pregnancy resulted from the fault (negligence), so they are to a substantial degree responsible (to blame) for it. [...] In these cases—4, 5, 6, and 7—the woman and her partner are therefore responsible for the pregnancy, and on the analogy with the case of the drowning swimmer who was pushed from the boat, they have a duty not to kill the fetus or permit it to die.

Cases 2 and 3 are more perplexing. In case 2, where the fault was entirely that of the manufacturer, the woman is no more responsible for being pregnant than in case 1 where she is the unwilling victim of a rape. [...] So in case 2, where the negligence of the manufacturer of the contraceptive is the cause of pregnancy, the woman cannot be held responsible for her condition, and that ground for ascribing to her a duty not to abort is not present.

Case 3 brings us very close to the borderline [...] This is a borderline case for the following reason. If we extend to this case the rule we applied to case 2, then we might be entitled to say that the woman is no more responsible than the fetus for the pregnancy. To reach that conclusion we have to judge the 1 percent chance of pregnancy to be a *reasonable* risk for a woman to run in the circumstances. That appraisal itself is a disguised moral judgment of pivotal importance, and yet it is very difficult to know how to go about establishing it. Nevertheless, *if* it is correct, then the woman is, for all practical purposes, relieved of her responsibility for the pregnancy just as she is in cases 1 and 2, and in that event the fetus's "right to life" does not entail a duty on her part to make extreme sacrifices.

[...]

These narrow restrictions on the right of the woman to an abortion will not satisfy many people in the proabortion camp. But if the assumption of the moral personhood of the fetus is false, as was argued in the first part of this essay, then the woman's right to bodily autonomy will normally prevail, and abortions at all but the later stages, at least, and for the most common reasons, at least, are morally permissible.

[...]

Questions

1. Feinberg and Levenbook examine three standard rights which *might* justify a woman's having an abortion, even if the "fetus is a moral person and thus has a valid claim to life." What are those three standard rights?
2. Go through the Feinberg/Levenbook analysis and explain why they believe each of those rights provides either no justification, or very limited justification, for having an abortion.
3. Feinberg and Levenbook list cases of pregnancy ranging from the "totally involuntary" to the "completely voluntary." In which of these cases do they believe abortion could be justified? Explain.

Note

1. Judith Jarvis Thomson, "A Defense of Abortion," *Philosophy and Public Affairs* 1 (1971), pp. 48–9.

Jane English thinks a moderate position on abortion can be justified, whether or not the fetus is conceived as a person

[…]

I argue that if a fetus is a person, abortion is still justifiable in many cases; and if a fetus is not a person, killing it is still wrong in many cases.

[…]

Let us consider what follows if a fetus is a person after all. Judith Jarvis Thomson's landmark article, "A Defense of Abortion,"[1] correctly points out that some additional argumentation is needed at this point in the conservative argument to bridge the gap between the premise that a fetus is an innocent person and the conclusion that killing it is always wrong. To arrive at this conclusion, we would need the additional premise that killing an innocent person is always wrong. But killing an innocent person is sometimes permissible, most notably in self defense. Some examples may help draw out our intuitions or ordinary judgments about self defense.

Suppose a mad scientist, for instance, hypnotized innocent people to jump out of the bushes and attack innocent passers-by with knives. If you are so attacked, we agree you have a right to kill the attacker in self defense, if killing him is the only way to protect your life or to save yourself from serious injury. It does not seem to matter here that the attacker is not malicious but himself an innocent pawn, for your killing of him is not done in a spirit of retribution but only in self defense.

How severe an injury may you inflict in self defense? In part this depends upon the severity of the injury to be avoided: you may not shoot someone merely to avoid having your clothes torn. This might lead one to the mistaken conclusion that the defense may only equal the threatened injury in severity; that to avoid death you may kill, but to avoid a black eye you may only inflict a black eye or the equivalent. Rather, our laws and customs seem to say that you may create an injury somewhat, but not enormously,

From "Abortion and the Concept of a Person," by Jane English, *Canadian Journal of Philosophy*, 5:2, October 1975. Copyright © *Canadian Journal of Philosophy*, reprinted by permission of Taylor & Francis Ltd, www.tandfonline.com on behalf of *The Canadian Journal of Philosophy*.

greater than the injury to be avoided. To fend off an attack whose outcome would be as serious as rape, a severe beating or the loss of a finger, you may shoot; to avoid having your clothes torn, you may blacken an eye.

Aside from this, the injury you may inflict should only be the minimum necessary to deter or incapacitate the attacker. Even if you know he intends to kill you, you are not justified in shooting him if you could equally well save yourself by the simple expedient of running away. Self defense is for the purpose of avoiding harms rather than equalizing harms.

Some cases of pregnancy present a parallel situation. Though the fetus is itself innocent, it may pose a threat to the pregnant woman's well-being, life prospects or health, mental or physical. If the pregnancy presents a slight threat to her interests, it seems self defense cannot justify abortion. But if the threat is on a par with a serious beating or the loss of a finger, she may kill the fetus that poses such a threat, even if it is an innocent person. If a lesser harm to the fetus could have the same defensive effect, killing it would not be justified. It is unfortunate that the only way to free the woman from the pregnancy entails the death of the fetus (except in very late stages of pregnancy). Thus a self defense model supports Thomson's point that the woman has a right only to be freed from fetus, not a right to demand its death.[2]

[…]

Several parallels arise between various views on abortion and the self defense model. Let's suppose further that these hypnotized attackers only operate at night, so that it is well known that they can be avoided completely by the considerable inconvenience of never leaving your house after dark. One view is that since you could stay home at night, therefore if you go out and are selected by one of these hypnotized people, you have no right to defend yourself. This parallels the view that abstinence is the only acceptable way to avoid pregnancy. Others might hold that you ought to take along some defense such as Mace which will deter the hypnotized person without killing him, but that if this defense fails, you are obliged to submit to the resulting injury, no matter how severe it is. This parallels the view that

contraception is all right but abortion is always wrong, even in cases of contraceptive failure.

A third view is that you may kill the hypnotized person only if he will actually kill you, but not if he will only injure you. This is like the position that abortion is permissible only if it is required to save a woman's life. Finally, we have the view that it is all right to kill the attacker, even if only to avoid a very slight inconvenience to yourself and even if you knowingly walked down the very street where all these incidents have been taking place without taking along any Mace or protective escort. If we assume that a fetus is a person, this is the analogue of the view that abortion is always justifiable, "on demand."

The self defense model allows us to see an important difference that exists between abortion and infanticide, even if a fetus is a person from conception. Many have argued that the only way to justify abortion without justifying infanticide would be to find some characteristic of personhood that is acquired at birth. Michael Tooley, for one, claims infanticide is justifiable because the really significant characteristics of person are acquired some time after birth.[3] But all such approaches look to characteristics of the developing human and ignore the relation between the fetus and the woman. What if, after birth, the presence of an infant or the need to support it posed a grave threat to the woman's sanity or life prospects? She could escape this threat by the simple expedient of running away. So a solution that does not entail the death of the infant is available. Before birth, such solutions are not available because of the biological dependence of the fetus on the woman. Birth is the crucial point not because of any characteristics the fetus gains, but because after birth the woman can defend herself by a means less drastic than killing the infant. Hence self defense can be used to justify abortion without necessarily thereby justifying infanticide.

On the other hand, supposing a fetus is not after all a person, would abortion always be morally permissible? Some opponents of abortion seem worried that if a fetus is not a full-fledged person, then we are justified in treating it in any way at all. However, this does not follow. Non-persons do get some consideration in our moral code, though of course they do not have the same rights as persons have (and in general they do not have moral responsibilities), and though their interests may be overridden by the interests of persons. Still, we cannot just treat them in any way at all.

Treatment of animals is a case in point. It is wrong to torture dogs for fun or to kill wild birds for no reason at all. It is wrong Period, even though dogs and birds do not have the same rights persons do.

[…]

It is crucial that psychological facts play a role here. Our psychological constitution makes it the case that for our ethical theory to work, it must prohibit certain treatment of non-persons which are significantly person-like. If our moral rules allowed people to treat some person-like non-persons in ways we do not want people to be treated, this would undermine the system of sympathies and attitudes that makes the ethical system work. […] Thus it makes sense that it is those animals whose appearance and behavior are most like those of people that get the most consideration in our moral scheme.

It is because of "coherence of attitudes," I think, that the similarity of a fetus to a baby is very significant. A fetus one week before birth is so much like a newborn baby in our psychological space that we cannot allow any cavalier treatment of the former while expecting full sympathy and nurturative support for the latter. Thus, I think that anti-abortion forces are indeed giving their strongest arguments when they point to the similarities between a fetus and a baby, and when they try to evoke our emotional attachment to and sympathy for the fetus. An early horror story from New York about nurses who were expected to alternate between caring for six-week premature infants and disposing of viable 24-week aborted fetuses is just that—a horror story. These beings are so much alike that no one can be asked to draw a distinction and treat them so very differently.

Remember, however, that in the early weeks after conception, a fetus is very much unlike a person.

It is hard to develop these feelings for a set of genes which doesn't yet have a head, hands, beating heart, response to touch or the ability to move by itself. Thus it seems to me that the alleged "slippery slope" between conception and birth is not so very slippery. In the early stages of pregnancy, abortion can hardly be compared to murder for psychological reasons, but in the latest stages it is psychologically akin to murder. Another source of similarity is the bodily continuity between fetus and adult. Bodies play a surprisingly central role in our attitudes toward persons. […] Even after death, when all agree the body is no longer a person, we still observe elaborate customs of respect for the human body; like people who torture dogs, necrophiliacs are not to be trusted with people. So it is appropriate that we show respect to a fetus as the body continuous with the body of a person. This is a degree of resemblance to persons that animals cannot rival.

[…]

Even if a fetus is not a person, abortion is not always permissible, because of the resemblance of a fetus to a person. I agree with Thomson that it would be wrong for a woman who is seven months pregnant to have an abortion just to avoid having to postpone a trip to Europe. In the early months of pregnancy when the fetus hardly resembles a baby at all, then, abortion is permissible whenever it is in the interests of the pregnant woman or her family. The reasons would only need to outweigh the pain and inconvenience of the abortion itself. In the middle months, when the fetus comes to resemble a person, abortion would be justifiable only when the continuation of the pregnancy or the birth of the child would cause harms—physical, psychological, economic or social—to the woman. In the late months of pregnancy, even on our current assumption that a fetus is not a person, abortion seems to be wrong except to save a woman from significant injury or death.

[…]

Questions

1. Explain English's view of the abortion-as-self-defense justification. Does she think it is ever successful? If so, in what cases?

2. For English, what is the crucial difference between abortion and infanticide in terms of justifying the first but not the second?

3. English thinks the look of the fetus has a legitimate role to play in our views on abortion? Why is this legitimate and how is it likely to influence our moral judgments regarding abortion at different stages of pregnancy?

Notes

1. J. J. Thomson, "A Defense of Abortion," *Philosophy and Public Affairs* 1 (1971).
2. Ibid.
3. Michael Tooley, "Abortion and Infanticide," *Philosophy and Public Affairs* 2 (1971).

Part VI

Animals

16

Animals
Fiction

The Trainers

1.

Ambio watched the gray sea as it smashed against the rocks, spewing foam high into the air. He liked the violence of the scene: It gave some semblance of life to this devastated world. Certainly there was little visible life behind him—just the gray thistles and scrub that covered the empty plain. There were organisms, of course, but it would have taken a microscope to see them.

A mile to the south was the shuttle craft that had brought him and his Amorphan crew from the mother ship, which was now in orbit some 250 miles above him—above "Earth," as the English-speaking inhabitants of this poor planet called it. Not far from the shuttle craft was the ocean pier his crew was repairing. An antique cruise ship—long ago repaired and refurbished—would be arriving from the islands in about a week. After that he and his crew could leave this planet.

The prospect of leaving neither pleased nor displeased him. There wasn't much here to engage him, but it was hardly more desolate than the emptiness of space. And at least here, for a time, he was *awake*. Like the rest of those on his ship, he spent much of his life in suspended animation. Even though the Amorphans could travel at 50 per cent of the speed of light and had natural life spans of three hundred Earth years, an

Amorphan space traveler would see almost nothing were he not able to quintuple his normal life span through slowing his life functions for long periods of time.

Not that Ambio could say he'd seen that much. What wonders he'd dreamed of as a young spacefarer! But the Universe—at least so far—had turned out to be much duller than his dreams. There were still no signs of parallel worlds, time travel had proved to be a contradiction, and wormholes, though real enough, had been impossible to keep open long enough to permit advanced life forms to slip through them. There was nothing to do but keep trying to increase speed, as well as to lengthen life spans through improved medical and sleep techniques; still, with all the advances they'd made thus far, space travel remained a tedious, lumbering process.

Perhaps if he'd been a physicist or astronomer he'd have found excitement enough in the endless data collection and subsequent theory revisions. But Ambio had been trained in what Earth people might have called anthropology—though, of course, his subject wasn't "anthro" (humans), but any intelligent life form. The problem was that few signs of intelligent life had been encountered during his two hundred years of space travel, and most of those forms had been fossils by the time the Amorphans found them.

Humans too might now be only fossils had the Amorphans not arrived when they did. As it was, the

Contemporary Moral and Social Issues: An Introduction through Original Fiction, Discussion, and Readings, First Edition. Thomas D. Davis.
© 2014 John Wiley & Sons, Inc. Published 2014 by John Wiley & Sons, Inc.

Amorphans' first visit had lasted just long enough to measure the high radiation levels below the dark stratospheric clouds that had covered most of the Earth. Returning fifty years later, the Amorphans had been sure that any semi-advanced life forms would be dead. Amazingly, a few humans were still alive on the islands. Still, those humans wouldn't have lasted much longer on their own: Diseased, reduced to a subsistence existence, having lost the knowledge that might have enabled them to survive in their ravaged surroundings, they would have died out within another ten years had the Amorphans not stepped in to help. Without the intervention of the Amorphans, there would no longer *be* human beings.

Not that the Amorphans had appeared as themselves. That would have been a needless complication, as well as a needless shock, for people already shocked almost beyond endurance. Fortunately humans—with their limited brains and primitive perceptual systems—had been easy enough to fool: Simple psychic projection was sufficient to make the Amorphans appear as nothing more than healthier, brighter human beings—humans who had supposedly arrived from another island to help. That illusion remained to this day. As humans grew stronger and healthier, the Amorphans kept enhancing their projected images so as to always seem superior and thus natural leaders. These projected images were known to humans as the "Trainers" and were much loved and emulated.

The Amorphan command considered a stay on an island as "Trainer" to be a hardship assignment. Ambio hadn't found it so during his posting. It's true that humans, as a lower life form, weren't of much interest to the average Amorphan: Being a Trainer was the equivalent of running a zoo or day-care. But being an anthropologist had given Ambio a professional interest in studying the creatures, and that had staved off boredom.

Ambio had spent time reading human writings prior to his time on the islands; there were huge intact libraries in many of the eerily deserted cities. He'd absorbed most human knowledge quickly—that had been easy enough. The challenge he'd set himself had been to "think like a human."

Thinking like another species was never an easy task; the lower the species, the more difficult it was. Still he kept trying to think like a human—made a point of practicing whenever he was on Earth—as he was doing right now.

Ambio supposed he'd managed some limited empathy with humans. Most Amorphans had contempt for *Homo sapiens* as a lower species; as an anthropologist, Ambio couldn't afford such a feeling: It would bias his understanding of his subject. Amorphans laughed at the way the humans had thrown away the future of their civilization through nuclear war. However, Ambio knew enough Amorphan history to know how close the Amorphans had come to doing the same thing; he'd also seen it happen on other worlds.

What continued to amaze Ambio was the tyranny of the body, the way the pure physicality of the Universe had defeated so many of the dreams that intelligent life forms had conjured up. There'd been human philosophers who—like early Amorphan philosophers—had dreamed of spirit breaking the bonds of the body and evolving into other dimensions. But it was not to be. It was amazing and disappointing the way the appetites and passions of the body remained insistent even in higher life forms, limiting evolution. One dead civilization he'd studied had tried to escape those passions by becoming machines, gradually replacing their fleshy parts with computers and mechanical devices. As far as Ambio had been able to ascertain, the farther those cyborgs had moved away from being flesh, the more a kind of mechanical pointlessness had settled in; the civilization had died from a lost will to live.

It seemed that even advanced civilizations would have to struggle to evolve while dragging the body along like a great weight. Still, who'd have ever imagined that a civilization as far along as the Amorphans would even now want.…Well, there was no point in dwelling on it.

Ambio looked out across the gray ocean in the direction from which the freighter would come. Somewhere out there were the green islands where humans still existed, thanks to the intervention of the Amorphans. Human life had been saved. Though, of course, salvation always comes at a price.

2.

Andrea was excited: She wanted the festival to begin. The lanterns atop the poles were already lit, forming a half-circle of light around the open area in front of her. Glancing up, she saw there were still streaks of red above the fringe of jungle at the top of the hill. Not quite sunset. Not quite time.

Andrea always loved festivals, but this one was special: It would be her last—at least here. It was a farewell party for her and the hundred or so other Candidates who would board the ship in the morning. Tonight she was going to have *fun*.

But her excitement was more about her future than about the party itself. Her years of hard work as a Novice were finally paying off. Recently she had been promoted from Novice to Candidate; tomorrow the ship would take her to another island where she would be transformed from Candidate to Trainer. She—a Trainer! She could hardly believe it! All her life she had been in awe of the Trainers and of the fantastic lives they led. Soon she would be living that life herself!

It did feel just a little sad to think she would never return to this place. Trainers were never assigned to the island where they'd grown up: She'd been told that familiarity might compromise the objectivity with which the Trainers must approach their jobs. Andrea was bound to miss this island and those she'd leave behind—not her parents, of course, who were so pathetic and ugly—nor her children, whom she barely knew. She'd miss those younger friends who were still Novices and would be here for a few more years. Still, she couldn't feel too sad. After all there were a hundred other Candidates going with her, many of them her friends. Anyway, whatever little sadness she felt now wouldn't withstand the palm wine they'd all be drinking tonight. "The palm is a balm" was the saying she'd heard often in school. Or, as the Novices liked to say, with a wink: "Let's get palm'd." Along with the wine would be singing and dancing and coupling, and she planned to enjoy it all.

With the growing darkness, the world had narrowed to the circle of light just in front of her, the light cast by lanterns sitting atop low stakes. Suddenly there was noisy applause, and cheers, as Trainers ran in.

Andrea leaned forward, excited, as she always was, by the sight of these magnificent people. How beautiful they were—tonight especially—with their red loin cloths, face paint, and leafy headdresses. Their dance costumes were a special treat, but what most excited her about them, as always, was their beautifully muscled bodies, now glistening with oil in the firelight.

Andrea glanced around at those with her in the audience—the Novices and her fellow Candidates. They were beautiful too—as was she—the men with their bulging biceps, massive pecs, and drum-tight abs—the women with their slightly gentler curves, but just as fit. The calisthenics, the lifting, the racing, and the games that went on from dawn to dusk had ensured this beauty. The near universality of beauty among their age group didn't spoil their appreciation of it. Their parents—and even more, their grandparents—were an ugly reminder, not so much of age, as of a time before the Trainers had come, when the people had all been weak and diseased. The elders were tended to kindly by Trainers, but were kept separate from the younger ones except for the ritual family visits in which you tried to be loving, while all the time fighting a vague nausea. The Trainers didn't seem to be bothered by the old, but then the Trainers were so much nicer than the Novices and the Candidates. The Trainers also tended to the children, who spent their lives in communal nurseries and schools. Seeing the children once or twice a week was always a pleasure, those beautiful little ones who began their physical training at a very young age. One tended to lose track of which children were one's own—let alone which man had fathered which one—but that was unimportant. It was the community that was important.

Andrea looked back at the Trainers. They were beginning gymnastic routines, which she knew would become more and complex, taking away your breath with the beauty of the movements and the skill of the execution. Tonight, with the costumes and the firelight and the drums that were just now starting a low beat, it would be almost unbearable to watch. In fact, it would have been unbearable—envy was there, no matter how hard you tried to squelch it—if Andrea hadn't known that soon she would become one of them. At the crack of dawn she and the other

Candidates would be paraded with cheers to the huge ship that would take them to another island; there they would undergo the rigorous training that would turn them into Trainers. After that they would be assigned to one of the other islands where they would oversee the administration of that island and the training of the Novices.

Andrea glanced up the hill where she knew the mansions of the Trainers were, though now nothing was visible but vague shadows. Novices were never allowed to visit the Mansions, though since childhood Andrea had heard stories of the beauty of the interiors and the delights that went with living there. Novices lived in dormitories with bunk beds (though special rooms were set aside for couplings); except, as now, on festival days, Novices ate plain, nutritious food, along with all the supplements necessary to develop strong bodies. The Trainers, it was said, slept on soft sheets and were allowed festival food whenever they wished. Pools of water from hot springs soothed their muscles after a hard day working out with the Novices. The Trainers were allowed such things because they had reached maturity and had the wisdom to enjoy them without becoming decadent and soft.

Andrea knew that most of the other Candidates aspired to be Trainers because of the life they led. But for her, the ultimate pleasure would be simply to *be* a Trainer, to have one of those bodies, not only for its strength and beauty, but for the coordination and control that went with it. As strong and as skillful as she already was, she could hardly believe that she could be transformed to Trainer level. But the Trainers had assured her—assured them all—that the secret regimens they had developed would indeed make it possible. She could hardly wait.

3.

Andrea didn't know if it had been the frightening dream or the faint acrid smell in the air that had woken her. For a moment she didn't remember where she was. Then the slight rocking of the ship brought it all back. She felt herself smile briefly at the memory of the festival and the parade to the ship, but the act of smiling seemed to exhaust her and she realized she felt slightly sick.

She forced herself to roll onto her side, then slide her legs onto the floor. With effort, she got herself into a sitting position and leaned forward toward the next lower bunk where her friend Sahel was sleeping. She whispered Sahel's name, then spoke it more loudly. When there was no response, she put her hand on Sahel's shoulder; it seemed so cold. She shook the shoulder, but still there was no response. What was wrong? And what was that smell? Andrea felt a stab of fear, a feeling she'd had rarely since childhood.

She was suddenly exhausted and fell back on her bunk. Then, surprisingly, she was overcome with a feeling of great peace and joy. Her fear was ridiculous—perhaps this was still part of her dream. She was on a ship heading for a new island and a new and better life. She was in the hands of the Trainers whom she trusted with her life. Andrea was headed for her destiny, and she was sure it would be greater than she could ever imagine.

Closing her eyes, she let herself drift off to sleep, barely conscious of the ferocious rumble of machinery starting up somewhere in the bowels of the ship.

4.

Ambio watched as his crew transferred the various crates and boxes from the cruise ship to the shuttle craft. It had been a good idea to fit the ship out as a processing plant, so as to get the work out of the way during the inevitably slow sea voyage. It would have been easier to convert an old freighter to their needs, but it would have defeated the illusion they were trying to maintain, and along with it, the kindness they were trying so hard to show. Ironically, the humans might have called this treatment "humane," a characteristic they had named for themselves, even though they had exhibited it so rarely.

There were a few Amorphans who were bothered by what was happening here, and though Ambio tried to understand their point of view, he couldn't sympathize. What was the problem? Humans were a lower species, too stupid to understand what was happening to them, and the Amorphans treated them with a kindness humans had never shown to what they considered lower species. The Amorphans had saved humans from extinction and could not continue to help them if they were not of *some* use.

The complaint that Ambio could understand was that this whole enterprise took so much time and effort. But what could you do? You lived with what you were. But it *was* odd: The Amorphans had developed an intelligence far beyond what even the brightest humans of former times could have ever conceived. They were mapping the universe, having vastly transcended the constraints of time and space. And yet, the animal still survived within them. After all this additional evolution, the Amorphans had still not outgrown their taste for meat.

Questions

(Please explain your answers, making specific reference to relevant passages in the story.)

1. According to the "The Trainers," who are the Amorphans? Who is Ambio? Who are the Trainers?
2. According to the story, what happened to degrade the condition of human beings? How did the Amorphans help humans?
3. Describe the life humans have on the islands. What do they do? How do they view their parents and their children? How are their parents and children tended to?
4. What does Andrea think is going to happen to her when she leaves the island? What does happen to her?
5. What does and doesn't bother Ambio about what the Amorphans are doing to humans? What is his reasoning?
6. Do you agree with Ambio's reasoning? If not, where does his reasoning go wrong?
7. If we come upon living creatures on another planet, what criteria should we use to decide if it is morally acceptable to raise them for food?

17

Animals
Discussion

The Trainers

"The Trainers," portrays an alien race—the Amorphans—who have made a colony of a nuclear-ravaged Earth at some time in the future. The Amorphans are much more advanced than human beings. Amorphans have the technology to travel the universe at enormous speeds; they can extend their three-hundred-year life spans through suspended animation. They have the ability to control human brains and perceptual systems through psychic projection.

Ambio, the alien narrator, was able to absorb human knowledge easily by spending time in some of the deserted libraries of Earth. The language of the narration isn't an indication of his advanced intelligence: He's narrating as if in baby-talk, as he practices trying to "think like a human."

Even at their best, humans would have been a lower life form compared to the Amorphans; however, humans are not at their best, having been reduced to an existence that focuses on little more than the body. According to the story, humans had virtually destroyed themselves through nuclear war; human life would now be extinct had it not been for the intervention of the Amorphans.

The humans who remain live on islands. They are under the supervision of the "Trainers," who are really Amorphans but appear to the humans as superior human beings. The focus of human life is on developing strong, beautiful bodies through constant workouts and competitions.

The young people believe that when they are old enough and can pass certain physical tests—thus becoming "Candidates"—they will board a ship and be taken to another island; there they'll become Trainers—not only becoming stronger and more beautiful, but also being allowed to lead the luxurious lifestyle the Trainers are reputed to live.

In fact, after the Candidates are on the ship, they are gassed, killed, and butchered. The Amorphans are raising humans for food.

Are the Amorphans "cannibals"? No. Cannibals are creatures who eat members of their own species; Amorphans are members of a more advanced species than human beings.

Is what the Amorphans are doing wrong? This issue parallels a real issue we face today—the issue of animal welfare or animal rights. Do we have the right to raise animals for food, as well as to hunt them, put them in zoos, and use them as subjects for medical experiments?

Like most of the animals we raise for food, the humans in the story would not exist were it not for their Amorphan keepers: The human race would have died out if the Amorphans hadn't intervened to save it. The Amorphans only bother to keep humans alive because they are valuable as a food source. The Amorphans haven't turned humans into

Contemporary Moral and Social Issues: An Introduction through Original Fiction, Discussion, and Readings, First Edition. Thomas D. Davis.
© 2014 John Wiley & Sons, Inc. Published 2014 by John Wiley & Sons, Inc.

brutes: The humans did that to themselves. The humans are healthier and happier now because of the intervention of the Amorphans. Why shouldn't the Amorphans use the humans as a resource?

Note that the process the Amorphans use in raising and killing humans for food is as kind as could be imagined. Humans are oblivious to what's happening to them. They are healthy; they enjoy their lives; they have hope for the future. Humans have no idea the "Trainers" are aliens; the Trainers appear to them as marvelous human beings. Humans don't know they are going to be killed; the killing process itself is virtually devoid of pain and fear. It's true Andrea does wake up and feel alarm, but she's too groggy to feel much fear; it looks as if the other humans with her never woke at all. The humans in the story are like animals raised on the kindest possible human farm and killed in the kindest possible slaughterhouse.

The Amorphans are a higher species cultivating a lower species for food, while treating that lower species as kindly as possible. Is what the Amorphans doing wrong or not? Imagine a human farm where animals are raised for food in the same benign way. Would the two situations be morally similar? Does consistency require us to make the same moral judgment in both cases—that is, to condemn both the Amorphan and human practices or accept them both? In the light of this, is the idea of humans raising animals for food morally acceptable or not? These are some of the questions we will be considering in this chapter.

Of course, the story focuses on the bare fact that the Amorphans are raising humans for food. The story would have had a broader focus if the third section had read like this:

Andrea woke from a frightening dream and for a moment didn't know where she was. Then a swaying movement of the floor reminded her she was on the ship. But something wasn't right. The bunk where she'd gone to sleep had been replaced by something harder—it felt like she was lying on wood. She realized that she'd assumed a fetal position. There was a slight cramp in her thigh. When she tried to stretch out her leg, her foot bumped into something thin and hard. She sat up and put out her hands, exploring. It felt like…she was in a cage. She tried to stand, but slammed her head and fell back. She reached up and felt what she now recognized

as the top of her cage. It was so small she wouldn't be able to stand up. She felt claustrophobic—waves of fear rising in her.

Or this:

Andrea woke from a horrible dream about being bound and gagged. Or maybe it was only a dream of waking because she still couldn't move. She was strapped to a large chair. There were wires attached to her body, and they all led to a large, gleaming machine with dials and gauges. She saw her partial reflection in the side of the machine: She saw her shaved head, saw that more wires were attached to it. Suddenly her whole body was alive with pain, as if a bolt of electricity was shooting through her. It was over in a few seconds, replaced by terror. She shifted her eyes—she couldn't move her head—but she could see no one. Then she heard a voice behind her say, "Everything checks out—I think we're ready to begin." She recognized the voice of a Trainer. Andrea tried to call out, but, though her mouth moved, only indecipherable sounds came out. Andrea felt and saw a hand touch her shoulder. "Don't bother," said the Trainer. "We've tied your vocal cords so we can't hear you scream."

We don't just raise animals for food on kindly family farms. We confine them in cramped cages and keep them in factory-like rooms where they may never see the sun, may never feel grass or earth; then we cram them into trucks where they can barely move and take them to slaughterhouses. We also use them for scientific experiments, at least some of which have been as terrible as the one to which Andrea is subjected in the supplementary paragraph above. Glimpsed from that perspective, what the Amorphans are doing to humans in the story seems highly moral by contrast. They are trying to treat humans "with a kindness humans had never shown to what they considered lower species."

Or could it be that those added fictional paragraphs amount to an absurd distortion of what animals experience? Are those fictional descriptions a matter of extreme anthropomorphizing, imagining that animals would feel just as we would feel in comparable situations, whereas their experiences would be totally different? Or perhaps animals don't really feel anything at all—this is a claim that has been made. Since the issue of animal experience has a philosophical as well as factual dimension, we shall take it up after we look at some facts and factual issues we'll need to be aware of if we're to make intelligent moral judgments regarding our current animal practices.

Facts and factual issues

In this section we will focus on information regarding animals used in research as well as animals raised for food under modern "factory farming" conditions. However, it's going to be difficult to present what the various sides would consider "neutral" information. For the purposes of our discussion, it's essential to present information related to the concerns of animal advocates, but this information, given within a short discussion, is going to seem distortion-by-emphasis to those on the other side. Also, to be frank, the public statements regarding factory farming by the food industry seem almost surreal in their sunny portrayal of the lot of factory-farmed animals, given even a bare-bones description of the conditions in which the animals are raised. In addition, factory farms are closed to the public, which means that the images that do appear via surreptitious videos by animal advocates are naturally going to emphasize the worst conditions.

Given the danger of distortion, I invite you to double-check the accuracy of my summaries and do your own research by consulting the "Notes and selected sources" section.

Research animals

Animals are used for medical and veterinary research and training, as well as to test drugs, cosmetics and other products. Though estimates vary widely, it appears that between 17 and 25 million animals are used each year in the United States for research, testing, and training; 100 to 200 million are used worldwide.

In the US 90% of the animals used for research are rats, mice, and birds. Other animals include primates, rabbits, guinea pigs, cats and dogs. The use of primates, cats, and dogs has been declining since the 1970s.

Most live animals used in research are bred in laboratories under controlled conditions in order to make sure they have whatever genetic make-up researchers

demand. Other animals are from various sources, including licensed dealers and animal shelters.

Cutting open live animals (with or without anesthetic) for research purposes is called "vivisection." (The term has also expanded to mean any invasive experimentation on live animals.) Vivisection has been practiced at least since the time of the Greeks, more than 2000 years ago. The teachings of the Greeks and Romans—especially those of the Greek physician, Galen, who did vivisection—formed the basis of medical science in the West during the Middle Ages.

The foundations of modern anatomy and medicine were laid down in the sixteenth and seventeenth centuries when such physicians as Andrea Vasalius and William Harvey challenged many of Galen's assumptions. Both men used animal vivisection in their studies, as well as dissections of human corpses.

The seventeenth-century philosopher, Descartes, argued that animals were machines that couldn't think or feel. On this view, one needn't have any qualms about using animals for experiments or demonstrations; their cries were nothing more than the squeaking of machinery. Other philosophers disagreed and through the eighteenth and nineteenth centuries there were debates about the morality of animal vivisection.

An anti-vivisection movement arose in Great Britain in the nineteenth century and spread to the United States. The movement gained force in the States in the mid-1960s. There was a widely publicized story of a dog named Pepper who disappeared from the backyard of the family house in Pennsylvania and ended up dead in a New York laboratory. In 1966 *Life* magazine published an article called "Concentration Camps for Dogs" about a police raid on the facility of a dealer who collected dogs and sold them to research laboratories. The story had photos of badly abused dogs kept in filthy cages. As a result of the public reaction to such stories, Congress that same year passed the Laboratory Animal Welfare Act requiring the licensing of dealers and the regulation of laboratory animals.

Animal Liberation, a book by philosopher Peter Singer that appeared in 1975, presented horrific stories of the way animals were treated in laboratory experiments (as well as on factory farms). For his stories on research animals, Singer only had to look at what scientists themselves had described in their journals. For example, in a related series of experiments having to do with induced psychopathy in monkeys, researchers would attach infant monkeys to mechanical mother-monsters, which would shake the infants violently, or throw them off, or repel them with spikes. Real mother-monsters were created by impregnating female monkeys who'd been reared in isolation: The mothers who did not ignore their infants would sometimes crush the infants' skulls with their teeth or smash their faces against the floor.

Countless experiments involved subjecting dogs and other animals to radiation and poisons and making careful records while the animals died what appeared to be slow and excruciating deaths. One of Singer's points was that the same experiments involving animal suffering were repeated over and over for the sake of demonstrations or PhD theses or journal articles—experiments which even other scientists concluded were mostly worthless.

Partly inspired by Singer's book, animal activists led a campaign against the testing of cosmetics on animals, especially the use of the Draize test, in which chemicals are tested by being put into the eyes of rabbits. Full-page ads against the cosmetics companies led to supportive public response, and companies like Revlon and Avon announced that they would cease animal testing and find alternatives.

Raids on animal research facilities by activists turned up evidence of gross animal mistreatment and callousness on the part of researchers. Alex Pacheco and Ingrid Newkirk, who founded People for the Ethical Treatment of Animals (PETA), did undercover work at a small private research institute, The Institute for Behavioral Research in Silver Springs, Maryland. After documenting what went on in the labs—including photos of monkeys with limbs that were bloody, chewed off, and infected—they gave the evidence to the police; this resulted in animal cruelty charges being brought against the Institute. In another case, PETA produced a video showing scenes from stolen researcher videos at a lab at the University of Pennsylvania. As Deborah Blum puts it in her book, *The Monkey Wars*:

> ...obviously the laboratory workers weren't just 'documenting' the research. Posing before the camera, young scientists held dazed baboons in silly 'say cheese'

poses; dangled them by crippled limbs, laughed when they struggled. Propping up one brain-damaged animal, whose paws quivered uncontrollably, researchers turned the camera on him and began a voice over: "Friends! Romans! Countrymen! [laughter] Look, he wants to shake hands. Come on.... He says, 'You're gonna rescue me from this, aren't you? Aren't you?'"

Public anger at revelations like these led Congress to toughen the protection under the Animal Welfare Act in 1985. The new act required researchers to minimize animal pain and distress whenever possible through the use of anesthesia, analgesics, and humane euthanasia. Other requirements were added regarding the care and welfare of dogs and primates used in research. The Animal Welfare Act regulations are enforced by the Animal Care unit of the USDA Animal and Plant Health Inspection Service.

Some animal researchers applaud these regulations, while others feel hemmed in by them. Many researchers feel harassed by the harangues of animal protesters and the threat of their research facilities being invaded. As a result animal researchers have become much more guarded in their relations to the public.

Those who support animal research in general insist that such research is vital to protect and enhance the health and life of human beings. They point to the following sorts of medical advances that came out of research with animals: Open-heart surgery, coronary bypass, and replacement of defective heart valves; kidney dialysis equipment and techniques; anticancer radiation therapies and drugs; vaccines for smallpox, measles and many other diseases; organ transplants; and blood transfusions. Animals are being used in research that is seeking cures for AIDS and Alzheimer's disease, spinal cord injuries and paralysis, and the genetic causes of cancer. Researchers also point out that animals have benefited from animal research, for example in the treatments for rabies, distemper, anthrax and in various surgical techniques.

Animal researchers say the regulations under the Animal Welfare Act are sufficient to guarantee an adequate level of animal welfare, given the necessity and desirability of using animals in research in the first place.

The US Department of Agriculture (USDA) keeps track of the occurrence of pain and distress in regulated animals. According to the USDA, in 2001, 57% of these animals experienced no pain or distress, 34% experienced pain or distress but were given drugs for relief, and 9% suffered pain and distress but were not given drugs for relief.

Animal welfare groups aren't convinced by these numbers, which are supplied by animal researchers themselves; welfarists believe the numbers are greatly underreported. One academic who studied animal research laboratories found that while anesthesia was given to animals in the same situations as with humans, pain relief was not.

One program to improve the use of animals in research originated in a book entitled *Principles of Humane Experimental Technique* by scientists William Russell and Rex Burch. The book suggested a program it called the "3 R's": Reduction, Refinement, and Replacement. Reduction is to be accomplished by improved statistical methods and avoiding unnecessary duplication of experiments. Refinement focuses on such means as reducing animal suffering and improving care practices. Replacement looks to substitute lower animal species for higher ones and to find alternatives to using animals at all. Though embraced by animal welfare organizations and the general public, the 3 R's are only recommendations and can be interpreted differently by both sides.

Factory farming

Though the use of animals for research has perhaps garnered the most publicity, the number of such animals—17 to 25 million in the US—is dwarfed by the number of farm animals slaughtered in the US each year for food: 5 billion.

There are people who are against the killing and eating of animals. There are other people who do accept the killing and eating of animals but complain that the current methods of raising and transporting animals are deplorable and getting worse.

In the last century, the methods of raising livestock have passed from the control of individual farmers to that of large corporations. These corporations have applied mass production techniques to the raising of animals, either employing those methods in their own facilities or pushing them on individual farmers who contract to provide the corporations with animals for slaughter.

More and more the raising of livestock involves industrial-style facilities called "factory farms." Large numbers of animals are raised in relatively small spaces and are fed, medicated and processed in the most efficient way possible. With the farming of many animals, the atmosphere is less like storybook images of the family farm than like a dark industrial plant.

While animal advocates say that factory farming is cruel, industry advocates, such as the American Meat Institute (AMI), deny this. The AMI says that livestock farmers practice humane animal treatment, both because such treatment is ethical and because it results in animals being calmer. Calmer animals result in better quality meat and mean a safer working environment.

As examples of factory farming practices, let's consider those related to the raising of hogs (full grown domestic pigs) and chickens.

Most of the hogs raised in the US are raised on factory farms. In some cases over 10,000 hogs are confined in buildings hundreds of feet long. The floors are typically slatted (allowing urine and manure to fall into pits below the floor) or made of concrete (for easy cleaning). Hogs are kept on short tethers, or in steel-barred cages. The producers don't want the hogs to get exercise, since that might toughen the meat.

The hogs suffer stress from close crowding and boredom. As a result the hogs can exhibit aggression toward other hogs, including tail chewing and biting. To prevent this, producers cut off the tails and clip the teeth. Large numbers of hogs suffer respiratory problems from high levels of dust and ammonia and suffer leg problems from confinement in crates and cages.

To keep the hogs calm, the confinement facilities are kept dark except when it's time to feed. Many hogs never see daylight until they're taken to auction or slaughter.

A problem for pork producers is Porcine Stress Syndrome (PSS), which can ruin the taste of the meat. The industry is funding genetic research with the aim of developing pigs which are less stressed by confinement.

The industry claims that factory farming is better for the animals than the natural environment, since there is less danger of predators, disease, and parasites. They claim that the animals have adapted well to this environment.

Sows (female hogs) are often artificially inseminated. The pregnant sow is confined in a "gestation crate," a steel-barred crate which is typically 6 or 7 feet long and 2 feet wide, hardly big enough for the sow to lie down and not big enough for her to turn around. She eats and defecates in that crate. She will stay there for just under four months. Such crates have been banned in Sweden and the United Kingdom, and will be phased out in the European Union over the next ten years. There are modest signs of such change in the US as well. Arizona voters approved the Humane Treatment of Farm Animals Act which prohibits the intensive confinement of breeding pigs, and Smithfield Foods has said it will end the use of gestation crates. For the most part, however, such crates continue to be used.

There are two types of "farmed" chickens, egg-laying chickens and "broilers" raised for eating. These two types are raised in different facilities.

Hatcheries for egg-laying chickens want only the females, of course. The males are not generally suitable for fattening as broilers. These male chickens are sorted out and then gassed, crushed or decapitated. A popular method is to stuff them in large plastic bags and let them suffocate. The remains are ground up, and the mush used as ingredients in animal feed supplements. Billions of baby chicks are killed this way every year.

The laying hens are typically kept in stacked battery cages. The average space allocated for each bird is 53 square inches—a little over half the size of a standard piece of notebook paper.

Broilers are raised in huge barns where tens of thousands of them may live crowded together. There's plenty of room when they arrive as chicks, but as they grow, there's barely space to move. Stress results from overcrowding and the unnatural manipulations of lighting to stimulate higher food consumption. The chickens suffer respiratory diseases due to dust and ammonia in the air and from "litter-burned" skin from the high moisture and ammonia content of the waste on the floor. A big problem is Marek's disease— a cancer connected with the stress of accelerated growth and overcrowding—which causes the meat to be condemned.

Unlike research animals, chickens have virtually no legal protections. What protections the larger farm animals have mostly have to do with slaughter. The Humane Methods of Slaughter Act of 1958 applies to slaughterhouses subject to federal inspection. It requires that animals (excluding chickens) must be made insensitive to pain before being slaughtered. The act is enforced by the USDA.

Animal welfare groups claim that in many cases the speed of the work, the fear of damaging the flesh of the animals, and the use of unskilled labor results in only the partial stunning of animals before slaughter. They claim that the USDA—frequently staffed by people who formerly worked in the farm animal industry—is often sloppy in their inspections.

What improvements there have been in the treatment of farm animals came initially from pressure put on retail food corporations by animal welfare groups. In 2003, PETA launched a campaign against Kentucky Fried Chicken (KFC) Corporation— calling it "Kentucky Fried Cruelty"—for the way its suppliers treated their chickens. That same year KFC instituted new guidelines for its suppliers, along with new auditing procedures, including video cameras in the slaughterhouses. McDonald's, Wendy's, and Burger King have also instituted policies for the more humane treatment of animals.

More recently there have been some legislative victories for those wanting to lessen the suffering of farm animals. In addition to the Arizona law already cited, California passed a ballot initiative in 2008 that will prohibit factory farms from keeping pregnant sows or egg-laying hens in pens or cages in which they can't turn around or stretch.

There is a small, but growing market for meat raised under much more humane conditions. These conditions are implied by such labels as "grass fed," "pasture raised," and "free range." Alternately, some people have adopted one of the vegetarian lifestyles, though sometimes such a diet is a matter of health concerns or religious belief, rather than concern for animals.

For those who deplore the general treatment of factory-farmed animals, the problem is getting worse, not better. Even if some improvements have been made to factory farming methods in Europe and the US, new factory farms are springing up all over the world. As economic conditions in developing nations improve, there is an increasing demand for meat; industrial farming methods are being applied to meet that demand.

Let's move on now to discuss different views regarding the morality of our treatment of animals.

Three moral views regarding our use of animals

We're going to consider three general categories of views regarding the use of animals in such areas as research and factory farming.

1. *Pro-Status Quo:* "There are no serious moral problems with the way we treat animals today. We are entitled to use animals to fulfill human needs, from using them for medical research to raising them for food. The way we currently deal with the animals we use in these areas is morally acceptable."
2. *Animal Welfare:* "There are serious moral problems with the way we treat animals today. Though we are entitled to raise animals for food and use them for medical research, our current practices involve far more animals and cause them far more pain than is morally justifiable. We ought to make substantial changes in the way we treat animals."
3. *Abolitionist:* "The way we treat animals today is morally wrong. Animals are entitled to a much higher moral status than we accord them: It is no more permissible for us to use animals for food or medical research than it would be for us to use human infants and mentally impaired adults for the same purposes. We need to radically change our treatment of animals, abolishing most of our current practices."

The *Pro-Status Quo* category, as I have defined it, covers a broad range of views. It covers people who think animals lack consciousness. It covers people who believe that animals do feel pain, but don't think that their pain should count for much when weighed against human needs. It includes certain conservationists, hunters, and food producers who are interested in the conditions of animals but only as a means to their continued survival value as aesthetic

components of public parks, or available targets for hunting, or as healthy resources for food. Since for one reason or another, these people aren't much concerned with animal pain (if they acknowledge it at all), let's call them *Status Quo/unsympathetic.*

However, Pro-Status Quo also includes people who would consider themselves "animal lovers," or at least people deeply concerned about the feelings of animals. These people—let's call them *Status Quo/ sympathetic*—might dote on their pets, get incensed at the idea of abusing a pet, and perhaps applaud the positive changes that have come about in the treatment of animals for medical research. They would probably see themselves as far removed from those in the Status Quo/unsympathetic category—much closer in spirit to animal welfarists.

Thanks to animal activists, we have come a long way in our treatment of animals. We have laws against animal abuse and even have "animal cops" to enforce those laws; we have animal shelters to help animals that are abandoned or abused. We lavish attention on pets as never before, spending tens of billions of dollars on their food, toys, medical care, and training. We have greatly diminished the use of primates in medical research and are more concerned than ever to avoid cruelty and unnecessary pain where the other research animals are concerned. Many of those in the Status Quo/sympathetic category would applaud all this as progress.

So why put Status Quo/sympathetic and Status Quo/unsympathetic in the same category? Whatever the relative moral merits of the two positions, both agree that no substantial changes are needed in our current treatment of animals. This puts them at odds with positions that insist we need substantial or radical change. Further the idea of those in Status Quo/ sympathetic being "animal lovers" comes under serious question in the area of factory farming. Even if in most other ways we have made considerable progress in the humane treatment of animals, factory farming seems a giant step backward.

Of course, many of those in the Status Quo/unsympathetic group would think of themselves as realists and all the others as "fuzzy-headed sentimentalists."

Since we have such a broad Pro-Status Quo category based on denying the need for change, why not combine the Animal Welfare and Abolitionist views into one category—those in favor of change? After all the vast majority of Americans would seem to fall into the Pro-Status Quo category, by acquiescence if nothing else, given the amount of factory-farmed meat they buy and consume. Those seriously holding views in the Animal Welfare and Abolitionist categories form a small minority of Americans.

There are a couple of reasons why I want to treat Animal Welfare and Abolitionism separately.

In the popular press, the Pro-Status Quo position is often defended by implying that the only alternative is Abolitionism—which seems too extreme to most people (especially after it has been thoroughly caricatured). But this is too easy: Animal Welfare presents another challenge to Pro-Status Quo.

The other reason for treating the views separately is that much of the philosophical literature on animals is engaged with some aggressive and powerful arguments that have been put forth specifically in support of Abolitionist views. These arguments deserve to be dealt with in detail.

However, before we discuss the morality of animal suffering, we'd better discuss the reality of it. How can we know what animals feel? How can we know whether, and to what degree, animals are suffering in situations in which we would suffer? Let's turn to the subject of animal minds.

Animal minds

The subject of animal minds is both fascinating and enormously complicated. We all have a natural tendency to anthropomorphize, to attribute human feelings and mental processes to animals. We've done this in fables for thousands of years. We certainly do this with pets. My wife and I have a Bernese Mountain Dog, named Augie (Augustus), who has five or six facial expressions. When his mouth is wide open with his tongue lolling to the side, he looks like the happiest goofball in the world. When his mouth is only partially open—especially when seen in profile—he has a sly, let's-see-what-I-can-get-away-with look. When his mouth is shut he has that classical stern-judge look that Berners have—unless he starts looking around, and then he seems anxious. When he rests with his chin on the floor—especially when his eyes follow us

around—he has the most pathetic, nobody-loves-me look that makes it hard to resist comforting him, even though we know that the chin-on-the-floor is just a preliminary to taking a nap.

Such "reading into" a pet's expressions is natural, fun and harmless—at least insofar as it doesn't interfere with what training the dog needs to fit in with the family "pack." Of course, many people take it much farther, talking as if they are intimately acquainted with their pets' incredibly rich mental lives.

If such anthropomorphism is innocuous when it comes to people and their pets, it would be a disaster for researchers who try to study the lives of animals scientifically. They want to study the animals themselves, after all, not what we project into animals. Suppressing anthropomorphism can be revealing: Often animal behavior we'd be inclined to explain in terms of, say, reflection, planning and deception, can be explained quite well in terms of instinctive behavior and rote learning.

However, many animal researchers take the anti-anthropomorphism stance much farther. They say we can't know—and never will know—whether animals have any conscious experiences at all, including sensations of pain; they sometimes add to this skepticism the claim that since we can't know if animals experience pain, we should assume they don't.

Doubts about whether or not the higher animals— for instance, the family dog and cat—have conscious experiences will strike most people as ludicrous. But let's step back a bit and ask what arguments could be given for the claim that animals are conscious. In what follows we will focus on animal pain, since this "experience" is the one most central to concerns about the humane treatment of animals.

What is pain? We know the various pain-related sensations from our own case. We learned pain-related words early on from parents and other caretakers, who were responding to our behavior, including our vocal sounds.

We judge pain in others by their behavior—such as crying out, yanking a hand back from a hot object, grabbing and protecting a limb, making grimacing and other facial expressions. Animals exhibit similar behaviors. One day Augie was running on a wet veranda, slipped and let out a yelp, got up and held his left front paw off the ground. We ran over to soothe him; we tested the limb gently and he pulled it away. We waited a little, then the paw went down, he limped a little, and later seemed all right. Allowing for his difference in physical form, he behaved pretty much as I would have behaved—minus the swearing. Judging from his behavior, it seems reasonable on the face of it to think he was in pain.

Beyond what we take to be behavioral signs of pain, physiologists tell us that vertebrate animals are analogous to humans in the neurophysiological and neuroanatomical mechanisms of pain. They also have the same mechanisms for modifying pain, including the release of endorphins. When such animals show serious pain behavior, they also show many of the same physiological symptoms we do; further, they react as we do to analgesics and anesthesia.

In evolutionary terms, the sensation of pain has obvious survival value and it would be odd, given the evolution of the nervous system, if conscious sensation (as opposed to higher thought) appeared for the first time with human beings.

This is a preliminary case for the claim that animals are conscious and can feel pain. What about the skeptical case?

One argument is this: *We can't observe the supposed private, subjective states of animals; therefore, we can't know they exist.*

The problem with this argument is that, by itself, it would imply that each one of us also ought to be skeptical of the existence of private subjective states in other human beings: We can't observe those states in other humans either. In the case of both other humans and animals, all we have to go by is behavior.

A modified version of the skeptical argument goes like this: *We can't observe the supposed private, subjective states of animals AND they have no language to describe those states to us; therefore, we can't know they exist.*

The problem with this modified argument is that, in the context of basic skepticism, language is nothing more than another piece of behavior. Once you grant that a creature is conscious, then language plays a special role in determining what those conscious states are. But prior to determining if another creature is conscious, language is just another behavior.

Consider a robot that is able to propel itself across the floor and do certain tasks with its mechanical arms and grippers; this robot is also built for speech recognition and speech synthesis. We can imagine programming the robot so that when we slap something metal against one of its mechanical arms, it says, "Ouch," draws the arm away and rubs the slapped arm with the other arm. When we ask, "What hurts?" the robot responds, "My arm hurts."

The point is that the robot's rudimentary "pain" speech is on a par with its rudimentary "pain" behavior. It's not as if its speaking gives us privileged information about the existence of pain in the robot.

So, to summarize, we can imagine animals behaving as if they are in pain, but not being in pain; in the same way, we can imagine all humans other than oneself behaving and speaking as if they are in pain but not being in pain. Denying the feeling of pain in animals seems as unreasonable as denying it in human beings.

Even if we did give language a privileged status in judging the existence of conscious states, we would have exactly the same grounds for doubting consciousness in very young pre-verbal children as we have for doubting consciousness in animals.

There's something else to consider: What if we followed the skeptics and were wrong? We'd add enormously to sum of animal pain.

It's important to see that the skepticism about animal minds wouldn't simply undercut the animal welfare and animal rights movements. It would undercut any concern for animal cruelty. Like the seventeenth-century followers of Descartes, you could cut open animals at will, marveling at the funny screams the "machines" made. If you saw your son burning a live cat in the backyard, you could puff out your chest and say, "I believe my boy's going to be a scientist; he's too smart to swallow that myth about animals having feelings."

It seems to me we ought to have awfully strong counter-evidence before we try to stifle our natural impulse to imagine that (at least) the higher animals have feelings—especially given what it might cost animals. I don't think the speculative skepticism of some philosophers and scientists comes close to the kind of counter-evidence we'd need.

Therefore, throughout the rest of this discussion, we will take it for granted that animals do feel.

However, the conclusion that animals are conscious and can feel pain certainly doesn't mean that we can decide what they're feeling by imagining ourselves in their position; it doesn't mean we're justified in approaching the subject of animal consciousness without considering empirical evidence.

As Marian Stamp Dawkins says,

Exactly what other animals find very pleasant or very unpleasant is left to experimental tests. In other words, the leap that we have to make from our skins to theirs takes into account the possibility that their suffering or their pleasure may be brought about by events quite different from those that cause them in us. We are not imagining ourselves shut up in a battery cage or dressed up in a bat suit when we try to find out what it is like to be a hen or a bat; we are trying to find out what it is like to *be* them....

She notes that the "animals' own preferences do sometimes produce surprises":

The Bramble Committee, which produced an important report on intensive farming in the UK, recommended that fine hexagonal wire should not be used for the floors of battery cages on the grounds that it was thought (by well-meaning humans) to be uncomfortable for the hen's feet. When allowed to choose between different floor types, however, the hens actually preferred the fine mesh to the coarse one which had been recommended by the Committee....

In the opening discussion of "The Trainers," I added two fictional paragraphs in which:

(i)   Andrea wakes up to find herself in a cage and becomes panicked with claustrophobia.
(ii) Andrea wakes up strapped into a chair; wires attached to her body are starting to deliver a series of painful electrical shocks. Her vocal cords are tied so she can't speak or scream.

Regarding *i*, we crate-trained our dog, Augie, using a large crate that is light and airy and easy to see out of. Such crates are generally used for house training, for keeping the puppy from destroying things, and as a safe place for him to sleep at night. In some ways, the crate is much like a crib or playpen for a child. Unlike older children, however, some older dogs seem to love

their crates as a secure, quiet place to rest. Waking up in a crate would hardly cause a dog the kind of panic reaction Andrea experiences in her "cage." (Of course, this is not to say that Augie would want to be in that crate all the time.)

We can't simply generalize from our own case as to what's going to cause an animal pain or distress; we need to consider evidence. Of course, something like Porcine Stress Syndrome seems to be evidence of distress.

Situation *ii* is something else entirely. Monkeys and dogs have endured experiments at least as potentially painful (and tying vocal cords is fairly standard practice with laboratory dogs to keep them from barking.) Even if we attribute to human beings all sorts of higher-order levels of anxiety and hopeless imaginings, what we know about the relatively similar physiologies of humans, monkeys, and dogs, as well as behavioral evidence, would tell us that experiments like the one Andrea is undergoing would likely also be terrible for a monkey or dog.

Let's now consider the three moral views mentioned above: the Pro-Status Quo, Animal Welfare and Abolitionist views.

Pro-Status Quo views

There are no serious moral problems with the way we treat animals today. We are entitled to use animals to fulfill human needs, from using them for medical research to raising and killing them for food. The way we currently deal with the animals we use in these areas is morally acceptable.

Here are some of the arguments given in support of the *Status Quo* position:

Argument A: Being "used" by humans is, overall, a good thing for animals; therefore it's all right for humans to use animals.

Argument B: Humans have "dominion" over animals, whether by divine decree or the natural order. Therefore we are entitled to use the animals as we see fit.

Argument C: The only way to justify morality is as an implied or hypothetical social contract among the people in a society. Since animals can't engage in such a contract, they have no moral status. Therefore there can be no moral objection to our using animals as we wish.

Regarding Argument *A*, the claim that being "used" by humans is, overall, a good thing for the animals, would be used primarily with reference to farm animals and would be supported by something like the following premises:

i.   The vast majority of farm animals owe their lives to the fact that they are being used by humans.
ii. Animals raised on farms have a good life—certainly a life as good as, if not better than, that of animals living in the wild.

Probably a lot of people find argument *A* appealing. Those herds of grazing cattle we see as we're driving along a rural highway simply wouldn't exist if we weren't willing to put time and expense into breeding and raising them; we wouldn't do that if they weren't of use. The same goes for the chickens pecking at the feed scattered for them in the backyard of some farmer's house. The cattle and the chickens have plenty to eat and for the most part are protected from predators; in the case of the cattle, their health is even monitored by veterinarians. These animals look like they have a pretty good deal. It's true that many of them are going to be killed for food, but they don't have the understanding to anticipate their death until just before it happens. (That this same argument is used in "The Trainers" to justify raising humans for food is a possible complication we'll take up later when we discuss the abolitionist position.)

The immediate problem with argument *A* is that it looks dated. Maybe it *was* a strong argument when most animals were raised on family farms. But factory farming methods bring premise *ii* into serious question. Representatives of the American meat industry vigorously argue for premise *ii*, but in spite of their sunny statements, the life of farm animals today seems, if not hellish, then pretty dismal. This is where the animal welfare objections would come in: We can justify raising animals for food only if we modify our current practices so that they are more "humane."

Argument *B*—that divine decree or the natural order entitles us to use animals as we see fit—is another popular argument.

Aristotle believed that there was a natural hierarchy of beings, with animals, lacking reason, ranking below humans and therefore being appropriate resources for humans to use. The medieval Christians adopted a similar view, bolstered by the belief that humans, but not animals, had immortal souls. Christians also inherited from the Jews God's injunction to human beings in Genesis, telling them:

> Be fruitful, and multiply, and replenish the earth, and subdue it; and have dominion over the fish of the sea, and over the fowl of the air, and over every living thing that creepeth upon the earth.

Whether dominion is taken as God's decree or just the natural order, no doubt that idea lies in back of much of our thinking and our practices related to animals. From very early in human history, humans have had a predator/prey relationship with many animals—hunting them for food and killing them to avoid being eaten. Later the use of animals was crucial to the development of agriculture. The fact that using animals is so natural to human beings is no doubt one reason why much of the criticism of these practices seems so odd to so many people.

That said, the animal advocates would point out that there are lots of human practices that are equally "natural" that we would consider morally abhorrent today, such as slavery. Aristotle defended slavery and the subordinate role of women, along with the use of animals, as part of the natural order.

If one believes that God created only humans with souls and created animals for our use, this view is bound to affect one's attitude toward animals. For instance, it's hard to imagine combining this view with a belief in animal rights.

Still, even if one believes that God intended animals for our use, there are still questions that can be asked about this "dominion" view. Do you suppose God has any compassion for animal pain? If He does, how would He view the worst of factory farming?

If one leaves God out of the picture and simply justifies our use of animals as part of the natural order, there are other questions that can be asked: If nature is cruel, and humans have been fortunate enough to come out on top of the food chain, is that sufficient reason to justify any pain we want to impose on animals? Or should it be one of our human ideals to introduce compassion into a world that would contain none without us?

Argument *C* appeals to a social contract view of morality and excludes animals from the province of morality because they are incapable of engaging in such a contract.

The primary question here, of course, is whether or not contractarianism is the most reasonable moral theory—and reasonable as the *whole* of moral theory. Contractarianism does provide a framework for the discussion of moral ideas among those who can't agree on much besides the need for *some* kind of social morality—one that will allow society to function and provide at least a modicum of general agreement. However, as we discussed in "Moral Theory," contractarianism seems incomplete as a full moral theory. If it is incomplete, then the fact that contractarianism doesn't cover animals isn't in itself a justification for excluding them from moral consideration.

These are some of the responses that the animal welfarists and abolitionists might make to the arguments in favor of the status quo. Let's go on now to discuss what we've defined as the *Animal Welfare* position.

Animal Welfare views

There are serious moral problems with the way we treat animals today. Though we are entitled to raise animals for food and use them for medical research, our current practices involve far more animals and cause them much more pain than is morally justifiable. We ought to make substantial changes in the way we treat animals.

Matthew Scully, an animal welfarist, may have put the animal welfare position best when, after visiting, and being sickened by, an industrial hog-raising facility, he wrote:

Turning to the question of animal rights, I confess that I could hardly care less whether any formal doctrine or theory can be adduced for these creatures. There are moments when you do not need doctrines, when even

rights become irrelevant, when life demands some basic response of fellow feeling and mercy and love.

Walking around a place like Farm 2149, I do not need some utilitarian philosopher to do the moral math for me, adding up and subtracting the suffering of the world to determine which lives have value and which do not. I do not need a contractualist philosopher to define for me an "appropriate object of sympathy." I do not need behavioral scientists or cognitive theorists to distinguish which pains are "real" pains and which are not. I do not need experts in evolutionary ecology or some other faddish field of the day to explain the hard and remorseless demands of natural selection. I require no advice from theologians on where mercy may be granted and where withheld. Confronted with this wholesale disregard and destruction of life, all attempts to justify it strike me as vain talk, miserable excuses that cannot cover the inequity, the ungodly presumption of it, the scale and the sorrow of it.

It seems as if most of the complex philosophical arguments are presented by those who hold the Pro-Status Quo or the Abolitionist positions. The Animal Welfare position becomes complex because it must be defended against the positions on either side of it. But at its heart, the position is fairly simple: It doesn't challenge the right of humans to raise animals for food or to use animals for research, even though this is bound to cause animals pain. But it views the pain of all creatures as mattering morally. It insists that the pain caused animals be kept to a decent minimum.

Philosopher Carl Cohen believes that our current use of research animals is morally justified. He is someone I would label as Status Quo/sympathetic, someone who cares about the welfare of animals but thinks their welfare is taken care of by the current laws and regulations. He says this:

Animal *welfare* is not at issue here. Basic care for animals is today a moral concern almost universally shared. Sentient animals must be treated with careful regard for the fact that they can feel pain; decent people will always exhibit that concern and will rightly insist that the animals we use be fed and housed properly, handled considerately. Regulations ensuring such humane treatment are not in dispute; they are entirely justified and (in this country) universally enforced. Principles of good animal husbandry rule, as they ought to rule, among the scientists who rely on animals in their investigations. Every medical center, every pharmaceutical company, every research institute using animals has (and under American law must have) its own Institutional Animal Care and Use Committee whose legal duty is to ensure that the animals in that facility are cared for properly and that experiments using those animals are conducted humanely. Frequent inspections by federal agencies, as well as by professional peers, enforce and reinforce high standards for animal care and use.

As we've seen from the "Facts and factual issues" section, animal welfarists would say that this paints far too rosy a picture of the situation regarding the use of research animals today. The welfarists would say there is much more work to be done in the area of the 3 R's: Reduction, Refinement, and Replacement.

In any case, whatever one's judgment about current scientific practices, there is still the issue of factory farming, which involves billions rather than millions of animals. The book from which the Carl Cohen quote is taken is a debate between Cohen and Tom Regan (discussed below) regarding animal rights. Interestingly, Regan tries and fails to get Cohen to take a position on factory farming. I can't say what Cohen was thinking, but one can see why someone in Cohen's position would be reluctant to reply: Whatever safeguards there may be for animals used in research, there is little that's comparable in the area of factory farming. One of the major efforts of animal welfare groups is to get substantial reforms in the area of raising animals for food.

Let's turn now to what we're calling the *Abolitionist* position.

Abolitionist views

The way we treat animals today is morally wrong. Animals are entitled to a much higher moral status than we accord them: It is no more permissible for us to use animals for food or medical research than it would be for us to use human infants and mentally impaired adults for the same purposes. We need to radically change our treatment of animals, abolishing most of our current practices.

I have tried to define the *Abolitionist* view so as to encompass two variations: an extreme utilitarian view, associated with philosopher Peter Singer, and an "animal rights" view, as presented by philosopher Tom Regan. Singer's view is sometimes called an "animal welfare" view, since it emphasizes animal pain rather than animal rights. However, there are two reasons why I think it best to group Singer's utilitarian view with an animal rights view. The implications of both views are extreme, demanding the abolition of most of our practices regarding animals. Further, both views share a central argument—what we'll call the "Speciesist Critique"—that we will turn to now.

The Speciesist Critique

What we're calling the "Speciesist Critique" argues that most of the ways in which we treat animals today are "speciesist" (and therefore wrong).

Speciesism can be defined as discrimination against another being solely on the basis of its being a member of a different species and is meant to suggest terms like "racism" and "sexism."

The Speciesist Critique consists of two related arguments we'll call the *Argument from Racism* and the *Argument from Marginal Cases*.

Peter Singer's original version of what we're calling the Argument from Racism seems to go like this:

1. Most of us agree that racism (as well as sexism) is wrong.
2. This agreement is based on the principle that all human beings are equal.
3. However, the "principle of equality of human beings is not a description of an alleged actual equality among humans…" since obviously all humans aren't equal in terms of intelligence and ability; rather the principle of equality "is a prescription of how we should treat human beings."
4. The principle of equality says that "the interests of every being affected by an action are to be taken into account and given the same weight as the like interests of any other being."
5. But if the principle of equality refers to interests, then it ought to apply to all beings with interests, and that includes animals.

To deny this equality of interests to a racial group is racism; to women, sexism; to animals, speciesism.

For Singer, equality of interests does not imply (as his sillier critics have claimed) that animals should have the right to vote, to marry, and so on. Equality of interests depends on what those interests are. Obviously animals have no interest in voting or marrying. But they do have an interest in not suffering—an interest that seems to be violated by many of our research and farming practices.

Most people reject the idea that the interests of animals are to be given the same moral weight as the interests of humans. They feel we have justifiable reasons for treating humans as having a higher moral standing than animals: Humans have all sorts of capacities that animals don't have, such as reason, complex emotions, spirituality, and artistic appreciation. (For simplicity of exposition, we'll use "reason" as a stand-in for this list.)

This sort of logic is the target of the *Argument from Marginal Cases*. "Marginal cases"—like the phrase that is sometimes used instead, "non-paradigmatic humans"—is intended to be a gentle (if jargonized) way of referring to those human beings who do not have the normal adult human capacities such as reason and complex emotions. "Marginal humans" ("non-paradigmatic humans") would include infants, those with severe mental retardation, and the senile.

The Argument from Marginal Cases can be put in the form of a dilemma:

a. As in arguments against racism (and sexism), we normally demand that differences in treatment between individuals be justified by pointing out morally relevant differences between the individuals.
b. Like individuals should be treated in a like manner: If one individual is treated a certain way because of having or lacking a certain characteristic, then other individuals having or lacking that characteristic should be treated the same way.
c. If animals are to be treated a certain way because they lack certain characteristics, like reason, then logical consistency requires that marginal humans who lack that characteristic must be treated the same way.

The dilemma here is this: If you think researchers are justified in experimenting on animals, you are committed to the view that it would be all right for them to experiment on infants and other marginal humans. If you think it's all right to kill animals for food, you are committed to the view that it's all right to kill infants and other marginal humans for food. The usual implication, of course, is that since you think it would be (horribly) wrong to experiment on or eat infants, you ought to consider it wrong to experiment on or eat animals.

The Argument from Marginal Cases is intended to show that (at least the higher) animals, like all humans, have inherent moral value (that is, value in and of themselves, apart from their value to others). Various phrases are used to convey this thought in the literature. Something has inherent moral significance or worth or standing; it is worthy of moral consideration (is "morally considerable").

The Argument from Marginal Cases claims that the burden of proof is on those who would discriminate against animals to justify their position by citing some characteristic that all marginal humans have that animals do not. For the traditionally religious, "souls" is the quick and easy answer, but many people who use animal products and support animal research aren't sure they believe in souls, at least not in a sense that would make all and only humans special.

A little perspective here: Singer does believe that there are lots of *indirect* reasons why, in general, experimenting on infants and other marginal humans would be much worse than experimenting on animals. "Indirect" here refers to effects on individuals other than the one being experimented on.

If you take an animal infant from its mother for research purposes, the animal-mother's grief (if any) seems brief, she has no conception of what's going to happen to the infant, and the other animal mothers aren't going to generalize from the incident to worry about their own infants (at least not for long). In contrast, human parents would suffer terrible grief over the loss, as well as terrible imaginings about what was happening to their child; other human parents would be in a panic about their children. Still, in the case of orphaned infants or senile persons without family, few, if any, of these indirect effects would apply. Do we want to say that research on orphans would be morally acceptable? If not, says Singer, we should say that research on animals isn't morally acceptable.

Some philosophers have argued that even if the Argument from Marginal Cases forces us to accept the moral equivalence of marginal humans and animals, there are still good indirect reasons for extending protections to marginal humans, while withholding them from animals. One argument is that experimenting on orphaned infants and senile persons without family would undermine respect for the life of all humans in a way that experimenting on animals does not. However, even if these indirect arguments work (and many would deny they do), a lot of people aren't comfortable with the idea that the protections morality affords marginal humans are all indirect—that there's nothing intrinsically wrong with, for example, experimenting on orphans.

What are we to make of the Speciesist Critique?

In his book, *The Expanding Circle*, Singer quotes with approval the following lines from W. E. H. Lecky's *The History of European Morals*:

> At one time the benevolent affections embrace merely the family, so that the circle expanding includes first a class, then a nation, then a coalition of nations, then all humanity, and finally, its influence is felt in the dealings of man with the animal world.

It does seem that over time there has been a general expansion of moral inclusiveness, even if the expansion has proceeded in fits and starts and has been honored more in theory than in practice. No doubt "benevolent affections" have played a role in this expansion, as have appeals to religious principles and certain standards of justice. But many of the causes have been more practical and self-interested: Increased familiarity with strangers, the desire to increase commerce and engage in other joint enterprises, and fears of revolts or revolutions if concession aren't made. Nonetheless, whatever the cause and effect, our moral reasoning has changed and here we want to focus on that.

Consider the arguments of those who protested the institution of slavery or the treatment of Native Americans; they can be seen as attempting to expand the circle of moral consideration. Many arguments for this expansion were religious: Africans and Native Americans were said to have souls (something earlier settlers had disputed) and were children of God "like us." Sympathetic observations of the lives of Native

Americans or African slaves made them recognizable as fellow humans and prompted a growing awareness of their suffering. Indian wars and slave rebellions also helped undercut any comfortable illusions that Native Americans and slaves were happy with the treatment they were receiving. Arguments were also given to the effect that they were perfectly capable of participating in the American political process.

Note that the arguments given against these extreme forms of racism don't imply anything about the wrongness of speciesism. Many of the reasons given for the inclusion of African Americans and Native Americans in the moral sphere—children of God," "fellow humans like us," "capable of participating in the American political process"—simply don't apply to animals.

Also the reasoning doesn't fit with the Argument from Marginal Cases. The arguments for expanding the circle were made primarily in terms of groups—should we include this group or that—and not in terms of individuals. And once a group is included in the moral sphere, the marginal humans in that group seem to be included automatically—a package deal, as it were.

Along these lines, one could see the animal welfare movement as an attempt to expand the circle of human compassion—to claim that the sufferings of animals should have weight in our moral deliberation—without extending to animals equal moral consideration. Again, if we're viewing animals as a group, they don't qualify for inclusion on the same sorts of grounds other humans have. From this perspective, it's not clear what the relevance would be of pointing out that adult animals have many of the same capacities as marginal humans.

All this is by way of arguing that an historical, expanding-circle view of ethics does not support the Speciesist Critique. The expanding-circle view seems to expand group by group, and animals as a group just aren't going to measure up.

What the Speciesist Critique needs, and what I think Singer would argue for, is something different. It needs the following background premises:

(i) Ethics is fundamentally concerned with individuals.

(ii) Ethics is universal in the sense that it could, in theory, apply to anything that exists in the Universe.

Given these premises, the burden of proof is on anyone who wants to exclude *any* beings from the moral circle; further, any criterion of exclusion must apply to individuals. This then sets up the claim of the Argument from Marginal Cases that any criterion you choose that excludes animals will have to exclude marginal humans as well.

In the next chapter we will see that premise *ii* is used by some environmentalists to argue that not only humans and animals, but all living things, belong within the circle of morality, having inherent moral worth. Abolitionists will argue back that sentience, not life, is the ultimate criterion of inherent moral worth. We'll take up the debate between the Abolitionists and those environmentalists in the next chapter.

What are we to say here about premises *i* and *ii*? They seem clearly stated and have a ring of fairness to them. That they may not accord with the historical course of ethical reasoning isn't necessarily a problem: For instance, one could argue that the historical steps taken to figure out a solution to a certain mathematical problem aren't equivalent to the solution itself. Perhaps the same is true of ethics.

However, one difficulty with the Speciesist Critique (backed by *i* and *ii*) is how extreme the consequences threaten to be. I don't mean extreme in the sense of leading to the Abolitionist position: that would be begging the question. What I mean is that most Abolitionists, having argued for the Speciesist Critique, almost immediately start backtracking from its implications, implications which *even they find extreme*.

We'll see this as we consider two Abolitionist positions: Peter Singer's utilitarian view and Tom Regan's animal rights view.

Singer and utilitarianism

As you may remember from the chapter on moral theory, we distinguished between the hedonistic and preference versions of utilitarianism. Singer is a preference-utilitarian, but let's talk about the hedonistic version first.

The hedonistic version of utilitarianism says that the only thing good in itself is pleasure and the only thing bad in itself is pain; the right thing to do is to act in such a way as to create the greatest balance of pleasure over pain.

Hedonistic utilitarians in the past didn't usually include animals in their utilitarian calculations, but you can see how hedonistic utilitarianism might lead naturally to a strong pro-animal ethic: Assuming that animals feel pleasure and pain *and* assuming that pleasure and pain are what matter morally, it seems as if the pains/pleasures of animals should have to count alongside the pains/pleasures of human beings in utilitarian calculations.

Singer and others have often quoted with approval a footnote in the writings of the nineteenth-century utilitarian philosopher Jeremy Bentham, who anticipated a day when serious moral consideration would be given to animals. In that footnote, Bentham says: "The question is not, Can they *reason*? nor Can they *talk*? but, Can they *suffer*?"

Earlier, in the context of the Speciesist Critique, we saw that Singer is willing to weigh the indirect effects of experimenting on human babies versus animal infants. This should make sense to you in terms of a consequentialist theory like utilitarianism. A consequentialist judges an action right or wrong in terms of all its effects, both direct and indirect.

Extending the hedonistic version of utilitarianism to animals leads to some startling conclusions. Imagine that somehow a lifeboat ends up holding the following seven creatures:

1. *Three* healthy young people with lots of hopes and plans for the future; all have families. (Their body weight ranges from 110 to 180 pounds.)
2. *One* cranky old man, with no family. He's in poor health, but with a stubborn will to live and a strong desire to finish a backyard gardening project he's started. (He weighs 130 pounds.)
3. *Three* gorgeous large-breed puppies who will eventually end up with three different families. (Each puppy weighs 35 pounds.)

The lifeboat is badly overloaded and unless at least a hundred pounds is jettisoned, the boat will sink and everyone will die. To survive, the group must get rid of one of the four people or all three of the dogs. All the humans are fair-minded, but no one is volunteering to jump overboard. What should the group do?

Despite the likely first impulse of some young dog-lovers—"Toss the old guy"—the considered view of most people is that we'd be morally obligated to sacrifice the dogs. The lives of humans have a much greater moral worth than that of animals.

What would the hedonistic utilitarian say? From a pleasure/pain standpoint, it looks as if a good utilitarian case could be made for throwing the old man overboard. The old man is in poor health, isn't likely to live that long, and doesn't seem very happy anyway. The puppies are full of high spirits and likely to live happy lives with families they will make very happy.

Oddly, Singer, a utilitarian and a strong animal advocate who is against factory farming and most animal research, would say that the puppies should be sacrificed. Singer holds a preference view of utilitarianism, but it seems as if this version too should recommend that the puppies, rather than the old man, should live: After all, it's three sets of preferences against one.

However, Singer appeals not just to the number (or even strength) of preferences, but also to their content. Human preferences involve future goals and projects (e.g., raising a family, advancing in one's job, achieving a certain level of athletic skill) that animal preferences do not. These future-regarding preferences give an adult human life a dimension that animal life doesn't have. So while animal suffering counts the same as (comparable) human suffering, animal life doesn't count the same as human life.

Other preference-utilitarians holding abolitionist views would reject this conclusion of Singer's. They would say: Humans prefer to live and animals prefer to live, and if you're going to give equal consideration to humans and animals, you should count these preferences equally, whatever their content. Killing an animal cuts it off from a future life just as killing a human does. Putting aside indirect effects, the animal's future enjoyment (fulfillment of preferences) should count the same as the human's future enjoyment (fulfillment of preferences). That the human might be finishing a gardening project while the animal is merely romping around should make no difference in a utilitarian calculation.

Regan and animal rights

The philosopher who is best known for supporting animal rights is Tom Regan. Regan argues for a rights view of morality in general, then argues that animals, as well as humans, qualify as having rights. As with humans, the rights view is supposed to give the individual animals stronger protections than does utilitarianism, rejecting the sacrifice of the individual to the greater good. Regan says of his position:

> I regard myself as an advocate of animal rights—as a part of the animal rights movement. That movement, as I conceive it, is committed to a number of goals, including:
> - the total abolition of the use of animals in science;
> - the total dissolution of commercial animal agriculture;
> - the total elimination of commercial and sport hunting and trapping.

Regan gives marginal humans stronger protections than does Singer. Since infants have no preferences regarding the future, Singer's theory doesn't give them any direct protection against being used for medical research. Regan wants none of that. He wants marginal humans to have the right not to be used for research or food. Further he believes that the same reasoning gives the higher animals the same rights.

What is it that marginal cases and at least the higher animals have in common? Regan says that each of us (normal humans, marginal cases, and at least the higher animals) is "the experiencing subject of a life, a conscious creature having an individual welfare that has importance to us whatever our usefulness to others." Each is said to have "inherent value," which, for Regan, is the basis for having rights.

There are a couple of oddities about Regan's position.

Regan's "subject of a life" criterion is supposed to include both marginal humans and higher animals, while excluding creatures whose total consciousness might consist of, say, nothing but perception of light and dark shapes; this is done by demanding at least a degree of self- consciousness. However, it looks like he is setting the bar too high to include the very youngest children.

Also, in spite of his going beyond Singer to give animals a right to life, his conclusion in our lifeboat case would be the same as Singer's. (Regan presents his own version of the lifeboat case.)

For Regan, all the creatures in our lifeboat would have a right to life. This is one reason he thinks it is wrong to kill animals for food.

Tossing someone overboard might be permissible on a rights view in a situation where everyone's life was in danger. But one would think that on an animal rights view, the puppies would have an equal right to live—or at the very least (given the weight that must be jettisoned) that the three puppies together ought to have the same chance to live as any of the humans. One would think it would be fair to draw lots, with the three puppies having a chance of staying in the boat.

However, Regan would say that it's the puppies that should be tossed. This would be true even if we had to choose between sacrificing one person or a million dogs. He says that because humans can aspire

to things, their lives are much more valuable than the lives of animals.

Other abolitionists, with perhaps greater consistency, would count the life of a (higher) animal as equal to that of a human. On the other hand, when your morality might require, say, two humans to jump off the lifeboat to save the lives of six dogs, perhaps you've achieved consistency at the price of absurdity.

All the Abolitionist views take us to extremes that few people find morally reasonable.

Still, if we reject the Speciesist Critique and the Abolitionist views, how can we protest when the Amorphans come for us?

Notes and selected sources

Facts and factual issues

SOURCES

For factual information I have relied most heavily on:

Kim Masters Evans. *Animal Rights. Information Plus® Reference Series*. Detroit, MI: Thomson Gale, 2010, chs. 1, 2, 4 & 5.

Some other sources regarding factual information:

Deborah Blum. *The Monkey Wars*. Oxford: Oxford University Press, 1994. (The quotation is from p. 118.)

Nancy Day. *Animal Experimentation: Cruelty or Science?* Hillside, NJ: Enslow Publishers, 1994.

David DeGrazia. *Animal Rights: A Very Short Introduction* by Oxford: Oxford University Press, 2002, chs. 1, 5, & 7.

Encarta: "Animal Experimentation." Microsoft® Encarta® 2006. © 1993-2005 Microsoft Corporation. All rights reserved.

Andrew Harnack (ed.). *Animal Rights. An Opposing Viewpoints series*. Detroit, MI: Greenhaven Press, 2005.

F. Barbara Orlans, et al. (ed.). *The Human Use of Animals: Case Studies in Ethical Choice*. Oxford: Oxford University Press, 1998. Introduction.

Peter Singer. *Animal Liberation* New York: Harper Collins/Ecco Paperback, 2002.

NOTES

"…obviously the laboratories…." Blum, p. 118.

Animal minds

SOURCES

Peter Carruthers. *The Animals Issue: Moral Theory in Practice*. Cambridge: Cambridge University Press, 1992, ch. 8.

Marian Stamp Dawkins, "Scientific Basis for Assessing Suffering in Animals," in ed. Peter Singer, *In Defense of Animals: The Second Wave*. Oxford: Blackwell Publishing, 2006.

David DeGrazia. *Animal Rights* (above), chs. 3 & 4.

Daniel Dennett. *Kinds of Minds*. New York: Basic Books, 1996.

Donald R. Griffin. *Animal Minds*. Chicago: University of Chicago Press, 1992.

Leslie J. Rogers. *Minds of Their Own: Thinking and Awareness in Animals*. Boulder, CO: Westview Press, 1997.

Matthew Scully. *Dominion: The Power of Man, the Suffering of Animals, and the Call to Mercy*. New York: St. Martin's Griffin, 2002, ch. 5.

NOTES

"…Exactly what other animals find…." Dawkins, p. 37.

"…The Bramble Committee…." Dawkins, p. 34.

Pro-Status Quo Views

SOURCES

Industry web sites include:

American Meat Association: http://www.meatami.com

National Association for Biomedical Research: http://www.nabr.org

US Sportsman's Alliance: http://www.ussportsmen.org

Carl Cohen and Tom Regan. *The Animal Rights Debate* Oxford: Rowman & Littlefield Publishers Inc, 2001.

Carruthers. *The Animals Issue* (above). (He holds a contractarian view.)

NOTES

"Be fruitful, and multiply…." Genesis 1:28.

Animal Welfare views

SOURCES
Matthew Scully. *Dominion* (above).
Carl Cohen and Tom Regan. *The Animal Rights Debate* (above).

NOTES
"…Turning to the question…" Scully, pp. 287–8
"Animal welfare is not at issue…." Cohen/Regan, pp. 5–6.

The Speciesist Critique

SOURCES
Peter Singer. *Animal Liberation*. New York: Harper Collins/Ecco Paperback, 2002. and the selection in
Peter Singer, *The Expanding Circle: Ethics and Sociobiology*. New York: Farrar, Straus & Giroux, 1981.

NOTES
For Speciesist Critique, see Singer, *Animal Liberation*, ch 1.
"principle of equality" and other quotes, Singer, *Animal Liberation*, p. 5.

"At one time the benevolent…." Quoted in Singer, *The Expanding Circle*, p. xiii.

Singer and utilitarianism

SOURCES
Peter Singer, *Animal Rights* (above).

NOTES
Singer, *Animal Rights*, pp. 1–19.

Regan and animal rights

SOURCES
Tom Regan. *The Case for Animal Rights* (Berkeley, CA: University of California Press, 1983).
Tom Regan in Cohen/Regan above.

NOTES
"I regard myself…" Regan in Cohen/Regan, p. 127.
"experiencing subject of a life," "inherent worth" etc.: Regan, pp. 235–50.
Regan and lifeboat cases: Regan, pp. 351–3.

Definitions

(Terms are defined in the order in which they appeared in the text.)

1. *Vivisection*: Cutting open live animals (with or without anesthetic) for research purposes; more generally, any invasive experimentation on live animals.
2. *Draize test*: The testing of chemicals for cosmetics by putting them into the eyes of rabbits.
3. *The 3 R's*: A proposed program to *reduce* animal experimentation in general, *refine* animal experiments to reduce suffering, and to *replace* higher animals with lower or all live animals with tissue testing and such.
4. *Factory farms*: Industrial-style facilities where large numbers of livestock are raised.
5. *Battery cages*: Plain-wire cages used for the confinement of most laying hens.
6. *Gestation crates*: Narrow pens for the confinement of pregnant sows.
7. *Pro-Status Quo view*: "There are no serious moral problems with the way we treat animals today. We are entitled to use animals to fulfill human needs, from using them for medical research to raising them for food. The way we currently deal with the animals we use in these areas is morally acceptable." *Status Quo/unsympathetic*: Animal pain not a concern. *Status Quo/sympathetic*: Animal pain a concern, but our current practices are humane enough.
8. *Animal Welfare view*: "There are serious moral problems with the way we treat animals today. Though we are entitled to raise animals for food and use them for medical research, our current practices involve far more animals and cause them far more pain than is morally justifiable. We ought to make substantial changes in the way we treat animals."
9. *Abolitionist view*: "The way we treat animals today is morally wrong. Animals are entitled to a much higher moral status than we accord them: It is no more permissible for us to use animals for food or medical research than it would be for us to use human infants and mentally impaired adults for the same purposes. We need to radically change our treatment of animals, abolishing most of our current practices."

10. *Anthropomorphism*: Attributing human-like characteristics to non-humans without proper justification.

11. *Dominion*: The idea that humans have the right of use over the natural world—a right based on divine decree or the natural order.

12. *Animal rights*: The idea that animals have certain natural rights that should be respected by humans. (This idea often underlies an Abolitionist position.)

13. *Speciesism*: A term implying that discrimination against animals on account of their species is comparable to discrimination against groups of humans based on skin color or gender.

14. *Marginal cases*: A phrase covering those human beings who do not have the normal adult human capacities such as reason and complex emotions. (Also referred to as "non-paradigmatic humans.")

Questions

(Please explain your answers, making specific reference to relevant passages in the discussion.)

1. What are some arguments in favor of using animals in medical research?

2. What are some of the complaints about the way research animals are treated?

3. There are now laws in place to protect animals used in research: What sorts of protections are these laws supposed to provide? Does everyone agree these protections are adequate?

4. What are the commercial advantages of factory farming?

5. What complaints have been made against the treatment of those animals that are factory-farmed.

6. What legal protections do factory-farmed animals have?

7. Define the "Pro-Status Quo," "Animal Welfare," and "Abolitionist" positions on the treatment of animals.

8. Which of those three positions most closely resembles your own position? What is your reasoning for holding the position you do?

9. "Being used by humans is overall a good thing for animals." Give an argument for this claim. What's a possible problem with the claim?

10. Is eating animals natural for humans? Does something being "natural" necessarily mean it is good? Explain.

11. Present an argument for an Animal Welfare view. How would those holding a Status Quo view respond? How would those holding an Abolitionist view respond?

12. What is the Abolitionist "Argument from Racism"? What are some possible problems with that argument?

13. What is the Abolitionist "Argument from Marginal Cases"? What are some possible problems with that argument?

14. Both Singer and Regan argue that if weight had to be jettisoned from a lifeboat to keep the boat from sinking, any animals aboard should be sacrificed before any humans. What is their reasoning? Do you find it consistent with their general views of the moral status of animals?

18

Animals
Readings

David DeGrazia presents the case for animals feeling pain

Cornered in the garage, the trembling racoon slowly backs up, focusing her eyes on the man who approaches with broom in hand. The man, who wants to chase the racoon out of the garage, sees the animal's behaviour as fearful. Her leg caught in a steel trap that has cut deep into the skin, a fox struggles for hours to free herself, to no avail, before slowly chewing off her leg and separating herself from the trap. A passerby who sees the fox just as she tears away from the trap—and her leg—perceives her as experiencing great pain and suffering. Staying at a kennel for the first time, as his human companion family takes a trip out of town, a dog is hypervigilant and jumpy, and urinates on the floor. The kennel worker assumes that the dog is anxious in this unfamiliar setting.

The attributions of fear to the racoon, pain and suffering to the fox, and even anxiety to the dog are natural enough, but are they well-grounded? Does available evidence support such interpretations of animals' behaviour? More generally, what sorts of mental lives do animals have? Although this question quickly leads into great complexity, both scientific and philosophical, this chapter offers only a preliminary and quite general discussion of the mental

From *Animal Rights: A Very Short Introduction*, by David DeGrazia. Oxford: Oxford University Press, 2002, ch. 3.

lives of animals—of what sorts of beings animals are, or what they are like. The chapter's central claim is that a wide range of animals, including most or all vertebrates and probably some invertebrates, possess a rich variety of feelings. Before going to the evidence, though, we should clarify a few key terms.

Some basic concepts

To have any mental states or mental life at all, a being must have some *awareness* or *consciousness*. But what is awareness? We may elucidate the term by reference to other familiar terms and by use of examples.

A human or animal is aware at a particular time if he or she is having any subjective experiences at that time. Such experiences include all states of consciousness when we are awake and even those confused modes of thinking and feeling known as dream experiences. A closely related concept is that of *sentience*—the capacity to have *feelings*. Feelings, in turn, include both *felt sensations*, such as pain and nausea, and *emotional states*, such as fear and joy. All sentient beings have states of awareness. For example, presumably all sentient animals can feel at least painful and pleasant sensations.

It is important to distinguish awareness from *nociception*. Nociception, the first event in a sequence that often involves pain, is the detection of potentially noxious, or tissue-damaging, stimuli by specialized neural end-organs – nociceptors – which fire impulses along axons (nerve fibres that serve as pathways). Such stimuli include cutting, pressure, pricking, heat, cold, inflammation of tissues, and muscle spasms. While nociception itself is not a state of awareness or consciousness, it often occurs together with such states, typically pain. With Bernard Rollin, one might think of nociception as 'the machinery or plumbing of pain', although in atypical cases there can be nociception without pain—as when a severed spinal cord permits a paraplegic to retain a withdrawal reflex but prevents the occurrence of pain, or in an animal under general anaesthesia.

While there is no perfect definition of 'awareness', our experience and common sense are sufficient to understand this basic concept. Whenever we are awake or dreaming, we experience subjective states; and we know that, in certain sleeping states and under general anaesthesia, we have no such subjective states. As we will see, empirical evidence strongly supports the common-sense judgement that many animals also have states of awareness, even if their consciousness is less complex, reflective, and language-laden than human consciousness typically is.

Evidence for pain and other sensations in animals

Although nearly everyone believes that many animals experience pain, a responsible discussion of animal mentality must consider whether evidence supports this or any other attribution. But here, as with other mental states, we need a working definition to clarify what we are looking for. Our own experience—or phenomenology—of pain combined with scientific study of the phenomenon supports roughly this understanding: *pain is an unpleasant or aversive sensory experience typically associated with actual or potential tissue damage.* (This definition doesn't cover 'emotional pain', a figurative extension of the most literal sense of 'pain'; 'suffering' is often an apt and more literal substitute for 'emotional pain'.)

Now, when we ask whether a particular sort of creature experiences a type of mental state, four kinds of evidence are relevant. First, human phenomenology helps to categorize mental states and informs us of what they feel like. From this starting-point, which can help to establish a working definition, we can

argue that non-human animals have a particular mental state on the strength of three other sources of information: animals' behaviour in context, their physiology, and functional-evolutionary considerations. The latter address the adaptive value of a type of mental state for a specific kind of creature living in a particular environmental niche.

Let us consider such evidence in connection with pain. Certainly, animals often behave as if in pain. Any of these three types of behaviour is at least somewhat suggestive of pain: (1) avoiding or escaping a noxious stimulus (for example, withdrawing a paw from a sharp object); (2) getting assistance (for example, crying out) after a noxious event; and (3) limiting the use of an overworked or injured body part to permit rest and healing (for example, immobilizing a pulled muscle and favouring another limb). The vast majority of animals, including insects, exhibit behaviours of type (1), though in some animals such behaviours may be due to nociception without pain or some similar type of non-conscious response to stimuli. Vertebrates and perhaps some invertebrates also display behaviours of type (3). Type (2), which may be relevant only to comparatively social animals, is common among mammals and birds. Evidence of learning and adaptation to novel circumstances strengthen the claim that behaviours of any of these three types indicate pain—and therefore sentience. Such evidence is found in the case of vertebrates and at least some invertebrate species such as octopuses and squid.

Turning now to physiological evidence for animal pain, there is extensive commonality across vertebrate species of the biological machinery apparently required for pain. Pain is associated with certain physiological changes, including measurable nerve impulses in specific pathways and metabolic and electrical activity in particular parts of the brain. In turn, these events elicit other physiological responses such as changes in the sympathetic adrenomedullary system and the hypothalamic-pituitary-adrenocortical system. Not only are the neurophysiology and neuroanatomy of pain quite similar in these animals; they also share the biological mechanisms for modulating pain, such as endogenous opiates. Moreover, anaesthesia and analgesia control what is apparently pain in all vertebrates and some invertebrates. Indeed, if animals were not significantly analogous to humans in the capacity for pain and other aversive mental states, it would be senseless to use animals as models for the study of these states in humans.

Consideration of pain's function in the context of evolutionary theory constitutes another form of evidence for animal pain. The biological function of pain is evidently (1) to provide an organism information about where tissue damage may occur, is occurring, or has occurred and (2) to motivate responses that are likely to avoid or minimize damage, such as rapid limb movement away from a noxious stimulus or immobilizing muscles to permit recuperation. Pain's unpleasantness provides the motivation for adaptive, life-preserving responses.

Then again, one might reply, perhaps nociception or some similar event—without pain or any conscious awareness—would function equally well to keep animals out of harm's way, in which case functional-evolutionary arguments might not support the case for animal pain. But evolution tends to preserve successful biological systems. And rather than spontaneously producing new creatures well-suited for particular niches, with no 'design constraints', evolution operates within the limits of the genetic endowment and anatomical systems inherited from evolutionary forebears. Now we know that in humans the ability to feel pain is important for functioning and survival. Humans with significantly impaired or no ability to feel pain, such as people with anaesthetic leprosy, are in danger of not surviving without extraordinary attention. The fact that neural structures similar to those that produce our consciousness are found in vertebrates—in combination with their pain behaviour—suggests that pain has a similar function for them and that natural selection has preserved the capacity for pain throughout the evolution of at least the vertebrates.

[...]

Evidence for distress, fear, anxiety, and suffering

While pain is sensory and therefore associated with specific body parts, distress, fear, anxiety, and suffering are emotional and therefore associated with the entire subject who experiences them. Before considering specific evidence for the occurrence of these states in animals, let us clarify the concepts themselves.

We may start with suffering, which has a sort of umbrella relationship to the others. Note that suffering differs from pain since either can occur without the other. If I pinch my hand, I have pain without suffering, whereas someone having a panic attack suffers without pain. Nor does suffering equal distress; if you are only mildly distressed due to a deadline, you do not suffer. *Suffering is a highly unpleasant emotional state associated with more-than-minimal pain or distress.* Since suffering is the defined in terms of pain and distress, the evidence for suffering is the same as that for pain or distress—or high degrees thereof. Pain we discussed earlier.

Distress is a typically unpleasant emotional response to the perception of environmental challenges or to equilibrium-disrupting internal stimuli. It can be caused by such diverse phenomena as the sight of approaching predators, the belief that one will fail, or diarrhoea. Distress can take the form of various more specific mental states, such as fear, anxiety, frustration, and boredom. While a thorough exploration of distress would investigate all such related mental states, here we will consider just fear and anxiety.

Fear motivates focused responses to perceived dangers and preparation for future responses. While perhaps mild fear can be pleasant, as with skiing, fear tends to be unpleasant. *Fear is a typically unpleasant emotional response to a perceived danger (usually in the immediate environment), a response that focuses attention to facilitate protective action.* By contrast, anxiety involves a generalized, as opposed to focused, state of heightened arousal and attention to the environment. It usually immobilizes our mental resources and inhibits our action, so we can attend to our environment until we have determined how to respond to any challenges that may arise. While fear and anxiety are closely related, anxiety serves especially well in unfamiliar situations, explaining why it is less focused than fear. Moreover, at least with humans, often the object of anxiety is possible damage to one's self-image. *Anxiety is a typically unpleasant emotional response to a perceived threat to one's physical or psychological well-being, a response that generally inhibits action and involves heightened arousal and attention to the environment.* Commonsensically, fear and anxiety have similar protective functions in complementary settings. For example, a cat may be anxious in the novel setting of a veterinarian's waiting room. In her second visit there, she may feel fear due to remembering a painful shot she received during the previous visit. But let us move beyond common-sense claims to rigorous evidence.

Consider the evidence for anxiety, which of the mental states under discussion is most likely to inspire scepticism. First, typical behavioural and physiological features of human anxiety are also found in many animals in circumstances that are likely to make animals anxious, if any would: (1) autonomic hyperactivity—pounding heart, sweating, increased pulse rate and respiration, etc.; (2) motor tension, as seen in jumpiness; (3) inhibition of normal behaviours in novel situations; and (4) hyperattentiveness, as seen in visual scanning. Consistent with the definition of anxiety, these findings add up to strong behavioural evidence and some physiological evidence for anxiety in animals. In addition, we have already seen the adaptive value, or evolutionary function, of anxiety: it permits a creature to inhibit action and attend carefully to the environment in preparation for protective action.

Further, human anxiety and some mental states in animals—which we infer to be anxiety—are mediated in similar ways by certain drugs that cause similar neurophysiological and neurochemical changes. In one kind of test, for example, randomly punishing thirsty rats causes reduced drinking, the inhibition of a normal behaviour. But giving the rats an anti-anxiety drug restores drinking to more normal rates. Another kind of test places animals in novel settings such as brightly lit open spaces. Animals who are given anti-anxiety drugs beforehand exhibit what is apparently less anxious behaviour than animals who are not given these drugs. Moreover, when drugs that *induce* anxiety in humans are given to animal subjects, they display the behaviours and physiological responses associated with anxiety.

Since most of the subjects of these latter studies were mammals, the following findings are of special interest. Scientists have long known that benzodiazepine receptors, which in humans are the substrate for nearly all known anti-anxiety agents, are also found in mammals. More recent research demonstrated that none of the five invertebrates tested, nor the one cartilaginous fish (an animal at the border between vertebrates and invertebrates), had these receptors. Yet all the other species examined—including three species of birds, a lizard, frog, and turtle, and three species of bony fishes—had such receptors, providing some additional evidence that at least most vertebrates can experience anxiety.

While the available evidence, taken together, supports this conclusion, it does not imply that human anxiety and animal anxiety are qualitatively similar beyond a common unpleasantness and heightened arousal and attention. Undoubtedly, the language-laden complexity of human thought produces anxious experiences very different from those of animals. The present claim is that animals representing a wide range of species are capable of having anxious states, as captured in our definition of 'anxiety'.

Given the close relationship between anxiety and fear, as explained above, one would expect that animals capable of being anxious are also capable of being afraid. Supporting this common-sense judgement is the fact that all vertebrates have autonomic-nervous and limbic systems, which contain the basic substrates of fear and anxiety. And, of course, such animals often behave as if in fear—a state that has great adaptive value from an evolutionary standpoint.

But if certain animals can experience fear and anxiety—which are forms of distress—there is no further question of whether they can experience distress. Can they suffer, though? Suffering, again, is a highly unpleasant emotional state associated with more-than-minimal pain or distress. We have already argued that vertebrates can experience pain and distress. But if some animals can experience these states only *minimally*—that is, not very intensely—that would imply that they cannot suffer. It is unclear what would count as evidence that certain animals could have only minimal pain and distress, beyond the general speculation that the most primitive sentient creatures have dim mental lives. In any case, since apparently all vertebrates and at least some invertebrates are sentient, I recommend the tentative assumption that at least most vertebrates can suffer.

Responding to some sceptical arguments

The evidence we have considered supports the thesis that a wide range of animals, including most or all vertebrates and probably some invertebrates, possess a variety of feelings. It will not be possible, however, to discuss evidence for more sophisticated mental phenomena that animals may or may not share with humans—such as thinking or reasoning, language, and autonomous decision-making. (I have discussed these elsewhere.) But it will be worthwhile to identify and rebut several alleged grounds for scepticism about animals' mental lives.

[…]

Some philosophers have argued that because *language* is necessary for awareness, animals must lack awareness. Granting the implicit assumption that presently existing animals lack language—although a few highly trained Great Apes and dolphins may constitute exceptions—the argument remains unsound. While language is certainly necessary for verbal expression of one's states of awareness, there is no reason to think that language is always or even typically necessary for *having* those states. If it were, then human babies would be incapable of experiencing pain, pleasure, and fear before they acquired language—a notion whose implausibility is almost universally recognized today. It is true that some specific manifestations of feelings, such as fear *of one's own mortality*, involve such abstract thinking that they may require linguistic ability just to form the associated thoughts (for example, of mortality). But that in no way suggests that creatures lacking language have no feelings.

One also sometimes hears the claim that a high degree of *rationality* is necessary for states of awareness, including feelings. But there is no good reason to accept this claim. Certainly, a high degree of rationality is necessary for complex reasoning in response to certain feelings—such as devising elaborate plans for improving your health, thereby reducing the pain and distress caused by your illness. But to experience pain, distress, and other feelings we have discussed does not require sophisticated reasoning.

A sceptic might also attempt to challenge the thesis that animals have awareness by arguing that they lack *self-awareness*. But such an argument either fails to distinguish awareness and self-awareness or supposes that the former depends on the latter. But note that, conceptually, self-awareness is more specific and complex than basic awareness, involving the concept of a self. And, factually, there is no clear reason why all awareness must involve awareness of oneself. To see a tree requires awareness—assuming we use the term 'see' in a way that implies conscious experience—but this visual experience doesn't seem to require any conscious noting of who is doing the seeing. Thus, we typically think that even very young infants can have some feelings, such as painful and pleasant sensations, long before they achieve any significant form of self-awareness.

Then again, one might argue that, even if animals have some mental states, their lack of self-awareness entails that they lack some specified mental states such as suffering. Perhaps the previously stated definition of 'suffering' is incomplete; according to Eric Cassell, suffering involves a sense of oneself as existing over time and, in suffering, one feels a threat to the integrity of the self. While such sceptics tend to leave terms like 'integrity of the self' unhelpfully vague, let us grant the assumption that suffering involves a sense of oneself as existing over time—that is, *temporal self-awareness*.

The chief difficulty with this case for scepticism about animal suffering is that there are very good reasons to think that many animals possess temporal self-awareness. Consider, for example, our assertion—which probably few people will deny—that vertebrates experience fear. Fear, I suggest, is impossible unless the subject has some awareness of persisting into the future. After all, one fears something that might happen to one—in the (possibly very near) future. One might, of course, preserve scepticism about temporal self-awareness, and suffering, in animals by insisting that they are incapable of fear. But we presented evidence for fear in animals and we have seen no evidence or arguments supporting the claim that animals lack temporal self-awareness.

Further considerations, including the following two, bolster the attribution of temporal self-awareness to many animals. First, the growing field of cognitive ethology—which examines animal behaviour in the context of evolutionary biology—tends to support the attribution of beliefs, desires, and intentional actions to many animals. The central claim is that the *best explanation* of their behaviour, given everything we know about them, requires these attributions. But if Rufus the dog wants (desires) to go outside to bury a bone, and intentionally does so, that suggests that Rufus has some awareness of himself as persisting over time; desires usually concern states of affairs involving oneself in the future, and intentions are carried out over time. Second, there is considerable independent evidence that vertebrate animals have memories as well as expectations for the future. For example, it has been rigorously demonstrated that many birds have extensive recall of where they have hidden food. Now if, as seems likely, any of an animal's memories or expectations include representations of the *animal herself*, as in a memory of being hurt, that would entail some temporal self-awareness. In conclusion, while suffering—along with certain other feelings, including fear—may require a degree of temporal self-awareness, there is a strong case that at least most vertebrates have such self-awareness.

[…]

Questions

1. According to DeGrazia, what sort of evidence supports the claim that animals can feel pain?
2. Critics have argued that animals can't suffer because they (a) lack language, (b) lack rationality and/or (c) lack self-awareness. How does DeGrazia argue against each of these claims?

Robert Nozick asks what moral constraints there are, if any, on the behavior of humans toward animals

We can illuminate the status and implications of moral side constraints by considering living beings for whom such stringent side constraints (or any at all) usually are not considered appropriate: namely, nonhuman animals. Are there any limits to what we may do to animals? Have animals the moral status of mere *objects*? Do some purposes fail to entitle us to impose great costs on animals? What entitles us to use them at all?

Animals count for something. Some higher animals, at least, ought to be given some weight in people's deliberations about what to do. It is difficult to *prove* this. (It is also difficult to prove that people count for something!) We first shall adduce particular examples, and then arguments. If you felt like snapping your fingers, perhaps to the beat of some music, and you knew that by some strange causal connection your snapping your fingers would cause 10,000 contented, unowned cows to die after great pain and suffering,

From *Anarchy, State, and Utopia*, by Robert Nozick. New York: Basic Books, 1974, pp. 35–47. Copyright © 1974 Robert Nozick. Reprinted by permission of Basic Books, a member of the Perseus Books Group.

or even painlessly and instantaneously, would it be perfectly all right to snap your fingers? Is there some reason why it would be morally wrong to do so?

Some say people should not do so because such acts brutalize them and make them more likely to take the lives of *persons*, solely for pleasure. These acts that are morally unobjectionable in themselves, they say, have an undesirable moral spillover […] But why *should* there be such a spillover? If it is, in itself, perfectly all right to do anything at all to animals for any reason whatsoever, then provided a person realizes the clear line between animals and persons and keeps it in mind as he acts, why should killing animals tend to brutalize him and make him more likely to harm or kill persons? Do butchers commit more murders? (Than other persons who have knives around?) If I enjoy hitting a baseball squarely with a bat, does this significantly increase the danger of my doing the same to someone's head? Am I not capable of understanding that people differ from baseballs, and doesn't this understanding stop the spillover? Why should things be different in the case of animals?

[…]

My purpose here […] is to pursue the notion of moral side constraints, not the issue of eating animals. Though I should say that in my view the extra benefits Americans today can gain from eating animals do *not* justify doing it. So we shouldn't. One ubiquitous argument, not unconnected with side constraints, deserves mention: because people eat animals, they raise more than otherwise would exist without this practice. To exist for a while is better than never to exist at all. So (the argument concludes) the animals are better off because we have the practice of eating them. Though this is not our object, fortunately it turns out that we really, all along, benefit them! (If tastes changed and people no longer found it enjoyable to eat animals, should those concerned with the welfare of animals steel themselves to an unpleasant task and continue eating them?) I trust I shall not be misunderstood as saying that animals are to be given the same moral weight as people if I note that the parallel argument about people would not look very convincing. We can imagine that population problems lead every couple or group to limit their children to some number fixed in advance. A given couple, having reached the number, proposes to have an additional child and dispose of it at the age of three (or twenty-three) by sacrificing it or using it for some gastronomic purpose. In justification, they note that the child will not exist at all if this is not allowed; and surely it is better for it to exit for some number of years. However, once a person exists, not everything compatible with his overall existence being a net plus can be done, even by those who created him.

[…]

What about persons distinguishes them from animals, so that stringent constraints apply to how persons may be treated, yet not to how animals may be treated? Could beings from another galaxy stand to *us* as it is usually thought we do to animals, and if so, would they be justified in treating us as means à la utilitarianism? Are organisms arranged on some ascending scale, so that any may be sacrificed or caused to suffer to achieve a greater total benefit for those not lower on the scale? Such an elitist hierarchical view would

distinguish three moral statuses (forming an interval partition of the scale):

Status 1: The being may not be sacrificed, harmed, and so on, for any other organism's sake.

Status 2: The being may be sacrificed, harmed, and so on, only for the sake of beings higher on the scale, but not for the sake of beings at the same level.

Status 3: The being may be sacrificed, harmed, and so on, for the sake of other beings at the same or higher levels on the scale.

If animals occupy status 3 and we occupy status 1, what occupies status 2? Perhaps *we* occupy status 2! Is it morally forbidden to use people as means for the benefit of others, or is it only forbidden to use them for the sake of other *people*, that is, for beings at the same level? Do ordinary views include the possibility of more than one significant moral divide (like that between persons and animals), and *might one come on the other side of human beings?* Some theological views hold that God is permitted to sacrifice people for his own purposes. We also might imagine people encountering beings from another planet who traverse in their childhood whatever "stages" of moral development our developmental psychologists can identify. These beings claim that they all continue on through fourteen further sequential stages, each being necessary to enter the next one. However, they cannot explain to us (primitive as we are) the content and modes of reasoning of these later stages. These beings claim that we may be sacrificed for their well-being, or at least in order to preserve their higher capacities. They say that they see the truth of this now that they are in their moral maturity, though they didn't as children at what is our highest level of moral development. […] Do our moral views permit our sacrifice for the sake of these beings' higher capacities, including their moral ones?

[…]

Questions

1. "If you felt like snapping your fingers, perhaps to the beat of some music, and you knew that by some strange causal connection your snapping

your fingers would cause 10,000 contented, un-owned cows to die after great pain and suffering, or even painlessly and instantaneously, would it be perfectly all right to snap your fingers? Is there some reason why it would be morally wrong to do so?" Answer these questions of Nozick's, giving your reasons.

2. "Some say people should not do so [as in #1] because such acts brutalize them and make them more likely to take the lives of *persons*, solely for

pleasure. These acts that are morally unobjectionable in themselves, they say, have an undesirable moral spillover." What is Nozick's criticism of this idea?

3. Do you agree that if we lived in a universe with much higher life forms, that it would be all right for those higher beings to sacrifice us just as we sacrifice animals?

Peter Singer argues that all creatures who are capable of suffering are entitled to equal concern

[…]

[O]ne might cling to the view that the demand for equality among human beings is based on the actual equality of the different races and sexes. Although, it may be said, humans differ as individuals, there are no differences between the races and sexes as such. From the mere fact that a person is black or a woman we cannot infer anything about that person's intellectual or moral capacities. This, it may be said, is why racism and sexism are wrong. The white racist claims that whites are superior to blacks, but this is false; although there are differences among individuals, some blacks are superior to some whites in all of the capacities and abilities that could conceivably be relevant. The opponent of sexism would say the same: a person's sex is no guide to his or her abilities, and this is why it is unjustifiable to discriminate on the basis of sex.

The existence of individual variations that cut across the lines of race or sex, however, provides us with no defense at all against a more sophisticated opponent of equality, one who proposes that, say, the interests of all those with IQ scores below 100 be given less consideration than the interests of those with ratings over 100. Perhaps those scoring below the mark would, in this society, be made the slaves of those scoring higher. Would a hierarchical society of

this sort really be so much better than one based on race or sex? I think not. But if we tie the moral principle of equality to the factual equality of the different races or sexes, taken as a whole, our opposition to racism and sexism does not provide us with any basis for objecting to this kind of inegalitarianism.

There is a second important reason why we ought not to base our opposition to racism and sexism on any kind of factual equality, even the limited kind that asserts that variations in capacities and abilities are spread evenly among the different races and between the sexes: we can have no absolute guarantee that these capacities and abilities really are distributed evenly, without regard to race or sex, among human beings. So far as actual abilities are concerned there do seem to be certain measurable differences both among races and between sexes. These differences do not, of course, appear in every case; they appear only when averages are taken. More important still, we do not yet know how many of these differences are really due to the different genetic endowments of the different races and sexes, and how many are due to poor schools, poor housing, and other factors that are the result of past and continuing discrimination Perhaps all of the important differences will eventually prove to be environmental rather than genetic. Anyone opposed to racism and sexism will certainly hope that this will be so, for it will make the task of ending discrimination a lot easier; nevertheless, it would be dangerous to rest the case against racism and sexism on the belief that all significant differences are environmental in origin. The opponent of, say, racism who takes this line will be unable to avoid conceding that if differences in ability did after all prove to have some genetic connection with race racism would in some way be defensible.

Fortunately there is no need to pin the case for equality on one particular outcome of a scientific investigation. The appropriate response to those who claim to have found evidence of genetically based differences in ability among the races or between the sexes is not to stick to the belief that the genetic explanation must be wrong, whatever evidence to the contrary may turn up; instead we should make it quite clear that the claim to equality does not depend on intelligence, moral capacity, physical strength, or similar matters of fact. Equality is a moral idea, not an assertion of fact. There is no logically compelling reason for assuming that a factual difference in ability between two people justifies any difference in the amount of consideration we give to their needs and interests. *The principle of the equality of human beings is not a description of an alleged actual equality among humans: it is a prescription of how we should treat human beings.*

Jeremy Bentham, the founder of the reforming utilitarian school of moral philosophy, incorporated the essential basis of moral equality into his system of ethics by means of the formula: "Each to count for one and none for more than one." In other words, the interests of every being affected by an action are to be taken into account and given the same weight as the like interests of any other being. A later utilitarian, Henry Sidgwick, put the point in this way: "The good of any one individual is of no more importance, from the point of view (if I may say so) of the Universe, than the good of any other." More recently the leading figures in contemporary moral philosophy have shown a great deal of agreement in specifying as a fundamental presupposition of their moral theories some similar requirement that works to give everyone's interests equal consideration—although these writers generally cannot agree on how this requirement is best formulated.[1]

It is an implication of this principle of equality that our concern for others and our readiness to consider their interests ought not to depend on what they are like or on what abilities they may possess. Precisely what our concern or consideration requires us to do may vary according to the characteristics of those affected by what we do: concern for the well-being of children growing up in America would require that we teach them to read; concern for the well-being of

pigs may require no more than that we leave them with other pigs in a place where there is adequate food and room to run freely. But the basic element—the taking into account of the interests of the being, whatever those interests may be—must, according to the principle of equality, be extended to all beings, black or white, masculine or feminine, human or nonhuman.

[…]

It is on this basis that the case against racism and the case against sexism must both ultimately rest; and it is in accordance with this principle that the altitude that we may call "speciesism," by analogy with racism, must also be condemned. Speciesism—the word is not an attractive one, but I can think of no better term—is a prejudice or attitude of bias in favor of the interests of members of one's own species and against those of members of other species. […][2]

Many philosophers and other writers have proposed the principle of equal consideration of interests, in some form or other, as a basic moral principle; but not many of them have recognized that this principle applies to members of other species as well as to our own. Jeremy Bentham was one of the few who did realize this. In a forward-looking passage written at a time when black slaves had been freed by the French but in the British dominions were still being treated in the way we now treat animals, Bentham wrote:

> The day *may* come when the rest of the animal creation may acquire those rights which never could have been withholden from them but by the hand of tyranny. The French have already discovered that the blackness of the skin is no reason why a human being should be abandoned without redress to the caprice of a tormentor. It may one day come to be recognized that the number of the legs, the villosity of the skin, or the termination of the *os sacrum* are reasons equally insufficient for abandoning a sensitive being to the same fate. What else is it that should trace the insuperable line? Is it the faculty of reason, or perhaps the faculty of discourse? But a full-grown horse or dog is beyond comparison a more rational, as well as a more conversable animal, than an infant of a day or a week or even a month, old. But suppose they were otherwise, what would it avail? The question is not, Can they *reason?* nor Can they *talk?* but, Can they *suffer?*[3]

In this passage Bentham points to the capacity for suffering as the vital characteristic that gives a being the right to equal consideration. The capacity for suffering—or more strictly, for suffering and/or enjoyment or happiness—is not just another characteristic like the capacity for language or higher mathematics. Bentham is not saying that those who try to mark "the insuperable line" that determines whether the interests of a being should be considered happen to have chosen the wrong characteristic. By saying that we must consider the interests of all beings with the capacity for suffering or enjoyment Bentham does not arbitrarily exclude from consideration any interests at all—as those who draw the line with reference to the possession of reason or language do. The capacity for suffering and enjoyment is *a prerequisite for having interests at all*, a condition that must be satisfied before we can speak of interests in a meaningful way. It would be nonsense to say that it was not in the interests of a stone to be kicked along the road by a schoolboy. A stone does not have interests because it cannot suffer. Nothing that we can do to it could possibly make any difference to its welfare. The capacity for suffering and enjoyment is, however, not only necessary, but also sufficient for us to say that a being has interests—at an absolute minimum, an interest in not suffering. A mouse, for example, does have an interest in not being kicked along the road, because it will suffer if it is.

Although Bentham speaks of "rights" in the passage I have quoted, the argument is really about equality rather than about rights. Indeed, in a different passage, Bentham famously described "natural rights" as "nonsense" and "natural and imprescriptible rights" as "nonsense upon stilts." He talked of moral rights as a shorthand way of referring to protections that people and animals morally ought to have, but the real weight of the moral argument does not rest on the assertion of the existence of the right, for this in turn has to be justified on the basis of the possibilities for suffering and happiness. In this way we can argue tor equality for animals without getting embroiled in philosophical controversies about the ultimate nature of rights.

In misguided attempts to refute the arguments of this book, some philosophers have gone to much trouble developing arguments to show that animals do not have rights. They have claimed that to have rights a being must be autonomous, or must be a member of a community, or must have the ability to respect the rights of others, or must possess a sense of justice. These claims are irrelevant to the case for animal liberation. The language of rights is a convenient political shorthand. It is even more valuable in the era of thirty-second TV news clips than it was in Bentham's day; but in the argument for a radical change in our attitude to animals, it is in no way necessary.

If a being suffers there can be no moral justification for refusing to take that suffering into consideration. No matter what the nature of the being, the principle of equality requires that its suffering be counted equally with the like suffering—insofar as rough comparisons can be made—of any other being. If a being is not capable of suffering, or to experiencing enjoyment or happiness, there is nothing to be taken into account. So the limit of sentience (using the term as a convenient if not strictly accurate shorthand for the capacity to suffer and/or experience enjoyment) is the only defensible boundary of concern for the interests of others. To mark this boundary by some other characteristic like intelligence or rationality would be to mark it in an arbitrary manner. Why not choose some other characteristic, like skin color?

Racists violate the principle of equality by giving greater weight to the interests of members of their own race when there is a clash between their interests and the interests of those of another race. Sexists violate the principle of equality by favoring the interests of their own sex. Similarly, speciesists allow the interests of their own species to override the greater interests of members of other species. The pattern is identical in each case.

[…]

Animals can feel pain. As we saw earlier, there can be no moral justification for regarding the pain (or pleasure) that animals feel as less important than the same amount of pain (or pleasure) felt by humans. But what practical consequences follow from this conclusion? To prevent misunderstanding I shall spell out what I mean a little more fully.

If I give a horse a hard slap across its rump with my open hand, the horse may start, but it presumably feels little pain. Its skin is thick enough to protect it against a mere slap. If I slap a baby in the same way, however, the baby will cry and presumably feel pain, for its skin is more sensitive. So it is worse to slap a baby than a horse, if both slaps are administered with equal force. But there must be some kind of blow—I don't know exactly what it would be, but perhaps a blow with a heavy stick—that would cause the horse as much pain as we cause a baby by slapping it with our hand. That is what I mean by "the same amount of pain," and if we consider it wrong to inflict that much pain on a baby for no good reason, then we must, unless we are speciesists, consider it equally wrong to inflict the same amount of pain on a horse for no good reason.

Other differences between humans and animals cause other complications. Normal adult human beings have mental capacities that will, in certain circumstances, lead them to suffer more than animals would in the same circumstances. If, for instance, we decided to perform extremely painful or lethal scientific experiments on normal adult humans, kidnapped at random from public parks for this purpose, adults who enjoy strolling in parks would become fearful that they would be kidnapped. The resultant terror would be a form of suffering additional to the pain of the experiment. The same experiments performed on nonhuman animals would cause less suffering, since the animals would not have the anticipatory dread of being kidnapped and experimented upon. This does not mean, of course, that it would be *right* to perform the experiment on animals, but only that there is a reason, which is *not* speciesist, for preferring to use animals rather than normal adult human beings, if the experiment is to be done at all. It should be noted, however, that this same argument gives us a reason for preferring to use human infants— orphans perhaps—or severely retarded human beings for experiments, rather than adults, since infants and retarded humans would also have no idea of what was going to happen to them. So far as this argument is concerned nonhuman animals and infants and retarded humans are in the same category; and if we use this argument to justify experiments on nonhuman animals, we have to ask ourselves whether we are also prepared to allow experiments on human infants and retarded adults; and if we make a distinction between animals and these humans, on what basis can we do it, other than a bare-faced—and morally indefensible— preference for members of our own species?

There are many matters in which the superior mental powers of normal adult humans make a difference: anticipation, more detailed memory, greater knowledge of what is happening, and so on. Yet these differences do not all point to greater suffering on the part of the normal human being. Sometimes animals may suffer more because of their more limited understanding. If, for instance, we are taking prisoners in wartime, we can explain to them that although they must submit to capture, search, and confinement, they will not otherwise be harmed and will be set free at the conclusion of hostilities. If we capture wild animals, however, we cannot explain that we are not threatening their lives. A wild animal cannot distinguish an attempt to overpower and confine from an attempt to kill; the one causes as much terror as the other.

It may be objected that comparisons of the sufferings of different species are impossible to make and that for this reason when the interests of animals and humans clash the principle of equality gives no guidance. It is probably true that comparisons of suffering between members of different species cannot be made precisely, but precision is not essential. Even if we were to prevent the infliction of suffering on animals only when it is quite certain that the interests of humans will not be affected to anything like the extent that animals are affected, we would be forced to make radical changes in our treatment of animals that would involve our diet; the farming methods we use; experimental procedures in many fields of science; our approach to wildlife and to hunting, trapping, and the wearing of furs; and areas of entertainment like circuses, rodeos, and zoos. As a result, a vast amount of suffering would be avoided.

So far I have said a lot about inflicting suffering on animals, but nothing about killing them. This omission has been deliberate. The application of the principle of equality to the infliction of suffering is, in theory at least, fairly straightforward. Pain and suffering are in themselves bad and should be prevented or minimized, irrespective of the race, sex, or species of the being that suffers. How bad a pain is depends on how intense it is and how long it lasts, but pains of the same intensity and duration are equally bad, whether felt by humans or animals.

The wrongness of killing a being is more complicated, I have kept, and shall continue to keep, the question of killing in the background because in the present state of human tyranny over other species the more simple, straightforward principle, of equal consideration of pain or pleasure is a sufficient basis for identifying and protesting against all the major abuses of animals that human beings practice. Nevertheless, it is necessary to say something about killing.

Just as most human beings are speciesists in their readiness to cause pain to animals when they would not cause a similar pain to humans for the same reason, so most human beings are speciesists in their readiness to kill other animals when they would not kill human beings.

[…]

This does not mean that to avoid speciesism we must hold that it is as wrong to kill a dog as it is to kill a human being in full possession of his or her faculties. The only position that is irredeemably speciesist is the one that tries to make the boundary of the right to life run exactly parallel to the boundary of our own species. Those who hold the sanctity of life view do this, because while distinguishing sharply between human beings and other animals they allow no distinctions to be made within our own species, objecting to the killing of the severely retarded and the hopelessly senile as strongly as they object to the killing of normal adults.

To avoid speciesism we must allow that beings who are similar in all relevant respects have a similar right to life—and mere membership in our own biological species cannot be a morally relevant criterion for this right. Within these limits we could still hold, for instance, that it is worse to kill a normal adult human, with a capacity for self-awareness and the ability to plan for the future and have meaningful relations with others, than it is to kill a mouse, which presumably does not share all of these characteristics; or we might appeal to the close family and other personal ties that humans have but mice do not have to the same degree; or we might think that it is the consequences for other humans, who will be put in fear for their own lives, that makes the crucial difference; or we might think it is some combination of these factors, or other factors altogether.

Whatever criteria we choose, however, we will have to admit that they do not follow precisely the boundary of own species. We may legitimately hold that there are some features of certain beings that make their lives more valuable than those of other beings, but there will surely be some nonhuman animals whose lives, by any standards, are more valuable than the lives of some humans. A chimpanzee, dog, or pig, for instance, will have a higher degree of self-awareness and a greater capacity for meaningful relations with others than a severely retarded infant or someone in a state of advanced senility. So if we base the right to life on these characteristics, we must grant these animals a right to life as good as, or better than, such retarded or senile humans.

[…]

Questions

1. "Equality is a moral idea, not an assertion of fact." What does Singer mean by that? What would be the problems if we based moral equality on factual equality?
2. According to Singer, what is "speciesism"?
3. Singer talks about equal consideration of interests? What does he mean by "interest" here? What sorts of beings do and do not have interests in this sense?
4. Do you think Singer is endorsing "animal rights"? Explain your answer with specific reference to the text.
5. Does Singer give animal pain the same moral weight as human pain? Does he give animal life the same moral weight as human life?

Notes

1. For Bentham's moral philosophy, see his *Introduction to the Principles of Morals and Legislation*, and for Sidgwick's see *The Methods of Ethics*, 1907 (the passage is quoted from the seventh edition; reprint, London: Macmillan, 1963).
2. I owe the term "speciesism" to Richard Ryder.
3. *Introduction to the Principles of Morals and Legislation*, chapter 17.

Tom Regan argues the case for animal rights

[...]

We begin by asking how the moral status of animals has been understood by thinkers who deny that animals have rights. Then we test the mettle of their ideas by seeing how well they stand up under the heat of fair criticism. If we start our thinking in this way, we soon find that some people believe that we have no duties directly to animals, that we owe nothing to them, that we can do nothing that wrongs them. Rather, we can do wrong acts that involve animals, and so we have duties regarding them, though none to them. Such views may be called indirect duty views. By way of illustration: suppose your neighbour kicks your dog. Then your neighbour has done something wrong. But not to your dog. The wrong that has been done is a wrong to you. After all, it is wrong to upset people, and your neighbour's kicking your dog upsets you. So you are one the one who is wronged, not your dog. [...]

How could someone try to justify such a view? Someone might say that your dog doesn't feel anything and so isn't hurt by your neighbour's kick, doesn't care about the pain since none is felt, is as unaware of anything as is your windshield. Someone might say this, but no rational person will, since, among other considerations, such a view will commit anyone who holds it to the position that no human being feels pain either—that human beings also don't care about what happens to them. A second possibility is that though both humans and your dog are hurt when kicked, it is only human pain that matters. But, again, no rational person can believe this. Pain is pain wherever it occurs. If your neighbour's causing you pain is wrong because of the pain that is caused, we cannot rationally ignore or dismiss the moral relevance of the pain that your dog feels.

Philosophers who hold indirect duty views—and many still do—have come to understand that they must avoid the two defects just noted: that is, both the view that animals don't feel anything as well as the

Reproduced with permission from "The Case for Animal Rights," by Tom Regan, in *In Defense of Animals*, ed. Peter Singer. Oxford: Basil Blackwell, 1985, pp. 13–23.

idea that only human pain can be morally relevant. Among such thinkers the sort of view now favoured is one or other form of what is called *contractarianism*.

Here, very crudely, is the root idea: morality consists of a set of rules that individuals voluntarily agree to abide by, as we do when we sign a contract (hence the name contractrarianism). Those who understand and accept the terms of the contract are covered directly; they have rights created and recognized by, and protected in, the contract. And these contractors can also have protection spelled out for others who, though they lack the ability to understand morality and so cannot sign the contract themselves, are loved or cherished by those who can. Thus young children, for example, are unable to sign contracts and lack rights. But they are protected by the contract none the less because of the sentimental interests of others, most notably their parents. So we have, then, duties involving these children, duties regarding them, but no duties to them. Our duties in their case are indirect duties to other human beings, usually their parents.

As for animals, since they cannot understand contracts, they obviously cannot sign; and since they cannot sign, they have no rights. Like children, however, some animals are the objects of the sentimental interest of others. You, for example, love your dog or cat. So those animals that enough people care about (companion animals, whales, baby seals, the American bald eagle), though they lack rights themselves, will be protected because of the sentimental interests of people. [...]

When it comes to the moral status of animals, contractarianism could be a hard view to refute if it were an adequate theoretical approach to the moral status of human beings. It is not adequate in this latter respect, however, which makes the question of its adequacy in the former case, regarding animals, utterly moot. For consider: morality, according to the (crude) contractarian position before us, consists of rules that people agree to abide by. What people? Well, enough to make a difference—enough, that is, *collectively* to have the power to enforce the rules that are drawn up in the contract. That is very well and good for the signatories but not so good for anyone who is not asked to sign. And there is nothing in contractarianism of the sort we are discussing that guarantees or requires that everyone will have a chance to participate equally in framing the rules of morality. The result is that this approach to ethics could sanction the most blatant forms of social, economic, moral and political injustice, ranging from a repressive caste system to systematic racial or sexual discrimination. [...]

The version of contractarianism just examined is, as I have noted, a crude variety, and in fairness to those of a contractarian persuasion it must be noted that much more refined, subtle and ingenious varieties are possible. For example, John Rawls, in his *A Theory of Justice*, sets forth a version of contractarianism that forces contractors to ignore the accidental features of being a human being—for example, whether one is whiter or black, male or female, a genius or of modest intellect. Only by ignoring such features, Rawls believes, can we ensure that the principles of justice that contractors would agree upon are not based on bias or prejudice. Despite the improvement a view such as Rawls's represents over the cruder forms of contractarianism, it remains deficient: it systematically denies that we have direct duties to those human beings who do not have a sense of justice—young children, for instance, and many mentally retarded humans. And yet it seems reasonably certain that, were we to torture a young child or a retarded elder, we would be doing something that wronged him or her, not something that would be wrong if (and only if) other humans with a sense of justice were upset. And since this is true in the case of these humans, we cannot rationally deny the same in the case of animals.

Indirect duty views, then, including the best among them, fail to command our rational assent. Whatever ethical theory we should accept rationally, therefore, it must at least recognize that we have some duties directly to animals, just as we have some duties directly to each other. The next two theories I'll sketch attempt to meet this requirement.

The first I call the cruelty-kindness view. Simply stated, this says that we have a direct duty to be kind to animals and a direct duty not to be cruel to them. Despite the familiar, reassuring ring of these ideas, I do not believe that this view offers an adequate theory. To make this clearer, consider kindness. A kind person acts from a certain kind of motive—compassion or concern, for example. And that is a virtue. But there is no guarantee that a kind act is a right act. If I am a generous racist, for example, I will be inclined to act kindly towards members of my own race, favouring their interests above those of others. My kindness would be real and, so far as it goes, good. But I trust it is too obvious to require argument that my kind acts may not be above moral reproach—may, in fact, be positively wrong because rooted in injustice. So kindness, notwithstanding its status as a virtue to be encouraged, simply will not carry the weight of a theory of right action.

[...]

Some people think that the theory we are looking for is utilitarianism. A utilitarian accepts two moral principles. The first is that of equality: everyone's interests count, and similar interests must be counted as having similar weight or importance. White or black, American or Iranian, human or animal—everyone's pain or frustration matter, and matter just as much as the equivalent pain or frustration of anyone else. The second principle a utilitarian accepts is that of utility: do the act that will bring about the best balance between satisfaction and frustration for everyone affected by the outcome.

As a utilitarian, then, here is how I am to approach the task of deciding what I morally ought to do: I must ask who will be affected if I choose to do one thing rather than another, how much each individual will be affected, and where the best results are most likely to lie—which option, in other words, is most likely to bring about the best results, the best balance between satisfaction and frustration. That option, whatever it may be, is the one I ought to choose. That is where my moral duty lies.

The great appeal of utilitarianism rests with its uncompromising *egalitarianism*: everyone's interests count and count as much as the like interests of everyone else. The kind of odious discrimination that some forms of contractarianism can justify—discrimination based on race or sex, for example—seems disallowed in principle by utilitarianism, as is speciesism, systematic discrimination based on species membership.

The equality we find in utilitarianism, however, is not the sort an advocate of animal or human rights should have in mind. Utilitarianism has no room for the equal moral rights of different individuals because it has no room for their equal inherent value or worth. What has value for the utilitarian is the satisfaction of an individual's interests, not the individual whose interests they are. A universe in which you satisfy your desire for water, food and warmth is, other things being equal, better than a universe in which these desires are frustrated. And the same is true in the case of an animal with similar desires. But neither you nor the animal have any value in your own right. Only your feelings do.

[…]

Serious problems arise for utilitarianism when we remind ourselves that it enjoins us to bring about the best consequences. What does this mean? It doesn't mean the best consequences for me alone, or for my family or friends, or any other person taken individually. No, what we must do is, roughly, as follows: we must add up (somehow!) the separate satisfactions and frustrations of everyone likely to be affected by our choice, the satisfactions in one column, the frustrations in the other. We must total each column for each of the options before us. That is what it means to say the theory is aggregative. And then we must choose that option which is most likely to bring about the best balance of totalled satisfactions over totalled frustrations. Whatever act would lead to this outcome is the one we ought morally to perform—it is where our moral duty lies. And that act quite clearly might not be the same one that would bring about the best results for me personally, or for my family or friends, or for a lab animal. The best aggregated consequences for everyone concerned are not necessarily the best for each individual.

That utilitarianism is an aggregative theory— different individuals' satisfactions or frustrations are added, or summed, or totalled—is the key objection to their theory. My Aunt Bea is old, inactive, a cranky, sour person, though not physically ill. She prefers to go on living. She is also rather rich. I could make a fortune if I could get my hands on her money, money she intends to give me in any event, after she dies, but which she refuses to give me now. In order to avoid a huge tax bite, I plan to donate a handsome sum of my profits to a local children's hospital. Many, many children will benefit from my generosity, and much joy will be brought to their parents, relatives and friends. If I don't get the money rather soon, all these ambitions will come to naught. The once-in-a-lifetime opportunity to make a real killing will be gone. Why, then, not kill my Aunt Bea? Oh, of course I *might* get caught. But I'm no fool and besides, her doctor can be counted on to co-operate (he has an eye for the same investment and I happen to know a good deal about his shady past). The deed can be done … professionally,

shall we say. There is *very* little chance of getting caught. And as for my conscience being guilt-ridden, I am a resourceful sort of fellow and will take more than sufficient comfort—as I lie on the beach at Acapulco—in contemplating the joy and health I have brought to so many others.

Suppose Aunt Bea is killed and the rest of the story comes out as told. Would I have done anything wrong? Anything immoral? One would have thought that I had. Not according to utilitarianism. Since what I have done has brought about the best balance between totalled satisfaction and frustration for all those affected by the outcome, my action is not wrong. Indeed, in killing Aunt Bea the physician and I did what duty required.

This same kind of argument can be repeated in all sorts of cases, illustrating, time after time, how the utilitarian's position leads to results that impartial people find morally callous. It *is* wrong to kill my Aunt Bea in the name of bringing about the best results for others. A good end does not justify an evil means. Any adequate moral theory will have to explain why this is so. Utilitarianism fails in this respect and so cannot be the theory we seek.

What to do? Where to begin anew? The place to begin, I think, is with the utilitarian's view of the value of the individual—or, rather, lack of value. In its place, suppose we consider that you and I, for example, do have value as individuals—what we'll call *inherent value*. To say we have such value is to say that we are something more than, something different from, mere receptacles. Moreover, to ensure that we do not pave the way for such injustices as slavery or sexual discrimination, we must believe that all who have inherent value have it equally, regardless of their sex, race, religion, birthplace and so on. Similarly to be discarded as irrelevant are one's talents or skills, intelligence and wealth, personality or pathology, whether one is loved and admired or despised and loathed. The genius and the retarded child, the prince and the pauper, the brain surgeon and the fruit vendor, Mother Teresa and the most unscrupulous used-car salesman— all have inherent value, all possess it equally, and all have an equal right to be treated with respect, to be treated in ways that do not reduce them to the status of things, as if they existed as resources for others. My value as an individual is independent of my usefulness to you. Yours is not dependent on your usefulness to me. For either of us to treat the other in ways that fail to show respect for the other's independent value is to act immorally, to violate the individual's rights.

Some of the rational virtues of this view—what I call the rights view—should be evident. Unlike (crude) contractarianism, for example, the rights view *in principle* denies the moral tolerability of any and all forms of racial, sexual or social discrimination; and unlike utilitarianism, this view *in principle* denies that we can justify good results by using evil means that violate an individual's rights—denies, for example, that it could be moral to kill my Aunt Bea to harvest beneficial consequences for others. That would be to sanction the disrespectful treatment of the individual in the name of the social good, something the rights view will not—categorically will not—ever allow.

The rights view, I believe, is rationally the most satisfactory moral theory. It surpasses all other theories in the degree to which it illuminates and explains the foundation of our duties to one another—the domain of human morality. [...]

But attempts to limit its scope to humans only can be shown to be rationally defective. Animals, it is true, lack many of the abilities humans possess. They can't read, do higher mathematics, build a bookcase or make *baba ghanoush*. Neither can many human beings, however, and yet we don't (and shouldn't) say that they (these humans) therefore have less inherent value, less of a right to be treated with respect, than do others. It is the *similarities* between those human beings who most clearly, most non-controversially have such value (the people reading this, for example), not our differences, that matter most. And the really crucial, the basic similarity is simply this: we are each of us the experiencing subject of a life, a conscious creature having an individual welfare that has importance to us whatever our usefulness to others. We want and prefer things, believe and feel things, recall and expect things. And all these dimensions of our life, including our pleasure and pain, our enjoyment and suffering, our satisfaction and frustration, our continued existence or our untimely death—all make a difference to the quality of our life as lived, as experienced, by us as individuals. As the same is true of those animals that concern us (the ones that are eaten and trapped, for example), they too must be viewed as the experiencing subjects of a life, with inherent value of their own.

Some there are who resist the idea that animals have inherent value. 'Only humans have such value,' they profess. How might this narrow view be defended? Shall we say that only humans have the requisite intelligence, or autonomy, or reason? But there are many, many humans who fail to meet these standards and yet are reasonably viewed as having value above and beyond their usefulness to others. Shall we claim that only humans belong to the right species, the species *Homo sapiens*? But this is blatant speciesism. Will it be said, then, that all—and only—humans have immortal souls? Then our opponents have their work cut out for them. I am myself not ill-disposed to the proposition that there are immortal souls. Personally, I profoundly hope I have one. But I would not want to rest my position on a controversial ethical issue on the even more controversial question about who or what has an immortal soul. That is to dig one's hole deeper, not to climb out. Rationally, it is better to resolve moral issues without making more controversial assumptions than are needed. The question of who has inherent value is such a question, one that is resolved more rationally without the introduction of the idea of immortal souls than by its use.

Well, perhaps some will say that animals have some inherent value, only less than we have. Once again, however, attempts to defend this view can be shown to lack rational justification. What could be the basis of our having more inherent value than animals? Their lack of reason, or autonomy, or intellect? Only if we are willing to make the same judgement in the case of humans who are similarly deficient. But it is not true that such humans—the retarded child, for example, or the mentally deranged—have less inherent value than you or I. Neither, then, can we rationally sustain the view that animals like them in being the experiencing subjects of a life have less inherent value. *All* who have inherent value have it *equally*, whether they be human animals or not.

Inherent value, then, belongs equally to those who are the experiencing subjects of a life. Whether it belongs to others—to rocks and rivers, trees and glaciers, for example—we do not know and may never know. But neither do we need to know, if we are to make the case for animal rights. We do not need to know, for example, how many people are eligible to vote in the next presidential election before we can know whether I am. Similarly, we do not need to know how many individuals have inherent value before we can know that some do. When it comes to the case for animal rights, then, what we need to know is whether the animals that, in our culture, are routinely eaten, hunted and used in our laboratories, for example, are like us in being subjects of a life. And we do know this. We do know that many—literally, billions and billions—of these animals are the subjects of a life in the sense explained and so have inherent value if we do. And since, in order to arrive at the best theory of our duties to one another, we must recognize our equal inherent value as individuals, reason—not sentiment, not emotion—reason compels us to recognize the equal inherent value of these animals and, with this, their equal right to be treated with respect.

That, *very* roughly, is the shape and feel of the case for animal rights.

[…]

[H]aving set out the broad outlines of the rights view, I can now say why its implications for farming and science, among other fields, are both clear and uncompromising. In the case of the use of animals in science, the rights view is categorically abolitionist. Lab animals are not our tasters; we are not their kings. Because these animals are treated routinely, systematically as if their value were reducible to their usefulness to others, they are routinely, systematically treated with a lack of respect, and thus are their rights routinely, systematically violated. This is just as true when they are used in trivial, duplicative, unnecessary or unwise research as it is when they are used in studies that hold out real promise of human benefits. We can't justify

harming or killing a human being (my Aunt Bea, for example) just for these sorts of reason. Neither can we do so even in the case of so lowly a creature as a laboratory rat. It is not just refinement or reduction that is called for, not just larger, cleaner cages, not just more generous use of anaesthetic or the elimination of multiple surgery, not just tidying up the system. It is complete replacement. The best we can do when it comes to using animals in science is—not to use them. That is where our duty lies, according to the rights view.

As for commercial animal agriculture, the rights view takes a similar abolitionist position. The fundamental moral wrong here is not that animals are kept in stressful close confinement or in isolation, or that their pain and suffering, their needs and preferences are ignored or discounted. All these *are* wrong, of course, but they are not fundamentally wrong. They are symptoms and effects of the deeper, systematic wrong that allows these animals to be viewed and treated as lacking independent value, as resources for us—as, indeed, a renewable resource. Giving farm animals more space, more natural environments, more companions does not right the fundamental wrong, any more than giving lab animals more anaesthesia or bigger, cleaner cages would right the fundamental wrong in their case. Nothing less than the total dissolution of commercial animal agriculture will do this, just as, for similar reasons I won't develop at length here, morality requires nothing less than the total elimination of hunting and trapping for commercial and sporting ends. The rights view's implications, then, as I have said, are clear and uncompromising.

[…]

Questions

1. First, Regan wants to show that a rights view of morality fits our moral intuitions about the proper treatment of people better than a contractarian or utilitarian view. What are his general arguments against contractarianism? Against utilitarianism?

2. Second, Regan wants to show that any reasonable rights view of morality must accord rights to animals. What is his argument for this?

3. In what sense, and to what degree, is Regan an "Abolitionist" when it comes to our treatment of animals?

Carl Cohen defends the use of animals in medical research

We humans use animals. We eat them, play with them, and wear their skins. Most important, we use them as the subjects of experiments in advancing medical science. Animals of many species—rabbits, dogs, pigs, monkeys, but in overwhelming proportion mice and rats above all—have long been used in scientific research. Such research has led to discoveries that have saved millions of human lives and have contributed to the safety and well-being of hundreds of millions of other lives, animal and human. In experiments aimed at the *discovery* of new drugs or other therapies to promote human health, animal subjects are essential. They are also indispensable in *testing* the safety of drugs and other products to be used by humans. Anesthetized, the animals serving in this way are seldom caused pain. Some do experience distress, however, and many are killed.

Animals are not stones. They live and they may suffer. Every honest person will agree that treating animals in some ways is inhumane and unjustified. But the good that has been done by medical investigations that could not have been undertaken without animal subjects is so very great as to be beyond calculation; this, also, every honest person must acknowledge. Using animals is an inescapable cost of most successful medical research. Bearing that in mind, we ask, Is this use of animals in medicine morally right?

Other uses of animals are common, obviously. Animals give companionship, provide transportation, serve as food and clothing, and so on; and within each kind of use there is an enormous variety of specific uses. For each specific use, as for each kind of use, it may always be asked, *Should* that be done? Is it right? The answer in medical science is very clear. Investigators there *cannot* do without animal subjects. All over the world medical centers and individual scientists, pharmaceutical companies and great research institutes, rely heavily—and must rely—on the use of animal subjects in testing candidate drugs for safety, searching for new cures, widening and deepening biological knowledge. This arena gives us the most powerful lens with which

Reproduced with permission from *The Animal Rights Debate*, by Carl Cohen and Tom Regan. Oxford: Rowman & Littlefield Publishers Inc, 2001, pp. 3–14, 61–3.

to examine the moral issues of animal use. The rightness or wrongness of using animals in medical science is the central focus of this book.

Critics contend that medical experiments unjustly infringe on the rights of animals. I ask, Do animals have rights? This philosophical question lies at the heart of the debate. We cannot evade it because, as we shall see, if animals do have rights, the use of them in medical experiments may have to be forgone. I emphasize: It is not the wearing of furs that is our chief concern here, or hunting for sport, or even the eating of meat. It is the use of animals in medical research, above all other uses, that compels us to think carefully about the moral status of animals.

Whether animals do have rights may be a provocative question, but is it of practical importance? Is it more than an exercise in theoretical dispute? The animal rights debate, some might say, is a set of quarrels so academic, so "philosophical," that it does not really concern most ordinary folks. After all, great industries and tens of thousands of jobs depend on animal use. Hundreds of millions of humans rely on animals as their food. Most humans in the world consume dairy products and fish and meat every day or every week; we wear leather shoes and wool clothing; we visit zoos and love our pets, and so on and on. Why take this "animal rights debate" seriously? Human reliance on animals is so pervasive, so deep and complete, that there would seem to be little point in asking whether animals have rights.

We have, in fact, very good reason to ask and answer that question. The morality of animal use is indeed a *philosophical* issue, but by no means is it arcane. Any position adopted regarding the alleged rights of animals will have a direct bearing on community policy and on the life of each of us.

The practical force of philosophical questions about animal rights is this: If what we (individually or as a society) are doing with animals is not morally justifiable, we ought to stop doing it, and we ought to seek to keep others from doing it. If animals really do have rights, those rights deserve protection, as do the rights of vulnerable humans. Laws may be adopted that forbid conduct that is now nearly universal; regulations may forbid acts and practices to which we have long been accustomed. Such laws and regulations may prove exceedingly inconvenient and very costly. But neither convenience nor cost can excuse us from fulfilling our obligations. I repeat for emphasis: If animals really do have moral rights, we humans have the moral duty to respect those rights. The controversy over the use of animals with which this book deals is therefore intensely practical. Whatever the moral status we conclude animals deserve, that conclusion will surely affect the range of things we are permitted to do with them—and will therefore play a significant role in guiding our personal lives.

I hold that most uses of animals in medical science, including some that result in the deaths of many animals, are fully justifiable. This position is very widely shared by ordinary folks. Defending this conclusion, formulating and explaining it, is a badly needed step in responding to emotional attacks on what animal rights advocates like to refer to as "vivisection." Those attacks by the defenders of "animal rights" are deeply and dangerously mistaken. Exposing and explaining their mistakes is an enterprise at once important and humane.

Animals do not have rights. This is not to say that we may do whatever we please to animals or that everything commonly done by humans to animals is justifiable. Not at all. It is morally right to use animals in medical research, but from this it does not follow that *any* use of them is right. Of course not. We humans have a universal obligation to act *humanely*, and this means that we must refrain from treating animals in ways that cause them unnecessary distress. Animals, to repeat what was said at the outset, are not lumps of clay, and they ought not to be dealt with as though they feel no pain.

[…]

Animal *welfare* is not at issue here. Basic care for animals is today a moral concern almost universally shared. Sentient animals must be treated with careful regard for the fact that they can feel pain; decent people will always exhibit that concern and will rightly insist that the animals we use be fed and housed properly, handled considerately. Regulations ensuring such humane treatment are not in dispute; they are entirely justified and (in this country) universally in force. Principles of good animal husbandry rule, as they ought to rule, among the scientists who rely on animals in their investigations. Every medical center, every pharmaceutical company, every research institute using animals has (and under American law must have) its own Institutional Animal Care and Use Committee whose legal duty is to ensure that the animals in that facility are cared for properly and that

experiments using those animals are conducted humanely. Frequent inspections by federal agencies, as well as by professional peers, enforce and reinforce high standards for animal care and use. Reasonable persons do not dispute the wisdom of this protective machinery. This book is not about animal welfare.

Advocates for animals, however, often demand regulations that would do very much more than enforce humane and thoughtful care. These critics object to any use of animals *categorically*. They aim to bring to an end all uses of animals, most certainly including all experiments in which animals are subjects. They seek, in their own words, "not larger cages, but empty cages." Such persons describe themselves, with respect to animal experimentation, as *abolitionists*. The growing popularity of this abolitionist position, and the danger of it, oblige us to reexamine here the arguments for and against the use of animals in medical science. I will argue that the abolitionist view is gravely mistaken, indefensible; it would (if enforced) seriously damage human well-being.

[…]

The astounding success of [the] first polio vaccine was announced at the medical center of the University of Michigan, only blocks from where I live in Ann Arbor. Its impact has been global. How many have been spared misery and death by this one great step in medical science we can hardly guess. But about this wonderful vaccine and its successors we do know one thing for certain: *It could not have been achieved without the use of laboratory animals.*

To prepare the culture from which the polio vaccine was made, animal tissue was indispensable. And with that new vaccine greatest caution was obligatory. Many candidate vaccines had earlier been tried and had failed. From those earlier vaccines some healthy children had actually contracted polio. That could not be allowed to happen again. To test the new vaccine before its administration to humans, animal subjects were absolutely essential.

This true story, close to us in time and place, is widely known. But there are a thousand stories like it of which we are mostly unaware: scientific victories over tuberculosis and typhus, the discovery of insulin rescuing diabetics from misery and death, the discovery of antibiotics and the development of anesthetics—uncountable advances that have proved to be of incalculable importance to human beings. All this and much more could not have been done without the use of animals in the key experiments.

[…]

Many wince at the thought of using animals in biomedical research because they think immediately of dogs and cats, whom they love. In this view we are misled. The controversy should be understood to be one that mainly concerns the use of rodents, and among rodents chiefly mice and rats. Dogs, pigs, and other mammals (almost always anesthetized) are also used when they are the most suitable models for the disease under investigation. But only in a small minority of studies is that the case. The number of dogs and cats killed each year as experimental subjects is less than one-fiftieth of the number of dogs and cats killed *in animal shelters by humane societies for convenience*, because we have no place for them. About ten million dogs and cats are put to death in the United States each year for no good reason save that nobody wants them. Bearing in mind this wholesale killing of strays and former pets in animal shelters, how ought we respond to academic philosophers like Tom Regan who strenuously protest the carefully limited use of mice by medical science? Of all the animals used in biomedicine, dogs and cats make up less than 1 percent and primates less than three-tenths of 1 percent. Pigs, rabbits, and chickens are used more—but they amount to an extremely tiny fraction of 1 percent of all those billions of pigs, rabbits, and chickens killed for use as human food.

The US Department of Agriculture recently estimated the number of animals used in medical and pharmaceutical research to be about 1.6 million, of which the vast majority, approximately 90 percent, were rats, mice, and other rodents. These animals would not have come to exist had they not been bred specifically for biomedical use.

Meanwhile, in the world of everyday life outside science, the extermination of rats and other vermin that infest our cities is a perennial objective, difficult to achieve but important for the sake of human health.

[…]

On the liberationist view, no species deserves preference over any other. All policies or acts supposing a moral inequality among the species are flatly wrong. *All species are equal*, they contend, and the interests of all in avoiding pain are therefore rightly given equal attention, equal concern. The principle expressing this equality was given its classical statement by Peter Singer in *Animal Liberation*:

> The racist violates the principle of equality by giving greater weight to the interests of members of his own race when there is a clash between their interests and the interests of those of another race. The sexist violates the principle of equality by favoring the interests of his own sex. Similarly the speciesist allows the interests of his own species to override the greater interests of members of other species. The pattern is identical in each case.[1]

This argument is worse than bad. It *assumes* the equality of species, which is the very point at issue, and therefore can prove nothing, of course. But it serves (as it is meant to serve) as a rhetorically effective accusation because the label with which Singer brands his opponents carries very nasty overtones. This is deliberate.[2] The word *speciesism* was *chosen* to convey the thought that its practitioners exhibit moral insensitivity no less crude, no less brutal and perhaps more brutal, than that of racists or sexists. […]

But the cases are *very* far from parallel; the analogical argument is insidious. Racism is evil because humans really are equal, and the assumption that some races are superior to others is false and groundless.

[…]

"Speciesism" may be taken as one way of expressing the recognition of these differences—and in this sense speciesism, in spite of the overtones of the word, is a correct moral perspective, and by no means an error or corruption. We incorporate the different moral standing of different species into our overall moral views; we think it reasonable to put earthworms on fishhooks but not cats; we think it reasonable to eat the flesh of cows but not the flesh of humans. The realization of the sharply different moral standing of different species we internalize; that realization is not some shameful insensitivity but is rather an essential feature of any moral system that is plausible and rational. In the conduct of our day-to-day lives, we are constantly making decisions and acting on these moral differences among species. When we think clearly and judge fairly, we are all speciesists, of course.

If a neighbor of ours were to insist on exhibiting the same moral concern for rats as for human beings, we would be likely to think him unbalanced. A neighbor who would have us treat dogs as we treat worms we would find abhorrent; we would have her arrested.

The liberationist denial of fundamental differences among species is a terrible mistake; it is a gruesome moral confusion that encourages insensitivity, interferes with reasoned conduct, and may lead to unwarranted cruelty. We *ought not* respect rats as we respect humans; we *ought not* treat dogs as we treat worms.

Although the analogy drawn between "speciesism" and "racism" is insidious, it does often succeed in winning converts. The emotional overtones injected by the insinuating words interfere with sound moral thinking. If we are to act justly, we *need*, to recognize the morally relevant differences among species and to incorporate that recognition into our habits and patterns of conduct. Making balanced judgments about what we owe to others *requires* some grasp of the nature of the beings to whom those things are owed. Therefore, the moral view that urges us to refrain from attending to these moral differences is pernicious; if adopted, it must result in our failing to apprehend our true obligations—obligations to human beings that differ very greatly from the obligations we owe to rodents or to chickens.

If all species of animate life—or only vertebrate animal life?—must be treated equally, and if therefore in evaluating a research program the pains of a rodent count equally with the pains of a human (as Singer explicitly contends), we are forced to conclude either (1) that what we may not do to humans we may not do to rats or (2) that what we may do to rats we may do to humans also. At least one of these two propositions must be defended by those who insist on the moral equality of species. Both are absurd, and the animal liberation movement affirms them both.

I certainly do not mean to suggest that the pain of animals is unworthy of consideration. Their pain *is* morally *considerable*, of course; animals are not machines. I note this again with emphasis. But in making a calculation of long-term utility, it is one thing to say that the pains of animals must be *weighed*, and another thing entirely to say that all animal and human pains must be weighed *equally*. Accepting the truth that lower animals are sentient surely does not oblige one to accept the liberationist conviction that animal experiences are morally equivalent to the experiences of humans.

Humans, I submit, owe to other humans a degree of moral regard that cannot be owed to animals. I love my dog very much, but it would be very wrong for me to protect my dog at the cost of the life of my neighbor's child or of any human child. Obligations are owed to humans that are not owed to dogs.

[…]

Questions

1. Why does Cohen think it is crucial to use animals in medical research?
2. What does Cohen say we should do if we conclude that animals have rights? Does he think animals do have rights?
3. Cohen says that Singer's argument "assumes the equality of species, which is the very point at issue, and therefore can prove nothing." Look back at Singer's argument(s). Does Singer simply assume the equality of species or does he argue the point?
4. Cohen seems more concerned with the pain of dogs than of rats. How does he (would he) justify this?

Notes

1. Singer, *Animal Liberation* (New York: Avon, 1975) 9.
2. "[T]he attitude that we may call 'speciesism,' by analogy with racism, must also be condemned....It should be obvious that the fundamental objection to racism and sexism....apply equally to speciesism. If possessing a higher degree of intelligence does not entitle one human being to use another for his own ends, how can it entitle humans to exploit nonhumans for the same purpose?" Singer, *Animal Liberation*, 7.

Matthew Scully pleads for animal welfare, speaking particularly to fellow conservatives and Christians

[…]

[I]n a strange way mankind does seem to be growing more sentimental about animals, and also more ruthless. No age has ever been more solicitous to animals, more curious and caring. Yet no age has ever inflicted upon animals such massive punishments with such complete disregard, as witness scenes to be found on any given day at any modern industrial farm. […]

When a quarter million birds are stuffed into a single shed, unable even to flap their wings, when more than a million pigs inhabit a single farm, never once stepping into the light of day, when every year tens of millions of creatures go to their death without knowing the least measure of human kindness, it is time to question old assumptions, to ask what we are doing and what spirit drives us on.

[…]

Animals are more than ever a test of our character, of mankind's capacity for empathy and for decent, honorable conduct and faithful stewardship. We are called to treat them with kindness, not because they have rights or power or some claim to equality, but in a sense because they don't; because they all stand unequal and powerless before us. Animals are so easily overlooked, their interests so easily brushed aside. Whenever we humans enter their world, from our farms to the local animal shelter to the African savanna, we enter as lords of the earth bearing strange powers of terror and mercy alike.

Dominion, as we call this power in the Western tradition, today requires our concentrated moral consideration.

[…]

When did you last hear any Christian minister caution against cruelty to animals? It comes up about as often as graven images, even though animal welfare actually began, in both the United States and Britain,

as the cause of nineteenth-century Christian reformers who founded the Royal Society for the Prevention of Cruelty to Animals and its American counterpart. Often they were the same people […] behind the abolition of slavery and child labor. […]

Religious thinkers rightly caution against the ideas of theorists like Peter Singer. They might also ask themselves what alternative they profess—what their own standards are for the care of animals, and whether these standards are taught and applied. Our laws concerning animals are inconsistent and permissive. Behind these laws are religious and moral standards almost as empty. They are prescriptive, too seldom prohibitive. They are lofty generalities, admitting of easy and endless adaptation, so that […] even the commonest gut-shooter may today call himself a "Christian sportsman" without fear of correction.

[…]

The result, in the doctrines of so many churches, is an array of options without obligations, two worlds often bearing no relation at all to one another—as in a place […] in North Carolina, where you can find a factory farm, a captive hunting ranch, and a Baptist church literally neighboring one another. For many Christians, there is this one world in which man made in the image of God affirms the inherent goodness of animals, feeling himself the just and benevolent master. And then there is this other world, the world of reality in which people and industries are left free to do as they will without moral restraint or condemnation.

[…]

I suppose I am an unlikely friend to the animal advocates of our day in that I count myself a conservative, and conservatives tend to view the subject with suspicion. But the whole matter can also be understood within the conservative's own moral vocabulary of ordered liberty and abuse of power. Are many people prone to abusing their power over the natural world and its creatures? Of course they are. This certainly happens in human affairs when the powerful forget the source of and justification for their authority. The power is corrupted, the abuses multiply, the governed suffer.

Even the folks at People for the Ethical Treatment of Animals (PETA) and other such groups, so frequently derided for their solicitude for mink and pigs and chickens, are, as a practical matter, usually just pointing out obvious and rectifiable wrongs even if one does not accept their whole vision of the world. Nobody, least of all the conservative, should be shocked or offended to be told that we are abusing dominion, the first and greatest power given to man on earth. It would be shocking if we didn't abuse our power.

[...]

I think using animals for milk and wool and the like is perfectly acceptable provided they and their young are treated humanely, as they are on smaller farms. This is probably a good example of what Saint Francis (not himself, I should note, a strict vegetarian) meant by dominion as domestication, like pruning the tree to make it grow. Indeed such animals would never know life at all were it not for these small businesses.

[...]

In some European countries they have "Green" butcher shops where the meat comes from animals raised by relatively humane standards, and here in the States we have similar options through various sellers like the Fresh Fields natural-food chain. I think that's a useful practice and I'm glad to see people caring enough to buy only "ranch-raised" flesh. This consumer option, however, only attests to the fact that meat from animals raised with any compassion at all has now become a sort of specialty food one has to look for. By far most pork or veal or beef for our burgers comes from the large-scale enterprises. Soon there will be even fewer factories of even greater size and scope.

They confront us with a choice we have been putting off for a while now. The only way of winding down the factory farms is by withdrawing our weight, each person, one act of conscience after another, from the momentum of consumer demand.

[...]

Few adults have any illusions about our modern factory farms and packing plants, or about the tender mercies accorded the creatures that creepeth therein: the bright, sensitive pig dangling by a rear hoof as he or she is processed along, squealing in horror; the veal calf taken from his mother, tethered and locked away in a tiny dark stall for all of his brief, wretched existence. If you could walk all of humanity through one of these places, 90 percent would never touch meat again. We would leave the place retching and gasping for air. We cringe at the thought of it, and that cringe is to our credit.

But there's a little bit of Safari Club in us all. We fall back on the lofty-sounding justifications. And so demand for the product only gets more furious. We push the image away, smite it, command it to leave, shrug it off, trusting that somehow it all comes out even, it is all redeemed by need, it's all a part of the natural order. And of course everyone else is doing it so what's the big deal? Only a few cranks question the necessity of it. So we tell ourselves.

Then, adding to the fantasy of it all, when it suits us we pour on the sentimental mush. With that distinctively modern mix of sentimentality and ruthlessness, we get all weepy over movies like *Babe*, while, back at the ranch, the intensity of consumer demand leaves no time for the least modicum of mercy. "What happened to Babe's mother?" the kids always ask. We make up some nice, comforting story because the little ones aren't ready for that yet. But if the movie itself suddenly flashed to Babe's mother hanging up there in the shackle squealing in agony, adult viewers would be as mortified as the children.

[...]

Questions

1. Scully says, "mankind does seem to be growing more sentimental about animals, and also more ruthless." What does he mean by this? What examples does he give?
2. What does Scully think of the Christian doctrine of "dominion"? Does he think this doctrine justifies our current treatment of animals?
3. What does Scully think of factory farming? Is he against raising animals for food?

Part VII

The Environment

19

The Environment
Fiction

Museum for a Dying Planet

Mernaz watched from the window of the landing craft as it slowly descended. She could barely contain her sense of awe and excitement. She was about to be among the first people from Earth ever to set foot on the planet Meraviglia.

"Meraviglia": She felt an involuntary smile at the name. It had been chosen by the Italian astronomer who'd discovered the planet more than three centuries ago. Impressed by the way the planet's gaseous cover seemed to dance with color, the astronomer had selected the Italian word for "marvel" or "wonder." The name "Meraviglia" had caused no end of frustration for American schoolchildren, who wanted to pronounce "vig" like "pig," rather than "vee." "*Mare*-ah-*vee*-lee-ah" the teachers had to keep repeating.

There had been no thought at the time that there might be "*Mare*-ah-*vee*-lee-ans." There had been, though they were gone now.

The planet below was beautiful in a rocky, semi-arid sort of way, pastel colors under a bright sun. A friend of hers who had lived in Indonesia and then had traveled to the American southwest had told Mernaz he felt as if he had seen the beginning of the world, and then the end of it. What Mernaz was seeing now really *was* the end of a world—at least the end of it for the intelligent life that had once been there.

One sign of civilization remained, and Mernaz could see it below. A distant photograph of the structure had reminded several crew members of a domed American football stadium. From this distance, though, its hemispherical roof appeared rough and patchy in color, suggesting a monstrous turtle shell. Except that this turtle looked as if it had been decorated for the holidays, its back twinkling with dots of light.

The huge structure was supposed to be a museum. It was ironic that most of the ship's crew wouldn't have crossed the street to visit a museum back on Earth, and here they'd traveled many light years to visit one. This museum was different, of course: It was a high-tech monument left by a dying civilization in memory of itself—a memorial to both its magnificence and its folly.

Apparently the structure had also served as a temporary habitat, giving a little more life and time to the workers and technicians who were completing the interior. Mernaz' fantasy was that some of the aliens were still in there, alive, and that she'd soon be meeting them. But she knew that was pure fantasy. The museum had been completed over a century ago: The last of the aliens would be long dead by now.

It was easy to get the time frame confused. When the crew had first picked up signals and located their probable source as the planet Meraviglia, it was assumed that the signals were a message from a still

Contemporary Moral and Social Issues: An Introduction through Original Fiction, Discussion, and Readings, First Edition. Thomas D. Davis.
© 2014 John Wiley & Sons, Inc. Published 2014 by John Wiley & Sons, Inc.

living civilization. Doubts emerged when computer analysis revealed that what they were receiving was a constantly repeating message. Then early in the translation process it was learned that while the mechanical source of the message remained, the beings who had sent it were long dead.

Even now, after months of computer work, translation of the signals was still rough and terribly incomplete. What had been learned was this: At the time the message was composed, the civilization on Meraviglia was dying off as a result of a series of environmental catastrophes, mostly of its own making. The Meraviglians had first ignored the warning signs, then taken them as less serious than they'd turned out to be. They'd reached what Earth scientists called a "tipping point"—a series of them actually—where events began to spin out of control at such an accelerated rate that even desperate measures could do no ultimate good. Soon even wishful thinking became impossible: The Meraviglians knew they were doomed.

The construction of the museum had been a last act of—what? Heroism? Grandiosity? Maybe both. The Meraviglians had intended the museum both as a tribute to what they saw as the magnificence of their world and an indictment of the folly that had led to such devastation.

What the crew from Earth found so frustrating was the incompleteness of the story. So far the plodding translation work had given few details either about what the people and their civilization had been like or what environmental disasters had caused their destruction.

One thing that was obvious—and, to Mernaz, heart-breaking—was how much the Meraviglians had loved the once flourishing beauty of their world. The signals from the planet had included passages of speech as well as electronic code. None of the crew would have known that the speech sounds were, in fact, speech, if the computer hadn't identified them as such. Mernaz could only describe the speech sounds as like a low, staccato humming. To Mernaz the "speech" sounded mournful, though that might simply have been her imagination.

One sentence had stayed with her, and it *was* mournful. It sounded something like, "Hmm-uh-eem-ooo-uuh." The computer had translated it as, "All beauty lost."

There was something else in the message that Mernaz found touching. The museum had been built in the hope that it would be seen by visitors from other worlds: It had a power source that would last for over two millennia. Yet the Meraviglians said they would have built the museum even if they had known that no one would ever visit it. They felt the universe would be a little better just for having a remnant of their world's beauty in it.

Mernaz thought that a people who could value beauty for its own sake must have been very special. To value unseen beauty would have seemed odd to the utilitarian, cost–benefit-minded inhabitants of Earth.

It certainly wasn't aesthetics that had led governments back on Earth to decide to spend a fortune diverting this spaceship toward Meraviglia, to use hours of valuable computer time to try to get a better translation of the signals coming from that planet. And it certainly wasn't an overwhelming curiosity about the history of a dead civilization. It was something much more practical.

Over the last sixty years Earth had experienced a series of environmental crises; it was still uncertain how much worse things might get, and how fast. The United States had lost up to ten miles of coastline in many sections of the country. There'd been even greater land loss in other areas of the world; some of the smaller, inhabited islands had simply disappeared. Storms all over the world had increased in size and ferocity. Skin cancer rates had doubled in the last few years, and more and more of the southwestern US was beginning to resemble Death Valley. Species of animals and plants were disappearing at an accelerated rate, with consequences that were only dimly understood. While many toxins had been removed from the air and water, others were now appearing as makeshift technologies were rushed in to avert this catastrophe or that, to try to keep life going in as normal a manner as possible.

How Earth had gotten to such a point was obvious enough, but what would happen next was not. There were so many factors to consider, human as well as environmental. Even now people were dragging their feet on making the most drastic life-style changes and were continuing to engage in wishful thinking. Some religious groups saw the disasters as God's will, which it would be blasphemous to oppose. The market, far from promoting a solution to this crisis, continued to subvert many of the reforms that seemed so obviously necessary. Narrow loyalties and limited foresight undercut many of the long-term, international reforms that had been proposed. It was so hard for humans to take a hard look at themselves and what they were doing, let alone care about future generations and Earth itself.

Among academics, a growing pessimism showed itself in the increasing number of scientific theories purporting to show how evolution must eventually produce an amalgam of characteristics that would work against each other, producing intelligent creatures made self-destructive by the residual instincts of their earlier evolution.

All these crises and questions made it invaluable to study an intelligent civilization that had not survived. Maybe something could be learned that would help Earth.

★★★★★

The landing party was walking toward the "Structure," as someone had dubbed it in bland officialese. Mernaz realized the name that kept running through her mind was absurd in an opposite way—"the Museum of Meraviglia"—as if it were already an item on a tourist map.

Mernaz and the others were moving slowly, weighed down by their space suits and the slightly stronger gravity on Meraviglia. They were also being cautious, testing the ground, taking readings of this and that, on the lookout for any movement around them.

The surroundings were beautiful, like the Painted Desert of Northern Arizona. Mernaz had a sudden urge to feel the sun on her face, an urge she laughed away. The temperature reading they'd just taken had shown 60° Celsius, or 140° Fahrenheit. Analysis of the air had shown far too little oxygen and too much of several other things to make trying to breathe the air healthy. She'd just stay right here inside her suit and mask, thank you very much.

They were close to the Structure now. It wasn't actually as big as a professional football stadium— more like a huge department store. But it was every

bit as strange looking as it had seemed a short while ago from the air. The walls had the same rough, patchy look as the roof. It wasn't clear what the outer materials were: They weren't metal, as one might have expected from a high tech civilization. They weren't stone or stucco or any of the materials with which Mernaz was familiar.

The building had a sort of half melted quality, as if the outer layer had partly liquefied, and then re-solidified. Yet it didn't look damaged: The building was more like some architectural whimsy from the mid-twentieth century.

The Structure had no windows Mernaz could see. Nor did it have any obvious doors. The crew had to walk halfway around the Structure before they found an area of wall that looked any different from the rest. The wall was covered with some unreadable symbols. Were they decoration? Instructions? Whatever they were, they didn't seem to mark any kind of a door.

The group circled the Structure twice, still finding nothing that looked like an entrance. The Structure was beginning to resemble an impregnable fortress. Yet they knew it had been built as a museum. There had to be some way in. Were they going to have to wait for further development of the message translation to figure out how to enter? Perhaps the symbols were the clue.

Cautiously a couple of the crew members moved closer to the wall to take photographs of the symbols. Suddenly there was a kind of watery wheezing sound, and a portion of the wall that had been indistinguishable from the rest, slid inward and then to the side.

Everyone moved back, waiting. The result was a gaping doorway, but everything was black inside. Mernaz would have expected some welcoming lights. Of course, you wouldn't want to leave the lights on for centuries if you were trying to conserve power. Still, wouldn't you key a light to the opening of the door? Perhaps it had malfunctioned.

There was much conferring between the landing party and the ship. It was decided that half the landing party would enter the Structure to take a preliminary look. Mernaz was one of those chosen to go in first. She felt a rush of both anxiety and excitement; she quickly took a few deep breaths to calm herself.

Mernaz and the others who would go with her moved closer to the Structure. Then, with some holding lights and others, weapons, they cautiously went inside.

Almost at once it was apparent that something had gone horribly wrong here: Either the Structure had been breached or something disastrous had happened to the internal systems.

All around them was swampy, watery rot that came up to their knees. There seemed to be putrid decay everywhere. Mernaz shuddered at the thought of how it must smell. Thank God for their masks.

They kept moving, the proportion of solid to liquid varying, so that sometimes they were wading, sometimes lifting their feet out of faintly sucking muck. They spread out, moving cautiously, worried most about the water suddenly deepening or the mud holding them fast. Mernaz sometimes had the creepy sense of small things slithering around her legs, but she was sure that was her imagination. There were strands of this and that in the water, but nothing so far that looked alive.

They would just take a preliminary look for now. They'd check out the whole Structure eventually, doing an analysis of the damage but also hoping that some sort of records had survived in waterproof containers. It was discouraging to think that the crew might have made this long voyage for nothing.

Mernaz heard one of the others say, "Light," just before she saw it herself. It was ahead and to the left, greenish, phosphorescent. Perhaps it marked a room that hadn't been ruined, a sanctuary from all this muck. Maybe they would find what they wanted after all.

As they got closer, Mernaz saw that the light source was coming from behind some mucky mound. The light was beginning to look bioluminescent. Perhaps it had a natural source; perhaps it meant nothing at all.

No, wait. There was something else. Mernaz could make out that now familiar low, staccato humming their computers had analyzed as speech. It seemed to be coming from the same direction as the light—a light which Mernaz now noticed was flickering.

Mernaz moved cautiously around to the other side of the mound, then stopped and gaped. What she was seeing was like a video screen, but the medium looked gelatinous and what surrounded it didn't look like any

machinery Mernaz had ever seen. Though perhaps it was all covered with ooze.

There seemed to be flickering images, but Mernaz had trouble making out what they were. The images seemed to be of a slightly brighter version of the black muck she had been wading through since she entered the Structure. Another problem was the speed and jerkiness of the images: It was like some sort of experimental movie juxtaposing this and that to prove the absurdity of something or other. If there was sense in this—and there had to be—the crew's technicians would have to find it. Mernaz certainly wasn't going to get it.

Yet, as she gave up, relaxing her mind and eye, Mernaz suddenly understood something. She realized that what she was seeing was not a movie, but a series of still images—a slide show. The problem was that it was running way too fast for her, perhaps because of some mechanical problem. Or even, possibly, because it was made by people who saw, or comprehended, visuals, at a different perceptual speed.

Mernaz found that she could get some of it, if she focused on a single image, then held that image in her mind for a few moments after it disappeared.

There was that staccato humming she knew to be speech. As it droned on, Mernaz got images of something close to the camera that looked … what? … almost like an eye. An eye-like aperture surrounded by a rough, wet surface.

There was a confusing alteration in the pictures, but then Mernaz understood that the perspective had changed, as if the recording device had moved back a few meters and refocused. What she was seeing now looked like a swamp—mud and water and thick, tangled vegetation of some sort. What did this have to do with anything? How she wished she could understand that incomprehensible narration!

There was something else now—it was a creature of some sort—a frog?—no, not quite. It was bipedal—at least could be sometimes—and seemed to be able to use its forelegs to manipulate things.

Were these creatures somehow the enemy? No, that wouldn't make any sense—the distress messages had all concerned environmental dangers. Was this some kind of nature film—showing up some life form that had once existed on this planet—a life form in its natural habitat? Mernaz wished she could understand.

There appeared lights among the dark forms on the screen—then more, and yet more—and it seemed to Mernaz as if she were getting a distant shot of some dark city. There were lights coming from what she might have taken to be buildings if they hadn't looked more like mounds; there were lights moving above the mounds as if from aircraft, and other lights moving among the mounds as if from vehicles moving along the ground. Still Mernaz wasn't sure of the scale, wasn't sure if she was seeing something vast or small.

There were changes again—this time as if the camera were closer to the mounds—and there were those frog things again—their strange faces silhouetted in the lights, as if one were staring from a window, another from a passing vehicle. It was like a city scene from some grotesque fairy tale, with frogs instead of people, and the objects all having a kind of gelatinous quality.

Then there was a shot of a blazing sun. The images seemed to grow lighter but they also seemed to speed up so it was still hard to catch what was happening. As the images grew brighter, the things in them seemed to dry up and crack, like so much mud in the heat. After a time the frogs ceased moving and lay down; their bodies became still and dry and cracked. In one of the last images, one of the creatures, facing toward the camera, made some kind of gesture with one foreleg, before collapsing. And suddenly Mernaz understood—with a mixture of wonder and pity and disgust—that these grotesque creatures in their swamp world had been the Meraviglians.

Then there was that Painted Desert scene again—the one their crew had seen on approaching the Structure—rock cliffs and barren plains bathed in pastels of pink and beige tinted with dark purples and red. As Mernaz looked at this picture of the Merviglians' dead world, the narration began to repeat over and over those words she did understand.

"Hmm-uh-eem-ooo-uuh," came the sounds.

"All beauty lost."

Questions

(Please explain your answers, making specific reference to relevant passages in the story.)

1. At the time the spaceship from Earth approaches the plant Meraviglia, what do the crew members know in general about the planet and its inhabitants? How have they gotten this information?

2. The Meraviglians have built a museum. What was their stated purpose in doing this?

3. What does the phrase "Hmm-uh-eem-ooo-uuh" mean in the Meraviglian language? How does that phrase connect to the purpose of the museum?

4. What does the planet Meraviglia look like when the spaceship arrives? What does the inside of the museum look like? What does Mernaz think has happened when she first sees inside the museum?

5. When Mernaz finally understands the moving images inside the museum, she reacts with a "mixture of wonder and pity and disgust." What is it that provokes this reaction in her? Do you find anything to criticize in her reaction?

6. What do you think of the view that beauty has value even if it isn't seen?

20

The Environment
Discussion

Museum for a Dying Planet

In "Museum for a Dying Planet" a spaceship from Earth begins receiving messages from the planet Meraviglia. At first the humans assume the signals are from a living civilization. Later they realize that the Meraviglians are long dead and that the messages are coming from some mechanical device the Meraviglians left behind.

The meaning of the messages emerges slowly, and then only partially. The Meraviglians suffered a series of environmental catastrophes of their own making. They ignored warning signs until events spun so far out of control that nothing could be done. At the time the messages were composed, the Meraviglians knew they were doomed.

The messages indicate that the Meraviglians were a people with a strong aesthetic sense. They loved the beauty of their world. Mernaz, a crew member, is touched by one mournful phrase in the messages, translated as "All beauty lost."

As the last act of their dying civilization, the Meraviglians built a museum, designed to last for centuries, a testament to their disappearing world. The Meraviglians valued beauty for its own sake and would have built the museum even had they known it would never be visited. "They felt the universe would be a little better just for having a remnant of their world's beauty in it."

The governments on Earth are devoting enormous financial resources to visiting Meraviglia. The motivation behind the space visit is much more urgent than any general scientific and historical curiosity. As the story says,

Over the last sixty years Earth had experienced a series of environmental crises; it was still uncertain how much worse things might get, and how fast. The United States had lost up to ten miles of coastline in many sections of the country. There'd been even greater land loss in other areas of the world; some of the smaller, inhabited islands had simply disappeared. Storms all over the world had increased in size and ferocity. Skin cancer rates had doubled in the last few years, and more and more of the southwestern US was beginning to resemble Death Valley. Species of animals and plants were disappearing at an accelerated rate, with consequences that were only dimly understood. While many toxins had been removed from the air and water, others were now appearing as make-shift technologies were rushed in to avert this catastrophe or that, to try to keep life going in as normal a manner as possible.

How Earth had gotten to such a point was obvious enough, but what would happen next was not. There were so many factors to consider, human as well as environmental. Even now people were dragging their feet on making the most drastic life-style changes and were continuing to engage in wishful thinking. Some religious groups saw the disasters as God's will, which it would be blasphemous to oppose. The market, far from promoting a solution to this crisis, continued to subvert many of the reforms that seemed so obviously necessary. Narrow loyalties and limited foresight undercut many of

Contemporary Moral and Social Issues: An Introduction through Original Fiction, Discussion, and Readings, First Edition. Thomas D. Davis.
© 2014 John Wiley & Sons, Inc. Published 2014 by John Wiley & Sons, Inc.

the long-term, international reforms that had been proposed. It was so hard for humans to take a hard look at themselves and what they were doing, let alone care about future generations and Earth itself.

What happened on Merviglia and is supposed to be happening on Earth in the story bears at least a superficial resemblance to what some are predicting will happen as a result of global warming.

Discussions of global warming focus primarily on possible effects on *people*. This is understandable given how dire some of the effects are predicted to be. However, traditionally, environmentalists have been concerned with damage to the environment, both for the sake of humans *and for the sake of the natural world itself*.

Many environmentalists believe that the natural world with its beauty and complexity has great value in and of itself. This, we've seen, is the view of the Meraviglians. Mernaz thinks that "a people who could value beauty for its own sake must have been very special."

As it turns out, what Mernaz finds is very different from what she was led to expect. From her perspective, the world with "beauty lost" looks lovely, like the Painted Desert of Arizona. The world that was supposed to have been beautiful looks rather disgusting—swampy and slimy—and the Meraviglians themselves look like bipedal frogs.

The point is not simply to bring up familiar questions about the relativity of beauty. The point is rather that if beauty is relative, what does that do to beliefs about valuing nature for its intrinsic beauty? What does that do to the Meraviglians' belief that even if no one ever saw it, "the universe would be a little better just for having a remnant of their world's beauty in it"?

Perhaps beauty isn't the best property to invoke when calling the natural world "good in itself." But what other properties might be relevant? Life? Complexity?

What things have value in and of themselves is a big issue in environmental philosophy; it is an issue we will discuss at length in the last sections of this chapter. First, however, we will discuss facts and factual issues related to environmental concerns, illustrated in part through a brief history of environmentalism

in the United States. Then we will talk about the methodology of environmental decision-making, with particular reference to how such methodology figures into the global warming controversy.

Facts and factual issues

Environmental problems

In its broadest sense, the term "environment" covers all the external influences on any organism; in this sense, "environmental problem" could refer to any problem an organism confronts in a particular environment, such as the difficulty of surviving in an especially cold climate.

However, we will restrict the phrase "environmental problems" to those having at least a partial human cause—human effects on the environment which pose a danger to human welfare and/or to the natural world itself. The issues will usually be ones in which it is claimed that humans should restrict or alter their activities because of such dangers. Environmentalists are those who view environmental problems as being of particular importance and urgency.

Some of what are typically claimed to be environmental problems are the following: endangered species; the depletion of natural resources; overpopulation; overconsumption; pollution; ozone depletion; and global warming.

Let's review some of the major environmental issues that have arisen in the United States since the mid-twentieth century.

A history of environmental issues in the US

In the years following World War II, Americans became more and more concerned about the visibly polluted air and rivers that were becoming a fact of life in many American industrial cities. In 1962, Rachel Carson published *The Silent Spring*, a bestseller warning against the indiscriminate use of pesticides. A 1968 book by Paul Ehrlich warned against the "population explosion" throughout the world; other books soon followed claiming that the future would bring a diminishing supply of resources and urging humans to change their lives.

Americans were made aware of the potential loss of such animals as grizzly bears, bald eagles, whales and dolphins through hunting/fishing, pollution or loss of habitat.

The sense of crisis coming out of the environmental literature—not to mention its implied critique of commerce and materialism—fit well with the counter-culture movement of the late sixties and the movements fed off each other. Environmental teach-ins and rallies were held at schools and colleges around the country. Organizations like the Environmental Defense Fund and Greenpeace were formed. In 1970 twenty million Americans showed up for "Earth Day" rallies, protesting abuse of the environment.

All this concern was having its effect on Congress. Clean air and water acts passed earlier in the sixties were updated under President Nixon. Congress passed the Endangered Species Act and set up the Environmental Protection Agency to set limits on pollutants and assess the environmental impact of proposed federally funded projects.

Through the 1970s and beyond, government regulation combined with citizen-led lawsuits resulted in enormous improvements in combating obvious environmental hazards—acid rain, filthy rivers, belching smokestacks, highly polluting vehicles, toxins dumped into oceans and streams, and disappearing species.

In the 1970s, scientists began to find evidence that the ozone layer above the Earth (which protects us from UV radiation) was being depleted, largely as a result of industrial chemicals. The prime culprit was CFCs (chlorofluorocarbons) which were used as propellants in aerosol sprays, as cleaning agents, and as coolants in air conditioners and refrigerators. In 1985 a historic agreement, called the Montreal Protocol, was signed by twenty-nine countries (including the US) to phase out the use of CFCs and other ozone-depleting chemicals. According to the UN, the agreement has resulted in a 95% reduction in the production and consumption of such chemicals.

By the 1990s, many of the environmental problems that were most obvious to the public and were the cheapest and easiest to fix had been improved. Public interest in the environment began to decline. A backlash against environmental regulation began to gain real force. Critics felt that there needed to be a balance between environmental and economic concerns and that the weight had shifted too far in the direction of the environment.

For example, whatever the general justification for protecting endangered species, specific outcomes of the Endangered Species Act often seemed absurd to a large portion of America: The Act might be used to block millions of dollars' worth of development and jobs for the sake of one or two obscure species said to be "endangered." The Tellico Dam in the Tennessee River basin was held up in the late 1970s because of concerns for a fish called the snail darter. In the 1990s logging was limited in the Northwest to protect the northern spotted owl.

Beyond that, environmental legislation and enforcement had become increasingly complex and confusing. Regulation by states became more difficult as problems spilled across state lines. The science involved was often complex and disputable, the assessment of risk often highly subjective.

There was a growing anti-regulatory movement that found a sympathetic hearing in the Reagan administration. In some cases Congress agreed to loosen the legislation. Where that didn't happen, conservatives found other ways to undercut environmental laws: Oversight and enforcement could be minimized by presidential directive or by cutting funding to regulatory agencies or by appointing industry-sympathetic figures to head the enforcing bodies—what is called "regulatory capture."

Even those in favor of strong environmental legislation agreed that the government regulations and their application by bureaucracies were often blunt, clumsy, arbitrary and inefficient. By the 1990s people on both sides were more open to market-based legislation. For example, 1990 amendments to the Clean Air Act allowed the Environmental Protection Agency (EPA) to use a market-based approach with regard to industrial plants releasing large amounts of sulfur dioxide—a cause of acid rain. Industrial plants were given allowances as to how many tons of sulfur dioxide they could release; extra allowances could be purchased from other plants that had reduced emissions enough that they had other allowances to sell. These transactions could be carried out through brokers as in a commodities market.

Of course, as we've moved into the twenty-first century, the environmental issue that has dominated all others is that of global warming (climate change).

Global warming

The theory of global warming should be familiar to most of you: There is a natural "greenhouse effect" that has existed on Earth for over four billion years. Certain gases in the atmosphere let sunlight in but trap much of the infrared heat reflected back toward space from the surface. This trapping has the effect of insulation, warming the Earth; it results in temperatures 33 °C (60 °F) higher than they would otherwise be, making possible life as we know it on Earth. The main greenhouse gas is water vapor, but others include carbon dioxide (CO_2) and methane.

The theory of anthropogenic (human-caused) global warming is that human activities which release additional amounts of greenhouse gases—primarily carbon dioxide through the burning of fossil fuels—are adding to the natural warming in ways that will have serious negative impacts on human beings and on the environment in general. Many scientists are advising us to make serious cutbacks on our use of fossil fuels, a move that might well have serious negative effects on the economy, at least in the near future. The argument is that these short-term losses are worth it in order to save ourselves from much worse consequences in the near and farther future.

In the United States, the issue of global warming has become a political circus.

For a number of years the oil industry has been funding a campaign against the science of global warming, using the same tactics (even some of the same scientists) used by the tobacco companies years before to try to discredit scientific claims about the harms of smoking. The oil industry has been joined in their distortions by anti-regulatory groups and right-wing radio.

On the other side, those arguing for global warming have hurt their case by exaggerating the immediacy and degree of the global warming threat, sometimes spinning out frightening scenarios that critics have labeled "climate porn." Also, in 2009, hacked e-mails of a group of British scientists showed, at the very least, that some of the scientists were trying to avoid sharing their data with critics of global warming.

Meanwhile the "Great Recession" of 2007–09 and its aftermath have diminished whatever enthusiasm there was among the public and politicians for taking costly action on global warming.

However, the issue is unlikely to go away: The basic science is too solid. Most scientists believe that the evidence shows that we are experiencing long-term anthropogenic global warming which will have serious consequences in the future. The serious debate these days seems to concern the following two issues:

1. How serious the negative effects of global warming are likely to be; and,
2. Whether the most rational strategy is to:
   a. Make substantial changes to our way of life in order to lessen global warming; or
   b. Go on as we are and use our resources to combat the effects of global warming as they come.

The debate involves economists as well as climate scientists since we need to estimate the costs of *2a* versus *2b*.

2a is often called a "mitigation strategy," a strategy to *lessen* global warming. The word "mitigation" is used because it is supposedly too late to avert (avoid) global warming altogether.

2b is called an "adaptation strategy." This strategy isn't to lessen global warming but counteract its effects (e.g., by building sea walls to block the advance of a rising warmer sea.)

There's what some people consider a third strategy, but it's more like a hope that both sides share: The hope is that we might come up with large-scale technological solutions that would save us the economic punishment foreseen for mitigation or adaptation. These technological solutions would be a form of "geoengineering."

The reason geoengineering is more of a hope than a strategy is that there are serious difficulties with the proposed fixes. Some have a bit of a science fiction cast and may turn out to be impossible or to have dangerous side effects. Others are technologically feasible, but still impractical: Currently they are either far too expensive or would use almost as much energy as they save.

Making decisions about how to approach any large-scale environmental problem is likely to involve answering different types of questions, including questions in the following topic areas: the assessment of risk; impacts on future people; environmental justice; and, cost–benefit analysis. Let's discuss these topics and see how they figure in the debates over global warming, especially in debates between those favoring a mitigation strategy ("mitigationists") and those favoring an adaptation strategy ("adaptationists").

Environmental decision-making

The assessment of risk

Sheila Jasanoff, a professor of science and public policy, says that the concept of "risk" has been crucial to the assessment of environmental hazards in the US. She says that risk "is commonly defined as the probability of a harm times the magnitude of its consequences." It was imported from the financial sector where, for instance, past data on fires, floods and automobile accidents could be used to quantify the probability of those events occurring in the future. However, "risk" took on a more elusive meaning as applied to environmental problems where it was difficult to do a "reliable estimate of the probability of harm."

Still, says Jasanoff, the concept of risk remains appealing because it "seems to render environmental problems more tractable precisely because it is measurable"; risks can be weighed against economic costs.

An alternative to risk-based assessment is the "precautionary principle," which underlies much European policy. As Jasanoff says, "It demands heightened caution in the face of uncertainty, to the point of inaction when the consequences of action are too unpredictable."

The most highly respected group making the case for serious anthropogenic global warming and assessing the risks associated with it is the Intergovernmental Panel on Climate Change (IPCC). The IPCC was established in 1988 by the United Nations Environment Program and the World Meteorological Organization

to consider the scientific information on climate change, judge the probable impact of such change, and recommend a response to the problem. (The IPCC itself does no independent research.) The IPCC issued reports in 1990, 1995, 2001, and 2007. The reports represented the contributions of first hundreds, then twenty-five hundred, international scientists.

In each report, as further data were collected and assessed, the predicted temperature increases have gone up, as has the likelihood that the warming is anthropogenic. The 2007 report concluded that a human cause was "very likely" (probability of 90–95%).

The 2007 report predicts a rise in temperature of 1.8–4 °C (3.2–7.2 °F) by the end of the century. Additional projections include: a rise in sea level by 28–43 centimeters (approximately 11–17 inches); the disappearance of Arctic summer sea ice in the second half of the century; a very likely increase in heat waves; and a likely increase in tropical storm activity.

We have gone from a pre-industrial level of 280 parts per million (ppm) of CO_2 to a current level of 380 ppm. What would be a reasonable level at which to try to cap CO_2 levels? At an international science meeting convened by the UK in 2005, it was decided that 2 °C increase over pre-industrial temperatures was a crucial number: Below 2 °C there might be some benefits as well as costs, but above 2 °C, everyone would lose. (There has been an 0.8 °C increase since 1860; we're likely to get an additional increase of 0.6 °C if we keep CO_2 levels where they are right now. That's already 1.4 °C of the 2 °C maximum.)

The scientists at the meeting decided that the absolute maximum CO_2 level we must allow is twice the 280 ppm level, or 560 ppm; however, we should try for something closer to 450 ppm. At the rate we're going, however, 560 ppm is the number we are likely to reach by 2050 if we continue as we are. Hence the need for drastic changes according to those advocating a mitigation strategy.

Some adaptationists say the evidence for the world reaching the mid- to high range of the IPCC predicted temperatures isn't nearly strong enough to justify hurting the economy by seriously restricting our use of fossil fuels. Remember that the IPCC's prediction of temperature rise is between 1.8–4 °C (3.2–7.2 °F) by the end of the century. The differences between the low end and the high end are considerable. Even in the opinion of the scientists at that UK meeting, up to a 2 °C rise there might be as many benefits as costs.

Other adaptationists argue that even if the world is facing the high end of the IPCC's temperature predictions, it's the case that a cost–benefit analysis favors an adaptation strategy. Before we discuss the cost–benefit debate, however, let's deal with two issues both sides must take account of: the welfare of present versus future people and environmental justice.

Present versus future people

A famous argument for the claim that we have responsibilities to future people was made by Richard and Val Routley in a paper discussing the risks of storing nuclear waste.

The Routleys ask us to imagine a Third World bus, carrying both passengers and freight, usually overcrowded, "as in Afghanistan, passengers riding on the roof, and chickens and goats in the freight compartment." The bus travels roads full of bumps and potholes and is subject to frequent breakdowns; the cargo is sometimes tampered with or stolen.

The Routleys ask us to imagine that this bus is on a very long journey which will involve changes of drivers and a constant change of passengers. They ask us to imagine further that someone is using the bus to ship a thin container full of a "highly toxic and explosive gas." They suppose that the shipper isn't intending to cause harm, but does know that shipping the package is risky, given the odds of accident, tampering or theft. "If the container should break, the resulting disaster would probably kill at least some of the people and animals on the bus, while others could be maimed or contract serious diseases." The Routleys say,

> This act of the manufacturer would widely be regarded as appalling, which nothing could excuse, let alone the claim that possibly no disaster will ever happen. Even if otherwise the manufacturer's firm would go out of business and his village undergo economic loss, this fails to justify his action...

The import of the argument is that we are responsible for the future and that our economic welfare now would be no excuse for acting, or failing to act,

in ways that might have dire consequences for those who follow us—whether in terms of nuclear waste disposal or any other large-scale environmental problem.

Most of us don't need much convincing to be concerned about the world we will bequeath to our children and grandchildren. But after that, it all gets a little vague. Very future peoples have been likened to people on a different planet, with whom we might feel little connection.

Even if we care about future people, there are complications. For one thing, future peoples will almost certainly have vastly superior technology: In that case, how much power do we really have to harm them? If they are sophisticated enough, perhaps they will have technological protections against, or fixes for, most environmental problems we could send their way (short of a nuclear winter). Some thinkers have argued—with respect to global warming as well as other environmental problems—that the best way to protect the future is to continue doing what we're doing, rather than cutting back to a simpler and less sophisticated style of life. This is because our present way of life is more likely to lead to technology that could be of use to future peoples in dealing with environmental problems.

Another complication is that future peoples are likely to be much better off financially than we are: If people in the future are to be much wealthier than we are, wouldn't our making great sacrifices now be a matter of the poor (us, relatively speaking) sacrificing for the rich (future richer people)? If so, what sense does that make?

We'll talk more about this issue when we discuss cost–benefit analysis, but first let's talk a bit about environmental justice.

Environmental justice

The EPA defines environmental justice as "the fair treatment and meaningful involvement of all people regardless of race, color, national origin, or income with respect to the development, implementation, and enforcement of environmental laws, regulations, and policies."

The EPA first acknowledged the issue of environmental justice back in 1990 when it issued a report agreeing with the long-time claims of protesters and a decade's worth of confirming studies that low-income persons and racial minorities had a greater frequency of exposure to environmental hazards.

Issues of environmental justice have become central in attempting to formulate global responses to global warming. In every global warming scenario, the worst consequences will fall on the developing and underdeveloped regions of the world—those that can least afford to cope.

Any serious attempt to mitigate global warming will require concerted action by all the nations of the world to reduce carbon emissions: Given current trends, unilateral cutbacks by the West wouldn't bring global warming under control. As the West attempts to work out a global treaty, it faces the following moral arguments by the other nations, arguments that fit under the rubric of environmental justice:

Argument 1. Unrestricted carbon emissions were a vital element in the economic development of the West. It's not fair to expect other nations to retard their growth now by restricting carbon emissions.

Argument 2. The West caused the problem of global warming and so bears responsibility for solving the problem. This means the West should:

a. Severely cut back its own carbon emissions;
b. Either let the developing nations proceed with development unimpeded or pay the developing nations the costs of making their economies more energy efficient;
c. Pay the bulk of the adaptation costs for the developing and underdeveloped nations until such a time as global warming is brought under control.

Some have countered that the West shouldn't be held responsible for anthropogenic global warming because no one in the West knew there was such a thing during most of its development. Others come back with an ignorance-is-no-excuse rebuttal.

Whatever the moral merits of the argument, the issue has so far stymied talks on global warming. The United States has done little to combat global warming and has consistently refused to sign any treaty which doesn't require comparable cutbacks by developing nations. Certainly it has shown no willingness to bear the astronomical costs implied by *2a*, *2b*, and *2c*.

Cost–benefit analysis

Trying to apply CBA to global warming is a complex and contentious matter, one that is complicated by various moral questions.

In the context of our earlier discussion, we want to compare the costs and benefits of a mitigation strategy to the costs and benefits of an adaptation strategy.

Adaptationists claim the mitigationist case includes crucial distortions: It emphasizes the negative impacts of global warming over very real positive impacts; it downplays the degree to which people are likely to adapt as climate change progresses (for instance, by planting crops better suited to warming weather); and it underestimates the costs of mitigation while overestimating the costs of adaptation.

For example, mitigationists have made much of the fact that global warming will result in many more heat-related deaths than now occur. The European heat-wave of 2003 involving over 30,000 deaths is seen as either the result of global warming, or, more cautiously, what we're going to see much of in the future if global warming continues. But some adaptationists like Bjorn Lomborg (see Readings) point out that there are many more cold-related deaths than heat-related deaths in Europe and that any global warming that reduced the former while increasing the latter would result in a net gain for human health.

Mitigationists claim that the negative effects would greatly outweigh the positive ones; they emphasize the difficulties much of the world will have adapting to climate change; and they claim that the costs of mitigating climate change (especially factoring in the partially offsetting benefits of a new green economy) would be much less than the costs of adaptation.

Economists, as a whole, tend to come down on the side of the adaptationists, recommending at most that we try for a modest slow-down in our use of fossil fuels.

One large issue (some would say it is *the* issue) between mitigationists and adaptationists regards the calculation of future costs, especially in the choice of a discount rate. What is worth more—$1000 right now or $1000 five years from now? Obviously $1000 five years from now is worth less than $1000 today: The future $1000 will be worth less due to inflation and it will not include whatever you could have made investing the money for five years. Thus we need a rate to discount that future $1000 versus $1000 today.

However, if you apply the sorts of discount rates you might apply for investment purposes, it turns out it's only worth paying a little bit now to avoid huge losses in the distant future. And the moral problem is that these losses are happening to future people.

The Stern Report on *The Economics of Climate Change* (2007) is the cost–benefit analysis that tends to be cited by the mitigationists. The Stern Report (done under the leadership of Nicholas Stern, an adviser on climate change to the UK government) argued that doing nothing on climate change could cost between 5% and 20% of world GDP every year, whereas doing what we need to do to reverse and adapt to climate change would cost us only 1% of world GDP (his estimate has now gone up to 2%).

Other economists have criticized the Stern Report on various grounds. They claim he seized on the worst IPCC scenario for the negative effects of climate change and has been way too optimistic about the likely costs. One of the most controversial stances taken by the Stern report is its choice of the appropriate discount rate:

> We have argued…that the welfare of future generations should be treated on a par with our own. This means, for example, that we value the impacts on our children and grandchildren, which are a direct consequence of our actions, as strongly as we value impacts on ourselves.

The Stern Report does take into account the likelihood that future people will be richer than we are today, but beyond that, future people are to count the same as present people. That includes not just our children and grandchildren, but people living two hundred years from now. To his critics, Stern's stance puts us too much in the position of being hostages to the future. And it doesn't include the likelihood that technology may change in a way that solves the problem of global warming for future people for whom we are to sacrifice our welfare. If we're really to count the welfare of people far into the future as equal to our own, that logic might require us to make huge sacrifices now to save future generations even minor inconveniences that go on for a sufficiently lengthy time.

Obviously we're arguing about more than simply costs and benefits here. When we bring in issues about future peoples and environmental justice, we're clearly dealing with moral matters.

One big difference between mitigationists and adaptationists is their view of the likelihood of the worst-case scenarios for global warming. But an interesting question here—which economics itself doesn't handle very well—is how to view a low-risk disaster scenario. Suppose scientists proved to you that there was a large meteor heading in the general direction of Earth, that it would arrive in our very general vicinity in the next ten years, and that there was a one in a thousand chance that it would strike the Earth and totally destroy all life. They further convinced you that they had a foolproof plan for diverting the meteor and that the plan would cost you and everyone else the equivalent of ten percent of your current after-tax income for the next ten years. Would you be willing to pay it? What if it were 20%? 30%? What if it were a one-in-a-hundred chance rather than one in a thousand?

How are we supposed to value the loss not only of our own life, but the lives of our family, friends and neighbors, of all Americans, of the entire human race? How would we even begin to do such a cost–benefit analysis? Is the prospect of the end of human life so momentous that any cost is worth paying? These are questions that are not at all easy to answer, and the answer is going to depend a bit on one's philosophy, temperament and outlook on life. Some people would embrace an extreme version of the precautionary principle that would endorse averting catastrophe at any cost. Others—especially those who don't do much forward-calculation in their own lives—would say, the hell with it, live for today and take your chances. What the rational middle ground might be is difficult to say.

What has inherent moral worth?

Humans? Animals? The natural world?

One of the biggest issues in philosophical environmental ethics is the moral standing of the natural world. Should the natural world figure into our moral calculations only insofar as it has effects on human beings, both present and future? Or does it have inherent moral worth (standing, significance), as the Meraviglians in the story claimed?

We will consider five different positions in environmental philosophy concerning the question, What has inherent moral worth?

1. Humans (only)
This is often referred to as the human-centered or anthropocentric view of the environment.

2. Sentient creatures (only)
This view "extends" inherent moral worth beyond humans to include all sentient creatures. It is sometimes referred to as the animal-centered view, but that's not quite correct: It's unlikely that animals such as sponges are sentient. The position might better be called the sentience-centered or senticentric view of the environment.

3. Living things (only)
This view—that living things (humans, animals, and plants) have inherent moral worth and non-living things do not—is generally referred to as the life-centered or biocentric view.

4. Natural things (only)
This view extends inherent moral worth to include all individual natural things, whether living or not. This view isn't pushed much and we won't attempt to give it a name.

5. Natural systems (e.g. ecosystems)
What has inherent moral worth on this view is the ecosphere or the ecosystems that make up the ecosphere. This view is called "holistic" or "ecocentric" and tends to emphasize the value of the whole (say, the interdependent system of plants and animals in a locale) over the value of the individual (plant or animal).

Let's consider these five positions in greater detail.

Humans (only)

A human-centered, or anthropocentric, view of the environment values the environment only in terms of its uses for human beings. According to this view, the environment can only have instrumental, not inherent, moral worth.

We touched on the notion of "dominion" in our discussion of animals—the idea that humans are lords of the Earth and that Earth's resources are there for our use. We saw that such a view is often backed by a certain interpretation of the Bible or simply by seeing humans as the highest order of natural beings. Obviously, if one believes humans have dominion over sentient animals, how much easier to believe humans have dominion over the nonsentient parts of nature—both living and non-living.

Anthropocentrism tends to get caricatured by environmentalists as having a let's-trash-the-planet-and-party attitude. It's true that some anthropocentrists embrace the crudest sort of commercialism, the kind that almost always favors strip malls, oil rigs and amusement parks over natural wonders. But other anthropocentrists love wilderness and wild animals, want us to be cautious in our use of natural resources for the sake of our children and future generations, and feel that nature is of potential spiritual importance to most human beings. What makes this latter view anthropocentric is that these people are still evaluating nature in human terms—just from a different set of human values and perspectives.

To see how radical an anthropocentric environmentalism can seem, think of the current global warming debate. To conservatives resisting the idea of anthropogenic global warming, the claim that we must make drastic cutbacks to our current lifestyle seems dangerously radical. Yet those who push such proposals are talking about grave dangers to human beings in the near and distant future. Most of the debate can be formulated solely in terms of human values.

Sentient creatures (only)

In the chapter on animals, we reviewed the arguments for considering not just humans, but all sentient creatures, as having inherent moral worth, even moral rights. With that chapter as background, it should be easy for you to understand that any environmentalism premised on the value of sentience will have a broader scope than would an anthropocentric environmentalism.

In the chapter on animals, we focused on complaints about the treatment of animals used for research and raised for food. But senticentric environmentalism would also be concerned with the welfare (or rights) of animals in the wild—those captured for zoos, hunted for meat or ivory or other byproducts, as well as animals whose habitats are threatened by development.

For purposes of illustration, consider some of the goals posted on the web site of the Born Free Foundation (located in the UK):

> Zoo check is at the heart of Born Free and takes action to stop captive animal suffering, challenge the multi-billion-pound global captive animal industry, and phase-out zoos and animal circuses.
>
> Born Free rescues individual lions, tigers and leopards from tiny cages and gives them lifetime care at sanctuaries, funds major lion and tiger conservation projects and fights hunting big cats for 'sport.'
>
> Born Free supports the UN's Great Ape Survival Project, rescues orphaned apes, fights the global ape "bushmeat" and exotic pet trades, protects wild gorillas and returns rescued monkeys to the wild.

Obviously senticentric environmentalists who believe in animal rights will take a more radical stance than those who emphasize animal welfare. For those who believe in animal rights, there can be no excuse for zoos of any kind. On the other hand, animal welfarists might accept zoos but only if the animals are well treated—meaning that the zoo habitats have many of the features of natural habitats. Since there are plenty of zoos around the world where the animals are treated miserably, both groups have common ground. For instance, there seems to be a strong movement to get elephants out of zoos—feeling that nothing a zoo could provide an elephant would remotely resemble its a natural habitat. For instance, because of such concerns, the Detroit Zoo announced in 2004 that it was sending its elephants to an elephant sanctuary.

Living things (only)

Just as a senticentric ethic argues for the "extension" of the category of inherent moral worth to all sentient creatures, so a life-centered, or biocentric, ethic extends intrinsic moral worth to all living things. And just as animal advocates have their charges of speciesism against the anthropocentrists, so the biocentrists have changes of "sentientism" and "vertebrate chauvinism" against those who want to limit inherent moral worth to sentient creatures.

A famous argument against anthropocentrism was given in a 1973 paper by Richard Routley (see Readings).

> The last man example: The last man (or person) surviving the collapse of the world system lays about him, eliminating, so far as he can, every living thing, animal or plant (but painlessly…). What he does is quite permissible according to basic [human] chauvinism, but on environmental grounds is wrong. Moreover one does not have to be committed to esoteric values to regard Mr. Last Man as behaving badly and destroying things of value….

Routley's point is this: Since most of us would feel what the Last Man does is wrong while an anthropocentric argument says what he does is morally acceptable, this shows that anthropocentrism is inadequate as an ethic.

Since we're dealing here with biocentrism, let's change Routley's Last Man scenario so its focus is solely on the extension of inherent worth to non-sentient living things. Let's call this the Last Woman scenario.

It is the future and our solar system is dying. The people on Earth have known for some time that their planet will be able to support life for no more than a thousand years.

For centuries nations have possessed almost unimaginable Doomsday weapons, but the threat of mutually assured destruction has kept the weapons from being used.

In a secret weapons location in Montana, the Last Woman has learned that a powerful suicide cult, which overthrew a government in Western Europe, has just set off Doomsday Weapon One, a weapon that will kill all sentient life by disrupting the nervous systems that control vital functions. Momentarily shielded from the effects of the weapon, the Last Woman looks out bitterly on the beautiful Earth, knowing it will never be seen by another sentient creature: The Earth is dying anyway, and a thousand years is far too short for other sentient life to evolve. She knows that the only extraterrestrial life is more than a thousand light years away.

"What's the point of it all if no one sees it," she thinks. As she feels herself dying, she angrily punches the button for Doomsday Weapon Two, a weapon that will incinerate the surface of the Earth, destroying the trees and the flowers and the grasses—all remaining living things.

The question is: Was it morally wrong for the Last Woman to set off Doomsday Weapon Two?

Note that Doomsday Weapon Two kills off only living things that are non-sentient. Further, no other sentient creatures will ever experience the things the woman is destroying. She is the last surviving sentient creature and is about to die. The Earth will be gone in a thousand years—too short a time for new sentient life to evolve or for creatures from another solar system to reach Earth. The question is: Do non-sentient living things have worth if they are never experienced?

Biocentrists expect most of us would agree that the Last Woman was morally wrong to set off Doomsday Weapon Two. This, they say, shows we believe that non-sentient living things do have worth in and of themselves.

The Last Man-style argument is rather impressionistic. Let's look at a detailed argument for biocentrism put forward by philosopher Paul Taylor.

Taylor argues that all living things have inherent worth and have it equally. Taylor says that what gives a being inherent worth is "not the capacity for pleasure or suffering but the fact that the being has a good of its own which can be furthered or damaged by moral agents." A being needn't be sentient to have a good of its own, but it must be living: Non-living things like water or rocks don't qualify.

Taylor says that each living thing is a teleological center of life.

> To say it is a teleological center of life is to say that its internal functioning as well as its external activities are all goal-oriented, having the constant tendency to maintain the organism's existence through time and to enable it successfully to perform those biological operations whereby it reproduces its kind and continually adapts to changing environmental events and conditions.

Senticentrists talk about sentient creatures having "interests"—meaning that they have desires, preferences. Taylor says that non-sentient living things don't have interests in this sense, but they do have things that are *in their interest*—that is, contribute to their well-being. We can say that it is in a person's interest (would do her good) to eat a low-fat diet, even though the person isn't interested in eating (has no desire to eat) such a diet. In the same way we can say it is in a plant's interest to get plenty of water and sun, without implying that the plant is interested in (has desires for) water and sun. On the other hand, Taylor would say, there is nothing that is in a rock's interest: Unlike living things, the rock has no innate goal.

For Taylor any being that has a good of its own (has things that are in its interest) has inherent worth; further all beings have it equally.

The claim that all living things have equal moral worth ("bioegalitarianism") would seem to have radical implications, even though Taylor doesn't draw them out. Given the destruction of nature humans have caused, an ethic like Taylor's would seem to imply that the world would be better with no humans in it—or at least far fewer of us. There are radical environmentalists who feel just that, who would agree with the misanthropic, nature-loving poet Robinson Jeffers who said that "the human race is a botched experiment that has run wild and ought to be stopped." There may be a bit of that feeling in a lot of us at one time or another: That may account for the unlikely popularity of the book, *The World Without Us*, which details what would happen to Earth if humans simply disappeared and wild nature began to destroy or cover everything humans left behind.

Nonetheless, even to most of those who believe that natural things do have inherent worth, the idea that every plant has the same worth as every human (or every gorilla, for that matter) seems preposterous. Most would insist on something much less extreme—only that nature be given *some* inherent worth in our personal and social decisions. Some philosophers have suggested an ethic that grants inherent worth to all living things, but gives bonuses according to levels of sentience and intelligence. (See the reading by J. Baird Callicot.)

Others reject biocentrism altogether, denying that an entity which doesn't feel or experience—which doesn't *care* what happens to it—can have inherent worth. Even if it's proper to speak of the good of a plant, it's not clear why we should care about its good. For instance, I might acknowledge that poison oak has a good of its own, and still have no moral qualms about eradicating it.

Let's look back at the Doomsday Scenario. The Last Woman—who is also the last sentient creature—sets off a weapon that will destroy all non-sentient life. Again, remember the stipulations of the example: The Earth will be destroyed anyway; there's not enough time for sentient life to re-evolve; and, no extraterrestrials are ever going to visit Earth. (If you find any loopholes, plug them up: We are simply after a hypothetical test case.)

Do we feel it's wrong for our Last Woman to destroy nature under these conditions? If we're inclined to say, yes, let's figure out why. What if our Last Woman was one of the Meraviglians and the beauty she was destroyed was a natural world of swamps and smells that would disgust us? Suppose further that when those natural things were destroyed, the result was what we would consider a beautiful world of landscapes with colored rocks and marvelous rock formations? Would what the woman did be bad in that case?

One of the central questions is this: If we condemn the Last Woman because it is wrong to destroy nature, are we thinking primarily of the destruction of plant life? Or might it be the destruction of beauty? If the latter, could anything be beautiful without an observer?

Natural things (only)

It's tempting to say that a beautiful rock formation has greater worth than a poison oak bush or a few mosquitos. Doesn't this show that if living things have inherent worth, so too do some non-living things?

The problem with this argument is that it seems to depend on an observer who appreciates beautiful rocks and dislikes poison oak rashes and mosquito bites. That is, the point might make sense from an anthropocentric perspective, but it needs a different argument if you remove the observer—which you must, in arguing for inherent worth. Whether you agree with Taylor or not, he did present an argument for the inherent worth of living things that did not depend on an observer. What argument would one give for the inherent worth of non-living things? The arguments I'm aware of are put in terms of

natural systems rather than individuals; we'll discuss these arguments next.

Natural systems

If we compare the Last Man scenario with the Last Woman scenario, we might find ourselves thinking that Last Man destroying as many plants as he can might be unfortunate but the Last Woman destroying all of Nature (even without sentient creatures) would be appalling. Think of your reaction if a lake and its surroundings become badly polluted or if a large forest is destroyed by arson. While we certainly value individual flowers and trees, perhaps what matters above all are systems of nature.

The term "ecosystem" is applied to a local system of living organisms and the environment they depend on, considered as an integrated whole. All the ecosystems of Earth are referred to as the "ecosphere". The word "ecology" refers to the study of organisms, their environment, and the relation between the two.

Most environmentalists who reject an anthropocentric or senticentric view of ethics tend to focus their environmentalism on natural systems more than individual natural things. They embrace what is called "ecological holism" or ecocentrism—valuing ecosystems and the ecosphere as a whole.

One of the inspirations for ecocentrists was Aldo Leopold, a naturalist and conservationist who worked with the US Forest Service. Leopold was a pioneer in applying environmental principles to wildlife management and was instrumental in having Gila National Forest designated as America's first national wilderness area in 1924. (There is now a wilderness area next to it that is named after Leopold.) Leopold later became professor of wildlife management at the University of Wisconsin. His *Sand County Almanac* was published after his death. Along with descriptions of his experiences in Wisconsin, the book puts forth a "land ethic" in which human beings no longer see themselves as conquerors of the land, but as members and citizens of it. According to Leopold, "We abuse the land because we regard it as a commodity belonging to us. When we see land as a community to which we belong, we may begin to use it with love and respect." Leopold's focus was often on the community, rather than the members of it, and his most famous quote emphasizes a holistic view: "A thing is right when it tends to preserve the integrity, stability, and beauty of the biotic community."

From the 1950s to the 1970s, prominent views in scientific ecology seemed to fit well with holism. According to historian Donald Worster, two ecologists, Eugene and Howard Odum, "believed that ecology must develop a unified theory of the ecosystem, described in precise mathematical and statistical terms, if the field was to be of any practical value. Such a theory must be holistic, not reductive." Eugene Odum developed a "view of nature as a series of balanced ecosystems" and this led him to take a strong stand in favor of preserving the landscape in as nearly natural condition as possible."

In 1969, James Lovelock presented his theory of Gaia. He claimed that life on Earth had not been an accident, but that life and the atmosphere had coevolved, with life shaping the Earth as much as the Earth shaping life. He called this process "Gaia," sometimes going beyond the science to imagine Gaia as a superorganism; he concluded from this that the basic principle of life was cooperation.

Scientists were always skeptical of Lovelock's more extreme claims. And further scientific research seemed to undermine the claim made by Lovelock, the Odums and others that nature is stable and harmonious. It became less clear what the "balance of nature" might amount to. Change seemed primary, not stability (which turned out to be relative to your viewpoint). A renaissance of evolutionary theory posited competition, rather than cooperation, as fundamental. Neo-Darwinists argued that evolutionary adaptation was a matter of individual organisms; the idea of ecosystems evolving and adapting was said to be wrong.

Some holists continue to cite science to support their view. But, as Worster says of earlier holists, "the ecological text they know and cite is either of their own writing or a pastiche from older, superseded models. Few appreciate that the science they are eagerly pursuing took another fork back yonder up the road."

Still, questionable science and metaphysics aside, it's hard to dismiss the idea of Nature having some sort of inherent worth. When we look up in the night sky at the heavens, when we think about the depths of the Universe that astronomy has so far revealed to us; when we contemplate quantum physics and the Big Bang that started the Universe we know; when we see photos of Earth from space, look at magnificent vistas of mountains, or forests or coastlines; or when we examine the myriad foliage and animal life with which we share the planet, it can be hard to see how human beings, watching our TV programs or working at our computers, fussing about our relationships and worrying about our neuroses, occasionally building magnificent structures that are still dwarfed by the natural things around us, often fighting and killing and destroying—that we and our little experiences are really the point of all this. Or, if there is no point, can we seriously believe that we little creatures scurrying around on one little planet have pride of place in this universe, which is simply here for us to cultivate or destroy as we see fit?

The minimum the biocentrists and ecocentrists are asking us is that we have some appreciation and respect for the Earth that is our source and our habitat, that we show some humility before its magnificence and some concern for its obvious vulnerabilities in the face of our growing, often uncontrolled power, that when we debate global warming and other environmental concerns, that we take into account species and ecosystems and simple living things, according them some inherent worth alongside the somewhat exaggerated worth we keep according ourselves.

Notes and selected sources

Facts and factual issues

SOURCES
For factual information I have relied most heavily on:
Kim Masters Evans. *The Environment: A Revolution in Attitudes.* Info Plus Series. Detroit, MI: Thomson Gale, 2006.

Donald Worster. *Nature's Economy: A History of Ecological Ideas.* 2nd edn. Cambridge: Cambridge University Press, 1994.

Some other sources regarding factual information:
Rachel Carson, *The Silent Spring.* Boston, MA: Houghton Mifflin Harcourt: 2002 (40th Anniversary Edition).

Paul Ehrlich, *The Population Bomb*. New York: Sierra Club/ Ballantine Books, 1968.

Bjorn Lomborg. *Cool It: The Skeptical Environmentalist's Guide to Global Warming*. New York: Alfred A. Knopf, 2007.

Mark Maslin. *Global Warming: A Very Short Introduction*. Oxford: Oxford University Press, 2009.

Gabrielle Walker and Sir David King. *The Hot Topic: What We Can Do about Global Warming*. Orlando, FL: Harcourt Inc., 2008.

Richard Wolfson. *Earth's Changing Climate*. Chantilly, VA: The Teaching Company, 2007, Part 1. (My interpretation/summary.)

Microsoft® Encarta® 2006. © 1993–2005 Microsoft Corporation.

NOTES

"Climb the mountains…" and "God has cared…" Muir in Microsoft® Encarta (above).

On Carson and Ehrlich, Worster, pp. 347–53.

Congressional acts and Montreal Protocol, Evens, Info, pp. 65–76.

Environmental decision-making

SOURCES

Dale Jamieson (ed). *A Companion to Environmental Philosophy*. Oxford: Blackwell, 2001.

Kim Masters Evans. *The Environment* (above).

A. Myrick Freeman III. "Economics." In Jamieson, pp. 277–90.

Sheila Jasanoff. "Law." In Jamieson, pp. 331–61.

Ernest Partridge. "Future Generations." In Jamieson, pp. 377–89.

Richard Routley and Val Routley. "Nuclear Energy and Obligations to the Future," *Inquiry* 21 (1978), 133–79. Reprinted in ed. Ernest Partridge, *Responsibilities to Future Generations: Environmental Ethics*. Buffalo, NY: Prometheus Books, 1981. pp. 277–85.

Nicholas Stern, *The Economics of Climate Change: The Stern Review*. Cambridge: Cambridge University Press, 2007.

NOTES

"…Sometimes the term…." Jasanoff, p. 334.

"…seems to render…." Jasanoff, p. 336.

"It demands heightened awareness…." Jasanoff, pp. 336–7.

"…the fair treatment…." Masters, p. 7.

"We have argued…." Stern, p. 663.

What has inherent moral worth?

SOURCES

Robin Attfield. *Environmental Ethics: An Overview for the 21st Century*. Cambridge, UK: Polity Press, 2003.

J. Baird Callicott, "The Search for an Environmental Ethic," in (ed.) Regan, *Matters of Life and Death*, pp. 322–82.

Robert Elliot, "Environmental ethics" in (ed.) Peter Singer, *A Companion to Ethics*. Oxford: Blackwell Publishing, 1993, pp. 284–93.

Robert Elliot. "Normative Ethics." In Jamieson, pp. 177–91.

Dale Jamieson (Ed). *A Companion to Environmental Philosophy*. (above).

Robinson Jeffers (& Tim Hunt). *The Selected Poetry of Robinson Jeffers*. Palo Alto, CA: Stanford University Press, 2001.

Hugh LaFollette (ed.). *The Oxford Handbook of Practical Ethics*. Oxford: Oxford University Press, 2003.

Richard Routley and V. Routley, "Human Chauvinism and Environmental Ethics," in D.S. Manson et al (eds.), *Environmental Philosophy*, Department of Philosophy, Research School of Social Sciences, Australian National University, Canberra, 1980.

Donald Scherer. "Anthropocentrism, Atomism, and Environmental Ethics," in Scherer/Attig, pp. 73–81.

Donald Scherer and Thomas Attig (eds.) *Ethics and the Environment*, Englewood Cliff, NJ, Prentice-Hall, 1983.

Kristin Shrader-Frechette. "Ecology." In Jamieson, pp. 304–15.

Kristin Shrader-Frechette. "Environmental Ethics." In LaFollette, pp. 189–213.

Paul Taylor. *Respect for Nature: A Theory of Environmental Ethics*. Princeton NJ: Princeton University Press, 1966.

Peter Singer, "Environmental Values" in Peter Singer, *Writings on an Ethical Life*. New York: Ecco Press, 2000, pp. 86–102.

Gary Varner. "Sentientism." In Jamieson, pp.192–203.

Alan Weisman. *The World Without Us*. New York: St. Martin's Press, 2007.

NOTES

The Detroit Zoo. Detroit Zoological Institute, PR Newswire, May 20, 2004.

"Last man example…" Routley & Routley, p. 124.

"To say it is a teleological…." Taylor, p. 121.

Taylor on interests, good of their own, Taylor, pp. 60–71.

Jeffers, p. 557.

On Aldo Leopold, Worster, pp. 284–90.

Worster on the Odums, Worster, pp. 364–9.

Lovelock and Gaia. Worster, pp. 379–87.

"the ecology text they know…." Worster, pp. 332–3.

Definitions

(Terms are defined in the order in which they appeared in the text.)

1. *Environment*: All the external influences on any organism; the natural world.

2a. *Environmental problem (broad)*: Any problem an organism confronts in a particular environment.

 b. *Environmental problem (narrow)*: Human effects on the environment which pose a danger to human welfare and/or to the natural world itself.

3. *Ozone layer*: An atmosphere layer above Earth that protects us from ultraviolet (UV) radiation.

4. *Chlorofluorocarbons (CFCs)*: Chemicals, used as propellants in aerosol sprays and coolants in air conditioners/refrigerators that many scientists believe cause depletion of the ozone layer.

5. *Montreal Protocol*: An international agreement to phase out the use of CFCs and other ozone-depleting chemicals.

6. *Regulatory capture*: Appointing industry-sympathetic figures to head regulatory bodies so as to diminish the enforcement of those regulations.

7. *Greenhouse effect* (natural): Certain gases in the atmosphere let sunlight in but trap much of the infrared heat reflected back toward space from the surface, thus warming the Earth to a habitable level.

8. *Anthropogenic*: Human-caused

9. *Global warming (anthropogenic)*: The theory that human activities which release additional amounts of *greenhouse gases*—primarily carbon dioxide (CO_2) through the burning of fossil fuels—are adding to the natural warming in ways that will have serious negative impacts on human beings and on the environment in general.

10. *Mitigation strategy*: A strategy to *lessen* global warming.

11. *Adaptation strategy*: A strategy not to lessen global warming but to counteract its effects.

12. *Geoengineering (re global warming)*: Technological fixes to counteract the warming effects caused by human-produced greenhouse gases.

13. *Mitigationists*: Those favoring a mitigation strategy.

14. *Adaptationists*: Those favoring an adaptation strategy.

15. *Risk*: "The probability of a harm times the magnitude of its consequences" (Jasanoff).

16. *Precautionary principle*: A principle which "demands heightened caution in the face of uncertainty, to the point of inaction when the consequences of action are too unpredictable" (Jasanoff). (Contrast with risk-based assessment.)

17. *The Intergovernmental Panel on Climate Change (IPCC)*: An organization established in 1988 by the United Nations Environment Program and the World Meteorological Organization to consider the scientific information on climate change, judge the probable impact of such change, and recommend a response to the problem.

18. *ppm*: Parts per million.

19. *EPA*: US Environmental Protection Agency.

20. *Environmental justice*: "The fair treatment and meaningful involvement of all people regardless of race, color, national origin, or income with respect to the development, implementation, and enforcement of environmental laws, regulations, and policies" (EPA definition).

21. *Cost–benefit analysis*: A method of evaluation that compares likely costs with potential benefits, usually translating both costs and benefits into monetary terms.

22. *Discount rate*: Calculated difference between the present value and the future worth of something likely to be worth less in the future.

23. *The Stern Report*: A report, *The Economics of Climate Change* (2007), done under the leadership of Nicholas Stern, an adviser on climate change to the UK government), that did a cost–benefit analysis of different approaches to global warming.

24. *Inherent moral worth*. Having moral value in and of itself, apart from its effects on human beings.

25. *Anthropocentric*: Thinking of worth relative to humans.

26. *Senticentric*: Thinking of worth relative to sentient (feeling) beings.

27. *Biocentric (life-centered)*: Thinking of worth relative to living beings.
28. *Ecocentric*: Thinking of worth relative to ecosystems. (Also *holistic*.)
29. *Bioegalitarianism*: The view that all living things have equal worth.
30. *Ecosystem*: A local system of living organisms and the environment they depend on, considered as an integrated whole.

31. *Ecosphere*: All the ecosystems of Earth.
32. *Ecology*: The study of organisms, their environment, and the relation between the two.
33. *Land ethic*: An ethic from Aldo Leopold in which human beings no longer see themselves as conquerors of the land, but as members and citizens of it.
34. *Gaia*: A system of coevolving life and Earth as conceived by James Lovelock.

Questions

(Please explain your answers, making specific reference to relevant passages in the discussion.)

1. List some of what are typically claimed to be environmental problems.
2. Why did the early environmental movement and the counter-culture movement (of the 1960s and 1970s) fit so well together?
3. What were some of the reasons for the backlash against the environmental movement in the 1990s?
4. What is the greenhouse effect? What is the theory of anthropogenic global warming?
5. What are the issues between those who argue for a mitigation strategy against global warming and those who argue for an adaptation strategy?
6. Roughly, what is the difference between risk-based assessment and the precautionary principle?
7. The Routleys ask us to imagine the journey of a Third World bus. Describe this journey. What argument do they make based on this image?
8. What are some possible problems with the idea that we have responsibilities not to harm future people?

9. What is "environmental justice"? How does this concept figure into the global warming debates?
10. How does the choice of a "discount rate" affect the cost–benefit analysis of our choices re global warming?
11a. What percentage of your income would you be willing to pay to eliminate a 1 in 20 chance that a meteor would destroy all life on Earth within 25 years? 50 years? 100 years?
   b. Does your answer here tell you what percentage of your income you should be willing to pay to avoid possible global warming catastrophes? Why or why not?
12. "Those who hold an anthropocentric view of the world can't possibly care about the environment." Why is this statement incorrect?
13. Summarize the "Last Woman scenario." What issue is this scenario intended to highlight?
14. For Paul Taylor, what sorts of things have "inherent worth"? What is his argument for this?
15. Explain Aldo Leopold's land ethic?

21

The Environment
Readings

Edmund O. Wilson describes
environmental problems and
presents two opposing views as
to how they should be approached

Imagine that on an icy moon of Jupiter—say,
Ganymede—the space station of an alien civilization is
concealed. For millions of years its scientists have closely
watched the earth. […]

The watchers have been waiting for what might
be called the Moment. When it comes, occupying
only a few centuries and thus a mere tick in geological time, the forests shrink back to less than half
their original cover. Atmospheric carbon dioxide
rises to the highest level in 100,000 years. The ozone
layer of the stratosphere thins, and holes open at
the poles. Plumes of nitrous oxide and other toxins
rise from fires in South America and Africa, settle in
the upper troposphere and drift eastward across the
oceans. At night the land surface brightens with
millions of pinpoints of light, which coalesce into
blazing swaths across Europe, Japan and eastern
North America. A semicircle of fire spreads from gas
flares around the Persian Gulf.

It was all but inevitable, the watchers might tell us
if we met them, that from the great diversity of large

Reproduced from "Is Humanity Suicidal?" by Edward O. Wilson.
© 1993 by *The New York Times*. Courtesy of E. O. Wilson.

animals, one species or another would eventually gain
intelligent control of Earth. That role has fallen to
Homo sapiens, a primate risen in Africa from a lineage
that split away from the chimpanzee line five to eight
million years ago. Unlike any creature that lived
before, we have become a geophysical force, swiftly
changing the atmosphere and climate as well as the
composition of the world's fauna and flora. […]

Darwin's dice have rolled badly for Earth. It was a
misfortune for the living world in particular, many scientists believe, that a carnivorous primate and not some
more benign form of animal made the breakthrough.

[…]

In the relentless search for more food, we have
reduced animal life in lakes, rivers and now, increasingly,
the open ocean. And everywhere we pollute the air and
water, lower water tables and extinguish species.

[…]

The human species is, in a word, an environmental abnormality. It is possible that intelligence
in the wrong kind of species was foreordained to
be a fatal combination for the biosphere. Perhaps a
law of evolution is that intelligence usually extin-
guishes itself.

This admittedly dour scenario is based on what
can be termed the juggernaut theory of human
nature, which holds that people are programmed by
their genetic heritage to be so selfish that a sense of
global responsibility will come too late. Individuals
place themselves first, family second, tribe third and

Contemporary Moral and Social Issues: An Introduction through Original Fiction, Discussion, and Readings, First Edition. Thomas D. Davis.
© 2014 John Wiley & Sons, Inc. Published 2014 by John Wiley & Sons, Inc.

the rest of the world a distant fourth. Their genes also predispose them to plan ahead for one or two generation at most. [...]

The reason for this myopic fog, evolutionary biologists contend, is that it was actually advantageous during all but the last few millennia of the two millon years of existence of the genus Homo. The brain evolved into its present form during this long stretch of evolutionary time, during which people existed in small, preliterate hunter-gatherer bands. Life was precarious and short. A premium was placed on close attention to the near future and early reproduction and little else. [...]

The rules have recently changed, however. Global crises are rising in the life span of the generation now coming of age, a foreshortening that may explain why young people express more concern about the environment than do their elders. The time scale has contracted because of the exponential growth in both the human population and technologies impacting the environment.

[...]

Yet, mathematical exercises aside, who can safely measure the human capacity to overcome the perceived limits of Earth? The question of central interest is this: Are we racing to the brink of an abyss, or are we just gathering speed for a takeoff to a wonderful future? The crystal ball is clouded; the human condition baffles all the more because it is both unprecedented and bizarre, almost beyond understanding.

In the midst of uncertainty, opinions on the human prospect have tended to fall loosely into two schools. The first, exemptionalism, holds that since humankind is transcendent in intelligence and spirit, so must our species have been released from the iron laws of ecology that bind all other species. No matter how serious the problem, civilized human beings, by ingenuity, force of will and—who knows—divine dispensation, will find a solution.

Population growth? Good for the economy, claim some of the exemptionalists, and in any case a basic human right, so let it run. [...] Species going extinct? Not to worry. That is nature's way. Think of humankind as only the latest in a long line of exterminating agents in geological time. [...] [R]esources? The planet has more than enough resources to last indefinitely, if human genius is allowed to address each new problem in turn, without alarmist and unreasonable restrictions imposed on economic development. So hold the course, and touch the brakes lightly.

The opposing idea of reality is environmentalism, which sees humanity as a biological species tightly dependent on the natural world. As formidable as our intellect may be and as fierce our spirit, the argument goes, those qualities are not enough to free us from the constraints of the natural environment in which our human ancestors evolved. [...]

At the heart of the environmentalist world view is the conviction that human physical and spiritual health depends on sustaining the planet in a relatively unaltered state. Earth is our home in the full, genetic sense, where humanity and its ancestors existed for all the millions of years of their evolution. Natural ecosystems—forests, coral reefs, marine blue waters—maintain the world exactly as we would wish it to be maintained. When we debase the global environment and extinguish the variety of life, we are dismantling a support system that is too complex to understand, let alone replace in the foreseeable future.

[...]

Questions

1. Summarize what Wilson sees as the pessimistic view ("the dour scenario") of the place of, and the future of, humans in the natural world.

2. Contrast this with the more optimistic view he calls "exemptionalism."

Gabrielle Walker and Sir David King present a mitigationist view re global warming

[…] [P]hotographs taken from satellites have now shown conclusively what scientists have been fearing for decades: The North Pole is melting. Each summer, the spread of the sea ice shrinks a little farther. It is vanishing from beneath the feet of the Arctic's polar bears. If we do nothing to stop it, by the end of the century the ice, polar bears and all, could be gone.

The story of global warming has progressed in the past few years from conjecture to suspicion to cold, hard fact. We now know for certain that on every inhabited continent on Earth, year by year and decade by decade, the world's temperature is rising. Something, or someone, is turning up the heat.

Should we care? After all, over the billions of years our planet has been around its climate has changed many times. In the geological past there have been ice ages, global floods, and heat waves. There have also been winners and losers throughout Earth's history— some species have become extinct while others have gone forth and multiplied.

But this time is different. If the current wave of change has its way with us, the polar bears will not be the only ones to suffer. Human civilization has never before been faced with a climate that is changing this fast or this furiously. […]

[…] [T]he amount of material focusing on the problem has multiplied. Books, newspapers, TV, radio—another day, another headline. It has become almost impossible to sort out what really matters.

Amid this cacophony there is a handful of voices that persists in arguing that warming isn't happening, or that it's not caused by humans, while others see disaster around every corner and indulge in gory scenarios that have been labeled "climate porn." We don't agree with either of these approaches. Climate change is happening, and humans are largely to blame.

However, we do not believe that disaster is inevitable. A few shiny new Priuses won't get humans out of this mess, nor will sticking our collective heads in the sand. But we still have time to tackle the worst aspects of climate change if we act fast and work hard.

[…]

The science of warming

It's not really warming
Yes, it is. […] Reconstructions of past temperatures using corals, ice cores, and other techniques show that the temperature is hotter now than it has been for at least one thousand years and probably longer […].

It was warmer during the Middle Ages than it is now
No, it wasn't. Temperatures are higher now than they have been for at least one thousand years […].

The ice cores show that temperature goes up before carbon dioxide at the end of ice ages, so CO_2 can't cause warming
The ice cores do show a time lag between the onset of warming and the rise of carbon dioxide at the end of each ice age. However, that doesn't mean that carbon dioxide doesn't cause warming. In fact, nobody thinks that carbon dioxide is what causes the ice ages to stop. Instead, a wobble in our planet's orbit changes the distribution of the sunlight we receive. That causes a little warming, which sets in motion other processes to release carbon dioxide.

[…]

Temperatures were going down in the middle of the twentieth century even though carbon dioxide was rising, so CO_2 can't cause warming
This is a very popular argument put forward by climate skeptics, but it skates over the fact that scientists can explain why temperatures dropped a little in the middle of the twentieth century in the northern hemisphere. In fact, burning dirty fossil fuels produces sulfur-containing particles called aerosols, which reflect sunlight back to space and thus help to cool the planet. They thus act in a sort of tug-of-war with carbon dioxide, creating cooling that offsets the greenhouse warming.

Researchers now believe that these aerosols were responsible for the slight cooling that took place between about 1940 and the late 1960s. The reason they didn't keep cooling is two-fold: We cleaned up our act by banning the fuels that were choking our cities, and carbon dioxide levels rose so high that they won the tug-of-war. Also, the reason this cooling was seen only in the northern hemisphere is that there was neither enough land mass nor enough industry in the southern hemisphere to produce enough aerosols to counteract the effect of carbon dioxide.

Humans aren't responsible for the warming—it's all been caused by a natural cycle/changes in the sun

In fact, the warming over the past few decades has human fingerprints all over it. There's no natural cycle that can explain what we've seen, and the sun has been going in the wrong direction. (Left to itself, the sun would have caused a slight cooling!) What's more, models tell us that the increased greenhouse gas concentrations that we have had should cause exactly the changes that we have already seen. There's no more room for doubt in this. Wedunnit [...].

Impacts of climate change

Earth's climate is constantly changing, so why should we worry?

Our planet's climate is certainly very restless, and in times past it has been both much warmer and much colder than it is today. But the whole of human civilization has been built around the climate we have now. For instance, just a few hundred thousand years ago, sea level was several feet higher than it is now, but back then there were no coastal cities waiting to be drowned [...].

A little warming could be a good thing

There are a few parts of the world where a little warming might indeed be a good thing. For instance, in the middle latitudes—northern Europe, the United States, and parts of Russia—a temperature rise of up to two degrees should actually increase overall crop yields. However, the problem with climate change is that you can't pick and choose its effects. Even for these countries, the increased food production will

also come with northward movement of the storm tracks (less rain, more fires and droughts), more intense individual rainstorms (risk of flooding), rising sea level, more intense storms coming in from the oceans (threats to coastal cities), and more intense heat waves (mass mortality and threat to crops). In the poorest parts of the world, the effects will be more severe with even a modest rise in temperature. In fact, that's already happening. Even if you didn't want to act on this for the sake of social justice, you'd need to realize that in a fully global economy, what affects some countries will eventually hurt the rest.

The chances are that we are already going to experience the effects of a few degrees' warming in any case—that much is too late to stop. But action that we take now could help us avert worse warming, in which even the richest, most northerly countries would suffer [...].

If the world warms, fewer people will die from the cold

It's true that there will be fewer extreme cold events in the world, and the reduction in deaths from cold will almost certainly outweigh the increase in deaths from heat waves. But that doesn't mean humans will survive better overall. As well as direct deaths from the heat, people will also be more vulnerable to flooding, infectious diseases, and starvation. The IPCC report [...] says clearly that in terms of numbers of lives these increased dangers far outweigh the reduction in deaths from the cold.

[...]

Economics

We can't afford to tackle climate change

In fact, tackling climate change turns out to be surprisingly cheap. Many of the strategies we need to employ to increase efficiency will actually save money where it has previously been wasted [...], and investment in new technologies could well lead to a growth spurt.

We'd be better off spending the money on aid

This is at best misguided. For one thing, if the money is not used for dealing with climate change, it's very unlikely to go to aid instead. [...]

Also, this is not about trying to solve all the troubles in the world—which is just as well, since that goal has spectacularly evaded us so far. Instead, it's about solving a specific problem faced by all of us, so we can leave behind a climate that our grandchildren will be able to weather.

The next two decades offer our only possible window of opportunity to rein in greenhouse gas levels to one that will achieve this goal. After that, no future generations of humans would be able to keep the greenhouse problem in check. For us, or our children, or our grandchildren, it would be too late.

[...]

Questions

1. What general position do Walker and King take on the issue of anthropogenic global warming? Do they believe that theirs is one of the less extreme views?

2. How do they respond to the claim that we can't afford to tackle global warming? To the claim that we'd be better off spending the money on other things?

Bjorn Lomborg presents an adaptationist case re global warming

[...]

[T]he media pound us with increasingly dramatic stories of our ever worsening climate. In 2006, *Time* did a special report on global warming, with the cover spelling out the scare story with repetitive austerity: "Be worried. Be *very* worried."[1] The magazine told us that the climate is crashing, affecting us both globally by playing havoc with the biosphere and individually through such health effects as heatstrokes, asthma, and infectious diseases. The heart-breaking image on the cover was of a lone polar bear on a melting ice floe, searching in vain for the next piece of ice to jump to. *Time* told us that due to global warming bears "are starting to turn up drowned" and that at some point they will become extinct.[2]

[...]

Over the past few years, this story has cropped up many times, based first on a World Wildlife Fund report in 2002 and later on the Arctic Climate Impact Assessment from 2004.[3] Both relied extensively on research published in 2001 by the Polar Bear Specialist Group of the World Conservation Union.[4]

From *Cool It: The Skeptical Environmentalist's Guide to Global Warming*, by Bjorn Lomborg. New York: Alfred Knopf, 2007, pp. 4–9.

But what this group really told us was that of the twenty distinct subpopulations of polar bears, one or possibly two were declining in Baffin Bay; more than half were known to be stable; and two subpopulations were actually *increasing* around the Beaufort Sea. Moreover, it is reported that the global polar-bear population has *increased* dramatically over the past decades, from about five thousand members in the 1960s to twenty-five thousand today, through stricter hunting regulation.[5]

[...]

The polar-bear story teaches us three things. First, we hear *vastly exaggerated and emotional claims* that are simply not supported by data. Yes, it is likely that disappearing ice will make it harder for polar bears to continue their traditional foraging patterns and that they will increasingly take up a lifestyle similar to that of brown bears, from which they evolved.[6] They may eventually decline, though dramatic declines seem unlikely. But over the past forty years, the population has increased dramatically and the populations are now stable. The ones going down are in areas that are getting *colder*. Yet we are told that global warming will make polar bears extinct, possibly within ten years, and that future kids will have to read about them in storybooks.

Second, polar bears are *not the only story*. While we hear only about the troubled species, it is also a fact that many species will do *better* with climate change. [...]

The third point is that *our worry makes us focus on the wrong solutions.* We are being told that the plight of the polar bear shows "the need for stricter curbs on greenhouse-gas emissions linked to global warming."[7] Even if we accept the flawed idea of using the 1987 population of polar bears around Hudson Bay as a baseline, so that we lose 15 bears each year, what can we do? If we try helping them by cutting greenhouse gases, we can at the very best avoid 15 bears dying. We will later see that realistically we can do not even close to that much good—probably we can save about 0.06 bears per year. But 49 bears from the same population are getting shot each year, and this we can easily do something about.[8] Thus, if we really want a stable population of polar bears, dealing first with the 49 shot ones might be both a smarter and a more viable strategy. Yet it is not the one we end up hearing about.[…]

The argument in this book is simple.

1. *Global warming is real and man-made.* It will have a serious impact on humans and the environment toward the end of this century.
2. *Statements about the strong, ominous, and immediate consequences of global warming are often wildly exaggerated*, and this is unlikely to result in good policy.
3. *We need simpler, smarter, and more efficient solutions for global warming* rather than excessive if well-intentioned efforts. Large and very expensive CO_2 cuts made now will have only a rather small and insignificant impact far into the future.
4. *Many other issues are much more important than global warming.* We need to get our perspective back. There are many more pressing problems in the world, such as hunger, poverty, and disease. By addressing them, we can help more people, at lower cost, with a much higher chance of success than by pursuing drastic climate policies at a cost of trillions of dollars.

These four points will rile a lot of people. We have become so accustomed to the standard story: climate change is not only real but will lead to unimaginable catastrophes, while doing something about it is not only cheap but morally right. We perhaps understandably expect that anyone questioning this line of reasoning must have evil intentions. Yet I think—with the best of intentions—it is necessary that we at least allow ourselves to examine our logic before we embark on the biggest public investment in history.

We need to remind ourselves that our ultimate goal is not to reduce greenhouse gases or global warming per se but to improve the quality of life and the environment. We all want to leave the planet in decent shape for our kids. Radically reducing greenhouse-gas emissions is not necessarily the best way to achieve that. As we go through the data, we will see that it actually is one of the least helpful ways of serving humanity or the environment.

[…]

Questions

1. Explain in what ways Lomborg thinks claims that global warming will soon wipe out the polar bears are wrong. What lessons does he think we can draw from such claims?

2. What does Lomborg believe the most sensible approach to global warming would be?

Notes

1. *Time*, 2006, April 6. Be Worried. Be Very Worried.
2. "And with sea ice vanishing, polar bears—prodigious swimmers but not inexhaustible ones—are starting to turn up drowned. 'There will be no polar ice by 2060,' says Larry Schweiger, president of the National Wildlife Federation. 'Somewhere along that path, the polar bear drops out'" (Kluger, 2006).

[Kluger, J. (2006, April 3). Polar Ice Caps Are Melting Faster Than Ever…More and More Land Is Being Devastated by Drought…Rising Waters Are Drowning Low-lying Communities…by Any Measure, Earth Is at…the Tipping Point. *Time*. Retrieved 6-11-06, from http://www.time.com/time/magazine/article/0,9171, 1176980,00.html.]

3. Berner et al., 2005; Hassol, 2004.

[Berner, J., Symon, C., Arris, L., Heal, O. W., Arctic Climate Impact Assessment, National Science Foundation (US), et al. (2005). Arctic Climate Impact Assessment. New York: Cambridge University Press. Retrieved 7-11-06, from http://www.acia.uaf.edu/pages#scientific. html. Hassol, S. J. (2004). Impacts of a Warming Arctic: Arctic Climate Impact Assessment. New York: Cambridge University Press. Retrieved 7-11-06, from http://www.acia.uaf.edu/pages/overviewhtml.]

4. The World Conservation Union is also known as the IUCN; the Polar Bear Specialist Group website is http://pbsg.npolar.no/default.htm (IUCN Species Survival Commission, 2001).

[IUCN Species Survival Commission. (2001). Polar Bears: Proceedings of the 13th Working Meeting of the IUCNISSC Polar Bear Specialist Group, 23–28 June 2001, Nuuk, Greenland. Retrieved 6-11-2006, from http://pbsg.npolar.no/docs/PBSG13proc.pdf.]

5. The IUCN counts twenty groups, but most commentators mention about nineteen subpopulations (IUCN Species Survival Commission, 2001:22).

6. The Arctic Climate Impact Assessment finds it likely that disappearing ice will make polar bears take up "a terrestrial summer lifestyle similar to that of brown bears, from which they evolved." It talks about the "threat" that polar bears would become hybridized with brown and grizzly bears (Berner et al., 2005:509).

7. Eilperin, 2004.

[Eilperin, J. (2004). Study Says Polar Bears Could Face Extinction. *The Washington Post*. Retrieved 7-11-06, from http://www.washington post.com/wp-dyn/ articles / A35233-2004Nov8.html.]

8. This is based on a simple model starting in 2000 with a population of one thousand, a reduction of 1.5 percent (fifteen bears first year), and the full Kyoto Protocol reducing global warming by about 7 percent in 2100 (Wigley, 1998).

[Wigley, T. M. L. (1998). The Kyoto Protocol: CO2, CH4 and Climate Implications. *Geophysical Research Letters*, 25(13), 2285–8.]

Timothy Taylor discusses the problem of how to discount the future, especially in the case of low-probability, high-risk events

[…]

It's easy to find scientists who argue that the IPCC forecasts are overstated and have been hyped up to some extent by governments. The conclusion I draw from all this controversy is that the extent of uncertainty is probably understated. In other words, things could be better than the best IPCC scenario; they could be worse than the worst, as well.

As someone who is not a climate scientist, I know one thing for sure: A very large number of climate scientists do believe that global warming is a real and dangerous phenomenon, and a smaller minority disagrees. Maybe the small minority will eventually turn out to be right (it wouldn't be the first time that a small minority turned out to be right), but when the bulk of experts in a certain area believe something, it's wise to assume that there is at least some probability that the majority is correct. We can quarrel over whether the probability that they're correct is 99%, or 90%, or 50%, but I don't see how one can reasonably say that there is zero probability that the majority of experts aren't correct about something. They probably are onto something.

When there's a risk of something bad happening, the standard economic response is to think about whether it's possible to buy insurance, and in fact, policies about global warming are a kind of insurance. Just as you pay for insurance on your home or your car, and you hope the bad thing doesn't happen or isn't as bad as you fear, we need to think about what kind of insurance it makes sense to buy for global warming in a public policy sense. And, of course, we'll hope the bad thing doesn't happen or isn't as bad as we'd feared. Of course, to make sensible decisions about insurance, you have to decide how bad the risk is and how much insurance it makes sense to buy. It doesn't mean, of course, you just buy huge amounts of insurance against relatively small risks, but taking out zero insurance is not usually a sensible approach if you're confronted with risks that are real.

Evaluating the problem of climate change involves some difficult questions of how to value costs and benefits. [...] [M]y underlying approach here, following the standard IPCC estimates, is to say that the most likely scenario for climate change right now is one of moderate warming with moderate costs. And we would deal with this with some combination of moderate strategies, a mix of, say, reducing energy usage and paying to mitigate some of the other problems that arise, like flooding or changes in agricultural yields, as they happen. If it's a middle-range problem, it's not a world-changing problem. But the IPCC evidence also suggests there is some lower-probability chance that the most likely scenario isn't what happens, and there will be either very high warming or very high costs resulting from moderate warming. And I think actually that much of the concern over climate change isn't about the moderate scenario; it's about the risk of something perhaps less likely but very, very bad happening. How do we think about these kinds of risks?

Richard Posner [...] posed this question a few years back in a book called *Catastrophe* [that] was about how you should respond to low-risk, high-cost events. And he includes global warming as being in this category. He also uses the useful law professor approach of trying out some other examples to draw out our intuition on the overall issues here. For example, what's the chance of a large asteroid hitting the globe in the next 100 years? Maybe there's one chance in 100 million of, say, 1.5 billion people dying—small chance, large, bad outcome if it does happen. What about a chance of a severe bioterrorist attack? Say there's one chance in 100,000 that an attack like that will kill 100 million Americans at some point in the next 100 years. What's the appropriate policy response to lower-probability, high-cost events?

You would, of course, make some generic statements here. If the probability of the event gets bigger, you should spend more to avoid it. If the probability is smaller, spend less. If the potential cost is bigger, you should spend more to avoid it. If the potential cost is smaller, you should spend less. You can also note that people often are not very good at thinking about these kinds of low-probability risks. People either tend to overspend because they base all their actions on the fear of the biggest possible loss, or they brush it aside and they spend nothing because they say there's not very much chance it's going to happen. The more rational approach has to balance these two possibilities. You would search for ways to reduce the mega-risk because it's so big, but you wouldn't try to eliminate all risk because there's a relatively low chance of that worst outcome happening. Stick to relatively low-cost approaches in the present, but build up over time.

For example, think about what one might do if one took the asteroid risk seriously. You might start an agency, for example, that would formulate a plan for disrupting the flight of an asteroid. You would start early monitoring of possible asteroids, so we would know they were coming sooner. Eventually, the goal of this agency would be to act in the time we have available for early warning if we knew an asteroid was likely to hit. We might also have that agency think about what steps the globe would take if an asteroid was on its way. They could produce an annual report for what concrete steps we might take for dealing with the aftereffects. These policies might have useful spinoffs. Monitoring asteroids might well have some scientific benefits. Emergency plans for an asteroid strike might also be useful if, say, a major tidal wave, or an earthquake, or a volcanic eruption occurred.

Notice this plan doesn't eliminate the risk of a huge asteroid strike. Maybe instead of its being something that [has a] one in 100 million [chance] of happening, maybe we could do something that would make it be one in 1 billion instead. Or, instead of something that would cause 1.5 billion people to die, maybe only 100 million people would die when the asteroid hit. In other words, the risk doesn't go away, but you need to balance the reduction in risks against the costs you're incurring. In the realm of climate change and global warming, we need [to cultivate] a sense of these catastrophe scenarios in this way, and we need to do something to think about them. But nothing is particularly gained by making a really broad claim that most scientists agree that catastrophes are near term and high probability. That's not what the IPCC reports say. Most scientists do agree that global warming is a real problem with high costs that extend off into the future, but that's very different from believing that it's a high-probability catastrophe just about to happen. The broad approach would be to balance costs of action with reductions in risk and reductions in harm.

Let me [...] consider another big problem with comparing costs and benefits of climate change. The costs of dealing with climate change are incurred relatively close to the present. The benefits are much further off in the future. In fact, the benefits might be hundreds of years into the future. One prominent report on climate change that came out in 2006 by a very eminent British economist named Nicholas Stern estimated that climate change would reduce world GDP by an average of 1% per year over the next century, but the total loss over time would be equal to 14% of world GDP. How do you get from 1% average over the next century to 14% average over time? It turns out that when you look at Stern's calculations more closely, half of the losses he suggests will happen from climate change happen after the year 2800. Yes, that's 2800, about eight centuries from now.

Ask yourself a question: If we're going to have costs of reducing carbon emissions right now and if it's worth the benefits, should we be paying attention to benefits that are more than 800 years off in the future? I think the answer is obviously yes, we should pay attention to benefits that far off in the future, but it's a yes that comes with a bit of an asterisk. I would argue, in common with most economists, that while you definitely want to count benefits in the future, the further off the benefits are in the future, the less you want to count them. In other words, benefits that arrive next year or in a decade should be counted as worth more than benefits that arrive several centuries off in the future.

A lot of noneconomists don't like doing this. How can you say a life in the future is worth less than a life in the present? All lives are equal. You can hear the rhetoric, right? Other people say we just don't want to mess up the environment—not now, not ever. It doesn't matter to me the timeline or how far off the future is. I think that view is something that people might not really believe if they thought about it more closely. Do you really want to place the same value on someone who lives three generations from now or 50 generations from now as you place on someone who's alive today? There are so many future generations out there. Is it really the problem of this generation to pay for every possible reaction that might affect the entire future of the human race? Sure, maybe we have a responsibility to start in the right direction, but don't they have some responsibilities, too? I mean, after all, the odds are good that people in the future will have vastly better energy technology, vastly better health care, vastly longer lives, and a higher standard of living Shouldn't they have some responsibility, as well?

[…] The amount by which you count the future less than the present is what economists call the "discount rate." If you ignore the difference between the present and the future, basically, you're saying your discount rate, the amount you discount the future, is zero, and as a result, anything happening eight centuries from now should count just as much to you as something happening this week. If you think that sounds a little crazy, you don't believe the discount rate ought to be zero. We could argue over what the discount rate ought to be—1% a year, 2% a year, 3% a year—but saying it should be zero is a very extreme choice.

[…]

A zero discount rate has the natural effect that it makes it very important to deal right now with big problems that could be a ways off in the future. Almost any positive discount rate—1, 2, 3% a year—means that you end up just not worrying too much about anything that's several hundred years off in the future. What discount rate you choose is probably more important for your thinking about climate change policy than all the rest of the uncertainty in the economic and meteorological models about costs and benefits put together.

[…]

Questions

1. Why does Taylor believe that anthropogenic global warming is real? Why does he believe that there is a low, but very real, probability that the effect of global warming will be very, very bad?
2. How does Taylor think we should approach low-risk, high-cost events? (Refer to his asteroid example.)
3. How does Taylor think we should deal with costs close to the present versus costs in the more distant future? With the welfare of those close to us in time versus the welfare of those much farther in the future?

William Baxter argues for an anthropocentric view of the environment

[...]

I start with the modest proposition that, in dealing with pollution, or indeed with any problem, it is helpful to know what one is attempting to accomplish. Agreement on how and whether to pursue a particular objective, such as pollution control, is not possible unless some more general objective has been identified and stated with reasonable precision. We talk loosely of having clean air and clean water, of preserving our wilderness areas, and so forth. But none of these is a sufficiently general objective: each is more accurately viewed as a means rather than as an end.

With regard to clean air, for example, one may ask, "how clean?" and "what does clean mean?" It is even reasonable to ask, "why have clean air?" Each of these questions is an implicit demand that a more general community goal be stated—a goal sufficiently general in its scope and enjoying sufficiently general assent among the community of actors that such "why" questions no longer seem admissible with respect to that goal.

If, for example, one states as a goal the proposition that "every person should be free to do whatever he wishes in contexts where his actions do not interfere with the interests of other human beings," the speaker is unlikely to be met with a response of "why." The goal may be criticized as uncertain in its implications or difficult to implement, but it is so basic a tenet of our civilization—it reflects a cultural value so broadly shared, at least in the abstract—that the question "why" is seen as impertinent or imponderable or both.

I do not mean to suggest that everyone would agree with the "spheres of freedom" objective just stated. Still less do I mean to suggest that a society could subscribe to four or five such general objectives that would be adequate in their coverage to serve as testing criteria by which all other disagreements might be measured. One difficulty in the attempt to construct such a list is that each new goal added will conflict, in certain applications, with each prior goal listed; and thus each goal serves as a limited qualification on prior goals.

Without any expectation of obtaining unanimous consent to them, let me set forth four goals that I generally use as ultimate testing criteria in attempting to frame solutions to problems of human organization. My position regarding pollution stems from these four criteria. If the criteria appeal to you and any part of what appears hereafter does not, our disagreement will have a helpful focus: which of us is correct, analytically, in supposing that his position on pollution would better serve these general goals. If the criteria do not seem acceptable to you, then it is to be expected that our more particular judgments will differ, and the task will then be yours to identify the basic set of criteria upon which your particular judgments rest.

Reproduced with permission from *People or Penguins: The Case for Optimal Pollution*, by William F. Baxter. New York: Columbia University Press, 1974. Columbia University Press.

My criteria are as follows:

1. The spheres of freedom criterion stated above.
2. Waste is a bad thing. The dominant feature of human existence is scarcity—our available resources, our aggregate labors, and our skill in employing both have always been, and will continue for some time to be, inadequate to yield to every man all the tangible and intangible satisfactions he would like to have. Hence, none of those resources, or labors, or skills, should be wasted—that is, employed so as to yield less than they might yield in human satisfactions.
3. Every human being should be regarded as an end rather than as a means to be used for the betterment of another. Each should be afforded dignity and regarded as having an absolute claim to an even-handed application of such rules as the community may adopt for its governance.
4. Both the incentive and the opportunity to improve his share of satisfactions should be preserved to every individual. Preservation of incentive is dictated by the "no-waste" criterion and enjoins against the continuous, totally egalitarian redistribution of satisfactions, or wealth; but subject to that constraint, everyone should receive, by continuous redistribution if necessary, some minimal share of aggregate wealth so as to avoid a level of privation from which the opportunity to improve his situation becomes illusory.

The relationship of these highly general goals to the more specific environmental issues at hand may not be readily apparent, and I am not yet ready to demonstrate their pervasive implications. But let me give one indication of their implications. Recently scientists have informed us that use of DDT in food production is causing damage to the penguin population. For the present purposes let us accept that assertion as an indisputable scientific fact. The scientific fact is often asserted as if the correct implication—that we must stop agricultural use of DDT—followed from the mere statement of the fact of penguin damage. But plainly it does not follow if my criteria are employed.

My criteria are oriented to people, not penguins. Damage to penguins, or sugar pines, or geological marvels is, without more, simply irrelevant. One must go further, by my criteria, and say: Penguins are important because people enjoy seeing them walk about rocks; and furthermore, the well-being of people would be less impaired by halting use of DDT than by giving up penguins. In short, my observations about environmental problems will be people-oriented, as are my criteria. I have no interest in preserving penguins for their own sake.

It may be said by way of objection to this position, that it is very selfish of people to act as if each person represented one unit of importance and nothing else was of any importance. It is undeniably selfish. Nevertheless I think it is the only tenable starting place for analysis for several reasons. First, no other position corresponds to the way most people really think and act—i.e., corresponds to reality.

Second, this attitude does not portend any massive destruction of nonhuman flora and fauna, for people depend on them in many obvious ways, and they will be preserved because and to the degree that humans do depend on them.

Third, what is good for humans is, in many respects, good for penguins and pine trees—clean air for example. So that humans are, in these respects, surrogates for plant and animal life.

Fourth, I do not know how we could administer any other system. Our decisions are either private or collective. Insofar as Mr Jones is free to act privately, he may give such preferences as he wishes to other forms of life: he may feed birds in winter and do with less himself, and he may even decline to resist an advancing polar bear on the ground that the bear's appetite is more important than those portions of himself that the bear may choose to eat. In short my basic premise does not rule out private altruism to competing life-forms. It does rule out, however, Mr Jones' inclination to feed Mr Smith to the bear, however hungry the bear, however despicable Mr Smith.

Insofar as we act collectively on the other hand, only humans can be afforded an opportunity to participate in the collective decisions. Penguins cannot vote now and are unlikely subjects for the franchise—pine trees more unlikely still. Again each individual is free to cast his vote so as to benefit sugar pines if that is his inclination. But many of the more extreme assertions that one hears from some conservationists amount to tacit assertions that they are specially appointed representatives of sugar pines, and hence that their preferences should be weighted more heavily than the preferences of other humans who do not enjoy equal rapport with "nature." The simplistic assertion that agricultural use of DDT must stop at once because it is harmful to penguins is of that type.

Fifth, if polar bears or pine trees or penguins, like men, are to be regarded as ends rather than means, if they are to count in our calculus of social organization, someone must tell me how much each one counts, and someone must tell me how these life-forms are to be permitted to express their preferences, for I do not know either answer. If the answer is that certain people are to hold their proxies, then I want to know how those proxy-holders are to be selected: self-appointment does not seem workable to me.

Sixth, and by way of summary of all the foregoing, let me point out that the set of environmental issues under discussion—although they raise very complex technical questions of how to achieve any objective—ultimately raise a normative question: what *ought* we to do? Questions of *ought* are unique to the human mind and world—they are meaningless as applied to a nonhuman situation.

I reject the proposition that we *ought* to respect the "balance of nature" or to "preserve the environment" unless the reason for doing so, express or implied, is the benefit of man.

[...]

Questions

1. What are the "four goals" Baxter generally uses in "attempting to frame solutions to problems of human organization"? To what extent do you agree or disagree with these goals? Do you believe these are sufficient as the main goals in framing solutions to the environmental problems we face?

2. Suppose the majority of the people in a society decided that "we ought to preserve penguins for their own sake" and instituted policies to protect penguins.
   (a) Could Baxter consistently argue that such policies were wrong?
   (b) Could he consistently argue that the thinking behind such policies was wrong?

Richard Routley argues against an anthropocentric view of the environment

It is increasingly said that civilization, Western civilization at least, stands in need of a new ethic (and derivatively of a new economics) setting out people's relations to the natural environment, in Leopold's words "an ethic dealing with man's relation to land and to the animals and plants which grow upon it."[1] It is not of course that old

From "Is There a Need for a New, an Environmental Ethic?" by Richard Routley (later Richard Sylvan). This essay was originally published in *Proceedings of the XV World Congress of Philosophy*, Varna, Bulgaria, 1, 1973, pp. 205–10.

and prevailing ethics do not deal with man's relation to nature; they do, and on the prevailing view man is free to deal with nature as he pleases, i.e., his relations with nature, insofar at least as they do not affect others, are not subject to moral censure.

[...]

[E]*thic* is ambiguous, as between a specific ethical system, a *specific* ethic, and a more generic notion, a super ethic, under which specific ethics cluster. An ethical system S is, near enough, a propositional system (i.e. a structured set of propositions) or theory which includes (like individuals of a theory) a set of values and (like postulates of a theory) a set of general evaluative judgments concerning conduct, typically of what is obligatory, permissible and wrong, of what are rights, what is valued, and so forth. A general or lawlike proposition of a system is a principle; and certainly if systems S_1 and S_2 contain different principles, then they are different systems. It follows that any environmental ethic differs from the important traditional ethics outlined, Moreover if environmental ethics differ from Western ethical systems on some *core* principle embedded in Western systems, then these systems differ from the Western super ethic (assuming, what seems to be so, that it can be uniquely characterized)—in which case if an environmental ethic *is* needed then a new ethic is wanted. It suffices then to locate a core principle and to provide environmental counter examples to it.

It is commonly assumed that there are, what amount to, core principles of Western ethical systems, principles that will accordingly belong to the super ethic. The fairness principle inscribed in the Golden Rule provides one example. Directly relevant here, as a good stab at a core principle, is the commonly formulated liberal principle of the modified dominance position. A recent formulation runs as follows:

> The liberal philosophy of the Western world holds that one should be able to do what he wishes, providing (1) that he does not harm others and (2) that he is not likely to harm himself irreparably.[2]

Let us call this principle *basic (human) chauvinism*—because under it humans, or people, come first and everything else a bad last—though sometimes the principle is hailed as a *freedom* principle because it gives permission to perform a wide range of actions (including actions which mess up the environment and natural things) providing they do not harm others. In fact it tends to cunningly shift the onus of proof to others. It is worth remarking that *harming others* in the restriction is narrower than a restriction to the (usual) interests of others; it is not enough that it is in my interests, because I detest you, that you stop breathing; you are free to breathe, for the time being anyway, because it does not harm me. There remains a problem however as to exactly what counts as harm or interference. Moreover the width of the principle is so far obscure because "other" may be filled out in significantly different ways: it makes a difference to the extent, and privilege, of the chauvinism whether "other" expands to "other human"—which is too

restrictive—or to "other person" or to "other sentient being"; and it makes a difference to the adequacy of the principle, and inversely to its economic applicability, to which class of others it is intended to apply, whether to future as well as to present others, whether to remote future others or only to non-discountable future others and whether to possible others. The latter would make the principle completely unworkable, and it is generally assumed that it applies at most to present and future others.

It is taken for granted in designing counter examples to basic chauvinist principles, that a semantic analysis of permissibility and obligation statements stretches out over ideal situations (which may be incomplete or even inconsistent), so that what is permissible holds in some ideal situation, what is obligatory in every ideal situation, and what is wrong is excluded in every ideal situation. But the main point to grasp for the counter examples that follow, is that ethical principles if correct are universal and are assessed over the class of ideal situations.

(i) The *last man* example. The last man (or person) surviving the collapse of the world system lays about him, eliminating, as far as he can, every living thing, animal or plant (but painlessly if you like, as at the best abattoirs). What he does is quite permissible according to basic chauvinism, but on environmental grounds what he does is wrong. Moreover one does not have to be committed to esoteric values to regard Mr Last Man as behaving badly (the reason being perhaps that radical thinking and values have shifted in an environmental direction in advance of corresponding shifts in the formulation of fundamental evaluative principles).

(ii) The *last people* example. The last man example can be broadened to the last people example. We can assume that they know they are the last people, e.g. because they are aware that radiation effects have blocked any chance of reproduction. One considers the last people in order to rule out the possibility that what these people do harms or somehow physically interferes with later people. Otherwise one could as well consider science fiction cases where people arrive at a new planet and destroy its ecosystems, whether with good intentions such as perfecting the planet for their ends and making it more fruitful or, forgetting the lesser traditions, just for the hell of it.

Let us assume that the last people are very numerous. They humanely exterminate every wild animal and they eliminate the fish of the seas, they put all arable land under intensive cultivation, and all remaining forests disappear in favour of quarries or plantations, and so on. They may give various familiar reasons for this, e.g. they believe it is the way to salvation or to perfection, or they are simply satisfying reasonable needs, or even that it is needed to keep the last people employed or occupied so that they do not worry too much about their impending extinction. On an environmental ethic the last people have behaved badly; they have simplified largely destroyed all the natural ecosystems, and with their demise the world will soon be an ugly and largely wrecked place. But this conduct may conform with the basic chauvinist principle, and as well with the principles enjoined by the lesser traditions. Indeed the main point of elaborating this example is because, as the last man example reveals, basic chauvinism may conflict with stewardship or co-operation principles. The conflict may be removed it seems by conjoining a further proviso to the basic principle, [to] the effect (3) that he does not willfully destroy natural resources. But as the last people do not destroy resources willfully, but perhaps. "for the best of reasons," the variant is still environmentally inadequate.

(iii) The *great entrepreneur* example. The last man example can be adjusted so as to not fall foul of clause (3). The last man is an industrialist; he runs a giant complex of automated factories and farms which he proceeds to extend. He produces automobiles among other things, renewable and recyclable resources of course, only he dumps and recycles these shortly after manufacture and sale to a dummy buyer instead of putting them on the road for a short time as we do. Of course he has best of reasons for his activity, e.g. he is increasing gross world product, or he is improving output to fulfill some plan, and he will be increasing his own and general welfare since he much prefers increased output and productivity. The entrepreneur's behavior is on the Western ethic quite permissible; indeed his conduct is commonly thought to be quite fine and may even meet Pareto optimality requirements given prevailing notions of being "better off."

Just as we can extend the last man example to a class of last people, so we can extend this example to

the *industrial society* example: the society looks rather like ours.

(iv) The *vanishing species* example. Consider the blue whale, a mixed good on the economic picture. The blue whale is on the verge of extinction because of his qualities as a private good, as a source of valuable oil and meat. The catching and marketing of blue whales does not harm the whalers; it does not harm or physically interfere with others in any good sense, though it may upset them and they may be prepared to compensate the whalers if they desist; nor need whale hunting be willful destruction. (Slightly different examples which eliminate the hunting aspect of the blue whale example are provided by cases where a species is eliminated or threatened through destruction of its habitat by man's activity or the activities of animals he has introduced, e.g. many plains-dwelling Australian marsupials and the Arabian oryx.) The behavior of the whalers in eliminating this magnificent species of whale is accordingly quite permissible—at least according to basic chauvinism. But on an environmental ethic it is not. However, the free-market mechanism will not cease allocating whales to commercial uses, as a satisfactory environmental economics would; instead the market model will grind inexorably along the private demand curve until the blue whale population is no longer viable—if that point has not already been passed.

In sum, the class of permissible actions that rebound on the environment is more narrowly circumscribed on an environmental ethic than it is in the Western super ethic. But aren't environmentalists going too far in claiming that these people, those of the examples and respected industrialists, fishermen and farmers are behaving, when engaging in environmentally degrading activities of the sort described, in a morally impermissible way? No, what these people do is to a greater or lesser extent evil, and hence in serious cases morally impermissible. For example, insofar as the killing or forced displacement of primitive peoples who stand in the way of an industrial development is morally indefensible and impermissible, so also is the slaughter of the last remaining blue whales for private profit. But how to reformulate basic chauvinism as a satisfactory freedom principle is a more difficult matter. A tentative, but none too adequate beginning might be made by extending (2) to include harm to or interference with others who would be so affected by the action in question were they placed in the environment and (3) to exclude speciecide. It may be preferable, in view of the way the freedom principle sets the onus of proof, simply to scrap it altogether, and instead to specify classes of rights and permissible conduct, as in a bill of rights.

[…]

An environmental ethic does not commit one to the view that objects such as trees have rights (though such a view is occasionally held, e.g. by pantheists. But pantheism is false since artifacts are not alive). For moral prohibitions forbidding certain actions with respect to an object do not award that object a correlative right. That it would be wrong to mutilate a given tree or piece of property does not entail that the tree or property has a correlative right not to be mutilated (without seriously stretching the notion of a right). Environmental views can stick with mainstream theses according to which rights are coupled with corresponding responsibilities and so with bearing obligations, and with corresponding interests and concern; i.e. at least, whatever has a right also has responsibilities and therefore obligations, and whatever has a right has interests. Thus although any person may have a right by no means every living thing can (significantly) have rights, and arguably most sentient objects other than persons cannot have rights. But persons can relate morally, through obligations, prohibitions and so forth, to practically anything at all.

The species bias of certain ethical and economic positions which aim to make principles of conduct or reasonable economic behavior calculable is easily brought out. These positions typically employ a single criterion p, such as preference or happiness, as a *summum bonum;* characteristically each individual of some *base* class, almost always humans, but perhaps including future humans, is supposed to have an ordinal p ranking of states in question (e.g. of affairs, of the economy); then some principle is supplied to determine a collective p ranking of these states in terms of individual p rankings, and what is best or ought to be done is determined either directly, as in act-utilitarianism under the Greatest Happiness principle, or indirectly, as in rule-utilitarianism, in terms of some optimization principle applied to the collective ranking. The species bias is transparent from the selection of the base class. And even if the base class is extended to embrace persons, or even some animals (at the cost, like that of including remotely future humans, of losing testability), the positions are open to familiar criticism, namely that the whole of the base class may be prejudiced in a way which leads to unjust principles. For example if every member of the base class detests dingoes, on the basis of mistaken data as to dingoes' behavior, then by the Pareto ranking test the collective ranking will rank states where dingoes are exterminated very highly, from which it will generally be concluded that dingoes ought to be exterminated (the evaluation of most Australian farmers anyway). Likewise it would just be a happy accident, it seems, if collective demand (horizontally summed from individual demand) for a state of the economy with blue whales as a mixed good, were to succeed in outweighing private whaling demands; for if no one in the base class happened to know that blue whales exist or cared a jot that they do then "rational" economic decision-making would do nothing to prevent their extinction. Whether the blue whale survives should not have to depend on what humans know or what they see on television. Human interests and preferences are far too parochial to provide a satisfactory basis for deciding on what is environmentally desirable.

These ethical and economic theories are not alone in their species chauvinism; much the same applies to most going meta-ethical theories which, unlike intuitionistic theories, try to offer some rationale for their basic principles. For instance, on social contract positions obligations are a matter of mutual agreements between individuals of the base class; on a social justice picture rights and obligations spring from the application of symmetrical fairness principles to members of the base class, usually a rather special class of persons, while on a Kantian position which has some vague obligations somehow arise from respect for members of the base class persons. In each case if members of the base class happen to be ill-disposed to items outside the base class then that is too bad for them: that is (rough) justice.

Questions

1. What general strategy does Routley use to try to show that there is the need for a new ethic that gives value to the environment independently of human desires?

2. How do Routley's imaginings of the "last man" and "last people" work within this strategy?

3. Routley doesn't believe that an environmental ethics commits one to "the view that natural objects such as trees have rights." Why not? How does he see such an ethic working?

Notes

1. Aldo Leopold, *A Sand County Almanac with Essays on Conservation from Round River* (New York: Ballantine, 1966). p. 238.

2. P.W. Barkley and D.W. Seckler, *Economic Growth and Environmental Decay: The Solution Becomes the Problem* (New York; Harcourt, Brace, Jovanovich, 1972.)

Paul Taylor argues that all living things can be said to have a "good of their own" and are worthy of respect and moral consideration

Let us now take an overall view of the theory of environmental ethics which is to be propounded and defended in this book. Like the theory of human ethics just outlined, it is made up of three components: a belief-system, an ultimate moral attitude, and a set of moral rules and standards. These elements stand in relation to each other in the same way that the three components of human ethics are interrelated. The belief-system supports and makes intelligible the adopting of the attitude, and the rules and standards give concrete expression to that attitude in practical life. A brief summary of each component will bring out this parallel with human ethics.

The belief-system [...] constitutes a philosophical world view concerning the order of nature and the place of humans in it. I call this world view "the biocentric outlook on nature." When one conceives of

From *Respect for Nature: A Theory of Environmental Ethics*, by Paul Taylor. Princeton, NJ: Princeton University Press, 1986, pp. 44–6, 60–8. © 1986 Princeton University Press. Reprinted by permission of Princeton University Press.

oneself, one's relation to other living things, and the whole set of natural ecosystems on our planet in terms of this outlook, one identifies oneself as a member of the Earth's Community of Life. This does not entail a denial of one's personhood. Rather, it is a way of understanding one's true self to include one's biological nature as well as one's personhood. From the perspective of the biocentric outlook, one sees one's membership in the Earth's Community of Life as providing a common bond with all the different species of animals and plants that have evolved over the ages. One becomes aware that, like all other living things on our planet, one's very existence depends on the fundamental soundness and integrity of the biological system of nature. When one looks at this domain of life in its totality, one sees it to be a complex and unified web of interdependent parts.

The biocentric outlook on nature also includes a certain way of perceiving and understanding each individual organism. Each is seen to be a teleological (goal-oriented) center of life, pursuing its own good in its own unique way. This, of course, does not mean that they all seek their good as a conscious end or purpose, the realization of which is their intended aim. Consciousness may not be present at all, and even when it is present the organism need not be thought of as intentionally taking steps to achieve goals it sets for itself. Rather, a living thing is conceived as a unified system of organized activity, the constant tendency of which is to preserve its existence by protecting and promoting its well-being.

Finally, to view the place of humans in the natural world from the perspective of the biocentric outlook is to reject the idea of human superiority over other living things. Humans are not thought of as carrying on a higher grade of existence when compared with the so-called "lower" orders of life. The biocentric outlook precludes a hierarchical view of nature. To accept that outlook and view the living world in its terms is to commit oneself to the principle of species-impartiality. No bias in favor of some over others is acceptable. This impartiality applies to the human species just as it does to nonhuman species.

These are the implications of accepting the biocentric outlook. A full argument justifying the acceptance of that outlook will be presented [...]. For the moment we shall simply assume its justifiability and consider how its acceptance supports and makes intelligible a moral agent's adopting the attitude of respect for nature. It can be seen from the foregoing account that insofar as one conceives of one's relation to the whole system of nature through the conceptual framework of the biocentric outlook, one will look at members of nonhuman species as one looks at members of one's own species. Each living thing, human and non-human alike, will be viewed as an entity pursuing its own good in its own way according to its species-specific nature. (For humans this will include not only an autonomous, self-directed pursuing of one's good, but also the self-created conception of what one's true good is.) No living thing will be considered inherently superior or inferior to any other, since the biocentric outlook entails species-impartiality. All are then judged to be equally deserving of moral concern and consideration.

Now, for a moral agent to be disposed to give equal consideration to all wild living things and to judge the good of each to be worthy of being preserved and protected as an end in itself and for the sake of the being whose good it is means that every wild living thing is seen to be the appropriate object of the attitude of respect. Given the acceptance of the biocentric outlook, the attitude of respect will be adopted as the only suitable or morally fitting

attitude to have toward the Earth's wild creatures. One who takes the attitude of respect toward the individual organisms, species-populations, and biotic communities of the Earth's natural ecosystems regards those entities and groups of entities as possessing inherent worth, in the sense that *their value or worth does not depend on their being valued for their usefulness in furthering human ends* (or the ends of any other species). When such an attitude is adopted as one's ultimate moral attitude, I shall speak of that person as having *respect for nature*.

The third component of this theory of environmental ethics is the set of standards and rules considered to be morally binding upon everyone who has the capacities of a moral agent. These norms are principles that guide a moral agent's conduct with regard to how such an agent should or should not treat natural ecosystems and their wild communities of life. They are valid norms, according to the present theory, because they embody the attitude of respect for nature. To say that a rule or standard embodies that attitude is to say that a moral agent's complying with the rule or fulfilling the standard is a genuine manifestation of that attitude in conduct or character. Indeed, sincerely adopting that attitude as one's ultimate moral attitude *means* (among other things) that one is disposed to use those rules and standards as normative directives upon one's choice and conduct.

[...]

The concept of the good of a being

Some entities in the universe are such that we can meaningfully speak of their having a good of their own, while other entities are of a kind that makes such judgment nonsense. We may think, for example, that a parent is furthering the good of a child by going on a camping trip with it. Our thinking this may be true or it may be false, depending on whether the child's good is actually furthered. But whether true or false, the idea of furthering the good of a child is an intelligible notion. The concept of entity-having-a-good-of-its-own includes in its range of application human children. Suppose, however, that someone tells us that we can further the good of a pile of sand by, say, erecting a shelter over it so that it does not get wet in the rain. We might be puzzled about what the person could mean. Perhaps we would interpret the statement to mean that, since wet sand is no good for a certain purpose, it should be kept dry. In that case it is not the sand's own good that would be furthered, but the purpose for which it is to be used. Presumably this would be some human purpose, so that if any being's good is furthered by keeping the sand dry, it is the good of those who have this purpose as one of their ends. Concerning the pile of sand itself, however, it is neither true nor false that keeping it dry furthers its good. The sand has no good of its own. It is not the sort of thing that can be included in the range of application of the concept, entity-that-has-a-good-of-its-own.

One way to know whether something belongs to the class of entities that have a good is to see whether it makes sense to speak of what is good or bad *for* the thing in question. If we can say, truly or falsely, that something is good for an entity or bad for it, without reference to any *other* entity, then the entity has a good of its own. Thus we speak of someone's doing physical exercise daily as being good for him or her. There is no need to refer to any other person or thing to understand our meaning. On the other hand, if we say that keeping a machine well-oiled is good for it we must refer to the purpose for which the machine is used in order to support our claim. As was the case with the pile of sand, this purpose is not attributable to the machine itself, but to those who made it or who now use it. It is not the machine's own good that is being furthered by being kept well-oiled, but the good of certain humans for whom the machine is a means to their ends.

[...]

In the light of these considerations, what sorts of entities have a good of their own? At first we might think that they are entities that can be said to *have interests* in the sense of having ends and seeking means to achieve their ends. Since piles of sand, stones, puddles of water, and the like do not pursue ends, they have no interests. Not having any interests, they cannot be benefited by having their interests furthered, nor harmed by having their interests frustrated. Nothing gives them either satisfaction or dissatisfaction. It would perhaps be odd to hold that they are indifferent to everything that happens to them or to say that nothing matters to them, for we ordinarily speak this way about people who are in special circumstances (such as being in a severe state of depression), and we are thus contrasting their present state of mind with their normal condition. But inanimate objects are never in a condition where things that happen to them *do* matter to them.

Although having interests is a characteristic of at least some entities that have a good of their own, is it true of all such entities? It seems that this is not so. There are some entities that have a good of their own but cannot, strictly speaking, be described as having interests. They have a good of their own because it makes sense to speak of their being benefited or harmed. Things that happen to them can be judged, from their standpoint, to be favorable or unfavorable to them. Yet they are not beings that consciously aim at ends or take means to achieve such ends. They do not have interests because they are not interested in, do not care about, what happens to them. They can experience neither satisfaction nor dissatisfaction, neither fulfillment nor frustration. Such entities are all those living things that lack consciousness or, if conscious, lack the ability to make choices among alternatives confronting them. They include all forms of plant life and the simpler forms of animal life.

To understand more clearly how it is possible for a being to have a good of its own and yet not have interests, it will be useful to distinguish between an entity having an interest in something and something being in an entity's interest. Something can be in a being's interest and so benefit it, but the being itself might have no interest in it. Indeed, it might not even be the kind of entity that can have interests at all. In order to know whether something is (truly) in X's interests, we do not find out whether X has an interest in it. We inquire whether the thing in question will in fact further X's overall well-being. We ask, "Does this promote or protect the good of X?" This is an objective matter because it is not determined by the beliefs, desires, feelings, or conscious interests of X.

[...]

Once we acknowledge that it is meaningful to speak about what is good or bad for an organism as seen from the standpoint of its own good, we humans can make value judgments from the perspective of the organism's life, even if the organism itself can neither make nor understand those judgments. Furthermore, we can conceive of ourselves as having a duty to give consideration to its good and to see to it that it does not suffer harm as the result of our own conduct. None of these ways of thinking and acting with regard to it presupposes that the organism values anything subjectively or even has an interest in what we may do for it.

All of the foregoing considerations hold true of plants as well as animals. Once we separate the objective value concept of a being's good from subjective value concepts, there is no problem about understanding what it means to benefit or harm a plant, to be concerned about its good, and to act benevolently toward it. We can intentionally act with the aim of helping a plant to grow and thrive, and we can do this because we have genuine concern for its well-being. As moral agents we might think of ourselves as under an obligation not to destroy or injure a plant. We can also take the standpoint of a plant and judge what happens to it as being good or bad from its standpoint. To do this would involve our using as the standard of evaluation the preservation or promotion of the plant's own good. Anyone who has ever taken care of flowers, shrubs, or trees will know what these things mean.

Nothing in the above ways of responding to and dealing with plants implies that they have interests in the sense of having conscious aims and desires. We can deny that subjective value concepts apply to vegetative life and yet hold that plants do have a good of their own, which can be furthered or damaged by our treatment of them.

[...]

Throughout the foregoing discussion of the good of living things, the sort of entity having a good of its own has always been understood to be an individual organism. Now, if individual organisms have a good that can be furthered, then *statistically* it is intelligible to speak of furthering the good of a whole species-population. The population has no good of its own, independently of the good of its members. To promote or protect the population's good, however, does not mean that the good of every one of its members is also promoted or protected. The level of a species-population's good is determined by the median distribution point of the good of its individual members. The higher this median, the better off is the species-population as a whole (when considered as an isolated unit). To benefit a whole species-population is to further the good of its individual members in such a way that the median level of their good-realization is raised. To cause this level to go down is to harm the species-population. Thus whenever the good, of an entire species-population is referred to, we must always keep in mind that it is individual organisms that alone comprise the actual entities that have a good definable independently of the good of any other entities. Their good, unlike the good of species-populations, is not analyzable into the good of any other kind of thing.

Questions

1. What, for Taylor, constitutes "the biocentric outlook on nature"?
2. According to Taylor, what sorts of things can, and cannot, be said to have "a good of their own"? What is the distinction he makes between (i) a being's having interests and (ii) something being in a being's interest?
3. What would Taylor say about the holistic or ecocentric views of inherent moral worth?

J. Baird Callicott discusses the land ethic of Aldo Leopold

[…]

According to Aldo Leopold, "All ethics so far evolved rest upon a single premise: that the individual is a member of a community of interdependent parts…. The land ethic simply enlarges the boundaries of the community to include soils, waters, plants, and animals, or collectively: the land."[1] Since ethics have evolved and changed correlatively to the growth and development of the putative social or communal organization, and since the natural environment is represented in ecology as a *community* or society, an ecocentric environmental ethic may be clearly envisioned.

Moral precepts—for example, against murder, robbery, treachery, etc.—may be regarded as the cultural specification or articulation of the limitations on freedom of action to which our social sentiments predispose us. Moral behavior has a genetic basis, but it is not "hard-wired." In the process of enculturation, we are taught both the appropriate forms of behavior and toward whom they should be directed. The people around us are socially classified. Some are mother, father, brothers, and sisters; others uncles, aunts, cousins; still others are friends and neighbors; and in former times, some were barbarians, aliens, or enemies. This representation plays on and provides substance to our "open" feelings toward others and produces subtly shaded moral responses. And should the cognitive representation of our relationships change, our moral responses would change accordingly. If one is told, for example, that a person previously thought to be a stranger is actually a long-lost relative, then one's feelings toward him or her are likely to be altered whether it is true or not. Or when religious teachers tell us we are all "brothers" and "sisters" beneath the skin, our moral sentiments are stimulated accordingly. How the social environment is cognitively represented therefore is crucial to how it is valued and to our moral response to it.

Now, the general world view of the modern life sciences represents all forms of life on the planet Earth

From "The Search for an Environmental Ethic," by J. Baird Callicott. Reproduced with permission from *Matters of Life and Death: New Introductory Essays in Moral Philosophy*, 3rd edn., ed. Tom Regan. New York: McGraw-Hill, 1993, pp. 363–8, 372.

both as *kin* and as fellow members of a social unit—*the biotic community*. The Earth may now be perceived not, as once it was, the unique physical center of the universe but rather as a mere planet orbiting around an ordinary star at the edge of a galaxy containing billions of similar stars in a universe containing billions of such galaxies. In the context of this universal spatial-temporal frame of reference, the planet Earth is very small and very local indeed, an island paradise in a vast desert of largely empty space containing physically hostile foreign bodies separated from Earth by immense distances. All the denizens of this cosmic island paradise evolved into their myriad contemporary forms from a simple, single-cell common ancestor. All contemporary forms of life thus are represented to be *kin, relatives, members of one extended family*. And all are equally members in good standing of one society or community, the biotic community or global ecosystem.

This cosmic/evolutionary/ecological picture of the Earth and its biota can actuate the moral sentiments of affection, respect, love, and sympathy with which we human mammals are genetically endowed. It also actuates the special sentiment or feeling (call it patriotism), noticed by both Hume and Darwin, that we have for the *group as a whole* to which we belong— the *family* per se, the *tribe*, and the *country* or *nation*. From the point of view of modern biology, the earth with its living mantle is our tribe and each of its myriad species is, as it were, a separate clan.

Thus the land ethic […] provides moral standing for both environmental individuals and and for the environment as a whole. In Leopold's words, "a land ethic changes the role of *Homo sapiens* from conqueror of the land community to plain member and citizen of it. It implies respect for fellow-members *and also* respect for the community as such."[2]

[…]

[A]s "The Land Ethic" proceeds, it becomes more and more holistic, that is, more and more concerned with the biotic community per se and its subsystems and less and less individualistic—less and less concerned with the individual animals and plants that it comprises. Toward the middle, Leopold speaks of the "biotic right" of species to continuance.[3] Finally, in the summary moral maxim of the land ethic, the individual drops out of the picture altogether, leaving only the biotic community as the object of respect and moral considerability: "A thing is right when it tends to preserve the integrity, stability, and beauty of the biotic community; it is wrong when it tends otherwise."[4]

The stress on the value of the biotic community is the distinguishing characteristic of the land ethic and its cardinal strength as an *adequate* environmental ethic. The land ethic directs us to take the welfare of nature—the diversity, stability, and integrity of the biotic community—to be the standard of the moral quality, the rightness or wrongness, of our actions. Practically, this means that we should assess the "environmental impact" of any proposed project, whether it be a personal, corporate, or public undertaking, and choose the course of action that will enhance the diversity, integrity, beauty, and stability of the biotic community. Quite obviously, then, environmental problems, from billboards and strip development to radioactive-waste generation and anthropogenic species extinction, are directly addressed by the land ethic. It is specifically tailored to be an *adequate* environmental ethic.

But, as with so many things, the cardinal strength of the land ethic is also its cardinal weakness. What are the moral (to say nothing of the economic) costs of the land ethic? Most seriously, it would seem to imply a draconian policy toward the human population, since almost all ecologists and environmentalists agree that, from the perspective of the integrity, diversity, and stability of the biotic community, there are simply too many people and too few redwoods, white pines, wolves, bears, tigers, elephants, whales, and so on. Philosopher William Aiken has recoiled in horror from the land ethic, since in his view it would imply that "massive human diebacks would be good. It is our species' duty to eliminate 90 percent of our numbers."[5] It would also seem to imply a merciless attitude toward nonhuman individual members of the biotic community. Sentient members of overabundant species, like rabbits and deer, may be (as actually presently they are) routinely culled, for the sake of the ecosystems of which they are a part, by hunting or other methods of liquidation. Such considerations have led philosopher Edward Johnson to complain that "we should not let the land ethic distract us from the concrete problems about the treatment of animals which have been the constant motive behind the animal liberation movement."[6] From the perspective of both humanism and its humane extension, the land ethic appears nightmarish in its own peculiar way. It seems more properly the "ethic" of a termitarium or beehive than of anything analogous to a human community. It appears richly to deserve Tom Regan's epithet environmental fascism.

Despite Leopold's narrative drift away from attention to members of the biotic community toward the community per se, and despite some of Leopold's more radical exponents who have confrontationally stressed the holistic dimension of the land ethic, its theoretical foundations yield a subtler, richer, far more complex system of morals than simple environmental holism. The land ethic is the latest step in an evolutionary sequence, according to its own theoretical foundations. Each succeeding step in social-moral evolution—from the savage clan to the family of man—does not cancel or invalidate the earlier stages. Rather, each succeeding stage is layered over the earlier ones, which remain operative.

A graphic image of the evolution of ethics has been suggested by extensionist Peter Singer. Singer suggests we imagine the evolutionary development of ethics to be an "expanding circle."[7] According to this image, as the charmed circle of moral considerability expands to take in more and more beings, its previous boundaries disappear. Singer thus feels compelled by the logic of his own theory to give as much weight to the interests of a person (or, for that matter, a sentient animal) halfway around the world as to the similar interests of his own children! "I ought to give as much weight to the interests of people in Chad or Cambodia as I do to the interests of my family or neighbors; and this means that if people in those countries are suffering from famine and my money can help, I ought to give and go on giving until the sacrifices that I and my family are making begin to match the benefits the recipients obtain from my gifts."[8] When he chooses to give preference to his own or his children's interests, he has, according to his own account, morally failed. This is because the basic moral logic of traditional Western humanism and its extensions rests moral considerability on a criterion that is supposed to be both morally relevant and *equally* present in the members of the class of morally considerable beings. Hence, all who equally qualify are *equally* considerable. The circle expands as the criterion for moral considerability is changed in accordance with critical discussion of it.

A similar but crucially different image of the evolution of ethics has been suggested by Richard Sylvan and Val Plumwood (formerly the Routleys). According to them,

> What emerges is a picture of types of moral obligation as associated with a nest of rings or annular boundary classes.... In some cases there is no sharp division between the rings. But there is no single uniform privileged class of items [i.e., rational beings, sentient beings, living beings], no one base class, to which all and only moral principles directly apply.[9]

The evolutionary development of ethics is less well represented by means of Singer's image of an expanding circle, a single ballooning circumference, within which moral principles *apply equally to all* than by means of the image of annular tree rings in which social structures and their correlative ethics are nested in a graded, differential system. That I am now a member of the global human community and hence have correlative moral obligations to all mankind does not mean that I am no longer a member of my own family and citizen of my local community and of my country or that I am relieved of the peculiar and special limitations on freedom of action attendant upon these relationships.

Therefore, just as the existence of a global human community with its humanitarian ethic does not submerge and override smaller, more primitive human communities and their moral codes, neither does the newly discovered existence of a global biotic community and its land ethic submerge and override the global human community and its humanitarian ethic. To seriously propose, then, that to preserve the integrity, beauty, and stability of the biotic community we ought summarily to eliminate 90 percent of the current human population is as morally skewed as Singer's apparent belief that he ought to spend 90 percent of

his income relieving the hunger of people in Chad and Cambodia and, in consequence, to reduce himself and his own family to a meager, ragged subsistence.

However, just as it is not unreasonable for one to suppose that he or she has *some* obligation and should make *some* sacrifice for the "wretched of the earth," so it is not unreasonable to suppose that the human community should assume *some* obligation and make *some* sacrifice for the beleaguered and abused biotic community. To agree that the human population should not, in gross and wanton violation of our humanitarian moral code, be immediately reduced by deliberate acts of war or by equally barbaric means does not imply that the human population should not be scaled down, as time goes on, by means and methods that can be countenanced from a humanitarian point of view. How obligations across the outermost rings of our nested sociomoral matrix may be weighed and compared is admittedly uncertain—just as uncertain as how one should weigh and compare one's to one's country.

[...]

The philosophical search for a fitting environmental ethic has also been criticized by allegedly more radical environmental thinkers, the deep ecologists [...], who think that *theories* of environmental *ethics* are more a part of the problem than the solution. The deep ecology alternative to environmental ethics, Self-realization, originated in a metaphysic—hyperholistic Hindu Advaita Vedanta—that is not in fact resonant with scientific ecology. To the extent that we remain inexpungibly separate and distinct individuals—however internally related to and mutually dependent upon other life forms, however embedded we may be in the biosphere—we shall need an ethic to guide our behavior with nonhuman others and nature as a whole.

[...]

Questions

1. According to Callicott, what is "the biotic community"? Who belongs to this commnity?
2. What is Aldo Leopold's "land ethic"? What does Callicott think is its greatest strength? Its greatest weakness?

3. What does Callicott think is wrong with Peter Singer's image of the development of ethics as an "expanding circle"? What image would Callicott put in its place? Explain Callicott's ethical disagreement with Singer and how that disagreement is reflected in this difference in images?

Notes

1. Aldo Leopold, *A Sand County Almanac with Essays on Conservation from Round River* (New York: Ballantine, 1966). p. 239.
2. Ibid, p. 240.
3. Ibid., p. 247.
4. Ibid., p. 262.
5. William Aiken, "Ethical Issues in Agriculture," in Tom Regan, *Earthbound: New Introductory Essays in Environmental Ethics*. New York: Random House, 1984, p. 269.
6. Edward Johnson, "Animal Liberation vs. the Land Ethic," *Environmental Ethics* 3 (1981), p. 271.
7. Peter Singer, *The Expanding Circle: Ethics and Sociobiology.* New York: Farrar, Straus & Giroux, 1982.
8. Ibid., p. 153.
9. Richard Routley and Val Routley, "Human Chauvinism and Environmental Ethics," in Don Mannison, Michael McRobbie, and Richard Routley, eds., *Environmental Philosophy*. Canberra: Department of Philosophy, Research School of the Social Sciences, Australian National University, 1980, p. 107.

Bill Devall and George Sessions discuss "deep ecology"

The term *deep ecology* was coined by Arne Naess in his 1973 article, "The Shallow and the Deep, Long–Range Ecology Movements."[1] Naess was attempting to describe the deeper, more spiritual approach to Nature exemplified in the writings of Aldo Leopold and Rachel Carson. He thought that this deeper approach resulted from a more sensitive openness to ourselves and nonhuman life around us. The essence of deep ecology is to keep asking more searching questions about human life, society, and Nature.

[…]

Many of these questions are perennial philosophical and religious questions faced by humans in all cultures over the ages. What does it mean to be a unique human individual? How can the individual self maintain and increase its uniqueness while also being an inseparable aspect of the whole system wherein there are no sharp breaks between self and the *other*? An ecological perspective, in this deeper sense, results in what Theodore Roszak calls "an awakening of wholes greater than the sum of their parts. In spirit, the discipline is contemplative and therapeutic."[2]

Reproduced with permission from *Deep Ecology, Living as if Nature Mattered*, by Bill Devall and George Sessions. Salt Lake City, UT: Peregrine, 1985, pp. 2–11.

Ecological consciousness and deep ecology are in sharp contrast with the dominant worldview of technocratic-industrial societies which regards humans as isolated and fundamentally separate from the rest of Nature, as superior to, and in charge of, the rest of creation. But the view of humans as separate and superior to the rest of Nature is only part of larger cultural patterns. For thousands of years, Western culture has become increasingly obsessed with the idea of *dominance*: with dominance of humans over nonhuman Nature, masculine over the feminine, wealthy and powerful over the poor, with the dominance of the West over non-Western cultures. Deep ecological consciousness allows us to see through these erroneous and dangerous illusions.

For deep ecology, the study of our place in the Earth household includes the study of ourselves as part of the organic whole. Going beyond a narrowly materialist scientific understanding of reality, the spiritual and the material aspects of reality fuse together. While the leading intellectuals of the dominant worldview have tended to view religion as "just superstition," and have looked upon ancient spiritual practice and enlightenment, such as found in Zen Buddhism, as essentially subjective, the search for deep ecological consciousness is the search for a more objective consciousness and state of being through an active deep questioning and meditative process and way of life.

Many people have asked these deeper questions and cultivated ecological consciousness within the context of different spiritual traditions—Christianity, Taoism, Buddhism, and Native American rituals, for example, While differing greatly in other regards, many in these traditions agree with the basic principles of deep ecology.

Warwick Fox, an Australian philosopher, has succinctly expressed the central intuition of deep ecology: "It is the idea that we can make no firm ontological divide in the field of existence: That there is no bifurcation in reality between the human and the non-human realms ... to the extent that we perceive boundaries, we fall short of deep ecological consciousness."[3]

From this most basic insight or characteristic of deep ecological consciousness, Arne Naess has developed two *ultimate norms* or intuitions which are themselves not derivable from other principles or intuitions. They are arrived at by the deep questioning process and reveal the importance of moving to the philosophical and religious level of wisdom. They cannot be validated, of course, by the methodology of modern science based on its usual mechanistic assumptions and its very narrow definition of data. These ultimate norms are *self-realization* and *biocentric equality*.

Self-realization

In keeping with the spiritual traditions of many of the world's religions, the deep ecology norm of self-realization goes beyond the modern Western self which is defined as an isolated ego striving primarily for hedonistic gratification or for a narrow sense of individual salvation in this life or the next. This socially programmed sense of the narrow self or social self dislocates us, and leaves us prey to whatever fad or fashion is prevalent in our society or social reference group. We are thus robbed of beginning the search for our unique spiritual/biological personhood. Spiritual growth, or unfolding, begins when we cease to understand or see ourselves as isolated and narrow competing egos and begin to identify with other humans from our family and friends to, eventually, our species. But the deep ecology sense of self requires a further maturity and growth, an identification which goes beyond humanity to include the nonhuman world. We must see beyond our narrow contemporary cultural assumptions and values, and the conventional wisdom of our time and place, and this is best achieved by the meditative deep questioning process. Only in this way can we hope to attain full mature personhood and uniqueness.

[...]

Biocentric equality

The intuition of biocentric equality is that all things in the biosphere have an equal right to live and blossom and to reach their own individual forms of unfolding and self-realization within the larger Self-realization. This basic intuition is that all organisms and entities in the ecosphere, as parts of the interrelated whole, are equal in intrinsic worth. Naess suggests that biocentric equality as an intuition is true in principle, although in the process of living, all species use each other as food, shelter, etc. Mutual predation is a biological fact of life, and many of the world's religions have struggled with the spiritual implications of this. Some animal liberationists who attempt to side-step this problem by advocating vegetarianism are forced to say that the entire plant kingdom including rain forests have no right to their own existence. This evasion flies in the face of the basic intuition of equality. Aldo Leopold expressed this intuition when he said humans are "plain citizens" of the biotic community, not lord and master over all other species.

Biocentric equality is intimately related to the all-inclusive Self-realization in the sense that if we harm the rest of Nature then we are harming ourselves. There are no boundaries and everything is interrelated. But insofar as we perceive things as individual organisms or entities, the insight draws us to respect all human and nonhuman individuals in their own right as parts of the whole without feeling the need to set up hierarchies of species with humans at the top.

The practical implications of this intuition or norm suggest that we should live with minimum rather than maximum impact on other species and on the Earth in general. [...]

A fuller discussion of the biocentric norm as it unfolds itself in practice begins with the realization that we, as individual humans, and as communities of humans, have vital needs which go beyond such basics as food, water, and shelter to include love, play, creative expression, intimate relationships with a particular landscape (or Nature taken in its entirety) as well as intimate relationships with other humans, and the vital need for spiritual growth, for becoming a mature human being.

Our vital material needs are probably more simple than many realize. In technocratic-industrial societies there is overwhelming propaganda and advertising which encourages false needs and destructive desires designed to foster increased production and consumption of goods. Most of this actually diverts us from facing reality in an objective way and from

beginning the "real work" of spiritual growth and maturity.

Many people who do not see themselves as supporters of deep ecology nevertheless recognize an overriding vital human need for a healthy and high-quality natural environment for humans, if not for all life, with minimum intrusion of toxic waste, nuclear radiation from human enterprises, minimum acid rain and smog, and enough free flowing wilderness so humans can get in touch with their sources, the natural rhythms and the flow of time and place.

[...]

Questions

1. What are the "two ultimate norms" that "Arne Naess has developed"? Explain each of these as far as you understand them.
2. What are a few of the similarities and differences between deep ecology and some of the other environmental philosophies we've discussed that give the natural world inherent value?

Notes

1. Arne Naess, "The Shallow and the Deep, Long-Range Ecology Movements: A Summary," *Inquiry* 16 (Oslo, 1973), pp. 95–100.
2. Theodore Roszak, *Where the Wasteland Ends* (New York: Anchor, 1972).
3. Warwick Fox, "Deep Ecology: A New Philosophy of Our Time?" *The Ecologist*, v. 14, 5–6, 1984, pp. 194–200.

Part VIII

Genetics

22

Genetics
Fiction

People of the Underground

1.

At night the landfill and the burnt-out factories became extensions of the caves, safe enough to move around in, though you always had to keep your eye out for patrols. As Gatt did now. Though the sky was clear, there was no moon yet, for which he was grateful. He'd be hard to spot tonight, dressed as he was in black from his boots to the cap he'd pulled down over his ears. He hadn't changed clothes for this night foray: He always dressed in black, as did the whole of P-tribe—as did most of the tribes living in the Underground. Gatt didn't know if the black clothing had evolved as style or as camouflage, or whether it had simply been the logical adaptation to living in dirt. That was part of the unwritten history of the People.

Power to the People of the Underground.

There was no sign of patrols. Off to his left was Border Hill; the sky beyond it reflected the silver glow of Chrome City. You couldn't see Chrome City, which was blocked from view by the Hill, and you didn't dare climb the Hill, not the way it was always crawling with patrols. It was Preacher, as always, who had given Chrome City its name—Preacher, with his love of silver-colored things, especially the old chrome wheels he built his hut out of and the crucifixes that hung from its metal walls. In one of his visions, Preacher

had seen the City built entirely of a chrome-like metal, its shapes bizarrely beautiful, tubes twisting through the sky like those old pneumatic tubes, shooting the Clenes from here to there on soft currents of air. "Clene" had been Preacher's term as well—the word formed from "clone" and "gene" to convey some of the manipulations that had transformed those once-human creatures. In some of Preacher's more recent visions, the Clenes had seemed cyborgean, their limbs replaced by silvery artificial parts. The few Clenes Gatt had seen from a distance hadn't looked silvery, but then they wouldn't have, not at night in their dark warrior outfits, slipping through the darkness in their black Humpback tanks. Gatt didn't know how much of what Preacher said he should believe. Preacher claimed his visions came directly from God, but the visions only came after a couple of hits of Sublime—to "open my soul," Preacher liked to say. Gatt had "visions" when he dropped too much Sublime, but his were always dark and violent, like the VR games he played. Preacher said that was because Gatt had a "punk soul—just like the rest of P-tribe." Maybe so, but Gatt would rather spend his life playing VR war games, than spend it in penitence and self-flagellation, like those in Preacher's C-tribe, praying for God to strike down the Clenes and create the New Earth. Fat chance. Anyway, Preacher's hope always struck Gatt as contradictory. There Preacher was, hiding out in the caves, railing against those who were trying to take the humanity out of people in the name of perfection, all the while dreaming of the day God would come and do the same thing. Gatt had called Preacher on that one time; Preacher, after stammering and failing to come up with an answer for once, had threatened to kick the hell out of Gatt. He could too—Preacher was huge—so Gatt had gotten out of there.

Let Preacher have his visions and contradictions. Better, like P-tribe, to play the hand you were dealt, play the last of your humanity until it, and you, were gone.

Gatt had been exploring the landfill for almost an hour. He was out there for the same reason he always was, trying to find discarded VR games and equipment. A few years earlier, the Clenes had been dumping VR war games by the truckload—man, it had been like Christmas every two or three months. Gatt figured the games had been banned in Chrome City; he had images of guys like himself getting rousted out of bed at night, having their games taken away by the black-suited Clene police. Of course, it was also possible the Clenes had been brain-washed into rejecting war games and playing only tame, boring games—if, indeed, they played anything anymore. Whatever the situation, Gatt was glad he lived in the Underground.

Tonight he'd come across some old wheels he'd tell Preacher about; it never hurt to get on the man's good side. But no war games. Truth was, they were getting harder to find; the Clenes obviously weren't making any new ones, and one day the supply of old ones would dry up. That in itself wouldn't be a disaster: P-tribe had made enough copies of the old ones to preserve them indefinitely. The problem would be maintaining the VR equipment: The equipment the Clenes were discarding now had already evolved beyond the technological level of the old war games. So far the tech-freaks of P-tribe had been able to modify the new equipment to maintain hybrid machines that would still play the games; however, Gatt could imagine a dismal, not-too-distant future in which the modifications would no longer work. Meanwhile, he'd just have to keep scavenging and hope.

Gatt had circled back toward the Caves to try a different direction when he came across a freshly dumped load of canned goods, clothing, and medical supplies. He cursed. The laws of the Underground required him to report these supplies immediately; that meant his search for games was over for tonight. It wasn't that he was oblivious to the value of such supplies; it was that they appeared with sufficient frequency and in sufficient quantity that he didn't feel a sense of urgency about them. But the law had been formulated in the early years, after the failed rebellion, when there had been urgency, and the early laws of the Underground rarely changed. In spite of his disappointment, Gatt felt no temptation to break the law now: A law punishable by death was not to be gambled with.

The regular appearance of the supplies was one of those on-going mysteries that would probably never be solved. Apparently, in the early days, the Underground People had been suspicious of the supplies, assuming either that the goods were poisoned or that they were bait set out by Clene patrols lying in wait. Once those suspicions were seen to be groundless, the new theories became more tenuous. Some wondered if the supplies might be charitable gifts—not from the Clenes in general—that theory was unacceptable—but by some in the Clene world who sympathized with the rebels. Another possibility was that they were a calculated move by the Clenes to make sure the Underground People did not become so desperate for food that they might attempt a suicide attack on the Clene world. There was no question of the People ever defeating the Clenes—they had already lost one civil war badly—but the People still possessed enough weaponry to do the Clenes some damage in a suicidal attack. That the People possessed such weapons—and, if attacked, could defend themselves effectively within the labyrinth of caves—was presumably the reason the Clenes had not attempted to stamp out the last of them.

2.

Back at the cave, Gatt reported the supplies to the guards at the entrance, then began to descend. Almost at once he could tell that C-tribe was conducting a service in the Silver Cave: The music was deafening. There were the deep pounding echoes of bass guitar and bass drums, but it was the voices that pierced him—voices chanting, crying, screaming. Gatt was used to loud music—it was one of the things he lived for. But the music of C-tribe creeped him out. It didn't have the raucous energy of the heaviest rock and roll, energy that turned bad feelings into good ones, or at least numbed the bad ones. The semi-musical screaming of C-tribe had too much reality to it, too much real pain. Which was not surprising since some of the screamers would be losing real skin and blood.

Gatt had to cover his ears as he reached the Silver Cave—man, they were going at it tonight! The Cave was something else, though: As many times as Gatt had seen it, it always got to him—the sheer brightness of the place—and in the Underground, no less. It was as if everything silvery thrown away by the Clene world had made its way down to this place. Silvery metal sheeting covered the walls of the cave; silvery goblets and candelabra and crucifixes were every-where. Arc lights gave the scene an intensity that was almost painful to look at. The People were lucky the Clenes had never cut off the electrical power to the old factories, power the People were able to divert into the caves for C-tribe's religious services, P-tribe's continuous VR games, and any other needs the vari-ous tribes might have. There were times Gatt almost felt grateful to the Clenes, but he knew that was absurd. Preacher said that if the Clenes were inten-tionally supplying the caves with power—if it wasn't just some administrative oversight—it must be a strat-egy designed to keep the rebels under the ground where they wouldn't be a threat. If the Clenes ever thought that turning the power off would be in their interest, they would do it. Gatt didn't want to think about that. The People had some old generators and a supply of fuel, but that wouldn't keep the power on for very long. How terrible life would be if the caves ever went dark!

Preacher was up on the table rock at the front of the Cave, glittering in the robe and cap he'd coated with some old aluminum foil. He was turned to the side, chanting with the audience, watching what eve-ryone else was watching. Five large boards—perhaps eight feet long and six feet wide—were propped up at a forty-five degree angle against a table-like rock and other nearby boulders. There was a penitent strapped

spread-eagle against each board; all were males, and each was wearing a white loin-cloth. The legs and chests of the men were bloody, the result of flogging by five other men, dressed in white robes, who were standing next to the penitents, wielding corded whips. All five whips struck in unison, eliciting screams of pain that were obviously genuine, but also ritualized, as if screaming rather than suppressing the pain was part of the ceremony. The floggers gave similarly ritu-alized grunts of effort, while the audience let out moans or cries in unison with the strokes of the whips. In the brief, relative quiet between groans, Preacher, in a deep bass voice that echoed around the walls, cried, "Redeem us, redeem us."

Gatt watched for a time in repulsed fascination, then moved on. Soon the sounds of C-tribe faded, to be replaced by the familiar sounds of P-tribe, the sounds of old rock videos played constantly on a giant screen affixed to one of the cave walls. It was Rebel Raunch, doing "Kick the S--t out of Sheila," the blows on the video in rhythm with the heavy back beat of the drums. Rebel Raunch were heroes—their long-ago hit song, "Misshapen and Proud," having been an anthem of the revolution.

There were rows of VR game machines, packed with people playing and watching. Several fights were going on, most between men, though there was one between two women who seemed to be pounding the hell out of each other. Fights broke out all the time here: There was just too much frenzy in too small a space. One man was kicking someone who was roll-ing on the floor, trying to cover his face: Gatt didn't know if that was a real fight or just a lost bet. Some guys like to bet a real beating on who won or lost a VR battle.

Gatt drank in the energy around him. He loved this place: It was like an ongoing rock party and carnival. *Everything* was going on here—not just the rock vid-eos and VR games, not just the couples groping each other in the shadows or dancing naked on the small stage—but the tarot card and palm readings, the tat-tooing and body painting, the muralists making their designs on the rock walls, the candy-makers cooking up their sugary treats and the chemists cooking up a new batch of Sublime.

He'd head off to the Crash Cave where he could get enough quiet for a little sleep, then he'd come back to party. And when night came, he'd head outside to search for games. Maybe tonight he'd get lucky and find some good ones.

3.

Gatt was outside in the dark landfill, on his knees, trying to push aside a piece of junk metal. He never heard the figure behind him. Suddenly a hand lifted Gatt up by the back of his shirt, lifted him until the toes of Gatt's boots were the only part of him touching the ground. Gatt might as well have been a small child for all the effect his hundred and fifty pounds seemed to have on that hand.

"Come with me," said a deep male voice.

There was no resisting the force of that hand. Gatt knew he would have been dragged had he not managed to move his feet fast enough to keep up with the man's long strides.

They reached the flatland and a Humpback patrol vehicle with two soldiers standing alongside it. Gatt wondered how the Clenes had ever gotten this close without his noticing. He'd seen the lights of one patrol go by half an hour before, but not the lights of this one. He'd spotted a copy of *Space Savages* in the middle of a pile of junk metal. In his excitement to dig out the game, he must have made too much noise, at the same time paying too little attention to his surroundings. Now he was going to be dead. Or worse.

Panicked, Gatt began to struggle; his struggling had no effect. The giant simply tightened his grip and extended his arm; Gatt managed nothing more than kicking and punching air. Then the giant released his grip and deposited Gatt in a heap in the dirt.

It took a few moments for Gatt to uncrumple himself and sit up, not because he was hurt (he wasn't), but because he was stalling. He told himself he was trying to give himself time to think, but he also knew there was nothing really to think about. What could he possibly do against these giants?

Sitting up, he looked up at his three captors. As he'd expected from past glimpses of patrols, the three were dressed in dark, tight-fitting black uniforms, wearing helmets and goggles that covered most of their faces. He realized that they weren't actually as big as he'd thought they were from the way he'd been handled. Gatt was a little over five-eight. The tallest of the three

soldiers was probably close to seven feet tall, but looked bigger from being so bulked up. Still, how had the man managed to pick him up like a doll? Then Gatt remembered the Preacher saying that the Clenes were cyborgs—part human, part machine: That arm that had picked Gatt up had probably been a piece of machinery. The voice he'd heard hadn't been machine-like, so it represented a human part of the soldier.

"Put him in back and let's get him to the station," said one of the soldiers.

The voice sounded female and confirmed what Gatt had guessed from the figure's slightly smaller, less angular build.

The man picked Gatt up, but this time didn't dangle him. He set Gatt on his feet and urged him forward. Gatt stumbled a little—from fear, he realized—but righted himself and moved toward the Humpback. The rear cargo door was opened and Gatt was pushed inside. It was a standard prisoner transport compartment, caged off from the front of the vehicle; Gatt took a seat on one of the two narrow benches. The vehicle started off.

It took him a moment to realize that though the vehicle was moving, he wasn't being jostled about. This was amazing, given the rocky terrain. The suspension in the vehicle had to be something else. He realized too that the bench he was sitting on wasn't the hardwood he'd taken it for. To his fingers, the surface felt like hard plastic, but it had a give to it that was actually comfortable. The black sides of the vehicle had the same give, and he could actually feel his body begin to relax.

But only for an instant. The thought of what was to come put the rigidity back into his muscles. Torture—no doubt, he'd be tortured. He tried to pump himself up with the idea of resisting. He muttered, "Power to the People," and tried to imagine himself being hailed as a martyr by those back in the Caves. But the idea didn't connect. He didn't have any images to trade on. In the VR games he played, he was always the one doing the torturing, and he'd always done it with relish. As for martyrdom, he didn't think those stoned comrades of his gathered around their games would be hailing anyone for anything. And the thought of being stoned reminded him of the time there'd been some vast screw-up in P-tribe, and they'd run short of Sublime and other drugs, and he remembered thinking during his withdrawal that he'd do almost anything to get a fix. And he was the guy who was going to resist torture? Hell, all they had to do was wait until he went into withdrawal, and he'd be telling them anything they wanted to know.

In fact, maybe it would be better to try to skip the whole pain thing—just start talking the minute he got to wherever they were taking him. Maybe he could tell them things that weren't true—throw them off completely—while still avoiding torture. Wouldn't that be a laugh on them. He'd…no, wait. Too risky. If they caught him in a lie they might just keep torturing him even when he told them the truth, figuring it too was a lie.

How much were they likely to know about the People and the Caves? Gatt wasn't the first to go missing. Some of the People had disappeared completely. There were rumors of some who'd gone missing and come back, but Gatt didn't know any such people. Their identities in the stories he'd heard were always a bit vague.

If the Clenes had talked to some of the People, then they had to have some information about the Caves. Which made trying to lie too dangerous. He should just tell them the truth, and maybe they wouldn't hurt him.

He felt the vehicle come to a stop. The door of his compartment opened, and Gatt was pulled out. This time he was marched slowly rather than dragged. He saw slivers of light suspended in front of him, and it took him a moment to realize they were fortress-like windows. The building itself was so black it blended into the dark hills behind it. Then the building's contours began to emerge. Gatt caught its low, square outline, and above, on the roof, towers, with antennae scanning the sky.

There was a whirring sound, and an electronic door opened in front of him. The bright light blurred his vision. He was escorted through—what?—some sort of scanner, he supposed, though he felt forced air against his face and smelled something sweet.

They were now in a reception area. The place was bare, antiseptic. There were black benches set into the gray walls, and one table, with chairs, in a corner of the room. It was hard to see much, scrunched as he was between two soldiers with the third just in front of him.

They stopped, and the soldier in front began talking to someone facing them through a reception window. Gatt glimpsed the soldier at the window and gawked. The man was dressed in the same black uniform as the other soldiers, but he wasn't wearing a helmet. The face was a shock: It was so…perfect. It was the face of some superhero out of his video games—chiseled features, jutting jaw, bright, intelligent eyes.

"We got your message," the man was saying to the other soldiers. "I'll tell the Captain you're here.

The man's eyes slid to Gatt and fixed on him.

"He give you any trouble?"

"Hardly."

"Take a seat."

Gatt was moved to a bench. As he sat down, his eyes scanned the room. All of a sudden he forgot about himself and his predicament. What he was looking at now was the equivalent of a video screen set into the wall, but the size of it—the clarity of the picture—the sense of depth—it was incredible! There was nothing much on the screen—just some boring nature scene at sunset—but the technology was something else. How amazing would it be to see a war game geared to that technology! If the People could ever get their hands on something like that! There was a musical background, he realized, seeming to come from all around him, soft but so clear. If you listened you could catch each detail of the instruments. The music was boring, like the pictures, but he could imagine how heavy metal would sound over such a system—like a live gig. What was wrong with these people, playing crap like this over a system like that?

The picture shifted now to what Gatt gathered was some sort of news show. Or maybe not. The people all looked like actors picked for their looks. Still it did sound like news of sorts.

"…*top stories.*

"*Man kills family in Iowa: Americans shocked by first multiple murder in twenty years…*

"*Today the President said it is a disgrace that one percent of Americans were still below the poverty line…*

"*Parkinson's finally defeated; Alzheimer's can't be far behind…*"

"Bor-ing," thought Gatt as he caught the words with half an ear.

His eyes drifted away from the screen, and suddenly he gaped. The female soldier had taken off her helmet, and Gatt couldn't believe it. She was gorgeous! Her dark hair wasn't much—cut short, a woman's military cut, he supposed—but her face…it was angular and strong, but also feminine and perfectly shaped—and those eyes of hers…large and brown—they seemed to flash. She looked so much like Freya, a female warrior in one of his favorite video games. She had been in so many of his dreams, she....

Gatt realized that Freya—that was his name for her now—was looking at him. He held her gaze for a moment, then dropped his eyes, feeling shame surge through him. For an instant he'd been the hero of his own dreams—before remembering who he really was and realizing how he must look to her—a shabby, dirty runt. Still he couldn't resist another glance a few moments later. He saw that Freya had turned away. A thought struck him. He'd thought those incredible-looking creatures on the television were all actors, but now, having seen the man behind the desk and this woman, he was beginning to think they all looked like that. Amazing.

"*President of France calls on the rest of the world to emulate the peace-loving Americans; asks for help from American genetic scientists….*"

"*Today the Roman Catholic Church officially merged with seven Protestant denominations to form the World Christian Church. During his dissolution-of-office ceremony, the Pope said his dream of a united Christianity had finally been realized. He called on people of other faiths to….*"

As the newscaster droned on, Gatt realized he'd learned quite a bit from his casual observation of those video pictures. Contrary to what Preacher had said, these people weren't cyborgs; they had no obvious metal parts. Nor was Chrome City colored silver. The city was weird, all right, looking like a dense collection of skyscrapers that were tightly connected with walkways to about two-thirds of their height, with only the upper thirds of the buildings distinct; however, the predominant colors were blues and grays. Tracks ran like exposed ribs along the sides of the buildings, guiding a series of shuttle cars. There was no sign of the pneumatic tubes Preacher had mentioned. How had Preacher gotten so much of it wrong? Gatt had never really believed in Preacher's visions, but Gatt assumed Preacher had real information about Silver City, perhaps from spies or escapees.

Gatt was going to have a lot to tell him. If he ever got out of here.

Wait. Wasn't the fact that Preacher knew so little, evidence that no one did get out of here?

Gatt's fear was just returning when a door opened and a man in a lab coat gestured toward them. Before Gatt could react, he felt hands propelling him up and forward.

Gatt saw that he was entering some sort of lab loaded with equipment, everything white or shiny metal. In front of him was a high-backed chair with arm and leg straps. Gatt began to tremble.

"Please don't torture me," said Gatt, in a voice he hardly recognized as his own. "I'll tell you everything you want to know."

"No one's going to torture you," said the man in the lab coat.

"My name is Gatt, I'm a member of P-tribe, and…"

"We'll get to all that in due course," said the man. I'm Dr Enerby. I'm in charge here."

"Please," Gatt pleaded.

Gatt was lowered into the chair. Before he realized what had happened, his arms and legs were clamped in place. His trembling grew worse.

"Please," he said again.

"No one's going to hurt you," said Dr Enerby. "In fact, you're going to have quite a nice time. We're going to give you something…."

"Truth serum," Gatt guessed.

"In part," said the doctor. "But it will also relax you. We have to do some tests…."

"No!"

"Nothing to worry about," said Enerby. "Nurse…."

Gatt realized that all the people around him now were in lab coats—the soldiers were gone. A man was placing what looked like the barrel of a space gun against the skin of Gatt's upper arm. Gatt tried to yank his arm away, but the arm wouldn't move.

"Is this going to…" Gatt started.

Before he could say, "hurt," the gadget was pulled away. He was puzzled. They hadn't done anything, yet they were all staring at him as if expecting some reaction. What did they think…?

Suddenly Gatt felt *very* relaxed. A voice inside him told him this feeling was dangerous, that he ought to fight against it, to stay on guard. But the voice had no effect.

"I feel good," said Gatt, though he hadn't planned on saying anything.

"You'll feel even better in a little while."

"What are you going to do to me?" asked Gatt, feeling curious in a detached sort of way.

"We need to give you a physical of sorts," said Enerby. "Nothing invasive, I can assure you. It's how we know what medications we need to include in the supplies we give to 'the People,' as you call yourselves."

"You don't give us the supplies," said Gatt. "You hate us. You want to destroy us."

Again, his words were abstract, with no feeling behind them.

"Hate you?" The doctor laughed. "Why would we hate you?"

"Because you can't control us and make us machines like everyone here," said Gatt. "Because we still represent true humanity."

Laughter erupted all around Gatt. A metal instrument dropped. A technician, giggling, leaned over to pick it up.

"Possibly you do," said Enerby, still smiling.

"You may have beaten us," said Gatt, "but we're safe from you where we are. Maybe not safe. Maybe you could kill us in the end. But you'd pay for trying, I can tell you that."

Abstractly, Gatt realized his words were defiant; but he felt no defiance. Abstractly, too, he realized it was pretty stupid for him to be saying the things he was. But that thought had no effect.

"You're safe, all right," said Enerby. "Actually, we have the means to kill you all without suffering a single casualty. But why would we want to? You're no threat to us, and we don't like fighting anymore. If we captured you, what would we do with you? You wouldn't fit in our world. We know. We've tried."

"Are you holding some of the People?"

"I wouldn't say, 'holding,' exactly," said Enerby. "They're in their own compound, but they work and they're comfortable enough. In fact, you may know one of their names. Mad Marcus?"

"The VR game guy?" asked Gatt, feeling a faint excitement stir within the pleasant fog. "But I thought...he was from years ago. I've read his name on lots of the old games."

"They're made in the old style and the boxes worked on to look used," said Enerby. "Marcus says that's the only way the People would accept

them—or be able to use them technologically. He fancies himself some kind of revolutionary, keeping the old culture alive. In any case, he's obviously satisfying a demand."

"He's the best," said Gatt. "I love his games."

"Well, then, since you're such an enthusiast...."

Enerby left the lab, but was back a moment later. He held up both hands.

"Which one?" asked Enerby.

Gatt couldn't believe his eyes. The doctor was holding up two VR games Gatt had never seen before. Gatt squinted at the covers. *Midnight on Deathstar* and *Sex Slaves Revolt.*"

"*Sex Slaves Revolt*," said Gatt, quickly. "But, I don't understand why you...."

"Live and let live," said Enerby. "We keep up on what goes on in the Caves from those who get caught by the patrols. We know what you want. For instance, some of the items your people produce in their compound are chrome wheels and aluminum foil. We haven't used those for ages, and the supplies would have dried up by now. Imagine: Aluminum foil. How bizarre."

"For Preacher."

"Yes. And Marcus tells us we need to start making some of the old VR equipment to 'throw away' so you don't run out."

"That would be great!" said Gatt.

Enerby glanced up at a clock.

"We've got to get to work," said the doctor. "We're going to put you under now. You won't mind, I can assure you. It may well be the best high you ever had. There certainly won't be any hangover."

"Then you'll let me go?" asked Gatt.

"Oh, yes," said Enerby. "In a couple of hours, in fact. It wouldn't do to have you gone any longer than that. We don't want to cause trouble for you."

"But what should I tell the People?"

"Tell them whatever you like," said Enerby. He smiled. "Tell them everything you remember."

4.

For a moment Gatt felt dizzy. He steadied himself and the dizziness passed. Feeling suddenly frightened, he glanced around the dark landfill, making sure no one was there. He let out a breath. It was all right: He was alone. He had to stay on his guard, though. The Clenes hadn't caught him yet, and he planned to keep it that way.

How long had he been out here? He wasn't sure, but he had the vague feeling he'd lost track of time. Maybe he'd better be getting back to the Caves. He hated nights like this when he hadn't found anything good…wait a minute—what was that?

It was just off to his left…half-sticking out of a pile of junk. He reached down, lifted up the case, and wiped off the grime. He still couldn't read the label, so he took out a small pen light. Carefully shielding the light he shone it on the case.

He saw the illustration first—a naked woman holding a rocket launcher, posed against a night sky with three moons. Then he caught the title: *Mad Marcus Presents: Sex Slaves Revolt.*

Gatt had to cover his mouth to keep from crying out with joy. It was an old game he'd never seen before. He was betting the rest of P-tribe hadn't seen it either. Were they going to have a time!

Man, sometimes life could be *good*.

Questions

1. Describe life in the "underground." How did people come to be living there?
2. Initially what are Gatt's beliefs about the Clenes and their world? Which of those beliefs turned out to be obvious falsehoods?
3. What attitudes do the people of the underground have toward life in the Clene world? What attitudes do the Clenes have toward the people of the underground?
4. What did you like/dislike about the world of the underground? What did you like/dislike about the world of the Clenes?
5. If you had to choose, which of the two worlds would you choose to live in? Which world would you choose for your children?

23

Genetics
Discussion

People of the Underground

"People of the Underground" supposes that at some time in the past society started a program of genetically altering human beings. Some people rebelled, were defeated, and retreated to caves where they have been living for years.

The rebels call themselves the "People of the Underground." They are divided into tribes, two of which are described in the story. One is P-tribe, which has a culture of rock music and violent virtual reality (VR) games; Gatt, the main character, is a member of P-tribe. The other is C-tribe, a religious group given to highly emotional worship, including self-flagellation. Preacher is the head of C-tribe.

Preacher has visions of the outside world and the people who inhabit that world. He calls those people the "Clenes," a word he made up by combining "clone" and "gene." Preacher's visions determine how others in the caves envision the Clenes—as cyborgs, part human, part machine. However, no one in the caves has actually seen the Clenes—except from a distance and only when the Clenes are wearing their patrol gear of black uniforms and night-vision masks.

Gatt spends his nights prowling the Clene refuse dumps not far from the caves, searching for old VR equipment and games the Clenes might have thrown away. One night Gatt is captured by Clene warriors and taken to a guard house to be interviewed. When the Clenes remove their gear, Gatt expects to see robotic monsters. Instead the Clenes look like people—but magnificent people—the kind Gatt might see in his video games.

As Gatt waits nervously with his captors, he is distracted by the room's incredible video system. There is a news program on and though Gatt doesn't pay much attention to the stories—he thinks they're "boring"—the stories give the reader some sense of what the Clene world is like. A reference to the first multiple murder in twenty years indicates that violent crime is much lower than it once was. The poverty rate is now only one percent. Parkinson's disease has been eliminated and there have been advances in defeating Alzheimer's. A headline about the Pope indicates that there's been great progress in reducing religious division.

Gatt expects to be tortured when he is hooked up to machines. But he is only being put through painless medical tests so the Clenes can learn what sorts of medicines they should leave for the People.

The medical staff tell Gatt things he won't remember; a drug he gets will blot out all memories of his "capture." Contrary to the stories circulating in the Underground, the Clenes have the capacity to wipe out all the People without any danger to themselves. But they have no desire to kill the People, nor any desire to capture them: the People would be misfits in the Clene world.

Gatt defiantly tells the Clenes that the People represent "true humanity." The Clenes laugh and concede, sarcastically, that the People probably do: Obviously the Clenes have had enough of that sort of "humanity."

"People of the Underground" begins as if expressing a familiar moral about genetic engineering: That we shouldn't tinker with human nature, that we shouldn't play God, that we should never risk the possibility of destroying our essential humanity.

Maybe you felt comfortable with that moral throughout your reading of the story. Perhaps, instead, you began to think that the "humanity" displayed in the story wasn't so wonderful; that the Clene world with beautiful nonviolent people, with minimal poverty and minimal religious strife, didn't look so bad.

Today we are developing technologies that may enable us one day to design human beings to make them stronger, healthier, more intelligent, less susceptible to disease—perhaps even kinder and less violent. Some would argue: Why not tinker with humanity if we can really make people so much better?

The story presents a distorted view of humanity for dramatic purposes: Obviously the "People" aren't your average people. Still, there are plenty of grounds for a pessimistic view of humanity. The world at this moment is plagued with poverty and disease, wars and corruption. For every person concerned with helping others, there are many more who are mainly interested in themselves and those close to them. Religion, which might inspire people to be kinder to others, seems to motivate intolerance and war as often as it motivates peace and altruism.

If we wanted to change humanity through science, what technologies would we have to develop to do that?

In a sense, we've been changing humanity through science for several centuries now. We've developed vaccines and sophisticated medical techniques, as well as crucial knowledge regarding nutrition and sanitary practices: All this has allowed vast numbers of humans to survive who wouldn't have survived earlier in human history.

Still, if we were trying to do something much more radical—to "redesign" human beings—how would we go about doing that?

Some futurists imagine (as Preacher does) that humans will become cyborgs, part human, part machine. Others doubt this. Why try to incorporate machinery into our bodies, when it would be more efficient and much less dangerous to "offload" the related tasks onto external machines like computers and robots? Why try to install mechanical memory in the brain, when you can have all the memory you want at your fingertips? Why try to give humans mechanical eyes, when an array of telescopes and microscopes could do far more than any improved "eye" could do?

Other futuristic scenarios imagine the extensive use of cloning: These scenarios are usually grim—envisioning clones used as slaves or for the "farming" of replacement body parts. Such scenarios do raise serious questions; however, they're irrelevant to the issue of designing new and better humans. Cloning is a conservative technique, giving you more of the same; it doesn't introduce any new genetic material.

What seems the most likely route to "designing humans" in the near future would involve some combination of in vitro fertilization (IVF), pre-implementation genetic diagnosis and screening (PGD), and human genetic engineering (HGE). We will discuss these technologies next.

Facts and factual issues

In vitro fertilization

In vitro fertilization (IVF) is a process in which eggs are removed from a female's ovaries, fertilized with semen in the laboratory, then implanted in the female's uterus.

IVF is one of a number of artificial reproductive technologies used to assist couples who cannot conceive in the usual way. Its success rate is good, but since it is unpleasant and expensive, couples often choose it as a last resort.

The fact that the in vitro process occurs outside the body in a laboratory opens up the possibility of genetically screening (PGD), or genetically altering (HGE), the eggs and sperm before fertilization or the embryos prior to implantation.

Pre-implantation genetic diagnosis (PGD)

Pre-implantation genetic diagnosis (PGD) involves removing one or two cells from an embryo created by IVF and analyzing the DNA of the cells removed. Such screening is done now to see if abnormalities that might lead to specific genetic disorders are present. Only those embryos not at risk for the disorder are implanted.

PGD was used in the early 1990s in England to screen for cystic fibrosis. It is now used to screen for sickle-cell anemia, Tay-Sachs disease, and Huntington's disease, as well as various other genetic and chromosomal conditions. It is bound to be extended to screen for risks of many other diseases.

Eventually scientists may be able to predict physical and mental traits, tendencies and capabilities. No one expects to find a gene or small group of genes for, say, criminality—as we have found for cystic fibrosis. But science may be able to identify the genetic bases for tendencies toward, say, sociopathy, lack of impulse control, and certain kinds of violence. They might be able to identify the genetic bases for tendencies toward emotional stability and empathy or for certain components of intelligence, such as good memory or the ability to do certain types of theoretical reasoning. They might find the bases for traits related to musical ability, such as perfect pitch and manual dexterity.

Geneticist Lee Silver imagines a future where parents can screen such profiles for, say, 84 of their (frozen) embryos—what he calls "virtual children"—and select the child they want to have. The profiles might include computer-generated images along with information about predispositions to disease, physical characteristics and "innate personality and cognitive characteristics."

Even if PGD were developed to the point that Silver envisions (and Silver says we have a long way to go), it would still have serious limitations in terms of choosing our children. Parents would be restricted in their choices to whatever embryos were actually produced. The characteristics they really want in a child might be missing. Or the combinations of characteristics might be less than ideal: The embryo with exceptional athletic coordination might be short, with a tendency toward obesity. The embryo most likely to be intelligent might be the one most likely to be lazy. (Imagine the parents as fussy shoppers who want just the "right" item with the "right" features.)

A much wider range of choices would result by genetically engineering the embryos produced by in vitro fertilization rather than by simply selecting from them.

Human genetic engineering (HGE)

The phrase, "human genetic engineering" (HGE), as used here, will refer to the deliberate manipulation of the genetic material in human cells in order to eliminate or produce certain characteristics in the human organism.

HGE can be done either as somatic-HGE or germline-HGE.

Somatic-HGE seeks to alter those body (soma) cells, which are not passed on through reproduction.

Germline-HGE would operate on the "germinal" cells—those related to reproduction—the sperm or the egg or, more probably, the fertilized embryo. Changes made by germline-HGE would be likely to be passed down to successive generations.

In theory, somatic-HGE could be done at any stage of a person's life, perhaps "turning off" a genetic disease or genetically altering tumor cells to counteract cancer. In practice, somatic gene therapy has not been approved for general medical use. It has been used in numerous clinical trials, but with limited success. The problem is considerable: finding a way to change the genetic material in millions of body cells.

Germline-HGE is, in theory, simpler than somatic-HGE because there are many fewer cells involved. However, it is potentially much more dangerous, given its likely effect on future generations.

Germline engineering with animals dates back to the 1980s when foreign DNA was injected in a mouse embryo and became incorporated into one of the embryo's chromosomes. The additional DNA got copied into every cell of the adult mouse and was passed on to the mouse's offspring.

Germline-HGE would be done in conjunction with IVF and PGD. Rather than simply screening embryos, new genetic materials could be introduced into them through the use of artificial chromosomes as the delivery system. The first artificial human chromosome was created by researchers in 1997.

Sophisticated germline-HGE may be a long way off. But let's suppose that the technical problems with IVF/PGD had been solved *and* that we had the genetic engineering technology to produce "made-to-order" children. Would the existence of such technology necessarily lead to changes on the scale of the Clenes in "Underground"? Would it lead to the "designing" of human beings?

It would do so only if it were imposed on, or chosen by, masses of people. Though there are fears that such technology would be imposed on people, in a society like ours it is much more likely that HGE would be offered through the free market—what philosopher Robert Nozick called the "genetic supermarket."

If only a few people took advantage of the technology, there'd be no great change in human nature: The characteristics would get lost in the general population. Germline-HGE would have to be chosen by large numbers of people over generations to make any great change in the general population.

One problem with the general adoption of germline-HGE would be its cost. If its pricing were established by the market, it's likely that there'd be a big discrepancy between what the rich and the less well off could afford.

However, if genetic engineering were made affordable to all through some combination of insurance and social services, its use through time might result in enormous changes, radically altering human beings and human civilization.

Such imaginings make people very nervous: Some propose that we ban the genetic engineering of human beings or strictly limit it to a few, carefully tested, disease-eliminating procedures.

If you look back at "Blessing of the Blastocysts" in the abortion chapter, you'll see that many of the issues we're going to discuss were anticipated there. Of course the society in the story had all the technology one would need to design future humans: All embryos were produced by IVF and subjected to PGD; the predictive power of their genetic science was amazing and could have been used for germline-HGE; and all embryos gestated in artificial wombs and so could be thoroughly monitored.

The society in the story is officially against designing humans, against any procedure that would "promote such characteristics as superior physical strength, musical ability, or intelligence." However there are voices saying that such design is probably inevitable.

> Elizabeth had read one interesting book…which had speculated, approvingly, that humanity was on a road that would lead it toward "designing" humans. The writer had said that once certain obvious disabilities

(like the tendency toward Parkinson's) had been removed from the population, another category, previously viewed as untouchable (as, for instance, tendencies toward alcoholism or obesity), would take their place and the same process would commence again….

In what follows we will consider objections to the idea of genetically engineering humans, objections that often conjure up nightmarish scenarios we might face if the use of HGE went wrong. We will then consider arguments in favor of HGE, along with counters to the initial objections. Finally we will weigh up the arguments on both sides.

The case against human genetic engineering

We will consider nine general objections to the use of HGE and/or PGD. Since PGD is not likely to be especially dangerous and is the less radical of the two in terms of making large-scale changes in human beings, most of the objections will focus primarily on HGE.

1. HGE would be too dangerous
2. HGE/PGD would be "playing God"
3. HGE/PGD wouldn't be limited to curing disease
4. HGE would lead to a "genetic arms race"
5. HGE could undermine religion and ethics
6. HGE could lead to totalitarianism
7. HGE could lead to Nazi-like eugenics
8. HGE could undermine human equality
9. HGE could undermine human freedom

Objection 1: HGE would be too dangerous

What seems extraordinarily dangerous to many people is germline-HGE, where any mistakes could be passed down to future generations. The development of the human species has taken millions of years. How can we pretend to know all the complex factors that have gone into this process of development? How could we know the full ramifications of our genetic heritage?

What if we made genetic changes designed to avert certain diseases and ended up creating worse diseases or vastly increasing mental disorders?

The process of developing HGE would at some point involve experimenting on human beings: How could such experiments be done without an ethically unacceptable degree of risk?

In his book, *Enough*, writer Bill McKibben (see Readings) quotes geneticist Stuart Newman to the effect that you're lucky if a biological experiment works 70–80 percent of the time. Then McKibben says of human engineering:

> …even if it appears to have worked, you won't know for generations: a germline-modified animal may appear completely unremarkable, but its progeny may, for instance, develop cancer at forty times the normal rate. Given our current attitudes toward lab mice and field animals, that doesn't represent an enormous problem. You just keep experimenting until you've figured it all out, and if you have a bunch of goofy batches—Doogie ["smarter"] mice that turn out to be Sumo [obese, lethargic] mice—you throw them out and start over. But people are more problematic: if you go into the clinic for a Doogie kid and the doctor gives you a hairy, cross-eyed fatso, you're going to sue. More than that, it's clearly unethical. How could you justify the unhappy life you'd created?

Objection 2: HGE/PGD would be "playing God"

The admonition against "playing God" can be advanced as a theological principle: There are certain powers that properly belong to humans and other powers that belong only to God; for humans to try to assume powers that belong to God would be a great sin.

The principle is often linked with a warning of danger on a cosmic scale: Playing God is likely to lead to catastrophe, either because God will punish us for the sin of pride or because in trying to play God we would be playing with awesome powers we are incapable of understanding or controlling.

Mary Shelley's nineteenth-century novel, *Frankenstein*, was a cautionary tale about a scientist creating life and being destroyed by his creation. (Today the image of Frankenstein is purposely invoked in the criticism of genetically altered crops or animals as "Frankenfoods.")

Early in our nuclear age, along with the not unrealistic fears that human beings would destroy themselves, there were fantasies like *Godzilla*, imagining terrible monsters created by nuclear explosions.

There's an analogous worry outside a religious context—that there may be a deep wisdom in Nature we don't understand, that in tampering with the human essence we may be opening ourselves to natural catastrophes. For instance, most of us deplore what we see as a human tendency toward excessive aggression and violence. However, can we be sure that if we tone down that tendency, we won't be toning down some other tendencies—the drive for mastery of the world or the willingness to fight against adversity—that might prove vital to human survival and welfare?

Objection 3: HGE/PGD wouldn't be limited to curing disease

A distinction is often made between using HGE/PGD for curing disease as against improving (or perfecting) humans. Other pairs of phrases express a similar contrast: "genetic therapy" versus "genetic enhancement"; "negative genetic engineering" versus "positive genetic engineering."*

People who put forward Objection 3 are usually saying that it might be all right to use PGD/HGE *if* we could confine their use to curing disease. But, they argue, there would be no realistic way to do this. Therefore we should avoid using these technologies at all.

Why believe we couldn't limit PGD/HGE to curing disease?

One argument is that the distinction between curing disease and improving humans is too fuzzy to begin with. What if scientists could safely improve the human immune system? Would that be enhancement or disease-avoidance?

Also the definition of disease keeps expanding. All sorts of conditions—excessive drinking and smoking and even sexual activity—have become "addictions," whereas earlier they were seen as simply bad behavior.

*For ease of exposition, we will use these contrasting phrases with reference to both HGE and PGD, but note they have to be taken loosely with regard to PGD: With PGD you're not really *curing* or *improving* any embryos; rather you're *selecting* embryos which lack the genes for certain diseases or which have the genes for certain desirable characteristics.

Even milder forms of irritability, nervousness, obsessive thinking, and being "down in the dumps" are seen by many as psychological conditions to be treated by medication. The more we find genetic bases for characteristics people don't like about themselves (so goes the argument), the more we'll be calling those "diseases" as well. So deciding that HGE/PGD will only be used for treating disease may not, in the end, leave out much.

Another argument is that even if we could draw a fairly firm line between curing disease and improving humans, the line would be too hard to hold against public and corporate pressure.

Suppose a genetic engineering technology was developed to help people with memory problems; suppose further that the technology turned out to improve normal memory to the degree that anyone whose memory had been so improved would have a decided competitive advantage against others. Think of the market potential. Think of the vast sums of corporate money that would be spent trying to influence politicians to approve a wide use of the technology, as well as the political pressure from all those who wanted to use it. Is that much pressure likely to be resisted long?

Even if the US government didn't approve the procedure right away, there could be the problem of what has been called "genetic tourism"—that is, people going to other countries where the treatments are legal. Genetic tourism would allow some Americans to avail themselves of the technology and put even more pressure on US politicians to legalize it.

Objection 4: HGE would lead to a "genetic arms race"

This objection is a kind of worst-case-scenario add-on to Objection 3: Not only would HGE not be limited to curing disease, it would spiral out of control, setting off a "genetic arms race."

Though "genetic arms race" suggests a war scenario, the phrase usually refers to something more like a genetic keeping-up-with-the-Joneses. The objection is that if technologies for genetic improvements come fast and furiously, few prospective parents will be able to resist. As Bill McKibben puts it:

…say you're not ready…. How long will you be able to hold the line if the procedure begins to spread among your neighbors? Maybe not so long as you think: if germline manipulation actually does begin, it seems likely to set off a kind of biological arms race. "Suppose parents could add 30 points to their child's IQ," asks economist Lester Thurow…. "Wouldn't you want to do it? And if you don't, your child will be the stupidest in the neighborhood." That's precisely what it might feel like to the parent facing the choice. Individual competition more or less defines the society we've built, and in that context love can almost be defined as giving your kids what they need to make their way in the world. Deciding not to soup them up…well, it could come to seem like child abuse.

As McKibben and others have pointed out (and here the "arms race" metaphor is more apt), the improvements in net welfare within each new engineered generation might be nil. We'd be running furiously to stay even. In our earlier discussion of happiness, we talked about positional goods, goods whose value comes from a comparison with what others have. If everyone becomes relatively more attractive, the same relative beauty rankings will hold. If everyone becomes relatively smarter, no one will have gained an advantage. We will have spent vast amounts of time and money and only stayed even.

Objection 5: HGE could undermine religion and ethics

In a world in which anxiety, a sense of incompleteness and perhaps the fear of death had all been engineered away, who would feel the need for religion? In a world in which, say, aggressiveness was toned down, while the desire to fit in was increased, what would be the need for ethics?

Francis Fukuyama warns us that through the use of genetic engineering we might someday lose our human essence, emerging on "the other side of a great divide between human and posthuman history":

…what is that human essence that we might be in danger of losing? For a religious person, human essence might have to do with the divine gift or spark that all human beings are born with. From a secular perspective, it would have to do with human nature: the species-typical characteristics shared by all human beings qua human beings. This is ultimately what is at stake in the biotech revolution.

There is an intimate connection between human nature and human notions of rights, justice, and morality. This was the view held by, among others, the signers of the Declaration of Independence. They believed in the existence of natural rights, rights, that is, that were conferred on us by our human natures.

Objection 6: HGE could lead to totalitarianism

Another fear is that HGE would give governments or small groups of elites too much control over people. One negative literary scenario of this type is Aldous Huxley's *Brave New World*, where the "Controllers" engineer people to fit the various classes of society. Those at the bottom of society are engineered with psychological traits that make them content with menial tasks and a more limited mental life.

Less dramatically one could imagine government-sponsored HGE which, in the name of limiting crime and violence, slowly tends to make the average citizen more accepting of authority and of the privileges of the upper classes. One doesn't have to imagine wild-eyed dictators in charge of the process: It could be "reasonable" people supposing that what is in their economic and social interest is what's good for everybody.

Objection 7: HGE could lead to Nazi–like eugenics

"Eugenics" refers to attempts to improve the genetic/hereditary characteristics of human beings. The term was coined by Francis Galton whose 1869 book, *Hereditary Genius*, discussed his studies of the families of eminent men and put forth the theory that "a highly gifted race of men" could be developed by the right sorts of marriages over several generations.

Intelligence tests were introduced in the early twentieth century and were taken to measure innate intelligence. People from deprived environments whose scores indicated a mental age of 12 or less were labeled "feebleminded"; such feeblemindedness was thought to be associated with criminality. Studies of

"degenerate" families purported to show how certain negative characteristics were derived from a single ancestor.

Eugenicists pushed for laws supporting sterilization of what were considered defective persons. Twenty-seven US states had passed such laws by 1931, Germany, Switzerland, and several Scandinavian countries, by 1935. (Early on, Hitler expressed admiration for the US sterilization laws.)

In Hitler's Germany, of course, millions of people were killed who were thought to be racially inferior. The horrors perpetrated by the Nazis brought eugenics into general disrepute. Today many people are upset at the idea of anything that smacks of eugenics.

HGE is clearly eugenics in that it would be an attempt to improve the genetic/hereditary characteristics of human beings. According to critics, the ability to change human beings through genetics would lengthen the current list of characteristics considered "undesirable" by society. Embryos that might have seen life and been valued as people would be discarded because of a tendency to slightly lower intelligence, excessive weight, shortness, or what are now considered fairly minor physical handicaps. People who were born with those characteristics would be looked down on as never before. And much of the diversity of human beings would likely be lost.

Objection 8: HGE could undermine human equality

Imagine that genetic enhancement technologies were made available through the free market and that each new breakthrough was initially priced out of the range of all but the wealthiest: Wouldn't the genetic advantages open to the wealthy increase exponentially the economic and other advantages they possess at present?

As biologist Lee Silver says,

> The isolation of the poor could become even more pronounced as well-off parents provide their children not only with the best education money can buy, and the best overall environment that money can buy, but the "best cumulative set of genes" as well. Emotional stability, long-term happiness, inborn talents, increased creativity, and healthy bodies—these could be the starting points chosen for the children of the upper strata. Obesity, heart disease,

hypertension, alcoholism, mental illness, and predispositions to cancer—these will be the diseases left to drift randomly among the families of the underclass

Silver imagines the development of a class he calls the "GenRich," a small, genetic aristocracy from which all the better athletes and scientists and artists and entrepreneurs and political leaders would emerge. Silver speculates that as the GenRich and the unenhanced others (the "Naturals") increasingly diverge, there would be less breeding between them. (Imagine how one of the Clene women in our story would react to the idea of mating with Gatt.)

Eventually the GenRich might even evolve into a different species. (One could easily imagine this happening with the Clenes and the people of the Underground.)

Objection 9: HGE could undermine human freedom

Some people are concerned that genetic engineering could undercut human freedom. Our everyday sense of freedom has to do with the range of opportunities open to us and our ability to take advantage of them. Part of it depends on mental and physical abilities: whether I can run fast, become adept at using a computer, learn calculus, or get through law school. Part of it has to do with having a broad enough range of likes and dislikes—and/or enough flexibility of desire—that I have a reasonable chance to find satisfactions. Part of it has to do with knowing enough about myself and the world to calculate the best course of action in a particular situation or for the long term.

A lot of people would agree that good parenting, in addition to teaching moral values, involves helping children develop a broad enough range of abilities and interests so that they are "free" to choose a life that suits them. Philosopher Joel Feinberg claims that children have a right to this sort of upbringing, what he calls the "right to an open future."

Some people think that a child's right to an open future would be undermined by genetic engineering.

Suppose parents dream of having a child who is a professional golfer or professional violinist. They might push an unengineered child in that direction. However, knowing there's no guarantee the child will have the appropriate abilities and interests, the parents are more likely to quit at a certain point if the child's abilities and interests differ radically from those necessary to achieve the "dream."

However, if the parents were able to have a child engineered to be a golfer or violinist, wouldn't they be remorseless about pushing their child in the engineered direction?

As for the child, if the self she was engineered to have didn't feel like a fit, wouldn't she feel trapped? Even if the self were more or less a "fit," wouldn't the child still have the feeling of being someone else's "creation"—less human and less free?

Such are the major objections to HGE. Let's now consider the case for it, including the replies to the objections we have just sketched.

The case for human genetic engineering

Humans have always struggled to avert or cure disease. This has certainly been one of the main projects of science for the last couple of hundred years. If we can continue the quest through genetic technologies, why not?

Throughout history, humans have admired those who have excelled in physical prowess or beauty, practical or intellectual accomplishment, and spiritual discipline. In today's world, many people are obsessed with self-improvement of one sort of another, seeking to improve their bodies, intellect, and moods through exercise, cosmetics (and cosmetic surgery), self-help books, education, and psychotropic medicines. If PGD/HGE could give us all better bodies and minds (without the painful work), why shouldn't we use such technologies?

Many of those who face up to the terrible toll of human cruelty, as well as the possibility that human beings might end up destroying themselves, wonder: If we could use PGD/HGE to produce kinder, less aggressive and more sensible human beings, why not do so?

It seems that at least a preliminary case can be made for the use of PGD/HGE. But what of the objections raised against them? Below are some of the replies that can be given.

Reply to Objection 1 that "HGE would be too dangerous"

If this objection is put forth in support of a ban on HGE, one counter is that the objection is premature. We won't know how dangerous germline-HGE is likely to be until we've done a lot more research and know a lot more. If it still looks too dangerous at that point, then, of course, we shouldn't use germline-HGE.

Reply to Objection 2 that "HGE/PGD would be 'playing God'"

In his 1967 book, *The Ghost in the Machine*, Arthur Koestler argued that "creativity and pathology" were two aspects of the human mind; the latter represented a "streak of insanity" that runs through the history of the human race and shows that "somewhere along the line of its ascent to prominence something has gone wrong."

Koestler said: "Nature has let us down, God seems to have left the receiver off the hook, and time is running out." We should look to science to find some way to modify the aggressive, self-destructive side of human nature. At the time, Koestler was imagining something on the order of psychotropic drugs, but similar sentiments are voiced now in regard to genetic engineering.

There are a number of thinkers, referred to as transhumanists, who want to see science (including genetic engineering) used to transcend human limitations. One such thinker, Max Moore, delivered the following "letter to Mother Nature" at a meeting of a group he founded, called the Extropians:

> Mother Nature, truly we are grateful for what you have made us. No doubt you did the best you could. However, with all due respect, we must say that you have in many ways done a poor job with the human constitution. You have made us vulnerable to disease and damage. You compel us to age and die—just as we are beginning to attain wisdom.... What you have made is glorious, yet deeply flawed.... Over the coming decades we will pursue a series of changes to our own constitution.... We will no longer tolerate the tyranny of aging and death.... We will expand our perceptual range...improve on our neural organization and capacity...reshape our motivational patterns and emotional responses...take charge of our genetic programming and achieve mastery over our biological and neurological processes.

Talk about embracing the role of "playing God"!

These, of course, are extreme views, the kind that are cited by opponents of HGE as evidence that such technology is likely to end up in the hands of mad scientists.

But others with much less extreme views are still unimpressed by the "playing God" objection; they see it as inconsistent with other practices most of us accept. As Gregory Stock says,

> As for playing God, by the measure of earlier ages, we do just that every time we give our children penicillin, use birth control, fly in an airplane or telephone a friend. We embrace technologies that tame and harness nature because we think they improve our lives, and we will accept or reject human genetic manipulation on the same grounds.

Even some theologians would reject the playing-God objection. They would argue that in using our intelligence to improve human lives through science, we are simply using our God-given gifts in the way God intended.

Reply to Objection 3 that "HGE/PGD wouldn't be limited to curing disease"

There are two sorts of responses to this objection: One response agrees with the background assumption that PGD/HGE should be limited to curing disease; however, it argues that such a limitation would be possible. The other response rejects the background assumption, arguing that PGD/HGE shouldn't be limited to curing disease, that they should be used for improving humans.

Political scientist Francis Fukuyama (see Readings) gives the first sort of reply. He is in favor of using HGE only for curing disease, but thinks we could limit the use of HGE in this way.

> It has often seemed to me that the only people who can argue that there is no difference between disease and health are those who have never been sick: if you have a virus or fracture your leg, you know perfectly well that something is wrong.
>
> And even in cases where the borderline between sickness and health, therapy and enhancement, is murkier, regulatory agencies are routinely able to make these distinctions in practice.

Fukuyama gives the example of Ritalin and its use for attention-deficit/hyperactivity disorder (ADHD): This is a case, he says, where there are controversial cases in the middle range, but still "regulatory agencies *make and enforce this distinction all the time.*"

Fukuyama agrees that the battle to set and maintain limits will be a difficult one, that we will probably have to modify our current regulatory apparatus if it is to be up to the task. But he thinks it can be done.

Jonathan Glover (see Readings) is someone who argues that we shouldn't worry about the curing/enhancing distinction in the first place; he argues that the distinction has no great moral importance.

In *What Sort of People Should There Be?*, Glover points out that many parents work hard to instill their religious, moral and cultural values in their children. They educate them at home and in schools and otherwise try to give them "advantages" that will help them thrive and succeed in the world.

> Home and schools would be impoverished by attempting to restrict their influence on children to the mere prevention of physical and mental disorder. And if we are right here to cross the positive-negative boundary, encouraging children to ask questions, to be generous or imaginative, why should crossing the same boundary for the same reasons be ruled out absolutely when the means are genetic?

Reply to Objection 4 that "HGE would lead to a 'genetic arms race'"

For those few people who look forward to a post-human future, a "genetic arms race" couldn't occur soon enough or go fast enough: If there's a better future ahead, let's race toward it.

Those with a more moderate interest in PGD/HGE argue that the "genetic arms race" scenario is pure fantasy. Given the difficulties with IVF and all the complexities likely to be involved in developing PGD/HGE, the idea that new and substantially improved genetic modifications will be offered with the frequency of new clothing styles or new car models seems unreal.

If there ever does come a time when a genetic arms race is threatened, society will have had a lot more experience with genetic engineering and will be better

able to deal with that problem. For us to ban or severely limit genetic technologies now out of fear of a genetic arms race would be absurdly premature.

There are also problems with the claim that if we all improved in beauty and intelligence, we would have put in all that effort only to remain relatively the same. It may be decisive against improvements in beauty, but not against improvements in intelligence. Even if no individual gained relative to others, wouldn't the human race as a whole improve? Wouldn't the overall increase in intelligence be likely to pay huge dividends to the human race as it seeks medical breakthroughs and faces such challenges as global warming? (Think of the accomplishments of the Clenes in the story.)

Reply to Objection 5 that "HGE could undermine religion and ethics"

A similar response could be made here as was made to the "genetic arms race" objection—namely, that the objection seems premature. Think how many changes would have to take place through human engineering before people would have no need for, or curiosity about, God, before they had no need of ethical rules to guide their interactions. It's not clear this will ever be a problem: If it is, it's one for future peoples to evaluate and deal with.

Also there's something supremely ironic about the argument that we shouldn't make people nicer because if they were a lot nicer, they wouldn't need ethics anymore. What is ethics, if not an attempt to make people nicer? Isn't it unethical to claim that we should leave the nastiness in people so they'll need ethics?

Reply to Objection 6 that "HGE could lead to totalitarianism"

This objection is perhaps a bit dated, imagining fascism using genetics to design a "super race" or communism using genetics to design the perfect workers. As mentioned earlier, it calls to mind Aldous Huxley's *Brave New World* in which central planners engineer people for the various class and work strata of society, making their abilities and moods match their roles.

It's not that something like this couldn't happen in the future, but it seems unlikely that genetic engineering itself would be the force that would bring about a totalitarian state.

If genetic engineering does become a reality in the United States, its use is likely to be shaped by a free market—Nozick's "genetic supermarket"—where the use of genetic enhancements is left to the decisions of parents who are able to pay for those benefits.

If there does turn out to be a genetic supermarket, we still need to decide what the role of government should be: Almost no one would be in favor of a totally laissez-faire market. What if certain children were engineered to be ideal sexual objects? Or to show a degree of obedience to parental authority that most would consider pathological? At the very least, we should have laws analogous to those we have now against child abuse.

As for the larger society, parents collectively might be swayed by fashion or conceive the child's (or their own interests) in a way that might impact the larger society. Suppose that 50% of the parents engineered their children to excel at professional sports. Suppose 70% of embryos in a certain generation were engineered to be male. Suppose parents, perceiving society as highly competitive and feeling obligated to engineer their children to succeed in it, left out certain moral qualities necessary to balance out the competitiveness.

Jonathan Glover proposes that, instead of either centralized planning or laissez-faire genetics, society adopt a "mixed system" that would at least give the government veto power over individual choices that seemed abusive or over collections of choices that seemed obviously detrimental to society.

Reply to Objection 7 that "HGE could lead to Nazi-like eugenics"

If the word, "eugenics," merely refers to attempts to improve the genetic characteristics of mankind, then it is irrational to use it as a scare word conveying all the horrors done under that label. What was wrong with Nazi eugenics (as well as less extreme programs) is that the program was a coercive, eventually murderous, attempt to get rid of persons considered racially or otherwise inferior.

Phillip Kitcher claims that eugenics involves four types of decisions:

> First, eugenic engineers must select a group of people whose reproductive activities are to make the difference to future generations. Next, they have to determine whether these people will make their own reproductive decisions or whether they will be compelled to follow some centrally imposed policy. Third, they need to pick out certain characteristics whose frequency is to be increased or diminished. Finally, they must draw on some body of scientific information that is to be used in achieving their ends.

Kitcher argues that the morality of eugenics will vary depending on what sorts of decisions are made.

> Greater evils seem to be introduced if we move in particular directions with respect to the four components. More discrimination in the first, more coercion in the second, focusing on traits bound up with social prejudices in the third, using inaccurate scientific information in the fourth.

The Nazi program was horrible because it involved massive discrimination and coercion and because it involved the worst sort of social prejudices backed up by inaccurate scientific information.

But the eugenics we're contemplating is likely to be of the laissez-faire or the "mixed system" variety—individuals taking the best genetic information and deciding how to apply it in their own cases, with minimal government oversight and interference. There are serious moral issues regarding the use of such genetic technology, but labeling it "eugenics" is not a cogent moral argument—just rhetorical shorthand that seeks to avoid the hard thinking.

Reply to Objection 8 that "HGE could undermine human equality"

We talked earlier about Lee Silver's vision of society developing into two classes—the GenRich and the Naturals—as those who could afford the expensive new genetic improvements became increasingly superior to the other members of society.

The general drift toward inequalities resulting from genetic engineering would seem especially likely in a system of laissez-faire genetics. On the other hand, we don't have a pure laissez-faire system now: We redistribute income and other benefits to the poorest Americans through progressive taxation. If we applied redistributive principles in a way that gave the less well off access to genetic services, that could keep genetic inequality from becoming too disproportionate.

How much redistribution Americans would be willing to approve and how much this redistribution would limit growing genetic inequality are serious questions. However, the issue of genetic engineering should at least be discussed within the context of those redistributive possibilities.

Reply to Objection 9 that "HGE could undermine human freedom"

We talked about Feinberg's claim that a child has the "right to an open future"—the right not to have her options narrowed prematurely by failing to provide her with the life experiences and education necessary to develop her abilities and interests and to understand the possibilities that her society does, and doesn't, offer.

It's not clear that HGE by itself would violate the child's right to an open future. What would violate this right is an excessive narrowing of options through HGE. If HGE ever got to the point where one could "make" a would-be concert pianist or professional ball player—a person who wasn't capable of doing or wanting to do anything else—most of us, I think, would agree that such HGE would threaten human freedom and would have to be seriously restrained. But simply engineering in a love of music or physical activity wouldn't seem to narrow the person any more than natural genetics does at the moment.

We also mentioned the worry that children subject to HGE as embryos would feel more like creations than free creatures, feel more responsible for fulfilling the desires of their parents. This concern is not about freedom per se, but the child's feeling of freedom.

It seems to me this is a legitimate concern, but one that would be difficult to decide apart from empirical study. If HGE started and built slowly, perhaps it would just seem normal. Would children who were engineered to have some athletic ability and were pushed into athletics by their parents feel any more like creations than those who now have athletic ability and are mercilessly pushed in that direction by their parents? Again, it's a legitimate concern, but

one that would require empirical research, not off-the-top-of-one's-head guesses.

Concluding remarks

Obviously there are many questions you need to think about here:

How likely is it that human genetic engineering will become a serious possibility in the near future?

Are you open to HGE for curing humans? Enhancing humans? Both?

If you're inclined to allow HGE only for curing humans, what would we need to do to draw and enforce the line between curing and enhancing? Could we do so effectively?

If you're inclined toward the use of HGE for enhancing humans, how likely do you find the various nightmare scenarios, such as GenRich and Naturals becoming different species? Do such scenarios imagine an unrealistic degree of success with HGE? If not, do you think there are good social methods for avoiding such extremes?

Whatever your views on PGD and HGE, presumably you'd agree that there should be a public dialogue about whether, and how, they should be used. You might assume that there is bound to be such a discussion at the appropriate time. But this assumption may well be false.

Consider people who run large corporations with a huge financial stake in developing HGE. Or transhumanists who are anxious to move as fast as possible toward a "post-human future." Or those with great faith in scientific progress who think scientific developments should be left to the experts.

Such people may want the public kept out of the decision-making process on HGE as much as possible. They'll figure that if the debate goes public, they're going to have to deal with "vague" religious objections, *Frankenstein*-style fears of science, and a host of misconceptions and misunderstandings. How much easier just to move the whole process along by committees of "scientific experts."

Remember that the introduction of genetically modified foods in the US (as opposed to Europe) proceeded without public debate, and it's very likely to be the same with PGD/HGE.

It's not that "ethical concerns" are being ignored altogether. Three percent of the three billion dollars of funding for human genetics goes for "ethical, legal, and social implications" (ELSI). But, as a number of writers have pointed out, these bioethicists often have the same scientific orientation as the scientists, and the fact that they are being supported by a portion of the funds devoted to scientific research doesn't encourage them to resist it.

As Barbara Katz Rothman says in her book, *Genetic Maps and Human Imaginations*, "bioethics becomes a translator, sometimes an apologist, sometimes an enabler, of scientific 'progress.'"

Rothman talks about how sociologist John R. Evans traced the way a presidential commission under President Carter dealt with theologians' concerns that human genetic engineering would be "playing God."

What Evans shows is the way the process of translation into a "common" tongue ends up leaving people speechless. At each point the theologians' concerns were translated, and lost everything in the translation. The commission objected to "vague" concepts, which meant just about everything the theologians might say. If your concerns are on the level of principles, values and morals, then they're vague. If you're worried about safety tolerances, you can be specific. To eliminate vagueness, "playing God" is translated as acting without knowing the consequences, taking risks. So controlling the risks becomes the solution. Bacteria are being genetically engineered and that creation of a new life form is playing God? Playing God is taking risks? Put more filters on the lab hoods and then you're not playing God? Somehow, that was not what the theologians intended.

There are some issues those involved in the funded ethics discussions do worry about in addition to safety. One issue is the autonomy of the child. Though the ethicists assume parents have the right to make genetic decisions about their children, they are concerned about the problem of consent on the part of the engineered child. Some scientists have discussed the possibility of developing genes with chemical on/off switches. If the parents opted for a gene for patience and the child decided she didn't want that quality, that gene could be chemically turned off.

One biomedical conference did talk about the worry that HGE would allow the rich to gain advantages over the poor, but concluded there was no easy technical fix for that.

However, many of the larger questions we have discussed about the impact of HGE on society in the long run never get discussed in any serious way. Obviously if we want them discussed, we're going to have to become politically aware and involved.

Notes and selected sources

Facts and factual issues

SOURCES

Phillip Kitcher. *The Lives to Come: The Genetic Revolution and Human Possibilities.* New York: Simon & Schuster, 1996.

Robert Nozick. *Anarchy, State and Utopia.* New York: Basic Books, 1974.

Lee M. Silver. *Remaking Eden: How Genetic Engineering and Cloning Will Transform the American Family.* New York Perennial/HarperCollins, 1997.

Gregory Stock. *Redesigning Humans: Choosing Our Genes, Changing Our Future.* New York: Houghton Mifflin Co., 2003.

Barbara Wexler. *Genetics and Genetic Engineering.* Detroit, MI: Thomson Gale, 2004. Information Plus Reference Series.

NOTES
Scenario for "virtual children": Silver, p. 233.
Genetic supermarket, Nozick, p. 315n.

The case against human genetic engineering

SOURCES

Joel Feinberg. "The Child's Right to an Open Future" in Joel Feinberg. *Freedom and Fulfillment: Philosophical Essays.* Princeton, NJ: Princeton University Press, 1992.

Francis Fukuyama. *Our Posthuman Future: Consequences of the Biotechnological Revolution.* New York: Farrar, Straus and Giroux, 2002.

Aldous Huxley. *Brave New World.* New York: Perennial Classics, 1989.

Bill McKibben. *Enough: Staying Human in an Engineered Age.* New York: Times Books, 2003.

(See also Kitcher, Silver and Stock above.)

NOTES

"...even if it appears to have worked...." McKibben, pp. 41–2.

"...say you're not ready...." McKibben. pp. 33–4.

"...what is that human essence...." Fukuyama, p. 101.

"The isolation of the poor could...." Silver, pp. 263–4.

"GenRich" vs. the "Naturals." Silver, pp. 4–8.

The case for human genetic engineering

SOURCES

Jonathan Glover. *What Sort of People Should There Be?* New York: Penguin Books, 1984.

Arthur Koestler. *The Ghost in the Machine.* New York: Macmillan Co., 1967.

(See also Kitcher, Silver, Stock, and Fukuyama above.)

NOTES

"creativity and pathology" and other quotes in this paragraph, Koestler, p. xi.

"Nature has let us down..." Koestler, p. 339.

"Mother Nature, truly we are grateful...." Max Moore, quoted in Stock, pp. 158–9.

"As for playing God...." Stock, p. 131.

"It has often seemed to me...." Fukuyama, pp. 209–10.

"regulatory agencies make and...." Fukuyama, p. 210.

"Home and schools..." Glover, p. 53.

Glover's "mixed system," Glover, pp. 45–56.

"First, eugenic engineers..." and next quote, Kitcher, p. 193.

Concluding remarks

SOURCES

Barbara Katz Rothman. *Genetic Maps and Human Imaginations: The Limits of Science in Understanding Who We Are.* New York: 1998.

NOTES

"What Evans shows...." Rothman, pp. 35–9.

Definitions

(Terms are defined in the order in which they appeared in the text.)

1. *Cyborg*: A being that would be part human, part robot.

2. *Cloning*: Creating a genetically identical organism (called a *clone*).

3. *In vitro fertilization (IVF)*: A process in which eggs are removed from a female's ovaries, fertilized with semen in the laboratory, then implanted in the female's uterus.

4. *Pre-implantation genetic diagnosis (PGD)*: A process that involves removing one or two cells from an embryo created by IVF and analyzing the DNA of the cells removed.

5. *Human genetic engineering (HGE)*: The deliberate manipulation of the genetic material in human cells in order to eliminate or produce certain characteristics in the human organism.

6. *Somatic-HGE*: HGE that seeks to alter those body (soma) cells which are not passed on through reproduction.

7. *Germline-HGE*: HGE which operates on the "germinal" cells—those related to reproduction.

8. *Genetic supermarket*: Genetic engineering distributed via the free market. (From Robert Nozick.)

9. *Genetic therapy*: HGE/PGD intended to cure disease.

10. *Genetic enhancement*: HGE/PGD intended to improve (perfect) humans.

11. *Negative genetic engineering*: HGE/PGD intended to cure disease.

12. *Positive genetic engineering*: HGE/PGD intended to improve (perfect) humans.

13. *Genetic arms race*: The image of an out-of-control race for more and better genetic improvements.

14. *Eugenics*: A systematic scientific attempt to improve the genetic/hereditary characteristics of human beings.

15. *GenRich*: An imagined genetic aristocracy (contrasted to the *Naturals*). (From Lee Silver.)

16. *Right to an open future*: A supposed right children have not to have their futures unduly limited by HGE. (From Joel Feinberg.)

17. *Transhumanists*: A name given to those who want to see science (including genetic engineering) used to transcend human limitations.

18. *Extropians*: A particular group of transhumanists.

19. *ELSI*: A term referring to the "ethical, legal, and social implications" of human genetics.

Questions

(Please explain your answers, making specific reference to relevant passages in the discussion.)

1. Why do many thinkers believe that any "redesign" of human beings would not be done through cloning or through making humans into cyborgs?
2. Explain how IVF and PGD might be used to redesign human beings?
3. Explain how IVF and HGE might be used to redesign human beings?
4. What is the difference between somatic-HGE and germline-HGE? Which one seems to hold the greater dangers and why?
5. For each of the claims below, give arguments for them and then arguments against them, referring to the discussion as you do so.

  (a) HGE would be too dangerous
  (b) HGE/PGD would be "playing God"
  (c) HGE/PGD wouldn't be limited to curing disease
  (d) HGE would lead to a "genetic arms race"
  (e) HGE could undermine religion and ethics
  (f) HGE could lead to totalitarianism
  (g) HGE could lead to Nazi-like eugenics
  (h) HGE could undermine human equality
  (i) HGE could undermine human freedom.

6. Why do some thinkers worry that the permissibility of human genetic engineering in the United States won't be decided democratically?

24

Genetics

Readings

Ronald M. Green discusses some of the fears of genetic enhancement displayed in literature and argues that these fears may simply reflect "status quo bias"

[...]

Genetic interventions raise many of our fears about biomedicine. Unlike stem cell research, which pits liberals against conservatives, left against right, genetic self-modification evokes opposition all across the political and cultural spectrum. Some liberal thinkers object to the expenditure of scarce research funds on what they regard as elitist genetic research. Others fear an emerging division between genetic haves and genetic have-nots. Some feminists who already see assisted reproductive technologies as a male usurpation of female reproductive powers join others opposed to the use of genetic testing for sex selection. The opposition includes environmental activists who believe that respect for untampered nature should extend to the human genome. In the United Nations, these constituencies have joined forces to help produce a UNESCO declaration calling the human genome the "heritage of humanity."

A glance at the work of some of our leading writers and filmmakers shows how broad this coalition of opposition is. In the novel *Oryx and Crake* (2003), the feminist writer Margaret Atwood depicts a not-too-distant future where bioengineering has produced an apocalypse. Genetically altered viruses have killed off most of the human population. Aggressive, genetically modified, superintelligent animal predators, from dogs to pigs, roam the planet. Only a handful of human beings remain, but gene modifications have made them too innocent and vulnerable to survive. Atwood's novel criticizes our excessive love of science and our environmental intrusiveness. Her fear is that we can never retain full control of our creations.

The same critical sentiment against human genetic self-modification is evident in Andrew Niccol's 1997 film *Gattaca*. The film was not a commercial success, but it lives on in bioethics classrooms around the country as the epitome of what is bad about human gene interventions. *Gattaca* begins with two acts of conception. The first takes place in the near future in the back seat of a Buick and produces Vincent, the love child of his young parents, Marie and Antonio. At birth, Vincent is diagnosed with a host of genetic maladies, including a heart problem that is predicted to end his life by age thirty.

Reproduced with permission from *Babies By Design: The Ethics of Genetic Choice*, by Ronald M. Green. New Haven, CT: Yale University Press, 2007, pp. 5–9.

The second conception occurs in the glistening laboratory offices of the Eighth Day Genetic Center and produces another son, Anton, one "worthy of his father's name." A counselor guides Marie and Antonio as they choose one of the embryos produced from their eggs and sperm through in vitro fertilization. He informs them of the modest genetic changes he has made in the embryos, including the eradication of genes for "prejudicial conditions" like premature baldness, myopia, alcoholism and addictive susceptibility, domestic violence, and obesity. When Marie and Antonio appear troubled by so much gene meddling, the counselor calms them, saying "You want to give your child the best possible start.... Keep in mind, this child is still you, simply the best of you. You could conceive naturally a thousand times and never get such a result." In a scene cut from the final version of the movie but available on the DVD, the counselor's speech to Marie and Antonio continues as he offers them a range of options. "For a little extra money," he says, "I could also attempt to insert [DNA] sequences associated with enhanced mathematical or musical ability." The couple decline the offer only when they learn that the cost is prohibitive.

Gattaca is meant to be a warning. Genetic manipulation leads to a nightmarish society obsessed with genetic perfection and disfigured by genetic discrimination. Vincent and other "nonengineered" people are scorned as "de-gene-erates" or "in-valids." They're consigned to the lowest rungs of society and shunned as mates. In the end, Vincent triumphs. Through hard work and determination, and with the help of other marginal people who evade the system, he achieves his dream of becoming an astronaut, proving that "there is no gene for the human spirit." But like so much science fiction dealing with genetics, the take-home lesson about human gene modification is wholly negative. In the film the deliberate manipulation of human genes threatens everything we hold dear: human individuality, freedom, justice, and love.

My aim in this book is to challenge the negative views that underlie works like *Oryx* and *Crake* and *Gattaca*. I do not intend to show that these visions are mistaken. No one can predict where our growing powers of genetic control will lead. The concerns voiced by artists, bioethicists, and others about genetics gone wrong are a healthy warning. In addition, the horrible eugenic abuses perpetrated by the Nazis that culminated in the Holocaust indicate how easily genetics can become an excuse for evil. Still, I believe that increased genetic control lies in our future and will make that future better. We will begin with gene selection aimed at reducing the likelihood that a child will be born with a genetic disease, and eventually include changes designed to permanently eliminate serious disorders like cystic fibrosis and sickle cell disease from a family line. Beyond this, gene modification will encompass the first hesitant steps to *improve* the genetic endowment of our children so they can flourish in new ways. This may include increased natural resistance to diseases like AIDS and cancer or to problems like diabetes or obesity. Somewhere down the line, we will see the emergence of what I call "cosmetico-genomics," as parents strive to give their children more attractive physical features, including normal height, good teeth, clear complexions, and pleasing faces. In the more distant future, we may see cognitive and neurological enhancements, ranging from reduced susceptibility to dyslexia, learning disorders, and depression to improved memory and enhanced IQ.

Some of these possibilities send chills down our spine because they raise so many scientific and ethical questions. What about mistakes and errors? Won't interventions carry unknown risks for the children themselves? Should we alter children's genes without their consent? What will these interventions do to the parent–child relationship? Will overzealous parents impose their vision of perfection on a child, creating psychological problems whether or not the child fulfills the parents' expectations? And what about social justice? Affluent parents have always been able to provide their offspring with advantages that enhance a child's chances of success. But now, in addition to better educational opportunities, a financial head start, and a network of well-placed friends, they could also confer "better genes." Will gene enhancement intensify and perpetuate the divide between society's winners and losers?

[...] [T]here are serious reasons for concern, but also some reasons to think that we will be able to adjust to (and even flourish in) a world where gene modification takes place. Above all, it is important to recognize how hard it is for us even to think about such new possibilities. Never before in history have we had anything like this ability to shape the biological inheritance of our children. Over millennia, we have become so accustomed to accepting our offspring as they are that the very idea of choosing their characteristics seems blasphemous and opposed to the way one human being should relate to another. These feelings and thoughts may be right. It could well be that the ability to choose another person's characteristics is a power that no human being should possess.

But our approach to this new power could merely reflect what social scientists call "status quo bias." Social science research has repeatedly shown that human beings resist change, even when there is no good reason to do so. In one study, researchers reported an episode that happened in Germany some years ago. The government found it necessary to develop an open pit coal mine, requiring the leveling of a village above the site, and offered to relocate the village to a similar valley nearby. Specialists developed planning options. Since the older village had evolved higgledy-piggledy over many centuries and was difficult to access by car, most of the new plans had

obvious advantages. But in the end, the townspeople chose their familiar if inconvenient layout.[1]

The results can be explained partly by the emotional attachments people form to what they know, but many other studies in finance and economics, where no such attachment is evident, point to the same result: people tend to resist change and favor the status quo. When faced with change, they greatly overestimate the advantages of the familiar and conjure up reasons for disliking and fearing innovations.

Where human reproduction is concerned, to what extent are we like the villagers, favoring dysfunctional patterns just because we have grown used to them? It is always easy to identify the benefits of existing patterns: that they are there and seem to work is an argument in their favor. Every proposed change invites suspicion. But what we miss in this approach to novelty is a balanced and reasoned assessment of both the present and the future. What are the negatives, as well as the positives, in our present arrangements? In what ways is the present dysfunctional? Can we see ourselves growing accustomed to new patterns and even coming to regard them as better than present ones?

[...]

Questions

1. Compare and contrast the negative visions conjured up by the films *Oryx and Crake* and *Gattaca*.

2. What is status quo bias? How does Green think it might be affecting our visions of genetically engineered humans?

Note

1. William Samuelson and Richard Zeckhauser, "Status Quo Bias in Decision Making," *Journal of Risk and Uncertainty* 1 (1988), 10.

Gregory Stock discusses the possibility of "redesigning humans" and argues it will likely happen

[...]

The arrival of safe, reliable germline technology will signal the beginning of human self-design. We do not know where this development will ultimately take us, but it will transform the evolutionary process by drawing reproduction into a highly selective social process that is far more rapid and effective at spreading successful genes than traditional sexual competition and mate selection.

[...]

Dismissal of technology's role in humanity's genetic future is common even among biologists who use advanced technologies in their work. Perhaps the notion that we will control our evolutionary future seems too audacious. Perhaps the idea that humans might one day differ from us in fundamental ways is too disorienting. Most mass-media science fiction doesn't challenge our thinking about this either. One of the last major sci-fi movies of the second millennium was *The Phantom Menace*, George Lucas's 1999 prequel to *Star Wars*. Its vision of human biological enhancement was simple: there won't be any. Lucas reveled in special effects and fantastical life forms, but altered us not a jot. Despite reptilian side-kicks with pedestal eyes and hard-bargaining insectoids that might have escaped from a Raid commercial, the film's humans were no different from us. With the right accent and a coat and tie, the leader of the Galactic Republic might have been the president of France.

Such a vision of human continuity is reassuring. It lets us imagine a future in which we feel at home. Space pods, holographic telephones, laser pistols, and other amazing gadgets are enticing to many of us, but pondering a time when humans no longer exist is another story, one far too alien and unappealing to arouse our dramatic sympathies. We've seen too many

apocalyptic images of nuclear, biological, and environmental disaster to think that the path to human extinction could be anything but horrific.

Yet the road to our eventual disappearance might be paved not by humanity's failure but by its success. Progressive self-transformation could change our descendants into something sufficiently different from our present selves to not be human in the sense we use the term now. Such an occurrence would more aptly be termed a pseudoextinction, since it would not end our lineage. Unlike the saber-toothed tiger and other large mammals that left no descendants when our ancestors drove them to extinction, *Homo sapiens* would spawn its own successors by fast-forwarding its evolution.

Some disaster, of course, might derail our technological advance, or our biology might prove too complex to rework. But our recent deciphering of the human genome (the entirety of our genetic constitution) and our massive push to unravel life's workings suggest that modification of our biology is far nearer to reality than the distant space travel we see in science fiction movies. Moreover, we are unlikely to achieve the technology to flit around the galaxy without being able to breach our own biology as well. The Human Genome Project is only a beginning.

[...]

Many bioethicists do not share my perspective on where we are heading. They imagine that our technology might become potent enough to alter us, but that we will turn away from it and reject human enhancement. But the reshaping of human genetics and biology does not hinge on some cadre of demonic researchers hidden away in a lab in Argentina trying to pick up where Hitler left off. The coming possibilities will be the inadvertent spinoff of main-stream research that virtually everyone supports. Infertility, for example, is a source of deep pain for millions of couples. Researchers and clinicians working on *in vitro* fertilization (IVF) don't think much about future human evolution, but nonetheless are building a foundation of expertise in conceiving, handling, testing, and implanting human embryos, and this will one day be the basis for the manipulation of the human species. Already, we are seeing attempts to apply this knowledge in highly controversial ways: as premature as today's efforts to clone humans may be, they would be the flimsiest of fantasies if they could not draw on decades of work on human IVF.

Similarly, in early 2001 more than five hundred gene-therapy trials were under way or in review throughout the world. The researchers are trying to cure real people suffering from real diseases and are no more interested in the future of human evolution than the IVF researchers. But their progress toward inserting genes into adult cells will be one more piece of the foundation for manipulating human embryos.

Not everything that can be done should or will be done, of course, but once a relatively inexpensive technology becomes feasible in thousands of laboratories around the world and a sizable fraction of the population sees it beneficial, it *will* be used.

[…]

Professional sports offers a preview of the spread of enhancement technology into other arenas. Sports may carry stronger incentives to cheat, and thus push athletes toward greater health risks, but the nonsporting world is not so different. A person working two jobs feels under pressure to produce, and so does a student taking a test or someone suffering the effects of growing old. When safe, reliable metabolic and physiological enhancers exist, the public will want them, even if they are illegal. To block their use will be far more daunting than today's war on drugs. An antidrug commercial proclaiming "Dope is for dopes!" or one showing a frying egg with the caption "Your brain on drugs" would not persuade anyone to stop using a safe memory enhancer.

Aesthetic surgery is another budding field for enhancement. When we try to improve our appearance, the personal stakes are high because our looks are always with us. Knowing that the photographs of beautiful models in magazines are airbrushed does not make us any less self-conscious if we believe we have a smile too gummy, skin too droopy, breasts too small, a nose too big, a head too bald, or any other such "defects." Surgery to correct these non-medical, problems has been growing rapidly and spreading to an ever-younger clientele. Public approval of aesthetic surgery has climbed some 50 percent in the past decade in the United States.[1] We may not be modifying our genes yet, but we are ever more willing to resort to surgery to hold back the most obvious (and superficial) manifestations of aging, or even simply to remodel our bodies. Nor is this only for the wealthy.[2] In 1994, when the median income in the United States was around $38,000, two thirds of the 400,000 aesthetic surgeries were performed on those with a family income under $50,000, and health insurance rarely covered the procedures. Older women who have subjected themselves to numerous face-lifts but can no longer stave off the signs of aging are not a rarity. But the tragedy is not so much that these women fight so hard to deny the years of visible decline, but that their struggle against life's natural ebb ultimately must fail. If such a decline were not inevitable, many people would eagerly embrace pharmaceutical or genetic interventions to retard aging.

The desire to triumph over our own mortality is an ancient dream, but it hardly stands alone. Whether we look at today's manipulations of our bodies by face-lifts, tattoos, pierced ears, or erythropoietin, the same message rings loud and clear: if medicine one day enables us to manipulate our biology in appealing ways, many of us will do so—even if the benefits are dubious and the risks not insignificant. To most people, the earliest adopters of these technologies will seem reckless or crazy, but are they so different from the daredevil test pilots of jet aircraft in the 1950s? Virtually by definition, early users believe that the possible gains from their bravado justify the risks. Otherwise, they would wait for flawed procedures to be discarded, for technical glitches to be worked through, for interventions to become safer and more predictable.

In truth, as long as people compete with one another for money, status, and mates, as long as they look for ways to display their worth and uniqueness, they will look for an edge for themselves and their children.

People will make mistakes with these biological manipulations. People will abuse them. People will worry about them. But as much could be said about any potent new development. No governmental body will wave some legislative wand and make advanced genetic and reproductive technologies go away, and we would be foolish to want this. Our collective challenge is not to figure out how to block these developments, but how best to realize their benefits while minimizing our risks and safeguarding our rights and freedoms. This will not be easy.

[…]

Our technology is evolving so rapidly that by the time we begin to adjust to one development, another is already surpassing it. The answer would seem to be to slow down and devise the best course in advance, but that notion is a mirage. Change is accelerating, not slowing, and even if we could agree on what to aim for, the goal would probably be unrealistic. Complex changes are occurring across too broad a front to chart a path. The future is too opaque to foresee the eventual impacts of important new technologies, much less whole bodies of knowledge like genomics (the study of genomes). No one understood the powerful effects of the automobile or television at its inception. Few appreciated that our use of antibiotics would lead to widespread drug resistance or that improved nutrition and public health in the developing world would help bring on a population explosion. Our blindness about the consequences of new reproductive technologies is nothing new, and we will not be able to erase the uncertainty by convening an august panel to think through the issues.

No shortcut is possible. As always, we will have to earn our knowledge by using the technology and learning from the problems that arise. Given that some people will dabble in the new procedures as soon as they become even remotely accessible, our safest path is to not drive early explorations underground. What we learn about such technology while it is imperfect and likely to be used by only a small number of people may help us figure out how to manage it more wisely as it matures.

[...]

Watson's simple question, "If we could make better humans ... why shouldn't we?" cuts to the heart of the controversy about human genetic enhancement. Worries about the procedure's feasibility or safety miss the point. No serious scientists advocate manipulating human genetics until such interventions are safe and reliable.

Why all the fuss, then? Opinions may differ about what risks are acceptable, but virtually every physician agrees that any procedure needs to be safe, and that any potential benefit needs to be weighed against the risks. Moreover, few prospective parents would seek even a moderately risky genetic enhancement for their child unless it was extremely beneficial, relatively safe, and unobtainable in an easier way. Actually, some critics, like Leon Kass, a well-known bioethicist at the University of Chicago who has long opposed such potential interventions, aren't worried that this technology will fail, but that it will succeed, and succeed gloriously.[3]

Their nightmare is that safe, reliable genetic manipulations will allow people to substantively enhance their biology. They believe that the use—and misuse—of this power will tear the fabric of our society. Such angst is particularly prevalent in western Europe, where most governments take a more conservative stand on the use of genetic technologies, even banning genetically altered foods. Stefan Winter, a physician at the University of Bonn and former vice president of the European Committee for Biomedical Ethics, says, "We should never apply germline gene interventions to human beings. The breeding of mankind would be a social nightmare from which no one could escape."[4]

Given Hitler's appalling foray into racial purification, European sensitivities are understandable, but they miss the bigger picture. The possibility of altering the genes of our prospective children is not some isolated spinoff of molecular biology but an integral part of the advancing technologies that culminate a century of progress in the biological sciences. We have spent billions to unravel our biology, not out of idle curiosity, but in the hope of bettering our lives. We are not about to turn away from this.

[...]

Questions

1. Stock seems to think it likely that we will slip easily into the practice of "redesigning humans." What current scientific practices does he think are leading us in this direction? What social practices?

2. Stock doesn't think that getting worked up now about the safety of eventual genetic manipulations makes much sense. Why not?

Notes

1. Bardo, S, 1998. "Braveheart, Babe, and the Contemporary Body." In *Enchancing Human Traits*. Edited by Erik Parens. Washington, DC: Georgetown University Press.
2. Siebert, C., 1996. "The Cuts That Go Deeper." *New York Times Magazine*, July 7, 20–6, 40–4.
3. Kass, L., 2001. "Why We Should Ban Cloning Now; Preventing a Brave New World." *New Republic*, May 21, 30–9.
4. Winter, S. 2000. "Our Societal Obligation for Keeping Human Nature Untouched," *Engineering the Human Germline: An Exploration of the Science and Ethics of Altering the Genes We Pass to Our Children*, edited by G. Stock and J. Campbell, 113–16. New York: Oxford University Press.

Jonathan Glover discusses a "genetic supermarket," positive versus negative genetic engineering and whether human nature should be sacrosanct

[...]

Some of the strongest objections to positive engineering are not about specialized applications or about risks. They are about the decisions involved. The central line of thought is that we should not start playing God by redesigning the human race. The suggestion is that there is no group (such as scientists, doctors, public officials, or politicians) who can be entrusted with decisions about what sort of people there should be. And it is also doubted whether we could have any adequate grounds for basing such decisions on one set of values rather than another.

This chapter is about the 'playing God' objection: about the question 'Who decides?', and about the values involved. I shall argue that these issues raise real problems, but that, contrary to what is often supposed, they do not add up to an overwhelming case against positive engineering.

From *What Sort of People Should There Be?* by Jonathan Glover. Middlesex, UK: Penguin Books, 1984, pp. 45–56. Reproduced by permission of Penguin Books Ltd and courtesy of Pr J. Glover.

Not playing God

Suppose we could use genetic engineering to raise the average IQ by fifteen points. (I mention, only to ignore, the boring objection that the average IQ is always by definition 100.) Should we do this? Objectors to positive engineering say we should not. This is not because the present average is preferable to a higher one. We do not think that, if it were naturally fifteen points higher, we ought to bring it down to the present level. The objection is to our playing God by deciding what the level should be.

On one view of the world, the objection is relatively straightforward. On this view, there really is a God, who has a plan for the world which will be disrupted if we stray outside the boundaries assigned to us. (It is *relatively* straightforward: there would still be the problem of knowing where the boundaries came. If genetic engineering disrupts the programme, how do we know that medicine and education do not?

[...]

When the objection to playing God is separated from the idea that intervening in this aspect of the natural world is a kind of blasphemy, it is a protest against a particular group of people, necessarily fallible and limited, taking decisions so important to our future. This protest may be on grounds of the bad consequences, such as loss of variety of people, that would come from the imaginative limits of those taking the decisions. Or it may be an expression of opposition to such concentration of power, perhaps with the thought: 'What right have *they* to decide what kinds of people there should be?' Can these problems be side-stepped?

The genetic supermarket

Robert Nozick is critical of the assumption that positive engineering has to involve any centralized decision about desirable qualities: 'Many biologists tend to think the problem is one of *design*, of specifying the best types of persons so that biologists can proceed to produce them. Thus they worry over what sort(s) of person there is to be and who will control this process. They do not tend to think, perhaps because it diminishes the importance of their role, of a system in which they run a "genetic supermarket", meeting the individual specifications (within certain moral limits) of prospective parents. Nor do they think of seeing what limited number of types of persons people's choices would converge upon, if indeed there would be any such convergence. This supermarket system has the great virtue that it involves no centralized decison fixing the future human type(s).'[1]

This idea of letting parents choose their children's characteristics is in many ways an improvement on decisions being taken by some centralized body. It seems less likely to reduce human variety, and could even increase it, if genetic engineering makes new combinations of characteristics available. (But we should be cautious here. Parental choice is not a guarantee of genetic variety, as the influence of fashion or of shared values might make for a small number of types on which choices would converge.)

To those sympathetic to one kind of liberalism, Nozick's proposal will seem more attractive than centralized decisions. On this approach to politics, it is wrong for the authorities to institutionalize any religious or other outlook as the official one of the society. To a liberal of this kind, a good society is one which tolerates and encourages a wide diversity of ideals of the good life. Anyone with these sympathies will be suspicious of centralized decisons about what sort of people should form the next generation. But some parental decisons would be disturbing. If parents chose characteristics likely to make their children unhappy, or likely to reduce their abilities, we might feel that the children should be protected against this. (Imagine parents belonging to some extreme religious sect, who wanted

their children to have a religious symbol as a physical mark on their face, and who wanted them to be unable to read, as a protection against their faith being corrupted.) Those of us who support restrictions protecting children from parental harm after birth (laws against cruelty, and compulsion on parents to allow their children to be educated and to have necessary medical treatment) are likely to support protecting children from being harmed by their parents' genetic choices.

No doubt the boundaries here will be difficult to draw. We already find it difficult to strike a satisfactory balance between protection of children and parental freedom to choose the kind of upbringing their children should have. But it is hard to accept that society should set no limits to the genetic choices parents can make for their children. Nozick recognizes this when he says the genetic supermarket should meet the specifications of parents 'within certain moral limits'. So, if the supermarket came into existence, some centralized policy, even if only the restrictive one of ruling out certain choices harmful to the children, should exist. It would be a political decision where the limits should be set.

[…]

A mixed system

The genetic supermarket provides a partial answer to the objection about the limited outlook of those who would take the decisions. The choices need not be concentrated in the hands of a small number of people. The genetic supermarket should not operate in a completely unregulated way, and so some centralized decisions would have to be taken about the restrictions that should be imposed. One system that would answer many of the anxieties about centralized decision-making would be to limit the power of the decision-makers to one of veto. They would then only check departures from the natural genetic lottery, and so the power to bring about changes would not be given to them, but spread through the whole population of potential parents. Let us call this combination of parental initiative and central veto a 'mixed system'. If positive genetic engineering does come about, we can imagine the argument between supporters of a mixed system and supporters of other decision-making systems being central to the political theory of the twenty-first century, parallel to the place occupied in the nineteenth and twentieth centuries by the debate over control of the economy.

My own sympathies are with the view that, if positive genetic engineering is introduced, this mixed system is in general likely to be the best one for taking decisions.[...]

If this mixed system eliminates the anxiety about genetic changes being introduced by a few powerful people with limited horizons, there is a more general unease which it does not remove. May not the limitations of one generation of parents also prove disastrous? And, underlying this, is the problem of what values parents should appeal to in making their choices. How can we be confident that it is better for one sort of person to be born than another?

Values

The dangers of such decisions, even spread through all prospective parents, seem to me very real. We are swayed by fashion. We do not know the limitations of our own outlook. There are human qualities whose value we may not appreciate. A generation of parents might opt heavily for their children having physical or intellectual abilities and skills. We might leave out a sense of humour. Or we might not notice how important to us is some other quality, such as emotional warmth. So we might not be disturbed in advance by the possible impact of the genetic changes on such a quality. And, without really wanting to do so, we might stumble into producing people with a deep coldness. This possibility seems one of the worst imaginable. It is just one of the many horrors that could be blundered into by our lack of foresight in operating the mixed system. Because such disasters are a real danger, there is a case against positive genetic engineering, even when the changes do not result from centralized decisions. But this case, resting as it does on the risk of disaster, supports a principle of caution rather than a total ban. We have to ask the question whether there are benefits sufficiently great and sufficiently probable to outweigh the risks.

But perhaps the deepest resistance, even to a mixed system, is not based on risks, but on a more general problem about values. Could the parents ever be justified in choosing, according to some set of values, to create one sort of person rather than another?

[...]

The positive–negative boundary may seem a way of avoiding objectionably God-like decisions, on the basis of our own values, as to what sort of people there should be. Saving someone from spina bifida is a lot less controversial than deciding he shall be a good athlete. But the distinction, clear in some cases, is less sharp in others. With emotional states or intellectual functioning, there is an element of convention in where the boundaries of normality are drawn. And, apart from this, there is the problem of explaining why the positive–negative boundary is so much more important with genetic intervention than with environmental methods. We act environmentally to influence people in ways that go far beyond the elimination of medical defects. Homes and schools would be impoverished by attempting to restrict their influence on children to the mere prevention of physical and mental disorder. And if we are right here to cross the positive–negative boundary, encouraging children to ask questions, or to be generous and imaginative, why should crossing the same boundary for the same reasons be ruled out absolutely when the means are genetic?

It may be said that the genes–environment boundary is important because environmentally created changes can be reversed in a way that genetically based characteristics can not. But this perhaps underrates the permanence of the effects of upbringing. It may be that the difference is at best a matter of degree. And it is also hard to believe that irreversibility can be our main objection to crossing the genes–environment boundary. In bringing up our children, we try to encourage kindness and generosity. Would we really stop doing this if we were so effective that cruelty and meanness became impossible for them? It is not clear that our concern to develop their autonomy requires keeping open *all* possibilities, at whatever cost to our other values.

[...]

Changing human nature

Positive genetic engineering raises two issues. Could we be justified in trying to change human nature? And, if so, is genetic change an acceptable method? Most of us feel resistance to genetic engineering, and these two questions are often blurred together in our thinking. One aim of the discussion has been to separate the different sources of our resistance. Another has been to try to isolate the justifiable doubts. These have to do with risks of disasters, or with the drawbacks of imposed, centralized decisions. They need not justify total rejection of positive engineering. The risks are good reasons for extreme caution. The other drawbacks are good reasons for decentralized decisions, and for resisting positive genetic engineering in authoritarian societies. But these good reasons are quite separable from any opposition in principle to changing human nature.

The idea of 'human nature' is a vague one, whose boundaries are not easy to draw. And, given our history, the idea that we must preserve all the characteristics that are natural to us is not obvious without argument. Some deep changes in human nature may only be possible if we do accept positive genetic engineering. It is true that our nature is not determined entirely by our genes, but they do set limits to the sorts of people we can be. And the evolutionary competition to survive has set limits to the sorts of genes we have. Perhaps changes in society will transform our nature. But there is the pessimistic thought that perhaps they will not. Or, if they do, the resulting better people may lose to unreconstructed people in the evolutionary struggle. On either of these pessimistic views, to renounce positive genetic engineering would be to renounce any hope of fundamental improvement in what we are like. And we cannot yet be sure that these pessimistic views are both false.

Given the risks that positive genetic engineering is likely to involve, many people will think that we should reject it, even if that means putting up with human nature as it is. And many others will think that, quite apart from risks and dangers, we ought not to tamper with our nature. I have some sympathy with the first view. The decision involves balancing risks and gains, and perhaps the dangers will outweigh the benefits. We can only tell when the details are clearer than they are now, both about the genetic techniques and about the sort of society that is in existence at the time.

It is less easy to sympathize with opposition to the principle of changing our nature. Preserving the human race as it is will seem an acceptable option to all those who can watch the news on television and feel satisfied with the world. It will appeal to those who can talk to their children about the history of the twentieth century without wishing they could leave some things out. When, in the rest of this book, the case for and against various changes is considered, the fact that they *are* changes will be treated as no objection at all.

Questions

1. Glover gives two interpretations of the claim that "we shouldn't play God" by genetically engineering people. What are those interpretations?
2. For Glover what are the advantages of a "mixed system" as compared to an unregulated genetic supermarket or centralized planning?
3. What are Glover's objections to the positive–negative boundary as marking off unacceptable versus acceptable genetic manipulations?
4. What are Glover's objections to the idea that we shouldn't change human nature?

Note

1. *Anarchy, State and Utopia.* New York, 1974, p. 315.

Francis Fukuyama warns against genetics leading us into a "post-human" future. He thinks genetic engineering should be limited to curing disease and outlines the regulatory changes the US would need to make to accomplish this

[...]

Embryo research is only the beginning of a series of new developments created by technology for which societies have to decide on rules and regulatory institutions. Others that will come up sooner or later include:

- *Preimplantation diagnosis and screening.* This group of technologies, in which multiple embryos are screened genetically for birth defects and other characteristics, is the beginning point of "designer babies" and will arrive much sooner than human germ-line engineering. Indeed, such screening has already been performed for children of parents susceptible to certain genetic diseases. In the future, do we want to permit parents to screen and selectively implant embryos on the basis of sex; intelligence; looks; hair, eye, or skin color; sexual orientation; and other characteristics once they can be identified genetically?

- *Germ-line engineering.* If and when human germ-line engineering arrives, it will raise the same issues as preimplantation diagnosis and screening, but in a more extreme form. Preimplantation diagnosis and screening is limited by the fact that there will always be a limited number of embryos from which to choose, based on the genes of the two parents. Germ-line engineering will expand the possibilities to include virtually any other genetically governed trait, provided it can be identified successfully.

  [...]

- *New psychotropic drugs.* In the United States, the Food and Drug Administration (FDA) regulates therapeutic drugs, while the Drug Enforcement Administration (DEA) and the states regulate illegal narcotics such as heroin, cocaine, and marijuana. Societies will have to make decisions on the legality and extent of permissible use of future generations of neuropharmacological agents. In the case of prospective drugs that improve memory or other cognitive skills, they will have to decide on the desirability of enhancement uses and how they are to be regulated.

Regulation is essentially the act of drawing a series of red lines that separate legal from proscribed activities, based on a statute that defines the area in which regulators can exercise some degree of judgment. With the exception of some die-hard libertarians, most people reading the above list of innovations that may be made possible by biotechnology will probably want to see some red lines drawn.

[...]

One obvious way to draw red lines is to distinguish between therapy and enhancement, directing research toward the former while putting restrictions on the latter. The original purpose of medicine is, after all, to heal the sick, not to turn healthy people into gods. We don't want star athletes to be hobbled by bad knees or torn ligaments, but we also don't want them to compete on the basis of who has taken the most steroids. This general principle would allow us to use biotechnologies to, for example, cure genetic diseases like Huntington's chorea or cystic fibrosis, but not to make our children more intelligent or taller.

The distinction between therapy and enhancement has been attacked on the grounds that there is no way to distinguish between the two in theory, and therefore no way of discriminating in practice. There is a long tradition, argued most forcefully in recent years by the French postmodernist thinker Michel Foucault,[1] which maintains that what society considers to be pathology or disease is actually a socially constructed phenomenon in which deviation from some presumed norm is stigmatized. Homosexuality, to take one example, was long considered unnatural and was classified as a psychiatric disorder until the latter part of the twentieth century, when it was depathologized as part of the growing acceptance of gayness in developed societies. Something similar can be said of dwarfism: human heights are distributed normally, and it is not clear at what point in the distribution one becomes a dwarf. If it is legitimate to give growth hormone to a child who is in the bottom 0.5 percentile for height, who's to say that you can't also prescribe it for someone who is in the fifth percentile, or for that matter in the fiftieth?[2] Geneticist Lee Silver makes a similar argument about future genetic engineering, saying that it is impossible to draw a line between therapy and enhancement in an objective manner: "in every case, genetic engineering will be used to add something to a child's genome that didn't exist in the genomes of either of its parents."[3]

While it is the case that certain conditions do not lend themselves to neat distinctions between pathological and normal, it is also true that there is such a thing as health. As Leon Kass has argued, there is a natural functioning to the whole organism that has been determined by the requirements of the species' evolutionary history, one that is not simply an arbitrary social construction.[4] It has often seemed to me that the only people who can argue that there is no difference in principle between disease and health are those who have never been sick: if you have a virus or fracture your leg, you know perfectly well that something is wrong.

And even in the cases where the borderline between sickness and health, therapy and enhancement, is murkier, regulatory agencies are routinely able to make these distinctions in practice. Take the case of Ritalin. [...] [T]he underlying "disease" that Ritalin is supposed to treat, attention deficit-hyperactivity disorder (ADHD), is most likely not a disease at all but simply the label that we put on people who are in the tail of a normal distribution of behavior related to focus and attention. This is in fact a classic case of the social construction of pathology: ADHD was not even in the medical lexicon a couple of generations ago. There is, correspondingly, no neat line between what one might label the therapeutic and enhancement uses of Ritalin. At one end of the distribution, there are children almost anyone would say are so hyperactive that normal functioning is impossible for them, and it is hard to object to treating them with

Ritalin. At the other end of the distribution are children who have no trouble whatsoever concentrating or interacting, for whom taking Ritalin might be an enjoyable experience that would give them a high just like any other amphetamine. But they would be taking the drug for enhancement rather than for therapeutic reasons, and thus most people would want to prevent them from doing so. What makes Ritalin controversial is all the children in the middle, who meet some but not all of the diagnostic criteria specified in the *Diagnostic and Statistical Manual of Mental Disorders* for the disease and who nonetheless are prescribed the drug by their family physician.

If there was ever a case, in other words, where the distinction between pathology and health in diagnosis, and therapy and enhancement in treatment, is ambiguous, it is ADHD and Ritalin. And yet, regulatory agencies *make and enforce this distinction all the time*. The DEA classifies Ritalin as a Schedule II pharmaceutical that can only be taken for therapeutic purposes with a doctor's prescription; it clamps down on Ritalin's recreational (that is to say, enhancement) use as an amphetamine. That the boundary between therapy and enhancement is unclear does not make the distinction meaningless. My own strong feeling is that the drug is overprescribed in the United States and used in situations in which parents and teachers ought to employ more traditional means of engaging children and shaping their characters. But the current regulatory system, for all its faults, is better than a situation in which Ritalin is either banned altogether or else sold over the counter like cough medicine.

Regulators are called on all the time to make complex judgments that cannot be held up to precise theoretical scrutiny. What constitutes a "safe" level of heavy metals in the soil, or sulfur dioxide in the atmosphere? How does a regulator justify pushing down the level of a particular toxin in drinking water from fifty to five parts per million, when he or she is trading off health consequences against compliance costs? These decisions are always controversial, but in a sense they are easier to make in practice than in theory. For in practice, a properly functioning democratic political system allows people with a stake in the regulator's decision to push and shove against one another until a compromise is reached.

Once we agree in principle that we will need a capability to draw red lines, it will not be a fruitful exercise to spend a lot of time arguing precisely where they should be placed. As in other areas of regulation, many of these decisions will have to be made on a trial-and-error basis by administrative agencies, based on knowledge and experience not available to us at present. What is more important is to think about the design of institutions that can make and enforce regulations on, for example, the use of preimplantation diagnosis and screening for therapeutic rather than enhancement purposes, and how those in stitutions can be extended internationally.

[...]

Let us suppose that Congress legislatively distinguishes between therapeutic and enhancement uses of preimplantation diagnosis and screening. The FDA is not set up to make politically sensitive decisions concerning the point at which selection for characteristics like intelligence and height ceases to be therapeutic and becomes enhancing, or whether these characteristics can be considered therapeutic at all. The FDA can disapprove a procedure only on the grounds of effectiveness and safety, but there will be many safe and effective procedures that will nonetheless require regulatory scrutiny. The limits of the FDA's mandate are already evident: it has asserted a right to regulate human cloning on the legally questionable grounds that a cloned child constitutes a medical "product" over which it has authority.

[...]

A second reason that existing institutions are probably not sufficient to regulate biotechnology in the future has to do with changes that have taken place in the research community and the biotech pharmaceutical industry as a whole over the past generation. There was a period up through the early 1990s when virtually all biomedical research in the United States was funded by the NIH or another federal government agency. This meant that the NIH could regulate that research through its own internal rule-making authority, as in the case of rules concerning human experimentation. Government regulators could work hand in glove with committees of scientific insiders [...] and be reasonably sure that no one in the United States was doing dangerous or ethically questionable research.

None of this holds true any longer. While the federal government remains the largest source of research funding, there is a huge amount of private investment money available to sponsor work in new biotechnologies.[...]

This means that any new regulatory agency not only would have to have a mandate to regulate biotechnology on grounds broader than efficacy and safety but also would have to have statutory authority over all research and development, and not just research that is federally funded. Such an agency, the Human Fertilisation and Embyology Authority, has already been created in Britain for this purpose. Unification of regulatory powers into a single new agency will end the practice of complying with federal funding restrictions by finding private sponsors and, it is hoped, will shed a more uniform light on the whole biotech sector.

What are the prospects for the United States and other countries putting into place a regulatory system of the kind just outlined?[5] There will be formidable political obstacles to creating new institutions. The biotech industry is strongly opposed to regulation (if anything, it would like to see FDA rules loosened), as is, by and large, the community of research scientists. Most would prefer regulation to take place within their own communities, outside the scope of formal law. They are joined in this by advocacy groups representing patients, the elderly, and others with an interest in promoting cures for various diseases, and together these groups form a very powerful political coalition.

[...]

We may be about to enter into a posthuman future, in which technology will give us the capacity gradually to alter that essence over time. Many embrace this power, under the banner of human freedom. They want to maximize the freedom of parents to choose the kind of children they have, the freedom of scientists to pursue research, and the freedom of entrepreneurs to make use of technology to create wealth.

But this kind of freedom will be different from all other freedoms that people have previously enjoyed. Political freedom has heretofore meant the freedom to pursue those ends that our natures had established for us. Those ends are not rigidly determined; human nature is very plastic, and we have an enormous range of choices conformable with that nature. But it is not infinitely malleable, and the elements that remain constant—particularly our species-typical gamut of emotional responses—constitute a safe harbor that allows us to connect, potentially, with all other human beings.

It may be that we are somehow destined to take up this new kind of freedom, or that the next stage of evolution is one in which, as some have suggested, we will deliberately take charge of our own biological makeup rather than leaving it to the blind forces of natural selection. But if we do, we should do it with eyes open. Many assume that the posthuman world will look pretty much like our own—free, equal, prosperous, caring, compassionate—only with better health care, longer lives, and perhaps more intelligence than today.

But the posthuman world could be one that is far more hierarchical and competitive than the one that currently exists, and full of social conflict as a result. It could be one in which any notion of "shared humanity" is lost, because we have mixed human genes with those of so many other species that we no longer have a clear idea of what a human being is. It could be one in which the median person is living well into his or her second century, sitting in a nursing home hoping for an unattainable death. Or it could be the kind of soft tyranny envisioned in *Brave New World*, in which everyone is healthy and happy but has forgotten the meaning of hope, fear, or struggle.

We do not have to accept any of these future worlds under a false banner of liberty, be it that of unlimited reproductive rights or of unfettered scientific inquiry. We do not have to regard ourselves as slaves to inevitable technological progress when that progress does not serve human ends. True freedom means the freedom of political communities to protect the values they hold most dear, and it is that freedom that we need to exercise with regard to the biotechnology revolution today.

Questions

1. What reasons does Fukuyama give for his claim that we could make a sensible legal distinction between the use of genetics for "therapy" and for "enhancement"?

2. What regulatory changes would the US need to make in order to effectively regulate such a legal distinction?

3. Why does Fukuyama believe it is dangerous for genetics to alter "human nature"? What bad consequences does he think might follow from such altering?

Notes

1. Michel Foucault, *Madness and Civilization: A History of Insanity in the Age of Reason* (New York: Pantheon Books, 1965).
2. The biotech firm Genentech has in fact been accused of trying to push the envelope for use of its growth hormone on children who are short but not hormonally deficient. See Tom Wilke, *Perilous Knowledge: The Human Genome Project and Its Implications* (Berkeley and Los Angeles: University of California Press, 1993), pp. 136–9.
3. Lee M. Silver, *Remaking Eden: Cloning and Beyond in a Brave New World* (New York: Avon, 1998), p. 268.
4. Leon Kass, *Toward a More Natural Science: Biology and Human Affairs* (New York: Free Press, 1985), p. 173.
5. Stuart Auchincloss, "Does Genetic Engineering Need Genetic Engineers?," *Boston College Environmental Affairs Law Review* 20 (1993): 37–64.

Bill McKibben argues that human genetic engineering will end up limiting human freedom and that it's our responsibility—not that of geneticists, doctors and bioethicists—to decide its future course

[…]

We are all tempted to leave things in the hands of wiser people who manage to make troubling phenomena—designer children, robots merging with people—seem benevolent, inevitable. It's always nice not to have to think. But it would be extremely unwise to let scientists walk away with that much power. In the first place, non-scientific concerns can cloud scientific judgment. Money, for instance: bio-tech has become one of the strongest magnets for venture capital in recent years, and any biologist worth his centrifuge is awash with stock options. In 2001, "a survey of medical experts who write guidelines for treating conditions like heart disease, depression, and diabetes has found that nearly nine out of ten have financial ties to the pharmaceutical industry, and the ties are almost never disclosed."[1][…]

But there's a deeper reason to give no special weight to the judgment of scientists: in truth, they have no better idea how we should proceed than anyone else who's thought about these issues. The devil is not in the details; it's the basic *thrust* of these technologies that's diabolical. Understanding which chromosomes are responsible for the expression of which proteins doesn't give you any added insight into whether designer babies are a good idea, any more than figuring out how to make an atom bomb turns you into an expert on when or where you should drop it.

[…]

If we don't dare abdicate the power to make decisions to research scientists, then perhaps we could turn to doctors. We're used to deferring to their judgment: if they produce a patient and say, "This person

Reproduced from *Enough: Staying Human in an Engineered Age*, by Bill McKibben. New York: Henry Holt and Company, 2003, pp. 181–91.

might be helped by this procedure," it's tempting just to go along. But as we've seen, there are many other routes toward treatment of genetic disorders that don't entail species-changing revolutions. And, in fact, it's the doctor's admirably total dedication to her *individual* patients that makes her just the wrong person to figure out what makes sense for the society. The dedication to an individual leaves little room for larger considerations; as anyone who's ever watched a parent kept "alive" in a tangle of machinery can attest, sometimes doctors can't even think clearly about the deeper needs of their own patients.

Doctors' struggles with deciding when to stop intervening against death helped lead to the creation of a makeshift profession, "bio-ethics" Though "anyone who cares to hang out a shingle"—a lawyer, a philosopher, an anthropologist, a doctor, a theologian—can join, "bioethicists" are nonetheless "quoted almost daily in the media, testify before Congress, and advise the president." They are, in the words of the journalist Nell Boyce, a kind of "secular priest"—and they are the last line of defense for those who would like "someone else" to make these decisions about these new technologies.[2] But that, alas, is an idle dream as well.

For one thing, all sides in these debates have "their" bioethicists, whom they use for cover. When President George W. Bush appointed a panel to advise him on cloning, for instance, he was widely accused of stacking it with conservatives who would tell him what he wanted to hear. In general, however, bioethicists have been captives of science and industry, for a variety of structural reasons. One, perhaps the least important, is simply self-interest: all the big bio-tech companies have ethics boards, and some of them pay their advisers with stock options or hand them checks for $2,000 a day.[3]

In a broader sense, bioethicists come from the same intellectual background as most of the people whose projects they're supposedly judging. Daniel Callahan, the president of the Hastings Center on bioethics, remarks that "most of those who have come into the field have accepted scientific ideology as much as most scientists, and they have no less been the cultural children of their times, prone to look to medical progress and its expansion of choice as a perfect complement to a set of moral values that puts autonomy at the very top of moral hierarchy." Most bioethicists thus don't ask questions about society or the species—they ask questions about individuals. Is this drug trial safe? Did everyone sign the informed-consent form? "Bioethicists have, on the whole, become good team players," says Callahan, "useful to help out with moral puzzles now and then and trustworthy not to probe basic premises too deeply."[4] So, for instance, when Advanced Cell Technology was planning to clone human embryos, the chairman of its ethics board outlined the "extreme precautions" the company was taking: the eggs would be kept in a secure location, access to which required permission from two ACT technicians; the eggs would be repeatedly counted, photographed, and videotaped; and so on. Nothing untoward would happen to the eggs—but the society that was about to be dramatically changed by this new development would have to fend for itself.[5]

Even the language of moral inquiry quickly turns technical. The sociologist Barbara Katz Rothman describes how, early in the history of genetic engineering, one group of theologians began by worrying about people "playing God"—that is, taking control over parts of life that they felt people had no business controlling. When they expressed their concerns to President Carter, he formed a commission of ethicists—but in draft after draft of their report they kept reducing the moral questions to technical ones. "Playing God" was too vague; it was translated as "acting without knowing the consequences, taking risks." So the response was to control risks—to put more filters in the lab's safety hoods; to write better informed-consent forms. The moral dilemma became somehow manageable.[6] The question isn't whether "playing God" is a sufficient objection; I've tried to show that bioengineering raises fundamental issues of meaning that don't depend on one's theology. But "ethicists" rarely do more than scratch the surface.

And how could they do any more? There are no all-knowing, all-seeing oracles to tell us the truth about these technologies. I think genetically engineering our children will be the worst choice human beings ever make—but I've explained *why* I think that, just as I would if I were writing about welfare reform or nuclear power or drug addiction. And I understand, intellectually if not emotionally, why others might want to engineer "improved" children; they weigh the costs and benefits differently. When we're deciding about a tax increase, we don't consult

"tax ethicists." We listen to economists who offer predictions about effects; we look at our schools and roads and judge their condition; we look at our paychecks and gauge what we can afford; and then we go vote. All that thinking may eventually boil itself down to an ideology—we become generally "anti-tax" or "pro-spending"—and that's all right, just as it's all right to feel generally queasy about genetic manipulation or generally gung-ho about technology. But you can't take a pass on the work of decision making, can't hope that some wizard from Oz will appear to explain in a booming voice precisely what should be done. "Forums and commissions can't settle these disputes," writes the essayist William Saletan. "Nor can ethicists. It's not their job. It's yours."[7]

Happily for us, we have a system for dealing with competing ideas. It's called politics. As always, we're going to have to make choices, basing them on some mix of knowledge and thought and intuition. We will have to *choose*.

True hard-core libertarians are few in number; the party's candidate for president doesn't win many votes, in part because people deeply devoted to individualism tend to be bad at organizing in groups. But if you held the election among high-tech CEOs, he'd have a fighting chance.

Paulina Borsook, a technology journalist, published a remarkable book titled *Cyberselfish* a few years ago, right at the height of the Internet boom. She began to chronicle Silicon Valley libertarianism when she noticed "maybe for the tenth time" a particular kind of personal ad in the local paper. "It didn't say he was buffed or liked walks along the beach or was into caring and sharing.... Instead, 'Ayn Rand enthusiast is seeking libertarian-oriented female for great conversation and romance. I am a very bright and attractive high-tech entrepreneur.'" At technical conferences and trade shows and in Santa Cruz barrooms, Borsook spent the next months "trying to make sense of the libertarianism I found all around." Some of it was pure Randian capitalist devotion; some of it an almost New Age belief that these new technologies were so complicated that they defied regulation ("The Economy Is a Rainforest" read one Bay Area bumper sticker). And some of it came from the simple overweening pride of the techies in their own amazing dynamism—the hard work, the serial bankruptcies, finally the stunning success. (It also had something to do with how most of these men spent their working days: "as the sole commander of one's own computer.")[8] A lot of it was also pretty dumb, of course—the Internet, after all, began as a government-funded invention.

But if you read the bulletin boards where true believers in the emerging technologies congregate, it's clear how influential this school of thought has become. There's a profound conviction that trying to direct or regulate or slow down any of these species-changing projects is despotism of the worst sort. "Any attempt to stop the Extraordinary Future, even if democratically decided, will be a form of tyranny, trapping minds in human bodies when alternative venues are available," writes one futurist.[9] "Just as Winston Churchill identified an Iron Curtain of totalitarianism that was falling across Europe half a century ago, I see an Iron Triangle of opposition to meaningful progress in the human condition vying for control of the cultural scene," another speaker told a 2001 gathering of technophiles.[10] When I published an op-ed piece in the *Times* questioning cloning, my e-mail in box filled within an hour. "The imposition of moral strictures on one's fellows to me is a *vile repudiation of everything American,*" ran one of the more reasonable notes.

When this libertarian streak is applied in normal, everyday politics, most of the overstatement drops away, being replaced by the constant, mantralike use of one of the most seductive words in the modern vocabulary: "choice."

In the endless buffet line that constitutes modern consumer culture, we've learned to think of choice as our highest value. We have five hundred channels—we can choose what we want to watch. We have twenty thousand new products annually in the supermarket—we choose what we want to buy. We have every compact disc on earth trading constantly across our hard drives—we choose what we want to hear. We can get anywhere we want in eighteen hours on a plane—we choose where we'll live. We have access to every culture on the planet—we choose how we want to dress, whose food we want to eat, whose tribal jewelry we want to copy. Why shouldn't we choose what we want our kids to be like? If I want my daughter to stand six feet tall, run two-hour marathons, and remember every e-mail address on Yahoo!, how is that any different from deciding I want to dine

on Honey Nut Cheerios? Gregory Stock has proposed changing the name of germline engineering to "germinal choice technology."[11]

The advocates of these technologies are at pains to announce that they don't believe in "eugenics," in anything that smacks of Nazis and Aryans and government policies. Instead of Huxley's vision in *Brave New World* of a "worldwide political state" controlling our breeding, Lee Silver stresses that "it is individuals and couples—Barbara and Dan and Cheryl and Madeleine and Melissa and Curtis and Jennifer, *not governments*—who will seize control of these new technologies."[12] And he's right. Strain as hard as you will to hear, there's no sound of jackboots clomping up the stairs. Most of our governments have spent the last few decades falling over themselves to disappear, to get out of the way of corporate and individual choice. In fact, say the proponents, the politicians will be behaving in totalitarian fashion only if they try to *stop* anyone from breeding his own little Einstein. As Dr Watson remarked not long ago, "I don't believe we can let the government start dictating the decisions people make about what sorts of families they'll have."[13]

These positions are attractive to the left as well as the right, for liberals have their own reasons to fear overreaching by the government. The "pro-choice" movement, after all, is what we call the campaign for abortion rights; one of its most popular slogans has always been "Keep Your Laws off My Body." It was the California Democrat Dianne Feinstein who inserted a letter from biotech giant Genentech into the *Congressional Record* arguing that cloning regulators shouldn't trifle with "the legal rights of persons to free expression and inquiry in the private market."[14] (Feinstein later joined with Ted Kennedy to lead the fight against any restrictions on "therapeutic" cloning.) Gay people rightly detest the long history of government efforts to limit their choice of whom to love.

All in all, in other words, choice is a powerful rhetorical device. It is for biotech, and it will be for the other species-changing technologies that are following behind it. ("I think it boils down to the question of choices," says the nanotech pioneer Ralph Merkle. "If you have better technology, then you're no longer constrained in the range of choices of what you can do.")[15]

Which is why it's so important to say: *These are the most anti-choice technologies anyone's ever thought of.* In widespread use, they will first rob parents of their liberty, and then strip freedom from every generation that follows. In the end, they will destroy forever the very possibility of meaningful choice.

To understand why, imagine what will happen when the first few hundred parents on New York's Upper East Side decide that they will indeed spend some of their spare cash on upgrading their offspring. Almost immediately, at precisely the moment the first cover story on the subject appears in *New York* magazine, every other well-off couple of childbearing age in Manhattan will be forced to decide whether, like it or not, they're going to have to follow suit. If not, their kids may *lose*—may not get into the right preschool, may not get into Brearley, may not get into Harvard. What choice will those parents have? Only the choice to keep up with the neighbors, or the choice to put their kids behind from the start. A "choice" that will spread from Manhattan to Scarsdale, and so on down the line, as the enhancements get cheaper and as the competition gets more heated. Remember the words of Lester Thurow [...]: "Suppose parents could add 30 points to their child's IQ. Wouldn't you want to do it? And if you don't, your child will be the stupidest in the neighborhood."[16] That's your choice.

We can see such "choices" in action already. Consider sports. Very few kids grow up thinking, "I'm going to do steroids so I can hit home runs." But at some point young athletes reach a level at which a couple of other kids are sticking needles in their butts to build their biceps, and as a result they're hammering it over the fence, and as a result they're moving up to the majors. You have a *choice*, sure. But really it was only the first few guys who had a *free* choice. In the words of one Olympic coach, "Most of the athletes didn't really want to do drugs. But they would come to me and say, 'Unless you stop the drug abuse in sports, I have to do drugs. I'm not going to spend the next two years training—away from my family,

missing my college education—to be an Olympian and then be cheated out of a medal by some guy from Europe or Asia who is on drugs."[17]

Eventually, even the possibility of choosing may all but disappear. Say you have a family tendency toward fatness. Many other people have started to engineer it out of their children, to the point where the insurance company decides to make such a "choice" a prerequisite for coverage. Eugenics in that kind of world won't take a Hitler; as the bioethicist Arthur Kaplan puts it, it will only require people saying, "You can have a kid like that if you want, but I'm not paying."[18] Even if legislation could prevent such a scenario, what happens when your unenhanced child grows up and goes to get a job? "On the merits," maybe he gets to take out the trash. Hey, but it's your choice. No one's making you do it.

Bad as it is, however, this kind of coercion is barely half the story. The person left without any choice *at all* is the one you've engineered. You've decided, for once and for all, certain things about him: he'll have genes expressing proteins that send extra dopamine to his brain to alter his mood; he'll have genes expressing proteins to boost his memory, to shape his stature. He'll be putty in your (doctor's) hands. Since embryos, even enhanced ones, can't sign informed-consent forms, you'll be taking this on your own shoulders, exercising infinitely more power over your child than your parents did over you. Sure, they tried to raise you a certain way. They sent you to a particular school, tried to pick your friends, shared with you their prejudices. But you could walk away from some of that; doubtless you did. Maybe you turned your back entirely. *Of course* the effects of your upbringing linger—that's what it means to be a social species. But that's nothing like choosing your kid out of a catalogue; the engineered child won't have that same ability to walk away from you. If you get the proteins right, it may never occur to him to do so.[...]

Questions

1. Why does McKibben think we ought *not* to leave decisions about whether or not "designer babies are a good idea" to scientists? To physicians? To bioethicists? How does he think such decisions should be made?

2. Libertarians and others argue for unregulated biotechnology and unregulated individual use of such technology in the name of "choice" and "freedom." Why does McKibben think that "choices" and "freedom" are just what such technology threatens to undermine?

Notes

1. Sheryl Gay Stolberg, "Study Says Clinical Guides Often Hide Ties of Doctors," *New York Times*, Feb. 6, 2002.

2. Nell Boyce, "And Now, Ethics for Sale? Bioethicists and Big Bucks. Problem City?" *U.S. News & World Report*, July 30, 2001.

3. Sheryl Gay Stolberg, "Bioethicists Find Themselves the Ones Being Scrutinized," *New York Times*, Aug. 2, 2001.

4. Daniel Callahan, "Calling Scientific Ideology to Account," *Society*, May/June 1996, p. 19.

5. William Saletan, "The Ethicist's New Clothes," www.slate.com, July 17, 2001.

6. Barbara Katz Rothman, *Genetic Maps and Human Imaginations* (New York: 1998), p. 37.

7. William Saletan, "Ethicist's New Clothes." (www.slate.com, July 17, 2001).

8. Paulina Borsook, *Cyberselfish* (New York: 2000), pp. 35, 32, 16.

9. Gregory S. Paul and Earl Cox, *Beyond Humanity: CyberEvolution and Future Minds* (Rockland, Mass.: 2001), p. 427.

10. Greg Burch, "Progress, Counter Progress, and Counter Counter Progress," speech, Extro 5, June 16, 2000, www.gregburch.net.

11. Gregory Stock, *Redesigning Humans* (New York, 2003), pp. 110–11.

12. Lee Silver, *Remaking Eden* (New York, 1999), pp. 8–9.

13. Richard Lemonick, "Designer Babies," *Time*, Jan. 11, 1999.

14. William Saletan, "Fetal Positions," *Mother Jones*, May/June 1998, p. 59.

15. Ed Frauenheim, "Small Changes," *Techweek*, Feb. 7, 2000, www. techweek.com.

16. Lester Thurow, *Creating Wealth: The New Rules for Individuals, Companies, and Nations in a Knowledge-Based Economy* (New York: 1999), p. 33.

17. Michael Baumberg and Don Yaeger, "Over the Edge," *Sports Illustrated*, April 14, 1997.

18. Martine Rosenblatt, *Unzipped Genes* (Philadelphia: 1997), p. 66.

The President's Council on bioethics gives its analysis of some of the ethical issues regarding future use of PGD

Ethical analysis

The technologies we have just considered range from the well-established (prenatal "screening out," using amniocentesis and abortion) to the speculative (embryonic "fixing up," using direct genetic modification of embryos or gametes), with special attention to the new and growing ("choosing in," using

From *Beyond Therapy: Biotechnology and the Pursuit of Happiness*, by The President's Council on Bioethics, United States Government Printing Office, October 2003.

preimplantation genetic diagnosis followed by selective embryo transfer). It bears emphasis that genetic technologies have been and are being devised mainly with the intention of producing healthier children—not "enhanced children" or "super-babies," but children who are better only in the sense of being free of severe disease and deformity. As we have suggested, we have our doubts whether these powers will soon be widely employed for any other purpose. Yet there are ample reasons why we should not become complacent or take these matters lightly.

Powers to screen and select for one purpose are immediately available to screen and select for another purpose; the same is true for powers of directed genetic change. And, as already noted, it is sometimes hard to distinguish between desirable traits that one would call "healthy" and those that one would call "good in some other way": consider the case of leanness (non-obesity) or perfect pitch (non-tone-deafness) or attentiveness (non-distractibility). Moreover, there is ample reason to take stock of the ethical and social issues related to present and anticipated practices of screening and selection even if, as we have indicated, there is no reason for alarm regarding "designer babies." For the confluence of ever more sophisticated techniques of assisted reproduction with ever greater capacities for genetic screening and manipulation is already increasing the intrusion of science and technology into human procreation, yielding to scientists and parents ever growing powers over the beginnings of human life and the native capacities of the next generation. In addition to welcome consequences for the health of children, such practices may have more ambiguous or worrisome consequences for our ideas about the relation of sex and procreation, parents and children, the requirements of responsible parenthood, and beliefs in the equal worth of all human beings regardless of genetic (or other) disability.

Before one can decide whether these changes should be welcomed enthusiastically, tolerated within limits, or met with disquiet, one must try to think through what they mean—for individuals, for families, and for the larger society. In what follows, we shall examine, first, the reasons why many people welcome these technologies; second, concerns that might be raised about the safety of these procedures and about equality of access to their use; and, finally, more profound ethical questions regarding how these technologies might affect family life and society as a whole.

1 Benefits

There is no question but that assisted reproductive technologies have, over the past few decades, enabled many infertile couples to conceive and bear children, and that the more recent addition of PGD holds the promise of helping couples conceive healthy children when there is a serious risk of heritable disease. The widespread practice of prenatal screening in high-risk pregnancies has enabled numerous couples to terminate pregnancies when severe genetic disorders have been detected. It is the natural aspiration of couples not only to have

children, but to have healthy children, and these procedures have in many cases lent crucial assistance to that aspiration. People welcome these technologies for multiple reasons: compassion for the suffering of those afflicted with genetic diseases; the wish to spare families the tragedy and burden of caring for children with deadly and devastating illnesses; sympathy for those couples who might otherwise forego having children, for fear of passing on heritable disorders; an interest in reducing the economic and social costs of caring for the incurable; and hopes for progress in the overall health and fitness of human society. No one would *wish* to be afflicted, or to have one's child afflicted, by a debilitating genetic disorder, and the new technologies hold out the prospect of eliminating or reducing the prevalence of some of the worst conditions.

Should it become feasible, many people would have reason to welcome the use of these technologies to select or produce children with improved natural endowments, above and beyond being free of disease. Parents, after all, hope not only for healthy children, but for children best endowed to live fulfilling lives. At some point, if some of the technical challenges are overcome, PGD is likely to present itself as an attractive way to enhance our children's potential in a variety of ways. Assuming that it became possible to select embryos containing genes that conferred certain generic benefits—for example, greater resistance to fatigue, or lowered distractibility, or better memory, or increased longevity—many parents would be eager to secure these advantages for their children. And they would likely regard it as an extension of their reproductive freedom to be able to do so; they might even regard it as their parental obligation. In a word, parents would enjoy enlarged freedom of choice, greater mastery of fortune, and satisfaction of their desires to have "better children." And, if all went well, both parents and children would enjoy the benefits of the enhancements.

2 Questions of safety

[...]

To date, ethical thinking about the hazards of the techniques of assisted reproduction has often been incomplete, partly as a result of the perceived desirability of the end. IVF and PGD are undertaken with the intention of producing healthy, fit children; put this way, the enterprise would seem to be much like other medical practices and, as such, amenable to the same ethical standards. But a medical procedure designed to *produce* a healthy person has a different character from procedures aimed at safeguarding or healing a patient who is already alive. Yet here our thinking is ill-served owing to a noticeable lacuna in our approach to the ethics of risky therapies and (especially) the ethics of research using human subjects.

Ordinarily, when new technologies are introduced into medical practice or when medical research is undertaken with human subjects, the safety of the patients or subjects is of paramount ethical concern. However, in the case of IVF, with or without PGD, the children who are produced as a result of these procedures are not considered subjects at risk, for the simple reason that the embryos being handled, tested, and manipulated are not regarded as human subjects. Thus, blastomere biopsy performed on a tiny eight-cell embryo is not treated as an experiment on a *human subject* or as diagnosis of a *patient*, even though the future health and well-being of the child are very much at stake. Instead, the ethics of IVF and PGD are generally dealt with as though the only patient involved were the mother. Whether or not one believes that the embryo here manipulated is a fully human being worthy of moral and legal protection, it is certainly the essential (and fragile) beginnings of the child who will be born and whose health and well-being should therefore be of overriding concern.

A deeper safety question connected with the goal of genetic screening is whether the normal ethical standard—"the best interests of the patient"—can be said to apply if and when PGD is used to select a "better" child. Even when PGD is used only to screen out genetic diseases—and all the more when it is employed to select positive traits—the parents are in effect choosing a particular genotype for their child. The question is, will this unprecedented power in the hands of the parents necessarily be used for the good of the child? Should parents be willing to gamble the safety of their children for the chance to make them "better than well"? What risks to their health and safety are worth taking in pursuit of improvement or perfection?

Ordinarily, in most matters regarding children, our society accepts the principle that each set of parents has authority and responsibility for the well-being of their own children. Yet there are circumstances that lead the state to step in to protect a vulnerable child against abusive or negligent parents. In such cases, the best of parental intentions do not exonerate. How should our society view parental (and biotechnical) discretion to seek to produce "better children" through procedures carrying unknown hazards to those children?

These questions take on greater poignancy once we recognize a novel but morally significant feature of embryo selection using PGD, absent in *prenatal* diagnosis. In intrauterine genetic screening, there is one fetus being tested, and the question at issue is a binary choice of "keep" or "destroy." In contrast, in preimplantation screening a whole array of embryos are scrutinized and tested, and the choice is not the either-or "yes or no" but rather the comparative choice of "best in the class." For if one is going to the trouble of doing IVF supplemented by preimplantation diagnosis, why not get "the best"—the healthiest and, perhaps soon, the "better-than-healthiest"? But in order to get the best, or even in order to get a non-diseased child, one must conceptually "bundle" all the separate embryos and regard them as if they were a single precursor. All will be subjected to testing so that the one who is chosen will be disease-free or better. Yet to make sure that the child who is to be born is the fittest, rather than his diseased or inferior brother or sister, the anointed one must bear potential risks (imposed during the testing) *that he would not have borne in the absence of the parental desire for quality control.* For the sake of which benefits *to the child* can we justify imposing on him what kinds and what degrees of risk?

Before leaving the subject of safety and the concern for the health of children, we observe an ironic feature of the search for better babies with he aid of genetic screening. What if, as a result of widespread genetic screening of adults and improvement in diagnostic screening of embryos, the practice of IVF with PGD came to be seen as *superior* to natural procreation in offering a greater probability of obtaining a healthy child? If the procedures became sufficiently routine and inexpensive (to the point, say, where they are covered by ordinary health insurance), prospective parents interested in healthier (or otherwise better) children might increasingly be tempted to consider IVF with PGD. Furthermore, couples who would then elect PGD in order to screen out genetic diseases might well be tempted to engage at the same time in some positive trait selection. In that case, what began modestly as a means to help the infertile bear children and continued as a way to screen out the worst genetic defects might ultimately stand as a competitor to natural reproduction altogether, with significant consequences for the family and for society at large.

As this discussion indicates, the issue of health and safety proves, on further reflection, to concern more than safety. When biomedical technology permits the substitution, for natural procreation and the rule of chance, of a procedure in which parents begin to control their child's genotype, reproduction becomes to some extent like obtaining or making a product to selected specifications. Even if the parents are guided by their own sense of what would be a good or perfect baby, their selection may serve to satisfy their own interests more than that of the child. The new technologies, even when used only to screen out and get rid of the sick or "imperfect," imply a changed attitude of parents toward their children, a mixture of control and tacit expectations of perfection, an attitude that might grow more pronounced as the relevant techniques grow more sophisticated. Apparently good intentions—to improve the next generation, to enhance the life of our descendants—will not guarantee that genetic screening will be an unqualified blessing for parents and children. (We return to this subject shortly.)

3 Questions of equality

Many observers have noted with concern that, owing to the sheer expense of IVF and PGD—a successful assisted pregnancy costing, on average, roughly $20,000–$30,000—not all couples who could benefit from these procedures have unfettered access to them. If PGD were to become an established option, but only for the affluent, one envisages the troubling prospect of a society divided between the economically *and* genetically rich, on the one hand,

and the economically *and* genetically poor on the other. Severe inherited diseases might disappear except among the poor, while genetic enhancement through screening and selection might be a privilege enjoyed exclusively by the rich. These concerns would, of course, diminish (though they would not disappear) if, as seems likely, the costs of the procedures in question come down and access to these services grows wider.

Yet these legitimate concerns about equality of access rest, ironically, on certain *inegalitarian* assumptions that need to be brought to light. First, the goal of eliminating embryos and fetuses with genetic defects carries the unspoken implication that certain "inferior" kinds of human beings—for example, those with Down syndrome—do not deserve to live. The assumption that the genetically unfit ought to be prevented from being born embodies and invites a profoundly denigrating and worrisome attitude toward those who *do* get to be born. How will we come to regard the many people alive today who carry genetic defects that in the future will be screened out, or the many people, even in a future age of more widespread screening, who will still be born with the abhorred disabilities and diseases? The worry over unequal access to PGD is, in effect, a worry about the inability of the *economically* poor to practice the ultimate discrimination against the *genetically* poor.

Second, when new techniques permit parents to be the partial authors of their child's genetic makeup, the inequality between parents and children is substantially increased. Parents thereby acquire the power, not just of giving life to their children, but of shaping (or trying to shape) the character of that life. Of course, through education and upbringing parents have always had an enormous influence on the lives of their children; but inasmuch as the consequences of genetic screening are imposed before birth and are carried as the child's permanent biological destiny, the inegalitarian effect of the new technology is unprecedented and irreversible.

In response to these concerns, it will be pointed out, rightly, that genes are not exactly destiny, and that it will prove very difficult to intervene genetically at the embryonic stage in ways that will guarantee the appearance of the desired "improvements" in one's children. But much mischief can be done to a child simply from the enhanced parental expectations, all the more so if the child fails to attain the superior native gifts for which he was selected. And as we shall soon see, we are already witnessing certain subtle forms of genetic discrimination even though the technology of screening is still very undeveloped.

4 Consequences for families and society

Beyond questions of safety and equal access, there is reason to believe that the advent of expanded genetic screening and its uses in reproduction could have a profound impact on human procreation, family life, and society as a whole. At present, fewer than 10,000 children have been born following PGD, and the screening procedure itself is being used to diagnose only a limited number of chromosomal and genetic ailments. For these reasons, it is both difficult to predict and also easy to underestimate the societal import of marrying genomic knowledge with established techniques of assisted reproduction, should the practice become widespread.

To make vivid the possible implications, it may therefore be helpful to imagine a future time at which all external barriers to the use of these procedures have been largely removed. Suppose that, a decade from now, IVF and PGD have been perfected to the point where preimplantation screening is safe and effective, not prohibitively expensive, and capable of identifying a wide range of markers for heritable disorders. Suppose, in other words, that prospective parents (perfectly fertile) routinely have the option of using these technologies in order to select an essentially disease-free embryo for transfer to the mother's womb.

Under such circumstances—admittedly quite hypothetical—might not the practice become moderately widespread? Could many people come to regard using IVF plus PGD as safer (for the child) than the randomness of sex, and therefore preferable to natural procreation even when there is no particular history of genetic disease? In societies in which people are limited—or limit themselves—to only one child, might they not increasingly turn to these techniques to ensure that their child might be as "perfect" as possible? And, should this procedure begin to compete with or even to supplant sex as the more common route to conceiving children, in what ways would the meaning of childbearing be altered?

The hypothetical case just sketched may seem like science fiction, but the important questions it raises are, in fact, implicated in the current practice of genetic screening. Even though the practice of PGD is still in its infancy, its availability has begun to influence our thinking about childbearing. Already the goals of assisted reproductive technologies are changing, from the original modest aim of providing children for the infertile to the novel and more ambitious aim of producing healthy children for whoever needs extra assistance in obtaining them. Anticipating the coming of augmented powers of genetic screening and selection, people are expanding the idea of "a healthy child" and therewith almost certainly the aspirations of prospective parents. In his presentation to the Council, Dr Gerald Schatten, a leading researcher in the field of reproductive biology, stated that the overall goal of assisted reproductive technology is "to help prospective parents *realize their own dreams* of having a *disease-free legacy*" (emphasis added). The dream of a disease-free legacy—as stated, a goal that looks beyond merely the next generation—seems rather different from the merely hopeful wish for a healthy child. And even without such a broad ambition, the intervention of rigorous genetic screening into the order of childbearing will likely involve raising the standard for what counts as an acceptable birth. The likely significance of this fact is subtle but profound. The attitude of parents toward their child may be quietly shifted from unconditional acceptance to critical scrutiny: the very first act of parenting now becomes not the unreserved welcoming of an arriving child, but the judging of his or her fitness, while still an embryo, to become their child, all by the standards of contemporary genetic screening. Moreover, as the screening technology itself grows more refined, more able to pick out serious but not life-threatening genetic conditions (from dwarfism and deafness to dyslexia and asthma) and then genetic markers for desirable traits, the standards for what constitutes an acceptable birth may grow more exacting.

With genetic screening, procreation begins to take on certain aspects of the *idea*—if not the practice—of manufacture, the making of a product to a specified standard. The parent—in partnership with the IVF doctor or genetic counselor—becomes in some measure the master of the child's fate, in ways that are without precedent. This leads to the question of what it might mean for a child to live with a chosen genotype: he may feel grateful to his parents for having gone to such trouble to spare him the burden of various genetic defects; but he might also have to deal with the sense that he is not just a gift born of his parents' love but also, in some degree, a product of their will.

These questions of family dynamics could become even more complicated when preimplantation genetic screening is used to select embryos for some desirable traits. While current negative screening is guided by the standard of a healthy or disease-free baby, the goals of prospective positive use are in theory unlimited, governed only by the parents' ideas of what they want in their child. Today, parents using PGD take responsibility for selecting for birth children who will not be chronically sick or severely disabled; in the future, they might also bear responsibility for picking and choosing which "advantages" their children shall enjoy. Such an enlarged degree of parental control over the genetic endowments of their children cannot fail to alter the parent-child relationship. Selecting against disease merely relieves the parents of the fear of specific ailments afflicting their child; selecting for desired traits inevitably plants specific hopes and expectations as to how their child might excel. More than any child does now, the "better" child may bear the burden of living up to the standards he was "designed" to meet. The oppressive weight of his parents' expectations—resting in this case on what they believe to be undeniable biological facts—may impinge upon the child's freedom to make his own way in the world. Here we see one of the ethically paradoxical consequences of the new screening technologies: designed to free us from the tyranny of our genes, they may end up narrowing our freedoms as individuals even further.

In addition to changes in the parent–child relationship, there are reasons to be concerned about the wider social effects of an increased use of genetic screening and selection. There is, first of all, the prospect of diminished tolerance for the "imperfect,"

especially those born with genetic disorders that could have been screened out. It is offensive to think that children, suffering from "preventable" genetic diseases, should be directly asked, "Why were you born?" (or their parents asked, "Why did you let him live?"). Yet it is almost as troubling to contemplate that "defective" children and their parents may be treated contemptuously and unfairly in light of such prejudices, even if they go unspoken. Already, parents who have a child with Down syndrome are sometimes asked, "Well, didn't you have an amnio? How did this happen?" Many of these parents are people who, for their own ethical reasons, have chosen to proceed with the pregnancy even after learning the results of genetic screening, electing to love and care for the children that it has been given to them to love. Yet as the range of detectable disorders increases, as adult screening becomes ubiquitous and every pregnancy is tested, and as the economic cost of caring for the afflicted remains high, it may become difficult for parents to resist the pressure, both social and economic, of the "consensus" that children with sufficiently severe and detectable disabilities must not be born.

In all likelihood parents will increasingly feel pressure to conform to shifting social standards of what is genetically fit. Along with the freedoms bequeathed, by the new technologies comes a certain danger of social coercion and tyranny of public opinion. Furthermore, as our table of detectable genetic markers grows more complete, there is the prospect of using genetic screening to weed out not only the most devastating genetic disorders but also heritable conditions that are bad but manageable, or even merely inconvenient. In practice, it is likely to prove very hard to draw a bright line between identifiable defects that might justify discarding an embryo or preventing a birth and those defects that parents might (or should) be able to find acceptable. It is not clear what resources our society will be able to draw upon to assist parents in making such important decisions.

Should PGD and IVF, contrary to current expectations, ever become widely used for positive screening of desirable traits, the impact on society could be even greater. Our knowledge of the human genome and our powers of genetic selection might grow so great as to unleash competition among parents eager to bear children who are biologically destined to be taller, thinner, brighter, or better-looking than their peers.

It should be noted that the social consequences of the widespread use of genetic screening alone are likely to outstrip the actual biological enhancements: those "unfortunate" enough to be born with genetic "defects" that might have been detected by screening might well be subject to discrimination, even without waiting to see how they turn out. The thoughtful (if not quite scientifically accurate) film *Gattaca* explores some of the chilling social implications of a human future in which genetic screening of children has become the norm. To the careful observer of current practices, the risks of such discriminatory implications are already evident.

[...]

Questions

1. According to the Council, what are some of the potential benefits of IVF with PGD? What are some of the potential safety concerns?
2. According to the Council, should limits be placed on the sorts of selections parents could make through the use of IVF and PGD? What limits are now in place?
3. If children are eventually "designed," how might this change the parent–child relationship, according to the Council? How might it change social attitudes toward those with genetic disorders or toward those with less desirable traits?